The Sino-Soviet Split

D0420412

PRINCETON STUDIES IN INTERNATIONAL
HISTORY AND POLITICS

SERIES EDITORS

G. John Ikenberry and Marc Trachtenberg

RECENT TITLES

The Sino-Soviet Split: Cold War in the Communist World
by Lorenz M. Lüthi

Nuclear Logics: Contrasting Paths in East Asia and the Middle East
by Etel Solingen

Social States: China in International Institutions, 1980–2000
by Alastair Iain Johnston

Appeasing Bankers
by Jonathan Kirshner

The Politics of Secularism in International Relations
by Elizabeth Shakman Hurd

Unanswered Threats: Political Constraints on the Balance of Power
by Randall L. Schweller

*Producing Security: Multinational Corporations, Globalization, and the
Changing Calculus of Conflict*
by Stephen G. Brooks

Driving the Soviets up the Wall: Soviet-East German Relations, 1953–1961
by Hope M. Harrison

*Legitimacy and Power Politics: The American and French Revolutions
in International Political Culture*
by Mlada Bukovansky

*Rhetoric and Reality in Air Warfare: The Evolution of British and
American Ideas about Strategic Bombing, 1914–1945*
by Tami Davis Biddle

*Revolutions in Sovereignty: How Ideas Shaped Modern International
Relations*
by Daniel Philpott

*After Victory: Institutions, Strategic Restraint, and the Rebuilding of
Order after Major Wars*
by G. John Ikenberry

The Sino-Soviet Split

COLD WAR IN THE COMMUNIST WORLD

Lorenz M. Lüthi

PRINCETON UNIVERSITY PRESS

PRINCETON AND OXFORD

Library of Congress Cataloging-in-Publication Data

Luthi, Lorenz M., 1970–
    The Sino-Soviet split : cold war in the communist world / Lorenz M. Luthi.
      p. cm. — (Princeton studies in international history and politics)
    ISBN: 978-0-691-12934-1 (cloth : alk. paper) — ISBN: 978-0-691-13590-8 (pbk. : alk.
paper) 1. China—Foreign relations—Soviet Union. 2. Soviet Union—Foreign relations—
China. 3. Communism—History—20th century. I. Title.
    DS740.5.S65L88   2008
    327.4705109'045—dc22   2007033119

British Library Cataloging-in-Publication Data is available

This book has been composed in Sabon

Printed on acid-free paper. ∞

press.princeton.edu

Printed in the United States of America

10 9 8 7 6 5 4 3 2 1

FOR MY PARENTS

In memory of my brother

Contents

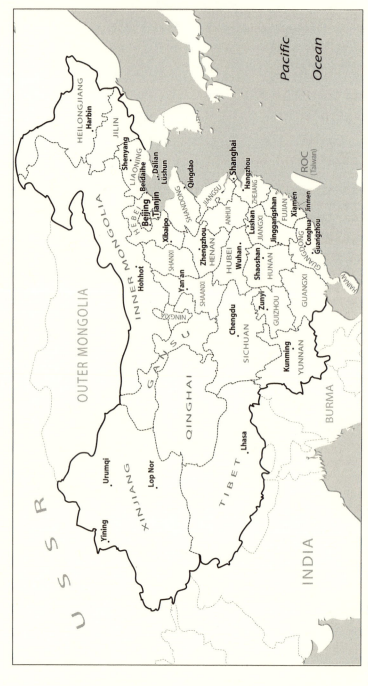

Figure 1. China: Provinces and Towns

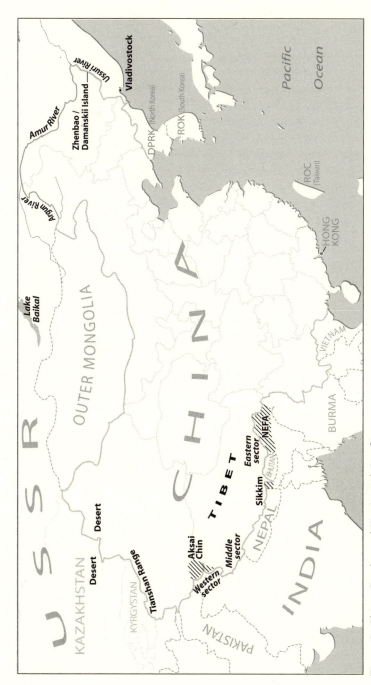

Figure 2. China: Border and Territorial Conflicts

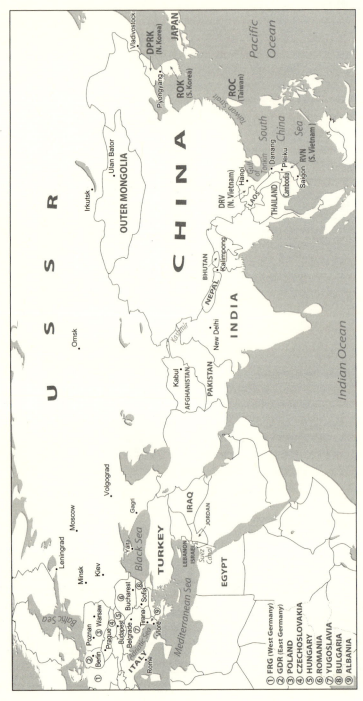

Figure 3. Eurasia

Acknowledgments

WITHOUT THE SUPPORT of numerous individuals and institutions, I would not have been able to write this book. I apologize in advance to those I have forgotten to include. During my graduate studies, I benefited from advice from John Gaddis, Jonathan Spence, and Paul Kennedy. My travels to Russia, China, Hong Kong, Germany, Poland, Hungary, the Czech Republic, Bulgaria, Italy, Boston, and Washington for language training and research have been generously supported by grants from the Smith Richardson Foundation, the Council on East Asian Studies (Yale), the Richard U. Light Fellowship (Yale), the Fox Fellowship (Yale), the Henry Hart Rice Fellowship (Yale), internal SSHRC grants (McGill), the National Security Fellowship at the Olin Institute (Harvard), and the membership at the Institute for Advanced Study. Often, my parents have generously added substantial amounts of money.

Numerous persons have been very gracious with their time and assistance during my research. I am grateful to Jean Hung and the staff of the USC; Sieglinde Hartmann, Sylvia Gräfe, and the staff at SAPMO-BArch; B. Kmezik and Ulrich Geyer at the PAAA; the staff at BArch-Freib; Galina Albertovna and Oleg Khlevniuk at GARF; Elisaveta Guseva and the staff at AVP RF; the staff at RGANI and RGASPI; Adam Dąbrowski at AAN; Szczepan Ciborek at AMSZ; the staff at MOL; Alena Nosková, Vladimír Waage, and the staff at SÚA; Galina Mindikova, Mariana Lecheva, and the staff at TsDA; Borislav Staminirov at AMVnR; Paul Lydon and the staff at the JFK Library and Museum; the staff at JSSDAG; Silvio Pons and Giovanna Bosman at FIG; and Peter Filardo at Taminent Library.

Niu Dayong, Hou Xiaojia, Wang Xiaoying, Jasper Becker, Kurt Spillmann, Vladimir Pechatnov, Aleksei Voskressenkii, Andrea Graziosi, Christian Ostermann, Wanda Jarzabek, Krzysztof Persak, Magdolna Baráth, János Rainer, William Taubman, Oldřich Tůma, Jordan Baev, Niu Jun, Cai Jiahe, Andy Kennedy, Mao Xiaosong, Liu Jing, Iwa Nawrocki, Malgorzata Gnoinska, Valerie Maymen, and Phyllis Rudin have helped me to organize research trips or interviews, facilitated access to archives, or assisted in other important ways in the research process. Gerhard Wettig, David Holloway, Amy Dunkle, Vladimir Zubok, Priscilla Roberts, Sergey Radchenko, Bruce Adams, Fredrik Logevall, and Mark Edele have provided important sources or references to literature. Mike Hornacek translated valuable Czech documents. Sebastian Caquard produced the maps. Many thanks to Mary Sharp, Mat Emerson, Heather McAllister,

Jonathan Winkler, Karin Schiebold, Werner Richtering, and Reinhard Wolf, who provided me with food and shelter while doing research near their homes.

I greatly appreciated the comments of those who have read the manuscript as a whole or in parts. In no specific order, I owe thanks to Paul Bushkovitch, Laura Engelstein, Timothy Snyder, Jonathan Winkler, Charles Lansing, Brian Rohlik, Andrew Preston, Mark Edele, Ben Kiernan, Fredrik Logevall, Balazs Szalontai, Hang Nguyen, Peter Vámos, Jan Rowiński, Ioan Romulus Budura, Andrea Graziosi, James Hershberg, Vojtech Mastny, Chen Jian, O. Arne Westad, Robert Ross, Terry Martin, the Olin fellows of 2004-5, M. Taylor Fravel, Mark Kramer, Chris Gosha, the China Group of Montreal, Tsuyoshi Hasegawa, Stephen Rosen, Thomas Christensen, Wang Dong, Adrienne Edgar, David Welch, Geoffrey Hosking, Jeff Bercuson, Ryan Griffiths, Catherine Lu, James Krapfl, Chuck Myers, Ellen Foos, Cindy Crumrine, and three anonymous readers.

Catherine Lu sustained me with loving support and enduring patience during the difficult process of rewriting and publishing this manuscript.

I dedicate this book to my parents, who had to let their son go to many strange places to do research on peculiar people, and to my brother, who did not live long enough to see it researched and written. I am certain he would have been very proud of his little brother.

Abbreviations and Terms

AAN	*Archiwum Akt Nowych* (*Archive of Modern Records*, Warsaw/Poland)
a.e.	archivna edinitsa (Bulgarian: file)
AMSZ	*Archiwum Ministerstwa Spraw Zagranicznych* (*Archive of the Ministry for Foreign Affairs*, Warsaw/Poland)
AMVnR	*Arkhiv na Ministerstvoto na Vnshnite Raboti* (Archive of the Ministry of Foreign Relations, Sofia/Bulgaria)
APC	Archivio del Partito Comunista Italiano (Archive of the Italian Communist Party; in *FIG*)
AVPRF	*Arkhiv Vneshnei Politiki Rossiiskoi Federatsii* (*Archive of Foreign Policy of the Russian Federation*, Moscow/Russia)
BArch-Freib	*Bundesarchiv, Militärarchiv* (Federal Archives, Military Archives, Freiburg/Germany)
CB	*Current Background*
CC	Central Committee
CCP	Chinese Communist Party
CIA	Central Intelligence Agency
CLG	*Chinese Law and Government*
COMECON	Council for Mutual Economic Cooperation
CPSU	Communist Party of the Soviet Union
CP USA	Communist Party of the United States of America
CRSG	Cultural Revolution Small Group
CWIHP	*Cold War International History Project*
d.	delo (Russian/Bulgarian: collection)
DRV	Democratic Republic of Vietnam (official name for North Vietnam from 1945 to 1975)
f.	fond (Russian/Bulgarian/Czech/Hungarian: fund)

FIG	*Fondazione Istituto Gramsci* (Foundation Gramsci Institute, Rome/Italy)
FRUS	United States, Department of State. *Foreign Relations of the United States.* Washington: GPO, various years.
FYP	Five-Year Plan
GARF	*Gosudarstvennyi Arkhiv Rossiiskoi Federatsii* (*State Archive of the Russian Federation*, Moscow/Russia)
GDR	German Democratic Republic (East Germany)
Hongqi	*Red Flag*, CCP party journal (started in 1958)
ICBM	Intercontinental Ballistic Missile
IRBM	Intermediate Range Ballistic Missile
JFK	*John F. Kennedy Library and Museum* (Boston/United States)
JSSDAG	*Jiangsu Sheng Dang'anguan* (*Jiangsu Provincial Archive*, Nanjing/China)
JYMW	Mao Zedong. *Jianguo yilai Mao Zedong wengao* [*Mao Zedong's Manuscripts after the Foundation of the PRC*]. 13 volumes. Beijing: Zhongyang wenxian, 1987–1998.
KGB	Komitet Gosudarstvennoi Bezopasnosti (Russian: State Security Committee)
LNTB	Limited Nuclear Test Ban (treaty)
MAC	Military Affairs Commission
MLF	Multi Lateral Nuclear Force
MOL	*Magyar Országos Levéltár* (*Hungarian National Archives*, Budapest/Hungary)
MZDDG	Mao Zedong. *Mao Zedong daguan* [*Mao Zedong's Grand Sight*]. Beijing: Renmin daxue, 1993.
MZDSW	Mao Zedong. *Mao Zedong sixiang wansui* [*Long Live Mao Zedong Thought*]. No place: no publisher, 1969.
MZDW	Mao Zedong. *Mao Zedong wenji* [*A Collection of Mao Zedong's Works*]. 8 volumes. Beijing: Renmin, 1993–1999.

MZDX3	Mao Zedong. *Mao Zedong xuanji* [*Selected Works of Mao Zedong*]. Volume 3. Hong Kong: Mingbao yuekan she, 1971.
NARA	*National Archives and Record Administration* (Washington, D.C./United States)
NATO	North Atlantic Treaty Organization
NC	Xinhua tongxunshe [New China News Agency]. *Neibu cankao* [*Internal Reference Material*]. Beijing: Xinhua tongxunshe, 1949-.
NEP	New Economic Policy
NLF	National Liberation Front (South Vietnam, 'Vietcong')
NSA	*National Security Archive* (Washington D.C./United States)
NSC	National Security Council
NYT	*New York Times*
o.	opis (Russian/Bulgarian: inventory)
őe	őrzési egység (Hungarian: custody unit)
p.	papka (Russian: file)
PAAA-MfAA	*Politisches Archiv des Auswärtigen Amtes, Bestand: Ministerium für Auswärtige Angelegenheiten* (*Files of the Ministry for Foreign Affairs in the Political Archive of the Office for Foreign Affairs*, Berlin/Germany)
Pancha Shila	Five Sino-Indian Principles of Peaceful Coexistence
PCC	Political Consultative Committee (WAPA)
PDHNP	Wang Yanzhu, ed. *Peng Dehuai nianpu* [*A Chronicle of Peng Dehuai's Life*]. Beijing: Shijie zhishi, 1998.
PLA	People's Liberation Army
PR	*Peking Review*
PRC	People's Republic of China
RADD	Russian and East European Archive Documents Database (in *NSA*)
RG	Record Group
RGANI	*Rossiiskii Gosudarstvennyi Arkhiv Noveishei Istorii* (*Russian State*

	Archive of Contemporary History, Moscow/Russia)
RGASPI	*Rossiiskii Gosudarstvennyi Arkhiv Sotsialno-politicheskoi Istorii (Russian State Archive of Socio-Political History,* Moscow/Russia)
Renmin Ribao	*People's Daily,* CCP party newspaper
RVN	Republic of Vietnam (South Vietnam)
SAPMO-BArch	*Stiftung Archiv der Parteien und Massenorganisationen der DDR im Bundesarchiv (Archive of the Parties and Mass Organizations of the GDR in the Federal Archives,* Berlin/ Germany)
SCMP	Survey China Mainland Press
SED	Sozialistische Einheitspartei (Socialist Unity Party, GDR)
SEM	Socialist Education Movement
SLBM	Sea Launched Ballistic Missile
SRV	Socialist Republic of Vietnam (official name for Vietnam after 1975)
SS	MacFarquhar, Roderick, Timothy Cheek, and Eugene Wu, eds. *The Secret Speeches of Chairman Mao: from the Hundred Flowers to the Great Leap Forward.* Cambridge: Harvard University, 1989.
SÚA	*Státní Ústřední Archiv (Central State Archiv,* Prague/Czech Republic)
SW	Mao Zedong. *Selected Works.* 5 volumes. Beijing: Foreign Languages, 1961–1977.
TsDA	*Tsentralen Drzhaven Arkhiv* (Central State Archive, Sofia/Bulgaria)
TsPA	Tsentralen Partien Arkhiv (Central Party Archive; in *TsDA*)
U.S.	United States
USSR	Union of Socialist Soviet Republics
ÚV KSČ	Ústřední Výbor Komunisticke strany Československa (Central Committee of the Communist Party of Czechoslovakia)
VWP	Vietnamese Workers' Party

WAPA	Warsaw Pact
WFTU	World Federation of Trade Unions
WXL	Wu Lengxi. *Shinian lunzhan, 1956–1966: ZhongSu guanxi huiyulu* [*Ten Years of Debate, 1956-1966: recollections of Sino-Soviet relations*]. 2 volumes. Beijing: Zhongyang wenxian, 1999.
Xinhua	New China (News Agency)
ZELNP1/ZELNP2/ZELNP3	Zhonggong zhongyang wenxian yanjiushi bian. *Zhou Enlai nianpu, 1949–1976* [*A Chronicle of Zhou Enlai's Life: 1949–1976*]. 3 volumes. Beijing: Zhongyang wenxian, 1997.

Transliteration and Diacritical Marks

ANY RESEARCH PROJECT that operates in a multitude of languages faces transliteration problems. This book is no exception, although I aimed at consistency. I applied the following rules:

All European languages using the Latin alphabet (English, German, Polish, Czech, Hungarian, Romanian, Italian, and French) keep their diacritical marks.

For Cyrillic languages, I followed the transliteration tables generally used by the Library of Congress (ALA-LC Romanization table, see: http://www.loc.gov/catdir/cpso/roman.html), with the following exceptions: 1. Soft vowels such as ю, я, and ё are transliterated as yu (not: iu), ya (not: ia), and ye (not: ë). 2. The following signs and diacritical marks are dropped: ' for the soft sign ь, " for the Russian hard sign ъ, ŭ for the Bulgarian unstressed vowel ъ, ˇ on ĭ (й), ˙ on ė (э), and ⌢ above a cluster of Latin letters (ts, yu, ya), indicating that they jointly stand for one transliterated cyrillic letter (ц, ю, я).

Vietnamese and Korean names lose their diacritical marks.

For Chinese, the Pinyin system without tone marks applies.

I tried to keep exceptions to a minimum. Any name with a widespread English spelling that diverges from the correct transliteration is exempted from the above-mentioned rules, such as Moscow (not: Moskva), Khrushchev (not: Khrushchyev), Warsaw (not: Warszawa), Prague (not: Praha), etc. Some Chinese names retain their divergent but usual transliterations, such as Chiang Kai-shek (not: Jiang Jieshi).

East German or East European sources often contain Korean and Vietnamese names of lesser-known individuals and places that have been transliterated in an obviously distorted form. In some cases, I was unable to verify the correct transliteration.

The Sino-Soviet Split

Introduction

BEFORE OLEG TROYANOVSKII left his position as the last Soviet ambassador to the People's Republic of China, he met Wu Xiuquan for a chat about old times. The former vice-head of the Central Committee Liaison Department of the Chinese Communist Party remarked to the past adviser of Nikita Khrushchev: "When you now read the messages that our countries exchanged at a time not too long ago, you don't know whether to laugh or cry."[1] The pettiness and hyperbole of the Sino-Soviet polemics and their impact on the foreign and domestic policies of both countries, from the Great Leap Forward to the war scare of 1969, forces any contemporary observer to pause in incredulity. The Sino-Soviet Split was one of the key events of the Cold War, equal in importance to the construction of the Berlin Wall, the Cuban Missile Crisis, the Second Vietnam War, and Sino-American Rapprochement. The split helped to determine the framework of the second half of the Cold War in general, and influenced the course of the Second Vietnam War in particular. Like a nasty divorce, it left bad memories and produced myths of innocence on both sides.

Until very recently, much of the source material that could shed light on the dynamics of the Sino-Soviet Split was stashed away in inaccessible archives. While the literature on the topic is vast, much of it was written during the Cold War on the basis of selective published sources or tends to be speculative and theoretical. Since its slow opening in the early 1980s, China has produced a wealth of published primary and secondary sources and, recently, even made some archives accessible to foreign researchers. The collapse of the Soviet Union and communist East Europe threw open the doors of countless party and governmental archives.

The newly available documents point to the vital role of ideology in the Sino-Soviet Split. Both the Chinese Communists and the Soviets were true Marxist-Leninist believers. Discord between Beijing and Moscow arose over the method of establishing a socialist society domestically and over the direction of the joint policy of the socialist camp toward the capitalist world. Furthermore, while ideology was central, it increasingly became entangled in internal politics. Leadership conflicts led Mao

---

[1] Oleg Troyanovskii, *Cherez gody i rasstoyaniya* (Moskva: Vagrius, 1997), 348.

Zedong to exploit the worsening of Sino-Soviet relations for his goals abroad and at home.

The first point of ideological disagreement emerged in 1955 over the Stalinist socioeconomic development model. Facing a structural economic crisis, Mao replaced the development model that the People's Republic of China (PRC) had inherited from the late Iosif Stalin with a development strategy resembling earlier Soviet policies that had already been discredited in the Union of Socialist Soviet Republics (USSR). Despite its failure, Mao returned to their basic ideas in the Great Leap Forward of 1958–60, only to reap disaster.

De-Stalinization in the Soviet Union provided the second moment of ideological conflict. While Khrushchev's Secret Speech in February 1956 was rooted mainly in domestic necessities, it reverberated throughout the socialist world. As a result, over the course of 1956 and 1957, Mao and Khrushchev took up opposite positions on Stalin as a theoretician and practitioner.

Third, Sino-Soviet ideological disputes arose over the correct method of dealing with imperialism. Launched in early 1956 as well, Khrushchev's policy of peaceful coexistence with the United States did not cause immediate conflict with the Chinese Communists because they were preoccupied with de-Stalinization. From late 1957, however, tensions over this policy grew, and, by the mid-1960s, dominated Sino-Soviet relations.

Most other points of Sino-Soviet conflict were either the result of these ideological disagreements or of lesser importance. Security disputes—such as the Second Taiwan Strait Crisis in 1958—and economic disagreements—in particular trade and the sudden withdrawal of the Soviet specialists from China in 1960—arose as the consequence of ideological arguments. Similarly, territorial disputes that predated the Sino-Soviet alliance did not threaten the relationship until the two countries had developed their ideological disagreements. Finally, personality clashes contributed to but did not cause the existing ideological problems.

In the end, the new documents suggest that the Chinese side was far more active in pursuing ideological conflict. The PRC established itself through the alliance, in both positive and negative terms. Although China had sought the alliance in 1949 and 1950, Mao eventually pushed for its collapse after 1959, when he decided that it had run the full course of what he considered its usefulness to the country. Moreover, the Chinese leader increasingly linked Sino-Soviet disagreements with his internal disputes. In 1962, the struggle against domestic ideological revisionism merged with his battle against its counterpart in the policy of the socialist camp toward imperialism.

Previous Lines of Explanation

Before the end of the Cold War and the gradually increasing accessibility of new archival and documentary evidence, scholars offered four main explanations for the Sino-Soviet Split. First, some have argued that the split resulted from conflicts of national interest.[2] As early as 1952, one observer predicted the Sino-Soviet Split in light of the aspiration of Stalin's totalitarian regime to control its allies; inevitably, according to this line of thinking, this would violate their national interests.[3] Other authors identified nationalist conflicts, such as claims of fear of foreign domination or claims of cultural superiority, as a cause for the split.[4]

Second, the concept of the strategic triangle appealed to many observers, especially with the Sino-American Rapprochement since 1969. This theory posited that the United States, the Soviet Union, and China formed a triangular great power relationship; within this unique setup, the two weaker countries allied to balance against the strongest. Proponents of the strategic triangle tried to explain the Sino-Soviet Split as the result of relative changes in the military and political power of the three countries—changes that gradually questioned the rationale for the Sino-Soviet alliance and eventually triggered its collapse.[5]

Third, a small body of literature attempted to locate the source of the Sino-Soviet Split in domestic politics. Scholars have argued that unrelated Chinese domestic leadership conflicts had a negative impact on the Sino-Soviet alliance,[6] that Mao's anti-Soviet policies led him to undermine "the positions of all those [fellow] leaders who did not fully support

[2] Richard Lowenthal, "National Interests and the Orthodox Faith," Clement Zablocki, ed., *Sino-Soviet Rivalry* (New York: Praeger, 1966), 27–32. Richard Lowenthal, "The Degeneration of an Ideological Dispute," Douglas Stuart et al., eds., *China, the Soviet Union, and the West* (Boulder: Westview, 1982), 59–71.

[3] John Tashjean, "The Sino-Soviet Split," *China Quarterly* 94, 342–61.

[4] Klaus Mehnert, for example, made this argument, though not exclusively, in: *Peking and Moscow* (New York: Putnam, 1963).

[5] Donald Zagoria, "A Strange Triangle," Zablocki, *Sino-Soviet Rivalry*, 43–52. Michel Tatu, *The Great Power Triangle* (Paris: Atlantic Institute, 1970). Robert Scalapino, "The American-Soviet-Chinese Triangle," William Kintner et al., eds., *SALT* (Pittsburgh: Pittsburgh, 1973), 141–66. Harry Schwartz, "The Moscow-Peking-Washington Triangle," *Annals of the American Academy of Political and Social Sciences* 414, 41–54. William Griffith, "The World and the Great-Power Triangles," Griffith, ed., *The World and the Great-Power Triangles* (Cambridge: MIT, 1975), 1–33. Banning Garrett, "China Policy and the Strategic Triangle," Kenneth Oye et al., eds., *Eagle Entangled* (New York: Longman, 1979), 228–63.

[6] Richard Thornton, *The Bear and the Dragon* (New York: American Asian Educational Exchange, 1971).

his tough stance toward the USSR,"[7] or that the Chinese leadership attempted to use anti-Soviet policies to divert attention from internal legitimacy problems.[8] Others have focused on Soviet domestic politics by identifying factional infighting after Stalin's death as a source for the Sino-Soviet Split.[9]

Fourth, the role of ideology in the Sino-Soviet estrangement attracted scholarly attention as soon as public disputes started in 1960. In a seminal study published the following year, Donald Zagoria offered a multicausal interpretation that combined ideological with other causes (historical, personal, contextual, economic, and political).[10] Subsequent early authors saw the split as purely ideological,[11] or as the result of a mix of ideological and national interest factors.[12] Another interpretation promoted the idea that the split was not principally about ideology but merely articulated in ideological rhetoric.[13] Since the early 1980s, the "China under threat" interpretation garnered much academic interest; it promoted the idea that security concerns arising over an ideologically influenced threat perception shaped Chinese foreign policy behavior.[14] In a more general debate, early observers of the collapse of socialist unity after Khrushchev's Secret Speech argued that the intrinsic nature of Marxism-Leninism tended, over time, to create friction among its adherents. According to this argument, the absolute assertions of Marxism-Leninism (in the form of a dogma) and its promotion of hierarchical political structures (one leading communist party worldwide and one vanguard communist party within each country) made it liable both to degenerate into factional battles over the correct interpretation of Marxism-Leninism and, in the process, to increase competing claims to sole leadership of the international communist movement.[15]

The examination of the newly available evidence allows us to reconsider these arguments. Conventional wisdom defines national interest in terms

---

[7] Kenneth Lieberthal, "The Background in Chinese Politics," Herbert Ellison, *The Sino-Soviet Conflict* (Seattle: Washington, 1982), 3–28.

[8] Jürgen Domes, "Domestic Sources of PRC Policy," Stuart, *China*, 39–58.

[9] Vernon Aspaturian, "The Domestic Sources of Soviet Policy Toward China," Stuart, *China*, 59–72.

[10] Donald Zagoria, *The Sino-Soviet Conflict, 1956–1961* (Princeton: Princeton, 1962).

[11] Jean Baby, *La Grande Controverse Sino-Soviétique (1956–1966)* (Paris: Bernard Grasset, 1966).

[12] François Fejtö, *Chine-USSR: De l'alliance au conflit, 1950–1972* (Paris: Seuil, 1973).

[13] Franz Michael, "Common Purpose and Double Strategy," Zablocki, *Sino-Soviet Rivalry*, 15–16.

[14] Melvin Gurtov et al., *China under Threat* (Baltimore: Johns Hopkins, 1980).

[15] Richard Lowenthal, *World Communism* (New York: Oxford, 1964). Hans Morgenthau, *A New Foreign Policy for the United States* (New York: Praeger, 1969), 32–42.

of securing the physical survival of the country and developing its economic potential. There is no evidence that a clash of national interest emerged because one of the two partners entered the alliance with the intention of undermining the military or economic security of, or even of obtaining control over, the other. The major lines of Sino-Soviet conflict emerged over unrelated issues at a time, in 1955–57, when clashes of national interest, such as conflicts over unresolved territorial disputes, were irrelevant. Sino-Soviet debates over the correct handling of imperialism are the closest to a national interest interpretation, but they occurred only after ideological conflict had already emerged.

In any case, the discussion of the national interest interpretation must focus on China, since it was more active in pursuing the split. Starting in 1958, it was Mao who vigorously implemented policies that destabilized the alliance and eventually led to the country's self-imposed isolation from the world and its economic impoverishment by 1969. On the one hand, proponents of a national interest approach might object that this could have been the unexpected result of sensible, but ultimately unsuccessful, policies. However, belligerent self-isolation from the world and the insistence on ideological correctness rather than the pursuit of friendly external relations and economic prosperity were *conscious* policy choices by Mao. Barbara Tuchman called such a pursuit of policy contrary to the country's interest a "folly."[16] On the other hand, adherents of the national interest interpretation might argue that Mao misperceived China's national interest, but by doing so they merely acknowledge that national interest is dependent on another variable at the heart of the split. In essence, Mao's pursuit of what he considered to be China's global interests poses a methodological problem for existing academic definitions of national interest. Only if one accepts Mao's extreme conviction that China's national interest was its duty to spread world revolution aggressively or to follow his brilliant policy of withdrawing the PRC from a putrid world into the splendid isolation of a solitary model society, one might agree that Mao acted in the country's national interest.

Nationalism similarly seems not to have been a major contributing factor in the Sino-Soviet Split. Certainly, the Chinese Communists had been nationalists even before they became communists in the early 1920s, and Mao appealed to Chinese national feelings when he claimed that the PRC was the center of world revolution in the 1960s. These, however, were subsidiary aspects rather than central factors in his pursuit of policies that were designed to prove the ideological correctness of Chinese Communist—that is, his own—positions in the leadership conflict at home and in the struggle against Soviet ideological revisionism.

---

[16] Barbara Tuchman, *The March of Folly* (New York: Knopf, 1984).

Explanations that rely on the relative changes in the strategic triangle between the PRC, the USSR, and the United States also seem unsuccessful in explaining the Sino-Soviet Split. The vast majority of the literature focuses on the period after the late 1960s and thus is outside the scope of this book.[17] Although some authors have applied it to the post-1949 period,[18] others have suggested that the strategic triangle has limited or even no explanatory power because China was too weak to count as a great power during the years covered in this book.[19] I tend to agree with the critics of the triangular concept, though for different reasons. Despite its descriptive appeal, there is little evidence from the post-1949 period that can support its claims. While it is true that the Sino-Soviet alliance was directed against the United States, and that the Americans tried to drive a wedge into the partnership, no documentary evidence that the Chinese or the Soviets *thought* about their relationship within a triangular framework during the period covered in this book has surfaced. Maoist thinking from the 1940s to the 1960s proceeded from the assumption of a Sino-American conflict over the *intermediate zone*—basically, over the rest of the world.[20] Thus, when Mao's PRC turned away from the Soviet Union in the 1960s, it did not turn toward the United States but toward one of the two intermediate zones he had just redefined, claiming to be the head of, even the model for, the international movement of national liberation in the Asian-African-Latin American intermediate zone (the other intermediate zone, according to this idea, consisted of Europe and other developed countries). Similarly, in 1949, Moscow looked at Beijing as an asset in its world revolutionary enterprise that had fallen into its lap rather fortuitously. In the end, the triangular concept is, methodologically speaking, an ahistorical model that greatly limits the ability to explain the inner dynamics of the split.

[17] Schwartz, "Moscow-Peking-Washington Triangle." Griffith, "The World and the Great-Power Triangles." Garrett, "China Policy and the Strategic Triangle." William Hyland, "The Sino-Soviet Conflict," Richard Solomon, *The China Factor* (Englewood Cliffs: Prentice-Hall, 1981), 137–158.

[18] Zagoria, "Strange Triangle." Tatu, *Great Power Triangle*. Scalapino, "American-Soviet-Chinese Triangle." Richard Ashley, *The Political Economy of War and Peace* (London: Pinter, 1980). Harvey Nelson, *Power and Insecurity* (Boulder: Lynne Rienner, 1989). Gordon Chang, *Friends and Enemies* (Stanford: Stanford, 1990). Lowell Dittmer, *Sino-Soviet Normalization and Its International Implications, 1945–1990* (Seattle: Washington, 1992), 147.

[19] Gerald Segal, *The Great Power Triangle* (Houndsmills: Macmillan, 1982). Chen Min, *The Strategic Triangle and Regional Conflicts* (Boulder: Lynne Rienner, 1992). Chi Su even implied that China was too weak for most of the Cold War period to act as a true equal in such a triangular relationship: "The Strategic Triangle and China's Soviet Policy," Robert Ross, ed., *China, the United States, and the Soviet Union* (Armonk: Sharpe, 1993), 39–61.

[20] For an older, but still very good description: King Chen, *China and the Three Worlds* (White Plains: Sharpe, 1979).

In a related discussion, scholars have addressed the U.S. role in the Sino-Soviet Split. The focus on an outside factor, however, also tends to obscure rather than explain the inner dynamics of the split. There is no evidence that "the root cause of the Sino-Soviet dispute was . . . the fear of [a] potential [U.S.] nuclear attack that made the Soviet leadership ignore Chinese interests in favor of détente with the West," as one author maintained.[21] Similarly, the study of American policies toward the Sino-Soviet alliance tends to overestimate their effects on it.[22] In general, I contend that American policies—including the wedge strategy that attempted to split the alliance through a combination of punishments and enticements—only worked in the later stages of the Sino-Soviet breakup, thereby exacerbating a process that had started for independent reasons.

Those authors who have investigated the role of domestic politics in the split have pointed out important pieces of the puzzle. There is no doubt that Khrushchev's de-Stalinization, though launched mainly for domestic reasons, reverberated throughout the socialist world. The central question is why only Mao's China (together with Enver Hoxha's Albania) sought sharp conflict with the Soviet Union while most other socialist states and communist parties merely used de-Stalinization to enhance their autonomy. In my view, it was China's internal conditions that provided a ripe environment for ideological radicalism in the late 1950s and the manipulation of ideology for domestic aims throughout the 1960s.

The greater availability of primary documentation helps to refine the scholarly understanding of how domestic politics influenced Sino-Soviet relations. Roderick MacFarquhar's three volumes on the origins of the Cultural Revolution provided abundant evidence for the important role of Chinese domestic politics in the Sino-Soviet Split. While these tomes supplied many important details for this book, their focus was not primarily on the increasingly close links between internal and external Chinese behavior I identify during the 1956–66 period.[23]

Writing on Sino-American relations, Thomas Christensen asserted in the mid-1990s that Cold War powers manipulated foreign crises to mobilize their own citizens for domestic aims. In a case study on the Second Taiwan Strait Crisis, he argued that Mao exploited an international crisis in order to mobilize the Chinese people to support the launching of the

---

[21] Nelson, *Power and Insecurity*, 30.

[22] Chang, *Friends and Enemies*.

[23] Roderick MacFarquhar, *Origins of the Cultural Revolution*, 3 vols. (New York: Columbia, 1974–1997). Although the first two volumes are based on a wealth of public Chinese materials, only the third could take advantage of the greater availability of new Chinese sources.

radical Great Leap Forward.[24] More recently, Chen Jian has pushed this argument further, claiming that Mao's concerns over the revolution at home led him to create foreign enemies with the aim to keep the Chinese people mobilized.[25] Both thus argue that foreign policy was mustered for domestic objectives. Although my findings support both Christensen's and Chen's interpretations, I suggest that this process could work both ways. While domestic needs shaped foreign policy, as in the Second Taiwan Strait Crisis, events abroad, such as the Polish October or the Hungarian Revolution, greatly influenced Mao's thinking and his domestic policies. Even as Mao was willing to provoke crises in international affairs to mobilize the Chinese people—or at least to render pressure on internal opponents, real or invented—there were also instances where he mobilized domestic policies in order to influence international affairs. His attempts to create a model communist society during the Great Leap Forward were certainly supposed to underscore his claim to the leadership of the socialist camp.

THE ROLE OF IDEOLOGY

The story of the Sino-Soviet breakup cannot be told without a focus on ideology. I identify ideology broadly as a set of beliefs and dogmas that both construct general outlines—rather than a detailed blueprint—of a future political order, and define specific methods—though no explicit pathways—to achieve it. In line with this characterization, Marxism-Leninism envisioned the communist society as the final objective of history, and granted the communist party the exclusive vanguard role in this process, at the expense of all other political movements or even the democratic process itself. Although Marx and Lenin wrote in great detail about how communism would look like once it was achieved, they in fact left relatively few concrete cues on the exact path of transforming the bourgeois present into the communist future.

In daily politics, ideology functions both as a belief system and as a political tool. On the one hand, ideology is about the political commitments made by its adherents to its theoretical postulates. Consequently, ideological claims tend to be claims in principle. Similarly, ideological disagreements that arise within the general outlines or as the result of the contradictions within the theory often are disagreements in principle. The unsophisticated understanding of theoretical postulates by their believers can exacerbate ideological disagreements. On the other hand, ideology

---

[24] Thomas Christensen, *Useful Adversaries* (Princeton: Princeton, 1996).
[25] Chen Jian, *Mao's China and the Cold War* (Chapel Hill: North Carolina, 2001).

may be manipulated for short-term political, or even personal, objectives. Such manipulation might happen inside the general outlines of ideology when, for example, a leader exploits theoretical ambiguities or contradictions to his political or personal benefit. However, ideological claims might also be cynically used for objectives incongruent with theoretical postulates. Methodologically, these two forms of manipulation are not always easy to distinguish.

The available evidence suggests that both the Chinese Communists and the Soviets genuinely believed that they were working toward the realization of the communist dream. For the most part, in my view at least, neither used the high-sounding promises of Marxism-Leninism in purely cynical fashion. However, the theoretical ambiguities of Marxism-Leninism, combined with each side's underdeveloped understanding thereof, provided the two sides not only with ample opportunities for disagreement over their long-term domestic and foreign policies—both of which were at the root of the Sino-Soviet conflict—but also with a tool to achieve short-term political gains either against each other or against internal dissenters. Thus, although the ideological objective of Marxism-Leninism—the creation of a communist society—was clearly defined, the theoretically correct path to achieve it was sufficiently indeterminate to create discord both in principle and in daily political life.

Most previous authors tended to underestimate the disruptive role of ideology in the Sino-Soviet Split. In 1961, without the hindsight of history, Zagoria attributed great binding force to the shared ideology of the Sino-Soviet allies.[26] Similarly, interpretations of the Sino-Soviet Split that stress the rhetorical role of ideology or the ideologically influenced threat perceptions of a defensive China also seemed to undervalue the role of ideology itself.[27] Those authors who pointed out the intrinsic potential of dogmatic Marxism-Leninism to create discord correctly identified the ideological roots of the collapse of socialist unity in the period after Khrushchev's Secret Speech.[28] However, since most communist parties continued to maintain satisfactory, though not always cordial, relations with each other, disagreements on ideological principles alone cannot adequately explain the reasons for China's (and Albania's) split from the Soviet Union and, by extension, from the socialist world. Only specific internal conditions, such as the manipulative use of ideology, can achieve this.

My view of the role of ideology in the Sino-Soviet Split differs slightly from other interpretations that have previously benefited from the new

[26] Zagoria, *Sino-Soviet Conflict.*
[27] Michael, "Common Purpose and Double Strategy." Gurtov, *China under Threat.*
[28] Lowenthal, *World Communism.* Morgenthau, *New Foreign Policy for the United States.*

archival evidence. For example, I tend to give more weight to ideology than O. Arne Westad, who argued that it was "not sufficient to explain the breakdown in Sino-Soviet relations."[29] Without the vital role of ideology, neither would the alliance have been established nor would it have collapsed. Chen Jian's recent claim that the domestic mission of the revolution shaped its international mission and that foreign policy—even to the extent that "Mao acted to create an enemy" in international relations—functioned as a "source of domestic mobilization" is closer to the view presented in this book.[30] However, I take his interpretation even further, arguing that either policy realm, foreign and domestic, could influence—or even mobilize—the other. Moreover, I argue that Mao created international crises, not merely foreign enemies, for his domestic needs.

By the same token, the roles of security and economics in the Sino-Soviet Split cannot be understood without reference to ideology. It is true that, since the fall of 1950, American military might threatened China on the Korean peninsula. Equally, the military situation in the Taiwan Strait during the 1950s and in Indochina starting in the mid-1960s changed to China's disadvantage. However, these security threats were not the result of an inherent U.S. imperialist aggressiveness, as Mao and his comrades believed, but were largely the consequence of Chinese Communist commitments to world revolution since the 1920s—that is, to the overthrow of the imperialist international system that happened to be headed by the United States since 1945—and of Mao's assertive security policies since the late-1949 establishment of the PRC. Once Beijing recognized Hanoi diplomatically in early 1950 and committed itself to Pyongyang even before the Korean War, Washington's military and political responses turned Mao's beliefs about imperialist aggression into self-fulfilling prophecies. Furthermore, the Soviet policy of peaceful coexistence with the United States, which Khrushchev had been promoting since early 1956, did not undermine Chinese security (with regard to American military support for the Republic of China in Taiwan), as some observers have argued, but it was a point of ideological dispute between Mao and Khrushchev. By the late 1950s, firmly persuaded by the supposed might of the Soviet missile that carried Sputnik into space in 1957 and uncritically applying crude Leninist interpretations on the inherent inability of capitalists to cooperate with each other, Mao was convinced that imperialism was weak and internally split. Given this ideological preconception of the world, the Chinese leader simply could not understand why Khrushchev sought Soviet-American rapprochement.

[29] O. Arne Westad, "Introduction," Westad, ed., *Brothers in Arms* (Washington: Woodrow Wilson Center, 1998), 4.
[30] Chen, *Mao's China and the Cold War*, 7–8, 180.

Likewise, it is true that the structural economic problems the PRC faced in 1955 were genuine and that they threatened the material health of China. However, the solutions Mao proposed—first the Socialist High Tide, then the Great Leap Forward—were highly ideological, and ultimately poisonous for Sino-Soviet relations. I thus disagree with those authors who believed that "economics was never at the heart of the Sino-Soviet dispute."[31] On the contrary, I support, and even extend, Lowell Dittmer's contention that ideological disagreements over the economic model were a cause of the Sino-Soviet Split.[32] Similar to the ideological underpinnings of the Sino-Soviet economic debates in the second half of the 1950s, Moscow's withdrawal of its specialists from the PRC seems to be, at least superficially, an example of Soviet great power attempts at coercive or punitive diplomacy; in reality, however, it occurred only after antagonistic ideological campaigns by Beijing. Economic disagreements had deep ideological roots.

The findings of this book strengthen various interpretations put forward by New Cold War Historians. Ideology was significant to the policies of the socialist states, at least in the first half of the Cold War.[33] Equally, the Sino-Soviet relationship confirms empirical findings that smaller Cold War allies were often able to set the agenda of their superpower patrons on both sides of the Cold War divide.[34] Many of the arguments put forward by Vojtech Mastny and Malcolm Bryne in a recent study on the Warsaw Pact also apply to this book. Like the Sino-Soviet

[31] Dwight Perkins, "The Economic Background and Implications for China," Ellison, *Sino-Soviet Conflict*, 91–111.

[32] Dittmer, *Sino-Soviet Normalization*.

[33] Vladislav Zubok, *Inside the Kremlin's Cold War* (Cambridge: Harvard, 1996), 4–8. Chen Jian, *Mao's China and the Cold War*.

[34] Abraham Ben-Zvi, *United States and Israel* (New York: Columbia, 1993). Robert McMahon, *The Cold War on the Periphery* (New York: Columbia, 1994). Hope Harrison, *Driving the Soviets up the Wall* (Princeton: Princeton, 2003). A small number of political scientists have tried to assess bilateral, unequal alliances, but rarely addressed the agenda-setting capabilities of the smaller ally, see: Paul M. Johnson, "The Subordinate States and Their Strategies," Jan Triska, ed., *Dominant Powers and Subordinate States: The United States in Latin America and the Soviet Union in East Europe* (Durham: Duke, 1986), 285–309. James Morrow, "Alliances and Asymmetry: An Alternative to the Capability Aggregation Model of Alliances," *American Journal of Political Science* 35/4, 904–933. Some scholars have addressed small states in multilateral alliances and international organizations, see: Mancur Olsen et al., "An Economic Theory of Alliances," *Review of Economics and Statistics* 48/3, 266–79. Baldur Thorhallsson, "The Role of Small States in the European Union," Christine Ingebritsen et al., eds., *Small States in International Relations* (Seattle: Washington, 2006), 218–30. In comparison, the theoretical literature on the behavior of small states in international relations in general is quite developed, as two collections of seminal texts reveal. See several articles in: Triska, *Dominant Powers and Subordinate States*, and Ingebritsen, *Small States in International Relations*.

alliance, the principal socialist pact system ultimately collapsed as a result of the failure of ideology to provide clarity of purpose and unity of means.[35]

ADDITIONAL FACTORS

Apart from ideology, a range of other factors contributed to the Sino-Soviet Split. The PRC was more active in bringing about the breakup than the Soviet Union. Particularly in the 1960s, Beijing controlled the pace of the relationship's deterioration and its eventual collapse, while Moscow was often left having to react to recurring provocations.

This development was rooted in the nature of the Sino-Soviet relationship. The two countries never matched each other in real power or global influence, although Beijing claimed equality with Moscow in 1956–57. In truth, Khrushchev was heading a superpower with increasing commitments around the world, while Mao was running a regional power that was progressively getting poorer and more isolated as a result of his own blunders. For the PRC, the Sino-Soviet alliance it had sought in 1949–50 was *the defining moment* in its early history; for the Soviet Union, the partnership was just *another asset*, though an important one, in its world revolutionary mission. Little wonder that, once disagreements emerged, Beijing invested a lot of energy in reinventing and then divesting itself of the alliance, while Moscow became negligent in maintaining the partnership.

A number of other factors played notable, though less central, roles. The United States was not the immediate cause of the Sino-Soviet Split; its policies, while designed to strain the alliance, turned out to be effective only once Sino-Soviet disagreements had emerged over unrelated issues. Although territorial controversies predated the alliance, it was only the emerging ideological disputes that turned them into points of conflict and, eventually in 1969, into a cause for war.[36] Accidents, such as the U-2 Incident on May 1, 1960, or Soviet Defense Minister Rodion Malinovskii's drunken insult of Mao on November 7, 1964, wreaked havoc on the relationship, but it was the Chinese side that unduly exploited them for its own benefit. Finally, personality clashes contributed

[35] Vojtech Mastny and Malcolm Byrne, eds., *A Cardboard Castle?* (Budapest: Central European, 2005), 1, 73–74.

[36] The best current treatment of China's border problems: M. Taylor Fravel, *Strong Borders, Secure Nation* (Princeton: Princeton, 2008).

to but did not cause the Sino-Soviet Split.[37] Mao's and Khrushchev's strong personalities and their far-reaching, unchecked powers within their respective political systems had an undue, negative influence on the alliance.

IDEOLOGY AND ALLIANCE THEORY

This book further provides an empirical challenge to the theoretical literature on alliances. Political scientists who have explored alliances have mostly concentrated on their formation, which is not the focus of this book.[38] In comparison, the literature on alliance cohesion is less well developed. Because the Sino-Soviet Split occurred when the PRC and the USSR were still weaker than the United States, the implicit Realist assumption that changes in the balance of global power will trigger transformations in alliance systems seems not to apply to the partnership between Beijing and Moscow. Stephen Walt, one of the leading Realist alliance scholars, saw the collapse of the Sino-Soviet alliance not as the result of ideological disagreements but as the consequence of China's security concerns that defied any ideological consideration.[39] Mark Haas argued that while Mao's ideological radicalization during the Great Leap Forward was the "root cause" for the Sino-Soviet disagreements, conflicts resulting from their geographical proximity—territorial disputes and the militarization of the mutual border during the period after 1960—were ultimately responsible for the split.[40]

Although they are not connected to ideology, I concur, though with some qualifications, with several of the internal causes Glenn Snyder has proposed as to why alliances collapse. While the PRC indeed feared entrapment by the Soviet Union, this fear predated the alliance. Snyder's claim that allies try to restrain each other applies to several moments

[37] William Taubman, "Khrushchev vs. Mao," *CWIHP Bulletin* 8–9, 243–48. Aspaturian, "The Domestic Sources." Several Chinese memoirs contain colorful accounts on the personality clashes between Mao and Khrushchev.

[38] Hans Morgenthau, *Politics among Nations*, 6th ed. (New York: Knopf, 1985), 185–240, 360–91. Kenneth Waltz, *Theory of International Relations* (Reading: Addison-Wesley, 1979), 127. Stephen Walt, *The Origins of Alliances* (Ithaca: Cornell, 1987). John Mearsheimer, *The Tragedy of Great Power Politics* (New York: Norton, 2001). Glenn Snyder, *Alliance Politics* (Ithaca: Cornell, 1991), 44. Snyder, "The Security Dilemma in Alliance Politics," *World Politics* 36/4, 464. Dan Reiter, "Learning, Realism, and Alliances: The Weight of the Shadow of the Past," *World Politics* 46/4, 490–526. George Liska, *Nations in Alliance* (Baltimore: Johns Hopkins, 1962), 61–69. Mark Haas, *The Ideological Origins of Great Power Politics, 1789–1989* (Ithaca: Cornell, 2005).

[39] Stephen Walt, *Revolution and War* (Ithaca: Cornell, 1996), 323–27.

[40] Haas, *Ideological Origins*, 168, 174.

in the Sino-Soviet alliance. While it is true that China incited the Soviet Union to demonstrate greater anti-imperialist commitments, it did so not in order to make it fight the United States alone, as Snyder would argue, but in order to force it to join the PRC in such a struggle. Similarly, although Beijing often accused Moscow of failing to live up to alliance commitments, this usually happened over territorial conflicts with third parties that had occurred as a result of Chinese provocations or clumsy diplomacy.[41]

In a twist on alliance theory, Thomas Christensen recently promoted an ingenious argument on the role of ideology in alliance cohesion. Looking at the Sino-Soviet alliance through the lens of U.S. containment, he argued that it was less radical in times of great cohesion (1954–58) because Moscow was better at managing the partnership. In times of internal competition (1958–69), however, the alliance was more revolutionary because both partners vied for the allegiance of other socialist states or revolutionary movements.[42] While I do agree with his counterintuitive insight that ideological conflict might have led to an unintended congruence with the original alliance goals, I also must stress the great destructive force of such ideological competition within the Sino-Soviet alliance even before 1969. The rivalry between Beijing and Moscow for Hanoi's allegiance during the Second Vietnam War complicated Washington's attempts to contain communist expansion in East Asia, but, in my view, it simultaneously demolished the last vestiges of the alliance by 1966.

The Structure of the Book

Chapter 1 explores the background of the Sino-Soviet dispute. It includes accounts of the historical roots of the theoretical debates that rattled the alliance in 1955–66, Sino-Soviet relations since 1921, and the first six years of the alliance. The chapter ends with the emergence of the first major ideological disagreement in the Sino-Soviet relationship—the Socialist High Tide of 1955.

The impact of Khrushchev's Secret Speech of February 1956 on the Sino-Soviet relationship stands at the center of chapter 2. Although the speech briefly checked Mao's preeminence in China's domestic politics, its catalytic effect on Poland and Hungary provided the Chinese leader with an opportunity to rethink the role of Stalinism in China's political and economic development. Over the course of 1957, political developments in the PRC—the failure of Mao's attempt at political liberalization—and

[41] Snyder, *Alliance Politics*, 307–71.
[42] Thomas Christensen, "Worse Than a Monolith," *Asian Security* 1/1, 80–127.

in the Soviet Union—the failure of the remaining Stalinist stalwarts in the Soviet leadership to stop de-Stalinization by overthrowing Khrushchev—set the two countries on paths of political development that were diametrically opposed to one another. Nevertheless, both Beijing and Moscow sought to obscure these disagreements at the Moscow Meeting of the world communist movement in late 1957.

Chapter 3 addresses Mao's double challenge to Khrushchev's leadership of the socialist camp in 1958. The Chinese leader rejected both the contemporaneous Soviet development model in favor of a more radical economic policy—the Great Leap Forward—and peaceful coexistence for a confrontational stance during the Second Taiwan Strait Crisis in August of 1958. Ultimately, the two events were closely linked; military conflict off the coast of the PRC was supposed to help Mao mobilize the Chinese people to participate in the radical policies of the Great Leap Forward.

The connection between domestic and foreign policy was less tangible in the following year (chapter 4). Mao's refusal to address the congenital problems of the Great Leap Forward and his suppression of criticism further radicalized China's political discourse, and thereby produced a negative context for the development of Sino-Soviet relations throughout the year. Although Beijing had not openly provoked the Tibetan Uprising, nor had it started the ensuing Sino-Indian Border War, its clumsy way of dealing with these crises alienated Moscow in the period before Khrushchev's seminal visit to Washington. At the end of the year, both the Chinese Communists and the Soviets reassessed their relationship. Each side nursed misgivings about the other.

Chapter 5 revolves around China's so-called Lenin Polemics and the collapse of economic relations. Mao's decision to make the ideological disagreements public on the occasion of Lenin's ninetieth birthday in April of 1960 reflected his mounting ideological disagreements with Khrushchev. The U-2 Incident on May 1 seemed to confirm his opinion of the inherent aggressiveness of U.S. imperialism. An ideological campaign against the Soviet Union, both within and outside of China, provoked Khrushchev into the punitive action of withdrawing all Soviet advisers from the PRC in July. Although, as a result, economic relations broke down, the eventual collapse of the Great Leap Forward in China and the failure of Soviet-American rapprochement forced Beijing and Moscow to seek reconciliation during the Second Moscow Meeting in late 1960. The ideological compromise reached at the meeting, however, was only temporary.

From early 1961 to mid-1962, Sino-Soviet relations experienced a period of ambiguity (chapter 6). The collapse of the Great Leap Forward had limited Mao's prerogatives to set China's domestic and foreign policies. The country's internal needs led to sound economic reform policies, promoted by other Chinese leaders against Mao's desires, and even to related Sino-Soviet cooperation. At the same time, Mao tried to seize on Sino-Soviet disagreements over de-Stalinization and Albania in 1961 in order to keep pressure on Khrushchev. Ultimately, though, he was unable to prevent high-ranking party cadres from calling for a less radical foreign policy. While the PRC seemed to embark on moderate domestic and foreign policies in the first half of 1962, the sudden outbreak of ethnic conflict in Xinjiang and the mass flight of ethnic Central Asians and Russians to the Soviet Union taxed the relations between Beijing and Moscow.

The following two chapters cover the intertwined stories of the period from mid-1962 to mid-1963. Chapter 7 starts with Mao's political resurgence in the summer of 1962. After accusing his fellow leaders of propagating the reintroduction of capitalism in China's economy at the Beidaihe work conference, he was able to reclaim the preeminent position in daily policy making. Subsequently, he terminated the relaxation of Sino-Soviet relations and exploited Khrushchev's public humiliation during the Cuban Missile Crisis. By early 1963, Mao had decided to work actively for the Sino-Soviet Split, though he sought to achieve it in ways that would force Khrushchev to assume responsibility.

Chapter 8 deals with U.S. President John Kennedy's attempt to instrumentalize the rift for the conclusion of the Limited Nuclear Test Ban (LNTB) treaty that, among other aims, was supposed to prevent China from acquiring nuclear know-how or even isolate the PRC internationally. In the summer of 1963, Sino-Soviet reconciliation talks, requested by the Vietnamese Communists, and the Soviet–British–American test ban negotiations were held simultaneously in Moscow. While the former failed as a result of Mao's uncompromising position, the Soviet Union and the United States were able to make a sufficient amount of concessions to reach a minimal agreement.

The final two chapters address the collapse of Sino-Soviet party and military relations. Internationally isolated after the LNTB treaty, Mao increased the ideological attacks on the Soviet revisionists in propaganda and at the five communist party congresses in Europe in the period from mid-1963 to mid-1964 (chapter 9). The shrill and redundant anti-Soviet claims were related to his goal of pressuring domestic opponents, real and invented, into ideological and political acquiescence. Firm in his belief that Khrushchev's fall would mean a return of the Soviet comrades to correct—that is, to his own—theoretical positions, Mao misunderstood the October 1964 leadership changes in Moscow. When he realized that the new Soviet leaders had hardly modified Khrushchev's foreign policies, he knew that anti-Soviet propaganda had failed to cow his domestic opponents into political submission. Starting in early 1965, Mao thus used anti-Soviet positions to prepare for a purge of what he called revisionists and capitalists within the party leadership. With that, the collapse of the Sino-Soviet partnership had become a function of domestic politics. The mid-1966 launch of the party purge in the Cultural Revolution thus required the complete abrogation of Sino-Soviet party relations.

This ideological development set the stage for the collapse of Sino-Soviet military relations over the early Second Vietnam War (chapter 10). The U.S. escalation of the Indochina conflict paralleled the leadership changes in Moscow. Khrushchev's hands-off policy toward Vietnam was among the few policies the new Soviet leaders revised completely and quickly. Although the U.S. escalation and the sudden Soviet willingness to provide massive military aid to North Vietnam created security problems for China in early 1965, Mao's unconstructive response was ideologically predetermined. The Sino-Soviet military relationship collapsed in 1965–66 not because of Moscow's failure to honor the alliance's anti-imperialist spirit, but as a result of Beijing's attempt to redefine it as a tool for radical policies that reflected Mao's distinct, ideological goals.

Historical Background, 1921–1955

THE OCTOBER REVOLUTION in 1917 was Vladimir Lenin's opening shot for world revolution. Once power was consolidated, the Bolshevik party faced two new tasks: deepening the revolution at home and extending it abroad. Socialist construction was supposed to make the revolution irreversible in Russia. As described in the first part of this chapter, it promised a socioeconomic development alternative to the allegedly exploitative characteristics of capitalism. From 1921 to 1941, three major development models emerged: the *New Economic Policy* (*NEP*) in the 1920s, *Revolutionary Stalinism* in the late 1920s and early 1930s, and *Bureaucratic Stalinism* afterward. The last was the model the Soviet Union exported to its East European satellite states after 1945.

The second part of this chapter addresses the impact of Lenin's call to export world revolution to China. The Comintern, Lenin's International of Communist Parties that was founded in 1919, was supposed to foment anti-capitalist revolutions in Europe; in the colonial world, it aimed at provoking anti-imperialist insurgencies, designed to overthrow imperialism and thereby contribute to anti-capitalist revolutions in Europe. For that purpose, the Comintern sponsored the foundation of the Chinese Communist Party (CCP) in 1921. Yet, by the late 1920s, when Iosif Stalin refashioned the Comintern from a revolutionary internationalist organization into a tool for Soviet security, its offshoot parties throughout the world fell victim to narrow Soviet interests or outright indifference. In China, the CCP gradually developed its own brand of ideology. After the Second World War, it reemerged as a powerful party in the impending final act of the Chinese civil war, with clear ideas about its position in the world at large.

With the establishment of the Sino-Soviet alliance, as covered in the third part of this chapter, the newly founded People's Republic of China (PRC) became a part of the socialist camp. Unlike the East European states, China voluntarily joined on the assumption that only the anti-capitalist and anti-imperialist Soviet Union would support the PRC in its struggle to regain prosperity and international standing. The end of this chapter and the next chapter show that the Stalinization of the Chinese political and economic system as well as Beijing's overestimation of Moscow's anti-imperialist commitments provided one source for the Sino-Soviet disagreements.

Soviet Development Models

As a result of the civil war following the October Revolution in 1917 and Lenin's erratic economic policies, Soviet Russia was on the brink of economic collapse in 1921. Sounding a temporary retreat from revolution, the Bolshevik leadership decided to embark on the New Economic Policy. Low taxes-in-kind, market mechanisms, and various forms of rural organizations were supposed to stimulate peasant and artisan production and thereby fuel its surplus into the development of the whole economy. In view of Maoist rural development strategies in the 1950s, it is important to focus on the rural communes (*kommuna*). Lenin had promoted them as early as 1919 as the form of social organization closest to the Paris Commune of 1871, which Marxist-Leninists considered to be the prototype of a communist society. Common characteristics in most of the communes were the absence of personal property, collective labor, and communal living. Scarce evidence suggests that most communes did not work well. Once forced collectivization started, they lost their political viability.[1]

From its very start, NEP was the focus of fierce ideological debates among the Bolsheviks. Leftist critics saw rural liberalization as a threat to what they believed to be the essential equilibrium in the development pace of all economic sectors—heavy industry, light industry, and agriculture.[2] But Nikolai Bukharin, the primary architect of NEP, rejected the proposed compulsory grain requisition as war against the peasants. He hoped that a slow development pace of all economic sectors would eventually forestall the problems raised by his critics.[3]

After Lenin's death in 1923, Stalin supported Bukharin, solely because he needed him to oust the leftist critics of NEP for unrelated reasons.[4] Once they were gone, Stalin adopted their political platform and turned against Bukharin.[5] The Soviet leader justified this sudden change by warning of capitalist restoration: "Either *back*—to capitalism, or *forward*—to

---

[1] Dmitri Volkogonov, *Lenin* (New York: Free, 1994), 309. Martin Malia, *Soviet Tragedy* (New York: Free, 1994), 97, 105, 143-47, 153. Viktor Danilov, *Sovetskaya dokolkhoznaya derevnya* (Moskva: Nauka, 1977), 107. Richard Stites, *Revolutionary Dreams* (New York: Oxford, 1989), 207–12.

[2] Evgenii Preobrazhenskii, *Crisis of Soviet Industrialization* (White Plains: Sharpe, 1979).

[3] Kenneth Tarbuck, *Bukharin's Theory of Equilibrium* (London: Pluto, 1989), 6–33, 126–44. Alexander Ehrlich, "Stalinism and Marxian Growth Models," Robert Tucker, ed., *Stalinism* (New York: Norton, 1977), 141–42. Stephen Cohen, *Bukharin and the Bolshevik Revolution* (New York: Knopf, 1973), 160–212.

[4] Tarbuck, *Bukharin's Theory*, 6–33, 126–44. Cohen, *Bukharin*, 160–212.

[5] Robert Tucker, *Stalin in Power* (New York: Norton, 1990), 69, 81. Malia, *Soviet Tragedy*, 22–223.

socialism." His long-term aim, as he wrote in 1929, was to develop agriculture with the aim to fuel the growth of socialist industry.[6]

Revolutionary Stalinism,[7] the model following NEP, combined unbalanced (or shocklike) development in agriculture and industry and the use of force against whole groups of the population.[8] Stalin justified his policies with an appeal to Lenin: "When the New Economic Policy was introduced, Lenin said: We are now retreating . . . in order to prepare for a longer *leap forward*."[9] The brutality of forced collectivization left peasants demoralized and rural production depressed.[10] In his notorious "Dizzy with Success" article of March 1930, Stalin shifted the blame for excesses onto low-ranking officials.[11] Mao Zedong would do the same in 1959 when his Great Leap Forward in the PRC faltered. The costs of forced collectivization in the Soviet Union were as staggering as they would be in China three decades later: millions of displaced peasants and deadly famines.[12]

Forced collectivization paralleled the hurried development of socialist industry. Bolshevism always upheld the dogma of developing heavy industry first. But state-sponsored voluntarism and the storming mentality of shock work produced imbalanced giant projects that seldom functioned, individually or collectively. Despite the existence of a Five-Year Plan (FYP; 1929–33), Revolutionary Stalinism sacrificed planning.[13] The Chinese Great Leap Forward, thirty years later, would suffer from similar problems. But unlike Mao in the late 1950s, Stalin soon realized that state-sponsored enthusiasm was not capable of replacing petty material incentives for proletarians. In 1931, he claimed that the hitherto sacred Bolshevik dogma of an egalitarian society "breaks with Marxism, breaks with Leninism."[14] Scaled wages according to individual productivity and skills were reintroduced.[15]

---

[6] Iosif Stalin, "Concerning Questions of Agrarian Policy in the USSR," 12/27/1929, Stalin, *Works*, vol. 12 (Moscow: Foreign Languages, 1954), 151–52.

[7] I drew this term from Tucker, *Stalin in Power*.

[8] Moshe Lewin, "Baseline," Robert Daniels, ed., *Stalin Revolution*, 4th ed. (Boston: Houghton Mifflin, 1997), 37–40.

[9] Stalin, "Socialist Drive," Daniels, *Stalin Revolution*, 60 (italics mine).

[10] Malia, *Soviet Tragedy*, 195–97. Tucker, *Stalin in Power*, 182–86, 195–215. Sheila Fitzpatrick, *Stalin's Peasants* (New York: Oxford, 1994), 48–62.

[11] Stalin, "Dizzy with Success," 3/2/1930, Stalin, *Works*, vol. 12, 197–205. Leszek Kolakowski, *Main Currents of Marxism*, vol. 3 (Oxford: Oxford, 1978), 39.

[12] Fitzpatrick, *Stalin's Peasants*, 69–76. Malia, *Soviet Tragedy*, 198–99.

[13] Malia, *Soviet Tragedy*, 184–89, 195–96, 206. Lewin, "Baseline," 36–40. Chris Ward, *Stalin's Russia* (London: Edward Arnold, 1993), 77–82.

[14] Stalin, "New Conditions—New Tasks in Economic Construction," 6/23/1931, Iosif Stalin, *Leninism* (London: Lawrence and Wishart, 1942), 207.

[15] Malia, *Soviet Tragedy*, 204–6.

Similar to the Great Leap Forward (1958–60) and the Cultural Revolution in the PRC (1966–76), Revolutionary Stalinism used negative and positive propaganda to elicit popular compliance. As to the first, in 1927–28 Stalin used the collapse of Soviet-British relations, the breakdown of economic negotiations with France, and the bloody end of the united front in China in 1927 to create a war scare that was designed to help implement the radical changes described above.[16] With regard to positive incentives, a cultural revolution launched in early 1928 aimed at grooming a proletarian awareness in the Soviet working class. Similar to the Chinese Cultural Revolution, its primary method was to tap into the socioeconomic frustrations of the traditionally underprivileged in an effort to destroy old customary habits and beliefs. As in China four decades later, the persecution of political dissenters and show trials against alleged wreckers not only served to liquidate opponents within and outside of the party, but it also functioned as a mobilization strategy.[17]

Already many of the characteristics of Revolutionary Stalinism were fading away before the seventeenth party congress in early 1934 officially announced "Socialism Victorious."[18] Imbalanced and leaplike development was discarded because collectivization and industrialization had been completed, or so it was claimed. The second FYP instead launched "consolidation" as a new slogan.[19] The gradual return to a less irrational and more balanced economic development marked the start of what we shall call here *Bureaucratic Stalinism*. To be sure, it was not a static approach, but evolved over two decades and a world war, and endured far beyond Stalin's death in 1953. During the late 1930s, features of Revolutionary Stalinism continued to coexist with characteristics of the emerging Bureaucratic Stalinism.

The repudiation, in practice, of the Marxist-Leninist vision of a classless or even stateless society was one of the central characteristics that remained constant throughout Bureaucratic Stalinism. All spheres of economic and noneconomic life were exclusively run by a vast administrative system, as Stalin proclaimed in 1935: "Cadres decide everything."[20] In 1957, Milovan Djilas, the Yugoslav communist-turned-dissident, called this societal

[16] Malia, *Soviet Tragedy*, 191–92. Tucker, *Stalin in Power*, 74–80, 165–71.

[17] Sheila Fitzpatrick, "Cultural Revolution as Class War," Fitzpatrick, ed., *Cultural Revolution in Russia, 1928–1931* (Bloomington: Indiana, 1978), 8–40.

[18] "The Second Five-Year Plan of Development of the National Economy of the USSR (1933–1937)," CPSU, *Socialism Victorious* (New York: International, n.y.), 639.

[19] Manfred Hildermeier, *Geschichte der Sowjetunion, 1917–1991* (München: Beck, 1998), 480–506.

[20] Stalin, "Address to the Graduates of the Red Army Academies," 5/4/1935, Stalin, *Leninism*, 364.

stratification the new (bureaucratic or party) class.[21] This, and the intro-duction of multilayered wage differences, did not prevent Stalin from an-nouncing in late 1936 that class struggle had ended in the Soviet Union.[22] Bureaucratic Stalinism was a class society without class struggle.

While Revolutionary and Bureaucratic Stalinism implicitly rejected the Marxist-Leninist postulate of the state withering away, Stalin's rule wit-nessed the vanishing of the old Bolshevik party with its limited internal democracy. Conventional wisdom defines Stalin's personality cult as the all-pervasive worship of his person. By 1956, however, his successor, Khrushchev, considered the personality cult an arbitrary and criminal rule.[23] The cult legitimized Stalin's purging of rivals, their constituen-cies, and other real or imagined dissenters.[24] Mao similarly exploited his personality cult in the Cultural Revolution, ridding the CCP of real and invented opponents. The cult also helped Stalin to dispel any suspicions that had arisen about the legitimacy of his rule following Lenin's death. Starting in 1929, the date of its formal institutionalization, it was his manifest effort, driven by his emotional and psychological needs, to cre-ate genuine popularity. Ultimately, only victory over Nazi Germany in World War II helped to achieve this.[25]

Sino-Soviet Relations, 1921–1949

By the time the CCP established the PRC in 1949 after almost four de-cades of internal conflict, China had tried modernization for over a cen-tury. Despite the inability of the Qing Dynasty (1644–1911) to embrace political and economic changes, a number of Chinese officials and intel-lectuals had initiated reform debates, designed to restore China to former glory and power. The collapse of imperial governmental institutions at the beginning of the twentieth century prompted a burgeoning of com-peting political movements that all, to various degrees, sought to fuse past Chinese experiences with modern imported ideas. Among the many movements was a small, fractured leftist group in search of a political

[21] Milovan Djilas, *New Class* (New York: Praeger, 1957), 37–69.

[22] Fitzpatrick, "Cultural Revolution," 34–40.

[23] A. Artisov et al., eds., *Reabilitatsia* (Moskva: Mezhdunarodnyi fond 'Demokratiya,' 2000), 8–11.

[24] Malia, *Soviet Tragedy*, 183–84, 229, 243–70. Ward, *Stalin's Russia*, 108–49. Tucker, *Stalin in Power*, 2–3, 162–71, 366–409, 415–78. Robert Conquest, *Great Terror* (New York: Oxford, 1990), 438.

[25] Dmitri Volkogonov, *Stalin* (New York: Grove Weidenfeld, 1988), 76–84. Hildermeier, *Geschichte*, 788–800. Rudolf Pikhoya, *Sovetskii Soyuz* (Novosibirsk: Sibirskii Khronograf, 2000), 176, 233.

vehicle able to translate its nascent political ideas into reality. In 1921, Comintern agents, sent from Moscow to China to identify potential vanguard parties able to spark revolution, provided it with the Leninist party apparatus necessary for effective action. These Chinese leftists were particularly attracted by the ideological assessment that Lenin's Soviet Russia was the only proletarian, anti-imperialist, and anti-bourgeois country devoted to the liberation of other countries from the yoke of an unjust, imperialist international order.[26]

At the time of its foundation, CCP membership was tiny. To the dismay of Moscow's agents, the CCP could hardly agree on a program. The party developed only after the influx of radicalized work students returning from France, the emergence of a small working class in Guangzhou and Shanghai, and after its Comintern-induced entry into a united front with the dominant *Guomindang* (Nationalist Party) in 1923.[27] The united front collapsed in the summer of 1927 when the Guomindang bloodily turned on its smaller ally. The Comintern advised the remnants of the CCP to stage insurrections, which led to further decimation of the party. Three decades later, Mao Zedong and Zhou Enlai held Stalin personally responsible for these disasters. In reality, by 1927 the Comintern had become a plaything in the power struggles in Moscow.[28]

For Mao, the collapse of the united front was a chance to implement his own ideas of political mobilization. In late 1927, he found himself in the Jinggangshan area at the Hunan-Jiangxi border conducting radical land reform among impoverished peasants. The experiment and its collapse a year later put Mao in direct opposition to Stalin. His ultraleftist rural revolution stood in contradiction to the liberal NEP policies the Soviet leader had not yet abolished. The Jinggangshan experiment collapsed just when Stalin launched his own experiment in radical rural policies.[29]

---

[26] June Grasso et al., *Modernization and Revolution in China*, rev. ed. (Armonk: Sharpe, 1997), 34–71. Liao Kuang-sheng, *Antiforeignism and Modernization in China, 1860–1980* (Hong Kong: Chinese University, 1984), 21–37. Arif Dirlik, *Origins of Chinese Communism* (New York: Oxford, 1989). Tony Saich et al., eds., *Rise to Power of the Chinese Communist Party* (Armonk: Sharpe, 1996), 3. Michael Sheng, *Battling Western Imperialism* (Princeton: Princeton, 1997), 5–7.

[27] Alexander Pantsov, *Bolsheviks and the Chinese Revolution, 1919–1927* (Richmond: Curzon, 2000). Dirlik, *Origins*. Saich, *Rise*, 3–276. Hans van de Ven, *From Friend to Comrade* (Berkeley: California, 1991). Natalya Mamaeva, *Komintern i Gomindan, 1919–1929* (Moskva: ROSSPEN, 1999). Tony Saich, ed., *Origins of the First United Front in China*, 2 vols. (Leiden: Brill, 1991). Dan Jacobs, *Borodin* (Cambridge: Harvard, 1981).

[28] Saich, *Rise*, 277–330. Wu Lengxi, *Shinian lunzhan, 1956–1966* [WLX] (Beijing: Zhongyang wenxian, 1999), 12–13, 315. "Record of Conversation, Soviet Beijing Ambassador Pavel Iudin and Mao Zedong," 3/31/1956, Westad, *Brothers*, 336.

[29] Mao, "The National Revolution and the Peasant Movement," 9/1/1926, Stuart Schram, *Mao's Road to Power*, vol. 2 (Armonk: Sharpe, 1992), 387–88. Mao, "Remarks on the

In late 1928, the CCP decided to consolidate its fractured holdings in a couple of rural base areas in various parts of China. The most famous was the Jiangxi Soviet, where Mao soon arrived as well. Taking his own slogan "Seeking Truth from Facts" to heart, Mao concluded from the Jinggangshan experiment that only a gradual rural strategy would lead to success in the long term. He thereby found himself again in opposition, not only to Stalin's new policy of forced collectivization, but also to the CCP leadership that favored either the continuation of the urban insurrection strategy (Li Lisan, 1927–31) or followed the Comintern line of rural radicalism (Wang Ming, 1931–34).[30]

The Long March (October 1934–October 1935) from southern Jiangxi to another CCP base in the barren high plateau in Shaanxi, which would become the Yan'an base area, was not only *the formative experience* for the CCP but also witnessed the start of Mao's rise in the party. The Zunyi (Guizhou) party conference in January 1935 censured the previous CCP leadership for its mistakes in Jiangxi. In the following years, Mao slowly increased his power simply because he was not associated with the erroneous decisions made during the Jiangxi period. Officially a military assistant to Zhou Enlai, he superseded his superior and emerged as the chairman of the Military Affairs Commission (MAC), the most powerful organization in the CCP until 1949.[31]

The impoverished Yan'an base area did not possess any industry capable of fueling the Chinese Communist war effort against the Guomindang or the Japanese. Its only asset was its defensibility. The Yan'an decade nevertheless produced three powerful *myths* Mao would use for his own political needs in the Great Leap Forward and the Cultural Revolution. The first myth, people's war, was his response to the conventional military superiority of the CCP's enemies; it combined light armament, high mobility, the use of strategic depth, the human factor (political awareness), and the reliance on the civilian population for intelligence

---

Report of the Representative of the International at the August 7 Emergency Conference," 8/7/1927, Schram, *Mao's Road*, vol. 3, 31. Mao, "Hunan Problem," Schram, vol. 3, 11. Schram, *Mao's Road*, vol. 3, xxiv–xxxiv, xlii–xliii. John Rue, *Mao Tse-tung in Opposition, 1927–1935* (Stanford: Hoover, 1966), 59, 119–25.

[30] Robert North, *Moscow and the Chinese Communists*, 2nd ed. (Stanford: Stanford, 1963), 122–60. Saich, *Rise*, 341–654. Rue, *Mao*, 125–265. Schram, *Mao's Road*, vol. 3, xlii–xliv, vol. 4, xxviii–lxv. Richard Thornton, *Comintern and the Chinese Communists, 1928–1931* (Seattle: Washington, 1969). Thomas Kampen, *Mao Zedong, Zhou Enlai and the Evolution of the Chinese Communist Leadership* (Copenhagen: Nordic Institute for Asian Studies, 2000), 38–65.

[31] Rue, *Mao*, 266–86. Jonathan Spence, *Search for Modern China*, 2nd ed. (New York: Norton, 1999), 397–403. Frederick Teiwes, *Formation of the Maoist Leadership* (London: London, 1994), 43–47. Kampen, *Mao*, 66–77.

gathering, shelter, and supplies. Yet, people's war was hardly used in the conflict against the Japanese (besides sabotage acts behind enemy lines), and during the final years of the civil war against the Guomindang conventional warfare proved to be superior.[32] The second myth derived from the small-scale governmental administration and the military-style supply system that poverty and lack of resources at the Yan'an base area forced the CCP to adopt. During the Great Leap Forward, Mao declared this primitive form of survival to be the Chinese model of protocommunism.[33] The third myth revolved around the notion that the CCP was a party deeply rooted in the peasantry. In fact, the majority of the party members during the Yan'an years were urbanites and intellectuals, while the peasant mobilization, which Mao marshaled in support of his rural experiments during the Great Leap Forward, was almost nonexistent.[34]

Apart from the creation of these three myths, Yan'an also witnessed the emergence of Mao as a *revolutionary theoretician*. Since the late 1920s, he had been a revolutionary practitioner ready to discard ideological orthodoxy for experiments. His internal adversaries not only considered this to be un-Marxist but also tried to bring the CCP back under Comintern control. After the collapse of the Jiangxi Soviet, Wang Ming stayed in Moscow while many of his associates, the so-called Returned Students, ended up in Yan'an. In order to outmaneuver his rivals, Mao had to formulate a theory that fulfilled three requirements: it had to justify the correctness of his changing views since 1927, it had to be distinguishable from the ideology of the Returned Students, and at the same time it also had to be different from all anti-Stalinist heresies.[35]

Mao's two lectures "On Practice" and "On Contradiction" in the summer of 1937 were his first attempts at theory building.[36] While he endorsed the Marxist-Leninist idea of dialectical progress in history, he stressed to a much greater degree the central role of contradictions for the development of society. In "On Practice," Mao attacked the dogmatic application of Marxist-Leninist theory to reality by referring to Lenin's own rejection of

[32] Edward Dreyer, *China at War, 1901–1949* (London: Longman, 1995), 249–54, 312–70. Mao Zedong, "Problems of Strategy in China's Revolutionary War," Mao, *Selected Works*, vol. 1 (Beijing: Foreign Languages, 1961), 179–254.

[33] Chen Yung-fa, "Blooming Poppy under the Red Sun," Tony Saich et al., eds., *New Perspectives on the Chinese Communist Revolution* (Armonk: Sharpe, 1995), 263–98. Mark Selden, *China in Revolution* (Armonk: Sharpe, 1995).

[34] Mikhail Sladkovskii et al., eds., *Ocherki kommunisticheskoi partii Kitaya, 1921–1969* (Moskva: SSSR AN, Institut Dalnego Vostoka, 1971), 324. Richard Solomon, *Mao's Revolution and the Chinese Political Culture* (Berkeley: California, 1964), 269. Selden, *China*. Pauline Keating, *Two Revolutions* (Stanford: Stanford, 1997).

[35] Raymond Wylie, *Emergence of Maoism* (Stanford: Stanford, 1980), 7, 11–12, 37, 43–44, 47. Rue, *Mao*, 265, 273, 277–78.

[36] Wylie, *Emergence*, 53–59.

the mechanical use of theory during the October Revolution: *"Practice is higher than (theoretical) knowledge."*[37] "On Contradiction" tried to demonstrate the unsuitability of Soviet variations of Marxism—Leninism and Stalinism—to *Chinese* conditions, asserting that they were *russified* Marxism. Thus Marxism had to be *sinified* to be significant to China. Insuring against the possibility of the accusation that he promoted anti-Stalinist heresies, Mao endorsed basic ideas of Revolutionary Stalinism such as imbalanced development, class struggle, and the cultural revolution. At that time, he did not know that Stalin had already abandoned them.[38]

Wang's return to Yan'an in late 1937 was a mixed blessing for Mao. Although Wang conveyed Stalin's acceptance of Mao's de facto leadership of the CCP, the Soviet leader again criticized the Chinese leader's empiricism. Mao's sinification of Marxism became an even more delicate task with the 1938 publication of the Soviet *Short Course*—a Stalinist propaganda history of the Bolshevik party—which Wang promoted in a study campaign.[39] By late 1939, Mao published "Chinese Revolution and the Chinese Communist Party" and "On New Democracy," two essays trying to explain comprehensively the Chinese Revolution. Both rejected the *Short Course* as a model of a political and organizational program for China, though Mao was prudent enough not to oppose Stalin per se.[40] In his own interpretation of the Chinese Revolution, Mao stressed that the Soviet Union and the Chinese Revolution in Yan'an were in two different historical phases: "[T]he Chinese revolution at the present stage is not proletarian-socialist" directed against the exploitation of the proletariat but a "bourgeois-democratic" revolution struggling against colonial exploitation.[41] It implied, however, that the *Short Course* might be relevant to China once imperialism was overthrown. The party rectification campaign of 1942–44 gave Mao an opportunity not only to silence his critics but also to promote eighteen ideological writings of his own choice, most of them written by himself or by close supporters.[42]

After the defeat of Wang and the Returned Students, the seventh CCP congress in April 1945 buttressed Mao's preeminent leadership role. The "Resolution of the CCP CC on Certain Historical Questions" enshrined Mao's line since 1927 as the *only* correct line. The congress also created

[37] Mao, "On Practice," July 1937, *SW*, vol. 1, 297 (italics in original).

[38] Mao, "On Contradiction," August 1937, *SW*, vol. 1, 315–30, 336.

[39] Kampen, *Mao*, 78–98. Rue, *Mao*, 278, 285. Wylie, *Emergence*, 65–66, 110. Teiwes, *Formation*, 5–8.

[40] Wylie, *Emergence*, 114–18, 121–22, 124–25. Rue, *Mao*, 286.

[41] Mao, "Chinese Revolution and Chinese Communist Party," *SW*, vol. 2, 326–27. Also: Mao, "On New Democracy," *SW*, vol. 2, 339–84.

[42] Selden, *China*, 159–60. Complete list of documents in: Boyd Compton, ed., *Mao's China* (Seattle: Washington, 1952), 6–7.

the formal position of *Chairman of the CCP*—a position that did not exist in any other communist party—for Mao.[43] And finally, the incorporation of *Mao Zedong Thought* into the party constitution sanctioned an already existing personality cult that had developed during the Yan'an years on the basis of some genuine popularity. But unlike Stalin's model, Mao's cult was specifically adopted to serve as a rallying point for the impending civil war. Also distinct from the Soviet counterpart, the cult did not suspend collective decision making in the CCP Politburo (or even de facto abolish the Politburo itself, as in the Soviet case from 1937 to 1952), although the Chairman had the last say in all matters. His fellow leaders apparently hoped to be able to manipulate it for the greater good of the party.[44]

Despite Mao's emancipation from Stalin in theoretical affairs during the 1930s, collaboration in international affairs continued. The CCP at Yan'an stayed in contact with Moscow for the planning of the war against imperialist Japan. Stalin even prepared military shipments, which never materialized. In turn CCP propaganda supported the Soviet non-aggression pact with Nazi Germany in August 1939 and a similar treaty with Japan in May 1941, despite the obvious harm the latter brought to China by freeing Japanese troops in Manchuria for deployment farther south.[45] The only major disagreement was over the Comintern-promoted second united front against Japan in 1937–41. Its collapse not only justified Mao's earlier skepticism, but also provided additional arguments against Wang and his supporters in the rectification campaign.[46]

Japan's sudden defeat in August 1945 following the U.S. use of A-bombs triggered the race for the Japanese-built industrial base in Manchuria for the impending civil war. The CCP in Yan'an was in a much better position to slip through Inner Mongolia to the Northeast than the Guomindang, which the Japanese had pushed into the southwestern corner of China. Yet, after the Japanese had ruthlessly cleansed the territory of communists,

[43] CCP CC, "Resolutions of the CCP CC on Certain Historical Questions," 4/20/1945, in Saich, *Rise*, 1164–79. Kenneth Lieberthal, "The Great Leap Forward and the Split in the Yenan Leadership," Roderick MacFarquhar et al., eds., *Cambridge History of China*, vol. 14 (Cambridge: Cambridge, 1987), 328.

[44] Maurice Meisner, "Cult of Mao Tse-tung," Meisner, *Marxism, Maosim and Utopianism* (Madison: Wisconsin, 1982), 159–62.

[45] Niu Jun, "Origins of Mao Zedong's Thinking on International Affairs (1916–1949)," Michael Hunt et al., eds., *Toward a History of Chinese Communist Foreign Relations, 1920s–1960s* (Washington: Woodrow Wilson Center, n.y.), 3–14. Sheng, *Battling*, 15–56. Michael Hunt, *Genesis of Chinese Communist Foreign Policy* (New York: Columbia, 1996), 141–48. Dieter Heinzig, *Die Sowjetunion and das kommunistische China, 1945–1950* (Baden-Baden: Nomos, 1998), 26–44, 50–64.

[46] Hunt, *Genesis*, 136–38. Sheng, *Battling*, 45–50. Heinzig, *Sowjetunion*, 19–26, 44–50. Lyman van Slyke, *Enemies and Friends* (Stanford: Stanford, 1967), 48–121. Teiwes, *Formation*, 7–9. Tetsuya Kataoka, *Resistance and Revolution in China* (Berkeley: California, 1974).

the CCP spent much of 1945 and 1946 rebuilding the Manchurian party. Following initial setbacks against the Guomindang, the CCP in early 1948 gained the upper hand on the battlefield. The military and political ineptitude of the Guomindang made up for the lack of significant Soviet aid; by late 1949, the CCP swept to victory in China.[47]

In anticipation of final victory, Mao had thought systematically about China's post–World War II role in international relations. At the end of 1945, the Chairman came to see the United States as the greatest threat to his aspirations. He understood that East Asians were looking to the United States as the true liberator from Japanese militarism. American support for the Guomindang—in effect, the internationally recognized government in China, but in Mao's ideological worldview a puppet of U.S. imperialism—and the restoration of its authority in formerly Japanese Manchuria clashed with CCP plans to use the region for its own needs in the impending civil war. Soviet actions were no less exasperating. Military, political, and diplomatic support for the Chinese Communists in Yan'an and then in Manchuria was minimal and incoherent. Stalin also tried to extract territorial and economic concessions in Manchuria and Xinjiang from the Guomindang government in the Friendship and Alliance Treaty China signed in August 1945 under American and Soviet pressure in exchange for Soviet entry into war against Japan. Furthermore, Soviet troops removed Japanese-built industrial plants the Chinese Communists needed for the civil war effort. The emerging superpower conflict over Europe and over American intervention in the impending civil war in China led to Mao's ideologically influenced perception of basic U.S. imperialist aggressiveness toward the outside world in general, and toward the Soviet Union and China in particular.[48]

In August 1946, Mao for the first time promoted the theory of the intermediate zone, which envisioned a global united front against American imperialism. The Chinese leader saw the emerging superpower conflict as an American-Soviet contest for the intermediate zone—the capitalist, colonial, and semicolonial countries of West Europe, Africa, and Asia. He believed that the Soviet Union was the defender of world peace, and thus would support the global united front, without being a part of it.

---

[47] Steven Levine, *Anvil of Victory* (New York: Columbia, 1987), 87–248. Heinzig, *Sowjetunion*, 162–95. Lee Chong-Sik, *Revolutionary Struggle in Manchuria* (Berkeley: California, 1983). O. Arne Westad, *Decisive Encounters* (Stanford: Stanford, 2003), 1–258. Heinzig, *Sowjetunion*, 83–88.

[48] Niu Jun, *From Yanan to the World* (Norwalk: Eastbridge, 2005), 17–20, 190–93, 196, 217, 231–42, 262–64, 267, 278–79. O. Arne Westad, *Cold War and Revolution* (New York: Columbia, 1993). Sheng, *Battling*, 7. Levine, *Anvil*, 15–86. O. Arne Westad, "Introduction," Westad, *Brothers*, 7–8. Sergei Goncharenko, "Sino-Soviet Military Cooperation," Westad, *Brothers*, 142–45.

Conversely, the intermediate zone, including China, would not be a part of the socialist camp. Although Mao acknowledged the enormous economic potential of the United States for Chinese reconstruction, his ideological worldview and the developing civil war in China prevented him from seeking normalized relations with the United States.[49]

In 1949, the Chairman decided to "lean to one side." Despite two decades of unreliable support, Mao decided to seek rapprochement with the anti-imperialist Soviet Union. Given the perception of inherent U.S. imperialist aggressiveness, Mao's preferences between the two choices pointed toward socialism and proletarian dictatorship. The Chairman considered the ongoing anti-bourgeois campaigns in communist East Europe, which in reality were designed by Stalin to consolidate control, reason enough for China to isolate its own capitalist-bourgeois forces and to stand close to the supposedly progressive and peaceful forces of the Soviet Union. Existing U.S. hostility toward the Chinese Communists—mistaken as American imperialist aggressiveness toward all countries of the intermediate zone—necessitated the turn to the Soviet Union for economic aid and military assistance. Yugoslavia's expulsion from the socialist camp in 1948 made it politically imperative to stress close unity to the Soviet Union, lest Mao appear as a second Josip Broz Tito. Yet, within any alliance, China should preserve a high measure of self-reliance and *zili gengsheng* (regeneration through one's own efforts). Thus, the CCP in the 1950s would resist Soviet efforts to integrate China more closely into the socialist camp.[50] This and the very nature of the "lean to one side" decision suggest that Mao was seeking a long-term but nevertheless loose partnership with the Soviet Union that provided the PRC with sufficient room to maneuver.

The Chinese decision paralleled Soviet attempts of rapprochement in February 1949 when Stalin's emissary Anastas Mikoyan visited the Chinese Communist leadership in the North Chinese village of Xibaipo, then the provisional military headquarters of the CCP. The Chinese side reciprocated by sending Liu Shaoqi to Moscow in July, at which occasion Stalin admitted past mistakes in his treatment of the CCP and promised military and economic aid for the future. When the People's Republic was founded on October 1, 1949, relations between the Chinese and Soviet comrades had improved substantially.[51]

---

[49] Niu, *Yanan*, 286–89. Mao Zedong, "Talk with the American Correspondent Anna Lousie Strong," August 1946, *SW*, vol. 4, 97–101.

[50] Bo Yibo, "The Making of the 'Lean-to-One Side' Decision," *Chinese Historians* 5/1, 57–62. Niu, *Yanan*, 316–43. Steven Goldstein, "Nationalism and Internationalism," Thomas Robinson et al., eds, *Chinese Foreign Policy* (Oxford: Clarendon, 1994), 228. Sheng, *Battling*, 161–86.

[51] Chen Jian, *China's Road to the Korean War* (New York: Columbia, 1994), 69–78. Chen Jian, *Mao's China*, 44–45. Sergei Goncharov et al., *Uncertain Partners* (Stanford:

Many aspects of the CCP decision to stand close to the Soviet Union were based on its ideologically influenced worldview. The post–World War II United States was a powerful state, but it was not as inherently aggressive as Mao wanted to see it, especially in the immediate post–World War II years. While critical toward the United States, the CCP was also sensitive to the shortcomings of Soviet foreign policy, which had never treated Chinese interests as a priority. Nevertheless, it was unable to understand the imperial nature of Stalin's rule in Eastern Europe and the resulting implications for China.

THE SINO-SOVIET FRIENDSHIP, ALLIANCE AND MUTUAL ASSISTANCE TREATY

The treaty of February 14, 1950, and related economic agreements formed the basis of the new Sino-Soviet partnership.[52] For Stalin, the alliance was, to a certain degree, a utilitarian tool to obtain those concessions he had tried to extract from the Guomindang in 1945. For the newly founded PRC, the thirty-year alliance provided security against U.S. imperialism and economic aid for reconstruction.

Following a weeklong train trip to Moscow to attend Stalin's official seventieth birthday celebration, Mao's first meeting with the Soviet leader on December 16, 1949, revealed the asymmetrical character of the association the PRC was about to enter. His relationship with Stalin resembled that of a timid student quizzed by a daunting teacher. While Moscow provided the necessary underpinning for Beijing's foreign relations, the Soviet Union hardly needed China's military assistance and economic aid. Stalin was noncommittal when Mao cautiously broached his desire for a military alliance, since he feared repercussions for Soviet-American relations in East Asia. The Chairman was more outspoken with regard to his requests for loans designed for China's economic reconstruction, for increased trade, and for military assistance earmarked to liberate Taiwan.[53]

Stanford, 1993), 38–44, 61–75. Shi Zhe, "With Mao and Stalin," *Chinese Historians* 5/1, 35–46. Wu, *Eight Years*, 9–10. Niu Jun, "Origins of the Sino-Soviet Alliance," Westad, *Brothers*, 61–69. Westad, "Introduction," 8–9. Heinzig, *Sowjetunion*, 285–379. Mikhail Kapitsa, *Na raznykh parallelyakh* (Moskva: Kniga i biznes), 37–45.

[52] Documents reprinted in: Harold Hinton, *People's Republic of China, 1949–1979*, vol. 1 (Wilmington: Scholarly Resources, 1980), 123–26.

[53] For English translation of Russian transcript: "Conversation between Stalin and Mao, Moscow," 12/16/1949, Chen Jian et al., eds. "Stalin's Conversations with Chinese Leaders," *CWIHP Bulletin* 6–7, 5–7. For Chinese accounts: "Mao Zedong's Telegram to Liu Shaoqi," 12/18/1949, Chen Jian, ed., "Comparing Russian and Chinese Sources," *CWIHP Bulletin*, 6–7, 20–21. Shi Zhe et al., *Zai lishi juren shenbian*, rev./exp. ed. (Beijing: Zhongyang

After this thorny start, the Soviet leader let his Chinese guest wait in a dacha outside of Moscow until early January. Even Stalin's birthday party on December 21, a joint visit to *Swan Lake* in the Bolshoi that evening, and another personal meeting on the twenty-fourth did not lead to any breakthrough.[54] Why Stalin changed his hesitant attitude to commit the Soviet Union to the PRC is unclear.[55] On January 2, he eventually agreed to Mao's proposal to allow Zhou to come to Moscow for negotiations.[56] The prime minister[57] left Beijing by train on the tenth and arrived in Moscow on the twentieth.[58] During his trip, U.S. Secretary of State Dean Acheson declared on January 12 that the defense of South Korea and Taiwan were not among American vital strategic interests, which seemed to confirm Stalin's change of attitude.[59] It took Mikoyan and Zhou only three weeks to agree on the details of the Alliance and Friendship Treaty; the pact was officially directed against Japanese militarism and its allies, that is, the United States.[60]

The Sino-Soviet partnership was based on three elements: party, military, and economic relations. First, although a fellow communist party for more than a quarter of a century, the CCP was included in the customs of communist party internationalism—such as regular exchange of party delegations to the congresses of the fraternal parties in Stalin's socialist camp—only once the PRC had turned to the Soviet Union. Furthermore, Stalin's advice was central to the creation of China's one-party state in

---

wenxian, 1998), 392–94. Wu Xiuquan, *Eight Years in the Ministry of Foreign Affairs* (Beijing: New World, 1985), 8–9. Xu Zehao, *Wang Jiaxiang zhuan* (Beijing: Dangdai Zhongguo), 486–87. Zhu Zhongli, "Wang Jiaxiang waijiao shengya zong yi," Waijiao waijiaoshi yanjiushi bian, *Dangdai Zhongguo shijie waijiao shengya*, vol. 1 (Beijing: Shijie zhishi, 1994), 10–11.

[54] Shi, *Zai lishi*, 390–97. Wang Taiping, *Zhonghua renmin gongheguo waijiaoshi*, vol. 2 (Beijing: Shijie zhishi, 1998), 18–19. Heinzig, *Sowjetunion*, 460, 463–66, 469–74.

[55] O. Arne Westad, "The Sino-Soviet Alliance and the United States," Westad, *Brothers*, 170–71. Pei Jianzhang, *Zhonghua renmin gongheguo waijiaoshi*, vol. 1 (Beijing: Shijie zhishi, 1994), 19–20. Xu, *Wang*, 490–91. Shi, *Zai lishi*, 392–93.

[56] "Zhou Enlai to Go to the Soviet Union for Participation in Negotiations and Signing of Treaty," 2/1/1950, Mao Zedong, *On Diplomacy* (Beijing: Foreign Languages, 1998), 92–93.

[57] Technically, Zhou was the Chairman of the State Council. I decided to use the more customary title in this book.

[58] Shi, *Zai lishi*, 396–97.

[59] Goncharov, *Uncertain Partners*, 101–2, 130–54. John Gaddis, *We Now Know* (Oxford: Clarendon, 1997), 72–73. William Stueck, *Rethinking the Korean War* (Princeton: Princeton, 2002), 73.

[60] "Conversation between Stalin and Mao," 1/22/1950, Chen, "Stalin's Conversations," 7–9. Heinzig, *Sowjetunion*, 505–69, 594–99. Text of treaty in Hinton, *People's Republic*, vol. 1, 123–26.

the early 1950s.[61] The dispatch, on Mao's request, of Pavel Yudin, a Marxist-Leninist theoretician, was supposed to bring the Chairman's writings into the fold of Stalinist orthodoxy.[62]

Second, the military aspect of the Sino-Soviet alliance was supposed to provide the young and weak PRC with a strategic deterrent and military aid against U.S. imperialism at three fronts: Guomindang-held Taiwan, divided Korea, and Vietnam, where France tried to reassert its colonial control.[63] However, Mao's ideological worldview greatly affected China's security policies. The Chinese leader was convinced that U.S. imperialism would not accept the loss of China and thus would "wage war . . . in lieu of Chiang Kai-shek" or seek other ways to intervene and restore the old imperialist order in East Asia.[64] Consequently, since late 1949, Mao saw the three above-mentioned areas as conduits for a potential American attack.[65]

The Chinese leader decided to engage in an active defense. In Moscow, Mao asked Stalin, without success, to provide military assistance for the liberation of Taiwan.[66] The Chairman nevertheless committed much of his time during his stay in the Soviet Union to the planning of that operation.[67] Furthermore, since early 1949, Mao had thought about sending troops to Ho Chi Minh's Democratic Republic of Vietnam (DRV) to help in the fight against the French-supported counterrevolution.[68] At the beginning of 1950, Beijing agreed to deliver on large-scale military aid to Hanoi.[69] The PRC also was the first country to recognize diplomatically the DRV, on January 18.[70] Mao was instrumental in convincing the hesitant Stalin to follow suit on January 30.[71] Finally, Communist China committed itself to North Korea. Even before the PRC and the Soviet Union negotiated the treaty, Kim Il-sung had been planning the reunification of the Korean peninsula by military force. While Korea was not subject to

---

[61] Li Hua-yu, "Political Stalinization of China," *Journal of Cold War Studies* 3/2, 28–47.

[62] Shi, *Zai lishi*, 424.

[63] Chen, *China's Road*, 93–113.

[64] Quoted in Dangdai Zhongguo congshu, *Dangdai Zhongguo waijiao* (Beijing: Zhongguo shehui kexue, 1988), 4.

[65] Chen, *China's Road*, 93–94, 121.

[66] "Conversation between Stalin and Mao, Moscow," 12/16/1949, Chen, "Stalin's Conversations," 6. Chen Jian et al., "Chinese Politics and the Collapse of the Sino-Soviet Alliance," Westad, *Brothers*, 251.

[67] Xu, *Wang*, 489.

[68] Westad, "Sino-Soviet Alliance," Westad, *Brothers*, 169.

[69] William Duiker, *Communist Road to Power in Vietnam*, 2nd ed. (Boulder: Westview, 1996), 146.

[70] Mark Lawrence, *Assuming the Burden* (Berkeley: California, 2005), 260.

[71] Ilya Gaiduk, *Confronting Vietnam, 1954–1963* (Stanford: Stanford, 2003), 4–5. Westad, *Decisive Encounters*, 317.

Sino-Soviet treaty negotiations, Kim shortly afterward managed to convince Stalin and Mao to agree to the assault on South Korea. Although he misrepresented his case in rosy tones and under false pretenses, he found a sympathetic ear in Beijing. The Chinese leader saw the commitment to North Korea both as a defense against U.S. imperialism and as support for a fellow communist country.[72]

Mao's threat perceptions were, to a large degree, self-fulfilling prophecies. The Chinese leader based his strategic decisions on erroneous assumptions with regard to American military commitments in the region. Until late 1949, the United States had pursued a policy of disengagement from the East Asian continent, not one of imperialist revanchism. Neither mainland China nor Korea was at the center of American containment policy—Japan was.[73] France did not receive military aid for its war in Indochina.[74] The Truman Administration did not even consider Guomindang-held Taiwan an asset worth supporting.[75]

The establishment of the PRC on October 1 and Mao's subsequent actions in international relations led Washington to reconsider its policies. As a result of the PRC recognition of the DRV, the United States decided to provide France with military supplies.[76] The outbreak of the Korean War on June 25, 1950, finally triggered large-scale American commitments to South Korea, Taiwan, and the French military effort in Indochina. Although Harry Truman had concluded in spring 1950 that an assertive policy in East Asia would deter communist aggression, he feared that Congress would not agree to the necessary, steep budgetary increases. The Korean War eventually convinced a majority on Capitol Hill to follow the president.[77]

The Korean War had far-reaching consequences for the Cold War, in general, and for China, in particular. The American dispatch of troops and military aid to stop the North Korean assault cemented the stalemate in that country, persisting to this very day.[78] The stationing of the Seventh U.S. Fleet in the Taiwan Strait not only prevented China from

---

[72] Goncharov, *Uncertain Partners*, 136–48. Shen Zhihua, "Sino-North Korean Conflict and Its Resolution during the Korea War," *CWIHP Bulletin*, 14–15, 9. Kathryn Weathersby, "New Findings on the Korean War," *CWIHP Bulletin* 3, 1, 14–18. Stueck, *Rethinking*, 69–77. Chen, *China's Road*, 112.

[73] John Gaddis, *Strategies of Containment*, rev./exp. ed. (New York: Oxford, 2005), 40–42, 59, 68. Stueck, *Rethinking*, 79–80.

[74] Lawrence, *Assuming*, 276.

[75] Nancy Bernkopf Tucker, *Taiwan, Hong Kong, and the United States, 1945–1992* (New York: Twayne, 1994), 29–30.

[76] Lawrence, *Assuming*, 261–75. Chen, *China's Road*, 114.

[77] Gaddis, *Strategies of Containment*, 87–108.

[78] Stueck, *Rethinking*, 81–82.

liberating that island but also brought the U.S. military threat, which Mao had suspected to exist beforehand.[79] Also, the North Korean assault substantially increased the recently granted American military aid to French Vietnam.[80]

Since mid-1950, China's security problems were to some extent of its own making. Had the CCP not been a communist party committed to revolutionary and anti-imperialist goals, had the PRC not turned to the Union of Socialist Soviet Republics (USSR), and had Mao not embarked on assertive military policies at the turn of 1949/50, many of the subsequent security problems (the Korean War, the Taiwan Strait Crises, the Vietnam Wars) would likely have been less acute. Ironically, these problems also would haunt Sino-Soviet relations in the following two decades. In the hope to resolve the Taiwan issue, Mao provoked armed conflict in the Taiwan Strait in 1954 and 1958. Because Khrushchev hinted that the Soviet nuclear umbrella would not extend to the Taiwan Strait, the 1954 crisis convinced Mao to pursue his own nuclear weapons program, which was supported by, but separate from, the Soviet Union.[81] The Second Taiwan Strait Crisis, as we will see in chapter 3, undermined the Sino-Soviet alliance substantially.

As recounted at the end of this book, Vietnam ultimately broke the Sino-Soviet alliance. In 1954, the PRC had been instrumental in ending the First Vietnam War when the Chinese and Soviets cooperated closely to convince the victorious North Vietnamese to accept the temporary division of the country.[82] Yet, peace at Mao's southern front did not last. Ten years later, the U.S. escalation of the Second Vietnam War confronted the PRC with a security dilemma as grave as the Korean War. Renewed conflict in Indochina could have served as a rallying point for the restoration of the deteriorating Sino-Soviet military alliance. But the existing ideological disputes sounded the death knell of the partnership between Beijing and Moscow.

While the Sino-Soviet alliance formed the strategic bedrock for Mao's assertive policy at China's three fronts, Soviet aid and assistance were crucial to the strengthening of Chinese military capabilities. A total of 6,695 Soviet army personnel of all ranks went to China until their withdrawal in 1960; more than half went in the first three years of the alliance alone. Fifteen hundred Chinese military personnel went to the Soviet Union for

[79] Tucker, *Taiwan*, 32–40.

[80] Lawrence, *Assuming*, 276–77.

[81] John Lewis et al., *China Builds the Bomb* (Stanford: Stanford, 1997), 6–7, 26, 35–37. Zhang Shuguang, "Sino-Soviet Economic Cooperation," Westad, *Brothers*, 206.

[82] Zhai Qiang, *China and the Vietnam Wars, 1950–1975* (Chapel Hill: North Carolina, 2000), 49–64. Gaiduk, *Confronting*, 12–53.

advanced training. China also received massive transfers of military technology and defense-related industries ranging from missiles to modern aircraft to heavy artillery to small arms.[83] But in light of the decision to "lean to one side," the PRC resisted Soviet attempts at greater military integration, especially once the Warsaw Pact was founded in 1955.[84]

The start of the Korean War on June 25, 1950, put the military alliance to its first test. After a few months of fighting, Kim found himself with his back to the Sino–North Korean border, facing a formidable U.S.-led United Nations intervention force. Pressured by Stalin to rescue the embattled Korean comrades and fearing full-scale war at one of the three fronts, Mao dispatched volunteers. By early 1951, the battlefront had stabilized around the former line of division. Stalin's attitude during the whole conflict puzzled the Chinese. Having decided to stay out of the war himself in the fall of 1950, the Soviet dictator urged the Chinese to send their troops but was slow in dispatching the promised Soviet air cover. Afterward, he obstructed all attempts to bring the war to a negotiated end; only his death in March 1953 opened the way to a quick armistice. To add insult to injury, the Soviet dictator also made the Chinese pay—though at a discounted price—for Soviet military equipment used in Korea.[85]

Stalin's behavior during the Korean War and the nature of the "lean to one side" principle encouraged Mao's strategic attempts to break China's international isolation by turning toward the intermediate zone. Starting in 1952, China approached India with the aim to draw near one of the most important representatives of the Non-Alignment Movement. In 1954, the two countries enshrined *Pancha Shila*—the Five Principles of Coexistence (mutual respect for territorial sovereignty, mutual nonaggression, mutual nonintervention in internal affairs, equality and mutual benefit, and peaceful coexistence) among nations with different social systems—in their agreement on Tibet. With this agreement, India renounced all of its legal titles on Tibet, and China promised to respect the traditional form of government there. The invitation to attend the Bandung Conference in 1955 revealed Beijing's success in wooing the Non-Alignment Movement and in achieving a standing in world affairs that was not exclusively tied to the alliance with the Soviet Union.[86]

[83] Goncharenko, "Military Cooperation," 147, 152, 160.

[84] Pei, *Zhonghua*, vol. 1, 215. Liu Xiao, *Chushi Sulian banian* (Beijing: Dangshi ziliao, 1998), 109–10.

[85] Chen, *China's Road*. Goncharov, *Uncertain Partners*, 130–202.

[86] Harold Hinton, "China as an Asian Power," Robinson, *Chinese Foreign Policy*, 350–51. Zhou Enlai, *Selected Works*, vol. 2 (Beijing: Foreign Languages, 1981), 128. Xinhua, "Agreement between India and China on Trade and Intercourse between Tibet Region of China and India," 4/29/1954, Hinton, *People's Republic*, vol. 1, 165–66. William Tow, "China and the International System," Robinson, *Chinese Foreign Policy*, 125–26.

Third, apart from party relations and military security, economic assistance and trade formed the final of the three main components of the Sino-Soviet alliance. During Mao's seminal stay in Moscow, Stalin himself had promised the delivery of fifty projects for primary industrialization. The signing of the treaty also prompted a series of supplementary agreements. Among those agreements was a U.S. $300 million loan with a maturation period of ten years and an annual interest rate of 1 percent. The loan was to be repaid with a mixture of strategic materials, rubber, agricultural products, goods for daily use, and hard currency. Furthermore, Stalin used Soviet military and economic assistance pledges to extract concessions similar to those he had tried to get from the Guomindang government in 1945. These Chinese concessions, such as the lease of Dalian Harbor and the Lüshun naval base on Liaoning peninsula as well as mining, oil, and railroad concessions in Manchuria and Xinjiang furthered Soviet economic and strategic needs.[87] Finally, Stalin required Mao to accept the sovereignty of Outer Mongolia, although Mao would raise Chinese claims on that country in 1954 and in the 1960s.[88]

The economic disarray after the civil war and renewed economic pressures during the Korean War shaped recovery and reconstruction in the early years of the PRC. While the new Chinese regime could not tap into Soviet economic assistance immediately, because it needed some time to stabilize the war-torn economy, mutual trade nevertheless increased 6.5 times from 1950 to 1956. By 1955, over 60 percent of China's goods exchange was with the Soviet Union.[89] As early as mid-1951, the State Council considered the First Chinese Five-Year Plan with the purpose of utilizing promised Soviet economic aid. In August 1952, Zhou Enlai took the draft plan to Moscow for consultations with Stalin. Because the preparations for the nineteenth congress of the Communist Party of the Soviet Union (CPSU) gathered final momentum in late September, Zhou returned to Beijing without any concrete agreements.[90]

[87] Wu, *Eight Years*, 16–27. Xu, *Wang*, 488, 501. Pei, *Zhonghua*, vol. 1, 24, 41. About loan and debt repayment: "Soviet-Chinese Relations (Reference)," 2/13/1961, *Arkhiv Vneshnei Politiki Rossiiskoi Federatsii* [AVPRF], f.0100, o.54, d.27, p.470, 29–30.

[88] Viktor Zolotarev, ed, *Rossiya (SSSR) v lokalnykh voinakh i voennykh konfliktakh vtoroi poloviny XX veka* (Moskva: Kuchkogo Pole, 2000), 63. Shi, *Zai lishi*, 400–403. Xu, *Wang*, 497.

[89] Zhang, "Economic Cooperation," Westad, *Brothers*, 197. Pei, *Zhonghua*, vol. 1, 41.

[90] David Bachman, *Chen Yun and the Chinese Political System* (Berkeley: California, 1985), 27–33. Barry Naughton, "Deng Xiaoping," David Shambaugh, ed., *Deng Xiaoping* (Oxford: Clarendon, 1995), 131. Shi, *Zai lishi*, 460–61, 463–65. Waijiaobu waijiaoshi yanjiushi bian, *Zhou Enlai waijiao huodong dashiji, 1949–1975* (Beijing: Shijie zhishi), 34–36. Li Yueran, "Woguo tong Sulian shangtan," Pei Jianshang, ed., *Xin Zhongguo waijiao feng yun*, vol. 2 (Beijing: Shijie zhishi, 1991) 15. Vojtech Mastny, "From Consensus to Strains in

In early October, just before the opening of the congress, Stalin published what would become his last book. A work that influenced Mao in subsequent years, *Economic Problems of Socialism in the U.S.S.R.* was the Soviet leader's preliminary reply to some of the issues raised by the draft version of the textbook *Political Economy*, which summarized the economic model of Bureaucratic Stalinism and which was to be published in 1954. The aging Stalin considered the planned textbook as a guide for the world's "revolutionary youth" to carry on the struggle for socialism.[91]

In the last five weeks of his life in early 1953, Stalin eventually returned to the First Chinese FYP. In the fashion of Bureaucratic Stalinism, he urged the PRC to reduce the planned development speed to a mere annual growth of 13–14 percent, to keep in mind the equilibrium of the whole economy, and to plan individual projects in detail beforehand. The Soviet leader apparently had learned a lesson from his own mistakes two decades before. After his death on March 5, Zhou decided to use his visit of condolence to press forward the negotiations. When talks resumed on April 1, Beijing pushed for 150 Soviet industrial projects, but Moscow cut them down to 91 due to lack of sufficient data provided by the Chinese. Together with the 50 projects promised by Stalin in 1950, the final version of the First FYP included 141 Soviet (metallurgy, mining, oil, machinery, automobile, tractors, electricity, and defense) and 68 East European projects in a total of 694 planned. Three thousand Soviet advisers sent to China in subsequent years were directly tied to the First FYP. Adopted in late spring of 1953, five months after it had officially begun, the plan kicked off what the Chinese Communists considered the transition from the feudal/capitalist period to socialism.[92]

Stalin's death and Khrushchev's gradual ascent to power marked the start of a short-lived era in Sino-Soviet relations that historians have called the "golden years," the "high point of the Sino-Soviet alliance," or even the "honeymoon period."[93] The changes in Moscow initiated a general relaxation of Soviet foreign policy, resulting for example in the quick end of the Korean War (1953) and the Austrian State Treaty

the Sino-Soviet Alliance," *CWIHP Bulletin* 6–7, 20–21. Yuan Baohua, "Fu Sulian tanpan de riri yeye," *Dangdai Zhongguo shi yanjiu* 1996/1, 17–22.

[91] Iosif Stalin, *Economic Problems of Socialism in the U.S.S.R.* (New York: International, 1952), 31, 36 (quote). USSR, *Political Economy* (London: Lawrence and Wishart, 1957). Dmitri Volkogonov, *Autopsy of an Empire* (New York: Free, 1998), 138–39, 166–67.

[92] Yuan, "Fu Sulian," 23–26. Li, "Woguo," 15–18. Wang, *Zhonghua*, vol. 2, 40. Bo Yibo, *Ruogan zhongda juece yu shijian de huigu*, vol. 1 (Beijing: Zhonggong zhongyang dangxiao, 1991), 296, 299.

[93] Chen, "Chinese Politics," 257 (first quote). Westad, "Sino-Soviet Alliance," 172–73 (second quote). John Gittings, *Survey of the Sino-Soviet Dispute* (London: Royal Institute of International Affairs, 1968), 19 (third quote).

(1955).[94] In China's case, Khrushchev tried to improve relations to garner support against his rivals at home; most of them had been very close to Stalin.[95] The death of the Soviet leader also provided Mao with the opportunity to move against what he claimed were Soviet stooges in China. Yet, the affair around Gao Gang and Rao Shushi, the party bosses in Manchuria and Shanghai, respectively, is still shrouded in mystery.[96]

Khrushchev's visit to Beijing in the fall of 1954 thus was designed as a show of reassurance. According to his own claims, the Soviet leader realized that his predecessor had often tried to exploit his allies economically.[97] The PRC had come to regard some of the agreements of 1950—especially with regard to prices for Soviet goods that were higher than those charged East European countries, and with regard to low prices for Chinese goods to be exported to the Soviet Union—as unequal treaties, an allusion to the colonial treaties forced on imperial China a century before.[98] Similarly, the new Soviet leader wanted to terminate Stalin's secretive rule in China. In a gesture of goodwill he provided Mao's comrades with a list of all Chinese KGB (Komitet Gosudarstvennoi Bezopasnosti, State Security Committee) agents in the PRC. They all vanished quickly.[99] During Khrushchev's visit to Beijing, the two sides agreed on an extra fifteen industrial projects and another loan.[100] Nevertheless, relations between the two leaders were complicated. Although Khrushchev was not the potential threat Stalin had been, his personality irritated Mao.[101] Conversely, the Soviet leader found the Chinese ally and his culture unfathomable.[102]

Soviet economic assistance to China added up to the largest foreign development venture in the socialist camp ever. Sources from both sides provide different totals because various projects were merged, split, or canceled. One Soviet document lists 360 civilian projects agreed to in the period from February 1950 to February 1959. Two Chinese sources count

[94] Stueck, *Rethinking*, 73–81. Audrey Kurth Cronin, *Great Power Politics and the Struggle over Austria, 1945–1955* (Ithaca: Cornell, 1986), 121–59.

[95] Goncharenko, "Military Cooperation," 145–46. Interview with Sergei Khrushchev, Providence, 7/7/2003.

[96] Frederick Teiwes, *Politics and Purges in China* (White Plains: Sharpe, 1979). For Gao's contacts with the Soviets: Westad, "Introduction," 8–9, 17.

[97] Nikita Khrushchev, *Khrushchev Remembers: Glasnost Tapes* (Boston: Little, Brown, 1990), 142.

[98] Shi, *Zai lishi*, 399–400. Wu, *Eight Years*, 23–24. Zhang, "Economic Cooperation," 205–6. Also: Nikita Khrushchev, *Khrushchev Remembers: Last Testament* (Boston: Little, Brown, 1974), 283–84.

[99] Vladimir Semichastnyi, *Bespokoinoe serdtse* (Moskva: Vagrius, 2002), 334–35.

[100] WLX, 6. Pei, *Zhonghua*, vol. 1, 40.

[101] Harrison Salisbury, *New Emperors* (Boston: Little, Brown, 1992), 152.

[102] Taubman, "Khrushchev vs. Mao," 243–44, 247. Volkogonov, *Autopsy*, 229–31.

304 civilian and military projects overall. Two official Chinese history books claim that at the time of the collapse of economic cooperation in 1960 only around 150 projects were finished—a Soviet document counted a mere 134—with the remaining projects canceled in 1961 and 1965.[103]

Soviet loans financed Moscow's economic assistance to Beijing. A Soviet archival source records 1.413 billion rubles of loans granted from 1950 to 1960; Wu Lengxi mentions 1.52 billion rubles in his memoirs.[104] The loan agreements matured at different points in time. While the first was due as early as 1956, others ended as late as 1965. Except for the Stalin period, when hard currency was used for settlement, the PRC paid off its debt primarily through the delivery of strategic materials and agricultural products. Statistics on annual Sino-Soviet goods exchanges testify to the relative decrease of imports from the Soviet Union and the simultaneous increase in Chinese exports in the late 1950s, with 1956 being the year of balanced trade.[105]

Know-how transfers were similarly important to China's economic development. A study on Soviet experts counts 1,445 political advisers (*sovetnik*) and 9,313 technical specialists (*spetsialist*) sent to China until their sudden withdrawal in mid-1960. For political reasons, as told in chapter 2, the advisers were gradually withdrawn after late 1956. Specialists worked on annual contracts in ministries, enterprises, or on industrial projects. Many were highly qualified in their narrow fields, but ill-prepared for their tasks in China.[106] The Soviet side in the late 1950s increasingly considered the absence of their best people draining, and in 1957 started to request a gradual withdrawal—but to no avail.[107] Their

[103] "Reference of the Trade Representative of the USSR in the PRC," 9/22/1960, *AVPRF*, f.0100, o.53, d.24, p.457, 188–92. Su Shifang, "Guanyu 50niandai wo guo cong Sulian jinkou jishu he chengtao shebei de huigu," *Dangdai Zhongguo shi yanjiu* 1998/5, 14, 49–50. Dangdai, *Waijiao*, 29. Jiang Hongxun et al., "50niandai Sulian yuanzhu Zhongguo meitan gongye jianshe xiangmu de youlai he bianhua," *Dangdai Zhongguo shi yanjiu* 4 (1995), 13–14.

[104] "Soviet-Chinese Relations (Reference)," May [?] 1965, *AVPRF*, f.0100, o.56, d.22, p.498, 223–24. WLX, 336. Please note that loans granted in connection with the food emergencies in the early 1960s are not included. Also note that Wu provided a number ten times too high in his memoirs. The error is likely due to translating the Western numeric system based on multiples of thousands into the Chinese system, which is based on multiples of ten thousands.

[105] Bo, *Ruogan*, 299. Zhang Shuguang, *Economic Cold War* (Stanford: Stanford, 2001), 282–83.

[106] T. Zazerskaya, *Sovetskie spetsialisty i formirovanie voenno-promyshlennogo kompleksa Kitaya (1949–1960 gg.)* (Sankt Peterburg: Sankt Peterburg Gosudarstvennyi Universitet, 2000), 60, 67.

[107] Li Yueran, *Waijiao wutai shang de Xin Zhongguo lingxiu* (Beijing: Jiefangjin, 1989), 151. WLX, 167.

sudden withdrawal in 1960 occurred for unrelated reasons, as described in chapter 5. Thirty-eight thousand Chinese technicians and workers went to the Soviet Union for on-the-job training. More than 8,000 studied in large industrial enterprises, while the rest apparently were contract workers sent to Siberia to alleviate its acute labor shortages.[108]

Economic Roots of the Sino-Soviet Split

None of the Sino-Soviet disagreements that arose in the early 1950s, however, developed into a major factor in the bitter, public disputes that began in April 1960. *Neither* the Chinese disappointment about the Soviet reluctance to honor the alliance treaty in the Korean War *nor* the First Taiwan Strait Crisis can explain Mao's increasing ideological radicalization that started in late 1957. Pancha Shila did *not* prevent the Sino-Indian fallout over Tibet in 1959 that in turn taxed Sino-Soviet relations. And the occasional squabbles over Outer Mongolia did *not* lead to the border conflicts in the 1960s.

The *seminal* issue that triggered the deterioration of Sino-Soviet relations in the mid-1950s was the basic idea behind the First Chinese FYP. The Soviet economic development model China inherited caused a *structural crisis* between agriculture and industry, similar to the one NEP had triggered in the Soviet Union in the late 1920s. Right at the time when the Soviet side rewrote the First Chinese FYP, Stalin's last book, *Economic Problems of Socialism in the U.S.S.R.*, kicked off debates in China about the significance of Bureaucratic Stalinism to the PRC.[109]

The economic debates divided the Chinese leadership. Zhou Enlai's position was close to Yugoslav economic policy, which rejected the centralized and administrative characteristics of Bureaucratic Stalinism for a socialist market economy with limited competition.[110] Vice-Chairman of the PRC Liu Shaoqi and Vice-President of the Party Cadre School Yang Xianzhen used ideas of gradual and balanced development as promoted in *Economic Problems of Socialism in the U.S.S.R.* to advance NEP-style policies.[111] The economist Chen Yun was even closer to Bukharin with

[108] *Survey China Mainland Press* [SCMP] 1964, 32–34 and 2232, 42–45.

[109] Edward Friedman, "Maoism, Titoism, Stalinism," Mark Selden et al., eds., *Transition to Socialism in China* (Armonk: Sharpe, 1982), 173. Kolakowski, *Main Currents*, vol. 3, 143. Stalin, *Economic Problems*, 11, 18.

[110] Friedman, "Maoism," 160–70. Jan Prybyla, *Political Economy of Communist China* (Scranton: International, 1970), 111. Deborah Milenkovitch, *Plan and Market in Yugoslav Economic Thought* (New Haven: Yale, 1971), 62–77.

[111] Friedman, "Maoism," 174–76. Carol L. Hamrin, "Yang Xianzhen," Hamrin et al., eds., *China's Establishment Intellectuals*. (Armonk: Sharpe, 1986), 61–62.

his proposal to free rural production from state intervention, but he continued to advocate many of the core ideas of Bureaucratic Stalinism, such as scaled wages and central planning.[112]

In 1953, Mao rejected Zhou's Titoism for political reasons,[113] and Bukharinite ideas, like Stalin a quarter century before, out of fear they might slow down the revolution: "If socialism does not occupy the rural positions, capitalism inevitably will."[114] He also took issue with Chen Yun's stress of Bureaucratic Stalinism, warning of the danger that the CCP, entrenched in running vast bureaucracies and supervising still existing capitalist enterprises, was under threat of changing into a new bourgeois class. He thereby anticipated much of the criticism Milovan Djilas would raise in *The New Class* in 1957.[115] Practical fears led to Mao's rejection of Bureaucratic Stalinism, as well. China's rural parameters were different from those of the Soviet Union. While the USSR had reserves of arable land, China's agriculture was operating at its natural limits. Soviet loans fueled industrial expansion, while rural development lagged behind. The loans started to mature in 1956 without any prospects for more to be granted; at the same time Chinese repayment in strategic goods and rural products increased significantly. By then, Chinese agriculture had to be sufficiently developed to sustain the industrial sector *and* produce adequate additional quantities for debt settlement.[116]

The emerging malaise in agriculture threatened the implementation of the First FYP. In the spring of 1955, Mao Zedong characterized the situation in China's countryside as follows: "We now are faced with a task similar to the one the Soviet Union faced in the early years after its foundation. We want to change China's backward agriculture to advance China's industrialization; we face a Herculean task, [but] we have insufficient experience."[117] Like Stalin in the late 1920s, Mao eventually sought to cut the Gordion knot by embracing radical—Revolutionary Stalinist—ideas.

[112] Naughton, "Deng," 131. Bachman, *Chen Yun*, 33–34, 37–38, 48.

[113] Friedman, "Maoism," 160–70.

[114] Mao, "Two Talks on Mutual Aid and Cooperation in Agriculture," October and November 1953, *SW*, vol. 5, 132.

[115] Mao, "Combat Bourgeois Ideas in the Party," 8/12/1953, *SW*, vol. 5, 104. Lieberthal, "Great Leap," 303–4. Djilas, *New Class*, 37–69.

[116] About loan and debt repayment: "Soviet-Chinese Relations (Reference)," 2/13/1961, *AVPRF*, f.0100, o.54, d.27, p.470, 29, 30. WLX, 336. Nicholas Lardy, "Chinese Economy under Stress, 1958–1965," MacFarquhar, *Cambridge History of China*, vol. 14, 361. Zhang, *Economic Cold War*, 166–68, 282. Li Rui, *Li Rui wenji*, vol. 3/1 (Haikou: Nanfang, 1999), 37.

[117] Zhonggong zhongyang wenxian yanjiushi bian, *Mao Zedong zhuan (1949–1976)* (Beijing: Zhongyang wenxian, 1997), 508.

On July 31, 1955, Mao criticized the slow agricultural collectivization in public. In accordance with his perception of rural mass enthusiasm, Mao promised to provide "active, enthusiastic and systematic leadership" to the collectivization movement in China: "Although, as the . . . *Short Course* records, some local Party organizations in the Soviet Union became 'dizzy with success' during this period, the error was quickly corrected. Eventually, by a great effort the Soviet Union successfully accomplished the socialist transformation of the whole of its agriculture and at the same time achieved a massive technical reconstruction of agriculture. *This road traversed by the Soviet Union is our model.*"[118] Mao's ideas were finally formalized in January 1956 with the Twelve-Year Agricultural Program, which called for unrealistic overall production increases in an agriculture that already operated at the limits of its environmental capabilities.[119]

By late 1955, the Socialist High Tide (a.k.a. Little Leap Forward) had acquired its own inner dynamic. Responding to high-level directives, low-level cadres accelerated collectivization as much as possible.[120] Stimulated by quick successes on the ground, the CCP leadership set targets higher and deadlines earlier, exemplified in the slogan coined by Bo Yibo, Zhou Enlai, and Li Fuchun, and promoted by Mao himself: "More, Faster, Better, More Economical."[121] During the Sixth Central Committee (CC) plenum in October of 1955, the Chairman even announced Soviet-style collectivization to be carried out by early 1956. Simultaneously, the nationalization of all industrial enterprises was accelerated.[122]

The results of the Socialist High Tide resembled those of Soviet collectivization. Many collectives lacked experienced leadership, know-how, and technology for large-scale farming. Although poorer peasants willingly joined collectives since they received an immediate income in exchange for their meager possessions, well-off peasants, who had worked hard to improve their lot, experienced collectivization as expropriation. Although Mao's collectivization did not call for the smashing of the rich peasants as Stalin's had done, most of the peasants fell silent after some resisters had been labeled and ostracized.[123]

---

[118] Mao, "On the Cooperative Transition of Agriculture," 7/31/1955, SW, vol. 5, 184, 198–99 (italics mine).

[119] MacFarquhar, *Origins*, vol. 1, 15–29.

[120] Bachman, *Chen Yun*, 59–60.

[121] Quoted in MacFarquhar, *Origins*, vol. 1, 30.

[122] "Resolutions of the Sixth Plenary Session of the Party Central Committee," October 1955, Hinton, *People's Republic*, vol. 1, 240–48. Mark Selden, "Cooperation and Conflict," Selden, *Transition*, 69, 70.

[123] Edward Friedman et al., *Chinese Village, Socialist State* (New Haven: Yale, 1991), 186–87. Selden, "Cooperation," 70–73. Prybyla, *Political Economy*, 156.

The defects of the hasty development were powerfully driven home in early 1956. Agricultural production declined in size and quality. The closing of rural markets, introduced by Chen Yun just some years before, and the prohibition of the age-old peasant habit of secondary production caused scarcities of daily consumer goods. Industrial production in the cities collapsed partially because it had been redirected toward the manufacturing of 700,000 heavy but useless metal ploughs. This misguided allocation of scarce resources caused shortages of urgently needed semi-finished and finished goods. The Socialist High Tide also brought about a national deficit of 18.3 billion yuan for the year of 1956, raising the specter of inflation.[124] By the spring of 1956, famines raged through some provinces of China.[125] Expropriation and poor management led to demoralization, and the lack of technology for collectivized farming questioned the basic soundness of collectivization, while "gigantism" and "instantism" failed to solve any of the complex economic problems.[126]

Mao's hasty introduction of collectivization also destroyed the implicit agreement of 1945 among the CCP leaders on collective leadership. The seventh CCP congress in 1945 had agreed to build up Mao's personality cult in order to create a rallying point for the party and the masses in the impending civil war, but the party convention also made clear that the Chairman still had to submit to collective leadership. The 1945 agreement unraveled when Mao, in the second half of 1955, abused his by now full-fledged personality cult to push through the Socialist High Tide, accusing his fellow leaders of walking like "a woman with bound feet" and of "Right deviationist mistakes." His criticism aimed mainly at the Soviet-style economic planners—and above all at Liu Shaoqi and Zhou Enlai—who advocated slower and balanced development.[127]

In the years immediately after its foundation, the CCP was a part of the Soviet world system. The power struggles and ideological debates in Moscow influenced the fate and political life of the Chinese party. Yet,

---

[124] Craig Dietrich, *People's China*, 2nd ed. (New York: Oxford, 1994), 100–101. Jean-Luc Domenach, *Origins of the Great Leap Forward* (Boulder: Westview, 1995), 41, 43, 56. Friedman, *Chinese Village*, 192–203. Lowell Dittmer, *China's Continuous Revolution* (Berkeley: California, 1987), 17–18. MacFarquhar, *Origins*, vol. 1, 59, 347, n. 27.

[125] Xinhua tongxunshe, *Neibu cankao* [NC] 69, 766–67; 71, 828–29; 78, 165–67; 79, 191–92; 93, 490–91.

[126] Bachman, *Chen Yun*, 60. Selden, "Cooperation," 79–80. Prybyla, *Political Economy*, 156–58.

[127] Li Rui, "An Initial Study of Mao Zedong's Erroneous 'Left' Thinking in His Later Years [Part I]," *Chinese Law and Government* [CLG] 29/4, 24–28. Sladkovskii, *Ocherki*, 311–12. Meisner, "Cult," 160–61. Mao Zedong, "On the Co-operative Transformation of Agriculture," 7/31/1955, *SW*, vol. 5, 184, 190 (quotes).

these turbulences led to the emergence and eventually the consolidation of a more independent party around Mao Zedong. Once the CCP was on the verge of establishing political power in all of China in the late 1940s, it was confronted with the question of how to position the soon-to-be-founded PRC. The alliance with the USSR was designed to reestablish China as a world power, but it also made the PRC a part of the socialist camp. As a result, New China faced a series of security problems with which its predecessor had not been confronted. The first years of the alliance witnessed success in economic cooperation and, after Stalin's death, also in international politics. But Khrushchev was not able to remove completely the negative aura of his predecessor's legacy. Chinese memories of Stalin's Janus-faced policies during the Korean War and his insistence on unequal treaties were difficult to dispel. All of this, however, *cannot* explain the sharp ideological antagonism that would undermine and eventually ruin the alliance by 1966. It was only Mao's ideological radicalization, still inchoate in 1955, and Khrushchev's de-Stalinization in early 1956, the subject of the following chapter, that set a train of events into motion which eventually undermined the alliance.

CHAPTER 2

The Collapse of Socialist Unity, 1956–1957

AFTER THE FORMAL END of the twentieth CPSU congress, the delegates had just begun to relax when they were notified to attend immediately another, previously unannounced session. On February 25, 1956, past midnight, the first secretary of the CPSU, Nikita Khrushchev, spoke for more than four hours about terrible things that most of them remembered: terror, deportations, and summary executions. But the delegates were stunned to hear that these horrific events happened on the personal directives from the man most of them revered: the late Stalin.[1]

The twentieth congress established the ideological foundation for the disagreements that would rock the Sino-Soviet partnership in the years to come. Most importantly, de-Stalinization threatened to undercut Mao's domestic position. Since 1955, he had promoted policies similar to those of Stalin from a quarter of a century before—but with less severe effects. Khrushchev's criticism of Stalin's mistakes was potentially dangerous to Mao. While the Chairman tried to limit the range of the criticism and the scope of party discussions over the spring and the summer of 1956, he was unable to suppress them completely. The eighth CCP congress in September introduced policy reversals and checks on Mao's freedom of political action, though the Chairman still enjoyed preeminence among Chinese leaders.

The parallel political upheavals in Poland and Hungary in the fall of 1956 were the result of Khrushchev's criticism of Stalin's methods of rule and provided Mao with the opportunity to rethink de-Stalinization. In the spring of 1957, holding firmly to his belief that political liberalization would prevent the kind of disturbances that had rattled East Europe, the Chairman promoted the Hundred Flowers Campaign. While the campaign was supposed to harness the expertise of party members, technical experts, and bureaucrats for the improvement of China's political system, the criticisms voiced turned out to be far more severe than Mao had expected. Accordingly, the CCP leadership purged this rising dissent with the Anti-Rightist Campaign. The failure of the Hundred

---

[1] Hildermeier, *Geschichte*, 763–64. Pikhoya, *Sovetskii Soyuz*, 128. William Taubman, *Khrushchev* (New York: Norton, 2003), 270–75.

Flowers Campaign convinced Mao that not only was de-Stalinization incorrect but, paradoxically, China also needed more political and economic development along *Revolutionary Stalinist* lines. The sharp left turn in Chinese politics in the summer of 1957 paralleled the so-called Anti-Party Incident in Moscow, during which the Stalinist stalwarts in the CPSU Presidium tried to overthrow Khrushchev. Their failure, however, insured that de-Stalinization would continue in the Soviet Union. Thus by the late summer of 1957 China and the Soviet Union were setting out on diametrically opposed paths of ideological development.

Apart from de-Stalinization, the Soviet policy of peaceful coexistence with the United States, which was also announced at the twentieth congress, gradually undermined the Chinese rationale for the Sino-Soviet alliance. The relaxation of tensions with American imperialism was intended to reduce Soviet military and financial burdens in the superpower conflict in Europe. In the summer of 1956, China still supported peaceful coexistence with the United States in the hope that this would facilitate a solution to the Taiwan Question. However, by late 1957, once it had become clear that not only did peaceful coexistence fail to achieve this end, but Sino-American relations over Taiwan also worsened for unrelated reasons, the CCP notified the CPSU of its rejection of the Soviet policy.

While the Moscow Meeting of the world communist movement in late 1957 restored a semblance of unity in the socialist camp, it was clear that Moscow and Beijing were drifting apart. Given that de-Stalinization in the Soviet Union primarily affected the political system, Moscow came to believe that Beijing was opting out of the Bureaucratic Stalinist socioeconomic development model that was generally accepted in the socialist world. Meanwhile, Mao observed the Soviet Union moving away from what he saw as the anti-imperialist commitments of the alliance treaty.

THE TWENTIETH CPSU CONGRESS AND CHINESE REACTIONS

Even if we remember the twentieth CPSU congress mainly as the official start of de-Stalinization, we often forget that it also sanctioned peaceful coexistence with the nonsocialist world as a new Soviet approach to foreign relations. Harbingers of this new policy had already emerged after Stalin's death with the quick end of the Korean War. At the root of these changes was the fundamental insight that Cold War antagonism placed a burden on Soviet resources. Although China and India had enshrined the term "peaceful coexistence" in Pancha Shila two years before, Khrushchev's adaptation at the twentieth CPSU congress referred to a temporary truce with the capitalist world as proposed by Lenin during NEP in the 1920s.[2]

Examining Chinese reactions to the twentieth CPSU congress half a century later, we would expect Beijing's primary concern to have been Moscow's call for peaceful coexistence with Washington. The PRC had allied itself with the Soviet Union in the hope of garnering support against U.S. imperialism. While, as a result, the People's Republic had to give up any realistic hope of capturing Taiwan, it did also take on the Americans in Korea. As it turned out, however, the Chinese leadership was primarily occupied with de-Stalinization, and, for months, did not address peaceful coexistence and the related issue of Taiwan. On June 29, Zhou Enlai even announced that "the possibility of peacefully liberating Taiwan is increasing . . . *because international tensions are definitely easing.*"[3]

Over the following eighteen months, China's positive evaluation of Khrushchev's pursuit of peaceful coexistence evaporated because of the deadlock in the Sino-U.S. ambassadorial talks (which had originally started after the First Taiwan Strait Crisis), the October events in Poland and Hungary (see below), and the U.S. decision to introduce tactical nuclear missiles in Taiwan in the late spring of 1957. When the talks were suspended on December 12, 1957, the PRC believed it could no longer support the Soviet policy of peaceful coexistence with the United States.[4] It was a turning point that, as told in chapter 3, would lead to the Second Taiwan Strait Crisis.

In spite of the *lasting* influence of peaceful coexistence on the Cold War, de-Stalinization was of much greater *immediate* relevance to Sino-Soviet relations. The post-Stalin leadership quickly realized that terror was a dysfunctional form of rule. At the July 1953 plenum, Soviet Prime Minister Georgii Malenkov used the term "Stalin's personality cult"—meaning, in this context, his arbitrary and unlawful rule—for the first time. On February 9, 1956, a special commission investigating Stalin's bloody rule presented a shocking report, revealing that between 1935 and 1940 the late dictator had personally ordered the executions of many party members. Khrushchev proposed to include these findings in his speech to the impending twentieth congress. After acrimonious discussions, the Stalinist stalwarts—Vyacheslav Molotov, Lazar Kaganovich,

---

[2] Gaddis, *We Now Know*, 108, 207. Matthew Evangelista, "Why Keep Such an Army?" *CWIHP* Working Paper 19, 17–26. Hildermeier, *Geschichte*, 762–63. Adam Ulam, *Expansion and Coexistence* (New York: Praeger, 1968), 132.

[3] Zhou Enlai, "Taiwan Will Be Liberated," 6/29/1956, Zhou Enlai, *Zhou Enlai xuanji*, vol. 2 (Xianggang: Yishan tushu gongsi, 1976), 206 (italics mine).

[4] Steven Goldstein, "Dialogue of the Deaf?" Robert Ross et al., eds., *Re-examining the Cold War* (Cambridge: Harvard, 2001), 184–88. *SCMP* 1530, 11.

and Kliment Voroshilov—and the majority of the Presidium agreed that Khrushchev would read a sanitized version of the report to the congress *after* its official conclusion. But Khrushchev's final text—later known as the Secret Speech—went beyond the agreed limits, blaming Stalin for military mistakes during the Second World War, the expulsion of Yugoslavia from the socialist camp, and for a multitude of crimes during his last years.[5]

The Secret Speech had immediate repercussions inside and outside of the Soviet Union. Even before its official distribution to all CPSU members on March 5, the report had been circulated within the party and then quickly beyond.[6] By June, spontaneous demonstrations for and against Stalin forced the CPSU CC to adopt a resolution that acclaimed both the domestic achievements of the late leader and his revolutionary contributions abroad, while characterizing his crimes merely as abuses of power.[7] But nothing in the Soviet Union reached the level of explosive conflict that rocked East Europe over the course of 1956 (see below).

To understand the Chinese reaction to the twentieth CPSU congress, it is important to recall developments in China's domestic politics. The failure of the Socialist High Tide began to reveal itself in the spring of 1956. The policy had many of the characteristics of Stalin's bungled collectivization campaign. Khrushchev's criticism of Stalin's crimes was an unintended assessment of Mao's recent mistakes.[8]

The Secret Speech had not been totally unexpected. Since 1953, the ambassador in Moscow, Zhang Wentian, had written numerous reports on subtle changes in Soviet positions on Stalin.[9] The Chinese leaders had also started to work out their own criticism.[10] During the official sessions of the twentieth congress, Mikoyan criticized Stalin, however vaguely, and the CPSU distributed Lenin's so-called testament from 1923 demanding the removal of Stalin from his positions.[11] In turn, Zhu De, the head of the CCP delegation, lauded the CPSU in his official address for "maintain[ing] the Leninist principle of collective leadership" and for making "self-criticism."[12]

[5] Artizov, *Reabilitatsia*, 8, 11, 15, 317–48.

[6] Pikhoya, *Sovetskii Soyuz*, 128–29, also n. 81.

[7] Resolution in: Columbia University Russian Institute, ed., *Anti-Stalin Campaign and International Communism* (New York: Columbia, 1956), 275–306.

[8] MacFarquhar, *Origins*, vol. 1, 10, 59.

[9] Liu Ying, "Bu xunzhang de dashi," Waijiaobu waijiaoshi yanjiushi bian, *Dangdai Zhongguo shijie waijiao shengya*, vol. 2 (Beijing: Shijie zhishi, 1995), 23–24.

[10] Aleksei Brezhnev, *Kitai* (Moskva: Mezhdunarodnye otnosheniya, 1998), 47–49.

[11] Zhang Shude, "Sidalin shi Zhongguoren de pengyou," Chang Cheng et al., eds., Zhi-qingzhe shuo, 2nd series, vol. 2 (Beijing: Zhongguo qingnian, 1999) 153.

[12] *SCMP* 1231, 32.

The CCP Politburo began its discussions on March 17. The three-week delay was due to the lack of a reliable version of the Secret Speech. The delegation had returned to Beijing armed only with notes taken on February 27 after a Soviet liaison officer had read the speech to the Chinese delegation.[13] In mid-March, more information surfaced in Western newspapers which was reprinted in a special internal reference journal, *Neibu cankao*, for the Chinese central leaders to read.[14] The first round of the Politburo discussion revealed that Zhou Enlai and the Soviet specialists Wang Jiaxiang and Zhang Wentian had already identified several of Stalin's mistakes: collectivization, the wartime policies, the expulsion of Yugoslavia, and the blunders during the Chinese Revolution. Calling the Secret Speech a "surprise attack," Mao tried to nudge the discussion into a direction more in tune with his political needs. Still fairly ambiguous, he considered the criticism, which was made without prior consultation of the fraternal parties, Soviet "great power chauvinism," but was also happy that the Stalin "worship" within the socialist camp had ended.[15]

Two days later, Mao clarified his criticism. Stalin, he claimed, "had been correct in 70% [of his policies]; that means his principal mistakes make up 30%, but *these are less important*."[16] What exactly did the 30% include? Primarily, they included Stalin's failures during the *Chinese Revolution* and his condescending treatment of the Chairman in 1949–50. Since Stalin had committed all these mistakes *against* Mao personally, the Chairman tried to use them to bolster his *own* credentials. Criticism of Stalin's personality cult thus turned into support for his own cult.[17] On the same occasion, Mao proposed to write an article— "On the Historical Experience of the Proletarian Dictatorship"—which would re-evaluate the late Soviet leader in order to "make up for the one-sidedness of Khrushchev's secret report."[18] Because Mikoyan was due to arrive in Beijing on April 6, the Chairman pushed the writing committee to finish the article quickly in order to present it as a fait accompli.[19] The final version was a fusion of points made in the Secret Speech and Mao's own obsessions with Stalin's mistakes. Reintroducing

---

[13] WLX, 4–5.

[14] Wu Lengxi implied that *Xinhua* on a regular basis skimmed Western news reports: WLX, 4. I consulted the spring 1956 issues of *Neibu cankao*; at least one-third of the articles, many translations of Western news reports, were on the Secret Speech. The *New York Times* [NYT] started to report on 3/16/1956, 1, 6. The full text was published on 6/5/1956, 13–16.

[15] WLX, 3–12.

[16] WLX, 12 (italics mine).

[17] WLX, 12–20.

[18] WLX, 19.

[19] WLX, 20–30. Liu, *Chushi*, 22–23.

the Chairman's emphasis on contradictions within a society from the Yan'an years, the article also faulted the late Soviet leader for disregarding class struggle.[20]

"On the Historical Experience of the Proletarian Dictatorship" had several immediate political goals. Besides subtly reaffirming Mao's personality cult, it aimed to demonstrate that the Chinese comrades were superior at judging Stalin. For the Chairman personally, it was a jibe at Khrushchev who he lauded for having "the guts to confront Stalin" but nonetheless considered "immature."[21] At home, Mao did not want to arouse the "unhealthy interest" of the Chinese people.[22] A Soviet foreign ministry report from a year later stated that the Chinese leaders did not organize a single party meeting to discuss the Secret Speech and that low-ranking cadres had received only vague information. But the same document also reported that Khrushchev's Secret Speech "evoked hot arguments among the leading institutions of the party and a series of communists," including those on the local level.[23]

Mikoyan's visit to Beijing revealed that Mao's attempt at pre-empting discussions—at home and with the Soviet comrades—had been too rash. Officially, the Soviet leader came to Beijing to sign a long-planned agreement for more than fifty industrial projects.[24] In truth, Khrushchev had sent him as a troubleshooter. Never hesitant to use brute force to accomplish political ends themselves, the CCP leaders were nevertheless surprised by the extent of Stalin's criminal rule Mikoyan described. Although now in agreement over the reasons for the Secret Speech, Mao still insisted that it should have been more balanced.[25] In late May, he told the Soviet Ambassador Yudin that the Secret Speech had created "hot arguments among the Chinese cadres," but maintained that any free discussion was "too much" for ordinary party members. For official use, "the most acceptable correlation should be considered 30%."[26] A month later, Mao promoted his new evaluation: "Stalin was basically correct

[20] "On the Historical Experience of the Dictatorship of the Proletariat," Hinton, *People's Republic*, vol. 1, 322–37.

[21] First quote: Li Yueran, "Huiyi Mao Zedong Zhuyi," Pei, *Xin Zhongguo*, vol. 2, 11. Second quote: Yan Mingfu in Ding Ming, "Huigu ge sikao," *Dangdai Zhongguo shi yanjiu* 1998/2, 24.

[22] Sladkovskii, *Ocherki*, 322–23.

[23] "Soviet-Chinese Relations," 3/11/1957, AVPRF, f.0100, o.50, d.29, p.426, 26. Also: Brezhnev, *Kitai*, 49–50. Jan Rowin'ski, "China and the Crisis of Marxism-Leninism," Marie-Luise Näth, ed., *Communist China in Retrospect* (Frankfurt/Main: Lang, 1995), 71.

[24] WLX, 31.

[25] Salisbury, *New Emperors*, 135. Interview with Sergo Mikoyan, Reston, 6/6/2003.

[26] "Record of Conversation with Mao Zedong," 5/25/1956, AVPRF, f.0100, o.49, d.9, p.410, 129.

and had great meritorious achievements, but he also committed very big mistakes and did many things wrong."[27]

In late April, Mao's reassessment was also evident in his famous speech on the "Ten Major Relationships." The piece tried to address the ideological chasm the Secret Speech had created within the socialist camp, but also attempted to cover Mao's own flank. The Chairman acknowledged that the CCP, in the 1940s, had taken up "the bad aspect of Stalin's style of work" in party life, but he quickly shifted responsibility onto the actual victims of the purges. Mao also admitted that "Stalin [had] wrongly put a number of people to death." Although he promised "fewer arrests and executions," he continued to defend China's own record of suppressing "counterrevolutionaries in 1951–1952." Finally, the Chairman reproached the Soviet Union for "measures which [had] squeeze[d] the peasants very hard," concluding that "we must take greater care and handle the relationship between the state and the peasants well." It was an implicit acknowledgement that the Socialist High Tide had not worked.[28]

Regardless of its amorphous character, the "Ten Major Relationships" endorsed Zhou's January 1956 call to use the potential of China's intellectuals for the country's development.[29] But Mao cautioned against complete intellectual freedom: "Naturally, we mustn't pick up . . . [the] shortcomings and weak points" from other countries.[30] Some days later, the Chairman called on the Politburo to "let a hundred flowers bloom in art, let a hundred schools contend in science."[31]

Despite the commotions the Secret Speech had set in motion within the party, the vast majority of China's intellectuals remained suspicious of the Hundred Flowers Campaign. Nevertheless, it had one immediate success—in genetics. On May 3, only one day after Mao's official opening of the new campaign, Zhou castigated the "superstition in our studies" of the Soviet Union.[32] His announcement followed—or actually might have been triggered by—Trofim Lysenko's resignation as head of the Soviet All-Union Academy of Agriculture a month earlier.[33] Lysenko, a peasant-turned-charlatan who had gotten Stalin's attention with his application of dialectical materialism to genetics, had declared that the inherent charac-

[27] Mao, "Do not Blindly Believe that Everything Is Good in a Socialist Country," 6/28/1956, Mao, On Diplomacy, 185–86 (italics mine).

[28] Mao, "On the Ten Major Relationships," 4/25/1956, SW, vol. 5, 291, 298, 301.

[29] MacFarquhar, Origins, vol. 1, 33–35.

[30] Mao, "On the Ten Major Relationships," 303.

[31] "Summary Speech at the Enlarged PB Meeting," 4/28/1956, Mao Zedong, Mao Zedong Wenji [MZDW], vol. 7 (Beijing: Renmin, 1999), 54.

[32] Zhou, "Toward Studying the Strong Points of All Countries," 5/3/1956, Zhou Enlai, Zhou Enlai waijiao wenxuan (Beijing: Zhongyang wenxian, 1990), 161.

[33] NYT, 4/10/1956, 1, 10.

teristics of plants did not reside in their genes but—similar to the forging of political consciousness in proletarians through the vanguard party—could be changed by environmental influences.[34] In the early 1950s, China's adoption of this pseudo-agrobiology had only resulted in disaster.[35] It was in this context that, in early May 1956, Zhou specifically called for a critical reexamination of Lysenko's theories.[36] Three months later, at the Qingdao Genetics Symposium, Chinese scientists debunked Lysenkoism and, for the first time since 1949, discussed modern genetics freely.[37]

The breakthrough at Qingdao symbolized a turn in China's domestic politics. Mao's failed Socialist High Tide was his *first* substantial mistake since the Long March. It provided an opportunity to push the Chairman back into collective leadership at the impending eighth CCP congress in September, eleven years after the last one. Since the early 1950s, the structure of the CCP had changed because membership drives—designed to anchor the party in the countryside—had made the CCP less elitist. Critics of the Socialist High Tide expected that the majority of the delegates would support pragmatic economic policies.[38]

The outcome of the eighth CCP congress was a major success for Mao's detractors. The new party constitution—initiated by Marshal Peng Dehuai and worked out under Liu Shaoqi's and Deng Xiaoping's supervision—eliminated any reference to *Mao Zedong Thought*. The congress also declared the termination of class struggle in the PRC. In a reversal of the Socialist High Tide, it decided to stress a balanced and steady approach to economic development during the impending Second Five-Year Plan (1958–1962).[39] Deng Xiaoping summarized the results of the eighth CCP congress as follows: "The 20th CPSU congress provided a convincing explanation of the more important meanings of steady observance of the principles of collective leadership and of the fight against the personality cult . . . It is absolutely evident that individual decisions on important questions contradict the principle of party construction . . . and inevitably lead to mistakes."[40] Although Mao felt "slighted," he did not show it publicly.[41]

[34] Valery Soyfer, *Lysenko and the Tragedy of Soviet Science* (New Brunswick: Rutgers, 1994).

[35] Friedman, *Chinese Village*, 142–45.

[36] Zhou Enlai, "Toward Studying . . . ," 161.

[37] Laurence Schneider, "Lysenkoism in China," *CLG* 19/2, iv–xi. Schneider, "Learning from Russia," Denis Simon et al., eds., *Science and Technology in post-Mao China* (Cambridge: Harvard, 1989), 45–54.

[38] Sladkovskii, *Ocherki*, 324–26.

[39] Wu, *Eight Years*, 125. MacFarquhar, *Origins*, vol. 1, 100–101, 122–38. Documentation on the eighth CCP congress: Hinton, *People's Republic*, vol. 1, 359–458.

[40] Quoted in: Brezhnev, *Kitai*, 48.

[41] Li Zhisui, *Private Life of Chairman Mao* (New York: Random, 1994), 183.

POLAND AND HUNGARY

Outside of China, Khrushchev's Secret Speech set in motion a chain of events that led to both the Polish October and the Hungarian Revolution. The sudden death of Polish First Secretary Bolesław Bierut in March facilitated Władysław Gomułka's return to party leadership. The former first secretary had been dismissed from his position in 1948 because of his support for Tito. In late June, the political blossoming after the Secret Speech combined with the continuing decline of living standards in Poland triggered anti-Soviet workers' strikes in Poznań. Their brutal suppression paradoxically increased popular expectations for Gomułka's return to power.[42]

This rapid succession of events reached its climax in mid-October, when the entire Polish Politburo resigned. A commission under Gomułka, First Secretary Edward Ochab, Prime Minister Józef Cyrankiewicz, and Chairman of the State Council Aleksander Zawadski began to work out proposals for a new party leadership. But Moscow disliked the prospect of Gomułka's return to power and, in turn, the possible removal of Konstanty Rokossowski, the Russophile, Soviet-installed, and reviled Polish defense minister. On the evening of October 18, reports arrived in Warsaw that Soviet troops stationed in the country were advancing toward the capital. Early the next morning, Khrushchev, Mikoyan, Molotov, and Kaganovich unexpectedly arrived by plane for talks. Gomułka managed to have himself reinstalled as first secretary but he had to promise the Soviets that he would keep the country in the Warsaw Pact.[43]

Before the Soviet delegation flew to Warsaw, the CPSU had sent a circular to the fraternal parties about the current "basic questions of foreign and domestic politics" in Poland and their "significance . . . to the socialist camp."[44] In a Politburo meeting held in his bedroom on the afternoon of October 20, Mao maintained, according to Wu Lengxi's memoirs, that the Soviet threat of a military intervention was "inappropriate" for relations within the socialist camp: "Khrushchev criticized Stalin's policy toward Yugoslavia as incorrect, but his policy toward Poland is even more terrible than Stalin's." Still in pajamas, Mao summoned the Soviet ambassador. His message was as undiplomatic as his attire was

[42] Antoni Dudek, "Der Politische Umbruch von 1956 in Polen," Winfried Heinemann, *Das Internationale Krisenjahr 1956* (München: Oldenbourg, 1999), 27–36. A. Orlow, "Der Polnische Oktober," ibid., 44–47.

[43] Dudek, "Politischer Umbruch," 36–40. Orlow, "Polnischer Oktober," 47–55. Leo Gluchowski, ed., "Poland, 1956," *CWIHP Bulletin* 5, 38–45.

[44] "Decision of the CPSU CC Presidium on the Sending of a CPSU Delegation to Poland," 10/18/1956, Istoricheskii Arkhiv, "SSSR i Polsha," *Istoricheskii Arkhiv* 1996/5–6, 181–82.

inappropriate: "If the Soviet Union dispatches troops, we will support Poland." Khrushchev, as the Chinese realized later, learned about Mao's firm stance only after his return from Warsaw on October 20.[45] By then, the Soviet leader had already halted, though not called off, the advance of Soviet troops.[46]

The purpose of the CCP delegation that traveled to Moscow on October 23 and was headed by Liu Shaoqi and Deng Xiaoping, however, is baffling to the observer distant in time. Originally, on the twentieth, the Soviets had decided to invite high-ranking party representatives from Czechoslovakia, Hungary, Romania, East Germany, and Bulgaria, but *not* from China, to come to Moscow for talks on Poland.[47] Once invited the following day,[48] the CCP leadership, according to Wu's recollections, firmly believed that the comrades of the CPSU had requested it "to attend their negotiations" with the Poles after they had realized "our party's stand."[49] According to the Yugoslav ambassador to Moscow, Veljko Mićunović, however, the Soviet leaders only wanted to receive advice from comrades "further away" with a view on the situation unimpeded by the "inertia and habits of the past."[50] In any case, the Chinese Politburo decided to send a "mediating" mission for the purpose of talking to the Poles and Soviets individually; the Chinese leadership thereby intended neither to limit its "room to maneuver" in trilateral talks nor to forsake the opportunity to speak frankly in the bilateral meetings.[51]

Still fearing the resumption of Soviet military action, Mao twice reconfirmed to Yudin, on the twenty-first and the twenty-second, that the CCP "opposed military intervention" in Poland, or so a Chinese secondary source claims.[52] A Polish document based on Soviet information, however, is less categorical about Beijing's support for Warsaw; on October 22, the Chairman allegedly told the Soviet ambassador "that if the conditions are becoming so that it will be necessary to introduce Soviet troops to Poland, then this can be done."[53] Another Polish archival source suggests that only

[45] WLX, 35–36, 39, 44.

[46] Andrzej Paczkowski, *Spring Will Be Ours* (University Park: Pennsylvania State, 2003), 275. Aleksandr Stykalin, "The Hungarian Crisis of 1956: The Soviet Role in the Light of New Archival Documents," *Cold War History* 2/1, 119.

[47] "Protocol: Session of October 20, 1956," Aleksandr Fursenko, ed., *Prezidium TSK KPSS 1954–1964*, vol. 1 (Moskva: ROSSPEN, 2003), 174.

[48] "Protocol No. 47a: Session of October 23, 1956," Fursenko, *Prezidium*, vol. 1, 174, n. 2.

[49] WLX, 44.

[50] Veljko Mićunović, *Moscow Diary* (Garden City: Doubleday, 1980), 138.

[51] WLX, 44.

[52] Jin Chongji, ed., *Liu Shaoqi zhuan* (Beijing: Zhongyang wenxian, 1998), 804.

[53] Quoted in "Fragments of a Talk between Deng Xiaoping and F. Kozlov on the Topic of Polish-Hungarian-Russian Relations in 1956," [no date], *Archiwum Akt Nowych* [*AAN*], KC PZPR, XI A/5, 19. Thanks to Iwa Nawrocki, who found this document in *AAN*.

on October 27 did the CCP Politburo unequivocally support the "changes in Poland."[54]

Liu's and Deng's diplomatic activities in Moscow during the last week of October are equally mystifying. Although Wu claimed in his memoirs that "starting on October 23, the three delegations from the Soviet Union, Poland, and China, resembling a lantern of rotating shadow figures, bilaterally negotiated in turns,"[55] talks with "the Polish party headed by Gomułka"[56] must have been conducted over the phone or via embassy channels, if they occurred at all. No evidence has surfaced that the Polish leadership was in Moscow before the official talks with the Soviets started November 15.[57] Similarly, there is no indication that the Chinese delegation traveled from Moscow to Warsaw in late October.

Some Chinese secondary sources assert that, immediately after the arrival of the CCP delegation in the Soviet capital on the evening of October 23, Liu Shaoqi and Deng Xiaoping pressed Khrushchev for a peaceful resolution of the Polish crisis and called for an end to the military threats.[58] However, during a CPSU Presidium meeting the following day, obviously after the Soviet comrades had briefed him on the most recent developments, Liu lauded "the correct steps" taken by the Soviet leaders in Poland and "guaranteed" Chinese "unity with the CPSU CC" on the issue: "The USSR is the center of the socialist camp. There cannot be other centers."[59]

Whether it was Chinese pressure that convinced Khrushchev to relent thus is not clear from the available documentary record, but it is likely that Chinese advice supported Soviet decisions envisioned or already taken. As early as October 21, the CPSU Presidium had decided "to discard armed intervention" in Poland altogether.[60] In a letter to Gomułka the next day, Khrushchev agreed to recall all Soviet military officers from the Polish Army and all political advisers from the Polish government. In fact, Mikoyan had already discussed such measures with Ochab on September 11, that is, *before* the Polish October.[61] During a

---

[54] This is what Zhu De officially told the Polish ambassador, who was leaving for Poland, on Beijing airport: "Note," [no date], *AAN*, KC PZPR, XI A/30, 2. Thanks to Iwa Nawrocki, who found this document in *AAN*.

[55] WLX, 47.

[56] WLX, 46.

[57] "Protocol No. 48a: Session of October 23, 1956," Fursenko, *Prezidium*, vol. 1, 177, n. 5.

[58] Huang Zheng, ed., *Gongheguo zhuxi Liu Shaoqi* (Beijing: Zhonggong dangshi, 1998), 1043. Jin, *Liu Shaoqi zhuan*, 804. WLX, 46–47, 56–58.

[59] "Protocol: Session of October 24, 1956 (continuation)," Fursenko, *Prezidium*, vol. 1, 178–79.

[60] "Protocol No. 47a: Session of October 21, 1956," Fursenko, *Prezidium*, vol. 1, 175.

[61] "To Gomułka," 10/22/1956, *AAN*, KC PZPR, XI A/17–1, 178–79. Thanks to Iwa Nawrocki, who found this document in *AAN*.

long telephone conversation with Gomułka in the evening of October 23, Khrushchev reportedly also consented to the transfer of Soviets troops back to their bases in Poland.[62] The following day, the Polish government announced that this would happen "within two days."[63]

On October 30, the Soviet Union published a declaration on "the principles of full equality, respect of territorial integrity, state independence and sovereignty and non-interferences in the domestic affairs" in relations among socialist states.[64] While its release was triggered by the recent events in Poland, the declaration had been in the works since 1953.[65] Chinese memoirs nevertheless attributed its genesis to Chinese pressure on the Soviets to renounce their "great power chauvinism" and to accept Pancha Shila in relations among socialist states.[66] On November 1, Beijing issued a supporting statement.[67]

While Soviet attention focused on Poland, the Hungarian Revolution unfolded. As in Warsaw, events in Budapest revolved around a deposed leader. After Stalin's death and under pressure from Moscow, the Hungarian Stalinist Mátyás Rákosi agreed to appoint Imre Nagy as prime minister. Rákosi was quickly able to undermine Nagy politically. In 1955, the prime minister was forced to resign for alleged disrespect of collective leadership and was expelled from the party.[68] Not only did Khrushchev's Secret Speech provide implicit support for Nagy's political rehabilitation, but it also gave the so-called Petőfi Circle—a discussion club of young party members established in the spring of 1956—a political boost. Throughout July, Moscow seemed to support reforms in Hungary. Concerned over the violent uprising in Poznań, the CPSU leadership pressured the Hungarian party to replace Rákosi with Ernő Gerő. The new party leader, however, turned out to be unable to fulfill the hopes for change. Meanwhile, the Polish October triggered popular demands for reform and, eventually, for Nagy's return to power. Large-scale unrest erupted on October 23 when Hungarian State Security forces fired on demonstrators.[69]

[62] Telephone conversation mentioned in: "Protocol No. 48a: Session of October 23, 1956," Fursenko, *Prezidium*, vol. 1, 177, n. 5. The *NYT* reported that Gomułka and Khrushchev agreed during the phone call on "the end of all Soviet military measures in Poland by Thursday evening [October 26]"; see: *NYT*, 10/24/1946, 1, 8. No document on this telephone conversation was found in *AAN*.

[63] *NYT*, 10/25/1956, 1.

[64] Text of declaration in: *NYT*, 10/31/1956, 18.

[65] Csaba Békés, "1956 Hungarian Revolution and World Politics," *CWIHP* Working Paper 16, 5.

[66] WLX, 47. Shi, *Zai lishi*, 496–98.

[67] *SCMP* 1405, 22–23.

[68] Walentin Pronko, "Ungarn–UdSSR," Heinemann, *Krisenjahr*, 76–77.

[69] András Hegedűs, "Petőfi Circle," Terry Cox, *Hungary 1956* (London: Frank Cass, 1997), 110–27. Békés, "1956," 5. Mark Kramer, "New Evidence on Soviet Decision-Making and

The rapid developments in Hungary caught the Soviets by surprise. On the basis of embassy and KGB reports, the CPSU Presidium eventually decided to support Hungarian security forces through a military intervention. Due to Khrushchev's reluctance, as well as Mikoyan's opposition to the use of brute force, the CPSU Presidium also agreed to send Anastas Mikoyan and Mikhail Suslov to Hungary for talks.[70] They arrived in Budapest on October 24, just as Hungarian security forces were disintegrating in the face of the popular uprising. Simultaneously, the Soviet military intervention triggered bloody street warfare in the city.[71]

Events in Budapest unfolded faster than Moscow could react. On October 23, Mikoyan and Khrushchev had proposed to "recruit Nagy for political action" without allowing him to take over the government.[72] At that very moment, however, the Hungarian party decided to appoint him prime minister.[73] Once Moscow had accepted the inevitable, it hoped that Nagy could defuse the insurrection. But in the following days, the Soviet Union was forced to make one concession after the other. The CPSU Presidium gradually understood that the situation in Hungary was beyond Soviet military and political influence.[74] On October 30, the day it published the Chinese-backed declaration rejecting the Soviet right of intervention in the internal affairs of other states, it decided to call off any further military action.[75]

On October 31, as Soviet troops began to withdraw,[76] the Presidium suddenly questioned the wisdom of its decision to pull out on the basis of pessimistic reports pouring in from Budapest. The Soviet October 30 declaration on the principles of relations among socialist states had prompted Hungarian calls for withdrawal from the Warsaw Pact.[77] After Rákosi's removal in the summer, however, the Soviets had informed the Hungarians that they would not allow the front line of the socialist camp to collapse.[78] On October 26, Mikoyan and Suslov had warned Nagy again that a withdrawal from the socialist camp was simply out of question.[79] In fact, in the Polish October, the threat of a Soviet military

the 1956 Polish and Hungarian Crises," *CWIHP Bulletin* 8–9, 365–66. Pikhoya, *Sovetskii Soyuz*, 139. Stykalin, "Hungarian Crisis of 1956," 115.

[70] "Protocol No. 48a: Session of October 23, 1956," Fursenko, *Prezidium*, vol. 1, 177.

[71] Kramer, "New Evidence," 366–67. Pikhoya, *Sovetskii Soyuz*, 139–40.

[72] "Protocol No. 48a: Session of October 23, 1956," Fursenko, *Prezidium*, vol. 1, 177.

[73] Pronko, "Ungarn," 83.

[74] Békés, "1956," 11–12. Kramer, "New Evidence," 367–69.

[75] Pronko, "Ungarn," 85. Kramer, "New Evidence," 367–68.

[76] Pronko, "Ungarn," 87.

[77] Kramer, "New Evidence," 368–69.

[78] Békés, "1956," 5.

[79] Békés, "1956," 11.

intervention abated once Gomułka had promised to keep the country in the Warsaw Pact.[80] When, on October 30, Nagy endorsed popular calls for Hungary's departure from the Warsaw Pact, he signed the death warrant for the Hungarian Revolution.

In the Presidium meeting on October 31, Khrushchev used the concurrent Suez Crisis to justify the Soviet change of heart. Two days before, after French and British instigation, Israeli troops had occupied the eastern parts of Egypt—a Soviet friend in the Middle East—including the Suez Canal zone.[81] Although the United States had not known about Franco-British-Israeli preparations and subsequently pressured the three to withdraw, the Middle East crisis provided the Soviet Union with a pretext to intervene in Hungary. Khrushchev declared that "if we depart from Hungary, it will encourage the Americans, English, and French— the imperialists," and warned that "besides Egypt, we will give them also Hungary."[82] Even if the Soviet leadership issued orders to prepare for the return of Soviet troops to Budapest,[83] it made the final decision to intervene militarily after another twenty-four hours of hesitation, at a Presidium meeting in the morning of November 1.[84]

Before Soviet troops moved back into the Hungarian capital on the fourth, the Soviet leadership shored up support within the socialist camp for its new interventionist position. On a whirlwind tour, Khrushchev and Malenkov tried to convince the Poles, Czechs, Romanians, Bulgarians, and Yugoslavs.[85] With the exception of the Poles, who demanded that the Hungarian people solve their internal crisis by themselves, all agreed.[86]

How did China influence the Hungarian Revolution and its suppression? On the one hand, Mao had reportedly encouraged the Poles and Hungarians to follow the Yugoslav model during the eighth CCP party congress a month before; he thereby worked against Khrushchev's

[80] Kramer, "New Evidence," 362.

[81] Diane Kunz, *Butter and Guns* (New York: Free, 1997), 82–84.

[82] "Protocol No. 49 (sequel): Session of October 31, 1956," Fursenko, *Prezidium*, vol. 1, 191.

[83] "Protocol No. 49 (sequel): Session of October 31, 1956," Fursenko, *Prezidium*, vol. 1, 192. Taubman, *Khrushchev*, 298.

[84] "Protocol No. 50: Session of November 1, 1956," Fursenko, *Prezidium*, vol. 1, 193–95. "Protocol No. 50 from November 1 and 2: Decision of the CPSU CC Presidium 'On the Situation in Hungary,' November 1, 1956," Aleksandr Fursenko, ed., *Prezidium TSK KPSS 1954–1964*, vol. 2 (Moskva: ROSSPEN, 2006), 476. Nikita Khrushchev, *Khrushchev Remembers* (Boston: Little, Brown, 1970), 418.

[85] Khrushchev, *Khrushchev Remembers*, 419–22. Pikhoya, *Sovetskii Soyuz*, 142–43. Kramer, "New Evidence," 372–74. Békés, "1956," 13–14. Mićunović, *Moscow Diary*, 132.

[86] Orlow, "Polnischer Oktober," 55. János Tischler, "Die Führung der PVAP und die ungarische Revolution von 1956," Heinemann, *Krisenjahr*, 325–26. Khrushchev, Khrushchev Remembers, 419–22.

attempts to prevent precisely *that* from happening.[87] On the other hand, Soviet documentation and Chinese memoirs suggest that, until October 30, the Chinese delegation in Moscow was not involved in discussions on Hungary at all.[88] Its insistence on Pancha Shila with regard to the Polish October seemed to support a Soviet hands-off policy during the Hungarian Revolution.[89]

The Chinese position changed swiftly in the last days of October, although, as developments described below suggest, Mao and his representatives in Moscow only had a limited understanding of the rapidly unfolding events. Due to a lack of Hungarian speaking personnel, the embassy in Budapest did not comprehend the scope of the popular uprising until October 28, when it summoned Chinese students to translate newspaper articles and leaflets.[90] Two days later, in the morning, Yudin conveyed to the CPSU Presidium that the "Chinese comrades" had grown concerned that "Hungary leaves our camp," and that they even wanted to know: "Who is Nagy? Can we trust him?"[91] On the basis of reports from Budapest and news of continued Soviet concessions, Mao eventually concluded that Hungary had turned into a "battlefield for socialism."[92] Despite having reversed his own position on non-intervention so suddenly, Mao blamed Khrushchev's "zigzagging" for the crisis. Beijing then sent an urgent telegram to its delegation in Moscow to pressure the Soviets to keep troops in Hungary in order "to suppress the counter-revolutionary armed rebellion."[93]

In the later half of October 30, Liu briefly met with Khrushchev and Molotov to demand "that the [Soviet] troops must stay in Hungary and Budapest." But Khrushchev was indecisive, musing that there were "two courses" left to follow in Hungary: "The military one is the course of occupation, the peaceful one is the withdrawal of troops and negotiations." Molotov favored negotiations with Nagy's government on the withdrawal of troops.[94] In a subsequent meeting, the CPSU Presidium

---

[87] Gittings, *Survey*, 69. "Draw Historical Lessons and Oppose Big-Nation Chauvinism," September 1956, Mao, *On Diplomacy*, 195–203.

[88] Both Wu Lengxi and the Soviet record reveal that Liu Shaoqi was not involved in discussions on Hungary until October 30: WLX, 45–58. Fursenko, *Prezidium*, vol. 1, 176–87.

[89] Rowiński, "China," 81.

[90] Peter Vámos, "The Chinese Communist Party's Policy and the 1956 Hungarian Revolution," paper presented at the conference "New Central and East European Evidence on the Cold War in Asia," Budapest, Hungary, 10/30–11/2/2003, 6–9.

[91] "Protocol No. 49: Session of October 30, 1956," Fursenko, *Prezidium*, vol. 1, 187.

[92] Chen, *Mao's Diplomacy*, 155–56. WLX, 52 (quote).

[93] WLX, 52.

[94] "Protocol No. 49 (sequel): Session of October 30, 1956," Fursenko, *Prezidium*, vol. 1, 188. Wu Lengxi reports of a similar meeting on October 31, in which Liu Shaoqi strongly

reconfirmed its earlier decision to consider the withdrawal of Soviet troops from *all* socialist countries, in conformity with the declaration that rejected the Soviet right of intervention and that had just been released.[95]

Although Liu's intervention clearly preceded the Soviet October 31 decision to reverse the previous stance on non-intervention in Hungary, the available Russian evidence does not reveal a momentous Chinese influence on Soviet decision making.[96] The November 1 Presidium resolution to intervene militarily was adopted solely on the basis of the troubling reports on the deteriorating situation in Budapest.[97] Furthermore, Khrushchev's memoirs suggest that the hard Chinese position on intervention actually softened after Liu's appeal. The Soviet leader reminisced that he, together with other Presidium members, spent the night from October 31 to November 1 with the CCP delegation in Stalin's former dacha at Lipky outside of Moscow discussing the situation in Hungary.[98] The conversation revolved around the benefits and disadvantages of an outright military intervention. Liu repeatedly called Mao on the phone for advice, but the Chairman "approved whatever Liu Shao-chi recommended." In the end, the Soviet hosts and his Chinese guests parted in the wee hours of November 1 with an agreement "*not* to apply military force in Hungary." It was only a CPSU Presidium meeting a couple of hours later that sanctioned a military intervention given the deteriorating situation in Budapest.[99]

---

urged Khrushchev to keep troops in Hungary. Given the contents of Liu's words, it seems that Wu, who was not present in Moscow, mistook the October 30 meeting for the meeting the following evening (described below in text), see: WLX, 51–52.

[95] "Protocol No. 49 (sequel): Session of October 30, 1956," Fursenko, *Prezidium*, vol. 1, 188–90.

[96] Chen Jian, who wrote from a Chinese perspective, suggests that Chinese influence was decisive: *Mao's China*, 156–57. János Rainer et al., who worked with Soviet and Hungarian documents, maintain that Chinese influence was one of many factors: "Ungarische Revolution," András B. Hegedűs et al., eds., *Satelliten nach Stalins Tod* (Berlin: Akademie, 2000), 254.

[97] Interview with Sergo Mikoyan, Reston, 6/6/2003. Stykalin, "Hungarian Crisis," 138. Tofik Islamov, *Sovetskii Soyuz i vengerskii krizis 1956 goda* (Moskva: ROSSPEN, 1998), 467–68. Sergei Khrushchev, *Nikita S. Khrushchev and the Creation of a Superpower* (University Park: Pennsylvania State, 2000), 192–93. Khrushchev, *Khrushchev Remembers*, 418.

[98] Khrushchev, *Khrushchev Remembers*, 418. The October 31 Presidium meeting had decided to inform the Chinese delegation: "Protocol No. 49 (sequel): Session of October 31, 1956," Fursenko, *Prezidium*, vol. 1, 192.

[99] Khrushchev, *Khrushchev Remembers*, 418–19 (italics mine). Wu Lengxi confirms that a meeting occurred in the evening of October 31, but seems to quote Liu's words spoken the evening before, see: WLX, 51–52. Nikolai Bulganin informed the Presidium on November 1 about the talks at Lipky: "Protocol No. 50: Session of November 1, 1956," Fursenko, *Prezidium*, vol. 1, 194.

Regardless of the actual influence on the Soviet decision making process, the CCP presence in Moscow during these crucial October days raised the self-confidence of the Chinese comrades. Despite the ambiguity surrounding their role in the resolution of the double crisis in East Europe, the Chinese eventually convinced themselves that their rectitude and nerve had saved the socialist camp.[100] That the Soviet comrades had consulted their Chinese brothers-in-arms was an improvement over the "great power chauvinism" in the Stalin question at the twentieth congress. After informing the CCP delegation of its recent decision to intervene militarily, the *whole* CPSU Presidium—a rare honor—sent off the Chinese guests at the airport in Moscow on November 1.[101]

Rethinking the World, Reordering the Socialist Camp, Reforming China

The quick political and military resolution of the Polish October and the Hungarian Revolution concealed the long-term impact of these two crises on all communist countries—even on China. Upon the return of the CCP delegation, the Chinese leaders reconsidered the events and their implications. The discussions revolved around three questions: the Chinese ideological view of the world, the internal structure of the socialist camp, and economic and political liberalization in China.

With regard to the first—its ideological view of the world—the CCP leadership unambiguously blamed the CPSU for problems plaguing the socialist camp, asserting that the Soviets had committed three mistakes: first, their "great power chauvinism" since 1948 had produced tensions in Europe; second, Khrushchev's botched attempt at de-Stalinization had confused communists in Europe; and third, the Soviet Union had not understood the nature of the crises in Poland and Hungary. Moscow, claimed the CCP, had wanted to intervene in the anti-Soviet revolt in Warsaw but to withdraw in face of the counterrevolution in Budapest.[102]

Given this interpretation, the CCP leadership drew new conclusions about the twentieth CPSU congress. This new assessment took the form of Mao's reaffirmation of Stalin: "I think there are two 'swords': one is Lenin and the other Stalin. The sword of Stalin has now been discarded by the Russians. Gomulka and some people in Hungary have picked it up

---

[100] See below in text. Also: Khrushchev, *Khrushchev Remembers*, 419, n. 2.

[101] Khrushchev, *Khrushchev Remembers*, 419. WLX, 53–54, 56. Zhang, "Sidalin," 180.

[102] Zhonggong zhongyang wenxian yanjiushi bian, *Liu Shaoqi zhuan*, vol. 2 (Beijing: Zhongyang wenxian, 1998), 806. Zhang, "Sidalin," 180–81. Chen, *Mao's China*, 159. *SCMP* 1405, 22–23.

to stab at the Soviet Union and oppose so-called Stalinism . . . We Chinese have not thrown it away."[103] The Chairman turned against Khrushchev's de-Stalinization more decisively than ever before: "[Stalinism is] just Marxism . . . with shortcomings." He continued: "The so-called de-Stalinization thus is simply de-Marxification, *it is revisionism*."[104] Finally, the Chairman maintained that the Chinese comrades, "unlike some people who have tried to defame and destroy Stalin, . . . are acting in accordance with objective reality."[105] It was the *first* time that Mao clearly distinguished between the views of the subjectivist revisionists in Moscow and the objective Marxists in Beijing.

Before the end of the year, the CCP published these arguments in "Again on the Historical Experience of the Proletarian Dictatorship," a sequel to the April article.[106] The Chairman insisted that the new piece should neither mention too many details about the Hungarian Revolution nor defend the positive aspects of the twentieth CPSU congress but stress the Soviet evaluation of Stalin as too negative, support the policies of the CPSU in general while accentuating its numerous individual mistakes, and finally confirm that Stalin had been a great Marxist.[107] Like its predecessor, the article was selective and designed to confront the Soviets with a fait accompli.

In the days before the article's publication, Mao, however, chose not to include his criticism of peaceful coexistence. Khrushchev's policy, he asserted, failed to encompass the principle of nonintervention as defined in Pancha Shila, especially since the PRC maintained that U.S. imperialism interfered in Chinese internal affairs through its occupation of Taiwan. But the Chairman also believed that, at the moment, de-Stalinization was a greater menace to the socialist camp than peaceful coexistence, and thus he decided not to raise the matter publicly.[108]

In late 1956, there were additional ideological considerations that led the Chinese to reject Khrushchev's peaceful coexistence and its logical derivative: peaceful transition in the nonsocialist world. Despite the double crisis in East Europe, the Soviet leader still believed that communists could do well in free elections in nonsocialist countries.[109] According to the Chinese, however, the parliamentary road was revisionist since it

---

[103] Mao, "Speech at the Second Plenary Session of the Eighth CCP CC," 11/14/1956, *SW*, vol. 5, 341.

[104] WLX, 68 (italics mine).

[105] Mao, "Speech at the Second Plenary Session . . . ," 11/14/1956, *SW*, vol. 5, 341.

[106] "Again on the Historical Experience of the Dictatorship of the Proletariat," Hinton, *People's Republic*, vol. 1, 462–73.

[107] WLX, 59–60, 71–72.

[108] WLX, 80. *SCMP* 1233, 45.

[109] Li, *Waijiao*, 103.

rejected "proletarian dictatorship" for "capitalist class dictatorship." Implicitly, it not only discarded the "sword of Stalin" but also the "sword of Lenin." But Mao realized that such an absolute rejection would not have popular appeal in the world. The Chinese comrades thus decided to apply "dual tactics": "From a strategic point of view, [we] should prepare to adopt a policy of violent revolution to seize power, but for the sake of striving for the masses, from a tactical point, [we] should agree to peaceful transition."[110]

Despite the heightened nature of Sino-Soviet ideological disagreements in late 1956, the Chinese comrades considered ways to stabilize the socialist camp. Beijing was aware that it could not replace Moscow as the leader of the camp, as Liu Shaoqi had told the Soviets on October 24: "[T]he USSR is the center of the socialist camp. There cannot be other centers."[111] But this recognition did not prevent Beijing from devising policies to limit Moscow's authority and to push for greater equality among the socialist states. The Chinese comrades thus supported Gomułka's call for a withdrawal of Soviet military officers and political advisers—starting with the hated Rokossowski.[112] On October 30, Liu also explained to Yudin that it was time for the Soviet Union to withdraw all political advisers from other socialist countries. He was quick to add—obviously with the Chinese need for Soviet technology in mind—that "technical specialists" were welcome to stay.[113]

An investigation by the Soviet foreign ministry revealed a wide array of desires by fraternal countries ranging from calls for the withdrawal of individual Soviet advisers to more general pleas for better treatment by the Soviet Union. The PRC in particular wished for better foreign policy coordination, an improved exchange of information, and more personal contacts between Soviet and Chinese leaders.[114] Soviet foreign ministry documents from spring 1957 indicate that Moscow granted most of these wishes.[115] Some changes in Soviet policy were implemented

[110] WLX, 61, 70, 80. Mao Zedong, "Speech at the Second Plenary Session," 11/15/1956, SW, vol. 5, 341.

[111] "Protocol: Session of October 24, 1956 (continuation)," Fursenko, Prezidium, vol. 1, 178–79.

[112] For Polish demands: "Account of a Meeting at the CPSU CC, 24 October 1956, on the Situation in Poland and Hungary," Mark Kramer, "Hungary and Poland, 1956," CWIHP Bulletin 5, 53.

[113] "Record of Conversation with Liu Shaoqi," 10/30/1956, AVPRF, f.0100, o.49, d.9, p.410, 202.

[114] "Proposals," 11/23/1956, AVPRF, f.0100, o.49, d.37, p.414, 8–10. "On the Proposals and Critical Remarks" [12/12/1956], AVPRF, f.0100, o.49, d.37, p.414, 11–17.

[115] "List," 3/11/1957, AVPRF, f.0100, o.50, d.29, p.426, 13–19. "List," 3/11/1957, AVPRF, f.0100, o.50, d.29, p.426, 20–22. "To Khrushchev," 5/24/1957, National Security

almost immediately; in mid-November, a Chinese parliamentary delegation headed by Peng Zhen was wined and dined in Moscow.[116]

Meanwhile, the CCP designed policies meant to increase China's influence in the socialist world. In early November, Deng and Liu claimed that the Soviets had understood that "their one-sided" approach to East Europe was faulty.[117] The Chinese comrades also realized that helping Moscow to resolve tensions in East Europe required a subtle approach, as Mao explained in colorful tones: "We know that the Soviet Union wants to promote sausages by itself, it is not willing [to let] China promote its own sausages, too, because it wants to promote its own sausages [above all]."[118]

But new problems soon confronted the Chinese. In early November, Tito had acquiesced to the Soviet intervention in Hungary, but, after a fallout over the treatment of the deposed Nagy, the Yugoslav leader blamed Moscow in the so-called Pula speech of November 11 for the double crisis in East Europe.[119] In response, Khrushchev denounced Tito as a wiseacre in front of Yugoslav Ambassador Mićunović and the Chinese parliamentary delegation mentioned above.[120] Although the substance of the Pula speech was similar to the Chinese assessment of the Polish October and the Hungarian Revolution, the CCP leaders considered it counterproductive at this point.[121]

In late November, the new Chinese approach was finally given a chance to be implemented when Yudin invited Zhou to Moscow for talks in early 1957.[122] Khrushchev had earlier proposed the convention of a meeting of the world communist movement, apparently in order to provide it with a new sense of direction.[123] The Soviet leader obviously wanted to integrate the Chinese into the ongoing discussions; Zhou's visit to Moscow

Archive [NSA], Russian Archival Documents Database [RADD], 5/25/1957 (*RGANI*, f.5, o.3, d.230, 170–71).

[116] "Materials about the meeting of the members of the permanent commissions of the Supreme Soviet of the USSR with the parliamentarian delegation of the People's Republic of China," 11/15/1956, *Gosudarstvennyi Arkhiv Rossiiskoi Federatsii [GARF]*, f.7523, o.45, d.238, 18–21.

[117] WLX, 58. Zhonggong, *Liu Shaoqi zhuan*, vol. 2, 807. Chen, *Mao's China*, 158.

[118] WLX, 68.

[119] Peter Gosztony, "Die langfristigen Auswirkungen des ungarischen Volksaufstandes und aktuelle Reflexionen darüber," Heinemann, *Krisenjahr*, 503. "Speech by Comrade Josip Broz Tito in Pula," [11/11/1956], *Stiftung Archiv der Parteien und Massenorganisationen der DDR im Bundesarchiv [SAPMO-Barch]*, DY 30/IV 2/2.035/74, 47–59.

[120] Mićunović, *Moscow Diary*, 149–52, 161–66.

[121] Zhang, "Sidalin," 184–85. Li, *Waijiao*, 106.

[122] Xia Daosheng, "Yi Zhou Enlai zongli 1957nian fangwen Xiongyali," Pei, *Xin Zhongguo*, vol. 2, 24. Li Lianqing, *Lengnuan suiyue* (Beijing: Shijie zhishi, 1998), 257.

[123] Wang, *Zhonghua*, vol. 2, 208–9.

followed his own early January trip to Budapest for talks with the Hungarian, Bulgarian, Romanian, and Czechoslovak party leaders about the situation in Hungary.[124] Khrushchev was even willing to accommodate Chinese ideological viewpoints, calling himself a good "Stalinist" during the New Year's Eve gala at the Kremlin.[125] Half a year later, Molotov would mock Khrushchev for bending over backward to gratify the Chinese comrades.[126]

Before Zhou flew to Moscow, he interrupted an extended tour through Asia and returned to Beijing for preparations. Although the Chinese leaders had decided to stabilize the socialist camp, they maintained that this plan should not prevent them from "criticizing Khrushchev" if an opportunity should arise. Beijing's instructions for Zhou were vague; he was left with ample room to maneuver.[127]

On January 8, the first day of the Moscow talks, both sides agreed that the socialist camp was in urgent need of stability.[128] Accordingly, Khrushchev asked Zhou to fly to Hungary to shore up support for the new leadership. While the Chinese prime minister agreed to stop there briefly after his planned visit to Poland, he also wanted to talk to the new Hungarian leadership in Moscow before his departure.[129] In the night of January 10–11, Zhou, Khrushchev, János Kádár, and Ferenc Münnich, who had rushed to Moscow on short notice, discussed the situation in Hungary and relations with Yugoslavia. The Soviet leader proposed to invite Tito for tripartite talks in Budapest while Zhou was there, but the Chinese prime minister declined with the excuse that he had not yet consulted with Beijing.[130]

After arriving in Poland on January 11, Zhou listened to Gomułka, Cyrankiewicz, and Zawadski complain about past Soviet arrogance while trying to persuade his hosts to see the problems of the socialist camp from a broader perspective. If socialism was to succeed on a global level, he pleaded, then all socialist countries "should support each other, dispel

[124] Csaba Békés et al., eds., *1956 Hungarian Revolution* (Budapest: Central European, 2002), 489–93.

[125] Liu, *Chushi*, 23–24.

[126] "Third Session, evening June 24," N. Kovaleva, ed., *Molotov, Malenkov, Kaganovich, 1957* (Moskva: Mezhdunarodnyi fond 'Demokratiya,' 1998), 131.

[127] Li, *Lengnuan*, 257–58.

[128] Zhang, "Sidalin," 207–11.

[129] Xia, "Yi Zhou Enlai," 24–26. Li, *Lengnuan*, 259–61. Zhonggong zhongyang wenxian yanjiushi bian, *Zhou Enlai nianpu, 1949–1976*, vol. 2 [ZELNP2] (Beijing: Zhongyang, 1997), 4–7.

[130] Hao Deqing, "Waijiao gongzuo sanshinian," *Waijiaobu, Dangdai Zhongguo shijie*, vol. 2, 65–66. ZELNP2, 7. Also: "To Presidium of the CPSU CC, to Khrushchev," 1/10/1957, *NSA*, RADD, 1/10/1957. I could not find any archival material on Sino-Soviet-Hungarian talks.

mutual suspicions, because only unity will be advantageous." Given Poland's sufferings under Soviet occupation since 1944, however, Gomułka dismissed the Chinese evaluation of Stalin. In return, Zhou warned him not to band together with the Yugoslavs, who had sent a delegation to Warsaw in early January while Khrushchev had been in Budapest.[131] The final Polish-Yugoslav communiqué insisted on the principle of noninterference and on bilateral relations between communist parties as the most suitable form of interaction.[132] Zhou advised Gomułka against such unwise alliances; there was still only one center in the socialist camp, and that was Moscow.[133]

On January 16, Zhou flew to bullet-riddled Budapest for a twenty four hour stopover. The Hungarian comrades picked up the prime minister at a military airstrip, and drove him—in an armored car—past Soviet tanks to the trade union headquarters. There, he gave a rousing speech to the Hungarian party, followed by a night of talks with the new leadership about the different nature of the Polish October and the Hungarian Revolution. The next morning, Zhou left Budapest for a final three-day stay in Moscow.[134]

Back in the Soviet capital, the Chinese prime minister reported on his travels through East Europe. But once Zhou started to criticize the Soviet comrades for "great power chauvinism," Khrushchev turned to Suslov, remarking in a curt manner: "Zhou Enlai criticizes us, we cannot accept his lecture!" With talks stalled, the Chinese prime minister called the Chairman in Beijing on the phone for instructions. "If they don't finish listening to what we have to say," Mao advised, "then just forget it, don't speak about it again."[135]

Before Zhou left Moscow for Kabul to resume his tour through Asia, he tried to draw near the Yugoslavs. At a reception in the Kremlin on January 18, Zhou was demonstrably friendly to Belgrade's ambassador, Mićunović.[136] Later that evening, Zhou called Peng Zhen, whose parliamentary delegation had just arrived in the Yugoslav capital, and

[131] Zhang, "Sidalin," 210–11 (quote). "Notes of the Talks Held on January 11 and 12, 1957," Andrzej Werblan, ed., "Rozmowy Władysława Gomułki z Zhou Enlaiem w 1957 r.," Dzieje Najnowsze 29, 121–32. Sheldon Anderson, A Cold War in the Soviet Bloc (Boulder: Westview, 2001), 142.

[132] NYT, 11/26/1956, 1, 10; 1/1/1957, 1.

[133] "Notes of the Talks Held on January 11 and 12, 1957," 132.

[134] Xia, "Yi Zhou Enlai," 27–28. "Minutes of a Meeting between the Hungarian and Chinese Delegations in Budapest," 1/16/1957, Békés, 1956, 496–503.

[135] Li, Waijiao, 113–14. Also: Li, Lengnuan, 262–63. Li Yueran, "Wo zai Zhou Enlai shenbian gongzuo de pianduan huiyi," Pei, Xin Zhongguo, vol. 1, 93. Zhang, "Sidalin," 216.

[136] Mićunović, Moscow Diary, 196–97.

instructed him to seek a private talk with Tito in order to propose "a meeting of the world's communist parties, *sponsored by the CCP and the Yugoslav League of Communists.*"[137] The next day, Zhou repeated the proposal to Mićunović, and even hinted at a possible visit to Belgrade by himself if Tito would agree.[138] It was only on the plane to Afghanistan that Zhou broke the news of the Chinese initiative to the Soviet liaison officer.[139] Unfortunately for the Chinese, Tito told Peng that he preferred bilateral or even multilateral meetings over any international conference. The Chinese proposal had put the Yugoslavs into a delicate position: accepting it meant submission to Moscow's dominance of the socialist camp, while refusing it was a rejection of Beijing's goodwill. In the end, Belgrade preferred autonomy from the socialist camp over popularity in it.[140] Zhou's initiative had failed; he would not visit Belgrade.

It was at this point that Moscow stepped in. When Peng passed through the Soviet capital on his way home, Khrushchev informed him that the CPSU itself would organize the international meeting.[141] China and Poland quickly learned what this new Soviet assertiveness meant. The atmosphere between the Soviet and Chinese comrades had cooled considerably. Unlike in November, Peng's delegation was neither wined nor dined.[142] After the Polish side tried to draw close to the Chinese during an April state visit in Beijing, Khrushchev, a month later, bluntly told Gomułka and Cyrankiewicz to step back in line. The Soviet leader reminded his guests that Poland was economically too dependent on the Soviet Union and was thus not in a position to challenge it.[143]

In a report to the CCP leadership on his trip to Moscow, Warsaw, and Budapest, Zhou criticized the Soviets on several points. According to the prime minister, Soviet thinking failed to integrate all interests of the socialist camp in "an objective, far-sighted, and calm fashion." However, the comrades in Moscow "[have] not been truly convinced by our argument." And finally, the CPSU leaders were weak "in discussing strategic

[137] *ZELNP2*, 11–14. Zhang, "Sidalin," 216 (quote; italics mine).

[138] Mićunović, *Moscow Diary*, 197–99.

[139] "Record of Conversation with the Prime Minister of the State Council of the PRC Zhou Enlai," 1/19/1957, *AVPRF*, f.0100, o.50, d.3, p.423, 4.

[140] Wu, *Eight Years*, 118. Wang, *Zhonghua*, vol. 2, 348–49. Mićunović, *Moscow Diary*, 199–200. Li, *Waijiao*, 117–20.

[141] Li, *Waijiao*, 121–22. Yan Mingfu, "Huiyi liangci Mosike huiyi he Hu Qiaomu," *Dangdai Zhongguo shi yanjiu* 1997/3, 7.

[142] Li, *Waijiao*, 121–22.

[143] "Protocol," 4/8/1957, *Archiwum Ministerstwa Spraw Zagranicznych* [AMSZ], Departament V, Wydzial I, zespol 12, wiazka 4, teczka 83, 89–95. "Polish-Soviet Talks in Moscow from May 24–25, 1957," Andrzej Paczkowski, ed., *Tajne dokumenty Biura Politycznego* (London: Aneks, 1998), 31–84.

and long-term issues." Yet, despite this assessment, Zhou stressed that "Sino-Soviet relations are far better now than during Stalin's era." This change, Zhou claimed, was due to the Soviet insight that the socialist camp was facing a "grave enemy"—imperialism.[144]

Not only did the Polish October and the Hungarian Revolution affect China's outlook on international affairs and its approach to the socialist camp, it also influenced Chinese domestic politics. Mao tried to learn the lessons relevant for China, as he told the Central Committee in November 1956: "Failure is the mother of success."[145] The Chairman firmly believed that the inability of the Bureaucratic Stalinist model to deal with, or even diffuse, internal contradictions was at the heart of the problem.

As a result, Mao cautiously started to embrace economic liberalization. He admitted to the failure of the Socialist High Tide, and endorsed planning and balanced growth.[146] In reality, though, he was only following the economic thinkers in the Chinese leadership. In early November, Zhou had asserted that "the disturbances which occurred in . . . Poland [and] Hungary . . . cast doubt on Stalin's economic theory."[147] Recognizing this change in the political climate, Chen Yun immediately began to promote market mechanisms as the best means to allocate raw materials and to distribute goods. His policies clearly recycled many ideas of the NEP.[148] Even Mao now grudgingly agreed: "It seems that Lenin's New Economic Policy was correct, unfortunately this policy was terminated too early."[149]

Ultimately, political liberalization was more important to Mao than economic reconstruction. He was firmly convinced that a small number of counterrevolutionaries in Hungary—the Petőfi Circle—had "used the dissatisfactions of the masses" to overthrow party and government.[150] This discontent, in Mao's opinion, was largely due to the failure of the Hungarian comrades to adapt Soviet economic experience to the particular situation of the country.[151] The Chairman also blamed the Hungarian

---

[144] "Report: 'My Observations on the Soviet Union,' Zhou Enlai to Mao Zedong and the Central Leadership, 24 January 1957 (Excerpt)," Zhang Shuguang et al., eds., "The Emerging Disputes between Beijing and Moscow," CWIHP Bulletin 6–7, 153–54.

[145] Mao, "Speech at the Second Plenary Session . . . ," 11/15/1956, SW, vol. 5, 337.

[146] Mao, "Speech at the Second Plenary Session . . . ," 332–37.

[147] ZELNP1, 629–30.

[148] Nicholas Lardy et al., Chen Yun's Strategy for China's Development (Armonk: Sharpe, 1983), 7–22, 30–38. Bachman, Chen Yun, 117–30.

[149] WLX, 79. Mao made the same argument in March 1957: Mao, "A Talk with Literary and Art Circles," 3/8/1957, Roderick MacFarquhar et al., eds., The Secret Speeches of Chairman Mao [SS] (Cambridge: Harvard, 1989), 230.

[150] Zhang, "Sidalin," 187.

[151] "Speech to the Personages of Industrial and Commercial Circles," 11/8/1956, MZDW, vol. 7, 178.

party for leaving too many counterrevolutionaries at large: "And now they have to reap what they have sown, they have brought the fire upon their own heads."[152]

Consequently, Mao decided to launch yet another party rectification campaign to wipe out "subjectivism, sectarianism, and bureaucratism."[153] He embarked on an unusual path, however: the opening of political debate. Already in "Again on the Historical Experience of the Proletarian Dictatorship" Mao had formulated the ideas of antagonistic and nonantagonistic contradictions that he would further develop in the famous *Contradictions Speech* in late February.[154] While destructive criticism—the questioning of the system itself—was off-limits, constructive criticism—suggestions for the improvement of communist rule in China—should be encouraged. Mao's proposal was designed both as an outlet for popular dissatisfaction and as a means to uncover counterrevolutionaries. Although he admitted there were some malcontents in China,[155] Mao still remained convinced that "we don't have a 'Petőfi Circle' . . . we are better off than Hungary."[156]

Mao's new ideas ran into resistance among other central party leaders. Liu Shaoqi maintained that China's problems derived not from abstract ideas on relations between the party and the people but from its economic backwardness. Together with Peng Zhen, Deng Xiaoping, Peng Dehuai, and Chen Yun, he feared that even a limited liberalization of the political debate could not contain the spirit of counterrevolution.[157] But by late April of 1957, Mao was able to push his ideas through.[158] Even more troubling, though, was Mao's reintroduction of class struggle into the political discourse; it was clearly an attempt to overturn the decision of the eighth CCP congress that class struggle had been terminated in China.[159]

[152] Mao, "Speech at the Second Plenary Session . . . ," 342.

[153] Li, *Li Rui wenji*, 48. Li, "Study [I]," 36. Li, *Private Life*, 197–99. MacFarquhar, *Origins*, vol. 1, 169, 177–80.

[154] Hinton, *People's Republic*, vol. 1, 462–73.

[155] Mao, "Talks at a Conference of Secretaries of Provincial, Municipal and Autonomous Region Party Committees: Talk of January 18, 1956," Mao Zedong, *SW*, vol. 5, 352–53. Mao Zedong, "Talk at Yinian Tang," 2/16/1957, *SS*, 118.

[156] Mao, "On the Correct Handling of Contradictions among the People (Speaking Notes)," 2/27/1957, *SS*, 131–90.

[157] MacFarquhar, *Origins*, vol. 1, 191–92, 196–99. Salisbury, *New Emperors*, 136–37. Jürgen Domes, *Peng Te-huai* (Stanford: Stanford, 1985), 72–73.

[158] Hinton, *People's Republic*, vol. 1, 496–98. MacFarquhar, *Origins*, vol. 1, 201–8, 248–49.

[159] 'Hu Qiaomu Zhuan' bianxie zhubian, *Hu Qiaomu tan xinwen chuban* (Beijing: Renmin, 1999), 46.

FLOWERS WITHERED AND PARTIES PURGED

The Polish October and the Hungarian Revolution triggered domestic developments in both China and the Soviet Union that ultimately led to parallel catharses in the late spring and early summer of 1957. In the PRC, Mao's experiment with limited political liberalization ended in a humiliating defeat for the Chairman and in a protracted suppression of *all* criticism. Meanwhile, in Moscow, the disagreements among the Soviet leaders over de-Stalinization erupted into the so-called Anti-Party Incident. The resolution of these two crises set China and the Soviet Union on opposite paths of ideological development. At the time, both sides failed to realize the gravity of these new developments.

Since its inception in early 1956, the Hundred Flowers Campaign had hardly generated any echo outside the party. Although dissent in the PRC was rife,[160] fear of potential repressions kept many mouths shut. Starting in mid-March 1957, the Chairman tried to reassure skeptics that the campaign would *not* lead to any repercussions.[161] It was kicked off on May 1 with a public call to carry it out "as gently as a breeze or a mild rain."[162] In controlled meetings, those invited to speak tested the limits of the still unpublished Contradictions Speech. A significant number of people openly questioned the unchecked rule of the CCP, as well as the socialist system itself. Mao soon realized the magnitude of the menace he had provoked.[163] On May 15, he sent out an internal circular to high-ranking party cadres instructing them to allow criticism to continue. The Chairman wanted the "rightists" to expose themselves in full; he was not content in getting only the small fry because he wanted "to catch the big fish, [and] . . . dig . . . out the poisonous weed" once and for all.[164]

In early June, Mao decided that the party would "counterattack."[165] The Chairman boasted that he had set up a trap by breaking the whole campaign "into many small 'Hungarian incidents' . . . [to be] dealt with

[160] See, for example: Elizabeth Perry, "Shanghai's Strike Wave of 1957," *China Quarterly* 137, 1–27.

[161] Mao, "On Ideological Work," 3/19/1957, *SS*, 337. Mao, "Talk at the Meeting of Party Cadres in Shanghai," 3/20/1957, *SS*, 351–62. Mao, "Preserve in Plain Living and Hard Struggle, Maintain Close Ties with the Masses," 3/18–19/1957, *SW*, vol. 5, 436–39.

[162] "Why Must We Carry Out the Rectification Movement 'As Gently as a Breeze or a Mild Rain'?" 5/7/1957, Hinton, *People's Republic*, vol. 1, 501–4.

[163] Li, "Study [I]," 37–38. MacFarquhar, *Origins*, vol. 1, 218.

[164] Mao, "Things Are Beginning to Change," 5/15/1957, *SW*, vol. 5, 444.

[165] Wu Lengxi, *Yi Mao zhuxi* (Beijing: Xinhua, 1995), 40. "The Party's Decision to Counterattack Its Critics," June 1957, Hinton, *People's Republic*, vol. 1, 525–33.

individually."[166] Despite this belligerent claim, Mao's own position in the CCP Politburo had been severely weakened. The failure of the campaign validated the positions of his critics within the central party leadership. Although the Chairman tried to downplay the crisis, some of the other central leaders now advocated a severe purge.[167] After long discussions, the internally split CCP leadership decided on a compromise. Party rectification would be folded into the so-called Anti-Rightist Campaign designed to suppress *all* dissent.[168] It would last until late in the year, purging hundreds of thousands.[169]

The developments in Chinese domestic politics threatened to reopen the floodgates of East European criticism. Following Gomułka's acrimonious visit to Moscow in May, the Polish party leaked Mao's Contradictions Speech to the *New York Times* as a sign of support for Mao's liberalization policies.[170] By doing so, the Poles shot themselves in the foot. The publication of the speech forced the Chinese to come forward with their own official version, precisely at the time when they were trying to overcome its unfortunate consequences. The official version published on June 18 was amended; it retroactively included six criteria that significantly narrowed the limits of permissible criticism.[171] Nevertheless, the Poles had irritated their Chinese friends; after June 1957, Sino-Polish relations steadily worsened.[172]

The domestic impact of the failed Hundred Flowers Campaign and of the Anti-Rightist Campaign lasted well into the Cultural Revolution ten years later. In the summer of 1957, Mao again redefined his ideas on class and class struggle, endorsing ideas of Revolutionary Stalinism: the more developed socialism, the more acute the class struggle.[173] At the third CC plenum in the fall of 1957, Mao openly denounced the decision of the eighth Congress to declare an end to class struggle in China.[174]

[166] Mao, "Muster Our Forces to Repulse the Rightists' Wild Attacks," 6/8/1957, SW, vol. 5, 450.

[167] MacFarquhar, *Origins*, vol. 1, 263–65, 278–85.

[168] MacFarquhar, *Origins*, vol. 1, 253. Li, "Study [I]," 42–44.

[169] MacFarquhar, *Origins*, vol. 1, 270–310.

[170] MacFarquhar, *Origins*, vol. 1, 267.

[171] See editorial comment: Mao, "On the Correct Handling of Contradictions among the People," 2/27/1957, Hinton, *People's Republic*, vol. 1, 534. MacFarquhar, *Origins*, vol. 1, 265–66. Also: *NYT*, 6/19/1957, 1, 4.

[172] MacFarquhar, *Origins*, vol. 1, 267. Mercy Kuo, *Contending with Contradictions* (Lanham: Lexington, 2001), 127.

[173] Li Rui, "An Initial Study of Mao Zedong's Erroneous 'Left' Thinking in His Later Years [Part II]," *CLG* 29/5, 8

[174] Li Rui, "Study [Part I]," 43.

Equally important was Mao's decision to revive the leftist economic policies of the Socialist High Tide. The June collapse of the Hundred Flowers Campaign had not only compromised liberalization in China but also discredited the Bureaucratic Stalinist economic model. Those who by the nature of their professional training or scientific knowledge had sustained Bureaucratic Stalinism in China had betrayed Mao's trust by making undue criticism. Mao was thus convinced that China had arrived at a critical fork in its economic development.[175] But he couched his new ideas in terms of learning from the mistakes of the Soviet Union: "Can we not avoid the Soviet Union's detours and do things faster and better?"[176] The Chairman subsequently revived the notorious slogan of the Socialist High Tide: "Faster, Bigger, Better, and More Economical."[177] Although the CCP CC did not officially approve these changes, it did endorse one essential aspect: the construction of large-scale irrigation works in China's countryside with the help of tens of millions of peasants during the winter slack season.[178]

While the summer of 1957 saw a radical reversal of China's economic and political outlook, the outcome of the so-called Anti-Party Incident in the Soviet Union reconfirmed de-Stalinization. Since early 1957 the most rigorous critics of de-Stalinization—Molotov, Kaganovich, and Malenkov—had secretly prepared for Khrushchev's removal. They finally decided to move against the first secretary at a Presidium meeting on June 18. Khrushchev, however, was able to play on the indecision of the plotters. With the support of Marshal and Defense Minister Georgii Zhukov and of KGB leaders, he called a CC plenum that reviewed not only de-Stalinization but also the involvement of the plotters in Stalin's criminal activities. On June 29, it reconfirmed Khrushchev as party leader, while expelling his adversaries from their positions. The unexpected outcome of the Anti-Party Incident thus guaranteed the continuation of de-Stalinization in the Soviet Union.[179]

After the Anti-Party Incident, Khrushchev sent Mikoyan to China to explain the new situation.[180] Mao did not like what he heard. He believed

[175] MacFarquhar, *Origins*, vol. 1, 312–13, and vol. 2, 4.

[176] Li Rui, "Study [Part I]," 49.

[177] MacFarquhar, *Origins*, vol. 2, 16–17.

[178] Roderick MacFarquhar, "The Secret Speeches of Chairman Mao," *SS*, 14. Sladkovskii, *Ocherki*, 347.

[179] Pikhoya, *Sovetskii Soyuz*, 149–60. Taubman, *Khrushchev*, 310–24. For transcripts of June plenum: Kovaleva, *Molotov, 1957*. Anastas Mikoyan, *Tak bylo* (Moskva: Vagrius, 1999), 599–600.

[180] "From the Diary of P. A. Abrasimov, Secret, 9 July 1957, Memorandum of Conversation with the General Secretary of the CCP, Com. Deng Xiaoping, 3 July 1957," Chen Jian, ed., "Deng Xiaoping, Mao's Continuous Revolution, and the Path towards the Sino-Soviet Split," *CWIHP Bulletin* 10, 165–66.

the Soviet leader had gone too far in purging old party members who had participated in the October Revolution: "If they had opposed the party, how had they done it, and whose party had they opposed anyway?" The Chairman was equally unwilling to accept that they had conspired against Khrushchev: "They just had an opinion different from Khrushchev's."[181] He concluded that "the Soviet method of dealing with Malenkov, Kaganovich, [and] Molotov had some correct aspects but was over-all *incorrect*."[182]

Subsequently, Khrushchev decided to play the China card in order to shore up support within the CPSU and the socialist camp. Since his visit to Beijing in late 1954, the Soviet leader knew that the Chairman was interested in acquiring nuclear weapons. On his trip to China in August, Mikoyan offered Soviet assistance to the Chinese nuclear weapons program.[183] The official Sino-Soviet agreement of October 15, 1957, provided for the future delivery of a Soviet model A-bomb, along with relevant data, by 1959.[184]

In the early fall of 1957, the CPSU and the CCP were setting out on two different—ultimately irreconcilable—paths of ideological, political, and economic development. Mao had given up on Bureaucratic Stalinism for ideas closer to Revolutionary Stalinism, while the Anti-Party Incident in Moscow had removed the old Stalinist stalwarts in Moscow from power. Given Mao's claims about Stalin's poor treatment of China in the past, the purge of some of the late dictator's closest collaborators should have delighted the Chairman. It only angered him.

The Moscow Meeting, November 1957

On the eve of the Moscow Meeting of the world communist movement in November, Sino-Soviet relations seemed, at least on the surface, to be calm. Both sides made great efforts to present a picture of unity. This "show of force toward imperialism" rooted in the understanding that a façade of cohesion after twenty tumultuous months was essential.[185] Yet, a close look at the Sino-Soviet relationship reveals deep animosities. The Chinese comrades only grudgingly accepted an endorsement of the

---

[181] Salisbury, *New Emperors*, 138. Shi, *Zai lishi*, 509 (quotes).

[182] Liu, *Chushi*, 58 (italics mine).

[183] Li, *Private Life*, 206.

[184] "Record of Conversation with Liu Xiao," 8/8/1957, *AVPRF*, f.0100, o.50, d.3, p.423, 37–38. WLX, 205–6. Xinhua News Agency, *China's Foreign Relations* (Beijing: Foreign Languages, 1989), 460. MacFarquhar, *Origins*, vol. 2, 11–12. Zhang, "Economic Cooperation," 207. Wang, *Zhonghua*, vol. 2, 221. Liu, *Chushi*, 53–54.

[185] WLX, 96.

decisions of the twentieth CPSU congress, while the personal relationship between Mao and Khrushchev deteriorated.

By early June, despite his attempts to entice Mao with nuclear assistance after the Anti-Party Incident, Khrushchev had already approached Tito with the proposal to meet for talks about the organization of a meeting of all communist parties.[186] The two leaders met in Bucharest for friendly talks in early August; both sides agreed on the need for cooperation based on equality.[187] In mid-October, however, the Yugoslavs objected to a Soviet draft declaration to be published at the Moscow Meeting because it contained the term "socialist camp" and—in an effort to please Yugoslav *and* Chinese ideological views—the phrase "struggle against dogmatism and revisionism."[188] Belgrade immediately felt its political and ideological autonomy being threatened; Tito even refused to attend the Moscow Meeting himself.[189]

It was only after the Yugoslav refusal that the Soviets turned to the Chinese comrades, one week before the Moscow Meeting. Once again, Mao felt slighted—he was only Khrushchev's second choice.[190] To make matters worse, the Soviet draft was not at all to his liking. "Differences of viewpoints" led the Chinese comrades to draw up their own version and to fly to the Soviet capital early, on November 2, in order to "get rid of any harmful parts in the Soviet draft."[191] The Chairman instructed his secretary, Hu Qiaomu, to write a version that "contained as much as possible from the Soviet draft, but in the main points represented our views."[192]

Although Chinese sources do not specify the "differences of viewpoints," in the end, the Chinese delegation was forced to make significant concessions. Sino-Soviet talks, negotiations in the so-called Editorial Board (the French, Italian, and the thirteen ruling parties of the socialist camp), and, eventually, the meeting of all sixty-plus national delegations revealed that Chinese positions did not represent the majority view.[193]

---

[186] For Soviet June proposal: "[no title]," [no date], *Státní Ústřední Archiv [SÚA]*, Archiv ÚV KSČ, f.07/16, Antonín Novotný—Zahraničí, karton 52, Porada představitelů komunistických a dělnických stran (listopad 1957, Moskva), A-, 4–6.

[187] Mičunovič, *Moscow Diary*, 287–89. "Information about the Meeting of the Delegations of the CC of the CPSU and the CC of the YLC," [8/2/1957], *SAPMO-BArch*, DY 30/3642, 267–69.

[188] "Information by Comrades Ponomarev and Andropov," 10/15 & 18/1957, *SAPMO-BArch*, DY 30/3642, 97–102.

[189] Gittings, *Survey*, 85.

[190] Yan, "Huiyi," 7–8.

[191] WLX, 96.

[192] Yan, "Huiyi," 7–8.

[193] Chinese historiography tries to portray concessions as mutual, see: Ding Ming, "Huigu ge sikao," 24. WLX, 98, 100.

The final declaration not only called for unity but also confirmed the decisions of the twentieth CPSU congress. Despite this very public defeat of Chinese ideological positions, Mao tried to convince skeptics of the necessity of unity and of the socialist camp's need for, in a bipolar world, a "head"—the CPSU.[194]

The upbeat tone the Chairman tried to inject into the meeting also surfaced in the friendly boasting contest Khrushchev and Mao started in Moscow. As early as May, the Soviet leader had announced that, in a short time, the Soviet Union would surpass the United States in agricultural production.[195] In July, Mao responded with a call on China to surpass the American class enemy economically within the next fifty years.[196] During the early November celebrations for the fortieth anniversary of the October Revolution, Khrushchev announced the Soviet plan to overtake the American economy in fifteen years. In an impromptu speech, Mao boasted that China would surpass Great Britain in steel and heavy industrial production within the same period.[197]

Yet, this public display of Sino-Soviet harmony disguised political, ideological, and personal tensions. In the political sphere, Khrushchev and Mao squabbled over Tito and the Yugoslav refusal to sign the Moscow Declaration. Although the Chairman shared Soviet complaints about Belgrade's "bad manners," he admonished his host for failing to accept diversity and equality in the socialist camp.[198] Further disagreements arose over the Hundred Flowers Campaign and Stalin's mistakes in the Chinese Revolution. Far more serious, though, were differences linked to Khrushchev's pursuit of two essentially contradictory strategic goals: relaxation of relations with the West and a close partnership with anti-imperialist China.[199]

Given the gradual worsening of the situation in the Taiwan Strait since the summer of 1956—the stalled Sino-American ambassadorial talks, U.S. military support for the Guomindang on Taiwan, and the introduction of American tactical nuclear missiles on the island—the CCP refused to accept Khrushchev's pursuit of peaceful coexistence. Although the final papers of the Moscow Meeting endorsed the decisions of the

---

[194] WLX, 112–16. Also: Mao, "[Speech held in Moscow, 11/14/1957]," Mao Zedong, *Jianguo yilai Mao Zedong wengao* [*JYMW*], vol. 6 (Beijing: Zhongyang wenxian), 625–28.

[195] Pikhoya, *Sovetskii Soyuz*, 172–73.

[196] Li, *Private Life*, 209.

[197] Mao, "[Speech held in Moscow, 11/18/1957]," *JYMW*, vol. 6, 635. Li, *Li Rui wenji*, 53–54. Li, *Waijiao*, 162–63. Zhang, "Economic Cooperation," 203.

[198] Li, *Waijiao*, 150. Also: Wu, *Eight Years*, 150–55. WLX, 127. Mičunović, *Moscow Diary*, 319. Ding, "Huigu," 26. Li, "Huiyi," 12–13. On the Soviet treatment of the Yugoslav delegation: Mičunović, *Moscow Diary*, 315–17. Khrushchev, *Khrushchev Remembers*, 152–53.

[199] Li, *Waijiao*, 151. Khrushchev, *Testament*, 271–72; *Glasnost Tapes*, 150.

twentieth CPSU congress, the Chinese delivered a secret memorandum to the Soviets reiterating their disagreement with peaceful coexistence. It was the first time that Beijing told Moscow about its conflict with Soviet policy toward American imperialism.[200]

Theoretical disagreements also arose over the inevitability of nuclear war. Since the late 1940s, Mao had developed the opinion that nuclear weapons were nothing more than paper tigers. Given its the numerical superiority in population, Mao had told Indian Prime Minister Jawaharlal Nehru in late 1954, the socialist camp would survive a nuclear war while the imperialists would be totally wiped off the face of the earth.[201] Mao's strange logic received an additional boost when the Soviet Union launched Sputnik on October 4, 1957, a month before the Moscow Meeting. The Chairman was elated that the rocket carrying the tiny satellite into orbit seemed to have broken imperialist nuclear blackmail: "The correlation of forces in the international arena has seriously changed to our advantage."[202] Given his buoyant mood, the Chairman not only announced to all sixty-plus parties that the "East Wind was prevailing over the West Wind," but also once more expressed his strange beliefs on nuclear war: "The whole world has 2 billion 700 million people, possibly it will lose a third; or even more, possibly it will lose half . . . but there will be another half; the imperialists will be hit completely, [and] the whole world will become socialist; and after a couple of years, it will again have 2 billion 700 million people, probably more."[203]

The Soviets shared neither Mao's opinion that the imperialists were warmongers nor his belief that the Soviet Union had reached nuclear parity.[204] Khrushchev recollected that "the audience was dead silent" after Mao's speech. Władysław Gomułka and Antonín Novotný, the first secretary of the Czechoslovak party, voiced their disapproval almost immediately; while populous China might survive a nuclear war, they protested, their small countries would be completely destroyed.[205] In light of the recent Soviet promise to deliver a model A-bomb to the PRC, Mao's public promotion of his strange ideas on nuclear war must have made the Soviet comrades shudder.

---

[200] WLX, 138. Yan Mingfu, "Huiyi," 9. The Chinese published an outline of the memo in 1964: *Peking Review* [PR] 14, 4/3/1964, 22–23.

[201] Lewis, *China*, 6–7. Zhai Qiang, *The Dragon, the Lion, and the Eagle* (Kent: Kent State, 1994), 8–11. Mao, "Talk with the American Correspondent Anna Louise Strong, August 1946," *SW*, vol. 4, 100.

[202] "Record of Conversation with Mao Zedong," 10/11/1957, *AVPRF*, f.0100, o.50, d.5, p.423, 44.

[203] Mao Zedong, "[Speech held in Moscow, 11/18/1957]," *JYMW*, vol. 6, 630, 636.

[204] Chen, "Chinese Politics," 266.

[205] Khrushchev, *Testament*, 255.

Sino-Soviet tensions permeated personal relations between the leaders too. The Chairman lived up to his image as a difficult and rude person. Despite Khrushchev having made him the guest of honor,[206] and putting him up in the former residence of Empress Ekaterina, Mao complained to his personal physician: "Look how differently [from 1949] they're treating us now . . . Even in this communist land, they know who is powerful and who is weak. What snobs!"[207] Mao's personal jibes at Khrushchev were equally bad. At a dinner, the Soviet leader recalled Stalin's military mistakes during the world war at length, only to be cut short by his Chinese guest: "Comrade Khrushchev, I have already finished eating, have you finished your story?"[208] The Chairman also found it necessary to tell Khrushchev that he should work on the bad "dispositions" of his character.[209] Mao's arrogance derived from his belief in Khrushchev's "immaturity" and lack of "profound thinking."[210]

During 1956 and 1957, serious points of conflict in the Sino-Soviet relationship emerged for the first time. At the twentieth CPSU congress, Khrushchev's criticism of Stalin's rule called for the de-Stalinization of the political system, that is, the abrogation of arbitrary and unrestricted personal rule as well as the end of the use of terror, which had characterized especially but not exclusively Revolutionary Stalinism. The Soviet leader, however, did *not* call for the reform of the basic underpinnings of the Bureaucratic Stalinist economic system, such as the use of central economic planning or the socioeconomic organization of the USSR along party class lines. Although the call for political reform was rooted in domestic necessities, it seriously affected relations with many of the Soviet allies. Despite hidden disagreements on de-Stalinization, the CCP publicly supported the CPSU at the Moscow Meeting, attempting to heal the rifts that the upheavals in Poland and Hungary had caused. However, by then, Mao had decided not only to reject political and ideological de-Stalinization, but also to embark on economic policies that resembled Revolutionary Stalinism. Although, compared to de-Stalinization, peaceful coexistence did not rattle Sino-Soviet relations in the eighteen months after the twentieth CPSU congress, the worsening of Sino-American relations over Taiwan led the Chinese to abrogate, though only confidentially, its support for the new Soviet policy. By 1958, the disagreements over de-Stalinization

---

[206] Viktor Grishin, *Ot Khrushcheva do Gorbacheva* (Moskva: ASPOL, 1996), 20.

[207] Li, *Private Life*, 221.

[208] Ding, "Huigu," 36.

[209] Li, *Waijiao*, 152.

[210] Yan Mingfu in: Salisbury, *New Emperors*, 154 (first quote). Li, "Huiyi," 14 (second quote).

and peaceful coexistence, which had emerged by late 1957 for unrelated reasons, converged in Chinese politics into an explosive mix.

Throughout 1956–57, ideological disagreements thus permeated the Sino-Soviet relationship. At that time, Mao's use of ideology, however, had both instrumental and genuine characteristics. On the one hand, from the spring to the fall of 1956, Mao exploited ideology instrumentally to suppress a general debate on de-Stalinization and its implications for China. His aim was to protect his exposed flank against criticism from inside the party. On the other hand, his review of the world situation, the condition of socialist camp, and the state of China's internal affairs at the turn of 1956/57 revealed sincere concerns over the validity and failures of Stalinism. While he rejected Khrushchev's de-Stalinization of relations within the socialist camp, because it had created confusion among the East Europeans and led to misguided Soviet decisions with regard to Poland and Hungary, he was willing to allow a certain political liberalization at home during the Hundred Flowers Campaign of 1957. This was done in order to defuse the internal conflicts that the rigidity of Bureaucratic Stalinism had allowed to grow. Events in the international sphere thus influenced domestic politics to great effect. Mao's left turn after the failure of the Hundred Flowers Campaign thus contained genuine and instrumental aspects in his use of ideology. While he believed that there was only one alternative to both liberalization and Bureaucratic Stalinism—the radicalization of Chinese domestic politics—the purge of the Anti-Rightist Campaign he and his fellow CCP leaders implemented was designed to protect the party from further internal and external dissent.

Security concerns played only a secondary role in Sino-Soviet relations throughout most of this period. Even if, at the end of 1957, the CCP confidentially notified the CPSU that it no longer supported peaceful coexistence, this did not mean that the Soviet decision to pursue a policy of rapprochement with the United States itself had created an immediate security threat to China. While the gradual worsening of Sino-American relations over the Taiwan Question was unrelated, it did undermine the Chinese rationale for supporting peaceful coexistence. Nevertheless, in 1956–57, peaceful coexistence never grew into a point of disagreement in the way de-Stalinization did. In April and December of 1956, Mao had ordered the publication of two articles outlining his disagreement with Khrushchev's criticism of Stalin, but in December 1956 and November 1957, he twice decided to keep his criticism of peaceful coexistence out of the public sphere. Similarly, Mao did not reject peaceful transition, a derivative of peaceful coexistence, because it was a security threat to China, but because he was convinced that it rejected Stalinism in its support for bourgeois democracy. It was thus that by late 1957 notable cracks had opened under the seemingly smooth surface of Sino-Soviet relations.

CHAPTER 3

Mao's Challenges, 1958

IN LATE AUGUST 1958, the Frontline Commune came under crossfire during the artillery battles between the People's Liberation Army and Guomindang troops stationed on Jinmen Island at the center of Xiamen Bay. Chinese Communist propaganda blared across the water, demanding the surrender of the enemy troops stationed on the islet. During the intensive artillery exchanges of the Second Taiwan Strait Crisis, villagers took cover in shelters carved into the rock. In combat pauses, the commune members followed Mao's call to build the communist future. Public mess halls and communal quarters replaced individual living arrangements. Peasants turned into rural proletarians working in large brigades. After each Guomindang barrage, commune leaders sent the brigades out to collect shells that had landed in the fields for steel production in small brick smelters. The Chairman ordered the whole country to erect backyard blast furnaces to double steel production. It was a twin battle—a struggle to surpass imperialism in industrial production and a real war against its running dogs on Jinmen.[1]

The Second Taiwan Strait Crisis and the launching of the radical Great Leap Forward policies in late August 1958 were closely linked, though their roots were unrelated. The crisis, on the one hand, was the result of China's dissatisfaction with the development of Sino-American relations throughout the previous two years. It was not a response to an increasing American threat; Mao created it with the purpose of lashing out at the United States. The Great Leap Forward, on the other, had its origins in Mao's ideological left turn in the summer of 1957.

The radicalization of China's domestic politics over the spring and the summer of 1958, however, made its foreign policy more confrontational. Mao's rejection of Bureaucratic Stalinism in 1957 and his gradual embrace of socioeconomic policies resembling Revolutionary Stalinism led to the adoption of an anti-Soviet political tone that spread into other policy areas. Consequently, Mao reacted with hyperbole to Moscow's

---

[1] Huang Shu-min, *Spiral Road*, 2nd ed. (Boulder: Westview, 1998), 52–53, 57–59. *SCMP* 1844, 23. Wang Yanzhu, *Peng Dehuai nianpu* [*PDHNP*] (Beijing: Shijie zhishi, 1998), 698–99. Christensen, *Useful Adversaries*, 198. Chang, *Friends*, 195.

proposal of the so-called joint submarine proposal in July. Although the Chairman accused the Soviet Union of trying to control China, the ultimate goal of the proposal sought the stationing of Soviet nuclear-missile submarines in the PRC with the aim to deter the United States on a global scale. Eventually, in late July and early August, the Chairman was ready to use the planned crisis in the Taiwan Strait not only to lash out at the United States but also to confront the Soviet policy of peaceful coexistence.

The timing of the Second Taiwan Strait Crisis—late August—was a function of the Great Leap Forward. The ad hoc preparation of the radical domestic policies, intended to propel China from a backward country into the bright communist future, ended with their approval at the Beidaihe enlarged Politburo conference. The Second Taiwan Strait Crisis produced a domestic atmosphere that facilitated the mobilization of China's population for the implementation of these radical policies. Not only were both the crisis and the radical Great Leap Forward Mao's creations, but, by late August, they had also become an explicit double challenge to Soviet leadership in the world and within the socialist camp. Both undermined Sino-Soviet relations.

THE CONTINUOUS REVOLUTION: THE GREAT LEAP FORWARD CONCEIVED

Sino-Soviet relations seemed to flourish after the Moscow Meeting. A series of scientific and cooperation agreements were signed around the turn of the year 1957/58.[2] The Chinese supported Soviet initiatives to create a nuclear-free zone in East Asia, hoping to undermine U.S. alliances in East Asia.[3] Beijing publicly backed Moscow's proposal for a summit between the North Atlantic Treaty Organization (NATO) and the Warsaw Pact Organization (WAPA) on nuclear disarmament, while attacking the United States for announcing that it would not negotiate from a position of weakness after Sputnik.[4] Chinese support only wavered in May 1958 once Khrushchev agreed to U.S. President Dwight Eisenhower's proposal to negotiate on nuclear weapons.[5] The PRC instead publicly announced

---

[2] SCMP 1673, 46. Current Background [CB] 545, 3. "CPSU CC," 12/10/1957, GARF, f.9324, o.1, d.1, 2–3. "Soviet-Chinese Relations (Reference)," 2/13/1961, AVPRF, f.0100, o.54, d.27, p.470, 41. SCMP 1679, 40. CB 506, 3.

[3] CB 489, 25; 506, 29. SCMP 1674, 31–34; 1678, 42–43. MacFarquhar, Origins, vol. 2, 68–69. ZELNP2, 137.

[4] CB 506, 6. SCMP 1691, 28–29.

[5] MacFarquhar, Origins, vol. 2, 68, 70.

its desire to acquire nuclear weapons.[6] Chen Yi told the Soviet embassy that any U.S.-Soviet agreements would "not apply to China."[7]

Following Belgrade's aloof position during the Moscow Meeting, Sino-Soviet cooperation against Yugoslavia increased. In December, Suslov censured the Yugoslavs in the CPSU CC for their refusal to accept the concept of two hostile camps in world affairs.[8] Khrushchev informed Mao on April 2 that the CPSU would not send a delegation to the impending Yugoslav party congress because the draft program was anti-Marxist and revisionist.[9] Ambassador Yudin was instructed to talk with the Chinese comrades; at a meeting in Wuhan, Mao condemned Tito as an agent of U.S. imperialism.[10] The CCP refused to send a delegation to Belgrade.[11] After the congress, the Soviets and the Chinese launched a propaganda offensive against the Yugoslav revisionists. Polemics worsened to such a degree that Sino-Yugoslav diplomatic relations collapsed that summer.[12]

After Mao had returned from Moscow to Beijing, he started to plan what was to become the Great Leap Forward. His ambitions stemmed from his optimistic assessment of the international and domestic situation. Sputnik apparently made socialism victorious abroad; the Anti-Rightist Campaign had seemingly produced popular enthusiasm for economic development at home.[13] The Chairman had mistaken enforced compliance for passionate voluntarism. The Anti-Rightist Campaign had crushed popular dissent; the CCP simply manipulated public opinion.[14] It was in this context that the CC officially adopted Mao's concept of Continuous Revolution. The Chairman was convinced that the Chinese Revolution was a series of distinct revolutions: anti-imperialist, anti-feudal, agricultural, socialist, and soon, technological. Believing that the Chinese

---

[6] MacFarquhar, *Origins*, vol. 2, 69.

[7] "Statements by Leaders of the PRC on Important Questions of Foreign Policy," 12/9/1960, *AVPRF*, f.0100, o.53, d.24, p.457, 236–37 (quote).

[8] "Stenographic Report of the CPSU CC Plenum, December 1957," *Rossiiskii Gosudarstvennyi Arkhiv Noveishei Istorii [RGANI]*, f.2, o.1, d.284, 43.

[9] Khrushchev's letter summarized in note 2: "Letter to Khrushchev on [Decision] not to send Delegation to 7th Party Congress of Yugoslav League of Communists," 4/8/1958, *JYMW*, vol. 7, 173.

[10] "Record of Conversation with comrade Liu Shaoqi," 4/4/1958, and "Record of Conversation with Mao Zedong," 4/5/1958, *AVPRF*, f.0100, o.51, d.6, p.432, 117–23.

[11] "Letter to Khrushchev on [Decision] not to send Delegation to 7th Party Congress of Yugoslav League of Communists," 4/8/1958, *JYMW*, vol. 7, 172.

[12] *CB* 519, 11; 519, 15. *SCMP* 1800, 1–3; 1785, 6–13; 1787, 9–12; 1795, 4–17. MacFarquhar, *Origins*, vol. 2, 73.

[13] Hu Qiaomu, *Hu Qiaomu huiyi Mao Zedong* (Beijing: Renmin, 1994), 14.

[14] Chen, "Chinese Politics," 265.

Revolution had to be pushed ahead relentlessly, Mao insisted that "it is better to strike while the iron is hot."[15]

The political scientist Lowell Dittmer identified four characteristics central to Mao's implementation of the Continuous Revolution: charismatic leadership, a salvational mission, mass mobilization, and an illegitimate authority structure that was the target of struggle.[16] Although some of these elements already shaped Mao's policies before 1958, they interacted closely just before the official launch of the Great Leap Forward at the second session of the eighth CCP congress in May 1958. Let us turn to the first three characteristics at the present juncture, and come back to the fourth later in this chapter.

Mao's personality cult as a form of charismatic leadership went through a revival in early 1958.[17] It was a means of obtaining control over the policy-making process.[18] At the Chengdu conference in March, he surmised: *"A team must worship its leader, not to worship him won't do."*[19] Mao even went further when he claimed that the CCP actually did not oppose Stalin's personality cult: "Khrushchev with one stroke finished Stalin. In the Chinese party the majority clearly does not agree."[20]

Mao's salvational mission, announced in Moscow in November of 1957, was to surpass economically Great Britain in fifteen years through a technological revolution, which he labeled the Great Leap Forward later that month. The technological revolution generated two central catchphrases. First, "Walking on Two Legs" symbolized Mao's belief in two types of industrial and agricultural development: indigenous, traditional methods and imported, modern methods.[21] Reflecting his emphasis on greater independence from Soviet thinking, this dual approach eventually led to paradoxical economic policies: the infamous backyard steel furnaces and simultaneous calls for more Soviet industrial assistance.[22]

---

[15] "Sixty Articles on Work Methods," 1/2/1958, Chen, "Chinese Politics," 267. Mao, "Speeches at the Supreme State Conference (Excerpts)," 1/28 & 30/1958, *CLG* 9/3, 66 (quote). Zhonggong, *Mao Zedong zhuan*, 762–63.

[16] Dittmer, *Continuous Revolution*, 4–5.

[17] Xiao Donglian, *Qiusuo Zhongguo*, vol. 1 (Beijing: Hongqi, 1999), 569–70.

[18] Li, "Study [II]," 61–62.

[19] Mao, "[Speech at the Chengdu Work Conference," 3/22/1958], Mao Zedong, *Mao Zedong daguan [MZDDG]* (Beijing: Renmin daxue, 1993), 605 (italics mine).

[20] Mao, "Speech at the Chengdu Conference," 3/10/1958, Mao Zedong, *Mao Zedong sixiang wansui [MZDSW]* (No place: no publisher, 1969), 162.

[21] Mao, "A Revolutionary Chronicle of Mao Zedong," *MZDDG*, 1086. Sladkovskii, *Ocherki*, 347. Mao, "From the Soviet Union's Experience We Should Choose Only the Good Things," 3/9/1958, Mao, *On Diplomacy*, 240–41.

[22] For calls for Soviet assistance: "Record of Conversation with Zhu De," 2/22/1958, *AVPRF*, f.0100, o.51, d.6, p.432, 81–82. "Record of Conversation with Zhu De,"

Mao justified the implicit rejection of the Bureaucratic Stalinist model with his call for learning from Stalin's mistakes.[23] Evoking theoretical postulates of Revolutionary Stalinism and the egalitarian myths of war communism in Yan'an, the Chairman faulted the late Soviet leader for emphasizing decision making by party cadres alone, for disregarding class struggle, and for using material incentives instead of popular enthusiasm.[24] Second, Mao recycled the 1955 slogan "Faster, Bigger, Better and More Economical" when he called for imbalanced and leaplike economic development.[25] He turned Marx's claims that historical developments have regular and protracted patterns on their head, declaring that "'rash advance' was Marxist, [while] 'opposition to rash advance' was non-Marxist."[26]

From the very beginning, the primary focus of Mao's industrial Great Leap Forward was on increased production of steel and its auxiliary products.[27] Heavy industry was central to Leninist ideas on economic growth, but Mao reduced that focus to steel. Consequently, steel targets dramatically increased from 5.35 million tons in late 1957 to 6.2 million tons in January 1958, to 8–8.5 million tons in May, and finally to 10.7 million tons in June—a doubling of the 1958 production quota with six months of that year left for its fulfillment.[28] Similarly, the time frame for economically surpassing Great Britain shrank from fifteen years to "shorter than fifteen years" in March, to "10–12 years" in April, to "seven years" in May, and then to "three years" in September.[29] The repeated target modification reflected the newly emerging political discourse. After the

3/9/1958, *AVPRF*, f.0100, o.51, d.6, p.432, 97–103. "Dear Comrade Khrushchev," 5/2/1958, *AVPRF*, f.0100, o.51, d.3, p.431, 40–41.

[23] Mao, "Speech at the Chengdu Meeting," 3/22/1958, Mao Zedong, *Mao Zedong xuanji*, vol. 3 [*MZDX3*] (Hong Kong: Mingbao yuekan, 1971), 182. "Record of Conversation with Mao Zedong," 2/28/1958, *AVPRF*, f.0100, o.51, d.6, p.432, 95.

[24] Li, "Study [II]," 63–65. Mao, "Speech at the Chengdu Meeting," 3/22/1958, *MZDX3*, 181–87.

[25] Li, "Study [II]," 18. *CB* 892, 1–14.

[26] Wu, *Yi Mao zhuxi*, 60–61. Also: Li, "Study [I]," 47. Chen, "Chinese Politics," 267–68.

[27] Zhang, "Economic Cooperation," 203–4. WLX, 156. Li, "Study [II]," 7–8.

[28] MacFarquhar, *Origins*, vol. 2, 89.

[29] First quote in: Chen, "Chinese Politics," 268. "Record of Conversation between Polish Delegation and PRC Leader Mao Zedong, Wuhan," 4/2/1958, Douglas Selvage et al., eds., "Polish Documents on Polish-Chinese Relations, 1957–1964," comp. and trans. for the conference "New Central and East European Evidence on the Cold War in Asia," Budapest, Hungary, 10/30–11/2/2003 (second quote). Mao, "Speech at the Conference of Heads of Delegations to the Second Session of the 8th Party Congress," 5/18/1958, Mao Zedong, *Miscellany of Mao Tse-tung Thought (1949–1968)* (Washington: JPRS, 1974), 123 (third quote). Mao, "Speech," 9/89/1958, *CLG* 9/3, 92 (fourth quote).

Anti-Rightist Campaign had removed all systemic checks and balances, no one was willing to resist unrealistic and potentially self-destructive policies.

Swift development of agriculture paralleled rash advance in heavy industry. The Chinese leadership had realized long before that the lack of agricultural mechanization routinely caused labor shortages during busy rural seasons. In early 1958, the Chairman used local reports to push the CC secretary for rural affairs, Tan Zhenlin, to systematize the use of indigenous and modern agricultural methods. In August, Tan proposed a list of sensible ideas, such as water conservancy, fertilizers, soil amelioration, better seed strains, pest prevention, better field management, and tools improvement. The methods Mao himself added were a much less sensible rehash of Lysenkoist ideas, such as the so-called genetic engineering through environmental changes, deep plowing, and close planting.[30] Given the bountiful spring harvest, the Chairman even worried that the weight of the expected greater fall harvest in China would make "the entire earth . . . turn upside down."[31]

Other central CCP leaders reacted to the unfolding follies of the agricultural Great Leap Forward in various ways. Zhou Enlai and the central planners kept silent after the Chairman had criticized them for opposing rash advance in early 1958. Peng Dehuai as late as April questioned Mao's use of the slogan "Faster, Bigger, Better and More Economical."[32] But Liu Shaoqi and Deng Xiaoping emerged as the most ardent supporters of the Continuous Revolution at the second session of the eighth CCP congress in May, which overturned the sensible economic decisions of the first session.[33] They apparently believed that Prime Minister Zhou's contemporaneous political decline meant more power to the party which they controlled through their constituencies.

The third characteristic in Mao's Continuous Revolution was mass mobilization. Since October 1957 Mao had been eager to exploit popular enthusiasm for "a grand upsurge" in economic development.[34] The successful use of mass labor in the water conservancy projects during the winter supported Mao's attack on Stalin's famous dictum of 1935 that "cadres decide everything." He stressed instead that "politics and the masses decide everything."[35] The Chairman also demanded the resurrection of Yan'an's "war communism" with its supposed "egalitarianism . . . , the abolition

[30] MacFarquhar, *Origins*, vol. 2, 122–24. *SCMP* 1834, 15–21.

[31] Li, "Study [I]," 48–49 (quote). MacFarquhar, *Origins*, vol. 2, 124.

[32] Domes, *Peng*, 82.

[33] *CB* 507, 1–25. MacFarquhar, *Origins*, vol. 2, 51–53.

[34] Li, "Study [I]," 46.

[35] Mao, *Miscellany*, 115.

of wages, and the reintroduction of a supply system" for daily goods.[36] Many of the ideas bore a close resemblance to Revolutionary Stalinism.

Mao's plan to use China's armed forces as a means to achieve his visions clashed with the positions of Defense Minister Peng Dehuai, who resisted political indoctrination as a substitute for military cooperation with the Soviet army.[37] For the Chairman, cooperation with China's ally was increasingly less interesting for another reason. In early 1958, following his jubilations on Sputnik months before, Mao realized that the future abundance of Soviet nuclear missiles would elevate the USSR to nuclear parity with the United States while marginalizing the PRC as a security asset to its ally. The fact that Khrushchev agreed to Eisenhower's proposal to discuss nuclear disarmament by May seemed to confirm such an assessment. Thus, because the Chairman expected that Moscow needed Beijing less and less for strategic reasons, he was more willing to risk a close Sino-Soviet military relationship in exchange for obtaining his domestic goals.[38] By early April, the Politburo followed Mao's vision for China's armed forces by approving new regulations on national defense work, which included the numerical reduction of the regular army with the purpose of freeing labor and equipment for economic production as well as the expansion of the people's militia and its use for labor projects.[39] Mao also promoted Lin Biao—a civil war hero loyal to the Chairman—as a long-term replacement for Peng.[40] He was attracted to Lin's idea of using the CCP MAC to indoctrinate the Chinese People's Liberation Army (PLA) with *Mao Zedong Military Thought*. Given the quick disintegration of the Hungarian army in October 1956, Lin was convinced that the PLA needed better ideological preparation for periods of internal tension.[41]

Lin's election to the Politburo Standing Committee—one party rank above Peng's—at the second session of the eighth CCP congress in mid-May forced the defense minister to compromise.[42] On May 24, the first day of an eight-week MAC conference, he announced the topics to be discussed: work styles, troop reorganization, Soviet experience, and Mao's military writings.[43] Although the majority of the PLA brass assembled did not heed such calls, Mao was able to force his line on the

---

[36] Li, "Study [II]," 63–65.

[37] MacFarquhar, *Origins*, vol. 2, 63, 95. *SCMP* 1719, 26–30. *CB* 506, 16.

[38] Christensen, *Useful Adversaries*, 206–7.

[39] "Ideas on National Defense Work," 4/8/1958, *Jiangsu Sheng Dang'anguan* [*JSSDAG*], 3011, zhang 412, 1–3.

[40] Domes, *Peng*, 81–82.

[41] Cong Jin, *Quzhe fazhan de suiyue* (Zhengzhou: Henan renmin, 1989), 286–88.

[42] MacFarquhar, *Origins*, vol. 2, 63–65, 75–76.

[43] *PDHNP*, 681–83.

armed forces.[44] The MAC also had to swallow Mao's idea of a "work-ers-peasants-soldiers" society in China: "Everybody should organize mi-litias, each person should have a gun, in order to realize *an entire nation in arms.*"[45] Calculating its costs, Peng realized that this alone "would bring us close to the annual military budget."[46] But Mao's nation-in-arms was a metaphorical picture designed to create the militarized atmosphere necessary for the implementation of the Great Leap Forward,[47] as he ad-mitted himself: "A little waste is . . . necessary. 'Everyone a soldier' helps boost morale and courage."[48]

The last pieces of the Great Leap Forward fell into place in mid-August, right before the Beidaihe conference. This enlarged Politburo conference at a Yellow Sea–side resort was originally scheduled to open on July 30, but Khrushchev's sudden visit to Beijing (see below) provided Mao with additional time to complete his ideas.[49] The day after Khrushchev had left Beijing on August 3, Mao went on a ten-day tour to Hebei, Henan, Shandong, and Tianjin, where he inspected the newest craze in Chinese economic politics: people's communes.[50] Earlier, the Chairman had called for the enlargement of agricultural cooperatives (formed in 1955) into larger units. His fellow central leaders had been reluctant, but Mao was able to convince provincial leaders to experiment locally. The first communes appeared in Henan in April 1958; by mid-August, 20 percent of Chinese peasants had joined them.[51] In July, Mao's close collaborator Chen Boda claimed that communes were ideal for the accomplishment of Mao's technological revolution. Large communes that would create self-sufficient economic, administrative, and military units complied with both Mao's earlier demands to decentralize China's government and the Marxist dogma of the state withering away in communism.[52] But it fun-damentally contradicted the experience of the failed Socialist High Tide. Nevertheless, in early August in Henan, on his visit to the first commune

[44] *PDHNP*, 681–90. Cong, *Quzhe*, 288–89. Mao, *On Diplomacy*, 247. *MZDW*, vol. 7, 375, 380. *MZDDG*, 608–9. *CLG* 1/4, 15–22.

[45] *PDHNP*, 688, 691 (italics mine).

[46] *PDHNP*, 697.

[47] Christensen, *Useful Adversaries*, 217–18.

[48] Mao, "Talk at Beidaihe Conference (Draft Transcript)," 8/17/1958, *SS*, 404.

[49] "Record of Conversation with Zhou Enlai and Peng Zhen," 7/28/1958, *AVPRF*, f.0100, o.51, d.6, p.432, 171.

[50] *WLX*, 175. MacFarquhar, *Origins*, vol. 2, 80. *CB* 519, 28.

[51] Domes, *Peng*, 78.

[52] Chen Boda, "New Society, New People," 7/1/1958, Hinton, *People's Republic*, vol. 2, 655–56. MacFarquhar, *Origins*, vol. 2, 77–80. Li, "Study [I]," 49–52. Li Rui, *Li Rui wenji*, vol. 3/1, 178. Mao, "Talk at Beidaihe Conference (Draft Transcript)," 3/19/1958, *SS*, 405–6. Mao, "Talk at Beidaihe Conference (Draft Transcript)," 8/21/1958, Afternoon, *SS*, 423.

to be established in the PRC, Mao commented: "French workers created the Paris commune when they seized power. Our farmers have created the people's commune as a political and economic organization in the march towards communism."[53]

On his way from Tianjin to Beidaihe, Mao prepared a list of seventeen topics to be discussed at the enlarged Politburo conference. Agriculture, economic production, communes, and militias made up more than two-thirds of the list.[54] When the conference met a few days later, the Chairman promoted a comprehensive vision of the radical Great Leap Forward policies to be launched. The nature of the decisions, more far-reaching than the decisions taken at the second session of the eighth CCP congress, revealed how much Mao's personality cult had already undermined regular party procedures. Mao simply appropriated the functions of a party congress to the Politburo—and through that, to himself.[55]

At Beidaihe, the Chairman again faulted Bureaucratic Stalinism for its emphasis on heavy industry: "We take a road opposite to that of the Soviet Union; [we] first take care of agriculture in order to facilitate industrial development; [we] first take care of the green leaves, then the red flowers."[56] Mao thereby resurrected basic tenets of Revolutionary Stalinism that demanded the establishment of a labor-saving agriculture prior to heavy industrial development. The agricultural techniques the Chairman endorsed at Beidaihe—a mix of Tan Zhenlin's indigenous methods, Lysenko's deep plowing and close planting, and so forth—made him euphoric about a plentiful future.[57] Grain production would increase 69 percent and cotton 100 percent over 1957, the Beidaihe Communiqué claimed.[58] The Chairman marveled: "In the future we'll establish a global committee, [and] make plans on global unification. Then wherever grain is short, we will supply it as a gift."[59]

Relying on his experience with local enthusiasm in agriculture, Mao called on the lower-level party ranks to "enlist . . . in the field of industry" and on the workers to "sleep on the work sites and beside the

[53] Li, *Private Life*, 269.

[54] Mao, "Problems to Be Prepared for Discussion at Beidaihe Enlarged Politburo Meeting," August 1958, *JYMW*, vol. 7, 343.

[55] Sladkovskii, *Ocherki*, 352.

[56] Mao, "Talk at Beidaihe Conference (Draft Transcript)," 8/21/1958, Afternoon, *SS*, 421 (brackets in original).

[57] MacFarquhar, *Origins*, vol. 2, 123. Mao, "Talk at Beidaihe Conference (Draft Transcript)," 8/21/1958, *SS*, 403.

[58] *SCMP* 1846, 1.

[59] Mao Zedong, "Talk at Beidaihe Conference (Draft Transcript)," 8/19/1958, *SS*, 410.

machines."[60] The steel target, however, remained at 10.7 million tons.[61] Mao hinted only vaguely at the backyard furnaces, which Shanghai party boss Ke Qingshi had promoted since April, but warned of an excessive "steel activism."[62] In early October, only after it had became clear that the 10.7 million ton target would not be reached, did *Renmin Ribao* (*People's Daily*) call for a mass smelting campaign.[63]

Apart from defining production targets, the Beidaihe conference also addressed the communization and militarization of society as innate organizational methods. Invoking the Yan'an myth of war communism, Mao emphatically endorsed "people's communes [that] have adopted a military organization" while denouncing bourgeois and even Soviet approaches to societal construction.[64] He also proposed "to eliminate private housing," to introduce "dormitories for workers and staff," and to construct "public mess halls" providing "free meals."[65] The Chairman was confident that China could quickly rid itself of imported Soviet lifestyles: "Luckily, . . . [their] roots are not deep; revolution is still easy to make."[66] He forecast a bright future for China: "The people's communes contain the sprouts of communism."[67]

Although Mao acknowledged the basic truth of Marx's postulate that the "first precondition for communism is plenty," he insisted that the lack thereof could be replaced by the "communist spirit."[68] In reality, the preconditions for communization in China were absent. The spontaneous conception of the Great Leap Forward led to structural deficits. No plans existed on how to build up communes or train their personnel.[69] The Great Leap Forward was an intentional leap into the dark designed to "realize some ideals of utopian socialism."[70] Mao himself started with a best-case scenario without taking unforeseen problems into account: "Some things are difficult to anticipate; blindness is unavoidable." Once the Great Leap Forward was proven successful, or so he claimed, "some of the problems in the theory of political economy and historical materialism should be

[60] Mao, "Talk at Beidaihe Conference (Draft Transcript)," 8/30/1958, SS, 438–39.
[61] SCMP 1846, 1.
[62] Domes, Peng, 78, 80.
[63] MacFarquhar, Origins, vol. 2, 114.
[64] Mao, "Talk at Beidaihe Conference (Draft Transcript)," 8/30/1958, SS, 436–37.
[65] Mao, "Talk at Beidaihe Conference (Draft Transcript)," 8/30/1958, SS, 430 (first quote). Mao, "Talk at Beidaihe Conference (Draft Transcript)," 8/21/1958, Afternoon, SS, 426 (remaining quotes).
[66] Mao, "Talk at Beidaihe Conference (Draft Transcript)," 8/30/1958, SS, 437–38.
[67] Mao, "Talk at Beidaihe Conference (Draft Transcript)," 8/21/1958, Afternoon, SS, 421.
[68] Mao, "Talk at Beidaihe Conference (Draft Transcript)," 8/30/1958, SS, 437–34.
[69] Domes, Peng, 80.
[70] Li, "Study [II]," 7.

written afresh."[71] The Soviet Embassy Secretary Aleksei Brezhnev in his memoirs agreed that the Great Leap Forward was a "profound conceptual review" but commented sardonically that it also "reflected the whole economic illiteracy" of the CCP leadership.[72] Mao's personal physician, Li Zhisui, speculated that the pills he had prescribed to the Chairman against recurring insomnia caused a drug-induced euphoria.[73]

The Soviet perception of the Great Leap Forward and its resemblances to Revolutionary Stalinism formed only slowly. In 1957 Moscow gradually recognized that the Chinese were no longer interested in the economic model they had inherited from Stalin.[74] Starting in May 1958, Soviet specialists complained about the bending of technical rules in Soviet-delivered factories,[75] the steel campaign, the "grain production satellites,"[76] and excessive production quotas.[77] In July, the Soviet chargé d'affaires in Beijing, S. F. Antonov, sent a detailed report on the changes in production targets to Moscow.[78] During Khrushchev's brief visit to Beijing (July 31–August 3), Mao bragged about the new steel quotas, the imminent problem of excess grain, and the people's communes. The Soviet guest did not comment officially, although he privately was angered by his host's claim that the PRC would enter communism before the Soviet Union.[79] It was a blow to his self-image as the leader of the most advanced socialist nation.[80] The head of the Soviet specialists in China, Ivan Arkhipov, however, bluntly told Chen Yun that the new quotas simply were "too high."[81]

Sino-Soviet Disagreements

Although the conception of the Great Leap Forward did not generate Sino-Soviet differences until late spring, the general radicalization

---

[71] Mao, "Talk at Beidaihe Conference (Draft Transcript)," 8/21/1958, Afternoon, SS, 420–21.

[72] Brezhnev, Kitai, 60.

[73] Li, Private Life, 265.

[74] Deborah Kaple, "Soviet Advisors in China in the 1950s," Westad, Brothers, 131.

[75] NC 2477, 17–18.

[76] Li, "Wo zai," 91.

[77] Bo, Ruogan, vol. 1, 704.

[78] Report mentioned in: David Wolff, ed., "'One Finger's Worth of Historical Events,'" CWIHP Working Paper 30, 49–51.

[79] Bo, Ruogan, vol. 1, 704. Mićunović, Moscow Diary, 421–23.

[80] Ding, "Huigu," 22, 31. Lev Delyusin, "Guanyu SuZhong chongtu qiyin de ruogan sikao," Dangdai Zhongguo shi yanjiu 1998/3, 101.

[81] Bo, Ruogan, vol. 1, 704.

of Chinese politics in early 1958 sparked discord. The squabble that emerged over Khrushchev's so-called joint submarine proposal in late July underscored how incongruent the military outlooks of the two allies had become. Khrushchev did not share Mao's perception of the international situation after Sputnik at all. Moscow's Intercontinental Nuclear Ballistic Missile (ICBM) force remained insignificant for years to come since the missile that launched Sputnik was huge, expensive, and unreliable.[82] Soviet nuclear strategy remained committed to bombers and to Khrushchev's decision to give up on Stalin's surface navy in favor of agile submarines.[83] In 1958, the first two diesel-powered, strategic submarines carrying nuclear missiles (SS-N-4 or SS-N-5 Sea Launched Ballistic Missiles [SLBM], modified Intermediate Range Ballistic Missiles [IRBM]) were commissioned.[84]

Washington worried about the supposed missile gap after Sputnik, especially once Khrushchev started to use it in order to squeeze political concessions from Eisenhower in unrelated Cold War conflicts in the Middle East and Europe.[85] In early 1958, the president decided to send IRBMs to Great Britain, Italy, and Turkey as stopgap measures.[86] Their stationing followed the delivery of tactical nuclear missiles to the Republic of China (ROC) on Taiwan and South Korea the year before.[87] The White House also decided on the continuation of the U-2 spy missions in Soviet airspace to assess the alleged Soviet ICBM force.[88]

Confronted with a threat of his own making, Khrushchev at a WAPA meeting in May 1958 complained that the stationing of IRBMs in Great Britain exceeded justified American defense needs. Moscow faced the conundrum that strategic parity could only be reached by moving Soviet missiles closer to U.S. territories. Deploying Soviet missiles in Cuba as in 1962 was still a future scheme; only strategic submarines carrying nuclear

---

[82] Gaddis, *We Now Know*, 240.

[83] Honoré Catudal, *Soviet Nuclear Strategy from Stalin to Gorbachev* (Berlin: Spitz, 1988), 45. Constantine Pleshakov, "Nikita Khrushchev and Sino-Soviet Relations," Westad, *Brothers*, 234–36.

[84] Norman Polmar et al., *Submarines of the Russian and Soviet Navies, 1718–1990* (Annapolis: Naval Institute, 1991), 288–89. Polmar, *Naval Institute Guide to the Soviet Navy*, 5th ed. (Annapolis: Naval Institute, 1991), 103.

[85] Walter McDougall, *Heavens and the Earth* (New York: Basic, 1985), 250–62. Gaddis, *We Now Know*, 239–41.

[86] Philip Nash, *Other Missiles of October* (Chapel Hill: North Carolina, 1997), 45–75.

[87] MacFarquhar, *Origins*, vol. 1, 316–17. Christensen, *Useful Adversaries*, 160–61. China complained about the missiles to the U.S.: "Telegram from Ambassador U. Alexis Johnson to the Department of State, Geneva," 5/15/1957, U.S. Department of State, *Foreign Relations of the United States* [*FRUS*] (Washington: GPO, 1986), *1955–1957*, III, 522–23. CB 480, 3.

[88] Gaddis, *We Now Know*, 244–48.

missiles could solve this problem.[89] The Soviet Navy Supreme Command had approached Khrushchev in early 1958 with an idea to base them in all oceans and to erect radio transmitter stations in southern India and on Hainan in China. The Soviet leader neither wanted to endanger nascent relations with India, nor did he believe that submarines in the Indian Ocean would enhance Soviet security. But he agreed to the Hainan option although he failed to appreciate that this might cause problems with his Chinese ally.[90]

On April 18, Soviet Defense Minister Rodion Malinovskii thus proposed to Peng Dehuai the construction of a joint radio transmitter station, offering equal usage rights while Moscow was willing to pay 70 of the 110 million rubles price tag. Fearing infringement on PRC sovereignty, the Chinese side demanded exclusive ownership.[91] Peng even proposed to the MAC that the Soviet Union should be allowed to use it only in wartime.[92] A month later, he suggested that China should limit cooperation with the Soviet Union only to collecting "samples, ready to be copied by ourselves."[93] This unexpected stinginess obviously derived from the most recent radicalization of Chinese domestic politics and, as a consequence, of military policies that both had strong anti-Soviet themes. Another Soviet request on the radio station in early June also was rejected. Mao even instructed Peng to "procrastinate" on further Soviet requests.[94]

Given Soviet proposals of late 1957 to deliver modern naval technology and Peng's new policy of collecting samples, the PRC asked the Soviet Union in late June for assistance in developing nuclear-powered submarines, probably destined to enhance China's naval power vis-à-vis Taiwan. These tactical attack submarines were the newest military vessels the USSR had developed; the first one would enter service not before August 1958.[95] Chinese sources claim that on July 21 Yudin approached Mao with the proposal to build a joint submarine fleet. Although the

[89] "Speech of the Head of the Soviet Delegation, N. S. Khrushchev, on the Conference of the Political Consultative Committee of the Warsaw Pact," 5/24/1958, *Politisches Archiv des Auswärtigen Amtes, Bestand: Ministerium für Auswärtige Angelegenheiten* [PAAA-MfAA], Konferenzen und Verhandlungen mit DDR-Beteiligung, Microfiche A 14702, 1349.

[90] Khrushchev, *Nikita S. Khrushchev* (University Park: Pennsylvania State, 2000), 266–68.

[91] Mao, *On Diplomacy*, 245–46, 480, n. 172. Dangdai, *Waijiao*, 112. PDHNP, 681. Wang, *Zhonghua*, vol. 2, 224.

[92] PDHNP, 680–81.

[93] PDHNP, 680.

[94] Wang, *Zhonghua*, vol. 2, 224–25.

[95] Wang, *Zhonghua*, vol. 2, 225. PDHNP, 689. Mao, *On Diplomacy*, 480, n. 172. Polmar, *Submarines*, 294. Polmar, *Naval Institute*, 123.

details of the Soviet request clearly referred to strategic submarines, the sources fail to mention which submarine type the Soviet ambassador spoke about.[96]

The next day, Mao ordered Yudin back to Zhongnanhai and accused the Soviet Union of trying to control "all of our coastline." After the Chairman had insinuated that the current Soviet proposal was only the first step to put "everything under joint operation," he threatened that the Chinese Communists would be "organizing guerilla forces" to wage war against the Soviet occupiers.[97] Mao's fierce reaction was based on a misunderstanding; either the ambassador had miscommunicated the original proposal or the Chairman had failed to understand the nuances in modern submarine warfare. But the Soviet offer also seemed to come at an inopportune time. Joint ventures of any kind did not fit China's emerging military doctrine. Mao opposed any outside control over Chinese submarines destined for the liberation of Taiwan. Finally, the Chairman must have had doubts about the sincerity of Soviet proposals in the nuclear sphere in general. Less than a year earlier, Khrushchev had promised to deliver a model A-bomb, but only recently had he agreed to negotiate with Eisenhower on policing nuclear weapons. In Mao's eyes, the joint submarine proposal must have appeared to be a Soviet attempt to control China's policy toward Taiwan for the sake of relaxing relations with the American imperialists.

After Yudin had cabled Moscow about Mao's outburst, Khrushchev decided to fly secretly to Beijing.[98] Before setting out, however, he instructed Yudin to ask "at which time it would be convenient to arrive."[99] How customs had changed in the socialist camp! Only some years earlier, Stalin had ordered his allies abroad to scramble to Moscow whenever he deemed it necessary. Once Khrushchev had arrived in the PRC on July 31 the Chinese comrades put him up in lodgings in the Fragrant Hills, which lacked air conditioning. When Khrushchev moved his bed to the terrace to escape his stuffy room he fell victim to a swarm of vicious insects.[100]

The mosquito bites were negligible compared to Mao's stinging criticism. Immediately after Khrushchev's arrival, the two leaders met to discuss the joint submarine proposal. The first secretary blamed his own

[96] WLX, 158. Ding, "Huigu," 28. Mao, *On Diplomacy*, 480, n. 177.

[97] Mao, "Talk with Yudin, Ambassador of the Soviet Union to China," 7/22/1958, Mao, *On Diplomacy*, 254.

[98] "Protocol No. 168: Session of July 24, 1958," Fursenko, *Prezidium*, vol. 1, 326. Khrushchev, *Testament*, 258–59. WLX, 162. Li, *Waijiao*, 167.

[99] "Record of Conversation with Zhou Enlai and Peng Zhen," 7/28/1958, AVPRF, f.0100, o.51, d.6, p.432, 170–71.

[100] Salisbury, *New Emperors*, 155–56.

ambassador for miscommunicating the proposal,[101] but Mao accused Khrushchev of "Russian nationalism" and threatened more "guerilla warfare."[102] After some bickering, the Soviet guest promised that "there will not be a joint fleet."[103]

On the second day, Mao humiliated Khrushchev at the swimming pool at Zhongnanhai. After a chat on international and domestic politics,[104] the Chairman—a renowned swimmer—suggested diving into the water.[105] His head covered with a "handkerchief with knots at all corners," and his body kept afloat with a "life belt," Khrushchev "paddled like a dog" while Mao executed the most skillful swimming and diving maneuvers.[106] The Chairman's deliberate insult to the first secretary seemed to have been lost on the Soviets.[107] Oleg Troyanovskii, who was present at the meeting, only remembered that "it was an unforgettable picture: The appearance of two well-fed leaders in swimming trunks, discussing questions of great policy under splashes of water."[108]

Following short talks over the next two days and the signing of an agreement to fund the radio station with Soviet loans, Khrushchev left for Moscow on August 3.[109] No real agreement had been reached on the Soviet proposals for a Pacific nuclear strategy—proposals that were reasonable given the Soviet strategic disadvantages vis-à-vis the United States. The Chinese side instead prided itself for having "stood up to Russian great power chauvinism."[110] Aleksei Brezhnev largely faulted the Soviet side for the lack of any tangible success: "Our side had been poorly prepared for the negotiations."[111] Khrushchev did not intend to control the Chinese coastline, as Mao claimed, but the Soviet leader showed a

[101] "First Conversation of N. S. Khrushchev with Mao Zedong, " 7/31/1958, Wolff, "Finger," 52. WLX, 162–63.

[102] WLX, 165.

[103] "First Conversation of N. S. Khrushchev with Mao Zedong," 7/31/1958, Wolff, "Finger," 54.

[104] Parts of the August 1 talk have been covered earlier in the section on Soviet views on the Great Leap Forward; another will be covered further below in the section on the Taiwan Strait Crisis: Li Yueran, *Waijiao*, 168–75. WLX, 168–70. Ding Ming, "Huigu," 26. Khrushchev, *Testament*, 260–61. Khrushchev, *Glasnost*, 147–50.

[105] Li Yueran, *Waijiao*, 175.

[106] Li Yueran, *Waijiao*, 175. Salisbury, *New Emperors*, 157.

[107] Li Zhisui, *Private Life*, 261.

[108] Troyanovskii, *Cherez*, 348.

[109] "Fourth Conversation of N. S. Khrushchev with Mao Zedong," 8/3/1958, Wolff, "Finger," 56–59. About the agreements: Mao, *On Diplomacy*, 480, n. 172. About assessment of Khrushchev visit: Lev Delyusin, "Nekotorye razmyshlenie o nachale sovetsko-kitaiskogo konflikta," paper presented at the conference "Sino-Soviet Relations and Cold War: International Scientific Seminar," Beijing, China, October 1997, 5.

[110] WLX, 173.

[111] Brezhnev, *Kitai*, 55.

lack of consideration toward Chinese sensitivities.[112] In the end, however, it was Mao who had pushed things. The domestic radicalization he had initiated in late 1957 as well as his personal dislike of Khrushchev had contributed considerably to the chilled atmosphere in Sino-Soviet relations. The Second Taiwan Strait Crisis—starting barely three weeks after Khrushchev's visit to Beijing—further cooled them.

THE SECOND TAIWAN STRAIT CRISIS

On August 23, the PRC began to shell Jinmen massively for thirteen days. After a pause of three days, the artillery bombardment resumed on September 7, but ended twenty-nine days later. Starting on October 25, the PRC fired only on odd days of each month—until January 1, 1979, the day of Sino-American diplomatic recognition. Washington immediately sent the Sixth Fleet from the Mediterranean to assist the Seventh Fleet in containing the conflict. It refrained from making further public commitments to keep the PRC guessing about further American intentions.[113] By late August, U.S. Secretary of State John Foster Dulles and the Central Intelligence Agency (CIA) were convinced that the shelling was a test of American commitments toward the Republic of China.[114]

On August 31, after days of factual reporting, a *Pravda* editorial notified the United States that any threat to the PRC would be considered a threat to the USSR.[115] Given Khrushchev's recent visit to Mao and Chinese propaganda on the liberation of Taiwan, Dulles warned Eisenhower on September 4 that Beijing and Moscow were implementing a long-planned campaign "to liquidate the Chinat [Chinese Nationalist] positions."[116] A public statement announced that "the President would not . . . hesitate" to defend ROC and to support the defense of Jinmen if "the Chinese Communists . . . leave us no choice but to react."[117] The vague wording neither ruled out the use of nuclear weapons nor announced plans to defend Jinmen.[118]

---

[112] Interview with Yan Mingfu, Beijing, 11/23/2000. Wang, *Zhonghua*, vol. 2, 227.

[113] "Memorandum of Meeting," 8/29/1958, *FRUS 1958–1960*, XIX, 73–74, 98. Chang, *Friends*, 186.

[114] Editorial Note, *FRUS 1958–1960*, XIX, 87. "Special National Intelligence Estimate, SNIE 100-9-58," 8/26/1958, *FRUS 1958–1960*, XIX, 81–82.

[115] *Pravda*, 8/26/1958, 3; 8/27/1958, 5; 8/28/1958, 3; 8/29/1958, 5; 8/31/1958, 4.

[116] "Memorandum Prepared by the Secretary of State Dulles," 9/4/1958, *FRUS 1958–1960*, XIX, 131.

[117] "White House Press Release," 9/4/1958," *FRUS 1958–1960*, XIX, 135–36.

[118] Zhang Shuguang, *Deterrence and Strategic Culture* (Ithaca: Cornell, 1992), 248. Christensen, *Useful Adversaries*, 196.

The causes for the Second Taiwan Strait Crisis were manifold and fluid. In 1954–55, the PRC had shelled Jinmen for months, with the sole result of informal Sino-American ambassadorial talks to start in Geneva. During the following two years of talks, the PRC neither achieved U.S. recognition as the legitimate government of China nor American promises to support its unification.[119] The talks collapsed on December 12, 1957—a month after Beijing had rejected Moscow's policy of peaceful coexistence with Washington—because the United States had downgraded the talks to the subambassadorial level. Since they had not produced a mutual renunciation of force in the Taiwan Strait, the United States considered talks on the ambassadorial level redundant.[120] Six days later, Mao ordered the PLA to transfer the Chinese Air Force to Fujian province (across from Taiwan) in order to confront increasing air space violations by Guomindang military planes.[121] In January, preparations for a renewed military action in the Taiwan Strait began and lasted until the early summer.[122] But no decision as to the *precise nature* and *timing* of the military confrontation had yet been made.

In May, Mao decided on a substantial artillery barrage of Jinmen but again left the precise date open.[123] This diffidence probably was due to new developments in the Taiwan Strait. In February, the Chairman told Yudin that American bases on Okinawa, the Philippines, and the Midway Islands were the greatest threat to China while "Taiwan and South Korea [only] represent *second-degree threats*, since less powerful military technology is concentrated there."[124] A May 2 American test-firing of tactical nuclear missiles introduced the year before did not elicit any reaction in Beijing although it revealed that they could hit targets several hundred miles away deep in the PRC.[125] However, Beijing's perception later that month that Washington was trying to create a joint U.S.-ROC military command increased its concerns that the island would be "cut off from the home-

---

[119] Chen, *Mao's China*, 167–71. Zhai, *Dragon*, 173–74. U. Alexis Johnson, *Right Hand of Power* (Englewood Cliffs: Prentice Hall, 1984), 260–61.

[120] Ronald Keith, *Diplomacy of Zhou Enlai* (Basingstoke: Macmillan, 1989), 90. Johnson, *Right Hand*, 236, 243, 260–61. Zhang Baijia et al., "Steering Wheel, Shock Absorber, and Diplomatic Probe in Confrontation," Ross, *Re-examining*, 187.

[121] "Notation, Mao Zedong on Chen Geng's Report," 12/18/1957, Li Xiaobing et al., eds., "Mao Zedong's Handling of the Taiwan Straits Crisis of 1958," *CWIHP Bulletin* 8–9, 215.

[122] Chen, *Mao's China*, 172. PDHNP, 689.

[123] Wang Fang, ed., "Mao Zedong bang le lao Jiang yi ba," Chang Cheng, ed., *Zhiqingzhe shuo*, vol. 1 (Zhongguo qingnian, 1995), 135. During May, the PRC shelled Jinmen at least twice with a over a hundred shells each: *NYT*, 5/18/1958, 2; 5/28/1958, 5.

[124] "Record of Conversation with Mao Zedong," 2/28/1958, *AVPRF*, f.0100, o.51, d.6, p.432, 89 (italics mine).

[125] *NYT*, 5/3/1958, 4.

[126] Wang, "Mao Zedong," 135.

land."[126] Thus not American threats to its security, but the prospect of a permanently divided China, seemingly promoted by U.S. policies, worried the PRC. Chen Yi told Soviet specialists in June: "We will never forget that the Americans . . . seized the Chinese island Taiwan. Time will come when we will settle accounts with the American imperialists for all their debt before us."[127] On June 30, the PRC demanded from the United States to resume ambassadorial talks within fifteen days, threatening to "liberate Taiwan" by force otherwise.[128] The United States let the deadline pass without an answer,[129] but on July 17 instructed its embassy in London to use British diplomatic channels to arrange an ambassadorial meeting in Geneva not earlier than the "second week of August."[130] The Chinese side did not reply to any diplomatic forays until September.[131] In the summer of 1958, the military action Beijing planned was designed to render diplomatic pressure on Washington to resume negotiations on Taiwan on the ambassadorial level. The PRC did not expect a direct military engagement resulting from the bombardment of Jinmen, as Zhou had told Yudin in April: "The USA will *not* render aid to the Chiang Kai-shekisti for the defense of . . . Jinmen," to say nothing of dispatching its own military forces.[132]

The July 14 revolution against the pro-Western Iraqi King Faisal changed the setting of the crisis radically. After the United States and Great Britain had sent troops to Lebanon and Jordan, respectively, to contain the revolution,[133] the PRC embarked on a public anti-American campaign.[134] On July 17 Mao ordered the armed forces to ready themselves quickly for combat in the Taiwan Strait.[135] The next day, he informed the MAC that he had decided "to support the Arab people in their struggle against aggression . . . [by] attacking Chiang Kai-shek . . . in order to contain American imperialism."[136]

After Khrushchev proposed a Soviet-U.S.-British-French-Indian summit conference on the Middle East on July 19,[137] Mao reassessed his

[127] "Statements by Leaders of the PRC on Important Questions of Foreign Policy," 12/9/1960, *AVPRF*, f.0100, o.53, d.24, p.457, 236.

[128] *NYT*, 7/1/1958, 13.

[129] Liu, *Chushi*, 78.

[130] "Telegram from the Department of State to the Embassy in the United Kingdom," 7/17/1958, *FRUS 1958–1960*, XIX, 31–32.

[131] *FRUS 1958–1960*, XIX, 34–35, 61. Christensen, *Useful Adversaries*, 198–99.

[132] "Record of Conversation with Zhou Enlai," 4/5/1958, *AVPRF*, f.0100, o.51, d.6, p.432, 138 (italics mine).

[133] MacFarquhar, *Origins*, vol. 2, 92. Chen, *Mao's China*, 175.

[134] *CB* 519, 24.

[135] *PDHNP*, 691.

[136] *PDHNP*, 692–93.

[137] *WLX*, 162.

decision to shell Jinmen, claiming now to be interested in finding a diplomatic solution as well.[138] Eisenhower initially welcomed Khrushchev's proposal but proposed on July 22 to submit the problem to the U.N. Security Council.[139] When the Soviet Union agreed, Beijing wrote bluntly to Moscow that China could not accept that Taiwan as a member of the Security Council would judge Middle Eastern countries that had recognized the PRC.[140] *Renmin Ribao* even called for the dispatch of Korean War–style volunteers to the Middle East. Moscow retracted its agreement.[141]

While Mao had worked himself up over the Middle East, Peng Dehuai on July 24 proposed to defer the shelling of Jinmen because he had received news about Taiwanese military reinforcements.[142] After three sleepless nights, the Chairman agreed because he wanted to "watch the situation" in the Middle East.[143] The delay provided Beijing with additional time to prepare the shelling, but, above all, a sudden Chinese-provoked military crisis during Khrushchev's impending visit would have been politically awkward. At the swimming pool meeting of August 1, Mao again raised the idea to "send a volunteer army."[144] Uneasy about this proposal, Khrushchev suggested an East-West division of work : "If we divide the work, we can deal more with European affairs, and you can deal more with Asian affairs." Mao rebuked Khrushchev for his "spheres of influence speech."[145]

Mao's belief that the Soviets were pursuing a policy of appeasing American imperialism in the Middle East and his conviction that the Soviets were trying to control China through the joint submarine proposal influenced Mao's decision *not* to inform Khrushchev on the planned shelling of Jinmen.[146] The Chairman claimed to his personal physician that the Soviets had attempted "to use China as a pawn in the . . . effort to improve relations with the United States." He concluded defiantly: "Good, we'll congratulate him [Khrushchev] with our

[138] WLX, 158. *PDHNP*, 693. Also: "Record of Conversation with Liu Xiao," 7/19/1958, *AVPRF*, f.100, o.45, d.5, p.180, 3.

[139] MacFarquhar, *Origins*, vol. 2, 92–93.

[140] Han Suyin, *Eldest Son* (London: Pimlico, 1994), 270.

[141] MacFarquhar, *Origins*, vol. 2, 93–94.

[142] *PDHNP*, 694.

[143] "Letter, Mao Zedong to Peng Dehuai and Huang Kecheng," 7/27/1958, Li, "Mao's Handling," 215–16.

[144] WLX, 170.

[145] Li, *Waijiao*, 174–75.

[146] The Chinese side emphasizes that Mao had not told Khrushchev about the shelling: Liu, *Chushi*, 86. Li, *Lengnuan*, 297. WLX, 186. Interview with Yan Mingfu, Beijing, 11/23/2000.

guns. . . . Maybe we can get the United States to drop an atom bomb on Fujian."[147]

Beijing must have known that the refusal to notify Moscow contradicted not only its own explicit desire—expressed after the Hungarian Revolution—for better information exchange on foreign affairs, but also Article Four of the alliance treaty which stated clearly that: "Both High Contracting Parties will *consult* each other in regard to all important international questions affecting the common interests of the Soviet Union and China, being guided by the interests of the consolidation of peace and universal security."[148] At the time, Mao disingenuously justified this violation with the claim that the shelling of Jinmen was an internal affair.[149] The Chinese side later insinuated that the PRC actually had informed the Soviet Union *shortly* before the start of the shelling. When Moscow investigated the matter after the crisis, Beijing asserted it had informed "the military counselor of the [Soviet] embassy" immediately before the start of the shelling, an explanation the Soviets dismissed because it was "in no way a *consultation*."[150]

Domestic developments *alone* determined the *timing* of the shelling of Jinmen. Once Mao had publicly supported the people's communes in early August, he was ready to use a foreign policy crisis to whip up popular enthusiasm for his grand vision of domestic transformation.[151] While he had been traveling from Tianjin to Beidaihe in mid-August, the shelling of Jinmen had *not* been on the list of seventeen points to be discussed at the enlarged Politburo meeting.[152] Also, none of those leaders responsible for propaganda and military affairs had been invited to attend. Only when Mao announced the impending shelling on August 17 were they hastily ordered to come to Beidaihe for instructions.[153] "He wanted *Renmin Ribao* and *Xinhua* to report intensely on the international situation," Wu Lengxi remembered, because "the center by then had already decided on the steel campaign, the people's communes, [and] the people's militias."[154]

[147] Li, *Private Life*, 262.

[148] Treaty text in: Hinton, *People's Republic*, vol. 1, 124.

[149] Si Fu, "Zhonggong duidai Duleise 'heping yanbian' zhanle de qianqian houhou," Chang, *Zhiqingzhe shuo*, vol. 8, 52. WLX, 177.

[150] "On the Exchange of Information between the USSR and the PRC," 9/10/1960, *AVPRF*, f.0100, o.53, d.24, p.457, 128 (italics mine).

[151] Mao, "Talk at Beidaihe Conference (Draft Transcript)," 8/17/1958, SS, 402. Also: "Statements by Leaders of the PRC on Important Questions of Foreign Policy," 12/9/1960, *AVPRF*, f.0100, o.53, d.24, p.457, 236.

[152] Mao, "Problems to Be Prepared for Discussion at the Beidaihe Enlarged Politburo Meeting," August 1958, *JYMW*, vol. 7, 343. Wang, "Mao Zedong," 136.

[153] Zhonggong, *Mao Zedong zhuan*, 854. Chen, *Mao's China*, 179–81.

[154] Wu Lengxi, *Yi Mao zhuxi*, 77–78.

The Soviet Embassy Secretary Brezhnev remembered that Mao wanted to create an atmosphere of a "besieged fortress" because the "non-economic methods of compulsion to work . . . demanded the creation of external conditions that could justify the use of extreme moral and physical measures to manipulate the workers."[155]

After Mao had announced his decision to shell Jinmen, he focused on the detailed planning for the artillery barrage. Although he failed to formulate clear objectives, he wanted to keep the crisis limited. On August 18, he barred Peng from any military maneuvers in Guangdong to prevent the British in Hong Kong from panicking.[156] On the twentieth, the Air Force started to harass Guomindang troops on Mazu, another island close to the mainland, as a diversionary maneuver.[157] Two days later, the Chairman ordered the shelling of Jinmen to start on August 23.[158] However, Mao told the Politburo on the twenty-fifth, the third day of the crisis, that he had not yet decided whether or not to take Jinmen. Decisions would be taken "as circumstances dictated."[159]

American reactions changed the nature of the crisis once more. On August 25, Eisenhower ordered the Seventh Fleet to protect Taiwanese supply ships; four days later, he authorized the fleet to enter, if necessary, the three-mile zone claimed by China as domestic waters.[160] The announcement astonished the PRC. In April, Zhou had been convinced that the United States would not commit itself to the defense of Jinmen.[161] Absorbed by the new situation, Mao did not pay much attention to the launching of the radical policies of the Great Leap Forward during the last five days of the Beidaihe conference.[162] On September 3, he ordered a stop to the shelling "to watch the developments."[163] The day after, Mao decided not to take Jinmen in order to "pull . . . the noose [around America's neck] tighter and tighter."[164] American commitments to the island had provided China with a tool to punish U.S. imperialist aggression everywhere in the world, the Chairman claimed. Mao instructed Peng to

[155] Brezhnev, *Kitai*, 55, 60.

[156] "Instruction, Mao Zedong to Peng Dehuai, 8/18/1958, 1:00 A.M.," Li, "Mao's Handling," 215.

[157] Wang, "Mao Zedong," 136.

[158] Li Xiaobing, "Making of Mao's Cold War," paper prepared for the Cold War International History Project Hong Kong Conference, 1/9–12/1996, 14.

[159] Wu Lengxi, "Memoir," Li Xiaobing et al., *CWIHP Bulletin* 8–9, 210.

[160] Li, "Making," 16.

[161] "Record of Conversation with Zhou Enlai," 4/5/1958, *AVPRF*, f.0100, o.51, d.6, p.432, 138.

[162] Wu, "Memoir," 210. Wu, *Yi Mao zhuxi*, 78.

[163] Si Fu, "Paoji Jinmen guocheng zhong xian weiren zhi de wangshi," Chang, *Zhiqingzhe shuo*, vol. 8, 86.

[164] Wu, "Memoir," 210 (brackets are in original).

tell the MAC the next day that the crisis would be "a complicated and long struggle."[165] On the same day, Dulles released Eisenhower's statement hinting at the use of nuclear weapons.[166] With that the crisis had reached a new dimension.

The outbreak of the Second Taiwan Strait Crisis was a surprise to the Soviets,[167] who believed that the Chinese had started the liberation of Taiwan.[168] The USSR decided to support the PRC by warning the United States in the *Pravda* statement of August 31.[169] As mentioned earlier, this triggered the oblique American threat of nuclear war.[170] On September 4, Beijing eventually notified Moscow, describing the crisis as a mere attempt to prevent the United States from dividing China.[171] Worried about Dulles's vague threats of nuclear war, Khrushchev ordered Chargé d'Affaires Antonov to meet with Zhou Enlai on September 5 and to announce Foreign Minister Andrei Gromyko's arrival in Beijing the following day. The prime minister tried to calm Soviet nerves: "If we get in trouble, China will assume all consequences, [and] will not drag down the Soviet Union into the water."[172] On the same day, Zhou backed up his promise by publicly announcing China's war aims: the resumption of ambassadorial talks.[173]

Once Gromyko had arrived in Beijing on September 6, Zhou offered another story. By now Mao's prophecy that nuclear war would lead to the end of the imperialist world had kicked in: "The PRC, [while] inflicting blows to the off-coast islands, takes into consideration the possibility of the rise in this region of a local war with the USA against the PRC and is now ready to accept on itself all serious blows right up to the atom bomb and to the destruction of our cities." The Soviet Union, Zhou's subsequent words implied, should then respond with a nuclear counterstrike on the United States.[174] Although Gromyko dismissed this course of action,[175] he nevertheless carried out the task for which he had been

---

[165] *PDHNP*, 699.

[166] "White House Press Release," 9/4/1958, *FRUS 1958–1960*, XIX, 135–36.

[167] Brezhnev, *Kitai*, 56.

[168] Khrushchev, *Testament*, 262.

[169] *Pravda*, 8/31/1958, 4.

[170] "White House Press Release," 9/4/1958, *FRUS 1958–1960*, XIX, 135–36.

[171] "Memo, [PRC] Ministry of Foreign Affairs to the Soviet Embassy in China," 9/4/1958, Zhang, "Emerging Disputes," 161–62.

[172] *ZELNP2*, 145.

[173] Liu, *Chushi*, 79–80.

[174] The quote is reprinted in an internal Soviet document: "Statements by Leaders of the PRC on Important Questions of Foreign Policy," 12/9/1960, *AVPRF*, f.0100, o.53, d.24, p.457, 238.

[175] Andrei Gromyko, *Memories* (London: Hutchinson, 1989), 251–52.

sent to Beijing. He had brought with him a draft letter to Eisenhower,[176] which faulted the United States for the tensions in the Far East, for review by the Chinese comrades. That night, Mao studied it, and the next morning at seven ordered Zhou to gather some people to make corrections.[177] Later the prime minister returned the modified draft to Gromyko, who, before he himself left Beijing, cabled it to Moscow to be handed over to the U.S. chargé d'affaires there.[178] Though the letter claimed that the USSR "would do everything to defend the security of both states," it did not endorse nuclear war to achieve that end.[179] After Eisenhower received Khrushchev's letter, he repeated the oblique September 4 nuclear threat, but also offered to resume ambassadorial talks in Warsaw on September 15.[180] Mao immediately instructed a reduction of the daily barrage of Jinmen to "two hundred to three hundred shells."[181]

Washington's renewed threat of nuclear war, however, made Moscow uneasy. In mid-September, the Soviet leadership decided to invite Liu Xiao to the family vacation homes of the Khrushchevs, Mikoyans, and Voroshilovs in Yalta.[182] The Chinese ambassador reminisced that the first secretary voiced concerns "on how to deal with situations before they get out of control" and offered "help."[183] In the following two weeks, Khrushchev cabled Mao twice with an offer to send anti-aircraft troops to Fujian—provided they would remain under Soviet command.[184] In order to mask this apparent attempt to supervise the Chinese ally on the battlefield, Vice–Foreign Minister Vasilii Kuznetsov approached the Chinese embassy with a new letter to Eisenhower explicitly threatening the United States with nuclear war.[185]

Both Washington and Beijing dismissed Moscow's correspondence as much-ado-about-nothing because Sino-American ambassadorial talks

[176] Wang, *Zhonghua*, vol. 2, 218–19.

[177] Summary of the draft letter and Mao's comments: *JYMW*, vol. 7, 404.

[178] "Record of Conversation with Liu Xiao," 9/8/1958, *AVPRF*, f.0100, o.51, d.3, p.431, 70.

[179] "Telegram from the Embassy in the Soviet Union to the Department of State," 9/7/1958, *FRUS 1958–1960*, XIX, 145–53.

[180] "Radio and Television Report," 9/11/1958, Dwight Eisenhower, *The Public Papers of the President*, vol. 6 (Washington: GPO, 1960), 699–700.

[181] "Letter, Mao Zedong to Zhou Enlai and Huang Kecheng," 9/13/1958, Li, "Mao's Handling," 221.

[182] Liu Xiao was in Yalta from 9/16–19/1958: *SCMP* 1858, 49. Liu, *Chushi*, 76–77.

[183] Liu, *Chushi*, 75–76.

[184] Li, "Mao's Handling," 223, n. 55. WLX, 187. Khrushchev, *Testament*, 261–62.

[185] Soviet letter in: "Telegram From the Embassy in the Soviet Union to the Department of State," 9/19/1958, *FRUS 1958–1960*, XIX, 231–38. Also: "Record of Conversation with the Ambassador of the PRC in the USSR Liu Xiao," 9/8/1958, AVPRF, f.0100, o.51, d.3, p.431, 70.

had already started and the Soviet Union had also accepted a U.S. offer to resume nuclear disarmament talks.[186] The Chinese side had understood that the American position at one of Mao's three fronts was purely defensive. Although the United States had unexpectedly rendered aid to ROC to defend Jinmen, it obviously wanted to avoid direct military conflict. Neither the U.S. Navy nor the U.S. Air Force, Zhou told the Bulgarian ambassador later, had violated even the twelve-mile zone claimed by Beijing in early September but immediately rejected by Washington.[187] Yet, U.S. attempts during the ambassadorial talks that started on September 15 to reduce tensions in the Taiwan Strait by demilitarizing Jinmen met sharp Chinese resistance. The PRC perceived this geographical disentanglement of mainland China and Taiwan on Jinmen as just another U.S. step toward the permanent division of China. Guomindang troops on the small island in Xiamen Bay symbolically linked the two parts of China.[188]

The Chinese reaction to Khrushchev's offer to send troops was similarly negative. Although Peng Dehuai on October 3 asked Mao to order 130 field guns and 40,000 shells from the Soviet Union to replenish quickly decreasing Chinese stocks,[189] the Chairman instructed Zhou Enlai "not to hurry with Soviet correspondence."[190] Later the Chinese told the Soviets that the "offer had offended them,"[191] but the Kremlin rejected a counterproposal to deploy the troops under PLA command.[192] Anyway, Mao could afford to play hardball, since, on the basis of a 1957 agreement, the PRC expected to receive SA-2 surface-to-air missiles from the USSR in November.[193]

The ease with which Beijing had nearly forced Moscow to commit itself to nuclear war troubled the Kremlin. The crisis and Soviet-American nuclear disarmament talks were both factors in the Soviet decision to rescind its October 1957 promise to deliver a model A-bomb in June

[186] Zhai, *Dragon*, 197–99. Li, *Lengnuan*, 297. WLX, 181.

[187] "Written Report by Petr Panchevski—Ambassador in the PRC," 11/12/1958, *Arkhiv na Ministerstvoto na Vnshnite Raboti* [AMVnR], o.14p, a.e.491, 158–61. For the Chinese claim: SCMP 1849, 1.

[188] Li, *Private Life*, 270. Zhang, "Steering Wheel," 189–90.

[189] PDHNP, 703.

[190] "Telegram to Zhou Enlai on the Questions of the Letter sent by the CPSU CC," 10/11/1958," JYMW, vol. 7, 449.

[191] Khrushchev, *Testament*, 262.

[192] WLX, 187.

[193] Fu Zhenguo, "Zuotian de mimi," Chang, *Zhiqingzhe shuo*, vol. 4, 109–14. ZELNP2, 145. "Letter 'Bushe' No. 0/152/58," 6/3/1958, AVPRF, f.0100, o.51, d.1, p.431, 12–13. "Letter 'Bushe' No. 0/162/58," 6/10/1958, AVPRF, f.0100, o.51, d.1, p.431, 17. "Dear Comrade Kuznetsov," 5/11/1958, AVPRF, f.0100, o.51, d.3, p.431, 51–52. "Ministry of Foreign Affairs of the PRC to the Chargé d'Affaires," 8/16/1958, AVPRF, f.0100, o.51, d.1, p.431, 20–21.

1959.[194] Although a cyclotron the Soviet Union had been building in China since early 1958 was put to use in late September,[195] the Chinese government realized in the fall that the Soviets were procrastinating over further nuclear technology transfers.[196] Aleksei Brezhnev called the decision to renege on the promised model A-bomb delivery a "blunder" since it came too late to stop China's nuclear weapons project and left the Soviet Union without any leverage.[197]

After the ruckus over the joint submarine proposal, the Second Taiwan Strait Crisis only further undermined the Sino-Soviet relationship.[198] Despite the Soviet nuclear bravado, Khrushchev did not want to wreck the fledgling relationship with Eisenhower.[199] Mao's actions in the Taiwan Strait were a challenge to Khrushchev's policy toward the United States and to Soviet leadership of the socialist camp. It reflected the Chairman's growing desire to be his own master in foreign relations. While Sino-Soviet cooperation on Yugoslavia had worked well earlier in the year, the Chinese leader was loath to consult with the Kremlin on foreign policy affairs after July.

THE CONTINUOUS REVOLUTION: THE RADICAL GREAT LEAP FORWARD LAUNCHED

The Chinese claim of U.S. imperialist aggression against the PRC served as a rhetorical device to mobilize the masses at home. This struggle against a supposedly illegitimate authority structure is the last of the four characteristics that Lowell Dittmer has identified as central to Mao's implementation of the continuous revolution.[200] In the early 1950s, Mao had already used propaganda about the supposed U.S. imperialist aggression in Korea as a means to push through mass campaigns aimed at the consolidation of his regime and the transformation of Chinese society.[201]

Mao was quite explicit about exploiting the ongoing Taiwan Strait Crisis to launch the radical Great Leap Forward policies, as he said in

---

[194] Kapitsa, *Na raznykh parallelyakh*, 61–63. Brezhnev, *Kitai*, 57–58. Westad, "Introduction," 21–22.

[195] "Soviet-Chinese Relations (Reference)," 2/13/1961, *AVPRF*, f.0100, o.54, d.27, p.470, 36. Goncharenko, "Military Cooperation," 157–59.

[196] Wang, *Zhonghua*, vol. 2, 221–22. Goncharenko, "Military Cooperation," 157. Zhang, "Economic Cooperation," 207.

[197] Brezhnev, *Kitai*, 58–59.

[198] Ding, "Huigu," 25.

[199] Westad, "Introduction," 22.

[200] Dittmer, *Continuous Revolution*, 4–5.

[201] Chen, *Mao's China*, 87–88, 116–17.

early September: "Crisis situations allow us to mobilize forces, mobilize backward strata, and mobilize middle-of-the-roaders to prepare for struggle."[202] While the shelling of Jinmen continued in the first three days of September, Chinese media pushed the commune movement into the spotlight.[203] On the fifth, *Renmin Ribao* called on the population to participate in the steel drive.[204] Three days later, the Chairman announced that "the framework for the people's communes will probably be set up by [the end of?] September."[205] On September 10, the CCP Central Committee issued five rural directives on ideological indoctrination, water conservancy, deep plowing, fertilizers, and pest prevention.[206] Similarly, Mao used Dulles's vague threats of nuclear war to launch the militia movement, designed to militarize daily life, on September 5: "[I]f [the enemy] is determined to fight, it is they who . . . will strike with atomic bombs. . . . If we have to fight, then we'll fight, and after we've fought, we'll rebuild. *For this reason we must now build up the militia.* . . . Everyone must be a soldier."[207] The final CC decision on the militia movement five days later explicitly used "imperialist aggression" as justification.[208] The movement quickly spread across China in the following two weeks.[209] At the end of the year, three hundred million Chinese—more than half the population—had joined.[210] The movement was accompanied by mass demonstrations against "America's aggressive war policy . . . in the Taiwan Strait."[211]

After the radical Great Leap Forward policies were launched, Mao went on an inspection tour from September 10 to 29 to east central China,[212] where he publicly endorsed the free-food supply system vociferously promoted by the Shanghai director for party propaganda, Zhang Chunqiao. Within a short while, communes introduced mess halls where peasants indulged on free food without thinking about leaner times ahead.[213] At the same time, *Neibu cankao* carried reports on food shortages, even in Shanghai.[214] Back in Beijing, Mao met other central leaders to talk about

[202] Mao, "Speech," 9/5/1958, *CLG* 9/3, 83. Zhou Enlai on this issue: "Written Report by Petr Panchevski—Ambassador in the PRC," 11/12/1958, *AMVnR*, o.14p, a.e. 491, 158.

[203] Hinton, *People's Republic*, vol. 2, 682–86.

[204] MacFarquhar, *Origins*, vol. 2, 114.

[205] Mao, "Speech of 9/8/1958—Concluding Remarks," *CLG* 9/3, 97.

[206] *SCMP* 1857, 1–16.

[207] Mao, "Speech," 9/5/1958, *CLG* 9/3, 88 (brackets in original, italics mine).

[208] "Decision by the CCP CC on the Question of the People's Militia," 9/9/1958, *JSS-DAG*, 3011, zhang 0401, 202–3a.

[209] *CB* 546, 5.

[210] Christensen, *Useful Adversaries*, 217–18.

[211] *WLX*, 178.

[212] *CB* 546, 5. Wu, "Memoir," 211.

[213] Li Zhisui, *Private Life*, 274–75.

[214] *NC* 2584, 16–19; 2596, 8–11.

the problems of the steel drive. Once it had become clear that the steel target for 1958 could not be achieved, *Renmin Ribao* called for a mass campaign on October 4. While only 19 percent of China's steel had been produced by backyard furnaces in September, their share rose to 49 percent the following month. Tens of millions of ordinary Chinese people—peasants, workers, office staff, students, pupils—participated.[215]

In October, full-blown famines were developing in Henan and Tianjin. Mao ordered an investigation into the situation in the province and personally inspected the city in mid-October. Once there, he dismissed reports that claimed the use of "deception and fraud" to cover up problems.[216] The Chairman failed to realize that the spectacle he saw from behind the windows of his personal train was staged. One of his secretaries, Lin Ke, told Li Zhisui in confidence that local party secretaries "had ordered furnaces constructed everywhere along the rail route, . . . [and had requested] to remove rice plants from faraway fields and transplant them along Mao's route."[217] At the same time, Peng Dehuai inspected Gansu and Henan, where he realized that labor shortages induced by the wasteful steel production with backyard furnaces had left the harvest rotting in the fields.[218]

Over the following six weeks, famine reports from Inner Mongolia, Hubei, Qinghai, Liaoning, and even Beijing reached the central leaders,[219] but *Neibu cankao* also carried propaganda reports about Soviet specialists supposedly praising the Great Leap Forward.[220] Eventually the severe economic distortions could no longer be ignored. Although the mass steel campaign led to the premature fulfillment of the 1958 target, it endangered food supplies for the winter.[221] On October 22, the central authorities issued an emergency directive for the shock collection of overdue crops.[222] Peasants and city people abandoned the backyard furnaces and rushed to the fields to save as much as possible, working around the clock for days.[223]

On October 25, Mao asked Chen Boda, Zhang Chunqiao, Tian Jiaying (one of his secretaries), and Wu Lengxi to investigate the Great Leap Forward in selected provinces. He instructed them to use "[the book] *Marx, Engels, Lenin, Stalin Discuss Communist Society* edited by the Chinese

[215] MacFarquhar, *Origins*, vol. 2, 114, 116.

[216] Xiao, *Qiusuo*, vol. 1, 437–39. NC 2609, 26–27.

[217] Li, *Private Life*, 278.

[218] Domes, *Peng*, 82–83. Xiao, *Qiusuo*, vol. 1, 497.

[219] NC 2605, 11, 14–17; 2606, 11–12; 2624, 6–8; 2627, 22–23; 2644, 8–11. Xiao, *Qiusuo*, vol. 2, 693.

[220] NC 2583, 24; 2614, 25–26; 2615, 5–8; 2617, 24–26.

[221] MacFarquhar, *Origins*, vol. 2, 114.

[222] CB 546, 19. SCMP 1886, 17–18. Li, *Li Rui wenji*, vol. 3/2, 342–44.

[223] MacFarquhar, *Origins*, vol. 2, 119–21.

People's University, [and] . . . Stalin's *Economic Problems of Socialism in the U.S.S.R.*" as guidance.[224] At the same time, Mao himself started to read economic texts by Marx and Stalin systematically—a task he had always shunned before.[225] In his own studies, he identified three conditions necessary for the success of the Great Leap Forward—the use of statistical data, changes in ownership and exchange patterns, and finally a high degree of literacy—which, he conceded, "are not easy to achieve."[226]

In late October and early November Chen, Zhang, Tian, and Wu reported to Mao. The first two, who had personally promoted the Great Leap Forward, now reported optimistically on Shandong. The other two had taken Mao's lifelong slogan "Seeking Truth from Facts" literally, but the truth they told the Chairman was not what he really wanted to hear.[227] The dysfunctional organization of the Great Leap Forward in Hubei had led to the complete expropriation and demoralization of rich peasants, the failure to bring in the harvest, and waste of food in the public mess halls, raising the specter of future famines.[228] Mao was ready to acknowledge excesses, but insisted that the Great Leap Forward was fundamentally sound.[229]

At the Politburo conference in Zhengzhou in early November, the Chairman was unwilling to admit that the Great Leap Forward had run aground. Like Stalin in his "Dizzy with Success" article, he criticized local cadres for promoting the "communist wind,"[230] and called for a rural responsibility system to increase accountability and forestall false reporting.[231] Mao also refused to see the heart of the problem; *he* had created a political system that provoked fraud and discouraged criticism. At least the Chairman was willing to downgrade his forecasts; China would enter communism a little later than planned, maybe in twelve to fifteen years.[232] He also called on the CCP to stop bragging because "our Soviet comrades would not understand this."[233]

Mao suffered a further blow during an inspection tour to Henan and Hubei in mid-November.[234] Finally, a low-level party official dared to tell

[224] Wu, *Yi Mao zhuxi*, 215.

[225] Salisbury, *New Emperors*, 132–33.

[226] Mao, "Remarks on the a Copy of Extracts of Material of Stalin's Theory," November 1958, *JYMW*, vol. 7, 596–97.

[227] Salisbury, *New Emperors*, 171–72, 195–96. Xiao, *Qiusuo*, vol. 1, 442.

[228] Wu, *Yi Mao zhuxi*, 98.

[229] Xiao, *Qiusuo*, vol. 1, 442–43. Wu, *Yi Mao zhuxi*, 100–103.

[230] Li, "Study [II]," 56.

[231] Mao, "Talk at First Zhengzhou Conference," 11/6/1958, *SS*, 454. Peng Dehuai, *Memoirs of a Chinese Marshal* (Beijing: Foreign Languages, 1984), 486.

[232] Mao, "Talk at First Zhengzhou Conference," 11/6/1958, *SS*, 444.

[233] Li, *Li Rui wenji*, vol. 3/2, 345.

[234] Wu, *Yi Mao zhuxi*, 105–6. Salisbury, *New Emperors*, 171.

him the whole truth. High rural requisition quotas based on excessive production targets had left people with "a hungry belly." The Chairman was shocked by the severity of the crisis, and finally "condemned himself" for the mistakes.[235]

From November 21 to December 10, the Politburo and the CC met in Wuhan to discuss the Great Leap Forward. Mao announced: "[I]n the last half of the year, everybody's brain was hot, including my own."[236] He called the long-term steel targets he had promoted subjectivism and demanded more prudence from all.[237] The Chairman revised the final tally for the 1958 harvest from 450 million to 375 million tons of grain,[238] which still was higher than a later Soviet estimate of 200 to 220 million tons.[239] He also agreed to the rectification of the communes to start in December.[240] But when Zhou Enlai, Wang Jiaxiang, Chen Yun, and Peng Dehuai urged him to lower future agricultural quotas, warning of famines in several provinces, Mao got testy.[241]

With his euphoria gone, the Chairman reconsidered his claims from the Beidaihe conference about China's impending entry into communism. He squarely admitted that the conditions in China for the transition to communism had not yet been achieved: "It seems that Khrushchev is still very cautious, he now speaks of preparing the conditions to enter communism in twelve years. . . . it is not good to think of entering [communism] *before the Soviet Union*."[242] In late 1958, Chinese media praised the recently published draft of the new Soviet Seven-Year Plan (1959–65) as the "correct solution for the preparation of conditions for transition toward Communism."[243]

Despite the public relations offensive promoting Soviet experience, Mao continued to criticize Bureaucratic Stalinism behind closed doors in an almost esoteric discussion designed to justify his deviations from Stalinist development theory. He condemned the late Soviet leader for his lack of clarity about the objective laws of economics, his failure to see

[235] Xiao, *Qiusuo Zhongguo*, vol. 1, 447–48.

[236] Wu, *Yi Mao zhuxi*, 110.

[237] MacFarquhar, *Origins*, vol. 2, 128. Mao, "Talk at Wuchang Conference," 11/21/1958, morning, *SS*, 485–86.

[238] MacFarquhar, *Origins*, vol. 2, 121. Mao, "Talk at Wuchang Conference," 11/21/1958, morning, *SS*, 484.

[239] Sladkovskii, *Ocherki*, 378.

[240] MacFarquhar, *Origins*, vol. 2, 136–37. Hinton, *People's Republic*, vol. 2, 720–30.

[241] Xu, *Wang*, 539. Hu, *Hu Qiaomu*, 15. Xiao, *Qiusuo*, vol. 1, 477–78. Peng, *Memoirs*, 486–87.

[242] Wu, *Yi Mao zhuxi*, 111–12 (italics mine).

[243] *SCMP* 1897, 42; 1919, 35, 36.

that "socialism contains the sprouts of communism," his concentration on heavy industry alone, and his failure to put politics in command.[244] Despite this criticism, the Chairman called on all party cadres to read Stalin's works: "He alone talks about socialist economy."[245] After Mao himself had finally started to read books on economics in late October, he also made the critical reading of the Soviet textbook *Political Economy*, Stalin's 1952 critique of its draft version—*Economic Problems of Socialism in the U.S.S.R.*—and other related texts mandatory reading for all party members.[246]

SOVIET REACTIONS TO THE GREAT LEAP FORWARD

The Soviet Union did not know details about events unfolding in China since late August 1958. After burning his fingers with the joint submarine proposal, Yudin did not want to create more misunderstandings by reporting any critical information. He even objected to the accurate translation of the term "Great Leap Forward" because he feared that its closeness to Stalin's "Leap Forward" from the early 1930s could "cause an allergy in Moscow."[247] Also, the Chinese government systematically cut off contacts to the Soviet embassy in the fall of 1958; the delivery of *Neibu cankao* was terminated.[248] Mao tried to prevent leaks when, in November, he accused unnamed comrades of "having illicit relations with foreign countries, [and] giving reports to embassies" that might alert the USSR about the situation in the PRC.[249]

Soviet experts had been critical of the emerging Great Leap Forward since May, as mentioned above. After the radical policies of the Great Leap Forward were launched in late August, they reported to Moscow about name calling because they had resisted demands to disregard technical norms of Soviet machinery. Khrushchev remembered that the USSR had promoted similar follies in the 1930s, "but there was no excuse for the Chinese to be repeating our own stupid mistakes."[250] Although the

[244] Mao, "Speech on the Book 'Economic Problems of Socialism,'" November 1958, Mao, *Miscellany*, 129.

[245] Mao, "Talks at First Zhengzhou Conference," 11/6/1958, *SS*, 462.

[246] Mao, "Talks at First Zhengzhou Conference," 11/6/1958, *SS*, 448. Xiao, *Qiusuo*, vol. 1, 444.

[247] Brezhnev, *Kitai*, 62–63.

[248] "On the Condition of the Exchange of Information," 2/18/1960, *AVPRF*, f.0100, o.53, d.24, p.457, 7–15, 19–24.

[249] Mao, "Talk at Wuchang Conference," 11/21/1958, morning, *SS*, 486.

[250] Khrushchev, *Testament*, 264–65.

Soviet leader internally condemned the Great Leap Forward,[251] Moscow refrained from public criticism.[252] The Soviet disapproval of the communes was mainly based on experience. Already in August, Khrushchev had told Mao that "in the USSR the communes had not worked out."[253] When commune rectification started in China later that year, Khrushchev alluded to his skepticism for the first time publicly in an interview with U.S. Senator Hubert Humphrey.[254] Yet, despite all the criticism, the Kremlin promised to deliver forty-seven industrial projects in August 1958 and another seventy-eight in early 1959.[255]

Mao's implicit assertion that China would surpass Great Britain before the Soviet Union could even catch up with the United States troubled Khrushchev. Allusions in the Chinese press in that regard surfaced at a time when the Soviet leader was sounding a *retreat* in Soviet economic development.[256] Contrary to Mao's claims, Khrushchev had well understood that agriculture was the principal economic problem in the USSR. After Stalin's death, he had launched the virgin soil campaign which extended acreage in Central Asia.[257] The average Soviet grain harvest for 1954–58 was 110.3 million tons, 20.4 million tons more than the average of the preceding five years. This apparent initial success led to huge increases in industrial production targets in the Sixth FYP (1956–60) and to Khrushchev's claim in May 1957 that the USSR would overtake the United States within fifteen years.[258]

Soil exhaustion, the lack of chemical fertilizer and crop rotation, a failed harvest in 1957 due to bad weather, and tiny growth rates in meat and milk production, however, made the fulfillment of the Soviet Sixth FYP impossible.[259] Ongoing governmental reorganizations, excessive investments in heavy industry, and unanticipated economic assistance to Poland and

---

[251] Delyusin, "Nekotorye," 4.

[252] "Short Record of Conversation," 12/4/1960, *AVPRF*, f.0100, o.53, d.6, p.453, 52. The Chinese side was aware that the Soviet leaders did not share their views: "Remarks on the Report by the Ambassador in the Soviet Union on all Occurrences in the Soviet Union since the Sino-Soviet Talks in Beijing," October 1958, *JYMW*, vol. 7, 486–87. Zhang Shuguang, "Economic Cooperation," 211–12.

[253] Referred to: "Short Record of Conversation," 12/4/1960, *AVPRF*, f.0100, o.53, d.6, p.453, 52.

[254] MacFarquhar, *Origins*, vol. 2, 135. WLX, 191.

[255] Wang, *Zhonghua*, vol. 2, 221.

[256] Khrushchev, *Khrushchev Remembers*, 473.

[257] Werner Klatt, "Fifty Years of Soviet Agriculture," *Survey* 65, 90–91. Malia, *Soviet Tragedy*, 329.

[258] Hildermeier, *Geschichte*, 791. Abram Bergson, *Economics of Soviet Planning* (New Haven: Yale, 1964), 83, 89.

[259] Hildermeier, *Geschichte*, 791. Malia, *Soviet Tragedy*, 330.

Hungary led to the abrogation of the plan in September 1957.[260] A year later—just when the Great Leap Forward was launched in China—the CPSU CC plenum decided to call for the extraordinary twenty-first party congress in late January 1959 in order to discuss the production targets of a special seven-year plan (1959–65; substituting the remainder of the Sixth as well as the Seventh FYP).[261] Soviet propaganda boasted publicly that the new—downwardly revised—figures would guarantee in 1970 the achievement of the highest living standard in the world.[262] They were still ambitious: anticipated production increases of 64 percent to 80 percent for various metals and of 85–88 percent for food during the *whole seven-year* period.[263] But they also were much more realistic than any of Mao's claims the same month, such as the doubling of steel output and the 69 percent increase in grain production for *1958 alone.*[264] It was ironic that the Chinese leadership—once it had recognized the excessive nature of the targets of the Great Leap Forward—decided to hail the comparatively humble Soviet seven-year plan as "a big step toward communism."[265]

Given Mao's challenges on economic and foreign policies in 1958, Khrushchev apparently wanted to know how serious the Chinese leaders felt about their claims from the Moscow Meeting in late 1957 that the Soviet Union was heading the socialist camp. Curiously, the invitation letter the CPSU CC sent out in September to all fraternal parties made no mention of the seven-year plan, but announced that the twenty-first congress would discuss whether or not to skip the phrase "the Soviet Union stands at the head of the socialist camp."[266] The reasons listed—alleged Yugoslav charges that the CPSU was striving for hegemony in the socialist camp—were plainly unconvincing; they sounded very much like Mao's recent censure of past Soviet behavior. The first secretary obviously demanded that the Chairman show his true colors.

The year 1958 witnessed two Chinese challenges to the Soviet Union. The first, the Great Leap Forward, was an ideological challenge to Soviet

---

[260] Bergson, *Economics*, 83. Harry Schwartz, *Soviet Economy since Stalin* (London: Gallancz, 1965), 85–95.

[261] "Stenographic Account of the CPSU CC Plenum," [11/5/1958], *RGANI*, f.2, o.1, d.332, 3a, 8a.

[262] *NYT*, 11/14/1958, 1; 1/27/1959, 32; 1/28/1959, 3.

[263] "Plenum of the CPSU CC," 11/12/1958, *RGANI*, f.2, o.1, d.336, 6–10.

[264] *SCMP* 1846, 1–2.

[265] *SCMP* 1897, 42; 1919, 35–36.

[266] "CPSU CC to the CCs of the Communist and Workers' Parties," [no date], *RGANI*, f.1, o.3, d.1, 21–22. However, a letter to the Czechoslovak party two months later spelled out the real reasons for the congress, see: "Letter by the CPSU CC to the KSČ CC," 11/3/1958, *SÚA*, Archív ÚV KSČ, f.100/3, Mezinárodní oddělení, 1945-1962, 181/611/129.

leadership in the socialist world. There is little doubt that by the fall of 1958, Mao hoped that the Great Leap Forward would propel China into the communist end of history before the Soviet Union, thereby helping him to supersede Khrushchev as the foremost communist leader in the world. This instrumental approach to the Great Leap Forward, however, obscures the fact that this radical development policy was deeply rooted in Mao's—obviously limited—understanding of communist development theory. The Great Leap Forward in its entire radicalism did not originally derive from Mao's wish to supersede Khrushchev but from his ideological left turn in the summer of 1957. The second challenge, the shelling of Jinmen, initially was the product of China's dissatisfaction with the Sino-American ambassadorial talks and, by extension, with the Soviet policy of peaceful coexistence. In time, however, it took on additional justifications, such as preventing the perceived division of China and punishing the United States over the Middle East. Although these two challenges to Soviet leadership had very different roots, they converged in August of 1958 when Mao launched the most radical Great Leap Forward policies and, simultaneously, initiated the Second Taiwan Strait Crisis.

The shelling of Jinmen was *not* the result of Chinese security concerns over U.S. support to Taiwan. Although the United States had introduced tactical nuclear missiles to Taiwan in 1957 and test-fired them in May of the following year, neither event caused the PRC to worry about an American attack. Beijing's hesitant planning for the Second Taiwan Strait Crisis similarly displayed its lack of concern over an immediate security threat. Instead, it was the possibility of a permanent division of China that was at the center of Beijing's worries. Mao decided to instigate a new crisis in late 1957 after the collapse of the ambassadorial talks in Geneva, where, for over two years, the PRC had tried to negotiate on Taiwan. A limited crisis over Jinmen was a perfect opportunity to pressure the United States into resuming the talks. This situation also explains Beijing's reaction to Moscow's joint submarine proposal. Although Mao misunderstood the Soviet intention to station submarines in China as a nuclear deterrent, his hyperbole nevertheless revealed the fear that the PRC would lose its freedom of action over the Taiwan issue to supposed Soviet control. Thus, the Second Taiwan Strait Crisis was both a challenge to the United States and the USSR.

The launching of the radical policies of the Great Leap Forward and the start of the Second Taiwan Strait Crisis did not merge until August of 1958. The timing of the crisis was irrelevant with regard to its external aim, that is, rendering pressure on the United States. Instead, Mao used the timing for internal purposes, such as the creation of a warlike atmosphere that allowed him to mobilize the Chinese people. Once the steel campaign, the communes, and the militia movement had been launched, the link between the Second Taiwan Strait Crisis and the Great Leap Forward weakened rapidly, although Mao would maintain the fiction of continued American aggression in domestic propaganda.

At the end of 1958, Mao could look back on a year characterized by mixed results. On the one hand, with regard to the United States, he had achieved the resumption of the ambassadorial talks while most of his fears about American intentions in Taiwan had evaporated. Indeed, considering the American attempt to demilitarize the Taiwan Strait, U.S. policy was focused on reducing conflict. These developments thus undermined, at least partially, China's opposition to the Soviet policy of peaceful coexistence. The PRC could well live in peaceful coexistence with the United States in the Taiwan Strait, which is what it has done to this very day. But, as we shall see in subsequent chapters, Mao continued to oppose peaceful coexistence for ideological rather than security reasons.

Relations with the Soviet Union, on the other hand, had suffered significantly in 1958. The lack of communication about the crisis in the Taiwan Strait led Moscow to question Beijing's reliability as an ally and facilitated the ongoing superpower rapprochement over nuclear weapons negotiations with Washington. The Great Leap Forward, with its outrageous claims of fast socioeconomic development, also irritated the Soviet Union. Although Khrushchev was highly critical of Mao's policies, he still supported Chinese economic requests loyally and refrained from any public comments until late 1958, after the PRC had started to admit to problems. Nevertheless, Beijing had overplayed its hand. With its invitation to the twenty-first CPSU congress in February of 1959, the CPSU demanded an oath of loyalty from the CCP. By late 1958, the cracks that had appeared in the alliance the year before still remained hidden beneath a smooth surface, but they had opened more.

CHAPTER 4

Visible Cracks, 1959

AFTER THE WUHAN CONFERENCE in early December 1958, Hunan's party boss Zhou Xiaozhou invited Mao to Changsha to attend the opera *The Board of Life or Death*. The plot concerned Hai Rui—a Ming dynasty official (1514–87)—who challenged the verdict of the Jiajing emperor (reign: 1522–67) by saving a falsely accused woman from execution. Peng Dehuai had liked both the opera during his inspection tour a short time before and Zhou's openness about the problems of the Great Leap Forward. The provincial party leader saw himself as an honest official willing to face an imprudent ruler. It was thus that this Ming dynasty official rose from obscurity into an unexpected second political career.[1]

Unlike the direct connection between the launching of the radical Great Leap Forward and the Second Taiwan Strait Crisis in late August 1958, the links between China's domestic and foreign policy in 1959 were merely contextual. The ideological radicalism in China and the emergence of leadership conflicts within the CCP created an environment conducive to the further deterioration of Sino-Soviet relations. Unrelated events such as the Tibetan Uprising, the Sino-Indian border war, and Soviet-American rapprochement worsened the tenuous situation even more. While Mao had been directly responsible for the problems in Sino-Soviet relations in 1958, he did not initiate most of the predicaments the year after.

Throughout 1959, problems and failures rattled the Great Leap Forward. Although the CCP moderated its claims on the viability of the Great Leap Forward and even admitted that the USSR was the most advanced socialist state, Mao, for selfish reasons, dragged his feet at reversing course in the first half of 1959. Yet, the suffering of ordinary Chinese people led to conflicts within the CCP leadership. At the Lushan conference in July, Peng Dehuai and a few like-minded high-ranking party members challenged Mao's standpoints. Although their criticism was constructive, designed to reform the Great Leap Forward, Mao feared an open debate and asserted that the criticism was a conspiracy of traitors against him and the party. The fact that the criticism came from people

[1] Li, *Private Life*, 285–86. About Peng's tour: Xiao, *Qiusuo*, vol. 1, 497–98. Peng, *Memoirs*, 487–88. Domes, *Peng*, 85–86.

with past Soviet connections, that it contained unflattering comparisons of Mao's personality cult to that of Stalin, that it was an account of mistakes similar to, though not as harsh as, those listed in Khrushchev's Secret Speech, and that the Soviet leader publicly but coincidentally censured the Great Leap Forward gave Mao's forceful response to the criticism at Lushan and his subsequent purge of the critics an anti-Soviet bent. The ensuing Anti-Rightist Campaign in the second half of 1959 not only ended free debate within most of the party, but also led to the strengthening of Mao's personality cult. Although the Chairman had initially promoted the cult in early 1958 for the purpose of achieving complete control over the decision-making process, by late 1959 it also worked as a shield against any dissent. At the same time, the Chairman relaunched the Great Leap Forward, without taking into account the constructive criticism voiced by Peng. This renewed ideological radicalism did not bode well for Sino-Soviet relations in 1959 and beyond.

Against this background, a series of international events continued to undermine Sino-Soviet relations. By itself, the Tibetan Uprising in March did not damage Beijing's alliance with Moscow. However, Mao's ideologically hard-line response, saturated with Great Leap Forward radicalism, destroyed the Sino-Indian friendship and irritated the USSR. Although, in August, New Delhi had initiated the Sino-Indian border war as a response to the militarization of the Sino/Tibetan–Indian border, Beijing's unnecessarily harsh diplomatic and rhetorical treatment of its southern neighbor after the Tibetan Uprising and its failure to inform Moscow on the ongoing border conflict led the Soviet government to believe that the PRC had created a new crisis similar to the one in the Taiwan Strait a year before. The fact that Khrushchev was scheduled to visit the United States the following month reinforced the erroneous Soviet perception that the Sino-Indian border war was yet another challenge to Soviet leadership of the socialist camp.

Finally, the Soviet-American rapprochement created further friction in the Sino-Soviet relationship. Despite the reduction of Sino-American tensions after the Second Taiwan Strait Crisis, Mao continued to oppose peaceful coexistence. The Soviet refusal to deliver a promised model A-bomb in June provided the PRC with supposed evidence to believe that Moscow was seeking rapprochement with Washington on Beijing's back. Although the Chinese comrades did not publicly disapprove of Khrushchev's visit to the American imperialists in September, they were apprehensive of its potentially negative impact on China. When the Soviet leader arrived in Beijing for the celebration of the tenth anniversary of the PRC on October 1, he met a critical Chairman who had just been radicalized by the Lushan conference. The ensuing talks plainly revealed the ideological disagreements on international relations.

At the end of 1959, Beijing and Moscow reassessed the supposed mutuality of their relationship. Still in a radical mood after Lushan, Mao nursed justified grievances against India and its Soviet friend, resented Moscow's breach of nuclear promises, and ridiculed Khrushchev for turning toward the United States without obtaining any American concessions. With the knowledge that most of the promised Soviet economic aid had been exhausted, and that the prospect of more was unlikely, Mao concluded that the Sino-Soviet alliance had lost much of its usefulness to China's security and economic development. Given his dislike of the revisionist Khrushchev, the Chairman decided that China should sail an independent course, designed to displace the current Soviet leadership at the helm of the socialist camp, in international affairs. Simultaneously, the CPSU reevaluated the Sino-Soviet relationship. Sickened by the extremism—real and perceived—of Chinese foreign policy and by Mao's Stalin-like personality cult, it decided to reassert its leadership in the socialist camp.

The Famines and Mao's Initial Retreat

The famines in 1959 and after were largely a result of the misguided Great Leap Forward policies. Citing widespread deception by low-ranking cadres, the Chairman himself claimed that he had been unaware of the depth of the crisis.[2] An evaluation of *Neibu cankao*—the internal reference news for the top party leaders—reveals that he must have known the terrible truth.

Rapid population growth made spring famines a recurrent phenomenon in early modern China. One of the great achievements of the newly established communist government was to reduce the frequency and scope of spring famines, although they did not disappear completely.[3] What set the spring famines of 1959 apart from those in previous years was their great number and early occurrence. Of the thirty administrative entities in the PRC (twenty-four provinces, three autonomous regions, and three municipalities), ten—according to *Neibu cankao*—were hit by famines in January alone (Gansu, Shandong, Henan, Sichuan, Yunnan, Hunan, Hubei, Tianjin, Guizhou, and Jiangxi),[4] three more in February (Liaoning, Inner Mongolia, and Hebei),[5] another five in March (Qinghai, Guangdong, Jiangsu, Shanxi, and Anhui),[6] three in April (Shanghai,

---

[2] "Internal Correspondence," 4/29/1959, *MZDDG*, 261–62.
[3] Jasper Becker, *Hungry Ghosts* (London: Murray, 1996), 1–57.
[4] NC 2681, 9–10; 2689, 9–11; 2694, 6–7; 2699, 10–11, 16.
[5] NC 2704, 12–14; 2705, 3–4; 2715, 13–14.
[6] NC 2718, 17; 2719, 8–10, 12–13; 2733, 6–7; 2739, 10–11.

Fujian, and Zhejiang),[7] two in May (Jilin and Guangxi),[8] and finally four over the summer (Beijing, Xinjiang, Shaanxi, and Hainan)[9]—twenty-seven in all. Only Tibet, Ningxia, and Heilongjiang did not report any famines. The 1959 famines were largely a rural problem, but they were not yet as deadly as those in 1960. Bo Yibo claimed that 25 million people suffered from famines in 1959.[10] Chinese statistics published in the 1990s suggest that 310,000 people died of famines in 1959, compared with a staggering 13.5 million in 1960.[11]

Mao's leadership was responsible for the disasters and the subsequent failure to alleviate them. For 1959, the Chairman had sown acreage reduced by 13 percent to prevent an anticipated excess harvest, but refused afterward to admit his culpability in the resulting severe food shortages. Fearing a loss of face, he insisted on keeping up with debt-in-kind repayment to the Soviet Union. That year, China exported 4.1575 million tons (2.8834 million tons in 1958) of grain, while it imported only 2,000 tons (223.5 thousand tons in 1958).[12]

The Chairman used the argument, which commune leaders brought forward as a tool to keep as much of the grain as possible, that natural disasters had wiped out the harvest, in order to explain away his responsibility for the disaster.[13] Again, *Neibu cankao* points to the opposite. Although parts of Zhejiang suffered hailstorms in February and two months later a famine,[14] in all other cases, natural disasters did *not* precede famines, but succeeded and thereby exacerbated them. In April, windstorms destroyed the fishing grounds off the Liaoning coast and hit Jiangsu, both already starving for at least one month.[15] Floods hit Hubei, which was suffering under famines since January.[16] In May, Henan, after enduring food scarcities since early in the year, was hit by hail.[17] Torrential rain struck Fujian, as its monthlong famine persisted.[18] In May and

[7] NC 2761, 13–15, 18–19.

[8] NC 2774, 10–11; 2775; 17–19.

[9] NC 2792, 10–12; 2815, 12–13; 2836, 14–15; 2842, 15–16.

[10] Bo quoted in: Becker, *Ghosts*, 85.

[11] Yao Shujie, "A Note on the Causal Factors of China's Famine in 1959–1961," *Journal of Political Economy* 107/6, 1366. Lardy, "Chinese Economy," 370; n. 27 acknowledges the relatively low level of mortality rates, and asserts that on average approximately 63 percent of the deaths were reported. Consequently, mortality rates per thousand would be: 17.6 (1956–57), 23.2 (1959), and 40.3 (1960).

[12] Lardy, "Chinese Economy," 381.

[13] Li, *Private Life*, 282–83, 385.

[14] NC 2717, 7; 2761, 18–19.

[15] NC 2753, 13–15; 2758, 11–12.

[16] NC 2761, 15–16.

[17] NC 2764, 10.

[18] NC 2784, 10.

June, flooding devastated parts of Hubei, Guangdong, Hunan, Guangxi, Jiangxi, Anhui, Fujian, and Guizhou—all of which had been affected by famines.[19] Liaoning and Hohhot (Inner Mongolia), both enduring famines since early in the year, were hit by flooding in July.[20] And in August, Guangdong reported torrential rain, its second natural disaster that year.[21] In early 1961, Liu Shaoqi declared that 70 percent of the famines were due to human errors, and not to natural disasters.[22]

The breakdown of industry followed the agricultural collapse. Nearly monthly, *Neibu cankao* reported shortages in coal production, the primary source of energy for individual consumption, railroad transport, and electricity production.[23] This problem led to shortages in light industrial production and price increases.[24] In January at Shenyang's Angang—China's largest steel mill—Mao realized that the backyard furnaces only consumed manpower and resources but did not produce utilizable steel. Despite his recognition that the technologically advanced, capitalist West produced steel in fuel- and labor-efficient large steel plants, Mao still refused to budge because he feared that a policy change would "dampen the enthusiasm of the masses."[25] By spring, the backyard furnace movement collapsed by itself.[26] Problems also rattled the modern, Soviet-style steel plants. *Neibu cankao* reported in April that a Qinghai steel factory hastily erected under the Great Leap Forward expansion was so shoddily built that it could not enter production.[27] A month later, Angang reported that it had to stop steel production because spare parts for the overused Soviet-built smelters had run out of stock before time.[28] Mao's steel drive was in peril, as a CC circular in mid-April revealed: overall steel production was short a third of the production plan.[29]

These failures moderated Mao's projections of China's future. As early as December 1958, *Hongqi* (*Red Flag*) stated that the PRC would enter communism only after the USSR.[30] In February 1959, Mao even recommended "to study humbly all advanced experience of the Soviet

[19] NC 2814, 9–11.

[20] NC 2827, 16–17; 2835, 11–13.

[21] NC 2840, 13.

[22] Sladkovskii, *Ocherki*, 387. Also: MacFarquhar, *Origins*, vol. 3, 63, 146, 152. Li, *Private Life*, 385.

[23] NC 2690, 4–5; 2707, 10–11; 2729, 11–12; 2762, 18–19; 2830, 17.

[24] NC 2701, 11–12; 2710, 9–11; 2764, 3–6.

[25] Li, *Private Life*, 290–91.

[26] NC 2772, 9–10.

[27] NC 2752, 11–12.

[28] NC 2778, 2–3.

[29] Cong Jin, *Quzhe*, 181. MacFarquhar, *Origins*, vol. 2, 166. NC 2764, 2.

[30] SCMP 1919, 34–37.

Union"—a reversal of his attitude of less than a year before.[31] A CC circular reminded party cadres to avoid arrogant behavior in relations with brotherly countries and demanded a "more respectful" attitude toward the USSR.[32]

Little wonder the Chinese side reconfirmed its earlier position that the Soviet Union *was* the "head of the socialist camp" at the twenty-first CPSU congress in February 1959, after the CPSU had invited all communist parties to attend the convention in order to discuss this question.[33] Zhou told the Soviet comrades several times that it was "inappropriate to abolish the formula of the socialist camp being headed by the Soviet Union."[34] Khrushchev had received a Chinese oath of loyalty. In turn, the Soviet leader was willing to mollify the Chinese side on ideological matters. He publicly announced that all socialist countries would enter communism *simultaneously.*[35] His conciliatory tone also extended to long-standing conflicts. The congress raised neither the Stalin issue nor Stalin's dogmatism; instead, it turned against Yugoslav revisionism as the primary danger to the socialist world.[36] It made the Chinese retreat a little less painful, although one major ideological difference remained: Khrushchev contradicted Zhou's claim of the inevitability of war with the imperialist camp.[37]

During the enlarged Zhengzhou Politburo conference (February 27 to March 5), Mao revisited agriculture and the communes. He now saw waste in the free mess halls and the concealment of harvests by peasants as the primary cause of the food scarcities, but he was not willing to use the word "famine."[38] Mao blamed party cadres for incorrectly implementing the rectification policies that had been approved at the Wuhan conference in late 1958, criticized the arbitrary transfer of wealth from rich to poor commune members that left the former frustrated and the latter without incentives to work harder, and condemned the wasteful

[31] "Remarks and Revisions on Draft Instructions to CC foreign affairs group and to CC," 2/13/1959, *JYMW*, vol. 8, 39.

[32] "CCP CC Instruction on the Correction of Appearances of Arrogant Behavior in Foreign Relations," 2/16/1959, *JSSDAG*, 3124, zhang 87, 27–28.

[33] "CPSU CC to CCs of the Communist and Workers' Parties," [no date], *RGANI*, f.1, o.3, d.1, 21. "CPSU CC to SED CC," 2/23/1959, *SAPMO-BArch*, DY 30/3533, 6–14.

[34] *ZELNP2*, 203–4. Also: Liu, *Chushi*, 92–95. *NYT*, 1/29/1959, 1, 2.

[35] "Soviet-Chinese Relations (Reference)," 2/13/1961, *AVPRF*, f.0100, o.54, d.27, p.470, 23. Also: "Report on the Control Numbers of the Development of the National Economy of the USSR in the Years 1959–1965," [1/27/1959], *RGANI*, f.1, o.3, d.17, 18–206, and d.18, 1–97.

[36] Pikhoya, *Sovetskii Soyuz*, 215. Kumara Menon, *Lamp and the Lampstand* (London: Oxford, 1967), 128–29.

[37] Kumara Menon, *Flying Troika* (London: Oxford, 1963), 232.

[38] *WLX*, 192. *CLG* 9/4, 42. MacFarquhar, *Origins*, vol. 2, 152.

use of labor for industrial and administrative work in the communes.[39] He even denied the existence of famines, claiming that rich peasants were hiding grain.[40] This had been Stalin's argument in 1928.[41]

Simultaneously, the Chairman warned against repeating Stalin's mistakes, asserting that the late Soviet leader had been overzealous during collectivization and had exploited the rural population: "We should make a comparison between Stalin's policies and our own. . . . With the peasants, he drained the pond to catch the fish. Right now we have exactly the same illness."[42] He concluded: "[If] this question is not resolved effectively, it's quite possible that [we will] commit Stalin's error, and then agriculture would not be able to develop."[43] However, like Stalin who in early 1930 had reproached Soviet officials in an article for being "dizzy with success," the Chinese leader still blamed lower-level party cadres for the excesses of the Great Leap Forward.[44] Linking his own refusal to abolish the communes to the Soviet experience in the 1920s, Mao also argued that abolishing communes would only halt the development of society and economy: "Why did Stalin change his approach to communes? They felt that the expenses were too much, that the systems of voluntary exchange and sale and of the collection of surplus grain were not capable of stimulating production, so then they changed back to a grain tax. For thirty long years Stalin never actually implemented a system of collective ownership; [they are] still [practicing] landlord extra-economic exploitation and are taking away 70 percent of the peasants' [production]."[45]

While Mao was procrastinating, the situation worsened. For most of March and April, the Chinese leaders did not focus on the economy, as the Tibetan Uprising absorbed much of their time (see below). Early in the year Mao had asked Chen Yun, Li Fuchun, Bo Yibo, and Li Xiannian for advice, but balked at their recommendation to lower production targets.[46] Nevertheless, Chen Yun in the March issue of *Hongqi* advocated a return to central economic planning.[47] Later that month, Mao agreed to reduce steel targets but refused to make them public[48] since he "was

[39] *CLG* 9/4, 20–28, 39–40, 41–42, 45–46, 50, 52–53. MacFarquhar, *Origins*, vol. 2, 146–49.

[40] *CLG* 9/4, 15, 20.

[41] Stalin, "Grain Procurements and the Prospects for the Development of Agriculture," January 1928, Stalin, *Works*, vol. 11, 7.

[42] *CLG* 9/4, 18. MacFarquhar, *Origins*, vol. 2, 151–52. Richard Levy, "New Light on Mao," *China Quarterly* 61, 102.

[43] *CLG* 9/4, 45–61. Also: MacFarquhar, *Origins*, vol. 2, 151–52.

[44] *CLG* 9/4, 30. MacFarquhar, *Origins*, vol. 2, 152.

[45] *CLG* 9/4, 82.

[46] Xiao, *Qiusuo*, vol. 1, 476–77.

[47] MacFarquhar, *Origins*, vol. 2, 163–65.

[48] Xiao, *Qiusuo*, vol. 1, 481.

afraid that the creative energies of the masses . . . would somehow be dampened."[49] Finally in May, after three months of investigations, Chen Yun, Li Fuchun, and Bo Yibo called for a steel target of 13 million tons for the current year (down from the 30 million in the plan of the fall of 1958) on the basis of the limited physical capabilities of China's industry.[50] Chen Yun also advocated population transfers from the cities to the countryside because the rushed establishment of industrial enterprises in previous months had swelled the urban population so dangerously that cities could not feed the newcomers while the countryside lacked their labor.[51] But Mao was still not willing to submit his high-flying dreams to sober economic analysis.[52]

Even as the top leadership was discussing production targets and population transfers, the agricultural Great Leap Forward disintegrated quickly in the face of the famines. In late April, Mao exhorted cadres to increase sown acreage to reduce grain consumption in favor of vegetables,[53] but peasants at that time had already been reduced to eating bark, tree leaves, roots, and herbs.[54] On May 7, the CC sent out an emergency directive reintroducing private plots that had been abolished during communization in the previous fall. On May 26, it even abandoned the provinces to their fate, announcing that "the central government is unable to deal with more than the grain crisis." On June 11, the CC also issued detailed regulations on family ownership of livestock and private plots.[55] Within some weeks, the agricultural Great Leap Forward had turned into a great retreat backward.

During a Politburo meeting attended by thirty people on June 12 and 13, Mao agreed to turn over economic management to Chen Yun because, as he announced, "he [himself] could not do economic affairs, . . . *he had not understood it during his whole lifetime.*"[56] The Chairman finally dropped the notion of leaplike development that had been so crucial to the Great Leap Forward. Given the depth of the crisis, Mao called for a meeting of all central and provincial leaders at Lushan—a holiday resort on a mountain in northern Jiangxi—for July 2, 1959.[57] Yet, although he admitted that "at the moment, our reputation is not very

[49] Li, *Private Life*, 294.
[50] Wu, *Yi Mao zhuxi*, 133. Cong, *Quzhe*, 183. MacFarquhar, *Origins*, vol. 2, 166–70.
[51] Xiao, *Qiusuo*, vol. 1, 761–62.
[52] Wu, *Yi Mao zhuxi*, 133. Cong, *Quzhe*, 183. MacFarquhar, *Origins*, vol. 2, 166–70.
[53] "Internal Correspondence," 4/29/1959, *MZDDG*, 261–62.
[54] NC 2771, 10, 11–12.
[55] Cong, *Quzhe*, 181–82.
[56] Hu, *Hu Qiaomu*, 15 (italics mine).
[57] Xiao, *Qiusuo*, vol. 1, 495.

good," he was still not ready to assume personal responsibility outside of the narrow circle of thirty people.[58]

Initially, the Soviets did not know about China's economic collapse. The isolation of the Soviet embassy and Yudin's failure to secure appointments with Mao and other top leaders served Moscow poorly.[59] Nevertheless, the start of commune rectification in late 1958 triggered Soviet public criticism.[60] And Zhou was willing to ask the Soviets, during the twenty-first CPSU congress, both for advice on fixing steel production and for more specialists to come to the country.[61] Although the Soviets maintained that the Chinese comrades "had been spitting into their face" with the Great Leap Forward, the atmosphere remained conciliatory.[62] Even Mao stressed afterward that "our relations with Khrushchev are like nine and one finger among ten fingers, there is only one finger that is unequal, the other nine fingers are alike."[63]

Following the congress, Beijing was somewhat more forthcoming about the disasters in China. In late February, Foreign Minister Chen Yi acknowledged to Yudin that China's cities suffered under food shortages.[64] Ten days later, Liu Ningyi, vice-head of the CCP CC Liaison Department, admitted grain shortages.[65] Nevertheless, Deng Xiaoping in late May told Yudin that the spring wheat harvest would be 20 percent higher than the previous one while attributing food shortages to flooding and drought.[66] Liu Shaoqi in June acknowledged that industrial enterprises erected randomly had increased the urban population far too quickly.[67] In mid-June, Zhou disclosed to a Soviet visitor "that in the four

---

[58] Wu, *Yi Mao zhuxi*, 139.

[59] Brezhnev, *Kitai*, 62–63. "On the Condition of the Exchange of Information in 1959," 2/18/1960, *AVPRF*, f.0100, o.53, d.24, p.457, 7–15, 19–24. Mikhail Prozumenshikov, "1960 god glazami sovetskikh i kitaiskikh rukovoditelei," paper presented at the conference "Sino-Soviet Relations and Cold War: International Scientific Seminar," Beijing, China, October 1997, 9.

[60] MacFarquhar, *Origins*, vol. 2, 135. WLX, 191. Mao Zedong, "Remarks on a Report by the Ambassador in the Soviet Union on some Philosophical Points of Yavchuk," 1/15/1959, *JYMW*, vol. 8, 5–7. NC 2679, 16; 2685, 16–17; 2688, 24–25.

[61] Khrushchev, *Testament*, 274, 275.

[62] Wang, *Zhonghua*, vol. 2, 228.

[63] WLX, 192.

[64] "Record of Conversation with Chen Yi," 2/20/1959, *AVPRF*, f.0100, o.52, d.7, p.442, 1–4.

[65] "Record of Conversation with Liu Ningyi," 3/3/1959, *AVPRF*, f.0100, o.52, d.7, p.442, 7–8.

[66] "Record of Conversation with Deng Xiaoping," 5/27/1959, *AVPRF*, f.0100, o.52, d.7, p.442, 86.

[67] "Record of Conversation with Liu Shaoqi," 6/1/1959, *AVPRF*, f.0100, o.52, d.7, p.442, 90–91.

months we made the Great Leap Forward last year we had not very good economic results."[68] And finally, in July, Chen Yi admitted that almost all of China was suffering from food shortages.[69] No one acknowledged the famines.

PENG DEHUAI, HAI RUI, AND "HUNGARY"

Because until early June Mao had refused to confront the basic problems of the Great Leap Forward, disagreements within the Chinese leadership steadily increased. Peng Dehuai's extensive inspection tours in March and April 1959 to Jiangxi, Anhui, and Hebei convinced him that the Great Leap Forward needed much greater revisions than Mao was willing to contemplate.[70] However, his major criticisms at the Shanghai Politburo conference in late March targeted Mao's personality cult.[71] Li Rui, one of Mao's secretaries, followed up with a frank letter to his boss urging forceful revisions of the Great Leap Forward.[72] Mao replied to the criticisms with a speech rejecting any "corrections" of his policies with the worn argument that "this would discourage the people."[73] He concluded with another version of the Hai Rui story—"Hai Rui Dismissed from Office"—in which the Ming emperor imprisoned his official for writing an excessively critical letter. During the Shanghai Politburo meeting, Mao's most loyal supporter in the city, Ke Qingshi, had operatically staged this particular version.[74] Li Zhisui recalled that the Chairman liked it because it reduced permissible criticism to "his own terms."[75]

The dilemma Peng faced became apparent during his friendship tour to East Europe, the USSR, and Outer Mongolia from April 24 to June 13. Some months later he would be accused of "illicit relations with foreign countries" and for plotting with Khrushchev to overthrow Mao.[76] In April, the Chinese ambassador to the Soviet Union, Liu Xiao, warned Peng that the Soviets were trying to make the PRC a bargaining chip in Soviet-American relations.[77] The defense minister took precautions against

[68] ZELNP2, 237–39.
[69] "On the Condition of the Exchange of Information," 2/18/1960, AVPRF, f.0100, o.53, d.24, p.457, 21.
[70] Domes, Peng, 86.
[71] Domes, Peng, 87.
[72] Li, Li Rui wenji, vol. 3/2, 446–48.
[73] Li, Li Rui wenji, vol. 3/2, 455–69.
[74] Li, Li Rui wenji, vol. 3/2, 469–70.
[75] Li, Private Life, 295–96.
[76] Bo, Ruogan, vol. 2, 879.
[77] Liu, Chushi, 108–9.

any political mishaps during the trip.[78] By a stroke of fate, however, he shared the plane to his first destination, Poland, with Zhang Wentian, who was on his way to a WAPA foreign ministers' conference.[79] Zhang, who would become Peng's closest ally against Mao in July, had studied Soviet economics while ambassador in Moscow from 1951 to 1955.[80] On several inspection tours, Zhang had come to conclusions similar to Peng's.[81] Emboldened, they began comparing Mao's personality cult with "Stalin's mistakes in his later years."[82]

Peng did not speak publicly about the Great Leap Forward during his European trip.[83] In East Berlin, however, he told the Chinese embassy staff: "Communists must not say falsehoods, must not cheat the people, and must not put on an act. Last year the Great Leap Forward was bombastic. . . . We must not abuse the party's and Mao's prestige."[84] After talking with János Kádár in Budapest about the Hungarian Revolution, he concluded: "The enemy by no means should be feared, but what should be feared most is a party's incorrect path and a party's work style separated from the masses." Peng was also shocked that the relatively well-off Hungarian people had revolted at all. After his return to China, he told the Central Committee that "the [Hungarian] people eat every year forty kilograms of meat [eighty-eight pounds], and they nonetheless produced the Hungarian incident."[85] Peng warned that the CCP was sitting on a time bomb: "If the Chinese peasants had hitherto not been so disciplined they would have followed the example of the Hungarians and already risen up." The remark infuriated Mao.[86]

Peng must have drawn distressing comparisons between the hated Stalinist regime in Hungary three years earlier and the contemporaneous situation in the PRC. Beijing's advice to Moscow to intervene in 1956 had also set a *precedent* for a similar course of action in China. Despite later accusations by Mao's entourage, there is no evidence that Peng broached the problems in China in his meetings with Khrushchev in Albania and Moscow in late May and early June, respectively.[87] On

[78] *PDHNP*, 726.

[79] CB 572, 29. SCMP 2004, 40; 2005, 45–48.

[80] Zhang Shude, "Wo shi gongchangdangyuan, yinggai jiang zhen huo!," Chang, *Zhiqing-zhe shuo*, 2nd ser., vol. 2, 79–80.

[81] Li, *Li Rui wenji*, vol. 1, 151.

[82] Zhang, "Wo shi," 100.

[83] Xiao, *Qiusuo*, vol. 1, 498.

[84] *PDHNP*, 727–28.

[85] Li Rui, *Li Rui wenji*, vol. 1, 115.

[86] Salisbury, *New Emperors*, 179.

[87] Domes, *Peng*, 85, 93–94. Li Rui, *Li Rui wenji*, vol. 1, 120. Peng Dehuai zhuanji bianxie zu bian, "Peng Dehuai mengyuan Lushan," *Renwu* 1995/5, 12–19. Peng Dehuai,

the contrary, he represented long-standing Chinese policies by declining politely Khrushchev's request that China join the WAPA.[88]

When Peng returned to Beijing on June 13, his chief of staff, Huang Kecheng, informed him about the worsening famine situation.[89] After catching up with *Neibu cankao* issues, he decided to go on an investigation to Hunan before traveling to the scheduled conference at Lushan.[90] Peng found support in a completely unexpected source—Hai Rui. Wu Han, a protégé of Beijing's mayor Peng Zhen, published a *Renmin Ribao* article on June 16 titled "Hai Rui Upbraids the Emperor," which quoted freely from an authentic memorial by the Ming official to the Jiajing emperor: "In earlier years you did quite a few good things, but how about now? . . . Your mind is set on occult arts, and you only want long life. Your mind is deluded, and you are too dogmatic and prejudiced. You think you are always right and refuse criticism. . . . The whole country has been dissatisfied with you for a long time and the inner and outer ministers and officers all know it."[91]

The starving refugees Peng saw from the train on the way to Hunan shocked him.[92] But the alleged self-discipline of the Chinese people still impressed the defense minister: "In Hungary each person each year on average eats forty pounds [kilograms?] of meat, yet, they rebelled against the revolution, the Soviet Army had to be called in to suppress the rebellion. Compared with that, we can see how good the Chinese workers and the peasants are. . . . *we don't need the big Red Army.*"[93] In his own native village, near Mao's birthplace Shaoshan, Peng listened to Zhou Xiaozhou's reports on food shortages and false statistics.[94] The findings were politically sensitive; famines existed in Mao's own patch.[95]

The Chairman decided to take measures to counter Peng's investigation, following him to Hunan on his own inspection tour.[96] After an early June visit to Hubei, where his staunch supporter Wang Renzhong had acknowledged a terrible famine, and to Henan, which was in slightly better shape due to Zhou Xiaozhou's more rational economic policies, the

---

"Weishenme yao xie xin gei Mao zhuxi," *Zhonggong dangshi ziliao* 28, 1–7. Dehuai, *Memoirs*, 493. Zhang, "Wo shi," 69. Salisbury, *New Emperors*, 175.

[88] Liu, *Chushi*, 109–11. Khrushchev, *Testament*, 268–69.

[89] Peng bian, "Peng," 5. Peng, *Memoirs*, 488–89.

[90] Tang Dihuai et al., "Huang Kecheng zishu (jiexuan)," *Renwu* 1994/4, 6.

[91] Quoted in: James Pusey, *Wu Han* (Cambridge: Harvard, 1969), 15–16. Merle Goldman, *China's Intellectuals* (Cambridge: Harvard, 1981), 33.

[92] Peng bian, "Peng," 6–7.

[93] Xiao, *Qiusuo*, vol. 1, 498 (italics mine).

[94] Tang, "Huang," 6. Salisbury, *New Emperors*, 177.

[95] Salisbury, *New Emperors*, 171.

[96] Salisbury, *New Emperors*, 171.

Chairman returned to Henan in late June on a political mission against Peng.[97] Even though Mao did not make any real investigations while he stayed in Shaoshan, he intended to use the encouraging conclusions he claimed to have found to confront his defense minister at Lushan.[98]

HIGH NOON AT LUSHAN

The Lushan work conference in July and subsequent CC plenum in August 1959 were among the most decisive leadership crises in the history of Mao's PRC. His victory over what he labeled a conspiracy had far-reaching consequences for political life in China. Afterward, the Chairman strengthened his personality cult, moved ideologically further to the left, relaunched an unreformed Great Leap Forward, and introduced class struggle into party life. Lushan marked a major switch in the track to the Cultural Revolution seven years later. As covered in the following chapters, it also had a great long-term impact on Sino-Soviet relations.

Mao opened the Lushan work conference on July 2 by playing down the disasters: "The achievements are great, there are some problems, but the future is bright." By enumerating nineteen narrow technical issues he deliberately *limited* the scope of the debate to problems of policy implementation.[99] He skirted the issue of personal responsibility by consistently using "we" instead of "I": "We have criticized Stalin for walking on one leg, but after we proposed to walk on two legs, we just walked on one."[100] And the Chairman even told the audience how to solve the problems: Chen Yun should run the economy, and the party should read the Stalinist textbook *Political Economy*.[101] With that, Mao split the participants into individual groups to discuss his plans. Despite all these machinations, the Chairman promised not to brand anyone with different views as a "rightist" or "counterrevolutionary."[102] He knew perfectly well that he was dodging the hard questions.

Peng soon criticized the continued exaggerations of the central leadership. Most in his group ignored the quarrelsome marshal. Frustrated by their apathy, Peng discussed the situation with Zhang Wentian and Zhou

---

[97] Li, *Private Life*, 298–300.

[98] Li, *Private Life*, 300. Xiao, *Qiusuo*, vol. 1, 495–96. Zhang, "Wo shi," 86.

[99] Mao, "Nineteen Problems to Be Discussed at the Lushan Conference," 6/29 & 7/2/1959, MZDW, vol. 8, 75–82. Peng bian, "Peng," 7–10.

[100] Mao, "Nineteen Problems . . . ," 77.

[101] Hu, *Hu Qiaomu*, 15.

[102] Quoted in: Domes, *Peng*, 89.

Xiaozhou.[103] A State Council Report of July 9 that was highly critical of the spontaneous conception and economic turmoil of the Great Leap Forward supported their dissent.[104] The next day Mao accused his critics of lacking "intraparty solidarity."[105] The Chairman attacked Stalin for covering up the Soviet abolition of the communes in *Political Economy*—the very Soviet textbook the Chairman had repeatedly urged the party to study.[106] Mao also instructed his secretary, Hu Qiaomu, to draft the decisions to be adopted on July 15 according to his own ideas. With that the conference was supposed to end.[107] Bo Yibo recalled the draft resolutions as "not very thoroughgoing" but a first step in the right direction.[108]

Peng was not happy about the abrupt end of discussions. His trip through East Europe, his own inspections tours, and the most recent *Neibu cankao* reports convinced him that Mao was not serious about reforming the fundamentally flawed Great Leap Forward.[109] He knew that other central leaders shared his views. But Liu Shaoqi's personal respect for Mao, Zhou Enlai's relative decline of influence since early 1958, and Deng Xiaoping's stay with a broken leg in a Beijing hospital convinced Peng that he was the only one capable of acting.[110] In the evening of July 12, Peng walked over to Mao's cottage with the intention of doing some plain talking. Security guards refused him entry because Mao had already gone to bed. It was in this situation that Peng Dehuai decided to write the famous July 14 letter that would greatly change the course of Chinese politics.[111]

Peng's letter highlighted the problems he believed had not attracted enough attention at Lushan: the economic bottlenecks stemming from the hasty industrial construction, the "chaotic" formation of the communes, the wasteful steel drive, the habit of exaggeration, and the mishandling of the 1958 fall harvest. Peng avoided accusing Mao personally when he wrote about "shortcomings and mistakes [that] appeared in *our* work" and when he insisted on "*no* investigation of personal responsibility." Yet, he criticized Mao's slogans as "a substitute for economic principles." His final conclusion—"Petty-bourgeois fanaticism renders us liable to commit 'left[ist]' mistakes"—referred to Lenin's "'Leftism' in

[103] MacFarquhar, *Origins*, vol. 2, 202–6. Peng, *Memoirs*, 490–93. Li, *Li Rui wenji*, vol. 1, 117–19.

[104] Paraphrased: *JYMW*, vol. 8, 386, n. 1.

[105] Mao, "Speech," 7/10/1959, *CLG* 1/4, 44–45.

[106] *MZDDG*, 621.

[107] Peng bian, "Peng," 12.

[108] Bo, *Ruogan*, vol. 2, 851–52.

[109] Li, *Li Rui wenji*, vol. 1, 111–16. Peng, "Weishenme," 1. Zhang, "Wo shi," 67–68.

[110] Peng bian, "Peng," 19. Domes, *Peng*, 93–94.

[111] Li, *Li Rui wenji*, vol. 1, 120. Peng bian, "Peng," 12–19. Peng, *Memoirs*, 494. Zhang, "Wo shi," 69.

Communism—an Infantile Disorder" (1920) which carped at impulsive and dogmatic revolutionary action.[112] After sending the letter on July 14, Peng believed the Chairman would talk with him *privately*, but did not expect the letter to "attract so much misfortune."[113]

Immediately resenting the letter, Mao alleged that it did not bring up anything new.[114] The Chairman loathed Peng's guts to label others—a prerogative he had reserved for himself.[115] More profoundly, Mao feared that he would be held responsible for mistakes similar to those over which his two predecessors as party leader, Li Lisan and Wang Ming, had fallen in so-called line struggles in the 1930s.[116] Although Peng or his supporters had neither the intention nor plans to remove Mao, the Chairman apparently wanted to seize the initiative to counter any potential threat. Claiming that the letter was "a deviation from the original restrictions" of July 2,[117] he declared Peng's criticism a "line struggle . . . spearheaded against the Politburo and the Chairman."[118]

On July 16, Mao hinted to his entourage that the party might split.[119] He ordered Peng Zhen, Huang Kecheng, Bo Yibo, Deng Xiaoping, and his staunch supporters Lin Biao and Kang Sheng to come to Lushan.[120] After his decision to continue the Lushan meeting with the distribution of Peng's letter to all participants on July 17, he instructed the daily reshuffling of the discussion groups in order "to avoid that one group would discuss along one tune only."[121] Some of the participants at Lushan realized that the Chairman was preparing a counterattack, and thus retreated from the debate; others misjudged the situation.[122] Peng himself demanded Mao withdraw his personal letter from public discussion.[123] The Chairman retorted disingenuously that the defense minister had not explicitly prohibited him from distributing it in the first place.[124]

---

[112] *SCMP* 4032, 1–5 (italics mine). MacFarquhar, *Origins*, vol. 2, 216.

[113] Zhu Ren, "Lishi zai zheli guaiwan," Chang, *Zhiqingzhe shuo*, 2nd ser., vol. 4, 122–23.

[114] Zhang, "Wo shi," 86. Zhu, "Lishi," 123.

[115] MacFarquhar, *Origins*, vol. 2, 216.

[116] Mao himself in September compared the purge of Peng with past line struggles: *CLG* 1/4, 79–84.

[117] Chen Shihui, "1959nian Lushan huiyi jishi," *Zhonggong dangshi ziliao* 28, 131.

[118] Tang, "Huang," 9.

[119] Li, *Private Life*, 315.

[120] Peng bian, "Peng," 20. Zhu, "Lishi," 123.

[121] Peng bian, "Peng," 20. Zhu, "Lishi," 123. *MZDDG*, 1001. Mao, "Proposals on how to change the Division of the Lushan Conference [and] the Participation in the Groups," 7/16/1959, *JYMW*, vol. 8, 355, 356.

[122] 'Hu' zhubian, *Hu Qiaomu*, 225–26.

[123] Peng, *Memoirs*, 492–502, 504.

[124] Li, *Private Life*, 317. Peng bian, "Peng," 25.

A bombshell, the publication of Peng's letter triggered open discussions in some of the groups.[125] Zhang Wentian, Zhou Xiaozhou, Huang Kecheng, and Li Rui openly supported Peng in their respective groups and in private talks with each other.[126] Peng asked why China "replicated" the Soviet experience of the communes. By quoting paragraphs from Stalin's *Political Economy* that discussed their economic infeasibility, he contradicted Mao's earlier claim that the late Soviet leader had dropped this issue from the book.[127] A majority at Lushan approved Peng's letter, with reservations about its harsh tone.[128] Hu Qiaomu, who knew about Mao's fury, cautioned Peng: "The wind is blowing more harshly now."[129] Only a few supported the Chairman openly, such as Ke Qingshi, who denounced the discussion as "not worth the effort."[130] Many of Mao's backers did not dare to speak up publicly.[131]

On July 21 Zhang Wentian dropped a second bombshell with a three-hour speech on the overall economic situation in China.[132] Despite the lack of statistical data, Zhang painted a coherent and detailed picture of the havoc the Great Leap Forward had wrought on China's economy. Its recovery, he warned, would take "several years." Zhang also dared to criticize Mao personally: "The Chairman has always said that we should seek truth from facts, but this dictum does not conform to the essence of what the Chairman says nowadays."[133]

On July 23, Mao counterattacked with a rhetorical masterpiece that aimed at the waverers at Lushan. The Chairman refused to carry responsibility alone, although he was willing both to admit to some (the steel drive and "rash advance") and to abolish those parts of the Great Leap Forward that did not work (the free mess halls). With the threat that the waverers were only "some 30 kilometers away from [being] rightists," however, the Chairman tried to cow the audience into obedience. With the same bluff he had hurled at Khrushchev in 1958, he announced his return to the mountains for another guerilla war if party and army

[125] Li, *Li Rui wenji*, vol. 1, 130–49.

[126] Zhang, "Wo shi," 71. Tang, "Huang," 7. Xu, *Wang*, 540–41.

[127] *PDHNP*, 742. I found two paragraphs that could refer to Peng's citation: USSR, *Political Economy*, 464, 467.

[128] Li, *Li Rui wenji*, vol. 1, 130–49. Li, *Private Life*, 315–16. Zhu, "Lishi," 123–27.

[129] 'Hu' zhubian, *Hu Qiaomu*, 225–26.

[130] Peng bian, "Peng," 22–23. Zhu, "Lishi," 123–27.

[131] Tang, "Huang," 7.

[132] Domes, *Peng*, 93. Li, *Li Rui wenji*, vol. 1, 153.

[133] Zhang Wentian, "Speech at Lushan Conference," 7/21/1959, Zhang Wentian, *Zhang Wentian wenji*, vol. 4 (Beijing: Renmin, 1989), 319–43.

would not follow him. Finally, he declared that the criticism raised at Lushan was a line struggle.[134]

After the speech, Peng met his supporters in his cottage. They wondered whether Mao had become "as dangerous as Stalin in his later years?"[135] And Zhou Xiaozhou commented on Mao's recent threat: "[W]e're only 50 steps away from being rightists."[136] Mao too met with his supporters to declare Peng Dehuai "just another Nagy" and to uncover other "rightists." When he got wind of the ongoing meeting at Peng's cottage, he used it as proof of a conspiracy against him.[137]

The Lushan conference continued somberly for a while.[138] Mao's opponents tried to save the situation by making amendments but they were not ready to retract the substance of their criticism.[139] Some central leaders also were unwilling to support the Chairman unequivocally. Meetings of the State Council had convinced Zhou Enlai that some criticism was justified.[140] Liu Shaoqi advocated a mild censure of Peng. Yet, when he insisted on publishing an article criticizing leftist mistakes, the politically cautious Hu Qiaomu refused to write a draft.[141]

Mao wanted the waverers to show their true colors when he accused Peng on July 26 of being the leader of the "Hunan clique"—the term "clique" referred to alleged counterrevolutionary activities—and of the "military club"—the word "club" (*julebu*) was used in Maoist polit slang exclusively for Petőfi Circle (*peiduofei julebu*).[142] The Chairman thereby had labeled his adversaries Hungarian-style counterrevolutionaries, who, on the evening of July 23, allegedly formed an anti-party organization directed against his person and against the Great Leap Forward.[143] He demanded everybody draw a line.[144] Afterward, most delegates attacked Peng, Zhang, and their supporters with unfounded accusations in a desperate scramble for their own political survival. The vicious attack on Peng for his supposed lifelong disloyalty to Mao was a deliberate political destruction of one of the Chairman's longest comrades-in-arms.[145] In

---

[134] Mao, "Speech at Lushan Conference," 7/23/1959, CLG 1/4, 28, 33–34, 35–36, 38–39, 41–42.

[135] Tang, "Huang," 9.

[136] Peng, *Memoirs*, 505.

[137] Li, *Li Rui wenji*, vol. 1, 159, 199–200, 208.

[138] Li, *Li Rui wenji*, vol. 1, 177–98.

[139] Zhang, "Wo shi," 87–88.

[140] Li Rui, "Lessons from the Lushan Plenum," CLG 29/5, 91.

[141] Hu, *Hu Qiaomu*, 15–16.

[142] Zhang, "Wo shi," 86–87, 89. Bo, *Ruogan*, vol. 2, 879. Cong, *Quzhe*, 302–3.

[143] Li, *Li Rui wenji*, vol. 1, 199–205. Zhu, "Lishi," 130.

[144] Zhu, "Lishi," 130.

[145] Zhang, "Wo shi," 86–87. Li, *Li Rui wenji*, vol. 1, 204–5.

this cacophony of sham accusations, the defense minister feared for the future: "This will develop into a situation similar to Stalin's later years. The ruler does not want to listen to adverse opinions."[146]

To drive his point home, Mao continued to seize new opportunities, such as the reports of Khrushchev's July 21 speech in Poznań (Poland) in which the Soviet leader stated that the communes had failed in the 1920s because "the political and material preconditions had not existed."[147] *Neibu cankao* carried it on July 26.[148] Three days later Mao circulated it at Lushan.[149] Khrushchev's speech was unrelated to the events at Lushan, but the Chairman was more than happy to use it as proof of Peng's collusion with the Soviets. In an attempt to display his apparent willingness to deal constructively with the criticism raised at Lushan, the Chairman asked the Soviet specialist Wang Jiaxiang to investigate the Soviet and Chinese communes. On the basis of research in Soviet archives and libraries, Wang published, in early October, a two-volume study that confirmed Khrushchev's analysis and concluded that "the establishment of big and public people's communes [in China] was extremely rash and inconsistent with the level of development of productive forces." At that time, however, the Chairman had already moved on, and the study had no impact at all.[150]

On July 30, Mao offered clemency to Huang Kecheng, Zhou Xiaozhou, and Li Rui on the condition that they draw a "clear line" between themselves and Peng."[151] They refused.[152] The same day, Nie Rongzheng and Ye Jianying tried to persuade Peng Dehuai to make a complete self-criticism. He too declined.[153]

During Politburo meetings on the following two days, Mao accused Peng of siding with Wang Ming in the 1930s and with Gao Gang and Rao Shushi in the early 1950s, and asserted that he had shown, since the 1920s, "30 percent of cooperation and 70 percent of non-cooperation" with the Chairman.[154] Mao even tried to marshal his personality cult to demonstrate how futile any attempt to overthrow him would be: "[W]hen I die, many people will fall into panic, [and] will not know how to handle this situation."[155] The Chairman received support from two of his staunchest

[146] *PDHNP*, 745.
[147] Reports in: *JYMW*, vol. 8, 367, 368–69. *Pravda*, 7/21/1959, 1 (quote).
[148] NC 2831, 19–20.
[149] MacFarquhar, *Origins*, vol. 2, 226–27.
[150] Xu, *Wang*, 541–45.
[151] Zhu, "Lishi," 132.
[152] Tang, "Huang," 10–13.
[153] Zhu, "Lishi," 132. Li, *Li Rui wenji*, vol. 1, 209.
[154] *MZDDG*, 1002.
[155] Zhu, "Lishi," 135.

followers. Kang Sheng submitted two Stalin speeches on how to handle rightist activities in the party.[156] Smelling "gunpowder" that could rid him of a longtime rival, Lin Biao charged the defense minister with having traveled to East Europe to plan with Khrushchev the ousting of Mao.[157] But Peng refuted these absurd accusations, and insisted on his right to criticize the Chairman on the ground that formerly Mao had criticized him as well.[158] He denied any mistakes simply because he did not want to be complicit in being labeled a "counterrevolutionary."[159] Nevertheless, the Politburo decided to replace Peng with Lin Biao as defense minister, to put him under house arrest, to dismiss Zhang Wentian, Huang Kecheng and Zhou Xiaozhou from their governmental positions, and to give Mao's secretary, Li Rui, an eighteen-year prison sentence.[160]

On short notice Mao convened a CC plenum at Lushan on August 2 to ratify the purge.[161] After paying brief lip service to the "break up [of] those unrealistic targets" of the Great Leap Forward, the Chairman spoke at length on the line struggle that supposedly had occurred.[162] Eight days later, Mao called his critics "capitalists" who "had planned to destroy the proletarian dictatorship," and asserted that "it was proven that they were members of the Gao-Rao clique that had plotted to rebel against the party."[163] Peng knew well that the Chairman sacrificed him for his own agenda.[164]

Given the repeated comparisons of Mao to Stalin that had surfaced at Lushan, the plenum addressed that topic as well. Zhang freely admitted that he and Peng had compared Mao with "Stalin in his later years."[165] But privately he realized that their criticism of Mao's personality cult had been futile: "Mao Zedong's prestige is not only his personal prestige, but also the prestige of the whole party; harming Mao's prestige is just harming the whole party's prestige."[166] Mao instructed Hu Qiaomu to draft

---

[156] Documents in: Hongdaihui Qinghua Daxue jinggangshan bingtuan jinggangshan zazhi she bian yin bian, *Lushan huiyi zhongyao wenxuan* (Beijing: Hongdaihui . . . , 1967), 39–44.

[157] Zhu, "Lishi," 134–36 (quote). Peng bian, "Peng Dehuai," 34. Salisbury, *New Emperors*, 184–85. MZDDG, 1002. PDHNP, 691. Bo, *Ruogan*, vol. 2, 879.

[158] MZDDG, 1002.

[159] Salisbury, *New Emperors*, 185.

[160] Salisbury, *New Emperors*, 185. MacFarquhar, *Origins*, vol. 2, 234.

[161] Zhu, "Lishi," 132. Peng bian, "Peng Dehuai," 32.

[162] Mao, "Speech at the Eighth Plenary Session of the Eighth CC," 8/2/1959, CLG 1/4, 60–63.

[163] Mao, "An Important Note," 8/10/1959, MZDSW 1967, 85.

[164] Peng, *Memoirs*, 507–8.

[165] Li, *Li Rui wenji*, vol. 1, 337.

[166] Zhang, "Wo shi," 97, 100–101.

a resolution, stating that "Mao always opposed the personality cult."[167] Many attending the plenum must have recognized this obvious sham, since they had also participated in the Chengdu conference in March 1958 where the Chairman had explicitly called for it.[168]

The CC adopted two more resolutions. The first on Peng quoted passages from his July 14 letter, but paraphrased incorrectly that in case of "a Hungarian incident" in China *it would have been necessary to invite Soviet troops in.*[169] The other praised the Great Leap Forward, but announced cuts in production quotas for steel, coal, grain, and cotton under the pretext of a "shortage of labor" and of "natural calamities."[170] None of the criticism raised at the work conference was incorporated.

Similarly misleading was the information the Chinese side provided to the Soviet comrades. Vice–Prime Minister Xi Zhongxun told a Soviet representative that some "rightist-opportunist" comrades had doubted the Great Leap Forward. "Real life confirmed the great vitality" of the communes, or so he claimed, and "not a single commune had suffered defeat." Although he admitted to "a series of mistakes," he hastened to add that they "existed only for some months" until Mao had "taken *decisive* steps" to fix them.[171] Khrushchev's memoirs reveal that the Soviet comrades were not easily fooled: "The Great Leap Forward and the creation of communes caused a great decline in China's industry and agriculture. . . . It was necessary for Mao to recognize his mistakes. But that was no more possible for him than for Stalin."[172]

The Lushan work conference and plenum revealed what Zhang Wentian had called "the defects in the political system of our party and state."[173] While the Hundred Flowers Campaign in 1957 had shut down popular disagreement, the drama at Lushan virtually destroyed open dissent within the party.[174] Mao's personality cult became "overt and legitimate" after Lushan.[175] The debate was neither about its desirability nor about its dispensability, but solely about the "*correct* personality cult." With Peng in mind, the Chairman criticized those who had followed the

---

[167] Li, *Li Rui wenji*, vol. 1, 345.

[168] *MZDDG*, 605.

[169] "CC Resolution on P'eng Te-huai," 8/16/1959, Hinton, *People's Republic*, vol. 2, 754 (italics mine).

[170] "CC Resolution on 'Increasing Production and Practicing Economy,'" 8/16/1959," Hinton, *People's Republic*, vol. 2, 760, 761.

[171] "Record," 8/28/1959, AVPRF, f.0100, o.52, d.5, p.442, 36–41 (italics mine).

[172] Khrushchev, *Glasnost*, 159.

[173] Quoted in: Li, "Lessons," 68. Also: Salisbury, *New Emperors*, 184. Bo, *Ruogan*, vol. 2, 878–81.

[174] Salisbury, *New Emperors*, 184. Sladkovskii, *Ocherki*, 378–79.

[175] Xiao, *Qiusuo*, vol. 1, 570.

"example of Khrushchev in opposing Chairman Mao's personality cult," and called their attitude "detrimental to the party, the proletarian revolution, and the cause of the people."[176]

The major vehicle for the promotion of Mao's personality cult was the PLA. In view of the PLA's lack of enthusiasm for studying *Mao Zedong Military Thought* in 1958 and its revulsion at the unwarranted sacking of the popular Peng Dehuai, Lin Biao spared no time in dismissing senior commanders he deemed ideologically unreliable.[177] In the fall, the PLA General Political Department published an article announcing the need "to carry out the spirit of the [Lushan] decisions." The article addressed the personality cult specifically with the words: "Fervent love for the leadership of Comrade Mao Zedong is identical with ardent love for the party and the undertakings of communism. Opposing the leadership of the party [and] destroying the prestige of the party's leadership is just criminal, anti-party behavior."[178]

Parallel to the relaunching of his personality cult, Mao reintroduced class struggle into the political discourse in China. Arguing that the criticisms leveled against him were nothing more than the "tools with which the bourgeois intellectuals wage their class struggle,"[179] the Chairman made the case for the existence of "class struggle within the party."[180] Mao's renewed emphasis on class struggle triggered another anti-rightist campaign designed to purge "reactionaries and . . . right opportunists."[181] As in 1957, many people within and outside of the party were branded rightist simply because they had dared to criticize the Great Leap Forward in some form. Some tried to forestall any harm by making preemptive retreats; on September 17, Wu Han published a *Hongqi* article replete with Marxist phraseology. He alluded that those who used Hai Rui to criticize Mao were opposing "those working for the people, those working for the cause of socialism."[182]

The cuts in production targets Mao had endorsed at Lushan perished quickly. Even before the end of the plenum, *Renmin Ribao* started a campaign against "a simple plan and low targets."[183] Peng's criticism of excessive targets now served Mao as a vehicle to relaunch the Great

[176] Li, "Lessons," 91 (italics mine).

[177] MacFarquhar, *Origins*, vol. 2, 242–43.

[178] Xiao, *Qiusuo*, vol. 1, 570–71.

[179] Mao, "Comments on 'How a Marxist Should Correctly Deal with Revolutionary Mass Movement,'" 8/15/1959, *CLG* 1/4, 70–71.

[180] Mao, "The Origins of Machine Guns and Mortars, etc.," 8/16/1959, *CLG* 1/4, 71.

[181] *CB* 611, 1.

[182] Pusey, *Wu Han*, 17–19.

[183] *SCMP* 2074, 4–6.

Leap Forward and reintroduce public mess halls.[184] Chen Yun, whom Mao had designated to run the economy in June, went on political sick leave.[185] Despite his efforts,[186] Zhou was unable to restrain Mao's intensification of the Great Leap Forward. In early September, the Chairman demanded that recalcitrant foreign specialists "should earnestly be persuaded over."[187] Mao mocked doubters of the Great Leap Forward as illiterate in Marxist-Leninist theory and "refuted rightist, opportunist viewpoints on imbalances in the national economy."[188] He pressed for a new "'leap forward' in the fourth quarter of 1959" through the restoration of the steel and coal quotas slashed at Lushan. Again, the focus on heavy industrial output occurred at the expense of food production. In 1959, total rural output dropped 13.6 percent and grain output 15 percent over the previous year.[189] Mao had still not given up his dream of a new society—even at the risk of new economic disaster.[190]

The consequences of Lushan for Sino-Soviet relations are obvious. Mao's attempts to construct both a conspiracy against him and a Soviet connection in Peng's criticism must have tarnished Moscow's image in the CCP. The relaunching of the Great Leap Forward did not mute Soviet criticism. The ideological radicalization in China after Lushan clashed with the ongoing political liberalization in the USSR. The events in the international sphere to which we now turn all bore this out. Despite Mao's claims in September that he wished "to unite with the Soviet comrades," the year 1959 would be a turning point in Sino-Soviet relations.[191]

SOVIET-AMERICAN RAPPROCHEMENT

Khrushchev's visit to U.S. President Eisenhower in early September 1959 marked the first time the United States became a major issue in the evolving Sino-Soviet disagreements. Even before the establishment of the People's Republic, the United States had developed a wedge strategy designed to split the Sino-Soviet alliance. Despite Khrushchev's attempts at peaceful coexistence, the United States rarely saw opportunities—except

[184] MacFarquhar, *Origins*, vol. 2, 247. Mao, "Comment," 8/5/1959, *CLG* 1/4, 64–65.

[185] Becker, *Hungry Ghosts*, 94.

[186] Zhou, "Report on the Economy," 8/26/1959, Hinton, *People's Republic*, vol. 2, 762–69.

[187] Mao, "Instructions," 9/4/1959, *JYMW*, vol. 8, 496.

[188] Mao Zedong, "Discussion of an Article," 9/6 & 10/1959, *JYMW*, vol. 8, 512–515.

[189] Xiao, *Qiusuo*, vol. 1, 567–68.

[190] Li, "Lessons," 82–83. Li, "Study [I]," 59–60.

[191] WLX, 204.

in the Taiwan Strait—to engage its strategy. The Hungarian Revolution, the Suez Crisis, and the Sputnik Shock prevented any Soviet-American rapprochement that could truly undermine the Sino-Soviet alliance.[192]

Khrushchev's willingness to establish a cooperative relationship with Eisenhower stemmed from his eagerness to gain recognition as an international statesman. His aspiration to international standing to some degree resembled Mao's insistence on equality in Sino-Soviet relations. But, so far, his initiatives had been either defeated by a series of Cold War crises or met with cool American responses. Khrushchev's frustrations about his continued exclusion from the illustrious circle of history's great statesmen rested to a certain degree on his inability to solve the complicated German Question.[193]

In November 1958, Khrushchev took drastic action. Egged on by East German leader Walter Ulbricht, who compared Jinmen with West Berlin,[194] Khrushchev hoped that an ultimatum on the legal status of divided Berlin and the announcement of a separate peace treaty for East Germany would force Eisenhower to negotiate personally. His gamble seemed to pay off. After Mikoyan's trip to the United States in January 1959, the talks on the German issue and preparations for Khrushchev's visit to the United States gathered momentum. Eisenhower was ready to invite the Soviet leader on the condition that the USSR made concessions in the Geneva negotiations on nuclear arms limitations that had stalled because of Soviet concerns about verification issues. After Soviet concessions in June, events proceeded quickly. On August 3, both sides announced the first visit to the United States by the highest Soviet leader six weeks later.[195]

The Chinese side was aware of the momentous shift in Soviet-American relations. Although Chinese propaganda backed Khrushchev's threats,[196] Beijing harbored suspicions. Its ambassador in Moscow, Liu Xiao, improbably insinuated that Khrushchev used that shift to rally the CPSU and the socialist camp behind him just before the twenty-first congress with the aim of "concentrating on the issue of the 'anti-party group.'"[197] On the basis of Soviet reports on Mikoyan's visit to the United States, the

[192] John Gaddis, *Long Peace* (New York: Oxford, 1987), 164–87. Chang, *Friends*, 46–48, 192–94. McGeorge Bundy, *Danger and Survival* (New York: Vintage, 1988), 330–34.

[193] Taubman, *Khrushchev*, 353, 396–99, 419–24. Chester Pach et al., *Presidency of Dwight D. Eisenhower*, rev. ed. (Lawrence: Kansas, 1991), 206.

[194] Harrison, *Driving*, 104. Christensen, "Worse Than a Monolith," 99.

[195] Taubman, *Khrushchev*, 403–19. Pach, *Presidency*, 206–7. Bundy, *Danger*, 332.

[196] CB 546, 29, 32, 35; 572, 5, 19. SCMP 1921, 45–47; 1941, 23–24; 1979, 29–31; 1980, 49–50; 2005, 45–48.

[197] Liu, *Chushi*, 96–97.

Chinese side was also apprehensive about "Khrushchev's enthusiasm . . . to relax relations with the West."[198]

Mao's dissatisfaction with Soviet-American rapprochement derived from his observations of international affairs. The Chairman believed that the Eisenhower administration was weak because it did not represent the American people and that his supposed "defeat" and failed "brinkmanship" policy in the Second Taiwan Strait Crisis had triggered increased class antagonism in American society and caused the Republican losses in the midterm elections in November.[199] This analysis confirmed his long-held view that American imperialism was a "paper tiger" in international relations.[200] Also, in late 1958, Mao forecast a split of the West.[201] Reading the chapter titled the "Inevitability of Wars between Capitalist Countries" in Stalin's *Economic Problems of Socialism in the U.S.S.R.*, he was convinced that the U.S.-British alliance could not survive the internal antagonisms that would appear "in the wake of the arrival of the economic crisis of the capitalist world."[202] The Chairman was hard-pressed to understand why Khrushchev wanted "to appease America" in this situation.[203] Like Stalin a decade before,[204] Mao had fallen victim to the crudeness of Leninist theory on the innate inability of long-term cooperation among capitalist states.

Mao's displeasure received an additional jolt when, on June 20, the Kremlin announced that it would not honor a previous agreement on the delivery of a Soviet model A-bomb. Russian historiography tends to see the Soviet decision as a result of Mao's nuclear gamble during the Second Taiwan Strait Crisis.[205] The official Soviet explanation was that the assembly of a bomb by China "could spoil" ongoing "international negotiations on the limitations of nuclear weapons," that nuclear weapons were too expensive for the Chinese economy, and that Soviet weapons

---

[198] Xiao, *Qiusuo*, vol. 1, 576.

[199] Mao, "Remarks on 'Good Aspects of Developments in American Politics,'" 11/27/1958, *JYMW*, vol. 7, 589–90. Also: "James E. Jackson Notes of His Interview with Mao Tsi Tung in China, December 4, 1959 [?]," *Tamiment Library & Robert F. Wagner Labor Archives*, 347 James E. Jackson and Esther Cooper Jackson Papers, box 23, folder 52.

[200] Mao, "On the Issue of Whether Imperialists and All Reactionaries Are Real Tigers," 11/25/1958, Mao, *On Diplomacy*, 281–83.

[201] Mao, "The Western World Will Inevitably Split Up," 11/25/1958, Mao, *On Diplomacy*, 280.

[202] Stalin, *Economic Problems*, 27–31. Mao Zedong, "Remarks and Revisions on a Text of a Speech by Zhang Wentian on the International Situation," 7/5/1959, *JYMW*, vol. 8, 339–40.

[203] Xiao, *Qiusuo*, vol. 1, 576.

[204] Gaddis, *We Now Know*, 195–96.

[205] Goncharenko, "Military Cooperation," 159. Kapitsa, *Na raznykh parallelyakh*, 61–63.

would protect the entire socialist camp.[206] In fact, the USSR feared that delivering a model A-bomb would set the precedent for the United States to arm West Germany, its nemesis in Europe, with nuclear weapons.[207] But for Beijing, the fuss about the model bomb, made right before the preparatory meeting for Khrushchev's visit to Eisenhower, assumed the notion of a *major* attempt by Moscow to improve relations with Washington on China's back.[208]

The news about the August 3 announcement of Khrushchev's impending visit to the United States arrived at Lushan just when the purge of Mao's internal adversaries was proceeding.[209] Official Chinese propaganda supported the visit as a "major victory for the Soviet Union's diplomacy of peace,"[210] but secretly the Chinese side was less than joyful. Khrushchev's supposed diplomatic victory was a *defeat* for China's foreign policy.[211] The Chinese side feared that, during his visit to the United States, Khrushchev would pursue policies that were contrary to China's positions.[212]

TIBET AND INDIA

Apart from the ideological disagreements before Khrushchev's seminal trip to the United States, Sino-Soviet relations underwent another straining test during the Tibetan Uprising and the ensuing Sino-Indian border conflict. The uprising led not only to the collapse of the Sino-Indian entente exemplified in the Pancha Shila formula, but also created tensions over their undemarcated border. The heavy-handed Chinese management of both crises put the Soviets into a dilemma: either back the Chinese ally at all costs or side with India, the most important Soviet friend outside the socialist bloc.

India and China had been entangled in struggle over control of Tibet for several centuries. Indian Buddhism had swayed great influence since the eleventh century, while the Qing emperors tried to incorporate Tibet politically. The collapse of imperial China in 1911 led to de facto Tibetan independence. The newly founded PRC thus had great difficulties establishing control over the territory in 1949. A Seventeen-Point Agreement

[206] Letter summarized: Kapitsa, *Na raznykh parallelyakh*, 63.
[207] Interview with Sergo Mikoyan, Reston, 6/6/2003.
[208] WLX, 206–7.
[209] MacFarquhar, *Origins*, vol. 2, 226.
[210] *SCMP* 2080, 40–41.
[211] Brezhnev, *Kitai*, 52.
[212] Li, *Lengnuan*, 297–98.

of 1951 between the new Chinese government and a Tibetan delegation promised Chinese respect for traditional forms of government while simultaneously announcing democratic reforms and Tibet's gradual admission to the PRC—two mutually exclusive visions for the future. The Sino-Indian agreement of 1954 not only comprised Pancha Shila but also terminated Indian claims on Tibet. Over the course of the 1950s, however, relations between Beijing and Lhasa deteriorated steadily. Unfounded rumors about the impending kidnapping of the Dalai Lama, the highest religious and political authority in Tibet, by the People's Liberation Army sparked a rebellion in Lhasa on March 12, 1959. The declaration of Tibetan independence by its leaders surprised the Dalai Lama as much as the Chinese government. Fearing for his own security, he fled in disguise to India on March 17.[213]

The Chinese leadership initially decided on a hands-off policy while it tried to determine "what to do if the Dalai Lama runs away."[214] In a Politburo meeting on March 17, Liu Shaoqi and Deng Xiaoping urged the implementation of democratic reforms, while Zhou accused the Indian, British, and American governments of exploiting émigré Tibetans in the Indian city of Kalimpong as tools for the revolt. The meeting also decided to shunt away the Dalai Lama politically: "If he actually goes, this also does not matter." Two days later, the PLA launched a massive "counterattack."[215] On March 23, it reestablished control over Lhasa, but fighting continued in inaccessible regions because Beijing had previously not stationed troops in most of Tibet.[216] The CCP Politburo in late March abrogated the Seventeen-Point Agreement of 1951 with the fictitious explanation that "the upper strata [in Tibet] had terminated the treaty with the central government," but decided to keep up the propaganda claim that "a Tibetan clique of armed rebels had kidnapped the Dalai"—a decision that allowed Beijing to keep all options open in case of "unforeseen circumstances." Mao also decided not to mention India, which he accused of masterminding the revolt, for the time being. China "could still settle scores later."[217]

The Dalai Lama's flight to India landed Nehru in a political minefield. The Indian prime minister was willing to grant asylum, but refused to

---

[213] Tsering Shakya, *Dragon in the Land of Snows* (New York: Columbia, 1999), 1–210. Melvyn Goldstein, *Snow Lion and the Dragon* (Berkeley: California, 1997), 1–36. Julian Weiss, "The PRC Occupation of Tibet," *Journal of Social, Political and Economic Studies* 12/4, 386–88.

[214] Wu, *Yi Mao zhuxi*, 119–20.

[215] WLX, 193–94.

[216] Shakya, *Dragon*, 203. WLX, 193–94.

[217] WLX, 194–95.

meet the famous Tibetan refugee because he did not want to jeopardize Sino-Indian relations. Except for the Indian communists, Tibet stirred nationalist passions and sympathies in India for the Buddhist brethrens north of the Himalayas. For some politicians the events in Tibet confirmed long-held anti-Chinese views; they had always favored military action against the Chinese in Tibet, and had willingly cooperated with the CIA and Tibetan émigrés in Kalimpong.[218] On April 8, Mao decided to counter international criticism, ordering *Renmin Ribao* to prepare a propaganda campaign against India, Great Britain, and the United States.[219] An editorial seven days later with the title "One Cannot Allow That the Sino-Indian Friendship Should Be Damaged" criticized "how imperialism and Indian non-governmental officials have attacked our suppression of the Tibetan rebellion," but welcomed Nehru's attempt at limiting frictions.[220] In April, Nehru continued to walk a tightrope when the Indian parliament made ample use of its right to question the prime minister on all political issues, including Tibet.[221]

Nehru's predicament worsened in late April when Mao gave up on his self-professed "restraint" and ordered the preparation of an article aiming at the prime minister's alleged role in the Tibetan uprising.[222] In his ideological worldview of contradictions, the Chairman maintained that he still wanted nothing less than "to struggle for unity" with India.[223] A *Renmin Ribao* article on May 6 accused the prime minister of violation of Pancha Shila.[224] The same day, Mao lectured the socialist ambassadors on the situation in India, portraying Nehru as a "middle-roader of the Indian bourgeoisie" who did "not reflect the opinion of four hundred million Indians."[225] Zhou added a distorted history of Sino-Tibetan relations that climaxed in the claim that Tibet had been Chinese territory "for the last seven hundred years."[226]

How did the Soviets react to the events in Tibet? Khrushchev had expended much time and energy reversing the policy of neglect by Stalin, who had not understood the emerging political role of nationalism and

[218] Shakya, *Dragon*, 213–14.

[219] WLX, 195.

[220] Wu, *Yi Mao zhuxi*, 122–23 (quote). WLX, 196–96. Si Fu, "Shi pengyou haishi diren," Chang, *Zhiqingzhe shuo*, vol. 8, 271.

[221] Shakya, *Dragon*, 212–20.

[222] WLX, 196, 198–202.

[223] Wu, *Yi Mao zhuxi*, 125–26.

[224] People's Daily, "The Revolution in Tibet and Nehru's Philosophy," 5/6/1959, Hinton, *People's Republic*, vol. 2, 814–23.

[225] Mao, "Speech to the Soviet and Other Delegations from 11 Countries and to the Diplomatic Envoys Stationed in China," 5/6/1959, *JYMW*, vol. 8, 247–48.

[226] Zhou, "The Tibet Problem and Sino-Indian Relations," 5/6/1959, Zhou, *Zhou Enlai waijiao wenxuan*, 269.

nonalignment in the Third World. Relations with India improved in 1953 when the United States started to arm India's arch enemy Pakistan with the aim to forestall Soviet expansion into the Near and Middle East. Nehru's visit to the USSR in June 1955 and Khrushchev's and Nikolai Bulganin's return visit five months later were clear signs that New Delhi had become one of Moscow's closest friends outside the socialist camp.[227]

After providing the PRC with intelligence relevant to the suppression of the rebels in Tibet,[228] Moscow decided to take up a middle position in the Sino-Indian dispute. Soviet newspapers were visibly reserved in their reporting; after two factual *Pravda* articles, Tibet disappeared from Soviet newspapers in early April.[229] The Soviet side also never publicly repeated Beijing's increasingly shrill accusations of Indian complicity in the Tibetan revolt. Later in the spring, Moscow defended Beijing's claims on Tibet at the United Nations, but since the PRC was not a member state and thus could not be punished, this action was more symbolic than substantial.[230]

Parallel to Mao's decision in late April to increase China's anti-Indian propaganda, the Chinese side embarked on a charm offensive to win Soviet support. Vice-Foreign Minister Zhang Hanfu told his Soviet counterpart, Georgii Pushkin, that the suppression of the Tibetan revolt certainly would not worsen, but, in fact, *improve* Sino-Indian relations since it eradicated those reactionary Tibetan elements that had been "undermining friendly relations between India and the PRC" all along.[231] In Moscow, Vice-Foreign Minister Zhang Wentian portrayed the most recent Chinese polemics against Nehru as a Maoist unity-struggle-unity process with the aim "to compel him to be more honest in the future." But he acknowledged that some Sino-Indian border questions were "unsolved."[232]

The Indians tried to cajole the Soviets as well. New Delhi's ambassador to Beijing told Yudin that the Indian response to the events in Tibet had "no political character" but was closely linked to India's religious

[227] Thomas Wersto, "Tibet in Sino-Soviet Relations," *Asian Affairs* 10/3, 73. Khrushchev, *Testament*, 306–7. S. Nihal Singh, *Yogi and the Bear* (London: Mansell, 1986), 1–18. Zafar Imam, *Ideology and Reality in Soviet Policy in Asia* (Delhi: Klyani, 1975), 1–179. Richard Remnek, *Soviet Scholars and Soviet Foreign Policy* (Durham: Carolina Academic, 1975), 1–25. McMahon, *Cold War*, 154–231.

[228] Chen Jian, "The Tibetan Rebellion of 1959 and China's Changing Relations with India and the Soviet Union," *Journal of Cold War Studies* 8/3, 91.

[229] *Pravda*, 3/31/1959, 3; 4/5/1959, 4.

[230] Shakya, *Dragon*, 220–37. A. Tom Grunfeld, *Making of Modern Tibet*, rev. ed. (Armonk: Sharpe, 1996), 145–46.

[231] "Record of Conversation with Zhang Hanfu," 4/20/1959, AVPRF, f.0100, o.52, d.5, p.442, 8.

[232] "Reception of Zhang Wentian," 5/4/1959, AVPRF, f.0100, o.52, d.5, p.442, 10–14, 16–18.

relations with Tibet. Displaying ignorance of Buddhist history, the highly decorated Marxist-Leninist theoretician flatly declared that "there is no closeness in religion" at all.[233] Two days later he even congratulated Zhou for the "well-written" *Renmin Ribao* article of May 6.[234] Chen Yi thanked Yudin for the first *official*—though not public—Soviet support for China against India.[235]

Chinese propaganda continued in mid-May when Chen Yi and Zhang Wentian told Yudin that Nehru's government was conducting a "slanderous campaign" using close historical Indian-Tibetan religious relations with the aim of establishing a "buffer zone" in the Himalayas. The two concluded that the PRC had always adhered to Pancha Shila.[236] Not only were the charges against India absurd, but the final assertion was also untrue. Mao in 1957 had resolved the obvious contradiction between the Chinese insistence on foreign noninterference in its internal affairs and Chinese clandestine support for communist parties outside of the socialist camp, as in the case of India, with the argument that "support for the communist parties not holding power in capitalist states" aimed at furthering world revolution and thus was exempt from Pancha Shila.[237]

Did the Soviets buy the Chinese argument on Indian aggression? In the absence of archival evidence this is difficult to gauge. According to the diary of the Indian ambassador to the USSR, Kumara Menon, Khrushchev, on April 30, assured him that Soviet-Indian relations "were so good that one can hardly wish them better." The Soviet leader also agreed that India had the right to grant asylum to the Dalai Lama, and discarded Chinese claims of Indian attempts to turn Tibet into a buffer zone: "Surely . . . India was the last country in the world to have expansionist ambitions."[238] One historian has suggested that Chinese propaganda against Nehru was specifically designed to vilify the Indian leader in world opinion and thereby undermine continued Soviet economic support for India.[239] If that is correct, then Chinese efforts were futile. Moscow and New Delhi continued to negotiate the hitherto largest Soviet industrial

[233] "Record of Conversation with Ambassador of India in the PRC Parthasarathi," 5/5/1959, *AVPRF*, f.0100, o.52, d.7, p.442, 32.

[234] Li, *Lengnuan*, 292–94.

[235] "Record of Conversation with Chen Yi," 5/5/1959, *AVPRF*, f.0100, o.52, d.7, p.442, 48–52.

[236] "Record of Conversation," 5/18/1959, *AVPRF*, f.0100, o.52, d.7, p.442, 61–70.

[237] WLX, 152.

[238] Menon, *Troika*, 235, 236.

[239] Richard Siegel, "Chinese Efforts to Influence Soviet Policy in India," Verinder Grover, *International Relations and Foreign Policy of India*, vol. 7 (New Delhi: Deep & Deep, 1992), 351.

development credit agreement (375 million U.S. dollars) outside of the socialist camp, which was finalized in September 1959.[240]

The Sino-Indian border conflict that emerged from the Tibetan Uprising revealed that China and India also had serious territorial disagreements. The disputes at the Sino-Indian border at Sikkim (between Nepal and Bhutan) and at the so-called Middle Sector (west of Nepal) were minor. The quarrel at the Eastern Sector (between Bhutan and Burma) went back to the 1914 Simla convention when the British proposed the so-called McMahon line, running roughly at the Himalayan crest line as the border between British India and Tibet. China, although it then lacked actual control over Tibet, refused to ratify it while claiming the traditional border line at the southern foothills of the Himalayas. After 1949, the PRC did *not* try to extend control over any territory south of the crest line, while India administered the contentious territory through the *North East Frontier Administration* (*NEFA*; today Arunachal Pradesh).[241] However, the initial aggravation of Sino-Indian relations that led to military clashes in 1959 stemmed from a more recent spat over Aksai Chin at the Western Sector (at Jammu and Kashmir). The legal status of this triangular high-altitude plateau squeezed in between India, Tibet, and Xinjiang, had an equally tangled history, but was smaller than NEFA and also totally unpopulated. In the early 1950s, China had started to build a road from Xinjiang into Tibet that passed through Aksai Chin. Although the road was opened in the fall of 1957, India did not claim the territory until August 1958.[242]

From August 1958 to March 1959, the Aksai Chin dispute spilled over to the other sectors. In letters to Zhou, Nehru claimed that India's maps were correct and accused China of "cartographic aggression" because it refused to recognize the McMahon line. Zhou responded by disputing that line, but offered to honor the status quo at all sectors. Nehru replied on March 22—just when the Chinese repression of the Tibetan revolt had started—insisting on the Himalayan crest line.[243]

The suppression of the Tibetan revolt militarized the disputed Sino-Indian border. Before spring 1959, Tibet had the right to patrol its own

[240] Arthur Stein, "India's Relations with the USSR, 1953–1963," Grover, *International Relations*, vol. 7, 86.

[241] Neville Maxwell, *India's China War* (London: Cape, 1970), 45, 53, 85, 107. Subramanian Swamy, *India's China Perspective* (New Delhi: Konark, 2001), 41–45, 54–67. Liu Xuecheng, *The Sino-Indian Border Dispute* (New York: Lanham, 1994), 26, 47–78. Mira Sinha, "China," *China Report* 15/2, 60.

[242] Swamy, *India's China Perspective*, 45, 53, 87. Liu, *Sino-Indian Dispute*, 19, 97.

[243] Swamy, *India's China Perspective*, 40, 75. Liu, *Sino-Indian Dispute*, 19–26, 187. Si, "Shi pengyou," 285. WLX, 209. Maxwell, *India's China War*, 78.

borders, but did not take the accompanying responsibilities seriously.[244] On April 25, Mao decided to subject the Sino-Indian borders to a stricter regime in order to prevent "the rebellious elements . . . [from] coming and going."[245] Ten days before, Nehru had defined the three factors governing India's Tibet policy as: (1) national security, (2) maintenance of friendly relations with China, and (3) deep sympathy for the Tibetan people. In accordance with point 1, Nehru implemented a military forward policy once Chinese border patrols had appeared in the Himalayas following Mao's April 25 decision.[246]

After Beijing and New Delhi had sent their troops to the contentious border, the ambiguity of the McMahon line plagued them. When Henry McMahon drew the line in 1914, he used a small map and a thick pen; the line thus was a quarter of a mile wide on the ground and frequently crossed valleys on both sides of the Himalayan watershed.[247] As a result of Indian assertiveness, skirmishes occurred at the Eastern Sector on August 7 and 25.[248] Both sides followed up with propaganda campaigns promoting their competing claims.[249]

The outbreak of the Sino-Indian border conflict caught the Soviets during their preparations for Khrushchev's visit to the United States. The Soviet leader recollected that the conflict was not accidental but that Mao "started the [border] war out of some sick fantasy" in the belief that he could "dictate to the Soviet Union" its foreign policy.[250] With no idea about the real state of affairs, the Kremlin scrambled to get as much information as possible from its own meager sources.[251] Menon personally informed Khrushchev on August 28,[252] while Beijing remained silent for another nine days. In fact, China's central leadership itself had no reliable information about the clashes.[253] Finally, on September 6, the Chinese Foreign Ministry informed the Soviet chargé d'affaires, Antonov, that

[244] WLX, 212.

[245] Wu, *Yi Mao zhuxi*, 126. Liu, *Sino-Indian Dispute*, 26.

[246] Liu, *Sino-Indian Dispute*, 25–26.

[247] Liu, *Sino-Indian Dispute*, 26. Maxwell, *India's China War*, 107.

[248] Liu, *Sino-Indian Dispute*, 26. Imam, *Ideology*, 181. Swamy, *India's China Perspective*, 67. WLX, 208–10.

[249] WLX, 210–12, 214–16. Imam, *Ideology*, 181. MacFarquhar, *Origins*, vol. 2, 259. CB 611, 3. Hinton, *People's Republic*, vol. 2, 826–29. Si, "Shi pengyou," 286–87. Swamy, *India's China Perspective*, 68.

[250] Khrushchev, *Testament*, 263, 307, 311.

[251] Brezhnev, *Kitai*, 69–71.

[252] Imam, *Ideology*, 181. "Letter by H. Fischer to Ambassador Schwab," 9/5/1959, *PAAA-MfAA*, 2. AEA/Sektor Indien, Ceylon, Microfiche A 13915, 47–50.

[253] Mao, "Remarks on a Situation Report of the Tibet Military Region," 9/4/1959, *JYMW*, vol. 8, 503.

New Delhi had initiated border conflicts with the aim of undermining Sino-Soviet relations.[254]

Moscow was not swayed. The shrill Chinese anti-Indian propaganda since the spring and the failure to inform Moscow about the Sino-Indian conflict for nine days had shaped a new Soviet perception. As Aleksei Brezhnev recalled, "[I]t was logical to think that the Chinese side had initiated the skirmishes. In favor of this proposition spoke the experience with the shooting in the Taiwan Strait. In 1958, Beijing had attempted to put before Khrushchev a choice: either the USA or China. And now, in 1959, this choice was expanded: either India and the USA, or China."[255] Convinced that Beijing had violated the alliance treaty for a *second* time through the lack of consultation (as stipulated in Article Four) within only thirteen months, Moscow decided to distance itself. In a TASS statement, the Chinese side had requested to be delayed without success,[256] the Soviet government in effect declared neutrality in the border conflict,[257] largely because Foreign Minister Gromyko wanted to have "a good tone" for Khrushchev's visit to the United States.[258] Beijing saw it as Moscow's signal to Washington and New Delhi that the USSR had turned away from its Chinese ally.[259] To add insult to injury, *Pravda* four days later announced the recently negotiated development credit to India.[260]

The Chinese side was not only disappointed by the lack of Soviet support, but also considered the statement a victory for both India's forward policy and the U.S. wedge strategy designed to split the Sino-Soviet alliance.[261] New Delhi's and Washington's reactions reconfirmed Beijing's assessment. Nehru called the TASS statement "unusual" and "very fair,"[262] and U.S. Secretary of State Christian Herter was more than happy—though only after Khrushchev had left the United States—to apply the wedge strategy publicly with the claim that the USSR had to accept coresponsibility for the belligerent actions of its ally.[263] Yet, Mao still believed

[254] WLX, 210. Si, "Shi pengyou," 285.

[255] Brezhnev, *Kitai*, 70.

[256] WLX, 213. Li, *Lengnuan*, 294.

[257] *Pravda*, 9/10/1959, 3.

[258] Kapitsa, *Na raznykh parallelyakh*, 63–64.

[259] WLX, 214.

[260] *Pravda*, 9/13/1959, 5.

[261] Mikhail Prozumenshikov, "The Sino-Indian Conflict, the Cuban Missile Crisis, and the Sino-Soviet Split, October 1962," *CWIHP Bulletin* 8–9, 25. MacFarquhar, *Origins*, vol. 2, 260.

[262] Quoted in: Imam, *Ideology*, 183.

[263] *NYT*, 10/7/1959, 1, 13.

that Sino-Soviet relations had not considerably worsened—and that the current setback was only "one unequal finger among ten."[264]

The deterioration of Sino-Soviet relations over India was as unnecessary as the Sino-Indian border conflict itself. Beijing could expect that Moscow would honor its treaty obligations because the conflict had technically started with Indian transgressions. But the PRC had fallen victim to its own inadequate foreign policy of the previous thirteen months. The tricky situation the Chinese leadership found itself in during the early fall of 1959 thus was largely of its own making. Mao's own words, with which he had blamed the Hungarian comrades in November 1956 for their failings to prevent the uprising, also applied to the Chinese Communists: "And now they have to reap what they have sown, they have brought the fire upon their own heads."[265] The parallels with Budapest in 1956 were even greater. As much as Moscow's intervention in Hungary had tarnished the Soviet image in the world, Beijing's actions in Tibet and during the Sino-Indian border conflict destroyed the appeal of "'five principles' of peaceful coexistence, for which they [the Chinese] had gotten applause from all continents."[266]

KHRUSHCHEV'S VISITS TO THE UNITED STATES AND CHINA

Thus, when Khrushchev flew to the United States on September 15, Sino-Soviet relations had worsened substantially. After a red carpet welcome and first talks with President Eisenhower, he went on a tour through the home country of capitalism.[267] Subsequent negotiations with the president at Camp David were disappointing. The primary reason why the Soviet leader had come to the United States—the German issue—was not resolved, although Khrushchev lifted the Berlin ultimatum for Eisenhower's commitment to a four-power summit.[268] The American side did not miss the opportunity to apply the wedge strategy.[269] Intelligence reports suggested Sino-Soviet tensions over Moscow's alleged refusal of Beijing's request to rescue the PRC from "economic chaos."[270] When Khrushchev "inquired about the U.S. policy toward the Chinese Government," Eisenhower accused China of "aggressive actions" against the United

[264] WLX, 204.

[265] Mao, "Speech," 11/15/1956, SW, vol. 5, 342.

[266] Brezhnev, Kitai, 69–70.

[267] Taubman, Khrushchev, 424–35.

[268] Pach, Presidency, 208–9. Taubman, Khrushchev, 425, 435–36, 439.

[269] Chang, Friends, 209.

[270] "Memorandum from the Director of the Bureau of Intelligence and Research (Cumming) to Secretary of State Herter," 9/24/1959, FRUS 1958–1960, XIX, 594.

States and defiance of the United Nations in the Taiwan Strait. After a tussle over the legitimacy of the PRC, the president returned to Berlin and compared divided China with divided Germany. While the Soviet leader had tried to bolster the division of Germany with the ultimatum, he now insisted on the unification of China under Beijing's leadership. Aware of the public discussion in the United States of American prisoners in China, Khrushchev also tried to end the Camp David talks on a positive note, offering to inquire about the fate of American prisoners during his impending visit to China.[271] In an attempt to sell wrinkled apples as shining oranges, Khrushchev publicly praised the Spirit of Camp David—a term Eisenhower himself "never used or deemed valid."[272] A CPSU memo to all fraternal parties called the visit a contribution to the "relaxation of tensions."[273] It did not mention that the international tensions around Berlin, as Eisenhower correctly remarked, had been "of Khrushchev's own making."[274]

Following a Soviet request for public backing before Khrushchev's visit, Mao and Zhou had decided to keep up the façade of "conditional support" but "not to cheer excessively."[275] Afterward, when the Chinese leaders read the official bulletin on the Camp David talks, they realized that "the talks had not reached any agreement." Eisenhower's public refutation of Khrushchev's assurance that the talks "had not touched on issues involving third countries" raised Chinese eyebrows. Beijing understood that Washington and Moscow had talked about the PRC.[276]

Khrushchev must have left Washington convinced that he had passed the rite of passage that elevated him to equality with Eisenhower, while Mao headed a country that was diplomatically isolated and economically broken by its own actions. Past Chinese claims for equality had turned into plain smoke. Mao's ideological radicalization after Lushan and rise to unchallenged leadership in China did not help facilitate Sino-Soviet relations.

The Soviet leader returned to Moscow on September 28 for a one-day stopover before his departure to Beijing. At a public rally with five thousand chosen workers he praised at length his contributions to world peace, and portrayed Eisenhower as a prudent leader who "sincerely wants to liquidate the conditions of the 'Cold War'" and who "enjoys the absolute support of the majority of the American people."[277] Mao must have been

[271] "Memorandum of Conversation," 9/26 & 27/1959, *FRUS 1958–1960*, XIX, 595–98. For public discussions of American prisoners: *NYT*, 9/23/1959, 27; 9/24/1959, 23.

[272] Dwight Eisenhower, *White House Years*, vol. 2 (New York: Doubleday, 1965), 448.

[273] "Confidential Information . . . ," [no date], *AAN*, KC PZPR, XI A/74, 756, 762–63.

[274] Eisenhower, *White House Years*, vol. 2, 448–49.

[275] Li, *Lengnuan*, 297. *SCMP* 2100, 47–49; 2110, 42–44.

[276] *WLX*, 218.

[277] Taubman, *Khrushchev*, 439. *Pravda*, 9/29/1959, 2–3 (quotes).

surprised by these words. Only some months before, he had argued the opposite.

Despite widespread famines in the country, Beijing staged a lavish show for the tenth anniversary of the PRC. Khrushchev would not be impressed. He flew to Beijing just in time for the peak of the celebrations. Arriving with some days' delay after the official Soviet delegation,[278] the reception at Beijing airport was a shadow of what he had experienced in Washington. No wonder that Khrushchev recalled: "The warmth . . . of our relations . . . had been replaced by a chill that I could sense as soon as I arrived."[279] For the lack of red carpet at the airport, the Soviet leader seemed to take revenge with a rambling and insolent speech six times longer than Zhou's welcome address. With one eye on the Taiwan Strait and the other on the Himalayas, Khrushchev lauded Eisenhower's acceptance of "peaceful co-existence," called on the socialist camp to "do all we can to exclude war as a means of settling disputed questions," and warned against "testing by force the stability of the capitalist system."[280] The Chinese hosts clearly understood these words as a slap in the face. After Mao read the draft the Soviet delegation had submitted in advance, he "refused to speak" to the gala at all.[281]

October 1 was the day of the big parade. Khrushchev spent the morning sandwiched between Mao Zedong and Lin Biao on top of Tiananmen reviewing the vehicles and airplanes that passed through the square below or roared past them above. A *Pravda* photograph shows Mao and Khrushchev standing wide apart and looking grimly into different directions.[282] Talking about "how Eisenhower hoped for peace,"[283] Khrushchev ruined Mao's holiday feelings. For the Chairman, the sermon about the greatness of the class enemy must have been especially offensive as it happened precisely during the anniversary celebrations of the country he had founded as a utopia of anti-capitalism and anti-imperialism. During a review of troops, Khrushchev remarked: "As to the building of the A-bomb, we decided that our specialists should return home."[284] The collapse of friendly relations between the two leaders was clearly visible to all present. A witness remembered Khrushchev's gloominess in Mao's company: "It was a distressing signal."[285]

[278] Li, *Waijiao*, 178. Liu, *Chushi*, 88.

[279] Khrushchev, *Testament*, 263, 308.

[280] *SCMP* 2112, 20–21.

[281] WLX, 220. Liu Xiao, *Chushi*, 88–89.

[282] *Pravda*, 10/2/1959, 1.

[283] WLX, 220.

[284] Si, "Shi pengyou," 292.

[285] Li Sha, "Goodbye, Elder Brother," Zhang Lijia et al., eds., *China Remembers* (Oxford: Oxford, 1999), 98.

Khrushchev started formal talks on October 2 in a good mood about the Camp David Spirit. Mao tersely replied: "In fact, this is not true."[286] When Khrushchev urged the Chinese to improve relations with the United States by reducing hostilities over Taiwan, the remark seemed to prove that Khrushchev had talked with Eisenhower about third countries and that he "had promised America to go to China as a paid intermediary." Zhou rejected this request with the long-standing argument that Taiwan was "a Chinese internal affair."[287] Once Khrushchev conveyed Eisenhower's request to release American prisoners as a sign of goodwill, the Chinese side retorted that they "all were criminals who had broken the Chinese penal code." They could not be released "until their terms had expired."[288] In fact, one American had languished in prison for years without facing a trial, only to be convicted in March 1960.[289]

The talk changed when the contentious issue that had rocked Sino-Soviet relations most recently arose. The Soviet leader urged the Chinese to "unite" with the Indians on the grounds that they too were "opposing imperialism." Chen Yi shot back: "We adopt unity and struggle toward nationalists, but this does not mean we adopt an appeaser's attitude." Khrushchev got the hint: "To criticize us as appeasers has no basis." Chen Yi retorted: "You publicly revealed that you are partial to India." On the defensive, the Soviet leader tried to refocus the discussion on Tibet, chiding the Chinese side that, as a result of the Dalai Lama's escape to India, "the border clash was stirred up, and neutral India joined the fire." Zhou cut Khrushchev short: "Comrade Khrushchev, your [comment] is totally irrelevant."[290] The talks ended on bad terms.

Frustrated that the meetings with Mao had not led to any accord, the Soviet leader left on October 4 for Vladivostok. "It's hard to make an agreement with an old boot. He can't forgive us for Stalin," the Soviet leader complained on the plane.[291] In a speech in the harbor city, the Soviet leader gave an upbeat assessment of the domestic situation and his trip to the United States. Touching on his visit to Beijing, he talked fictitiously about the "cordial, amicable meeting and talks" with the Chinese

[286] Li, *Waijiao*, 178–79. Li misdates talks, for correct date: Zhonghua, *Zhou Enlai waijiao huodong dashiji*, 261–62.

[287] WLX, 222.

[288] WLX, 223. Liu, *Chushi*, 89.

[289] SCMP 2223, 1–3, 3–5. CB 619, 20. MacFarquhar, *Origins*, vol. 2, 272.

[290] Si, "Shi pengyou," 288–92. For other but nevertheless substantially close versions: Li, *Waijiao*, 179–83. WLX, 223–27. "Record of Conversation of Comrade Khrushchev N. S. with CC CCP Chairman Mao Zedong, Vice Chairman CC CCP Liu Shaoqi, Zhou Enlai, Zhu De, Lin Biao, Politburo Members Peng Zhen and Chen Yi, and Secretariat Member Wang Jiaxiang," 10/2/1959, Wolff, "Finger," 65–68.

[291] Quoted in: Volkogonov, *Autopsy*, 233.

comrades, which supposedly had revealed that "our people go hand in hand in unity and with common goals ahead."[292]

After Khrushchev had left Beijing, the CCP Politburo also tried to assess the visit. Convinced that "Khrushchev had illusions about Eisenhower," Mao was concerned about the "revisionist leanings" of the Soviet leader, but urged patience in order "to let objective reality and the historical process teach him."[293] Studying the Vladivostok speech, the Chinese comrades found *one* short reference they interpreted as an implicit criticism of their uncompromising policy toward the United States and India: "It is unwise to long for war like a bellicose cock."[294] It is not clear whether Khrushchev had ever intended to give this sentence *that* particular meaning. No matter what, Mao maintained that disagreements "consist of just one finger out of ten, or more precisely, just half a finger."[295] PRC propaganda continued to hail Khrushchev's visit to the United States.[296]

REASSESSMENTS

After Khrushchev's visit to Beijing, the Sino-Indian border conflict flared up again. Nehru at first believed that Khrushchev had influenced Mao to relent on the border in the Eastern Sector; an October 6 Chinese telegram on the issue seemed to sound conciliatory. The situation changed when Chinese troops killed nine Indian border guards at the Lanak Pass in the Western Sector fourteen days later. The pass was one mountain range within Chinese-claimed territory; Nehru's forward policy had triggered the incident. Even senior Indian military officers condemned it as Indian expansionism.[297] The Chinese foreign ministry, apparently wiser after the diplomatic debacles in the previous months, informed the ambassadors of the socialist brother states immediately.[298]

Despite this clear case of Indian belligerence, Khrushchev decided not to give up his position of neutrality. On the thirty-first, in the Supreme Soviet, he "deeply regret[ted] the incidents that took place recently on the

[292] *Pravda*, 10/8/1959, 1.

[293] WLX, 227–28.

[294] *Pravda*, 10/8/1959, 1.

[295] "From the Journal of Antonov, S. F.," 10/21/1959, CWIHP, "Soviet Foreign Policy during the Cold War," *CWIHP Bulletin* 3, 56.

[296] *NYT*, 10/12/1959, 16.

[297] Imam, *Ideology*, 184–85, 195. Liu, *Sino-Indian Dispute*, 28.

[298] "Note on an Information on the Sino-Indian Border Issue on October 26, 1959, 15:00 P.M., in the Ministry for Foreign Affairs of the People's Republic of China," 10/27/1959, PAAA-MfAA, 2. AEA/Sektor Indien, Ceylon, Microfiche A 13915, 79–84.

frontier of the two states, both of which are our friends," and hoped that "the existing unsettled frontier question could be solved by friendly negotiations."[299] The Chinese side certainly could not be satisfied, but instead of berating its Soviet ally, it decided on a charm offensive. Some days later, Deng Xiaoping was waxing to Yudin about Khrushchev's contribution to world peace during his visit to the United States, but did not fail to warn that the "imperialists especially want to undermine the unity of our countries."[300]

In late 1959, Mao returned once more to assessing Soviet foreign policy. Moscow's renewed expression of neutrality in the Sino-Indian border conflict as well as the ongoing planning of the Soviet-American-British-French summit in Paris the following May raised new questions about Khrushchev's leadership of the socialist camp. Resting in Hangzhou in November, Mao started his review by studying three speeches by the recently deceased Dulles, who a year before had promoted constructive engagement with the USSR through low-level personal, cultural, and economic contacts with the aim to change the Soviet system from within.[301] For Mao, Dulles's "peaceful evolution" strategy was a new scheme that "supplemented" the U.S. "policy of strength" toward the socialist world.[302] He concluded that it was nothing other than "infiltration, corrosion, and subversion," which had the "wild ambition" of "preserving capitalism" and "eliminating socialism."[303]

Given this interpretation, Mao believed that Khrushchev's policies in 1959 had menacing consequences for the socialist camp. The Soviet leader in fact had fallen into Dulles's trap: "Khrushchev had already betrayed the Marxist, proletarian undertakings; he had changed into a *revisionist*." This interpretation of Soviet policies seemed to confirm his earlier suspicions that "the enemies inside and outside the party had linked up" at Lushan, and that they "had carried out *subversive* actions with Soviet support."[304]

Mao's new estimate of Khrushchev brought major changes in his assessment of Sino-Soviet relations. He was convinced "beyond doubt" that "Marxism-Leninism matures in China," while, in comparison, "Khrushchev does not understand Marxism, but is easily duped by imperialism." For the long term, the Chairman predicted: "If Khrushchev

[299] *Pravda*, 11/1/1959, 1–2.
[300] "Memorandum of Conversation with the General Secretary of the CC CCP, Deng Xiaoping," 11/6/1959, Chen, "Deng Xiaoping," 169–70.
[301] WLX, 230. Bo, *Ruogan*, vol. 2, 1142.
[302] Bo, *Ruogan*, vol. 2, 1142.
[303] Si, "Zhonggong," 59 (first quote). Bo, *Ruogan*, vol. 2, 1142 (remaining quotes).
[304] Si, "Zhonggong," 57–58 (all quotes except last). Mao Zedong, "Outline of a Speech on the International Situation," December 1959, *JYMW*, vol. 8, 600 (last quote; italics mine).

does not correct himself, he will go totally bankrupt after some years."[305] For this reason, the CCP should pass over the Soviet leader and concentrate instead on the "good" Soviet people and CPSU members who, alas, were currently led by "people with bad work styles . . . [and by] capitalist liberalism."[306] With hindsight of history, Mao's speculation on Khrushchev's possible fall seemed to be visionary, but the Chairman was wrong about its causes. To Mao's great frustration in late 1964, Khrushchev's *revisionism* outlived its creator almost unchanged, as told in chapter 9.

But what did Mao's assessment imply for the anti-imperialist alliance with the Soviets? Although Mao considered the differences with Khrushchev to be "a temporary phenomenon," he nevertheless deplored that "since March our friends have been organizing a big anti-Chinese chorus together with the imperialists and reactionary nationalists, and the Tito revisionists." The Chairman thus concluded that "in the long term, China will, on the one hand, be isolated, but on the other, gain the support of many Communist parties, many countries, and many peoples."[307] In short, the anti-imperialist alliance with the USSR had run its course for Mao; China would look for other partners to fulfill its anti-imperialist mission. Since the PRC had exhausted much of the military and economic aid the Soviet Union had offered anyway, this decision was not difficult to take. Advanced Soviet military assistance related to the nuclear program had been drastically curtailed, and economic relations, as the next chapter reveals, were in the process of breaking down as well.

Mao's belief that the Soviet leadership had turned revisionist paralleled his renewed ideological stress in domestic affairs. The Chairman urged "the whole party to be on guard" and to read again Stalin's *Political Economy*.[308] Study groups immediately formed in Beijing or fanned out into the farthest corners of the country.[309] The Chairman himself studied together with Chen Boda, Tian Jiaying, and Lin Ke in Beijing from December to February.[310] Because Mao had just criticized Khrushchev for his lack of theoretical knowledge, he apparently wanted to make sure that he understood Stalin's economic thinking correctly. His notes on *Economic Problems of Socialism in the U.S.S.R.*—Stalin's 1952 critique of the draft of *Political Economy*—provide a unique view into his thinking

[305] WLX, 233–34.

[306] Mao, "Outline of a Speech on the International Situation," December 1959, *JYMW*, vol. 8, 600.

[307] "An Outline for a speech on the international Situation, December 1959," Wolff, "Finger," 73–74.

[308] Si, "Zhonggong," 61–62.

[309] MacFarquhar, *Origins*, vol. 2, 293–94.

[310] WLX, 235. Wang Fang, ed., "Xiaosa moru Mao Zedong," Chang, *Zhiqingzhe shuo*, vol. 2, 102.

on economics. They repeatedly slight Bureaucratic Stalinism, scoff at the supposed rigidity in Soviet economic thinking, and scorn Stalin's alleged failure to put politics in command, to use class struggle and contradictions, and to understand communal ownership.[311] But Mao was unable to draw any concrete conclusions for the Great Leap Forward apart from the observation that "the last two years were a big experiment."[312] The Chairman also failed to mention that the guinea pigs of *that* experiment were real human beings with hungry stomachs to fill. The whole study of *Economic Problems of Socialism in the U.S.S.R.* revealed the absurdities of Mao's thinking. His belief that he could use Stalin's book review of the Soviet equivalent to an ECON 101 college textbook as the basis for running the whole Chinese economy expresses impeccably his misconceptions about the complexities of economics. Mao *still* did not understand economic affairs.[313]

While the Chairman reassessed Sino-Soviet relations, the Soviet comrades too reviewed the events of the year. With an eye on Mao's relaunching of the Great Leap Forward and another one on the perceived Chinese challenges to Soviet foreign policy, Khrushchev in early December demanded from all countries in the socialist camp "to synchronize our watches."[314] The CCP duly noted this appeal as an "allusive attack on the CCP."[315] The new Soviet ambassador to China, Stepan Chervonenko, spelled out to Liu Shaoqi what Khrushchev had meant: further Chinese attempts to sabotage Soviet foreign policy would affect all aspects of Sino-Soviet relations.[316] For the other ruling communist parties, the new Soviet course required them to step back in line. The East Germans, who had praised the people's communes beyond prudence, came under intense Soviet pressure in the following months to stop their domestic propagation of the Great Leap Forward.[317]

Behind the scenes, Soviet criticism of Chinese policies was even more strident. Suslov's official report to the Central Committee in mid-December harshly judged Chinese policies toward the United States (Mao's paper tiger theory was "boasting" and "a disregard for the threat of war"),

[311] MacFarquhar, *Origins*, vol. 2, 295–97. Levy, "New Light," 102. Notes in: Mao Zedong, *Mao Tse-tung: A Critique of Soviet Economics* (New York: Monthly Review, 1977), 129–47.

[312] *MZDDG*, 632.

[313] Hu, *Hu Qiaomu*, 15.

[314] Khrushchev made appeal during Hungarian Party Congress: *NYT*, 12/2/1959, 4.

[315] *WLX*, 230, 250.

[316] "Record of Conversation with Liu Shaoqi," 12/10/1959, *AVPRF*, f.0100, o.53, d.8, p.454, 5.

[317] Werner Meissner et al., eds., *DDR und China 1949 bis 1990* (Berlin: Akademie, 1995), 102–3.

in the Taiwan Strait Crisis ("a surprise for all countries in the socialist camp"), during the Tibetan Uprising (the personal attacks on Nehru were "regrettable"), and in the Sino-Indian border conflict ("a disruption of the Soviet pursuit of peace"). With regard to China's domestic situation, Suslov told the CC how the Chinese leadership lately had "gotten somewhat dizzy," that a sickening "atmosphere of the cult of personality of com. Mao Zedong" pervaded Chinese society, and that the Chairman had "come to believe in his own infallibility." Suslov concluded his verdict with words that could have been spoken by Peng Dehuai or Zhang Wentian half a year earlier: "This reminds us of the atmosphere that existed in our country during I. V. Stalin's last years of life."[318]

But Soviet criticism of Mao's personality cult sounded somewhat hollow. Since March 1958, when Khrushchev also assumed the position of prime minister,[319] a new Soviet personality cult had been in the making. When he issued the Berlin ultimatum later that year he had not consulted his fellow leaders.[320] And the then–Indian ambassador in Moscow recalled the "glowing tributes," the "reversion to idolatry," and the "revival of the cult of personality" during Khrushchev's birthday celebrations in April 1959.[321]

China's internal radicalism stemmed from Mao's unwillingness to acknowledge his mistakes and to change policies. Although the Chairman remained a self-declared Marxist-Leninist-Stalinist throughout 1959, his use of ideology in domestic politics was largely instrumental, designed to protect himself from possible attempts to remove him from power. He could barely concede his mistakes once the Great Leap Forward had run into trouble at the turn of the year 1958/59, nor accept well-founded criticism at the Lushan conference. Instead, the Chairman accused Peng and like-minded critics of a conspiracy against him. Despite the lack of evidence for such an audacious claim, he felt threatened. Mao was even willing to relaunch the extreme but disastrous Great Leap Forward policies after Lushan in order to reinforce his personal position within the Chinese political system.

Mao's domestic needs provided the context for, although only weak causal links to, his continued radicalism in foreign relations. Despite the alleviation of the Sino-American conflict over Taiwan in 1958, he continued

---

[318] "To the Presidium of the CPSU CC," 12/18/1959, *RGANI*, f.2, o.1, d.415, 19–33, 43–44.

[319] Technically, he assumed the position of Chairman of the Minister Council. I decided to use the more customary title in this book.

[320] Mikoyan, *Tak bylo*, 604.

[321] Menon, *Troika*, 235.

to reject peaceful coexistence. His conviction that the United States was on the losing side of history was a sincere expression of an ideologically influenced but nevertheless rudimentary understanding of the outside world. As a firm communist believer, he thus could not comprehend why Khrushchev sought rapprochement with the United States, was willing to sacrifice nuclear cooperation with China in the process, and even portray the failed meeting with the archimperialist Eisenhower as a success. No wonder that Mao looked down on Khrushchev at the end of 1959.

Although Mao instigated neither the Tibetan Uprising nor the Sino-Indian border war, his handling of both crises was clumsy. The self-righteous, harsh, and ideologically motivated treatment of India in the spring reflected his opposition to peaceful coexistence but also damaged bilateral relations beyond repair. The lack of diplomatic action during the Sino-Indian border war indicated China's surprise but also its failure to exploit international diplomacy for its own needs. On the contrary, it alienated the USSR, whose perception of Chinese unreliability was reinforced once more. Thus, internal factors, the Soviet-American rapprochement, failures in Chinese diplomacy, and Soviet misperceptions burdened Beijing's relations with Moscow greatly.

By late 1959, with both sides having reassessed the relationship, the Sino-Soviet alliance had reached an important turning point. In the economic sphere, disagreements had started even before Khrushchev's Secret Speech. In 1955, referring to the agricultural policies of Revolutionary Stalinism and Stalin's *Short Course*, Mao launched the Socialist High Tide in order to increase agricultural efficiency. The Secret Speech briefly undermined his economic radicalism, but in 1957 the Chairman returned to even more extreme economic policies after the Hundred Flowers Campaign had discredited liberalization and Bureaucratic Stalinism. The extraordinary growth claims of the Great Leap Forward irritated the Soviets; its subsequent failure confirmed their misgivings. Yet, Mao's continued radicalism in late 1959 made the collapse of China's economy inevitable the following year.

Khrushchev's call for de-Stalinization and Mao's excessive reaction put a heavy liability on Sino-Soviet party relations until late 1959. After Mao had slowed down, though not completely suppressed, the discussion on de-Stalinization within the CCP over the spring and summer of 1956, the political crises in Poland and Hungary in the fall provided him with the chance to articulate his distinction between the subjective Soviet revisionists in Moscow and the objective Chinese Marxist-Leninists in Beijing, with Mao himself at the center. Although, on the surface, the CCP and the CPSU worked for ideological unity in 1957, the following year Mao tried to implement his supposedly objective understanding of

Marxism-Leninism-Stalinism in an attempt to enter the communist and final stage of history before the USSR. The Great Leap Forward, however, turned out to be a fall backward. For instrumental reasons, Mao adhered to its radicalism throughout 1959, only to receive condescension from the Soviet comrades. By the end of that year, the leadership of both parties concluded that they represented real Marxism-Leninism, while the other had deviated from the truth. Time only would show which one was the heretic.

Finally, the Soviet policy of peaceful coexistence and Mao's opposition to it, which grew steadily from late 1956 to late 1959, did not help the Sino-Soviet alliance. Initially, the PRC did not object to peaceful coexistence, especially since, in 1954, Sino-Indian Pancha Shila had enshrined a similar concept of mutual toleration by two countries with different socioeconomic and political systems. Mao's support started to waver only once Sino-American relations over Taiwan, though never pleasant, worsened throughout 1956 and 1957, and once he realized that peaceful transition, a derivative of peaceful coexistence, threatened to subvert revolutionary action in capitalist states. By late 1957, the CCP confidentially informed the CPSU that it could no longer support peaceful coexistence. However, no specific American security threat triggered China's rejection of peaceful coexistence. The Second Taiwan Strait Crisis, which was initiated by Mao, expressed China's general dissatisfaction with American policy toward Taiwan. In 1959, Mao's opposition to peaceful coexistence was ideological, steeped in his crude understanding of the Marxist-Leninist historical interpretation of the rise and fall of capitalism and imperialism. His conception of world affairs clashed with the attempts of the superpowers to find negotiated solutions to the Germany problem and nuclear armament. The Sino-Soviet differences on global strategy thus raised the potential for friction in their alliance. For Mao, China's military links to the USSR, which turned out to be revisionist and deferential to U.S. imperialism, had become less important; for Khrushchev, the PRC, with its ideological radicalism and internal turmoil, became less central to Soviet global strategy. These developments left the alliance adrift in international politics—an easy prey for a crisis. By late 1959, the cracks that had opened in the Sino-Soviet alliance the year before had not only widened but had also become visible.

CHAPTER 5

World Revolution and the Collapse
of Economic Relations, 1960

THE SOVIET SPECIALIST MIKHAIL KLOCHKO arrived in Beijing in April of 1960 on his second tour to China. While he enjoyed the gigantic Labor Day spectacle in the Chinese capital, the Soviet downing of an American spy plane ruined the May 1 celebrations in his home country. Klochko also visited the new impressive government buildings erected since his departure two years prior. The Great Leap Forward seemed to have achieved miracles. Early in May, he took up his duties at the Kunming Institute of Metallurgy and Ceramics. On July 23, the Chinese Academy of Sciences in Beijing called by phone to tell Klochko to leave Kunming immediately for Beijing. After his return to the Chinese capital, his hosts put him up in a nice hotel and treated him in the most courteous manner. Only then did the flabbergasted Klochko realize that all fourteen hundred Soviet specialists in China were ordered to return home immediately.[1]

The Chinese publication of the so-called Lenin Polemics in April precipitated a shift in Mao's challenge to Khrushchev's leadership of the socialist camp from arguments over economic development theory and de-Stalinization, which had dominated Sino-Soviet ideological disputes in the late 1950s, to debates over the correct course of world revolution, which quickly grew to be a central point in the Sino-Soviet disagreements until Mao's death in 1976. With the Great Leap Forward having been steadily discredited as a viable economic alternative to Soviet economic thinking, the Chairman focused on his dissatisfactions with Khrushchev's foreign policy toward American imperialism. Good luck seemed to reward the audacious Mao. The downing of an American U-2 spy plane in Sverdlovsk on May 1 and Khrushchev's subsequent abrogation of the Paris Summit, for which he had worked so hard since his visit to the United States the year before, seemed to align with Mao's radicalized views on international affairs. Beijing tried to use the momentum

---

[1] Mikhail Klochko, *Soviet Scientist in Red China* (Montreal: International, 1964), 117–213.

not only to force its ideological views onto an international gathering of leftist trade unions in early June but also to pressure Soviet specialists in China to renounce Moscow's ideological positions.

In response, Khrushchev bullied the Chinese delegation to accept his ideological platform at the third Romanian Party Congress and decided to withdraw the Soviet specialists from the PRC afterward. Despite Chinese claims to the contrary, the economic damage of the withdrawal was minor. The political fallout, however, was enormous. As a result, economic relations broke down by late 1960.

Yet, both sides knew they could not go too far. By the fall, the Great Leap Forward had collapsed completely. By the same token, Khrushchev's visit to the United Nations in September revealed that Soviet-American relations remained frozen after the U-2 Incident. Thus, when, in early November, the international communist movement met in Moscow for a second time after 1957, the political foundations for the opposite ideological positions both sides had staked out had crumbled. Throughout tense negotiations, both the CCP and the CPSU tried to push through their ideological agenda but eventually reached a compromise. It would be only a temporary truce.

Deadly Famines

Nineteen sixty was the worst of the three famine years. Around three-quarters of what cautious estimates calculate to be 18.5 to 20 million excess deaths during 1959–61 occurred in that year alone.[2] Rural areas of Shandong, Henan, Shanxi, Anhui, Jiangsu, and Sichuan were particularly hard hit, while urban areas enjoyed better rationing.[3] But by June even the cities had to struggle with tight supplies.[4] The 1960 famine was largely a *manmade* disaster. The 1959 reversal of Mao's 1958 order to reduce the sown acreage could not prevent the severe food crisis.[5] The result was a 15 percent drop of grain production from 200 to 170 million tons in 1959, and another 15 percent drop to around 143.5 million tons in 1960.[6] At the same time, the central government continued

---

[2] Famine deaths are defined as excess deaths, that is, the difference between the actual death toll and the natural death rate. Yao Shujie claims 18.48 million deaths, Jasper Becker 19.5 million deaths: Yao, "Note," 1366. Becker, *Ghosts*, 272–74.

[3] Lieberthal, "Great Leap," 295. Lardy, "Chinese Economy," 372–76. MacFarquhar, *Origins*, vol. 3, 1–5.

[4] Xiao, *Qiusuo*, vol. 2, 626.

[5] Lardy, "Chinese Economy," 369–70.

[6] Yao, "Note," 1367. Lardy, "Chinese Economy," 381.

with the policy of exporting grain.[7] In 1959, 4.1575 million tons (1958: 2.8834 million tons) had been exported while only 2,000 tons (1958: 223.5 thousand tons) had been imported. For 1960, the corresponding numbers were 2.7204 million tons and 66.3 thousand tons.[8]

Unlike in 1959, *Neibu cankao* in 1960 remained eerily silent about the food crisis. It carried only *one* famine report for that year, as if famines had already been taken for granted.[9] But five reports in the spring on edema pointed to *prolonged* starvation.[10] Zhou was shocked when he heard about 126,000 edema cases in Jiangsu province alone.[11]

How did Mao react? At the January Politburo meeting in Shanghai, the Chairman claimed that "the internal situation is *good*."[12] Once the Chairman was confronted with the nationwide famines in late spring, he asserted that "a small number of class enemies had infiltrated the ranks for destructive purposes," and ordered a rectification campaign of the rural party in order to have "these scoundrels . . . disposed of."[13] But Mao's ideologically skewed views could not prevent China's agricultural collapse. On May 28, the CCP CC apparatus sent out an emergency directive to organize transportation for food deliveries to Beijing, Tianjin, Shanghai, and Liaoning provinces.[14] By early summer, the famines had also reached the central leadership compound in Beijing, as Li Zhisui remembered.[15]

At the Shanghai Politburo meeting on June 10–18, Zhou finally dared to tell Mao that China's agriculture was ruined. The prime minister cautioned that "after two years of famines due to crop failures [*sic!*]," China had to concentrate on rural reconstruction. He also warned that the political situation "will be completely dangerous until 1962." The central leadership thus should "lie low" for the rest of the year and publish production data not in December as usual but with a delay.[16] His words echoed Peng Dehuai's and Zhang Wentian's warnings a year before. Mao agreed but again denied personal responsibility. Instead, he claimed that "I and comrade Chen Yun" had been "uneasy" about the high steel targets all along, the "rightist" attack at Lushan had "essentially caused us to wake up," and

---

[7] I was unable to identify where exactly the grain was exported to, but the PRC provided food aid to the DRV in the 1950s and 1960s (chapter 10). In the summer of 1960, the PRC also decided to export grain to Albania, see text below.

[8] Lardy, "Chinese Economy," 381.

[9] NC 2994, 2–4.

[10] NC 2994, 8–9; 3002, 18–19; 3006, 20–22; 3037, 17–18; 3038, 22–23.

[11] Xiao, *Qiusuo*, vol. 2, 625.

[12] WLX, 243 (italics mine).

[13] Xiao, *Qiusuo*, vol. 2, 624.

[14] ZELNP2, 326, n. 1. Xiao, *Qiusuo*, vol. 2, 626.

[15] Li, *Private Life*, 339.

[16] Xiao, *Qiusuo*, vol. 2, 635–37 (quotes). MacFarquhar, *Origins*, vol. 3, 11. WLX, 277.

"we won a victory" afterward.[17] In reality, Chen had gone on political sick leave after Lushan, Mao continued to call for an increase of steel targets into *late 1960*, and the "victory" was a famine with millions dying.

What did the Soviets know about the internal situation in China? By late 1959, Stepan Chervonenko, who had replaced the dysfunctional Yudin as Moscow's ambassador in mid-October, shook the Soviet embassy out of its complacency. An internal embassy report identified two reasons reliable information had been lacking since late 1958: the Chinese side had been less forthcoming than before while the embassy had shown no initiative to remedy the situation. Embassy representatives also found it difficult to meet any of the Chinese leaders, the report stated; the best information sources were Soviet specialists who regularly reported on their meetings with Chinese leaders.[18] The Soviet foreign ministry responded to this tacit self-criticism with two lists of topics to be raised once the embassy had managed to arrange meetings with the Chinese leadership: the prevention of nuclear war, peaceful coexistence, problems within the socialist camp and its relations with "non-socialist countries" and "anti-imperialist and national liberation movements," improved mutual information exchange, the evaluation of Stalin's role in the Chinese Revolution and of "Mao Zedong Thought," the personality cult, and economic and border questions.[19]

But Chervonenko was still far from reaching any of his goals. The meetings with Mao and other central leaders in early 1960 were the last for several months.[20] By April, the Soviet ambassador decided to go on an inspection tour through China. He found only Potemkin villages set up by the Chinese hosts. Local cadres raved about what the Great Leap Forward had bestowed on Chinese women (kindergartens and nursing services), claimed that unemployment had been erased, and lauded the large dining halls. Chervonenko saw no signs of the famines.[21]

LENIN POLEMICS

While Chervonenko tried to remedy Sino-Soviet relations, Moscow was preparing for the impending Soviet-American-British-French summit in

---

[17] Xiao, *Qiusuo*, vol. 2, 630, 634–35.

[18] "On the Condition of the Exchange of Information," 2/18/1960, *AVPRF*, f.0100, o.53, d.24, p.457, 7–33.

[19] Both untitled lists are dated 3/9/1960: *AVPRF*, f.0100, o.53, d.24, p.457, 34–36, 37.

[20] Prozumenshikov, "1960," 10. For meetings with leaders: *AVPRF*, f.0100, o.53, d.8, p.454, 1–6, 19–42, 73–76; *ZELNP2*, 280; *SAPMO-BArch*, DY 30/3604, 8–9.

[21] Reports in: *AVPRF*, f.100, o.47, d.7, p.194, 1–7. Later reports confirm that the Chinese side organized tours: *AVPRF*, f.0100, o.55, d.24, p.483, 1–19.

mid-May. By late 1959 the four summit powers had agreed to a meeting in Paris. Because the antagonistic October 2 meeting with Mao had reconfirmed his decision to seek rapprochement with the United States,[22] Khrushchev tried to rally most of the socialist camp behind him. One of his letters to all ruling communist parties in early 1960 claimed that Moscow's most recent announcement on a unilateral conventional disarmament had put the war mongers in the West on the defensive. Henceforth, the socialist camp should seize the opportunity to push forward "peaceful coexistence" and "general and complete disarmament."[23]

Mao did not agree with this "un-Marxist" interpretation of world affairs.[24] At the Shanghai Politburo meeting in January, he claimed that the inherently aggressive attitude of American imperialism toward the world had not changed since 1945. Khrushchev's policy of "holding hands with Eisenhower" was a mistake. Therefore the CCP should make "proper confidential criticism" and "openly publish our opinions."[25] Even though Beijing supported Moscow's troop reductions publicly, it proclaimed that any disarmament agreement would not apply to the PRC.[26]

Mao's radical views on the outside world paralleled a campaign to enhance his personality cult at home. In January, the CC apparatus reintroduced the term "Mao Zedong Thought"—omitted from the CCP constitution in the fall of 1956—into the political discourse.[27] The campaign reached its peak in September 1960 with the long delayed publication of the fourth volume of Mao Zedong's *Selected Works*.[28] Since the tome covered the years 1945–49—the triumph of Mao's leadership in the civil war—it indirectly backed his larger claim to global leadership in the anti-imperialist struggle.

The Sino-Soviet confrontation over Khrushchev's foreign policy occurred at the one-day meeting of the Political Consultative Committee (PCC) of the Warsaw Pact in Moscow on February 4, 1960. Khrushchev explained the reasoning for the Paris Summit and called for a "correct line of unity" among the socialist countries.[29] Although its public

---

[22] Stephen Ambrose, *Eisenhower*, vol. 2 (New York: Simon & Schuster, 1983), 537–41, 567–70. Taubman, *Khrushchev*, 440, 447–48.

[23] "Letter by Khrushchev to Ulbricht," 1/8/1960, *SAPMO-BArch*, DY 30/3476, 1–6.

[24] Zhonggong, *Mao Zedong zhuan*, 1047.

[25] WLX, 236–46.

[26] *SCMP* 2181, 42–44. CB 619, 6.

[27] MacFarquhar, *Origins*, vol. 2, 318–19.

[28] Oleg Borisov et al., *Soviet-Chinese Relations, 1945–1970* (Bloomington: Indiana, 1975), 169–70. Lieberthal, "Great Leap," 337.

[29] Summary of Khrushchev's speech: "Protocol on the Meeting of the Politburo," 2/11/1960, *Tsentralen Drzhaven Arkhiv* [*TsDA*], Tsentralen Partien Arkhiv [TsPA], f.1B, o.5, a.e.416, 1–17.

declaration endorsed Soviet positions,[30] the Chinese observer delegation raised proper criticism as planned.[31] Mao's choice as head of the delegation, the ultraleftist Kang Sheng,[32] painted the United States as an untrustworthy and warmongering power that was trying to destabilize China. He ended with a veiled criticism of Khrushchev's rapprochement policies: "The imperialists, the modern revisionists, and the reactionaries of various countries continuously dream of changes in their favor within our countries, and of a crack in the unity of our ranks."[33]

Kang's speech and its advance publication in China triggered an éclat. At the banquet, Khrushchev chided the Chinese comrades for their policy of "harming the interests of the socialist camp."[34] Agitated by too much vodka, he gave his pent-up frustrations free rein, mocking China's insistence that the USSR was heading the socialist camp because that formula in fact was designed only to ridicule Moscow's policies.[35] He ended his tirade with an insult: Mao was nothing other than "a pair of worn-out galoshes standing discarded in a corner."[36] The next morning, the Soviet side orally warned the Chinese delegation not to go any further in publicly attacking Soviet policies—to no avail.[37] A *Renmin Ribao* editorial of February 6 misrepresented the outcome of the WAPA meeting as a victory for Chinese positions.[38]

Mao decided "to counter-attack."[39] He instructed a five-man team of central propaganda cadres to work on three pronouncements to be released on the occasion of Lenin's ninetieth birthday in April.[40] While frequently reviewing drafts,[41] the Chairman nevertheless began to worry about the danger of Chinese isolation in the world. True to his fashion of arguing away any problems, he eventually concluded that only 10 percent of the world's people "oppose us," while "the other 2 billion 430

---

[30] MacFarquhar, *Origins*, vol. 2, 266–67. *SCMP* 2194, 47–50.

[31] WLX, 241.

[32] MacFarquhar, *Origins*, vol. 2, 266.

[33] "Speech of Comrade Kang Sheng on the Meeting of the Political Consultative Committee of the Members of the Warsaw Pact," [2/4/1960], *SAPMO-BArch*, DY 30/3386, 87–99.

[34] WLX, 251.

[35] Wu Xiuquan, *Huiyi yu huainian* (Beijing: Zhonggong zhongyang dangxiao, 1991), 333–35. WLX, 251. Liu, *Chushi*, 93.

[36] WLX, 251.

[37] Wu, *Huiyi*, 335.

[38] *SCMP* 2194, 47–50.

[39] WLX, 241, 252–53.

[40] WLX, 253.

[41] WLX, 253–54.

million people who back us either do not oppose China or are temporarily duped by the enemy."[42]

The diatribe against Soviet revisionism—subsequently known as the Lenin Polemics—was published in the form of an *Hongqi* article titled "Long Live Leninism" on April 19, followed by a *Renmin Ribao* editorial and a speech by Lu Dingyi, the director of the CCP CC Propaganda Department, some days later.[43] They opened the public Sino-Soviet polemics that would last until Mao's death. "Long Live Leninism" was a rambling justification for the Chinese communes, a call to follow Lenin's anti-imperialism, a distorted rehash of the history of the USSR under Stalin, and the claim that real Marxist-Leninists must reject peaceful coexistence.[44] The *Renmin Ribao* editorial claimed thirty-six alleged American violations of the Camp David Spirit, which spoke against any "East-West Summit Conference."[45] Lu Dingyi's speech completed the triptych of Maoist invective, calling "revisionism . . . the product of the imperialist policy . . . of nuclear war blackmail."[46] Once the Chinese celebrations of Lenin's birthday had passed, the Chairman, however, decided "to suspend articles relating to modern revisionism" and "wait a little while and look for the response."[47]

The secretly prepared Lenin Polemics stunned the Soviets.[48] After catching his breath, Khrushchev fretted about Mao's audacious claim to the role of master theoretician in the socialist camp.[49] But the Soviet response was lame. Otto Kuusinen, a member of the CPSU Presidium, gave a speech at the Lenin birthday celebrations in Moscow marshaling some Lenin quotes and making a moral appeal for nuclear disarmament.[50] The Soviet comrades eventually republished Lenin's "'Leftism' in Communism—an Infantile Disorder" in mid-June, forty years after its original publication—a faint but unintentional echo of Peng Dehuai's use of the text at Lushan.[51] Chervonenko informed the East Germans in mid-May that the Soviet comrades officially would not reply to the Lenin Polemics.[52]

[42] Mao, "On the Anti–China Question," 3/22/1960, *JYMW*, vol. 9, 93.

[43] WLX, 258–59.

[44] CB 617, 1–29.

[45] CB 617, 30–45.

[46] SCMP 2246, 12.

[47] WLX, 265.

[48] Prozumenshikov, "1960," 3.

[49] Delyusin, "Guanyu," 102. Delyusin, "Nekotorye," 6, 7.

[50] MacFarquhar, *Origins*, vol. 2, 274–75.

[51] *Sovetskaya Rossiya*, 6/10/1960, 3.

[52] "Note on a Talk with the Soviet Ambassador, Comrade Chervonenko," 5/21/1960, *SAPMO-BArch*, DY 30/3604, 11–16.

Paris Summit

The Soviet downing of an American U-2 spy plane on May 1, 1960, was probably the most fortuitous event in the Sino-Soviet Split. Since late 1957, the U.S. spy missions had probed Khrushchev's bluffs with a Soviet ICBM fleet. As a result of the U-2 Incident, Khrushchev abrogated the Paris Summit. The Chinese were jubilant about this apparent vindication of their belligerence against U.S. imperialism. But much of their radicalism resulted from their ignorance of the true state of the Soviet ICBM program.

On May 1, Francis Gary Powers was on his way from Pakistan to Norway with his high-flying U-2 spy aircraft. Operating at its ceiling height of 72,000 feet over Sverdlovsk, the plane was hit by shrapnel from a recently improved Soviet SA-2 anti-aircraft missile exploding below. The plane crashed. Moscow had known for a long time about Washington's spy flights. Since 1959, the Soviets had fired SA-2s at the planes; some had come dangerously close. Neither Moscow nor Washington raised the issue. Khrushchev was unwilling to complain in public because this would have meant a tacit acknowledgment that the USSR still lacked the military means to shoot down these planes. Eisenhower wanted to keep the sensitive U-2 program secret for future missions.[53]

The timing of the incident—a fortnight before the Paris Summit—was politically treacherous. The Soviet military was still furious over Khrushchev's announcement of unilateral troop cuts, and proponents of a "China first" strategy grumbled over his supposed disinclination to keep the Sino-Soviet alliance alive.[54] The Soviet leader found himself in a dilemma: pursue Soviet-American rapprochement further or end it altogether. Eventually he tried to rationalize the U-2 Incident by convincing himself that rogue elements in the CIA had acted behind the back of his friend Eisenhower.[55] In truth, the president had for years personally endorsed every flight, although the one on May 1 was supposed to be the last before the Paris Summit.[56] Khrushchev "boiled over" when he heard Eisenhower publicly admitting to this on May 9.[57] Seven days later, in Paris, he demanded a public apology. Eisenhower was not eager to submit to a humiliation by the "son-of-a-bitch" whose nuclear bluffs essentially were responsible for the crisis. The summit was over before it began.[58]

---

[53] Michael Beschloss, *May-Day* (New York: Harper & Row, 1986), 13–28. Curtis Peebles, *Dark Eagles* (Novato: Presidio, 1995), 43–46. Khrushchev, *Nikita S. Khrushchev*, 152–62, 368–80. Taubman, *Khrushchev*, 443. Pach, *Presidency*, 215–16.

[54] Taubman, *Khrushchev*, 454.

[55] Taubman, *Khrushchev*, 446, 457.

[56] Pach, *Presidency*, 215–16.

[57] Taubman, *Khrushchev*, 458.

[58] Quoted in: Pach, *Presidency*, 216–20. Taubman, *Khrushchev*, 460–68.

Why did Khrushchev blow the summit? Some weeks later he explained to the fraternal communist parties that he had canceled the Paris meeting "in the interests of the preservation of unity with the Chinese comrades,"[59] but this was a politically opportune defense at a time of rapidly deteriorating Sino-Soviet relations. His personal foreign policy adviser, Oleg Troyanovskii, recalled that the Soviet reaction had to be sufficiently "harsh," since otherwise the hardliners in Moscow and Beijing would have exploited the incident.[60] But the main explanation for Khrushchev's destructive behavior in Paris seems to lie in his character. As at the WAPA meeting three months before, he was unable to control his anger.[61] The Paris debacle was most damaging to Khrushchev himself. He had put a lot of his domestic prestige behind the summit. And thanks to the recently exposed U-2 flights, the Soviet leader also must have realized that it was only a matter of time until Washington would reveal to the world that there was *no* missile gap.[62] Khrushchev had bluffed high since late 1957, and gambled even higher in May 1960. But he had lost everything by late spring.

The U-2 Incident came as a propaganda boon for the Chinese comrades. It added credibility to their most recent public invectives. Mao jeered at Khrushchev: "There were some people who said that Eisenhower is a peace-loving man, I hope that these people will gain some understanding from this event."[63] Deng Xiaoping told the CC secretariat that the U-2 Incident was a "fortuitous incident" for China: "After we had published the three articles 'Long Live Leninism,' Khrushchev could not be weak in the face of America."[64]

Following the abrogation of the Paris Summit, the Chinese shifted their propaganda efforts into high gear. On May 17, Deng told Chervonenko that Khrushchev's demand for an American apology was a "firm position."[65] The Politburo the same day decided on a huge propaganda campaign in "support of the Soviet Union."[66] A media blitz accused Eisenhower of complete unwillingness to reduce international tensions. Several million people attended organized rallies on Tiananmen Square from May 20 to 22.[67] Beijing doubled up the campaign at home with

---

[59] Quoted in: Prozumenshikov, "1960," 3.

[60] Troyanovskii, *Cherez*, 225.

[61] Taubman, *Khrushchev*, 468.

[62] Washington revealed the missile gap in 1961: Taubman, *Khrushchev*, 488.

[63] Zhonggong, *Mao Zedong zhuan*, 1075.

[64] WLX, 266–67.

[65] "From the Diary of Chervonenko S. V., June 1960, Top Secret, Copy No. 3, Memorandum of Conversation with the General Secretary of the CC CCP Member of the Politburo of the CC CCP, Deng Xiaoping," 5/17/1960, Chen Jian, "Deng Xiaoping," 170–72.

[66] WLX, 269.

[67] SCMP 2265, 21–25; 2267, 25–29. CB 631, 8.

one in the socialist world. In May, the Chinese comrades told East European and Soviet diplomats that the only way to secure world peace was to transfer nuclear weapons to the PRC.[68] Beijing's embassies in Moscow and East Berlin distributed propaganda material promoting Mao's radical new position.[69] The Soviets considered these actions illegal and repeatedly asked the Chinese embassy to stop them. But whenever they brought up the topic, the Chinese claimed that the texts "support[ed] the struggle of the Soviet people . . . against imperialism."[70]

Khrushchev's plunge in Chinese appreciation was not only related to Mao's new radicalism, but also to Moscow's failure to reveal the real state of affairs in Soviet missile technology. The Chinese comrades knew neither that Khrushchev's ICBM bluff was empty nor that the USSR had been unable to shoot down U-2 planes before May 1, 1960. Shortly after the first Sputnik in October 1957, Khrushchev instead had told them that "the Soviet Union's missiles undoubtedly [had] sobered the brains of the western leaders."[71] During the Beijing visit in 1958, Khrushchev bragged that the extended territory of the USSR was far too small for the testing of the newest version of long-range ICBMs.[72] And at the twenty-first CPSU congress, Khrushchev boasted that Moscow had started the "mass production of intercontinental ballistic missiles."[73] Little wonder the Chinese Foreign Minister Chen Yi told Chervonenko in early 1960 that "the USA remains behind the USSR in the production of modern missile weapons."[74] *Nothing* that Khrushchev had said was true; the USSR had only a very few and unwieldy ICBMs.[75]

Similarly, the Chinese had trusted Moscow's implicit claim of a Soviet anti-aircraft missile capability. In June 1959, two Taiwanese, U.S.-built RB-57D spy planes (a precursor to the U-2 with a ceiling height of 60,000 feet) appeared over Beijing.[76] The Chinese comrades were worried about a possible incident during the tenth anniversary celebrations of the PRC on October 1, 1959. Thus Ambassador Liu Xiao turned to Gromyko

[68] Pleshakov, "Khrushchev," 238–39.

[69] *AVPRF*, f.0100, o.53, d.6, p.453, 28, and d.24, p.457, 266. Meissner, *DDR*, 103.

[70] *AVPRF*, f.0100, o.53, d.1, p.453, 1–2, 3–5; d.2, p.453, 4–6, 9–11 (quote).

[71] Li, *Waijiao*, 117.

[72] "Fourth Conversation of N. S. Khrushchev with Mao Zedong," 8/3/1958, Wolff, "Finger," 56–57.

[73] *NYT*, 1/28/1959, 1, 3.

[74] "Record of Conversation of Chen Yi and Li Fuchun with the Ambassadors of the Socialist States in the PRC," 1/22/1960, *AVPRF*, f.0100, o.53, d.8, p.454, 40.

[75] Gaddis, *We Now Know*, 240. Khrushchev, *Nikita S. Khrushchev*, 282–83, 392.

[76] Mentioned: "Record of Conversation with Zhang Weile," 8/29/1959, *AVPRF*, f.0100, o.52, d.5, p.442, 35.

on July 7 with a request to deliver needed weapons systems,[77] but the Soviets equivocated since they obviously could not provide what they did not possess. Chargé d'Affaires Zhang Weile repeated the request with a tone of strained urgency on August 29.[78] By late September, the Soviets seemed to have delivered something because Liu profusely thanked Vice–Foreign Minister Pushkin for "the consolidation of Beijing's anti-aircraft defense."[79] Oddly enough, on October 7, the Chinese actually did bring down a Taiwanese RB-57D near Beijing. Like half a year later over Sverdlovsk, shrapnel damaged the airplane fatally. That the missile had not even hit the RB-57D, which had an operating ceiling of 12,000 feet lower than the U-2, did not matter.[80] The Chinese comrades must have felt reassured by the awe-inspiring anti-aircraft missile capabilities of the Soviet revisionists.

Unsurprisingly the Chinese leaders, in early May 1960, found that the American U-2 flights against a USSR seemingly armed to the teeth with ICBMs and powerful anti-aircraft missiles revealed the inherent belligerence of American imperialism, and by logical extension that their assertions in the Lenin Polemics had been completely correct. As much as Khrushchev's ICBM bluff had boomeranged by May 1960 in his relations with Eisenhower, his misinformation campaign toward China with regard to the nuclear and anti-aircraft missile capabilities greatly undermined his position in relation to Mao. In May 1960, Khrushchev had to pay *twice* a heavy price for his past bravado.

IDEOLOGICAL WARFARE IN BEIJING AND BUCHAREST

The Chinese comrades planned to use the momentum of the U-2 Incident and the abortive Paris Summit to promote their agenda at the Beijing meeting of the board of directors of the World Federation of Trade Unions (WFTU; an association of the state-sponsored unions in the socialist camp and fellow traveler unions elsewhere).[81] The meeting was supposed to open on May 30, but Liu Ningyi, the head of the Chinese delegation, requested so many changes in the draft report that the start was postponed repeatedly. On June 2, he even demanded a meeting of all

---

[77] "Reception of Liu Xiao," 6/7/1959, *AVPRF*, f.0100, o.52, d.5, p.442, 24.

[78] "Record of Conversation with Zhang Weile," 8/29/1959, *AVPRF*, f.0100, o.52, d.5, p.442, 35.

[79] "Reception of Liu Xiao," 9/25/1959, *AVPRF*, f.0100, o.52, d.5, p.442, 44.

[80] Curtis Peebles, *Shadow Flights* (Novato: Presidio, 2000), 248–50.

[81] MacFarquhar, *Origins*, vol. 2, 275.

member unions in order to adopt the Chinese line as laid out in the Lenin Polemics. The other delegations flatly refused.[82]

When Mao Zedong, Liu Shaoqi, and Zhou Enlai realized that Liu Ningyi had failed to force the Chinese line unto the WFTU, they quickly returned to Beijing from their inspection tours in China's provinces.[83] Liu Ningyi tried to raise the topic again on the fifth, but Viktor Grishin, the Soviet delegation head, left the hall demonstratively.[84] The same evening, the CCP announced that some selected foreign delegates were invited to an unspecified event that turned out to be a dinner with the CCP Politburo. Deng Xiaoping treated his guests to a surprise—a hundred-minute ideological diatribe against Soviet revisionism. In response, Grishin "demanded from the Chinese comrades to let them finally do their work."[85]

After the start of the official meetings, the Chinese delegation continued to deliver speeches unrelated to "the work of labor unions in China." The radical Chinese position found support only from the Indonesians and partially from the North Koreans, Japanese, and North Vietnamese.[86] When Beijing's top leaders realized that they had lost the gamble, they retreated to Shanghai for a Politburo conference to discuss China's ruined agriculture, as related above.[87] Taking over from Liu Ningyi, the moderate Wang Jiaxiang decided that Chinese compromises were necessary to get at least a final WFTU document.[88] The meeting nevertheless ended on bad terms on June 9.[89] Afterward, the CCP launched a media campaign portraying the gathering as a complete success for the Chinese line,[90] which the WFTU decried in November as a "misrepresentation of facts."[91]

The Chinese provocations at the WFTU meeting angered Khrushchev so much that he decided to use the impending Third Romanian Party Congress in Bucharest for retribution.[92] However, at the beginning of June, he had just agreed to meet there with all ruling parties to discuss the differences in a *calm fashion*. After a Presidium meeting on "unity of discipline

[82] "Report on the Preparation and Course of the 11th General Meeting of the WFTU," 6/9/1960, *SAPMO-BArch*, DY 30/3671, 16–24.

[83] Prozumenshikov, "1960," 4.

[84] WLX, 276.

[85] "Report on the Preparation . . . ," 6/9/1960, *SAPMO-BArch*, DY 30/3671, 26–28.

[86] "Report on the Preparation . . . ," 6/9/1960, *SAPMO-BArch*, DY 30/3671, 29–30.

[87] Yan Mingfu, "Peng Zhen zai Bujialeisite huiyi shang," *Dangdai Zhongguo shi yanjiu* 1998/3, 73.

[88] Xu, *Wang*, 545.

[89] Yan, "Peng," 73.

[90] *SCMP* 2278, 38–43.

[91] "About the Official Statement of the CCP Delegation," [no date], *SAPMO-BArch*, DY 30/3671, 43–55.

[92] Delyusin, "Guanyu," 102. Delyusin, "Nekotorye," 7–8.

by all" in the socialist camp,[93] the CPSU had sent out an invitation on the second to meet in Bucharest for talks about "our further, common line."[94] The Chinese comrades immediately wondered what the rationale behind Khrushchev's newest initiative was: "To approach jointly the enemy on the basis of the situation after the [Paris] summit, . . . [or] to make us suffer?"[95] Since they tried to exploit the WFTU meeting for their purposes right at that moment, the Chinese comrades concluded that Khrushchev wanted to use the Romanian congress for a similar end. Thus, on June 7, the CPSU agreed to a CCP proposal to meet for consultations *only*.[96]

It was only after the end of the WFTU meeting that Moscow's attitude toward Beijing changed. Just before the Soviet republication of "'Leftism' in Communism—an Infantile Disorder" on June 13, most of the delegations to the WFTU meeting stopped over in Moscow to report on the most recent Chinese provocations.[97] While a June 10 *Sovetskaya Rossiya* article had not even alluded to any Sino-Soviet disagreements, two days later *Pravda* criticized the Chinese comrades for ideological radicalism.[98] By mid-June, the Albanians had the impression the Soviets wanted to pressure them to participate in a "plot" against the Chinese.[99] Moscow also demanded from East Berlin to drop its lingering support of the communes; on June 17, the party organ *Neues Deutschland* disassociated itself from the Great Leap Forward.[100]

Although the CCP did not yet know about the sudden changes of the Soviet attitude by mid-June, it nevertheless felt a thunderstorm brewing. The CCP Politburo instructed the versatile Peng Zhen, who was chosen over the ultraleftist Kang Sheng as delegation head to the Romanian party congress, "to support unity, to support principle, . . . to gain mastery by counter-attacking, . . . [and] to allow for unforeseen circumstances."[101]

At an eight-hour stopover meeting in Moscow on June 17, Peng Zhen and Frol Kozlov, a CPSU Presidium member, battled over international politics. Kozlov repeatedly waved a thick document under Peng's nose. When the Chinese representative asked what it was, his Soviet opposite

[93] "Protocol No. 284: Session June 2, 1960," Aleksandr Fursenko, ed., *Prezidium*, vol. 1, 443.

[94] "Letter by Khrushchev to SED CC," 6/2/1960, *SAPMO-BArch*, DY 30/3476, 12.

[95] WLX, 273–74, 277.

[96] Yan, "Peng," 73–74. "Letter by Khrushchev to SED CC," 6/7/1960, *SAPMO-BArch*, DY 30/3476, 17–20.

[97] Li Danhui, "Genyu shijie gonglian Beijing huiyi de ruogan wenti," http://www.shenzhihua .net/muluzhong.htm, accessed on 11/15/2004.

[98] *Sovetskaya Rossiya*, 6/10/1960, 3. *Pravda*, 6/12/1960, 3.

[99] Enver Hoxha, *Khrushchevites* (Tirana: Nentori, 1980), 394–96.

[100] Meissner, *DDR*, 116.

[101] WLX, 278–79. Also: Yan, "Peng," 74.

equivocated by saying that "we will discuss that after we have arrived in Bucharest." The CCP delegation sent a telegram to Beijing about this "bad omen." Its gloomy speculation was on the spot; the document was a sixty-eight-page Soviet condemnation of Chinese policies.[102]

The charged atmosphere was plainly noticeable at the actual Romanian congress from June 20 to 22. The Romanian delegates clapped often during Khrushchev's rambling speech, while remaining "cold" through Peng's short address.[103] A Chinese telegram to Beijing speculated that "they might have organized an operation against us"; the reply wire warned "to be on guard."[104] The Soviets were indeed secretly making preparations.[105] On June 21, the CPSU distributed the sixty-eight-page condemnation to all the ruling parties attending—*except* the Chinese.[106] The piece accused the CCP of misunderstanding the recent historical period, questions of war and peace, and peaceful coexistence.[107] The Chinese were also cut by all other delegations; and Khrushchev repeatedly delayed a bilateral meeting.[108] Finally on June 22, he treated Peng to a six-hour stream of charges ranging from the failed Hundred Flowers campaign, the disastrous Great Leap Forward, the conflict with India, the publication of Kang Sheng's speech before the WAPA meeting, to "the anti-Soviet talks at the WFTU meeting."[109]

On June 23, Yurii Andropov, the head of the CC Liaison Department, finally provided Peng with the sixty-eight-page condemnation together with a draft bulletin, telling the Chinese that they should be prepared to discuss it the next day.[110] That very day, Mao convened the Politburo to discuss the first telegrams Peng Zhen had sent. It finally dawned on the comrades in Beijing how serious the situation was. Mao accused Khrushchev of making Sino-Soviet differences public—as if the CCP had never published Kang Sheng's WAPA speech or the Lenin Polemics. Beijing eventually sent a telegram to Bucharest warning of a possible Soviet "surprise attack."[111]

[102] WLX, 279–80. Also: Liu, *Chushi,* 98–100. Yan, "Peng," 74. For document: "To CC of the Hungarian Socialist Workers' Party, to Kádár," 6/21/1960, *Magyar Országos Levéltár* [MOL], 288 f.9/1960/38 ő e, 80–147.

[103] WLX, 280. Speeches in: *Pravda,* 6/22/1960, 1–3, and 6/24/1960, 3.

[104] WLX, 280.

[105] Khrushchev, *Testament,* 230.

[106] Liu, *Chushi,* 100–101. Prozumenshikov, "1960," 4. Delyusin, "Nekotorye," 7. Yan, "Peng," 76.

[107] "To CC of the Hungarian Socialist Workers' Party, to Kádár," 6/21/1960, MOL, 288 f.9/1960/38 ő e, 80–147.

[108] WLX, 280.

[109] Si, "Shi pengyou," 296.

[110] Yan, "Peng," 76. WLX, 285.

[111] WLX, 283–85.

The Soviet surprise attack came on June 24 at the meeting of the twelve ruling parties. Peng tried to "gain mastery by counter-attacking" when he took the floor to complain against the surprise attack *before* it happened.[112] The Bulgarian party boss, Todor Zhivkov, immediately requested to know why Peng did not want to discuss the disagreements within the socialist camp in Bucharest, especially after the Chinese party leadership had tried to force the same discussion onto the WFTU meeting three weeks before. Except for the Albanians, who regretted the Sino-Soviet quarrel, and the North Koreans and Vietnamese, who essentially remained silent, all other delegations condemned China's policies at length.[113] That evening, in the embassy, the Chinese delegation accused Khrushchev of violating what it called his supposed June 7 "promise" to meet for consultations *only*, and balked at signing the draft bulletin: "If we sign, then we surrender." Peng decided to ask Beijing for more instructions.[114]

The meeting of all fifty-one communist party delegations the next day was even worse. The delegates of the nonruling parties, one after the other, condemned Chinese policies; even the Indonesians and Japanese, who had supported the Chinese at the WFTU meeting, switched sides.[115] The CCP delegation was anxious as it had not received new instructions.[116] Peng Zhen responded in an impromptu speech, defending the CCP against the charges. It was a gallant but futile attempt to redress the situation.[117] Peng shortly afterward sent a report by telegram to Beijing with an urgent call for instructions.[118]

At that time the Albanian party was struggling over how to respond to the situation. A special plane was shuttling back and forth between Tirana and Bucharest with questions and directives. On June 25, the Albanian Politburo decided to instruct its delegation to agree to the proposed bulletin the next day—with reservations—and to disapprove strongly with the spirit and methods of the whole meeting.[119]

---

[112] "Note on the First Speech of Peng Zhen (given on June 25, 1960)," *Fondazione Istituto Gramsci [FIG]*, Archivio del Partito Comunista Italiano [APC], Anno 1960, vol. 474, 25–29.

[113] "Record of the Contents of the Meetings of Representatives of the Communist and Workers' Parties, which Convened at the Occasion of the 3rd Party Congress of the Romanian Workers' Party in Bucharest (Memory Protocol)," [no date], *SAPMO-BArch*, DY 30/J IV 2/201/613, 1–50. WLX, 285–88. Enver Hoxha, *Selected Works*, vol. 3 (Tirana: Nentori, 1980), 1–14.

[114] Yan, "Peng," 76–78.

[115] "Record of the Contents . . . ," 51–86.

[116] WLX, 291–93.

[117] "Record of the Contents . . . ," 87–89.

[118] Yan, "Peng," 78–79. MacFarquhar, *Origins*, vol. 2, 277.

[119] Hoxha, *Selected Works*, vol. 3, 5–18. WLX, 285–86. Hoxha, *Superpowers, 1959–1984* (Tirana: Nentori, 1986), 400–407.

June 25 ended in Bucharest with a tense banquet, which Peng left early to receive a telephone call from Zhou.[120] The Politburo advised the delegation to try to have the wording of the planned bulletin changed, and if that should prove impossible to hand out a statement of dissent that accused the Soviets of "pressuring us to surrender to their un-Marxist-Leninist points of view."[121] After the official instructions had arrived by coded telegram,[122] the Chinese delegation requested at 10 P.M. an urgent appointment with the Romanian party leader Gheorghe Gheorghiu-Dej.[123] Peng tried to get an additional meeting of the twelve ruling parties to discuss the Chinese proposals on the bulletin. But since the proposals were *three* times longer than the planned bulletin itself, Gheorghiu-Dej only agreed to an additional meeting to decide if the Chinese proposals should be discussed at a future gathering.[124]

On June 26, the last day of the Bucharest Meeting, the twelve ruling parties met briefly before noon to discuss the Chinese proposals. After a renewed clash between Khrushchev and Peng, it was settled that they would convene a second Moscow Meeting in November.[125] The Chinese also agreed to sign the bulletin reconfirming Soviet ideological positions,[126] but, to the surprise of all, distributed a written statement of dissent.[127] In the afternoon, when all fifty-one foreign delegations met to endorse the bulletin orally, the Albanians not only raised their disagreement with Soviet methods, but also chided the Chinese for their actions at the WFTU meeting.[128]

The Bucharest Meeting revealed that the Chinese were unbending. On the second day of the Beidaihe Politburo meeting from July 5 to August 10, Peng reported to Mao that the Romanian Congress had disclosed a "two-line struggle in the international communist movement, a struggle between Marxism and opportunism." Khrushchev was nothing but a "schemer" who used "intrigues" to pressure the Chinese. Peng concluded that the "struggle" with the Soviet opportunists would be long-lasting.

[120] Yan, "Peng," 79.

[121] WLX, 288–91.

[122] Yan, "Peng," 80–81.

[123] Interview with Ioan Romulus Budura, Bucharest, 7/10/2004.

[124] Yan, "Peng," 81–82. "Record of the Contents . . . ," 90. For Chinese proposal: *SAPMO-BArch*, DY 30/J IV 2/201/614, 1–6.

[125] "Record of the Contents . . . ," 91–99. For a different transcript: "Note on the Speech of Khrushchev (2nd session in the morning of May [June] 26)," *FIG*, APC, Anno 1960, vol. 474, 2511–26.

[126] *Pravda*, 6/28/1960, 1.

[127] WLX, 295. For Chinese statement: *SAPMO-BArch*, DY 30/J IV 2/201/615, 1–5.

[128] Hoxha, *Selected Works*, vol. 3, 1–18. "Record of the Contents . . . ," 113. Yan, "Peng," 78.

Mao immediately tried to apply the lessons learned at Bucharest to China's domestic situation. If Khrushchev had produced revisionism and opportunism in the USSR, then the PRC had been *correct* to embark on the "experiment" of the Great Leap Forward.[129] It was a chilling reminder that the Chairman still had not given up his own high-flying dreams.

A week later, Zhou delivered a three-day presentation of Soviet mistakes in the Chinese Revolution. It attempted to marshal historical evidence for the path of ideological isolation the CCP had taken most recently by arguing that the CCP had survived its many past travails only through *complete* ideological independence from Moscow while the USSR had been a *single* obstacle to the Chinese Revolution.[130] Indeed, the CCP was almost completely isolated—a situation Mao had warned of in April. But he was still convinced that "90% of the masses sympathize with and support us," and faced the reality that only the tiny Albanian party was willing to side with the CCP with stoicism: "One good friend is just enough."[131]

As the Chinese comrades were reassessing their relationship with the Soviet revisionists, the CPSU called a CC meeting to discuss its relations with the CCP. On July 16, the *very* day Zhou at Beidaihe talked about Sino-Soviet relations, Kozlov laid out at length the "major mistakes of the [CCP] leadership" since 1957. Khrushchev followed with a sketch of Mao's personality cult: "When I look at Mao Zedong, I just see Stalin, an exact copy."[132]

The Soviet leadership took three decisions to adjust to the new circumstances after Bucharest. It terminated all nuclear research collaboration in the PRC,[133] stopped the publication of the *Friendship* (*Druzhba*) journal,[134] and punished Albania for its refusal to back the Soviet position at Bucharest with a cut to economic aid.[135] When all other East European countries followed suit on the third issue in a matter of days, Albania—suffering under manmade famines in 1960 as well—had to turn to Mao

[129] WLX, 298–300, 308–14.

[130] The first two-thirds of the document (July 14 and 15) are printed: "Communist International and the Chinese Communist Party," 5/14–15/1960, Zhou, *Selected Works*, vol. 2, 306–19. Also summarized: WLX, 314–24.

[131] Mao, "Remarks on a Report of a Summary of Discussions with the Albanian Ambassador Stationed in Romania," July 1960, *JYMW*, vol. 9, 249.

[132] "Report," 7/16/1960, *RGANI*, f.2, o.1, d.484, 69–87a.

[133] Li, *Lengnuan*, 320. Nuclear cooperation with the Chinese in the Soviet Union was not affected: *SCMP* 3486, 32. *CB* 773, 31.

[134] "Basic Events in Soviet-Chinese Relations in 1960," 12/17/1960, *AVPRF*, f.0100, o.53, d.24, p.457, 266. Borisov, *Soviet-Chinese Relations*, 184.

[135] William Griffith, *Albania and the Sino-Soviet Rift* (Cambridge: MIT, 1963), 46–47. MacFarquhar, *Origins*, vol. 2, 124–25.

for economic assistance. The Chairman was more than happy to help out his only good friend.[136] The PRC agreed to provide grain aid to Albania.[137] But the Albanian position in Romania had not been as clear-cut as Khrushchev saw it; his hurried actions pushed Albania to side with China.[138]

According to Lev Delyusin, who worked in the Soviet foreign ministry at the time, Khrushchev did not want to break with the Chinese at Bucharest. He was angered by the Chinese attempt to depart from the position of unity he believed to represent in his dealings with the West.[139] The crudeness of his methods and his inability to restrain his anger at Chinese provocations since April only made the situation worse. Similar to his dealings with Eisenhower in Paris, he did not even try to provide the Chinese comrades with a face-saving way out of their political isolation.[140]

SOVIET WITHDRAWAL AND COLLAPSE OF ECONOMIC RELATIONS

On July 18, without prior warning, Moscow informed Beijing of the immediate withdrawal of all of the approximately fourteen hundred Soviet specialists.[141] The departure of civilian specialists was completed on August 24, the evacuation of their military counterparts, a week later.[142] The controversial nature of the withdrawal provided the Chinese side with the pretext to blame the Soviets for the disasters at home. Moreover, it served both as an excuse to terminate economic relations with the USSR, which had suffered under the Great Leap Forward, and as an opportunity to realign China's economy with the nonsocialist world.

The July 18 letter announcing the withdrawal listed a whole range of reasons: the long-standing Soviet desire that the specialists might return home, Chinese criticism of their work, the blatant Chinese disregard for Soviet technical advice, and CCP propaganda against the CPSU.[143] A

---

[136] Wang, *Zhonghua*, vol. 2, 342. Xiao, *Qiusuo*, vol. 2, 932.

[137] Christensen, "Worse," 100.

[138] Peter Danylow, *Die aussenpolitischen Beziehungen Albaniens zu Jugoslawien und zur UdSSR 1944–1961* (München: Oldenbourg, 1982), 163, 166.

[139] Delyusin, "Nekotorye," 20.

[140] Liu, *Chushi*, 113.

[141] "Note: The Soviet Embassy in Beijing to the Ministry of Foreign Affairs of the PRC," 7/18/1960, Chen Jian, ed., "A Crucial Step toward the Breakdown of the Sino-Soviet Alliance," *CWIHP Bulletin* 8–9, 249–50.

[142] "Basic Events in Soviet-Chinese Relations in 1960," 12/17/1960, *AVPRF*, f.0100, o.53, d.24, p.457, 269, 270.

[143] "Note: . . . ," Chen, "Crucial Step," 249–50.

Soviet circular to the East Europeans additionally claimed that the Chinese had purposely made the work of the Soviet specialists impossible.[144]

The deterioration of relations over the Soviet specialists had started some years before. Since early 1956, Moscow had called for their return home, but Beijing had always dragged its feet.[145] With the start of the Great Leap Forward, Soviet specialists complained to their embassy about ideologically motivated name-calling.[146] In September 1959, when Mao had announced that all foreign specialists in the PRC had to work for the Great Leap Forward, the situation turned even worse.[147] Following the Lenin Polemics, the CCP instructed Chinese specialists to influence their Soviet counterparts ideologically at the workplace.[148] The Soviet government had reacted to this gradual deterioration in working conditions even before July 18, 1960; by October 1959, Moscow started to withdraw some of its specialists inconspicuously.[149]

The trigger for the Soviet decision to withdraw *all* personnel was the Chinese attempt to pressure Soviet *military* specialists. Lin Biao's campaign to inoculate the PLA with *Mao Zedong Thought* reached its peak in June and July.[150] On June 10, General Colonel Fu Zhun delivered a speech to Soviet military specialists propagating the ideological line laid out in the Lenin Polemics. Chervonenko reported on the speech to Moscow on July 9. When Soviet Defense Minister Malinovskii saw a summary of the speech, he personally sent it to Khrushchev with his own critical remarks in the margins.[151]

The decision to withdraw all specialists was spontaneous. There is no indication that the CPSU CC plenum of July 13–16 was involved at all.[152] Some witnesses remember that Khrushchev personally made the

[144] "Khrushchev to SED CC," 6/18/1960, *SAPMO-BArch*, DY 30/3605, 21–27.

[145] Li, *Waijiao*, 151. WLX, 167–68.

[146] Borisov, *Soviet-Chinese Relations*, 142–43. Khrushchev, *Testament*, 264–65. Brezhnev, *Kitai*, 65–66.

[147] Mao, "Instructions of the CC on Uniting all Foreign Specialists," 9/4/1959, *JYMW*, vol. 8, 496. Borisov, *Soviet-Chinese Relations*, 210–11.

[148] Delyusin, "Guanyu," 102. Klochko, *Soviet Scientist*, 171, 178–79.

[149] Mark Kramer, ed., "The USSR Foreign Ministry's Appraisal of Sino-Soviet Relations on the Eve of the Split, September 1959," *CWIHP Bulletin* 6–7, 171. Interview with Xia Yishan, Beijing, 3/23/2000.

[150] For Lin's campaign: *Bundesarchiv, Militärarchiv* [BArch-Freib], VA-01/6384 Aktenvermerke des Militärattachés der DDR in der VR China über Gespräche, Besichtigungen und protokollarische Veranstaltungen, Band 2, 1–2, and VA-01/6385 Presseinformationen zu politischen und militärischen Ereignissen, 2–6.

[151] "[Letter by Chervonenko]," 7/9/1960, *AVPRF*, f.0100, o.53, d.24, p.457, 96–98. Prozumenshikov relates the Malinovskii story, but misdates it before the Bucharest Meeting: "1960," 5.

[152] "Report," 7/16/1960, *RGANI*, f.2, o.1, d.484, 69–89a.

decision;[153] others recall a collective judgment.[154] The withdrawal was hotly contested in the lower ranks. The foreign ministry warned that a similar decision in 1948 had not managed to subdue the Yugoslavs.[155] Chervonenko, whose embassy only half a year before had identified the specialists as the most important source for information, called the withdrawal plainly illegal, and advocated letting the specialists stay until their contracts expired.[156] The withdrawal was a self-defeating blunder; the USSR had committed a great amount of resources to the PRC for ten years but suddenly gave up its entire institutional and human leverage over the PRC.[157]

The sudden Soviet announcement to withdraw all specialists is to this day a convenient pretext for the PRC to deflect blame for the self-induced economic collapse. A recent government publication, for example, claims that the withdrawal meant that the Soviet government "scrapped . . . 600 contracts" and "stop[ped] dispatching more than 900 [additional] experts." It further alleges that Moscow "stopped supplying important equipment urgently needed in China's construction."[158] Statements from the time even blamed the USSR for the collapse of China's economy and for the famines,[159] or claimed that the Soviet Union demanded instant repayment of debts.[160] The historical reality, however, is more complicated.

The Soviet decision to withdraw came at a time when the Chinese leadership was discussing economics at Beidaihe anyway. The Politburo had already decided to make "agriculture the first battlefront." Industrial construction, which attracted most of the Soviet assistance, lost priority.[161] Despite this decision, Mao continued to demand another steel campaign involving 70 million people to raise annual production to 22 million tons in 1960. Few shared his ideas.[162]

[153] Delyusin, "Nekotorye," 8–9.

[154] Semichastnyi, *Bespokoinoe*, 321.

[155] Anatolii Khazanov, "Politika SSSR v otnoshenii Kitaya v period pravleniya Khrushcheva," paper presented at the conference "Sino-Soviet Relations and Cold War: International Scientific Seminar," Beijing, China, October 1997, 8–9.

[156] Brezhnev, *Kitai*, 67. Taubman, "Khrushchev vs. Mao," 247.

[157] MacFarquhar, *Origins*, vol. 2, 279, 281–82. Taubman, "Khrushchev vs. Mao," 247.

[158] Xinhua, *China's Foreign Relations*, 461.

[159] "Report by Khristo Ivanov—adviser," [no date], *AMVnR*, o.20a, a.e.1085, 18–24.

[160] "Note," 12/8/1961, *PAAA-MfAA*, Abteilung Ferner Osten—Sektor China, Microfiche A 6744, 1.

[161] Xiao, *Qiusuo*, vol. 2, 637–38

[162] MacFarquhar, *Origins*, vol. 3, 11–12.

Once the Soviet letter arrived, the Chinese leadership accused the USSR of "expanding the split in ideological matters to governmental relations."[163] In its narrow sense, the charge was correct, but it was the CCP itself that had carried the split in ideological matters out of the realm of party relations into the WFTU in the first place. Nevertheless, Soviet actions had given Beijing the *moral high ground* in the debate.

Mulling over the meaning of the withdrawal for China's place in the socialist world, Mao called for greater "self-reliance."[164] Nevertheless, on July 31, the Chinese asked the Soviets to reconsider their decision,[165] but Chen Yi warned Chervonenko some days later that if "you want to treat us as Yugoslavia, we will not accept it."[166] Moscow notified Beijing on August 26 that it had not changed its mind.[167] It did not surprise the Chinese. Pessimistic about this matter as early as August 8, Mao had told Deng and Liu that the Soviet party was essentially split from its own people: "Ninety percent of the Soviet people are good people." Nevertheless, it would take some time for them to grasp the truth; therefore "we should brace ourselves for the next ten years." Liu agreed, arguing that "without revisionism, Leninism cannot develop." He further asserted that the initial emergence of revisionism in the USSR in the late 1930s was all Stalin's fault: "After the elimination of counterrevolutionaries, salaries rose, material incentives were introduced, [and] this created a high salary class. When a high salary class occurs, revisionism occurs as well." The lesson, Deng concluded, was to be on guard against revisionism at home.[168] Also, Mao fretted that "Khrushchev did not give us any advanced technology."[169] In the fall, a propaganda campaign downplaying Soviet contributions to China's economic construction started.[170]

Be that as it may, the Chinese comrades did not let the Soviet specialists feel their disdain for the Khrushchevite leadership. In mid-August, at an official farewell dinner in Beijing, Zhou Enlai personally thanked a group of Soviet specialists for their "contributions to construct socialism in China," and claimed to see them off only "reluctantly."[171] Yet, the Chinese side broke diplomatic secrecy by reading the July 18 letter to all

---

[163] WLX, 308, 335.

[164] Mao, "Remarks on a Telegram about the Latest Changes in the Attitude to the Chinese Embassy," July 1960, *JYMW*, vol. 9, 252.

[165] "[Note]," 7/31/1960, *AVPRF*, f.0100, o.53, d.4, p.453, 61–69.

[166] "Record of Conversation," 8/4/1960, Westad, *Brothers*, 364.

[167] "[Note]," 8/26/1960, *AVPRF*, f.0100, o.53, d.3, p.453, 2–9.

[168] WLX, 339–42.

[169] *MZDDG*, 637–38.

[170] "Reference of the Trade Representative of the USSR in the PRC," 9/22/1960, *AVPRF*, f.0100, o.53, d.24, p.457, 188–92.

[171] *ZELNP2*, 341.

Soviet specialists.[172] The action was a successful maneuver to undermine their trust in their own government,[173] but also led to Soviet diplomatic complaints.[174]

What did the changes in Beijing's assessment of Moscow mean for China? In the days after July 18, Mao reviewed China's total debt to the Soviet Union. It was 1.52 billion transfer rubles (the bookkeeping unit in the socialist barter economy), of which 0.72 billion had already been paid off. After Zhou raised the problem of how quickly the remaining sum should be repaid, Mao decided for a short-term clearing: "Because this is the money of the Soviet people, we don't want to let down the Soviet people. . . . During the time in Yan'an, we also had such difficulties, we ate hot peppers and nobody died, the current time is quite similar, we want to fasten our belts, [and] to aim to pay the money back within five years."[175] In reality, China did not pay its debts with money but with raw materials and agricultural products that were in short supply anyway.[176] Also, the PRC was under *no* legal obligation to clear its debt in five years.

It is likely that the sudden withdrawal of specialists affected a number of industrial plants,[177] but the overall negative effect was far smaller than claimed—simply because China's economy had already been broken *before* July 18. According to Chen Yi's own admission in August 1960, *not one* of the Soviet specialists had worked directly in rural production, although the collapse of agriculture had caused China's economic problems.[178] In any case, it is hard to believe that the whole Chinese economy was dependent on fourteen hundred Soviet specialists. The Chinese assertion of Moscow's supposed termination, not only of planned short-term business trips of nine hundred specialists to the PRC, but also of the delivery of important industrial equipment, seems to be incorrect as well.[179] Soviet specialists continued to arrive in China on short-term assignments together with the equipment they were supposed to assemble even *after* the completion of the withdrawal in late August.[180]

[172] Liu, *Chushi*, 107.

[173] Klochko, *Soviet Scientist*, 178.

[174] "Record of Conversation," 8/4/1960, Westad, *Brothers*, 361–64.

[175] WLX, 334–37. Note that Wu provided a number ten times too high. The error probably is due to translating the Western numeric system based on multiples of thousands into the Chinese system based on multiples of ten thousands. See: "Soviet-Chinese Trade Relations," 11/3/1964, *AVPRF*, f.0100, o.57, d.29, p.512, 26. Wang, *Zhonghua*, vol. 2, 256–58.

[176] Interview with Yan Mingfu, Beijing, 11/23/2000.

[177] Su, "Guanyu," 50.

[178] "Record of Conversation," 8/4/1960, Westad, *Brothers*, 360–61. Also: Semichastnyi, *Bespokoinoe*, 320.

[179] Xinhua, *China's Foreign Relations*, 461. Wang, *Zhonghua*, vol. 2, 236.

[180] "Letter from Wandel to Florin," 10/9/1960, *PAAA-MfAA*, M B Schwab, Microfiche A 17258, 2.

Soviet specialists only stopped traveling to China when the PRC uni-laterally *suspended* all remaining supply contracts on October 31, 1960. The decision stemmed from the collapse of Sino-Soviet trade in 1960 and the resulting Chinese negative balance of payments of 2 billion transfer rubles.[181] Furthermore, after the Soviet withdrawal of specialists, Beijing was also unwilling to continue the practice of delivering strategic raw materials to Moscow at discount prices. The PRC knew it could charge more on the world market.[182]

The collapse of Sino-Soviet trade in 1960 was considerable. In absolute terms, the economic expansion during the first two Great Leap Forward years led to a final peak in trade in 1959, before the rapid decrease.[183] The 1959 Sino-Soviet goods exchange agreement stipulated trade worth 7.3831 billion transfer rubles (a 20 percent increase over 1958);[184] the 1960 agreement specified another 10 percent increase to approximately 8.1 billion.[185] In reality, trade in 1960 shrank approximately 20 percent to around 5.9 billion.[186] The numbers suggest that the Chinese negative balance of payment of 2 billion transfer rubles largely stemmed from China's inability to fulfill its trade obligations in 1960.

The Chinese side used the bad 1960 harvest and the illegal Soviet with-drawal as excuses for its own equally illegal abrogation of trade obli-gations and existing industrial orders. On October 31, Foreign Trade Minister Ye Jizhuang notified the Soviet embassy that existing Chinese deliveries of food and minerals and Chinese orders for Soviet civilian and military goods would be suspended, and that the 2 billion trade debt would be repaid in five years.[187] Seven weeks later, the Soviet for-eign trade ministry dismissed the Chinese excuse that invoked the Soviet withdrawal as a reason for the termination of trade agreements with the counterclaim that the PRC had failed to fulfill its trade obligations start-ing as early as 1959. Moscow also reminded Beijing that the 1960 trade agreement stipulated the clearing of trade debt within three months, but indicated willingness to talk about rescheduling.[188] The Chinese instan-taneously replied that article 33 of the trade agreement specified that the

[181] Wang, *Zhonghua*, vol. 2, 241.

[182] Zhang, *Economic Cold War*, 214, 257.

[183] Zhang, *Economic Cold War*, 282.

[184] "Soviet-Chinese Relations (Reference)," 2/13/1961, *AVPRF*, f.0100, o.54, d.27, p.470, 30.

[185] *CB* 619, 21.

[186] Wang, *Zhonghua*, vol. 2, 243. Zhang, *Economic Cold War*, 282.

[187] Wang, *Zhonghua*, vol. 2, 240–41. "Record of Conversation," 10/31/1960," *AVPRF*, f.0100, o.53, d.9, p.454, 70–81.

[188] Wang, *Zhonghua*, vol. 2, 241. "[Note]," 12/17/1960, *AVPRF*, f.0100, o.53, d.6, p.453, 58–63.

three-month deadline did not apply to "causes beyond human power"—a good argument, provided one accepted the fiction that this article applied to the ruinous Great Leap Forward policies.[189] The two sides eventually rescheduled the debt in early 1961.[190]

China's new emphasis on self-reliance meant a shrinking of Sino-Soviet trade and a simultaneous diversification of its international trading patterns. Since late 1958, the Chinese side had disapproved of Soviet pricing policies and the Soviet reluctance to provide advanced military technology.[191] The withdrawal of the specialists facilitated Beijing's decision to reorient its trade "away from the socialist camp toward the 'capitalist' camp," as Chen Yi frankly told Chervonenko in October.[192] Two months before, Beijing had proposed trade talks to Tokyo paired with an offer of "flexibility" over Japan's support of Taiwan.[193] Until 1965, the PRC established trade links with several West European countries and bought sixty-five complete sets of industrial enterprises in the capitalist world.[194]

Moscow was keenly aware of Beijing's changes in international trade patterns. Already in September 1960, as an internal report complained, the Chinese side had embarked on a propaganda campaign "degrading the significance of Soviet aid to China."[195] A quick review of the development of Chinese trade with the USSR, Japan, and some West European countries in the years after 1960 confirms that trade with the Soviet comrades fell sharply year by year (by 1965 it stood at one-sixth of the 1959 volume) while Chinese commerce with the class enemies generally grew in the early 1960s.[196]

BORDER PROBLEMS

In addition to open ideological conflict and the collapse of economic cooperation, border problems started to strain Sino-Soviet relations in 1960. The Sino-Indian border conflict in 1959 had alerted the Chinese

[189] Wang, *Zhonghua*, vol. 2, 241.

[190] "Note on a Talk with Chervonenko on March 3," 3/10/1961, *SAPMO-BArch*, DY 30/IV 2/20/123, 1–6. Liu, *Chushi*, 128. MacFarquhar, *Origins*, vol. 3, 121. Wang, *Zhonghua*, vol. 2, 242. Xiao, *Qiusuo*, vol. 2, 917. Zhang, *Economic Cold War*, 282.

[191] Zhang, *Economic Cold War*, 214–16, 232.

[192] "Record of Conversation with Chen Yi," 10/26/1960, *AVPRF*, f.0100, o.53, d.9, p.454, 62.

[193] Xiao, *Qiusuo*, vol. 2, 919.

[194] Xiao, *Qiusuo*, vol. 2, 919.

[195] "Reference of the Trade Representative of the USSR in the PRC," 9/22/1960, *AVPRF*, f.0100, o.53, d.24, p.457, 188–92.

[196] Zhang, *Economic Cold War*, 282, 289–93.

government to the necessity of settling the exact border lines with its many neighbors. From 1960 to 1963, the PRC resolved border disputes with Outer Mongolia, Burma, Nepal, Afghanistan, and Pakistan on the basis of mutual compromises. Apart from the maritime border with Vietnam, only the border problems with China's largest neighbors—India and the USSR—remained unresolved.[197]

As long as Sino-Soviet relations had remained amicable during the 1950s, the problem of their unsettled borders was politically negligible. In the eastern sector (from North Korea to Mongolia) disagreements revolved around the precise course—including some islands—of the ever-changing fairways of the Amur, Ussuri, and Argun rivers. In the western sector (from Mongolia to Afghanistan), the border line was running undemarcated through desert terrain and the Tianshan range.[198]

In an April 28 press conference in Katmandu (Nepal), Zhou declared that there were some disagreements between Chinese and Soviet maps.[199] Two months later, one hundred Chinese cattle breeders with fifteen thousand animals crossed the border near the Buz Aigyr pass (Tianshan) into Soviet Kyrgyztan. Soviet border guards asked them to leave, but the breeders refused because "the chairman of their people's commune" had ordered them to let cattle graze there.[200] They stayed into the winter, supplied by the Soviets with the necessary food.[201] Little wonder that, from August 17 to October 29, both sides staked out their claims on the territory near Buz Aigyr.[202]

The diplomatic showdown occurred on November 6. Chervonenko lodged a complaint with Vice-Foreign Minister Zeng Yongquan rejecting an earlier note by the Chinese side on the illegal withdrawal of the specialists in the summer. Zeng threw a fit in Maoist hysteria, accusing Moscow of following a "general plan" to pressure China, starting with the cessation of the *Friendship (Druzhba)* journal, Soviet complaints about

---

[197] Hinton, "China," 353.

[198] W. A. Douglas Jackson, *Russo-Chinese Borderlands*, rev. ed. (New York: Norstrand, 1968). Michael Strupp, *Chinas Grenzen mit Birma und der Sowjetunion* (Hamburg: Institut für Asienkunde, 1987), 221–378. An Tai Sung, *Sino-Soviet Territorial Dispute* (Philadelphia: Westminster, 1973), 25–57. Wu Cheng-Chi, *Über die Ursprünge des Chinesisch-Sowjetischen Grenzkonfliktes* (Bochum: Brockmeyer, 1988).

[199] Ginsburgs, *Territorial Dispute*, 12.

[200] "Basic Events in Soviet-Chinese Relations in 1960," 12/17/1960, *AVPRF*, f.0100, o.53, d.24, p.457, 264. Borisov, *Soviet-Chinese Relations*, 221.

[201] George Ginsburgs et al., *Sino-Soviet Territorial Dispute, 1949–1964* (New York: Praeger, 1978), 13.

[202] Dangdai, *Waijiao*, 122. Wang, *Zhonghua*, vol. 2, 237, 254. Li Danhui, "1969nian ZhongSu bianjie chongtu," *Dangdai Zhongguo shi yanjiu* 1996/3, 42. *AVPRF*, f.0100, o.53, d.3, p.453, 13–22; o.53, d.4, p.453, 118–20, 138–43; o.53, d.24, p.457, 270.

the Chinese embassy distributing propaganda material in the USSR, the Soviet withdrawal of the specialists, and the Soviet Union's "abnormal steps in trade with China," only to end with the charge that the "Soviet side had [also] staged border incidents." The ambassador reminded the vice–foreign minister that these issues should be addressed in the "interests of our friendship."[203]

The Buz Aigyr episode was only a prelude. Although the documentary evidence is inconclusive, the timing of the incident (late June) suggests a link to the ongoing deterioration of Sino-Soviet relations. Given the pattern of Chinese-provoked border incidents in 1960 and afterward, it is possible that it was also Beijing's attempt to bring the territorial dispute to Moscow's attention. The row intensified parallel to the Sino-Soviet negotiations in the run-up to the Moscow Meeting in late summer and early fall (see immediately below) and disappeared as soon as an agreement between the CPSU and CCP on ideological matters was impending at the meeting in the Soviet capital. Regardless, both sides had to prepare for future confrontations over the border issue. The diplomatic clash over Buz Aigyr was a turning point for Mao, who subsequently began to shift China's defense focus away "from the southwest to the north."[204]

MOSCOW MEETING

Despite all the conflict, both the CCP and the CPSU realized that they had to find at least a minimal common position at the Moscow Meeting in November. The final breakdown of the rapprochement with the United States in the early fall induced the USSR to seek a modus vivendi with the PRC. The ultimate collapse of the Great Leap Forward in early November undercut the radical positions China had taken up.

In late summer 1960, the Soviet and the Chinese comrades played their last cards from the Bucharest meeting. In mid-August, a CPSU circular to all fraternal parties condemned Chinese methods since the Lenin Polemics and public Chinese attempts to portray the majority opinions expressed in Bucharest as the splittist ideas of "comrade Khrushchev" alone.[205] The Chinese eventually replied to the sixty-eight-page CPSU condemnation at the Bucharest Meeting—in double length—in early September. A group of Chinese theoreticians had worked on it for two months, with Mao reviewing drafts frequently. It was a long-winded defense, complaining

---

[203] "Record of Conversation," 11/6/1960, *AVPRF*, f.0100, o.53, d.9, p.454, 91–97.

[204] Li Danhui, "ZhongSu guanxi yu Zhongguo de yuanYue kangMei," *Dangdai Zhongguo shi yanjiu* 1998/3, 115.

[205] "CPSU CC to CCP CC," 8/13/1960, *SAPMO-BArch*, DY 30/3605, 44–54.

about "the surprise attack" at Bucharest, and asserting that the Chinese revolution—especially its struggle against imperialism—was the correct model for the socialist camp.[206] Thus, the CCP explicitly laid a claim to a leading role in the history of the communist world.

By early August, however, the Chinese and the Soviets came to realize that they had to pull back from confrontation. Already on the first, Chen Yi proclaimed that U.S. imperialism, not Soviet revisionism, was still the main enemy.[207] Some days later, he told Chervonenko that "it was impossible even to think that our countries could be unfriendly."[208] The Chairman himself sent Liu Shaoqi to the Soviet ambassador to sound out what areas were still open to cooperation, especially in defense and military production.[209] The new Chinese flexibility was also apparent in Liu Ningyi's speeches in mid-August in Japan during commemoration proceedings of the fifteenth anniversary of the A-bomb droppings. In line with China's new trade requirements, Liu claimed that "the Chinese people consistently advocated peaceful coexistence; in relations with western countries, and also with the USA." The change of tone from his radical propaganda speeches at the WFTU meeting was so startling that Andropov personally drew Khrushchev's attention to it.[210]

The initial impetus for the Sino-Soviet rapprochement was North Vietnamese mediation. Ho Chi Minh did not agree to de-Stalinization and, given U.S. support for South Vietnam, the Soviet policy of peaceful coexistence. Hanoi, however, was also not willing to follow in Beijing's footprints. Ho understood that the DRV was dependent on cooperation between the USSR and the PRC in the Vietnamese conflict.[211]

Arriving at Beidaihe on August 8, Ho proposed to Mao to use his impending visit to Khrushchev "to run an errand" for the Chinese comrades. He "urged reconciliation" and unity against "the main enemy, American imperialism." Early the next morning, the two leaders thrashed out Ho's mission to Moscow while splashing in the Bo Hai Gulf.[212] But Mao still wondered why Sino-Soviet relations had gone amiss that year: "Khrushchev can cooperate with America, England and France. He can cooperate with India and Indonesia. He can even cooperate with Yugoslavia, but only with China is it impossible on the grounds that we have divergent

---

[206] WLX, 314, 351–57. "Response of the CCP CC to the Information of the CPSU CC," 9/10/1960, SAPMO-BArch, DY 30/3604, 18–153.

[207] MacFarquhar, Origins, vol. 2, 283.

[208] "Record of Conversation," 8/4/1960, Westad, Brothers, 362.

[209] Westad, "Introduction," 26.

[210] Quoted in: Prozumenshikov, "1960," 7.

[211] Gaiduk, Confronting, 105–17. "Telegram No. 165 from Claudius to Ulbricht and Schwab," 8/24/1960, SAPMO-BArch, DY 30/3667, 13–17.

[212] WLX, 344–49.

opinions."[213] Mao did not ask the reverse question: Why could *he* not cooperate with everybody else?

Immediately after his arrival in Moscow, Ho continued his flight to Yalta to see Khrushchev. Although the Soviet leader claimed that he had no differences with Mao about the need to fight against imperialism, he nevertheless insisted that Sino-Soviet ideological differences were numerous and mainly about China's internal policies.[214] When Ho passed through Beijing on his way home, this was precisely what he reported to Mao: "The Soviet side said that since 1958 in many affairs, China . . . had not talked with the Soviet Union. For example, during the Hundred-Flowers Campaign, the people's communes, the Great Leap Forward." Ho added that Khrushchev hoped for a success during the Moscow Meeting but said that it depended on the "Chinese attitude." Mao replied: "We will not relax."[215]

The North Vietnamese mediation nevertheless showed quick results. The Soviet comrades approached their Chinese brethren with two letters on August 15. One was the circular referred to above, but the other proposed a meeting between the two parties in order to start preparations for the planned Moscow Meeting.[216] The Chinese responded in kind. On September 10, they presented the Soviet embassy with the above-mentioned long reply together with a note that a CCP delegation would be ready to leave for negotiations with the CPSU in five days.[217] Both sides had incentives, mounting gradually during the fall, to pull back from the brink.

Soviet relations with the United States after the abortive Paris Summit were in a deep freeze. Khrushchev still could not swallow his anger. Instead, he put Francis Gary Powers on a public trial that was covered in *Pravda* in detail.[218] This unconstructive signal came right before his visit to New York to attend the fifteenth session of the United Nations General Assembly.

Khrushchev's second and last visit to the United States in early fall underscored the poor condition of relations. He had reasoned that his presence at the U.N. would force Eisenhower to attend as well and meet with him, but the atmosphere was poisoned from the very beginning.[219] Even before his arrival, Hungarian Americans picketed the residence of the Soviet U.N. delegation in Manhattan with placards such as "Welcome

[213] Fourth quote in: David Wolff, "In Memoriam," *CWIHP Bulletin* 10, 149.

[214] Delyusin, "Nekotorye," 4.

[215] WLX, 349–51.

[216] "Record of Conversation with Zhou Enlai," 8/15/1950, *AVPRF*, f.0100, o.53, d.8, p.454, 224–28.

[217] "Record of Conversation with Deng Xiaoping," 9/12/1960, *AVPRF*, f.0100, o.53, d.9, p.454, 22–24. WLX, 351, 357. ZELNP2, 341. Liu, *Chushi*, 113.

[218] *Pravda*, 8/18/1960, 2, and the following issues.

[219] Taubman, *Khrushchev*, 472.

Khrushchev? Then Why Not Heil Hitler."[220] The International Long-shoremen's Association vowed not to dock the ship *Baltika*, on which Khrushchev was to arrive on September 19.[221] The tugboat escorting the Soviet vessel into the harbor carried seventy union members holding up a big-lettered placard with the words: "Khrushchev, Butcher of Hungarian People."[222] Judging from his own experiences, Khrushchev was convinced that these demonstrations were government-sponsored.[223]

Tensions translated into the United Nations General Assembly as well. Even though Eisenhower refused to meet Khrushchev, he delivered a speech on September 22 on peace and disarmament. The Soviet leader listened in "stony silence," but later hinted that he would accept an invitation—to no avail.[224] Two days later, Khrushchev followed up with his own speech, rambling as usual, and four times longer, complaining about continued U.S. spy flights, calling for peaceful coexistence, and insisting on complete and rapid disarmament.[225] In a calculated attempt to be "not less anti-imperialist than the Chinese," he also made himself appear the champion of national liberation, claiming that the "Soviet Union has no colonies."[226] Several days later, Polish-American exile groups replied with a demonstration of 105,000 people, carrying placards such as "Poland is still in chains."[227]

After that, Khrushchev changed his tactics from statesmanship to rough play. During the September 29 speech of U.K. Prime Minister Harold Macmillan, Khrushchev yelled while pounding his desk: "You sent your planes over our territory, you are guilty of aggression."[228] Finally, when the Filipino delegation took up Khrushchev's call for immediate decolonization on October 12, remarking that past U.S. imperialism in the Philippines had been much more benign than present Soviet colonialism in East Europe, Khrushchev once more lost his temper, "pulled off his right shoe, stood up and brandished the shoe at the Philippine delegate on the other side of the hall. He then banged the shoe on his desk."[229]

---

[220] *NYT*, 9/12/1960, 4.

[221] *NYT*, 9/15/1960, 1, 12.

[222] *NYT*, 9/19/1960, 1, 15.

[223] Khrushchev, *Testament*, 466.

[224] *NYT*, 9/23/1960, 14.

[225] Nikita Khrushchev, "Disarmament, Colonialism, and Other International Problems," 9/23/1960, Khrushchev, *Khrushchev in New York* (New York: Crosscurrents, 1960), 11–57.

[226] Troyanovskii, *Cherez*, 229 (first quote). Khrushchev, "Disarmament, . . . ," 31 (second quote).

[227] *NYT*, 10/3/1960, 22.

[228] Quoted in: Taubman, *Khrushchev*, 475–76. *NYT*, 9/30/1960, 26.

[229] *NYT*, 10/6/1960, 1, 17; 10/13/1960, 1, 14 (quote).

As in previous years, the Soviet U.N. delegation also brought up the question of Chinese representation. In an apparent attempt to curry favor with China before the impending Moscow talks, Khrushchev pompously warned that the further exclusion of the PRC from the United Nations would lead to a "terrible" war.[230] His bravado brought neither success nor Chinese backing. Beijing's press was tight-lipped about his trip to New York.[231] Mao happily noted that all of Khrushchev's proposals at the U.N. had "suffered a crushing defeat."[232]

The trip provided an important impetus for Moscow to improve relations with Beijing. Troyanovskii recollected the "conditioned reflex" that afflicted the Kremlin at the time. When relations had been bad with the Chinese comrades in late 1959, Khrushchev had pressed for the Paris Summit. Conversely, in mid-October 1960 it was a "suitable time for new attempts to arrange things with Beijing."[233]

Simultaneously, the Chinese realized as well that they had overstretched their political and ideological credibility. Mao's Great Leap Forward radicalism was standing on a rapidly crumbling pair of clay feet. On August 16, Li Fuchun gave the first public hints of a retreat.[234] A week later, Zhou admitted to Chervonenko that the PRC was suffering under "many shortcomings," but he was still not willing to disclose the famines.[235] By September 30, Zhou eventually accepted Li Fuchun's warning from the Beidaihe meeting that the Chinese economy had to adjust. Even Mao, who had continued to promote another steel drive, now listened to advice urging drastic measures in agriculture.[236] The food crisis deteriorated so quickly in mid-October that the Chinese leadership sent out a directive to the provinces for the urgent collection of the harvest.[237] A week later, Chen Yun warned of a renewed famine in the coming winter.[238] By the end of the month, while Mao, Liu, and Deng were absorbed in preparations for the Moscow Meeting, Zhou regained operational control over

---

[230] Nikita Khrushchev, "Concerning Representation of the PRC in the United Nations," 10/1/1960, Khrushchev, *Khrushchev in New York*, 116–26.

[231] *NYT*, 9/26/1960, 15; 9/271960, 27; 9/30/1960, 1, 3; 10/9/1960, 1; 10/10/1960, 30.

[232] Mao, "Letter to Liu Shaoqi, Zhou Enlai, Zhu De," 10/14/1960, *JYMW*, vol. 9, 310–11.

[233] Troyanovskii, *Cherez*, 231–32.

[234] Li Fuchun, "March On! Hold High the Red Flag of the General Line," 8/16/1960, Hinton, *People's Republic*, vol. 2, 859–69.

[235] "Record of Conversation with Zhu De and Zhou Enlai," 8/23/1960, *AVPRF*, f.0100, o.53, d.8, p.454, 231–38.

[236] MacFarquhar, *Origins*, vol. 3, 11–12.

[237] "Directive of the CCP CC and the State Council on Launching of a Vigorous Campaign for Collection and Purchase of Autumn Farm Products," 10/14/1960, Union Research Institute, ed., *Documents of Chinese Communist Central Committee, September 1956 to April 1969* (Hong Kong: Union Research Institute, 1971), 681–83.

[238] Xiao, *Qiusuo*, vol. 2, 702.

agriculture. On November 3, the CCP CC sent out an emergency directive on rural work which legalized private plots, reduced the responsibilities and control of the people's communes, and called for the work brigade as the primary production unit. It was the de facto (but not legal) end of the communes.[239] With that the multiyear recovery that Zhang Wentian had forecast at Lushan began.

After a whole range of events had started to undercut the foundations for their antagonistic policies, the CPSU and the CCP were finally ready to talk from September 17 to 22 in Moscow. The Chinese delegation headed by Deng Xiaoping dwelled on alleged Soviet abuses and mistakes of the past, while the Soviet hosts under Suslov warned that the current, unconstructive Chinese attitude would only lead to a rebuke by the so-called Editorial Board, which was the framework for the next round of talks. Both bluffed so high that they were unable to move even an inch closer to each other.[240] Apparently, the need for a compromise was not yet pressing enough.

The two parties had two weeks to rethink their positions until the Editorial Board, consisting of the twelve ruling parties and the fourteen largest parties outside the socialist world, convened on October 1. The CPSU decided to prepare a draft statement since it wanted to commit the CCP to the written word. Its warning of the dangers of nationalism was clearly aimed at the CCP.[241] Mao advised his delegation to follow a hardline, convinced that the Soviets would buckle because they did not want a split.[242] The talks of the Editorial Board were as bitter as the Sino-Soviet negotiations before. For a while, partial agreements seemed to be possible until Khrushchev returned from New York.[243] The Soviet leader scolded Suslov for making "too many concessions 'during the Chinese scourge.'"[244] Also, the Soviet delegation had realized that the Chinese negotiation strategy was "offensive-defensive," designed to preserve as much of the Chinese position as possible. While Deng Xiaoping demanded that the Great Leap Forward be included as an integral part

---

[239] Text in: "Memorandum by Stefan Stoev," 11/3/1962, *AMVnR*, o.18p, a.e.540, 50–54. Also: MacFarquhar, *Origins*, vol. 2, 324–25.

[240] For Soviet versions: "Short Summary of the Negotiations between a Delegation of the CPSU and a Delegation of the CCP," 9/17–22/1960, *SAPMO-BArch*, DY 30/3605, 108–39. Delyusin, "Guanyu," 103. Delyusin, "Nekotorye," 8, 10. For Chinese versions: WLX, 357–64. Liu, *Chushi*, 168. Wu, *Huiyi*, 343.

[241] Delyusin, "Guanyu," 103–4.

[242] WLX, 364–65.

[243] WLX, 365–67. Also: "Records of the Session of the Editorial Board in Moscow," [no date], *AAN*, KC PZPR, XI A/8, 2–78.

[244] Troyanovskii, *Cherez*, 232 (quote). Also: "Report by Suslov: On the Results of the Meeting of the Chairmen of the Communist and Workers' Parties," 1/18/[1961], *RGANI*, f.2, o.1, d.535, 136a–137.

of the "collective experience of socialist construction," some members of the Chinese delegation "in private talks with Soviet staff" hinted that it had been a "failure." In the end, both sides did not want to break, and agreed to continue negotiating at the Moscow Meeting in November.[245]

When the CCP delegation left Beijing on November 5 for Moscow, the Great Leap Forward was comatose. The huge Chinese mission, headed by Liu Shaoqi and Deng Xiaoping, included Kang Sheng, Lu Dingyi, Peng Zhen, as well as CC personnel and an army of translators. It was housed in three state guesthouses on the Lenin Hills. Because the Chinese side feared Soviet bugging, the most important delegation members and all internal meetings were moved to the nearby embassy.[246]

On November 6, after the review of the obligatory military parade on Red Square, the CPSU provided a 127-page letter to the CCP summarizing Soviet positions.[247] The CPSU had realized that its tactics at Bucharest had been successful, and so this letter was again an attempt to frame the debate from the very beginning.[248] The Chinese side immediately understood that it "had to expect a rain storm,"[249] but knew to protect itself. Liu Shaoqi instructed Ambassador Liu Xiao to lobby other delegations,[250] and, during a courtesy call to Khrushchev, told the Soviet leader that a satisfying outcome on the conference would clear the way for a state visit by him afterward.[251] Yet, the Chinese delegation must have been aware that theirs was an uphill battle; the Albanians warned them that the Soviets and East Europeans were organizing "revolving attacks."[252]

Armed with these precautions, Deng Xiaoping and Peng Zhen received Suslov, Kozlov and Mikoyan at the Chinese embassy on November 9. The Soviets had decided to take the initiative and relax relations before the actual start of the conference,[253] but the CCP delegation was not convinced. Mikoyan's proposal to talk about economic aid and the return to the PRC of the specialists seemed to be another "nasty" Soviet trick.[254]

The official proceedings started on November 10. Khrushchev delivered the opening speech outlining Soviet points of view, and Suslov followed with a presentation on the work of the Editorial Board. While

---

[245] Delyusin, "Nekotorye," 15–16.

[246] WLX, 358, 370–71.

[247] "Letter of the CPSU CC to CCP CC," 11/5/1960, *SAPMO-BArch*, DY 30/3605, 160–300. WLX, 373.

[248] Prozumenshikov, "1960," 15. WLX, 374.

[249] WLX, 374.

[250] Liu, *Chushi*, 122–23.

[251] WLX, 372–74.

[252] Hoxha, *Superpowers*, 29–30. Hoxha, *Selected Works*, vol. 3, 72–83.

[253] "Report by Suslov . . . ," *RGANI*, f.2, o.1, d.535, 137a–138.

[254] WLX, 376–77.

neither report was excessively critical of or even belligerent toward Chinese positions,[255] the CCP delegation nevertheless discovered points that deviated from Chinese orthodoxy, interpreted them as attacks on the CCP, and thus decided to "raise the tune."[256] Deng's reply speech the following day dwelled on past Soviet mistakes and attacks on the CCP, but once more stressed the leading role of the CPSU in the international communist movement.[257]

Deng's words provoked passionate reactions. The Frenchman Maurice Thorez, for example, disputed China's claimed entitlement to spread its particular viewpoints after they had already been rejected by the vast majority of the parties.[258] But there was also a supporting voice. The Albanian party leader Enver Hoxha on November 16 attacked Khrushchev for perfidy, asserting that "while the rats could eat in the Soviet Union, the Albanian people were starving to death, because the leadership of the Albanian Labor Party had not bent to the will of the Soviet leadership."[259] Gomułka found the speech disgusting,[260] and the Spanish Civil War hero Dolores Ibárruri pointed out that "Hoxha was like a dog who bites the hand that feeds it."[261] This verbal misstep had come despite negotiations initiated by the Soviet leader some days earlier. During those meetings, Hoxha and his deputy Mehmet Shehu repeatedly yelled at Khrushchev, who remained uncharacteristically calm and composed.[262]

It was clear that the majority of parties did not share the ideological platform of the CCP. The East Europeans—save the Albanians—supported the Soviets, and most nonruling parties rejected China's dismissal of peaceful evolution because violent insurrections designed to seize power in their countries, as demanded by the Chinese comrades,

[255] "Speech by Khrushchev at the Meeting of the Communist and Workers' Parties," 11/10/1960, *SAPMO-BArch*, DY 30/J IV 2/201/636, 1–89. "Report to the Meeting of the Representatives of the Communist and Workers' Parties on the Draft Declaration Prepared by the Editorial Board," [no date], *SAPMO-BArch*, DY 30/J IV 2/201/638, 1–33. MacFarquhar, *Origins*, vol. 2, 286. Chinese sources claim Khrushchev's speech was a sharp attack, while they exempted Suslov's presentation from criticism: Liu, *Chushi,* 114–16. WLX, 377–80.

[256] WLX, 380.

[257] "Speech by Deng Xiaoping," 11/14/1960, *SAPMO-BArch*, DY 30/J IV 2/201/639, 1–93. MacFarquhar, *Origins*, vol. 2, 286–87.

[258] MacFarquhar, *Origins*, vol. 2, 287–89.

[259] "Albanian Party of Labor: Comrade Enver Hoxha (Excerpts)," [11/16/1960], *SAPMO-BArch*, DY 30/J IV 2/201/639, 19–20. MacFarquhar, *Origins*, vol. 3, 125.

[260] MacFarquhar, *Origins*, vol. 2, 288.

[261] Khrushchev, *Khrushchev Remembers*, 476.

[262] "Notes of a talk between the Delegation of the CPSU CC and the APL CC, which took place on November 12, 1960 in the CPSU CC," *SAPMO-BArch*, DY 30/J IV 2/201/642, 1–25.

were a sure recipe for political suicide.[263] Realizing that two-thirds of the delegations opposed its views, the CCP delegation decided on a two-pronged approach: to work more closely with the other "leftist delegations" and to ask Beijing to approve the strategy of actively wooing the middle-roaders.[264]

The Chinese delegation concluded that Khrushchev started to soften up once a Hungarian-Soviet proposal on November 21 to institute majority rule in decision making had failed to garner enough support.[265] Thus it decided that Deng's second speech the next day should also be "temperate."[266] The reduced fervor in Chinese opinions eased the worries of some parties about a possible split, but agreement remained elusive.[267] Moreover, discord seemed to run through the Chinese side. In internal debates, Liu suggested repeating the Bucharest method, signing a Soviet-sponsored statement, and issuing a dissenting opinion. But Mao in Beijing demanded a fight to the brink.[268]

The North Vietnamese decided to initiate mediation by themselves on November 25.[269] The CCP delegation agreed to meet its CPSU counterpart, but decided to play hardball during Mikoyan's and Kozlov's visit to Liu Shaoqi, Deng Xiaoping and Peng Zhen.[270] The next day, Ho again urged the Chinese to be more flexible, and on November 28, was able to move the CPSU to make one concession.[271] The following night, Ho pleaded once more with the CCP delegation to make some steps toward an agreement. The Vietnamese leader did not know that by then Beijing had already instructed its delegation in Moscow to make significant concessions. Masking China's own ideological vulnerability as concern for the unity of the communist movement, Mao had explained to his own delegation that many parties were not mentally prepared for a split and thus needed a unified platform to prepare for the struggle against Soviet revisionism. Still, the Chairman demanded that his delegation maintain a minimum position: the final statement must not include vocabulary endorsing Khrushchev's Secret Speech, nor a condemnation of (Chinese) factionalism and a censure of (Chinese) national communism.[272] The

---

[263] MacFarquhar, *Origins*, vol. 2, 286, 289.

[264] WLX, 385, 387–88.

[265] WLX, 389–90.

[266] WLX, 394–96. For the speech: "Comr. Deng Xiaoping (2nd speech)," [no date], *SAPMO-BArch*, DY 30/J IV 2/201/641, 1–16.

[267] WLX, 396–397.

[268] MacFarquhar, *Origins*, vol. 2, 289–90. Liu, *Chushi*, 115, 117.

[269] WLX, 398, 400–401. "Report by Suslov . . . ," *RGANI*, f.2, o.1, d.535, 141.

[270] WLX, 398–400.

[271] WLX, 402–5.

[272] WLX, 405–10.

following day, Peng and Kozlov met and quickly found common ground. The final text, however, showed that Peng had to make another concession: the Moscow Statement did endorse the decisions of the twentieth CPSU congress.[273] Deng and Suslov also agreed to suspend all unfriendly propaganda.[274]

After the Moscow Meeting, Liu stayed on for the state visit, which included a trip to Leningrad, to Minsk, back to Moscow, to Omsk, and to Irkutsk. The Chinese noted how stunned the Leningraders were to see Liu Shaoqi and Leonid Brezhnev, the president of the Supreme Soviet, celebrating unity after they had been fed with anti-Chinese propaganda.[275] Yet, the atmosphere was not euphoric. On the night train to Minsk, Brezhnev bluntly told Liu that the CPSU had never supported the people's communes because similar rural organizations had not worked in the USSR. Liu, who knew that Zhou had just ordered the de facto end of the communes, meekly replied that they had been a "temporary experiment."[276] But he had his glorious moment too. At a mass rally in Moscow, he talked about how his visit to the Soviet Union in the early 1920s had convinced him to join the CCP. It was a carefully prepared and successful propaganda speech.[277]

The Moscow Statement was a cosmetic truce. Afterward, both sides claimed that their positions had been confirmed, and neither felt bound to it. Khrushchev did not wish to be restrained, and Mao did not change his opinions about Soviet revisionism. After a temporary improvement of relations, propaganda quickly picked up again.[278] The CCP internally considered the Moscow truce "temporary"—an assessment that a KGB-intercepted directive from Beijing to the Chinese embassy confirmed.[279] The Soviet foreign ministry continued to compile lists of Chinese anti-Soviet statements.[280]

With the Moscow Meeting, 1960 ended on an upbeat note. During the course of that year, however, Sino-Soviet relations suffered great and

[273] WLX, 410–413. "Report by Suslov . . .," *RGANI*, f.2, o.1, d.535, 141.

[274] Liu, *Chushi,* 116–17. WLX, 428–29.

[275] WLX, 430–32.

[276] "Short Record of Conversation," 12/4/1960, *AVPRF*, f.0100, o.53, d.6, p.453, 41–53.

[277] *Pravda,* 12/8/1960, 2. Liu, *Chushi,* 125–26.

[278] Xiao, *Qiusuo,* vol. 2, 919. Troyanovskii, *Cherez,* 348–49. Liu, *Chushi,* 127. Ding, "Huigu," 25.

[279] WLX, 445. "Material on China," [no date], *Rossiiskii Gosudarstvennyi Arkhiv Sotsialno-politicheskoi Istorii [RGASPI],* f.522, o.3, d.12, 169–72.

[280] "Statements by Leaders of the PRC on Important Questions of Foreign Policy," 12/9/1960, *AVPRF*, f.0100, o.53, d.24, p.457, 235–42.

irreversible damage. Chinese provocations, based on Mao's radical vision of international politics that he had already formulated by late 1959, fueled the worsening of the relationship. Following the contentious WAPA meeting in February, Mao set out to teach the Soviet comrades a lesson in ideology, despite the fact that the radicalism in international relations that the Lenin Polemics were preaching stood in stark contrast to the tragedy Mao's radicalism had caused at home. The U-2 downing seduced the Chinese comrades to push their extreme plank even further at the WFTU meeting in early June. Eventually, Chinese provocations forced Khrushchev to respond lest he look weak. As with his reaction to the U-2 Incident, the Soviet leader overreacted and provoked a near-split with the Chinese at Bucharest. Irritated by Chinese ideological attacks, he decided to withdraw the Soviet specialists quickly.

The chasm these developments produced was difficult to bridge. The withdrawal of the Soviet specialists provided the Chinese with a pretext for reducing economic relations, which had already been strained by the economic failures of the Great Leap Forward. The second Moscow Meeting could not dispel the mutual mistrust; the ideological compromise it produced was empty. Both sides needed the semblance of unity once the bases for their opposite policies—rapprochement with the United States, on the one side, and the Great Leap Forward, on the other—had collapsed. Yet, the political misfortune of the CCP was greater in late 1960, and so it had to make more concessions to the CPSU than vice-versa.

The Moscow compromise did not address any of the real issues between the two sides. While Mao's radicalism in 1959 had been mostly instrumental, it was to a much greater degree genuine, though still misguided, in 1960. Whereas he still could not admit fully to the failures of the Great Leap Forward, he sincerely believed that peaceful coexistence was a mistake, given the inevitable fall of capitalism, as forecast by Marx, Lenin, and Stalin. Moscow's replies to Beijing's ideologically supercharged provocations throughout 1960 were both ideologically halfhearted and politically clumsy. In the end, neither side was able to convince the other because both spoke different languages. While Mao insisted on ideological correctness regardless of its political utility, Khrushchev was firm in his belief in the use of sheer power without principle.

For Khrushchev, 1960 was a turning point in his career. His dismissal of Mao as a pair of old galoshes in February was too much, even for some Soviet comrades.[281] Mikoyan and Troyanovskii in retrospect also chided the Soviet leader for his unnecessarily unconstructive behavior in Paris after the U-2 Incident.[282] Khrushchev's second use of shoe diplomacy at

[281] Grishin, *Ot Khrushcheva*, 20.
[282] Mikoyan, *Tak bylo*, 605. Troyanovskii, *Cherez*, 228.

the U.N. deepened the impression in Moscow that the Soviet leader was a liability in foreign relations.[283] Khrushchev passed the peak of his power in 1960, and Mao subsequently became quite aware of that.

For Mao, the year was a watershed as well. The Chairman convinced himself that the revisionist Khrushchevite leadership in Moscow was divorced from the Soviet people. Believing that, in the end, the Soviet people would share his—supposedly correct, anti-revisionist, anti-imperialist, Marxist-Leninist—vision of the world, the Chairman decided to circumvent the Soviet comrades and try to connect with the Soviet people directly. The attempts by the embassy in Moscow to disseminate Chinese propaganda in the USSR, the PLA speeches to the Soviet military specialists, the noble treatment of the specialists before they left for the USSR, as well as Mao's decision to repay the money that allegedly belonged to the Soviet people in a show of proletarian internationalism were all part of this strategy. In a romanticization of the Yan'an period, Mao also started to believe that the Chinese historical experience should serve as the model for the entire socialist world. In his mind, the CCP was a beacon of light in a world that had forsaken the truth of Marxism-Leninism. He apparently still had not understood that his brand of Marxism-Leninism was responsible for deadly mass famines in China and that few people in the world thought it attractive enough to be aspired to. By late 1960, the cracks in the Sino-Soviet Alliance had widened significantly.

[283] Arkadii Shevchenko, *Breaking with Moscow* (New York: Knopf, 1985), 108.

CHAPTER 6

Ambiguous Truce, 1961–1962

IN EARLY 1961, Wu Han's *Hai Rui Dismissed from Office* was staged for the first time in the Chinese capital, following several works by other authors who dared to criticize, however implicitly, Mao's shortcomings. Wu's play, which depicts Hai Rui standing up for a poor peasant family against the oppressive gentry, was an indictment of Mao's personality cult and its cancerous impact on China. At the time, the Chairman paid little attention to the play or to Wu's contemporaneous historical sketch that depicted a heroic defense minister who was dismissed and eventually executed for trying to redress popular grievances. But in late 1965, when Mao set out to launch the Cultural Revolution, the ideological zealots in his entourage accused Wu of disparaging the people's communes and the purge of Peng Dehuai.[1]

The publication of literary works implicitly critical of Mao testified to the relative decline of his political fortunes, which occurred despite his attempts to exploit his personality cult as a shield against political challenges. After the collapse of his brainchild—the Great Leap Forward—in late 1960, the Chairman had lost his preeminence in decision making for the following eighteen months. Simultaneously, Liu and Deng gradually introduced pragmatic rural policies, which Mao himself considered revisionist. The rollback of the Great Leap Forward and the need for food aid also led to some relaxation in Sino-Soviet relations. Still, the period from early 1961 to the summer of 1962 produced many conflicts within the CCP leadership. These issues would eventually dominate the political discourse in China from the late summer of 1962 to the Cultural Revolution.

In 1961, the Chairman twice tried to seize on events in the socialist camp in order to radicalize the domestic political discourse: one was the Soviet-Albanian split, the other a new wave of de-Stalinization at the twenty-second CPSU congress. Indeed, moderate Chinese leaders like Liu and Deng allowed Mao a certain degree of freedom in foreign relations. On the one hand, they were occupied with domestic policies; on the other, they shared with the Chairman the experience of the Soviet

---

[1] Ping Hao, "Reassessing the Starting Point of the Cultural Revolution," *China Review International* 3/1, 66–86. Clive Ansley, *Heresy of Wu Han* (Toronto: Toronto, 1971), 13–82. Pusey, *Wu Han*, 31–35. Spence, *Search*, 570–71.

strong arm tactics of 1960. By the end of 1961, the PRC had cut its institutional contacts with the socialist camp. Yet, Mao was unable to convert his achievements in foreign policy into an advancement of his domestic agenda. After his failure to exploit the January 1962 7,000-Cadres Conference as a platform for his ideological resurgence at home, some leaders within the CCP raised questions about the value of Mao's radical foreign policy. However, the simultaneous but coincidental aggravation of long-standing ethnic conflicts in Xinjiang, linked to Soviet citizenship issues, threatened to undercut the further relaxation of tensions between Beijing and Moscow. After the ups and downs in Sino-Soviet relations since early 1961, it was not clear in which direction relations between Beijing and Moscow would develop in the summer of 1962.

SINO-SOVIET RELATIONS AFTER THE COLLAPSE OF THE GREAT LEAP FORWARD

In 1961, the PRC exported 1.355 million tons of grain (1960: 2.7204 million) and imported 5.8097 million tons (66.3 thousand), mostly from Australia, Canada, and Argentina.[2] In each year from 1962 to 1965, China net-imported between 3.9887 and 4.7493 million tons. Yet, the net-import of 4.4547 million tons in 1961 as an emergency measure could not make up for the two-year decline of 56.5 million tons of annually harvested grain from 1958 to 1960.[3] Beijing lacked the hard currency reserves needed to pay for sufficient grain imports.[4] At least another 4.68 million people died of hunger in 1961.[5]

At the ninth CCP CC plenum in January 1961, Mao conceded that the famine situation was serious.[6] The gathering decided to return to the primacy of the central government in economic planning.[7] Although the decision corroborated the criticism at Lushan eighteen months earlier, Peng Dehuai was not rehabilitated. Just as in June 1960, when Zhou had advocated concealing the true state of affairs from the Chinese people, the central party leadership again decided to be parsimonious with the truth. The 1961 communiqué deflected attention away from the famines by referring to the "serious natural calamities of two successive years."[8]

---

[2] Lardy, "Chinese Economy," 381. MacFarquhar, *Origins*, vol. 3, 26–30. Philip Short, *Mao* (New York: Holt, 1999), 507.

[3] Lardy, "Chinese Economy," 381.

[4] Xiao, *Qiusuo*, vol. 2, 759–61.

[5] Yao, "Note," 1366.

[6] Sladkovskii, *Ocherki*, 381.

[7] MacFarquhar, *Origins*, vol. 3, 12–21.

[8] *CB* 644, 1–4.

In line with his call at the plenum to "seek truth from facts,"[9] Mao sent Tian Jiaying and Chen Boda on investigation tours.[10] In Zhejiang, Tian was devastated when he encountered famished peasants.[11] He later told the Chairman that neither "natural disasters" nor lack of revolution nor "class enemies" had caused the tragedy. Mao did not want to hear that kind of truth and, instead, warned his secretary "not to split hairs." Chen's positive report on communal egalitarianism was much more to his liking.[12]

At the Guangdong central work conference in late March, the Politburo discussed Anhui party boss Zeng Xisheng's policy of redistributing commune land for family farming. Mao rejected the so-called field responsibility system since he disliked the idea of reintroducing nonsocialist forms of agriculture. Nevertheless, he at least agreed to further investigations by the central leadership in the countryside.[13] In an undercover investigation, Liu Shaoqi realized the depth of the crisis in Hunan.[14] A Hubei farmer told Zhou Enlai: "If you [continue to] fool us . . . then you also will starve to death."[15] The Chairman finally conceded the seriousness of this assessment, but still did not accept personal responsibility.[16]

Mao retreated even further at the Beijing work conference in late May. There, Liu Shaoqi asserted that the mistakes of the Great Leap Forward were 70 percent due to human errors and 30 percent due to natural disasters.[17] The Politburo thus decided to restore the status quo ante of 1958 in the countryside, although the communes continued to exist formally. The CCP leadership also approved Chen Yun's proposal to resettle 10 million urban settlers to the countryside.[18] Chastising himself for "applying Stalin indiscriminately," Mao finally acknowledged mistakes, but, as in June 1959, only to a small circle. Although the Chairman still considered the purge of Peng Dehuai at Lushan correct, he admitted that the Anti-Rightist Campaign in late 1959 had been excessive: "Now we see

[9] Li, "Study [I]," 61.

[10] "Letter to Tian Jiaying," 1/20/1961, MZDW, vol. 8, 239–40.

[11] Salisbury, New Emperors, 197.

[12] Xiao, Qiusuo, vol. 2, 719–21, 753.

[13] Li, Private Life, 375–78. MacFarquhar, Origins, vol. 3, 39–47. Becker, Ghosts, 237–38.

[14] MacFarquhar, Origins, vol. 3, 50–61. Xiao, Qiusuo, vol. 2, 733, 738–39.

[15] Xiao, Qiusuo, vol. 2, 739–41, 743–44.

[16] Xiao, Qiusuo, vol. 2, 746. Short, Mao, 511.

[17] Liu Shaoqi, "Cause of the Present Economic Difficulties and Methods for Overcoming Them," 3/31/1961, Collected Works of Liu Shao-chi, vol. 3 (Hong Kong: Union Research Institute, 1969), 315. Also: Sladkovskii, Ocherki, 387. Li, Private Life, 385. MacFarquhar, Origins, vol. 3, 63.

[18] Xiao, Qiusuo, vol. 2, 759, 762–63. Li, Private Life, 378, 385. MacFarquhar, Origins, vol. 3, 61–71, 186.

that this was a mistake, made good people, people honestly speaking the truth into 'rightist opportunists,' even into 'counterrevolutionaries.'"[19]

Mao's self-criticism never reached the lowest levels of the party. Instead, the rectification of the rural party, which he announced at the May work conference, again shifted blame downward. The new campaign led to the Socialist Education Movement (SEM) in the fall of the following year, which quickly became the object of protracted political skirmishes between Mao and his more pragmatic fellow leaders Liu and Deng, as described in chapter 9.[20]

Facing the fallout from the failed Great Leap Forward, the Chairman temporarily withdrew from daily decision making on domestic affairs.[21] Though he hardly participated in the Lushan work conference in late summer 1961, he did still complain about Liu's and Deng's economic recovery program: "All the good party members have died. Those left are utterly worthless persons."[22] But these "worthless persons" rolled back Mao's radical economic ideas. In early summer of 1961, Liu had already criticized the "disregard for the investigation and study of objective reality" that had characterized Mao's reaction to the disasters of the Great Leap Forward two years earlier.[23] In the fall, he also admitted to the Hungarian Ambassador F. Martin that the Great Leap Forward had strong similarities to Revolutionary Stalinism: "The PRC has studied socialist construction in the Soviet Union and recognized that mistakes had been made. . . . we however . . . *repeated the mistakes of the Soviet Union*."[24]

Sino-Soviet relations seemed to enter 1961 on a relaxed note. The eleventh anniversary of the alliance treaty in mid-February was celebrated congenially.[25] In a gesture of goodwill, Moscow even offered designs of the MiG-21 fighter plane, which were eventually transferred to China by late 1962.[26] In the summer of 1961, Khrushchev twice assured Chen Yi,

[19] Mao, "Summarize Experience, Educate Cadres," 6/12/1961, *MZDW*, vol. 8, 273.

[20] Lieberthal, "Great Leap," 296, 320–21. Richard Baum et al., *Ssu-ch'ing* (Berkeley: California, 1968).

[21] Lieberthal, "Great Leap," 320.

[22] Li Zhisui, *Mao Zedong siren yisheng huiyilu* (Taibei: Shibao wenhua), 366.

[23] Liu Shaoqi, "Address at the Meeting in Celebration of the 40th Anniversary of the Founding of the CCP," 6/30/1961, Liu, *Collected Works*, vol. 3, 142.

[24] "Note on a Talk with the Hungarian Ambassador, Comrade Martin," 10/30/1961, *SAPMO-BArch*, DY 30/IV 2/20/123, 1 (italics mine).

[25] *CB* 653, 9; 647, 1–40.

[26] Liu, *Chushi*, 129–33. ZELNP2, 389–90. "To Embassy of the USSR in the PRC," 2/13/1961, *AVPRF*, f.0100, o.54, d.2, p.466, 4–5. "[To the Embassy of the USSR in the PRC]," 11/30/1961, *AVPRF*, f.0100, o.54, d.2, p.466, 10–12. "Record of Conversation with Zhou Enlai," 10/8/1962, *AVPRF*, f.0100, o.55, d.7, p.480, 59–60.

who passed through Moscow between Beijing and the Laos conference in Geneva, of his desire to improve relations with the Chinese.[27]

This relaxation of Sino-Soviet relations occurred despite the simultaneous bickering of the Chinese. In early 1961, Mao had a pamphlet published with the title "Don't Fear Ghosts." It had been in the works since spring 1959 and used old legends as parables for alleged Soviet mistakes.[28] At the same time, Beijing also disinvited the chairman of the Presidium of the Supreme Soviet, Leonid Brezhnev, claiming that domestic problems would interfere with the visit. This was a surprising gesture because Mao had personally invited the Soviet leader in December. Indeed, the domestic problems of 1961 did not prevent him from receiving the King of Nepal, the Queen of Belgium, or British Field Marshal Bernard Montgomery.[29]

Sino-Soviet relations in the first half of 1961 were thus a mix of positive and negative developments. A Soviet Foreign Ministry report in May concluded that, on the one hand, the PRC had reduced anti-Soviet polemics and improved cooperation on an international level; on the other hand, it noted China's continued support for Albania, its increased trade with the West, and no end to the border squabbles with India.[30] It seemed that Beijing chose cooperation when it needed Moscow's support, but that Mao was otherwise content to keep Sino-Soviet disputes simmering.

The ambivalent state of this relationship became evident in the way the PRC approached the USSR for help in solving its rural disasters. As we saw in chapter 5, Beijing indicated acute food shortages to Moscow only by the spring of 1960 but, at that time, continued to emphasize natural disasters. In late January 1961, Liu Xiao told Chervonenko that the recent CC plenum had addressed the rural problems but that, unfortunately, they had to face the quandary that "the weather prognosis for the next months is not comforting." The Soviet ambassador failed to ask how the Chinese comrades could possibly know "the weather prognosis *for the next months*."[31] A month later, Liu Shaoqi was more forthcoming when he hinted to Chervonenko that rural problems were due to weather *and* "shortcomings and mistakes in work." While he even suggested the possibility of a famine with "terrible" human losses, Liu nevertheless hoped that the emergency grain purchases abroad and a good spring harvest

[27] Liu, *Chushi*, 128. MacFarquhar, *Origins*, vol. 3, 121.

[28] MacFarquhar, *Origins*, vol. 3, 21–22.

[29] Borisov, *Soviet-Chinese Relations*, 218. Also: "Record of Conversation with Deng Xiaoping," 9/30/1961, *AVPRF*, f.0100, o.54, d.8, p.466, 175.

[30] "Positions of the Government of the PRC on Various Questions after the Moscow Meeting," 5/3/1961, *AVPRF*, f.0100, o.54, d.27, p.470, 52–58.

[31] "Record of Conversation with Liu Xiao," 1/29/1961, *AVPRF*, f.0100, o.54, d.7, p.466, 25.

would solve "temporary" food shortages.[32] Five days later, he admitted to more emergency purchases and announced that Beijing could not meet the year's debt-in-kind payments to Moscow.[33]

By early March, Chervonenko finally understood the implications of Liu's tortured admissions. The Soviet ambassador told his East German counterpart that the "Chinese comrades will find it very difficult to prevent people from starving to death this year."[34] Official statements on class struggle in the countryside as the primary reason for the food problems no longer fooled the Soviet ambassador and his Hungarian colleague, both of whom concluded "that the basic reasons for the difficulties, evidently, seem to be the miscalculations which the Chinese comrades had permitted in the economy," while "natural disasters only aggravated the situation."[35] In mid-June, Zhou finally admitted the obvious to Chervonenko: "Seeing objectively that *famines* have occurred in the last two years, and subjectively that our experience was insufficient, . . . we intend to adjust this year's plan and next year's plan."[36]

While gradually admitting to the existence and causes of the famines, Beijing started to ask for Moscow's advice on rural reconstruction. In early March, Ambassador Liu Xiao approached the Agricultural Department of the CPSU CC with detailed questions about the Soviet virgin soil campaign.[37] The timing of this inquiry was supremely ironic. Although the campaign had brought spectacular successes in the late 1950s, by the early 1960s rapid soil exhaustion and the lack of modern technology had condemned it to failure. Indeed, the January 1961 CPSU CC plenum had dealt extensively with the fruitless virgin soil campaign,[38] and Khrushchev himself spent much of February and March inspecting the country.[39] The situation was deteriorating so rapidly that, by 1962, the USSR was forced to import grain from abroad for the first time since the October Revolution.[40] The obvious failure of the virgin soil campaign, however, did not prevent the Chinese from trying it out in 1961 and 1962.[41]

[32] "Record of Conversation with Liu Shaoqi," 2/23/1961, *AVPRF*, f.0100, o.54, d.7, p.466, 57–64.

[33] "Record of Conversation with Liu Shaoqi," 2/28/1961, *AVPRF*, f.0100, o.54, d.7, p.466, 67–72.

[34] "Note on a Talk with Chervonenko on March 3," 3/10/1961, *SAPMO-BArch*, DY 30/IV 2/20/123, 4.

[35] "Record of Conversation with the Ambassador of the Hungarian People's Republic F. Martin," 3/17/1961, *AVPRF*, f.0100, o.54, d.7, p.466, 110.

[36] *ZELNP2*, 419 (italics mine).

[37] "Short Reference," 3/3/1961, *AVPRF*, f.0100, o.54, d.4, p.466, 14–16.

[38] "CPSU Plenum," 1/10–18/1961, *RGANI*, f.2, o.1, d.535.

[39] Taubman, *Khrushchev*, 481–82.

[40] Pikhoya, *Sovetskii Soyuz*, 176.

[41] NC 3297, 8–9; 3416, 4–5.

On February 27, 1961, Khrushchev made another gesture of good-will. Despite food shortages at home, he offered 1 million tons of grain and 500,000 tons of Cuban sugar on a loan basis.[42] On March 8, Zhou agreed to use the sugar loan and asked to keep the grain offer in reserve.[43] But the famine situation forced the PRC to use a part of the grain offer soon afterward.[44] In late March, Zhou also approached the Soviets with a request to deliver on loan another 300,000 tons of grain. These, he said, would be replaced in the fall by the direct delivery of Canadian wheat bought in advance by the PRC.[45] To alleviate the shortfall in the Chinese treasury due to increased grain purchases abroad, the USSR also agreed to buy from the PRC 1,000 tons of silver with hard currency.[46]

Early in the summer of 1962, Vice-Minister for Foreign Trade Li Qian approached Chervonenko requesting to buy more grain at low interest, hinting that lending rates on international financial markets were un-affordable. Having "bread difficulties in the USSR" in mind, the am-bassador pretended not to have understood.[47] Given its own need for grain purchases abroad and emergency deliveries recently provided to Poland, Moscow's willingness to render aid to Beijing had diminished.[48] Nevertheless, the Soviet government agreed to deliver 350,000 tons im-mediately in exchange for the delivery of 150,000 tons of rice later in the year.[49] With this, Soviet food aid ended.

Khrushchev's February 27, 1961, offer seemed to have broken the deadlock in the negotiations over debt rescheduling that had lingered on since late 1960.[50] In early April, the two sides settled on an interest-free debt-repayment-in-kind within five years.[51] In June, Moscow and Beijing also agreed to reduce outstanding civilian industrial projects to sixty-six,[52] which forced Moscow to foot the bill for equipment already

[42] Wang, *Zhonghua*, vol. 2, 242.

[43] "Record of Conversation with Zhou Enlai," 3/8/1961, *AVPRF*, f.0100, o.54, d.7, p.466, 92–95.

[44] "Record of Conversation with Zhou Enlai," 5/29/1961, *AVPRF*, f.0100, o.54, d.8, p.466, 81–84. Zhonghua, *Zhou Enlai waijiao huodong dashiji*, 311.

[45] "Record of Conversation with Zhou Enlai," 3/31/1961, *AVPRF*, f.0100, o.54, d.7, p.466, 166–172. It is not clear what happened to this request.

[46] Borisov, *Soviet-Chinese Relations*, 217.

[47] "Memorial on the Talk of Chervonenko with Li Qian," 6/13/1962, *AVPRF*, f.0100, o.55, d.6, p.480, 178–79.

[48] For the deliveries to Poland: *AAN*, KC PZPR, XI A/80, 50, 104–6.

[49] For the grain-rice exchange: *AVPRF*, f.0100, o.57, d.29, p.512, 4.

[50] Wang, *Zhonghua*, vol. 2, 242.

[51] Xiao, *Qiusuo*, vol. 2, 917. MacFarquhar, *Origins*, vol. 3, 121. Wang, *Zhonghua*, vol. 2, 242.

[52] Wang, *Zhonghua*, vol. 2, 242.

produced but not yet delivered.[53] The bargain also stipulated the return of Soviet specialists to work on the remaining projects; however, only a few arrived because China remained in economic agony.[54] In November, Beijing informed Moscow that it could not fulfill the obligations of that agreement.[55] A month later, the PRC even canceled the import of equipment arranged in June.[56] Thus, in 1961, trade fell 50 percent, with further decreases in the following years.[57] In May 1962, the two sides agreed to suspend construction of the remaining sixty-six projects until further talks in 1964.[58] The projects were canceled completely in early 1965.[59]

China's dire economic situation seriously curtailed the arrogant behavior of the Chinese leadership in their dealings with the Soviet comrades. In a private conversation, Li Fuchun apologized to Arkhipov in March for "their faults in the complications in Soviet-Chinese relations in 1960."[60] Despite these admissions, economic relations continued to decline.

ALBANIA

Although Mao watched the dismantling of the Great Leap Forward from the sidelines, the Soviet-Albanian split provided him with a new political opportunity. Since 1945, Albania's position in the communist world had been unpredictable. Until 1948, it was closely allied with Yugoslavia. In true Balkan fashion, however, Tirana used Moscow's 1948 expulsion of Belgrade to escape its neighbor's shadow. The political repositioning brought plenty of economic aid for Albania, while helping the USSR isolate Yugoslavia. But Khrushchev's Secret Speech undermined Soviet-Albanian relations. Not only did de-Stalinization threaten Hoxha's own position at home, but Khrushchev's review of Stalin's Yugoslavia policy undermined the Albanian raison d'être for improved relations with the Soviet Union.[61]

---

[53] "The Line of the Chinese Leadership on the Curtailment of Economic and Trade Links with the Soviet Union," 3/25/1964, AVPRF, f.0100, o.57, d.29, p.512, 2.

[54] Borisov, *Soviet-Chinese Relations*, 215–16.

[55] Xiao, *Qiusuo*, vol. 2, 917. "The Line of the Chinese Leadership . . . ," 4.

[56] Borisov, *Soviet-Chinese Relations*, 215.

[57] Zhang, *Economic Cold War*, 282.

[58] Su, "Guanyu," 50.

[59] Wang, *Zhonghua*, vol. 2, 278–79. ZELNP2, 706, 708.

[60] "Positions of the Government of the PRC on Various Questions after the Moscow Meeting," 3/3/1961, AVPRF, f.0100, o.54, d.27, p.470, 55.

[61] Lazar Dodic, *Historischer Rückblick auf die Stellung Albaniens im Welkommunismus (1941–1968)* (Trittau: Scherbarth, 1970), 15–21. Griffith, *Albania*, 14–34. Elez Biberaj, *Albania and China* (Boulder: Westview, 1986), 18–33, 41–42. Enver Hoxha, *Artful Albanian* (London: Chatto & Windus, 1986), 1–159. Danylow, *Aussenpolitischen Beziehungen*, 16–126.

Soviet-Albanian relations soured in 1960. Before the WAPA meeting in early February, Mikoyan informed Hoxha about the deterioration of Sino-Soviet relations, which Hoxha later dismissed as a Soviet attempt to "brainwash us against China." He was also unhappy about the Soviet rapprochement with the "American imperialists" before the impending Paris Summit.[62] But Albania's hesitations did not automatically mean a pro-Chinese stance. At the Bucharest meeting, the Albanian party remained neutral, as related in chapter 5.

It was only the outcome of the Albanian intraparty struggles in late summer that triggered a clear pro-Beijing line in Tirana's stance. The Bucharest meeting had a major impact on long-standing conflicts between Hoxha's pro-Stalinist wing and the pro-Khrushchevite faction, which eventually suffered defeat.[63] Moscow's cut in economic aid, including the withdrawal of some of its specialists, and its reluctance to supply grain for famine relief undermined the internal position of the pro-Khrushchevite wing in the Albanian party.[64] Ultimately, Hoxha's pro-Chinese policy was not the result of ideological concord but of intraparty struggles and Khrushchev's strong-arm tactics.[65]

Soviet-Albanian relations further deteriorated in the first eight months of 1961. At the fourth Albanian congress in mid-February, Hoxha revisited the intraparty conflict and charged his purged enemies of concocting a plot together with Yugoslavia, Greece, and the United States.[66] In several letter exchanges in late February and March with Albanian Defense Minister Beqir Balluku, Soviet General and Supreme Commander of WAPA Andrei Grechko asserted that alliance obligations required Albania to provide information about the alleged plot. He also complained that Albania had put its own small flotilla on high alert in November without notifying him, and had even tried to interfere with Soviet submarines stationed in Vlorë.[67] A March 27 letter from Grechko requested the termination of this "abnormal situation," or else the supreme command would request permission from the PCC of WAPA to withdraw all Soviet vessels.[68]

[62] Hoxha, *Superpowers*, 14–15.

[63] Dodic, *Historischer Rückblick*, 22–23. Danylow, *Aussenpolitischen Beziehungen*, 167.

[64] Danylow, *Aussenpolitischen Beziehungen*, 167. Dodic, *Historischer Rückblick*, 26. Hoxha, *Superpowers*, 26–27.

[65] Danylow, *Aussenpolitischen Beziehungen*, 168–72. Griffith, *Albania*, 45–59. Biberaj, *Albania and China*, 39.

[66] Griffith, *Albania*, 69–71. Dodic, *Historischer Rückblick*, 29.

[67] The letter exchange from late February could not be found, but is referred to in the following documents: "Albanian Memorandum on Incidents at Vlorë," 3/22/1961, and "Soviet Report on Incidents at Vlorë," 3/22/1961, both: http://www.isn.ethz.ch/php/documents/collection_3/PCC_docs/1961/1961_7.pdf and _8.pdf, accessed on 4/28/2004.

[68] "Letter by Grechko to Balluku," 3/27/1961, *SAPMO-BArch*, DY 30/3590, 16–23.

Balluku immediately protested against Soviet "pressure" and allegations of wrongdoing in Vlorë.[69] Despite these complaints, the late March WAPA PCC meeting in Moscow demanded that Tirana provide information about the alleged plot, as well as desist from subjecting Soviet submarines and torpedo boats to Albanian command.[70] While Tirana refused to budge to this pressure, it did declare that it would not prevent the removal of Soviet submarines.[71] On April 26, Vice–Prime Minister Aleksei Kosygin responded by announcing the departure of the vessels.[72] The withdrawal was completed in early June. However, despite earlier announcements to the contrary, Tirana suddenly claimed the Soviet-owned, but Albanian-manned, submarines its own, accusing Moscow of the "sabotage" of Albanian defense capabilities.[73]

The spat continued at the WAPA summit of August 3 to 5, which was convened to endorse formally the construction of the Berlin Wall, one of the most momentous events in Cold War history.[74] The East German leader Walter Ulbricht had asked for a summit to discuss the unilateral closing of the German-German borders.[75] He had suggested inviting all *first* party secretaries of the member states *except* Hoxha, but Khrushchev was only willing to convene the meeting if all were invited. When, in a show of contempt, Tirana sent a junior CC secretary, Ramiz Alia, Ulbricht demanded the exclusion of the Albanian delegation on the procedural ground that it was not "competent" enough to participate in such politically far-reaching deliberations. When the other first secretaries supported the proposal, the Albanian delegation was forced to leave on the first day.[76] Albania's estrangement continued with the Soviet recall of its ambassador on August 19 and a CPSU letter five days later accusing Albania of distorting facts with regard to the Soviet withdrawal from Vlorë.[77]

[69] "Letter by Balluku to Grechko," 3/28/1961, *SAPMO-BArch*, DY 30/3590, 24–28.

[70] "Decision by the Political Consultative Committee of the Warsaw Pact," [no date], *PAAA-MfAA*, Beratungen, Tagungen und Konferenzen, G-A 539, 1–3. "Secret Resolution on Albania," 3/29/1961, http://www.isn.ethz.ch/php/documents/collection_3/PCC_docs/1961/1961_0329.pdf, accessed on 4/28/2004. Wang, *Zhonghua*, vol. 2, 244.

[71] "[Letter by Shehu,]" 4/5/1961, *SAPMO-BArch*, DY 30/3590, 55–62.

[72] "Kosygin to the Albanian Minister Council," 4/26/1961, *SAPMO-BArch*, DY 30/3590, 86–108.

[73] Biberaj, *Albania and China*, 38. "Hoxha and Shehu to CPSU CC and the Minister Council of the Soviet Union," 7/6/1961, *SAPMO-BArch*, DY 30/3591, 2–67 (quote).

[74] Bernd Bonwetsch et al., eds., "Chruschtschow und der Mauerbau," *Vierteljahresheft für Zeitgeschichte* 48/1, 155–98.

[75] Klaus Schroeder, *SED Staat* (München: Hanser, 1998), 150.

[76] Bonwetsch, "Chruschtschow," 164–65.

[77] Griffith, *Albania*, 85. "CPSU CC to CC of the Albanian Party of Workers," 8/24/1961, *SAPMO-BArch*, DY 30/3592, 2–29. Delyusin, "Nekotorye," 17.

While relations between Moscow and Tirana continued to deteriorate, Mao tried to entice the Albanians to join forces against the revisionist Soviets. But Hoxha's view of the Chinese comrades had been ambivalent; since early 1956, he believed that they had not held Stalin's banner high enough.[78] In Hoxha's eyes, it was Mao who had come around to correct ideological positions in the last five years, and not vice-versa.[79] Although by the summer of 1960 Soviet strong-arm tactics had driven China and Albania closer together, Hoxha subsequently claimed that he was displeased with Chinese ideological concessions at the Moscow Meeting later that year.[80] And until 1965, the Albanian leader repeatedly chided the Chinese comrades for diluting their own ideological positions through tactical errors in their dealings with the Soviet revisionists.[81]

Despite these ideological differences, it was economic necessity, caused by Moscow's failed attempts to apply economic pressure, which drove Albania into an unequal alliance with China.[82] By late 1960, Albania's agriculture had fallen into shambles. Mao was more than happy to provide his good friend with emergency food aid.[83] The rapprochement, however, was hardly seamless, as Li Xiannian's visit to the fourth Albanian party congress in February of 1961 revealed. A moderate on ideological issues, Li pleaded with the Albanians not to split with the Soviets.[84] Although Hoxha spoiled everything by censuring the Soviet revisionists viciously,[85] an April agreement on twenty-five industrial projects and the financing of Canadian emergency grain deliveries to Albania was nevertheless signed, cementing the emerging Sino-Albanian partnership.[86] In the early 1960s, 80 percent of Beijing's development assistance went to four countries only: Vietnam, Korea, Outer Mongolia, and Albania.[87] Tirana joined this exclusive club largely because Mao valued its "anti-imperialist and anti-revisionist" credentials.[88] Aid for ideological reasons, however, had too

[78] Khrushchev, *Glasnost*, 107. Hoxha, *Artful Albanian*, 176.

[79] Biberaj, *Albania and China*, 45.

[80] Biberaj, *Albania and China*, 42, 45. Hoxha, *Khrushchevites*, 422–50. Dodic, *Historischer Rückblick*, 27–28. James O'Donnell, *A Coming of Age* (New York: Columbia, 1999), 49–52.

[81] Hoxha, *Reflections on China*, vol. 1, 8–12, 19–20, 23, 26–28, 33, 35–37, 39, 46–48, 50, 52–54, 71–94, 110–170, 177–85.

[82] Biberaj, *Albania and China*, 40.

[83] Xiao, *Qiusuo*, vol. 2, 932. Christensen, "Worse," 100.

[84] Liu Xiao, *Chushi*, 128–33.

[85] Hoxha, *Artful Albanian*, 244. "Report on the 4th Congress of the Albanian Workers' Party," 2/23/1961, *SAPMO-BArch*, DY 30/IV 2/20/96, 1–11.

[86] Xiao, *Qiusuo*, vol. 2, 920–21. Wang, *Zhonghua*, vol. 2, 342–44. Griffith, *Albania*, 78–79.

[87] Wang, *Zhonghua*, vol. 2, 343. Xiao, *Qiusuo*, vol. 2, 932–33.

[88] Xiao, *Qiusuo*, vol. 2, 933.

big a price tag for China in the long term; by 1965, Zhou decided to reduce economic assistance to Albania substantially.[89]

Ultimately, it was the Soviet withdrawal from Vlorë that opened the door for Mao. The March WAPA meeting had put the Chairman on alert. Having been victims of Soviet pressure politics themselves, the CCP leaders followed Mao's demand "to watch and observe." But it seems that the Chairman had been waiting for *any* opportunity to increase tensions with the Soviet revisionists. In July 1958, Mao had accused Khrushchev of "great power chauvinism" for his desire to *station* submarines in China. Three years later, Beijing charged Moscow with "great power chauvinism" because of its decision to *withdraw* submarines from Albania.[90]

Beijing instructed its observer of the August 1961 WAPA meeting, Liu Xiao, to support Tirana. Two days after August 3, when the Albanian delegation was denied admission, Liu registered a complaint that "no party has the right to reject the representative of another party to attend a meeting."[91] In their October 31 reply to Liu's protest, the Soviets claimed that rules and regulations would also apply to observing nonmembers like the Chinese in the future.[92] But a mid-October meeting between Chervonenko and Deng, who, together with Liu Shaoqi, tried to push through more rational economic policies in China at that time, revealed that not everybody shared Mao's new hard line. Deng deplored the Soviet-Albanian fallout while lauding the improvement of Sino-Soviet relations in recent months.[93]

THE TWENTY-SECOND CPSU CONGRESS

The unresolved Stalin issue and Albania received more attention at the twenty-second CPSU congress in late October 1961 than most observers had expected. The convention met to adopt a new party program to replace the old one from 1919. In 1958, Khrushchev formed a commission that eventually published the draft program on July 31, 1961.[94] Similar to the Great Leap Forward, though certainly less ambitious than Mao's failed brainchild, the new draft program envisioned the completion of the communist project. It announced that the USSR would create the

[89] Wang, *Zhonghua*, vol. 2, 342–45.

[90] WLX, 173, 457.

[91] Wang, *Zhonghua*, vol. 2, 244–45 (quote). Bonwetsch, "Chruschtschow," 165, 197–98.

[92] Wang, *Zhonghua*, vol. 2, 245.

[93] "From the Diary of S. V. Chervonenko, Top Secret, 12 October 1961, Copy No. 1, Transcript of Conversation with General Secretary of the CC CCP Deng Xiaoping, 30 September 1961," Chen Jian, "Deng Xiaoping," 174–75.

[94] Taubman, *Khrushchev*, 508–11.

"material and technical basis of communism" until 1970 by surpassing "the strongest and richest capitalist country, the U.S.A." Given the advanced state of socialism in the Soviet Union of 1961, it declared that "class antagonisms" had disappeared in Soviet society; the CPSU would open itself to all people. In the section on world communism, the program called for the "closest" unity within the socialist camp, termed the "line of socialist construction in isolation . . . theoretically untenable [and] . . . economically harmful," and predicted the impending collapse of "world capitalism." Finally, it called for the obligation "to ward off a thermonuclear war" through peaceful coexistence.[95] Although these positions contradicted current Chinese views, the program itself said nothing about the most recent ideological conflicts with the CCP.

Mao was not happy when he received the draft program seven days ahead of its official publication.[96] But much to the irritation of the CPSU, the CCP did not publicly react for two months.[97] Internally, on September 15, the Chairman told the Politburo: "This 'CPSU draft programme' is like the foot binding bandages of Wang's wife, not only long but also stinking." Lu Dingyi, the head of the CCP CC Propaganda Department, followed suit by claiming "that Khrushchev and his aides have renounced the fundamental principles of Marxism-Leninism," and ridiculed the idea of an end to class struggle in the USSR and of the CPSU being a "party for all people." Despite all the Chinese criticism, the Politburo decided to send a delegation, headed by Zhou Enlai and Peng Zhen, to the congress.[98] The CCP published both the new CPSU draft program and the old 1919 program without comment. As an East German document testifies, the meaning of this dual publication was not lost among other members of the socialist camp: "It was intended to create the impression that there were some contradictions between the two programs." Officially, the CCP denied having studied the program, claiming that all central leaders were on important errands in the country.[99]

The congress opened on October 17 with Khrushchev's formal report.[100] While he had not initially planned on attacking Stalin's personality cult,

[95] CPSU, *Programme of the Communist Party of the Soviet Union* (Moscow: Foreign Languages, 1961), 22, 24, 25, 54, 57, 61–62, 122–27.

[96] "Record of Conversation with Peng Zhen," 7/24/1961, *AVPRF*, f.0100, o.54, d.8, p.466, 156–63.

[97] "The Attitude of the Communist Party of China toward the CPSU Draft Program," 9/21/1961, *PAAA-MfAA*, Abteilung Ferner Osten–Sektor China, Microfiche A 6755, 1–6.

[98] WLX, 457–69.

[99] "Embassy of the GDR, Military Attaché Heim," 10/20/1961, *BArch-Freib*, VA-01/6383 Informationen und Berichte des Militärattachés der DDR in der VR China über militärpolitische und militärtechnische Probleme des Aufenthaltslandes, Band 2, 1961–64.

[100] "Summary Report of the CPSU CC," 10/17/1961, *RGANI*, f.1, o.4, d.89, 26–222 and f.1, o.4, d.90, 1–99.

a letter by the late leader's former right hand, Molotov, calling the new program "scandalous," forced Khrushchev, on rather short notice, to include de-Stalinization in his official report.[101] At the congress itself, Khrushchev found enough support to pass a resolution to rid the Lenin mausoleum of Stalin's body. On October 31, the coffin was removed and interred toward the rear at the Kremlin wall.[102] Khrushchev's criticism of Albania also entered his report to the congress rather spontaneously; for unknown reasons, the Soviet leader decided to rant against Hoxha while he was giving the official report.[103] The other speakers of the CPSU were surprised by the sudden change and, as a result, had to rewrite their own prepared addresses.[104]

Given Mao's mistrust of Khrushchev, the Chinese comrades had long expected that Khrushchev would raise de-Stalinization and Albania with the purpose "to attack" them.[105] After the formal report, Zhou returned to the embassy to cable Beijing for instructions. Liu Shaoqi proposed to the Politburo that the prime minister make a speech "indicating that the CCP does not agree with Khrushchev's attack on Albania." Mao, away from Beijing at the time, agreed on the phone. The two also concurred that, in the future, the CCP would no longer attend any international meetings that were platforms "to oppose China."[106]

Zhou's October 19 speech briefly lauded Soviet achievements since 1917, turned to a list of well-known Chinese positions on international relations, and finally complained about the "public, one-sided censure of a fraternal party" at the congress.[107] The assembled Soviet leadership did not applaud once during the speech.[108] Two days later, the CCP followed up with a political show on Stalin. The whole delegation paid homage to Lenin and Stalin who, at that time, were still lying side by side in the mausoleum. The wreath for the disgraced Soviet leader carried the words: "To J. V. Stalin, the great Marxist-Leninist."[109]

On October 22, Zhou met with the Soviet party leadership for a day of talks.[110] The premier "explained the CCP position and attitude on Soviet-Albanian relations, the CPSU 20th congress, the evaluation of

---

[101] Quoted in: Taubman, *Khrushchev*, 515. Condensed text of Khrushchev's speech: *NYT*, 10/18/1961, 16.

[102] Taubman, *Khrushchev*, 515. Pikhoya, *Sovetskii Soyuz*, 215, 217. Liu Xiao, *Chushi*, 25.

[103] Delyusin, "Nekotorye," 19. *NYT*, 10/18/1961, 16.

[104] Khrushchev, *Nikita S. Khrushchev*, 463.

[105] WLX, 458. *NYT*, 10/20/1961, 1.

[106] WLX, 471–75.

[107] *SCMP* 2605, 38–43.

[108] *NYT*, 10/20/1961, 1.

[109] *SCMP* 2605, 35. ZELNP2, 440–41.

[110] Zhonghua, *Zhou Enlai waijiao huodong dashiji*, 325–26.

Stalin, the anti-party incident."[111] Khrushchev replied bluntly: "We in the past needed very much your help, at that time the CCP's opinion carried weight for us. But now it is different."[112] Zhou decided to leave Moscow the next day, desiring to "express our party's serious stand."[113] In his closing remarks to the congress, Khrushchev acerbically declared: "We share the anxiety expressed by our Chinese friends and appreciate their concern for greater unity. . . . If the Chinese comrades wish to make efforts toward normalizing the relations of the Albanian Party of Labor and the fraternal parties, there is hardly anyone who can contribute to the solution of this problem more than the Communist party of China."[114]

Three days after Khrushchev's opening report, Tirana reacted with a monthlong propaganda campaign against the "Judas" Khrushchev.[115] On November 25, Moscow responded by demanding that Tirana withdraw its ambassador. A week later, it required the closing of the embassy while simultaneously shutting down its own in Albania.[116] The Warsaw Pact and the socialist Council on Mutual Economic Aid (COMECON) followed suit by excluding Albania from their meetings starting in 1962.[117]

For Mao, the developments in Soviet-Albanian relations since late October were an ideological boon. The Chairman personally went to the airport to greet Zhou upon his return from Moscow.[118] He also decided that this was a good occasion to publish an ideological polemic against the CPSU.[119] Internally, he launched educational measures designed to get the lower ranks of the party, as well as the people at large, in line and to deflect popular criticism after the Great Leap Forward. A tape of Zhou's ten-hour report to the CCP CC on the Soviet congress was distributed to all party organizations in China.[120]

Chinese behavior in international organizations reflected Mao's new hard line toward the Soviet comrades. On October 31, the CPSU and the East European parties sent letters informing the CCP that only first secretaries could attend WAPA PCC meetings.[121] Three weeks later, the CCP

---

[111] ZELNP2, 441.

[112] WLX, 474, 480.

[113] Wu, Huiyi, 345.

[114] NYT, 10/28/1961, 28.

[115] Danylow, Aussenpolitischen Beziehungen, 176. Quote in: Griffith, Albania, 100.

[116] Griffith, Albania, 113–14. Danylow, Aussenpolitischen Beziehungen, 176.

[117] Dodic, Historischer Rückblick, 31.

[118] Griffith, Albania, 94.

[119] WLX, 478–79.

[120] "Note on a Talk with Chervonenko," 1/11/1962, SAPMO-BArch, DY 30/IV 2/20/124, 1–2.

[121] Wang, Zhonghua, vol. 2, 356–57.

complained about this intervention into its internal affairs,[122] despite the fact that the Politburo had already decided *before*, on October 20, to boycott any WAPA and COMECON meeting to which the Albanians were not invited.[123]

As in earlier cases, both the CCP and the CPSU tried to assess the situation after the fact. The Chinese comrades claimed to be convinced "that the Soviet people and the majority of the CPSU totally do not go along with Khrushchev."[124] Similarly, the Soviets believed that "the people [in China] do not love Mao Zedong and Liu Shaoqi."[125] Soviet intelligence from China suggested that Mao was defeated in domestic policies and that the continued lack of Soviet aid would help to oust the Chairman. But Mao's ousting required a cessation of Soviet strong-arm tactics that ultimately united the Chinese leadership.[126] It was precisely these kinds of pressure tactics, however, that helped Khrushchev defeat the remaining Stalinist stalwarts at home.[127]

7,000-CADRES CONFERENCE

Mao's next opportunity to enhance his influence in the daily decision-making process came at the so-called 7,000-Cadres Conference from late December 1961 to early February 1962. The meeting went beyond the usual two hundred to three hundred central and provincial leaders who participated in such work conferences—hence the name.[128] All central leaders saw the conference as a defining moment, though for different reasons. Mao hoped to use it to stop what he perceived as the further corrosion of socialist values in China; his fellow leaders looked at it as an opportunity to draw lessons from the Great Leap Forward.[129]

The conference started with Deng's report on the twenty-second CPSU congress. Toeing Mao's hard line on foreign relations, the Chinese secretary general asserted that "Khrushchev's revisionism" threatened "the international communist movement . . . with the problem of a split." In the long term, "the ideological split will inevitably lead to an organizational

---

[122] "CCP CC to SED CC," 11/20/1961, *SAPMO-BArch*, DY 30/3386, 230–33.

[123] WLX, 476–77.

[124] WLX, 477.

[125] "Record of Conversation with Gheorghiu," 1/10/1962, *AVPRF*, f.0100, o.55, d.6, p.480, 4.

[126] Delyusin, "Guanyu," 108.

[127] Arbatov, *System*, 95–96.

[128] MacFarquhar, *Origins*, vol. 3, 137–38.

[129] Short, *Mao*, 510.

split" in many of the parties; and after some "setbacks," Deng claimed, the true Marxist-Leninist parties would emerge victorious.[130] Five weeks later, Liu Shaoqi confirmed Deng's assertions.[131] Subsequent developments suggest, however, that Deng and Liu both engaged in rhetorical posturing for tactical reasons.

If Mao himself had believed that his radicalized anti-revisionist foreign policy would help prevent the growth of domestic revisionism, he clearly miscalculated. Although little evidence on the monthlong discussions has surfaced, Liu Shaoqi's January 27 report reveals that rural revisionism was indeed on the march in China.[132] The report claimed that past "shortcomings and errors caused heavy losses to our economy. . . . Natural disasters can be blamed for some of our difficulties, but to a greater extent they were caused by mistakes in our work."[133] Mao still refused to accept this evaluation.[134]

Liu's report was ambivalent on Mao's personal responsibility, stating only that "although the Central Committee formulated correct policies, it did not check on them strictly or take effective measures to ensure their implementation."[135] But during the previous group discussions, low-ranking conference participants had demanded the accurate attribution of culpability. On January 18, Peng Zhen took up the task, first criticizing the Central Committee for its failures, but also charging the Politburo and, finally, the Chairman.[136] Liu's report, by contrast, was vague on all of these issues.

Although Mao vetoed the rehabilitation of Peng Dehuai, the fact that this topic reemerged at the 7,000-Cadres Conference spoke volumes about his standing in the party.[137] After three years of disaster, the Chairman could not react to criticism in the manner he had done in 1959; another Lushan-style purge was beyond his political powers.[138] The economic and political situation in the PRC did, however, force him to express a measure of self-criticism on January 30: "Any mistakes the Centre has made ought to be my direct responsibility, and I have also an indirect share in the blame because I am the Chairman of the Central Committee." Although Mao had finally admitted mistakes in front of a *large*

[130] WLX, 480–83.

[131] MacFarquhar, *Origins*, vol. 3, 131–33.

[132] MacFarquhar, *Origins*, vol. 3, 152–56.

[133] Liu Shaoqi, "Report to Working Conference of CPC," 1/27/1962, Liu, *Collected Works*, vol. 3, 333, 398. Also: Sladkovskii, *Ocherki*, 387.

[134] Li, *Private Life*, 385.

[135] Liu, "Report to Working Conference of CPC," 333.

[136] Short, *Mao*, 510. MacFarquhar, *Origins*, vol. 3, 156–57.

[137] Bo Yibo, *Ruogan*, vol. 2, 1091. Li, *Private Life*, 386. Sladkovskii, *Ocherki*, 386.

[138] Short, *Mao*, 511.

group of people, his mea culpa was disingenuous. He never said what his personal mistakes actually were. The Chairman also added that all provincial, district, county, and other secretaries present at the conference "must bear the responsibility for mistakes and shortcomings in the work" as well.[139] While Mao again shifted blame downward, he was almost completely isolated in this attitude. Lin Biao, who had the most to fear from the rehabilitation of Peng Dehuai, was one of the few persons to come out publicly in Mao's favor with a sycophantic confirmation of the personality cult: "The thoughts of the Chairman are always correct." Mao was grateful for the little support he got.[140]

The 7,000-Cadres Conference was a major setback for Mao. Indeed, he must have seen his worst fears confirmed given the economic liberalization promoted by Liu and Deng in the first half of 1962 (see below). According to his secretary, Hu Qiaomu, the Chairman started to oppose what he saw as "the restoration of capitalism" in China.[141] But, just as he refused to define the precise nature of Soviet revisionism, Mao never specified whether it was a political problem or class struggle.[142] It was simply a rhetorical weapon to discredit those who promoted ideas contrary to his own.[143]

In order to observe events developing in Beijing from afar, the Chairman withdrew to Wuhan.[144] In Mao's absence, the CCP leadership restored the basic economic ideas of the First FYP adopted in 1953.[145] Chen Yun and Zhou Enlai set out to rectify the deficit in China's national budget, to introduce agricultural reforms and "appropriate plans for both light and heavy industry," and to institute market mechanisms designed to improve the supply situation.[146] In July, Deng Xiaoping conducted a poll within the CC apparatus about the introduction of the field responsibility system promoted by Anhui party boss Zeng Xisheng in early 1961. The poll was politically dangerous given Mao's vehement and public opposition to nonsocialist forms of agriculture.[147] Even more explosive was the republication of Liu Shaoqi's *How to Be a Good Communist* the same

[139] Mao, "Talk at an Enlarged Central Work Conference," 1/30/1962, Schram, *Chairman Mao*, 167–87.

[140] Li Zhisui, *Private Life*, 387–88 (quote). MacFarquhar, *Origins*, vol. 3, 164, 166. Lieberthal, "Great Leap," 341. Zhonggong, *Mao Zedong zhuan*, 1197.

[141] 'Hu' zhubian, *Hu Qiaomu*, 60.

[142] Li, "Study [I]," 69–71.

[143] 'Hu' zhubian, *Hu Qiaomu*, 60. Li, "Study [I]," 63. Li, *Private Life*, 385–88.

[144] Lieberthal, "Great Leap," 329.

[145] MacFarquhar, *Origins*, vol. 3, 186–93. Lieberthal, "Great Leap," 329.

[146] Zhou, "Readjustment of the National Economy and Our Current Tasks," 3/29/1962, Zhou, *Selected Works*, vol. 2, 383–400. MacFarquhar, *Origins*, vol. 3, 199–203.

[147] Sladkovskii, *Ocherki*, 385–86. MacFarquhar, *Origins*, vol. 3, 209–34, 261–69.

month, twenty-three years after he had given the lectures in Yan'an.[148] It sold more than 18 million copies,[149] allegedly more than Mao's *Selected Works*.[150]

Maintaining the balance between a Maoist hard line in foreign relations and the kind of domestic reform proposed by Deng and Liu was indeed difficult. Early in 1962, a group of five communist parties (Vietnam, New Zealand, Great Britain, Sweden, and Indonesia) led by Ho Chi Minh proposed to terminate polemics and to convene another Moscow Meeting of the international communist movement.[151] North Vietnam deplored the Soviet-Albanian split and called for unity against the "common enemy, imperialism, with the United States as its head."[152] The CPSU took up the cause and, in late February, appealed to the CCP to terminate polemics.[153] With Mao absent, Liu and Deng had to choose between a hard and a conciliatory line. Avoiding overt confrontation, Deng told Chervonenko that "the larger party should take the initiative" when it came to Soviet-Albanian relations.[154] A Politburo meeting in late March, chaired by Liu Shaoqi, eventually decided to follow Mao's hard line and instructed that the same group of scholars that had drafted the Lenin Polemics in early 1960 to write a letter in reply.[155] The final product praised Beijing's past efforts to maintain unity and criticized Moscow's actions at meetings in 1960 and 1961. It endorsed the proposal of the five communist parties to convene an international meeting, only on the conditions, however, that all polemics in the socialist camp were terminated, that all problems between the various parties were overcome in bilateral talks beforehand, and that the CPSU yield to the demands of the Albanian party.[156] The Soviet response in late May was upbeat on the surface but refused to accept charges of Soviet great power chauvinism in its relations with Albania.[157] The Chinese comrades perceived the letter as "rejection of all our . . . proposals."[158]

But Mao's radical foreign policy line did not find undisputed support within the party apparatus. Wang Jiaxiang, a Soviet specialist, was

---

[148] Sladkovskii, *Ocherki*, 387–88.

[149] MacFarquhar, *Origins*, vol. 3, 262.

[150] Han Suyin, *Wind in the Tower* (London: Cape, 1976), 187.

[151] MacFarquhar, *Origins*, vol. 3, 271. Gittings, *Survey*, 169. Xiao, *Qiusuo*, vol. 2, 930.

[152] "The VWP CC to CC of Hungarian Socialist Workers' Party," 1/10/1964, MOL, 288 f.9/1962/31 őe, 7–9.

[153] "CPSU CC to CCP CC," 2/22/1962, SAPMO-BArch, DY 30/3606, 46–62.

[154] "Records of Conversations, Chervonenko and Deng Xiaoping," 3/1/1962, Westad, *Brothers*, 374–75.

[155] WLX, 492–94.

[156] "CCP CC to CPSU CC," 4/7/1962, SAPMO-BArch, DY 30/3606, 75–97.

[157] "CPSU CC to CCP CC," 5/31/1962, SAPMO-BArch, DY 30/3606, 115–56.

[158] Wang, *Zhonghua*, vol. 2, 246–47.

concerned about the self-imposed international isolation of the PRC.[159] During the 7,000-Cadres Conference, Wang gathered his fellow leaders of the CC Liaison Department to work out proposals for a more moderate Chinese foreign policy.[160] Once Zhou Enlai at that conference had called for a foreign policy without "illusions" and Mao had left for Wuhan, Wang felt politically secure enough to push the new ideas.[161] With Liu's support, he proposed that Zhou, Deng, and Chen Yi exploit Mao's idea of "striving for the majority, isolating the minority, using contradictions" as a means to promote his own policy initiative of the *sanhe yishao* (three reconciliations and one reduction). In light of domestic economic necessity, he advocated the improvement of relations with the USSR, the United States, and India, as well as a decrease in foreign aid granted for ideological reasons. The February 27 letter was cosigned by Wang's deputies in the CCP CC Liaison Department, Liu Ningyi and Wu Xiuquan.[162]

Despite Zhou's initial reservations, Wang continued to develop his own ideas in late spring. Mao's outright opposition to peaceful coexistence, he warned, "can be used by our adversaries" to caricature the Chinese comrades as nothing other than "war-cannot-be-avoided-people." Wang also argued that the absolute rejection of any negotiation with U.S. imperialism completely failed to mobilize the world's population.[163] His ideas finally seemed to catch on. During an Albanian state visit in late June, Liu told his guests to contribute to overcoming the disagreements with the Soviet comrades.[164] In the Chairman's absence, the Chinese central leadership also decided to bring Wang's ideas to the July World Peace Council in Moscow. Indeed, the sudden constructive behavior of the Chinese delegation led by Mao Dun completely surprised the Soviets.[165]

Xinjiang and the Abrogation of Sino-Soviet Consular Relations

With Beijing's attitude toward Moscow in limbo, Sino-Soviet relations suffered from sudden unrest in Xinjiang. The most western administrative

[159] Xu, *Wang*, 554–55.

[160] Li Jie, "China's Domestic Situation," Ross, *Re-examining*, 301.

[161] Xiao, *Qiusuo*, vol. 2, 932–33.

[162] Xu, *Wang*, 555–57. Xiao, *Qiusuo*, vol. 2, 926–29. MacFarquhar, *Origins*, vol. 3, 269–71, 273. Chen, "Chinese Politics," 275–76. For an analysis of Wang's ideas: Niu Jun, "1962," *CWIHP* Working Paper 48, 28–29.

[163] Xu, *Wang*, 557–63.

[164] Xiao, *Qiusuo*, vol. 2, 931.

[165] Xiao, *Qiusuo*, vol. 2, 929–30. Xu, *Wang*, 558–64. Wang Li, *Xianchang lishi* (Xianggang: Niujin daxue, 1993), 72. MacFarquhar, *Origins*, vol. 3, 271–72.

unit of the PRC harbored a dynamite keg of ethnic conflicts. The territory had come under Chinese control only in the late-eighteenth century. Russian influence started even later, in the 1830s, when Old Believers escaped religious persecution in Russia proper. While Chinese control waned in the early twentieth century, White Russians fleeing the civil war (1918–21) and then Bolshevik interests brought an even greater Russian element. In the late 1940s, Moscow granted Soviet citizenship to 20,000 ethnic Russians and 100,000 ethnic Central Asians in Xinjiang. Even after the establishment of the PRC, Stalin continued his attempts to keep Soviet influence alive.[166] Beijing countered by co-opting local elites, investing in infrastructure, and encouraging ethnic Chinese immigration. The simultaneous resettlement of USSR citizens into Soviet Central Asia started shortly after the establishment of the PRC, but seemed to have been stopped by Beijing in 1960, probably for fear of a steady loss of well-educated and trained people. In early 1962, Moscow's consulates in Yining (a.k.a. Ili or Kuldzha) and Urumqi started to distribute Soviet passports in order to facilitate emigration, apparently behind the back of Chinese authorities.[167]

It was against this background that the deterioration of Sino-Soviet relations led to the mass flight of 67,000 people from Xinjiang to Soviet Kazakhstan in spring 1962. Chinese sources do not cover the episode in great detail;[168] only one mentions food shortages due to the influx of famine refugees from other provinces and Soviet actions as causes for the problems.[169] According to an internal Soviet document from early 1962, the CCP in Xinjiang had, two years before, started an anti-Soviet campaign through the propagation of the Lenin Polemics and other anti-revisionist texts.[170] After the Soviet-Albanian split in 1961, the campaign

[166] David Wang, "Soviet Citizenship in Xinjiang," *Asian Studies Review* 19/3, 87–97. Anthony Harrigan, "Sinkiang: A Sino-Soviet Trouble Spot?" *Military Review* 43/5, 3–7. June Dreyer, "PLA and Regionalism in Xinjiang," *Pacific Review* 7/1, 40–41. Dreyer, "Ethnic Minorities in the Sino-Soviet Dispute," William McCagg et al., *Soviet Asian Ethnic Frontiers* (New York: Pergamon, 1979), 195–205. Donald McMillen, *Chinese Communist Power and Policy in Xinjiang, 1949–1977* (Boulder: Westview, 1979), 15–26.

[167] Dreyer, "PLA," 42–43. K. N. Ramachandran, "Tension and Conflict in Sinkiang," *China Report* 11/5–6, 11–13. Wang, "Soviet Citizenship," 93. Borisov, *Soviet-Chinese Relations*, 223. Dreyer, "Ethnic Minorities," 205, 209. An, *Territorial Dispute*, 68–73. Bruce Adams, "Re-emigration from Western China to the USSR, 1954–1962," paper presented at the workshop "Immigration, Forced Migrants, and Refugees in Central Eurasia," Kennan Institute for Russian Studies, Washington D.C., 2004–5.

[168] Xinhua, *China's Foreign Relations*, 462. WLX, 494–95. Li, "1969nian," 42. Dangdai, *Waijiao*, 122. Zhang Dequn, "Zai Mosike liunian ban," *Zhonggong dangshi ziliao* 58, 37. Wang, *Zhonghua*, vol. 2, 247.

[169] Li Danhui, "Dui 1962nian Xinjiang Yita shijian qiyin de lishi kaocha," http://www.shenzhihua.net/muluzhong.htm, accessed on 11/15/2004.

[170] "Some Facts on Manifestations of Non-Friendly Relations," 2/8/1962, *AVPRF*, f.0100, o.55, d.24, p.483, 23–24.

intensified.[171] Another Soviet document claims that since 1959 or 1960, the Chinese had refused to grant exit visas for those requesting repatriation; in 1961, "the Chinese authorities unilaterally imposed PRC citizenship on Soviet citizens," started to "annul" Soviet passports, and prevented the Soviet consulates from delivering travel documents. In early 1962, people who refused to accept Chinese citizenship were "dismissed from work, deprived of food rations, left without any means of subsistence, and, in case they lived in state housing, were expelled onto the street."[172] The first groups of refugees left for Kazakhstan in March.[173]

It was this situation that spurred Ambassador Chervonenko to call Vice–Foreign Minister Zhang Hanfu on April 24, requesting an urgent meeting to hand over a memorandum. Apparently, the Chinese sensed that the events in Xinjiang would be the topic of the discussion. After some delays, Zhang received the ambassador only to read him a prepared note. Chervonenko had the strong impression that Zhang's behavior was designed to validate the claim that "the PRC had raised the fact of the border crossings by people first."[174] The Chinese note accused the Soviet side of failing to guard its own borders and of facilitating the mass exit of 20,000 people with all of their belongings.[175] The Soviet memo, which Chervonenko was supposed to hand over, stated that the "Soviet border organs, which attempted not to allow the crossing into the territory of the USSR, were not in a condition to do that, given the large number of people."[176] Five days later, a Soviet reply note asserted that the Soviet government had experienced "serious perplexity and surprise" over Zhang's accusations.[177] For the following three weeks, accusations and counteraccusations were exchanged.[178]

The diplomatic deadlock worsened when, in late May, the problems in Xinjiang developed into a full-scale rebellion. According to a Western source, protesters in Yining surrounded, attacked, and set fire to party and government buildings and PLA barracks. Allegedly, the Soviet consulate quickly provided the necessary entry papers for the subsequent

[171] "Note by MID USSR," 9/19/1963, *AVPRF*, f.0100, o.55, d.1, p.480, 27.
[172] "[Note by MID USSR to Embassy of the PRC]," 10/31/1963, *AVPRF*, f.100, o.50, d.1, p.210, 68.
[173] Wang, *Zhonghua*, vol. 2, 247.
[174] "Record of Conversation with Zhang Hanfu," 4/24/1962, *AVPRF*, f.0100, o.55, d.6, p.480, 119–20.
[175] "Statement of the Government of the PRC," 4/24/1962, *AVPRF*, f.0100, o.55, d.2, p.480, 37–39.
[176] "Statement of MID USSR," 4/24/1962, *AVPRF*, f.0100, o.55, d.1, p.480, 3.
[177] "Memorandum of the Government of the USSR," 4/29/1962, *AVPRF*, f.0100, o.55, d.1, p.480, 4–8.
[178] *AVPRF*, f.0100, o.55, d.2, p.480, 44–46; o.55, d.6, p.480, 163–67.

flight to Kazakhstan.[179] A Chinese memoir blamed the Soviets for "engineering" the revolt.[180] By contrast, a Soviet archival source from 1963 claims that in the last days of May, the local Chinese authorities in Yining suddenly granted a large number of exit visas to those who already had Soviet entry papers, and even provided "tickets for transport by car to Khochen, 7 km away from the border." Apparently, twelve buses with forty to fifty people each left for the border day after day. The rebellion erupted only when the local Chinese authorities unexpectedly terminated the issuing of exit visas. Later that day, according to the testimony of the Soviet consul, shootings "by Chinese soldiers on a crowd of unarmed people" occurred in the city.[181]

Although the rebellion tapered off after 67,000 people had left,[182] it continued to exacerbate diplomatic tensions. In memoranda and meetings throughout June, the two sides blamed each other for the deterioration of Sino-Soviet relations over Xinjiang. Chervonenko accused the Chinese side of noncooperation in solving the matter; Zhang Hanfu refused to acknowledge the coresponsibility of Chinese border guards for the mass exit and continued to demand the forceful and immediate return of the refugees by Soviet authorities.[183] The situation changed slightly when, toward the end of June, Zhang fell ill; his substitute, the lower-ranking Ji Pengfei, freely admitted that "the Chinese border forces at the Sino-Soviet border are very small and far away from the Soviet border forces at that border."[184] Although Beijing eventually allowed the legal emigration of another 46,000 people between October 15, 1962, and May 1, 1963,[185] it continued to demand from Moscow the "return [of] all 60 thousand" that had fled in the spring of 1962.[186] But in the end, the

[179] Dreyer, "PLA," 43.

[180] Zhang, "Zai Mosike," 37.

[181] "[Note by MID USSR to Embassy of the PRC]," 10/31/1963, AVPRF, f.100, o.50, d.1, p.210, 72–75.

[182] "Soviet-Chinese Relations (Reference)," May [?] 1965, AVPRF, f.0100, o.56, d.22, p.498, 233.

[183] "Memorandum of the Government of the USSR," 6/8/1962, AVPRF, f.0100, o.55, d.1, p.480, 12–14. "Record of Conversation with Zhang Hanfu," 6/8 & 11/1962, AVPRF, f.0100, o.55, d.6, p.480, 170–73. "Statement of the Embassy of the USSR in the PRC," 6/11/1962, AVPRF, f.0100, o.55, d.1, p.480, 15. "Memorandum of the Government of the PRC," 6/26/1962, AVPRF, f.0100, o.55, d.2, p.480, 50–52.

[184] "Record of Conversation with Ji Pengfei," 6/26/1962, AVPRF, f.0100, o.55, d.6, p.480, 199–202.

[185] Borisov, Soviet-Chinese Relations, 1945–1970, 225. "Soviet-Chinese Relations (Reference)," May [?] 1965, AVPRF, f.0100, o.56, d.22, p.498, 233.

[186] "Oral Reply by MID PRC on the Memorial by MID USSR from May 25, 1966, Communicated to the Embassy of the USSR in the PRC on July 16, 1966," AVPRF, f.0100, o.59, d.2, p.525, 22–23.

events of 1962 solved the problem of Moscow's influence in Xinjiang. By 1965, according to a Soviet document, only 13,000 people with Soviet citizenship remained.[187]

Despite the de facto resolution of this issue, Sino-Soviet relations did not improve. On the contrary, the Chinese used the dispute to accuse Soviet consulates and other official organizations within the PRC of illegal and subversive activities. Beijing suspected, probably correctly, that Moscow's seven consulates did not cater solely to the needs of Soviet citizens.[188] On May 23, 1962, in order to solve "the problem of Soviet subversion in our country," the PRC annulled the bilateral consular treaty.[189] After the swift closing of the consulates, the Soviet embassy in Beijing also came under much stricter supervision by Chinese authorities.[190]

Beijing also decided to shut down Moscow's other official institutions in the PRC. Citing "irrefutable proof" that the "Society of Soviet Citizens" in Yining was involved in the events of 1962, the Chinese authorities closed all of its branches in Xinjiang, Inner Mongolia, and Manchuria.[191] In Harbin, Soviet sources claim, this was accompanied by police raids and arrests of Soviet citizens; one or two were killed or committed suicide in prison.[192] The PRC also demanded the liquidation of all Soviet trade offices in Xinjiang, Manchuria, Lanzhou, and Shanghai. By December 1962, Moscow was left only with its embassy.[193]

The period from early 1961 to mid-1962 witnessed a general relaxation of Sino-Soviet relations. China's domestic needs required a decrease in foreign policy radicalism. Moscow was ready to contribute to the improvement of the relationship with food aid and renewed military assistance. Although the signs for a recovery of Sino-Soviet relations were strong, especially in early 1961, both sides remained cautious. The accumulated mistrust was difficult to overcome and there were also points of renewed conflict. The Soviet-Albanian split, the twenty-second CPSU congress, and ethnic conflict in Xinjiang disturbed Beijing's relations with Moscow.

Because the PRC had been the victim of Soviet strong-arm tactics before, Mao was willing to push a confrontational line on Albania in the summer

[187] "Soviet-Chinese Relations (Reference)," May [?] 1965, *AVPRF*, f.0100, o.56, d.22, p.498, 233.

[188] Shi, *Zai lishi*, 399.

[189] Zhang, "Zai Mosike," 37.

[190] "On the Working Conditions of the Soviet Embassy and Consulates in the PRC and the Chinese Embassy in Moscow," 1/28/1964, *AVPRF*, f.0100, o.57, d.17, p.510, 14–23.

[191] Wang, *Zhonghua*, vol. 2, 247–48.

[192] "On the Anti-Soviet Expressions of the Chinese and the Albanians," [no date], *RGASPI*, f.522, o.3, d.13, 111–12. Borisov, *Soviet-Chinese Relations*, 225.

[193] Wang, *Zhonghua*, vol. 2, 247–48.

of 1961. He probably also hoped to exploit his renewed foreign policy radicalism in order to stop what he considered the growth of revisionism at home. But his unwillingness at the 7,000-Cadres Conference to acknowledge his own mistakes did not help him in this endeavor. On the contrary, it not only isolated him within the party but also provided renewed momentum for further economic reforms. While Mao complained about revisionism and the restoration of capitalism in China, the early 1962 political backlash against his radicalism even triggered concrete proposals for a more sensible foreign policy. The eighteen months from early 1961 to mid-1962 were thus a period of ambivalence in Sino-Soviet relations.

Had it not been for the inadvertent events of the twenty-second CPSU congress and ethnic conflict in Xinjiang, the period of domestic deradicalization in China might have produced the conditions for a genuine renaissance in Sino-Soviet relations. However, as a consequence of domestic needs and the inability to control his anger, Khrushchev raised de-Stalinization and Albania at the Soviet congress. Although the Soviet leader did not intend to make these issues the subject of a renewed debate with Chinese comrades, Mao happily seized the opportunity. Similarly, ethnic conflict in Xinjiang in the spring of 1962 stemmed from a combination of reasons—the Great Leap Forward, Chinese nativism, and citizenship issues. So far, no evidence that either Beijing or Moscow instigated the crisis has surfaced; it seems that local issues gradually drove the dispute toward its crisis point. Regardless, it greatly damaged the institutional links between the USSR and the PRC. Despite positive developments in Sino-Soviet relations since early 1961, cracks in the alliance remained, and, indeed, new ones opened.

CHAPTER 7

Mao Resurgent, 1962–1963

IN LATE 1962, the *New York Times* reported that Zhao Fu, a twenty-seven-year-old security officer for the Chinese delegation in Stockholm, had defected and been debriefed by West German intelligence. According to his testimony, Mao had recently asserted that "whoever is against Stalin is against Mao." Zhao further claimed that the Chairman was hoping for an uprising in the USSR against the anti-Stalinist and anti-communist Khrushchev, "leaving the way free for China to take over as leader of world Communism."[1]

At the late summer of 1962 Beidaihe meeting, Mao staged a brilliant comeback in daily policy making. He used this momentum to stamp his mark on Chinese foreign relations. The impending Yugoslav-Soviet rapprochement was only a prelude to the Sino-Soviet fallout over the Second Sino-Indian Border War and the Cuban Missile Crisis. By late October, Chinese propaganda was blasting the Soviet revisionists for the betrayal of the communist cause and for capitulating to U.S. imperialism. At the turn of the year, the five party congresses in Bulgaria, Hungary, Italy, Czechoslovakia, and East Germany revealed the depth of the ideological disagreements. In early 1963, pressure from within the socialist camp pushed the CCP and the CPSU to agree to a July meeting designed to resolve the ideological dispute. While skeptical about a possible reconciliation, the Soviet comrades were ready to give it a chance. Mao, in comparison, was determined to exacerbate the split, while trying to blame it on the revisionist Khrushchev.

Although Mao was genuinely dissatisfied with Soviet foreign policy toward the imperialist United States, the hyperbolic nature of his anti-Soviet propaganda served a domestic purpose. In fact, Mao launched his comeback over disagreements on rural policies within the party leadership. By accusing his internal opponents of being close to Khrushchev's domestic revisionism, he exploited rhetorical anti-Sovietism even further. Until the start of the Cultural Revolution, the Chairman applied these kinds of tactics with increasingly destructive effectiveness.

[1] *NYT*, 11/3/1962, 2.

THE BEIDAIHE WORK CONFERENCE AND THE TENTH CC PLENUM

By the summer of 1962, Mao was clearly discontented with the ideological softening in rural and foreign policies that had occurred since the spring. During his self-imposed exile in Wuhan, the Chairman developed a practice that would become typical of his political style in the following years: politicking outside official party and governmental structures. While gradually mobilizing those who shared his views—Chen Boda, Kang Sheng, his own wife Jiang Qing, and Lin Biao, for example—he turned away from long-trusted advisers.[2] When, for instance, his personal secretary Tian Jiaying started to support the field responsibility system, Mao began to lose faith in him.[3] Similarly, after the Chairman heard about Mao Dun's appeasement policies at the World Peace Council, he decided to turn against Wang Jiaxiang.[4]

Mao believed in a close connection between foreign and domestic policy. As he said in July of 1962: "International and domestic [affairs] share the same set of problems, that is, whether the revolution is led by the proletariat or the bourgeoisie."[5] The continued deterioration of relations with the Soviet revisionists over Xinjiang, as related in chapter 6, was a political bonus for the Chairman. By then, he had probably already decided to counter what he perceived to be the revisionism of his fellow leaders Liu, Deng, and their constituents.

Despite a dearth of evidence, it is possible to outline Mao's political comeback at the Beidaihe work conference from July 25 to August 24.[6] While the gathering was scheduled to discuss economic issues, Mao jettisoned the agenda by demanding to talk about class struggle and about the revisionists in the Chinese leadership.[7] Since the Chairman knew that he lacked the political capital to push through a purge of his internal adversaries similar to the one after Lushan in 1959, he framed his attack solely in rhetorical terms.[8] He started by distributing *Xinhua* reports on the economic problems in revisionist Yugoslavia coupled with an ominous question: "Is the path walked by the Yugoslavs good, or is the Marxist-Leninist path good?"[9] The dichotomous phrasing of the question naturally pointed to Mao's own conclusions. The Chairman then turned against the

---

[2] Lieberthal, "Great Leap," 332. Li, *Private Life*, 390–93.

[3] Salisbury, *New Emperors*, 197. MacFarquhar, *Origins*, vol. 3, 263–67.

[4] Xiao, *Qiusuo*, vol. 2, 933. Wu, *Huiyi*, 374–75. Xu, *Wang*, 565.

[5] Zhonggong, *Mao Zedong zhuan*, 1235.

[6] Bo, *Ruogan*, vol. 2, 1071.

[7] Niu, "1962," 33.

[8] Li, *Private Life*, 394.

[9] "Remarks on a Report by Xinhua News Agency regarding the Economic Situation in Yugoslavia," 8/2/1962, *JYMW*, vol. 10, 129.

"dark wind"—nonsocialist family farming in China.[10] He exploited his long-standing depiction of Khrushchev as a revisionist in order to crush the liberalization of rural policies at home: *Did Khrushchev dare to call publicly for the abolition of the collective farmsteads?*[11] The question made the rural reformers like Liu and Deng look worse than Khrushchev. Using words similar to Stalin's dictum of 1929 ("Either *back*—to capitalism, or *forward*—to socialism"),[12] Mao believed that China had reached a fork in the road: "Either we go to socialism, or we go to capitalism."[13] He thus called on the party to fight revisionist and bourgeois thinking in the countryside. The Socialist Education Movement was supposed to rectify the rural party of its revisionist and capitalist tendencies.[14]

The tenth plenum, from September 24 to 27, revealed the extent of Mao's capacity to set the agenda.[15] Still against decollectivization, the Chairman warned that the field responsibility system would encourage those groups he most vehemently opposed—landlords and rich peasants who would restore the reactionary, pre-1949 society.[16] He asserted that Lenin had forecast the danger of bourgeois restoration after the Bolshevik Revolution, maintained that China's struggle against Soviet revisionism dated back to "1945 when Stalin tried to prevent the Chinese Revolution," and demanded that the CCP "deal with the problem of revisionism and the problem of the bourgeoisie within itself."[17]

The day after the tenth plenum, Mao revised his vision of the intermediate zone. In 1946, as described in chapter 1, he believed that the emerging superpower conflict was a Soviet-American contest over the intermediate zone. Given the anti-imperialist nature of the USSR, the Chairman had decided to "lean to one side"; eventually, the alliance treaty with the Soviet Union made the newly founded PRC a part of the socialist camp. However, as a result of the past years of disagreement over peaceful coexistence, supposed Soviet-American collusion against China, and his belief that East and West European countries tried to escape the shadow of their respective Soviet and American hegemons, Mao now sought to redefine China's role in the world. Seeing two intermediate zones—"one is Asia, Africa, Latin America, one is Europe"—he called on China "not

[10] Cong, *Quzhe*, 507–8.

[11] *MZDDG*, 642 (italics mine).

[12] Stalin, "Concerning Questions of Agrarian Policy in the USSR," 12/27/1929, Stalin, *Works*, vol. 12, 151–52.

[13] Bo, *Ruogan*, vol. 2, 1087.

[14] Lieberthal, "Great Leap," 333.

[15] Lieberthal, "Great Leap," 333.

[16] Lieberthal, "Great Leap," 334. Short, *Mao*, 514–15.

[17] Mao, "Speech at the Tenth Plenary Session of the Eighth CC," 9/24/1962, *CLG* 1/4, 85–93.

to rely on the leader of a big country" any longer.[18] Instead, as he had told the plenum on the twenty-fourth, "we have the anti-imperialist task, as well as the task of supporting the movement of national liberation. This means that we must support the broad masses of people in the three continents of Asia, Africa, and Latin America."[19]

With this, Mao turned to the revisionist nature of *sanhe yishao* (three reconciliations and one reduction) promoted by Wang Jiaxiang.[20] He called it "a position amiable with imperialism, a position polite towards the reactionaries, a position courteous towards revisionism, a position of little support for the Asian-African-Latin American people, [in short, a position] equaling the 'revisionist path.'"[21] Wang was forced to make a public self-criticism and—branded as a "domestic revisionist"—soon disappeared from political life.[22] The Sixth All-Country Foreign Affairs Conference, which the tenth plenum instructed to be convened, translated Mao's new radicalism into the policies to be followed by both party and government in foreign relations: the intensification of the anti-revisionist struggle through the propagation of *Mao Zedong Thought* abroad, the cooperation with socialist states and capitalism only in the spheres of economy and science, and a greater focus on Asia, Africa, and Latin America.[23]

Also, at the Beidaihe conference Mao admitted once more that "during the 1959 anti-Rightist struggle, wrong was done," and promised that there would be no new Anti-Rightist Campaign.[24] It was another empty assurance; instead, he asserted that "it would seem to be better for China's right opportunism to change its name to Chinese revisionism."[25] This linguistic modification allowed the Chairman to place any domestic critic under the category of revisionism. In line with his rejection of Wang Jiaxiang's *sanhe yishao*, Mao also insinuated that those critical of his policies were connected to China's enemies—the *sanni yitie* (three *ni*'s and one *tie*: John Kennedy [Ke-*ni*-di], Nikita Khrushchev [*Ni*-ji-ta He-lu-xiao-fu], Jawaharlal Nehru [*Ni*-he-lu], and Josip Tito [*Tie*-tuo]).[26]

Although the Beidaihe work conference and the tenth plenum represented a defeat for domestic reformers—and would later stand as the crucial turn of events that led to the Cultural Revolution—the resolutions

---

[18] "Two Intermediate Zones (1963/9, 1964/1, 7)," *MZDW*, vol. 8, 343–44.

[19] Mao, "Speech at the Tenth Plenary Session of the Eighth CC," 86.

[20] Xiao, *Qiusuo*, vol. 2, 929–30, 933. Niu, "1962," 33–34.

[21] Zhonggong, *Mao Zedong zhuan*, 1236.

[22] Xu, *Wang*, 566. Mao, "Remarks on the 137th Issue of the Foreign Affairs Bulletin," 9/29/1962, *JYMW*, vol. 10, 199 (quote).

[23] "Communication of the Main Points of the 6th All-Country Foreign Affairs Conference," [no date], *JSSDAG*, 3124, zhang 145, 2–13.

[24] Bo, *Ruogan*, vol. 2, 1092.

[25] Mao, "Speech at the Tenth Plenary Session of the Eighth CC," 90.

[26] MacFarquhar, *Origins*, vol. 3, 290.

and the official plenum communiqué that the meetings produced were by no means unambiguous. Mao had been able to stop what he called revisionist or even capitalist reforms, but he had not come up with any workable alternative. The official documents were accordingly riddled with inconsistencies; while they embraced Mao's ideological concerns, they continued to promote methods and policies that had been worked out before the Chairman's political resurgence.[27]

After the tenth plenum, Mao tried to implement his brand of leftist policies at home.[28] According to the Chairman, the mild economic recovery of 1962 was evidence that more nonsocialist emergency measures were redundant, that they were actually capitalist restoration: "We have to oppose our own domestic revisionism, the forces of evil capitalism."[29] In the fall, he launched the SEM, which subsequently became the primary ideological battlefield within the CCP leadership. The struggle developed, however, *outside* of traditional decision-making organs; Mao, who had preeminence in calling CC plena, did *not* convene a single plenum until the start of the Cultural Revolution in August 1966. He tried to implement his policies through directives, while his domestic opponents used the party, which they controlled, to stop him.[30]

One of the main weapons in Mao's ideological arsenal was the call to fight revisionism everywhere with the slogan *fanxiu fangxiu* (oppose revisionism abroad, prevent revisionism at home), closely linking foreign and domestic policies to each other.[31] Anti-Soviet and anti-Yugoslav polemics began after the tenth plenum,[32] insinuating that Beijing was the world's revolutionary center and the vanguard of national liberation in Asia, Africa, and Latin America.[33] The sudden changes in Chinese propaganda since the later summer did not go unnoticed in Moscow.[34]

[27] For resolutions: Union, *Documents*, vol. 1, 185–205. Lieberthal, "Great Leap," 335. Cong, *Quzhe*, 517.

[28] MacFarquhar, *Origins*, vol. 3, 334. Short, *Mao*, 515.

[29] Xu, *Wang*, 567.

[30] Lieberthal, "Great Leap," 296–97, 325–26, 348–51. Baum, *Ssu-ch'ing*. MacFarquhar, *Origins*, vol. 3, 325–26. Sladkovskii, *Ocherki*, 397–400.

[31] Cong, *Quzhe*, 518–22, 576.

[32] "Decision of the 10th Plenum of the CC of the 8th Party Congress of the CCP," [September 1962], *BArch-Freib*, VA-01/6385 Presseinformationen zu politischen und militärischen Ereignissen, 4.

[33] "Note number 13/62 on the Discussion with the Military Attaché of the USSR," 10/18/1962, *BArch-Freib*, VA-01/6384 Aktenvermerke des Militärattachés der DDR in der VR China über Gespräche, Besichtigungen und protokollarische Veranstaltungen, Band 1, 1–2.

[34] "Note on a Talk with the Embassy Counselor Mokhulskii," 10/20/1962, *PAAA-MfAA*, VS-Hauptstelle, G-A 338, 1–3. "To Gromyko," 10/12/1962, *AVPRF*, f.0100, o.55, d.24, p.483, 197–209.

These polemics paralleled Leonid Brezhnev's friendship visit to Yugo-slavia from September 24 to October 5. Despite Tito's words about the clearing of the "fog" in the relationship, the visit did not restore complete amity. While ideological disagreements remained, it at least cleared the way for a return visit in December.[35]

CRISES IN THE HIMALAYAS AND THE CARIBBEAN

In October, fate seemed to reward the Chairman. The parallel crises of the Second Sino-Indian Border War and the Cuban Missile Crisis con-firmed his views on Soviet revisionism, whereas Khrushchev was con-fronted with a twofold predicament: in the Himalayas, the Soviet leader had to balance Soviet-Indian friendship with the Sino-Soviet alliance while, in the Caribbean, the revelation of his risky policy of stationing nuclear IRBMs behind the back of the Americans forced him into a pub-licly ignominious retreat under U.S. pressure. Mao was more than happy to carp at the Soviet archrevisionist for his wobbly support of revolution-ary China against bourgeois India and for his weakness in dealing with American imperialism in Cuba. Similar to the U-2 Incident in May 1960, unrelated events in international affairs provided Mao with just the po-litical boost he needed.

In light of his rejection of Wang Jiaxiang's *sanhe yishao*, Mao set out to implement an assertive policy designed to forestall Nehru's renewed for-ward policy in the Himalayas. On October 20, the PLA launched an attack in the Western Sector that pushed up to 160 kilometers into Indian territory though, on average, the Chinese did not advance more than 25 kilometers. China's simultaneous intrusions at the Eastern Sector were much smaller. The rout of Indian troops was humiliating; the PRC had de facto removed the military basis of Nehru's forward policy within only weeks. On No-vember 21, China declared a unilateral cease-fire and proposed the mutual withdrawal of all troops twenty kilometers behind the 1959 line of actual control in the Western Sector and behind the McMahon line (*sic!*) in the Eastern Sector. Although Nehru refused, China had nevertheless achieved its immediate aim; India never again resumed the forward policy.[36]

During the crisis, close Soviet-Indian diplomatic contacts influenced Moscow's reaction to the renewed Himalayan conflict. From August to

[35] *NYT*, 9/24/1962, 7, 28; 9/26/1962, 5 (quote); 9/27/1962, 4; 9/30/1962, 42; 10/1/1962, 21; 10/4/1962, 1, 2; 10/5/1962, 8; 10/6/1962, 2.

[36] Maxwell, *India's China War*, 173–443. Liu, *Sino-Indian Dispute*, 31–40. Swamy, *In-dia's China Perspective*, 87–91. MacFarquhar, *Origins*, vol. 3, 298–312. Maharaj Chopra, "Himalayan Border War," *Military Review* 43/5, 8–16.

December, leaders of the anti-Chinese majority faction of the Communist Party of India, high-ranking government officials, and even the prime minister were in frequent contact with the Soviets.[37] Sino-Soviet contacts, in comparison, occurred less frequently, usually on a much lower level, and, at times, only after Soviet requests.[38] China's own ambassador in Moscow, Liu Xiao, did not resurface in diplomacy until October 13. Despite previous Indian lobbying, Khrushchev told the ambassador he had advocated a peaceful solution all along and supported Chinese diplomatic protests against India's forward policy. In his memoirs, Wu Lengxi claimed that Khrushchev's backing stemmed only from his need for Chinese support during the impending Cuban Missile Crisis (see below).[39]

The next day, the CPSU Presidium received Liu for a lavish farewell dinner. The Soviets tried to convince him that the USSR would not support India in the impending border conflict.[40] The next day, October 15, Mikoyan briefed Liu on the situation in the Caribbean and requested the information be conveyed to the Chinese leaders.[41] But Beijing still did not care about close diplomatic cooperation. After Liu's departure on October 24, ending eight years in the Soviet capital, it took seven weeks for his successor—coincidentally, the ambassador to New Delhi, Pan Zili—to arrive in Moscow.[42] Following China's October 20 notification of the outbreak of hostilities,[43] the Chinese side also rarely informed the Soviet ambassador in Beijing, Chervonenko.[44] In comparison, Soviet-Indian diplomatic contacts remained intensive during the four weeks between outgoing Indian Ambassador S. Dutt's late September departure and the October 24 arrival of his successor, T. N. Kaul.[45]

Despite this apparent lack of diplomatic interest, Beijing made sure to complain about Moscow's promised deliveries of the MiG-21, which the

[37] See extensive documentation on Soviet-Indian contacts in *NSA*, RADD (all documents from: *AVPRF*, f.090, o.24, d.3–6).

[38] For Sino-Soviet communications: *NSA*, RADD, 7/4/1962, 7/7/62, 10/10/1962, and "Record of Conversation with Zhou Enlai," 10/8/1962, *AVPRF*, f.0100, o.55, d.7, p. 480, 59–70. I. Benediktov, "Diary Entry, 1/17/1962," James Hershberg, ed., "New East-Bloc Documents on the Sino-Indian Conflict, 1959 and 1962," *CWIHP Bulletin* 8–9, 263. *JYMW*, vol. 9, 252,n. 1.

[39] WLX, 497–98. Si, "Shi pengyou," 298–99. Soviet transcript: "Reception by Khrushchev of Liu Xiao," 10/13/1962, *AVPRF*, f.0100, o.55, d.4, p.480, 20–37.

[40] Liu, *Chushi*, 146–54.

[41] Wang, *Zhonghua*, vol. 2, 248–49.

[42] *SCMP* 2849, 26–27; 2880, 35.

[43] "Record of Conversation with Zhang Hanfu," 10/20/1962, *AVPRF*, f.0100, o.55, d.7, p.480, 105–6.

[44] Chinese information about border war: *AVPRF*, f.0100, o.55, d.7, p.480, 109–12, 119–20, 123–26.

[45] Soviet-Indian diplomatic contacts between late September and October 24: *NSA*, RADD, 10/2/1962; 10/8/1962; 10/18/1962; 10/22/1962; 10/23/1962; 10/28/1962.

PLA had already received the year before, to New Delhi.[46] On October 14, Khrushchev placated the Chinese by offering a delay of the Soviet-Indian MiG-21 agreement.[47] Six days later, the same day the Chinese informed the Soviets about the outbreak of the war, Moscow notified New Delhi of the suspension of the MiG-21 agreement.[48]

The Second Sino-Indian Border War had begun just when one of the most dangerous crises of the Cold War suddenly erupted. On October 22, U.S. President Kennedy announced that the USSR had stationed SS-4 and SS-5 nuclear IRBMs on Cuba, threatening U.S. national security. While Khrushchev has subsequently received much criticism for his adventurism, in fairness, the dangerous game made some sense at the time. His ICBM bluff after the October 1957 Sputnik launch had led to the subsequent transfer of American IRBMs to Great Britain, Italy, and Turkey as stopgap measures.[49] Since the new American threat increased Soviet insecurity, Moscow proposed a joint Sino-Soviet submarine fleet in the Pacific in 1958. Mao's refusal, however, did not solve the Soviet strategic dilemma.[50] It was only the Cuban Revolution in early 1959 that provided the USSR with the opportunity to counter American IRBMs along Soviet borders with its own IRBMs off the U.S. coast.

On October 28, under Washington's pressure and faced with the possibility of nuclear war, Moscow agreed to the publicly humiliating withdrawal of the missiles. The withdrawal undermined Khrushchev's standing in the Soviet party. Upon his removal from office in October 1964, for example, the CPSU Presidium accused him of "adventurism" in Cuba, bringing "the world to the edge of nuclear war," and inflicting "damage to the prestige of our country."[51] It also affected his relationship with Fidel Castro—a relationship developed, partially, because of his desire to exclude Chinese revolutionary influence in Latin America. In his anger, the Cuban leader refused to thank Moscow for obtaining Washington's pledge not to act militarily against Havana in the future.[52] Khrushchev was also deprived of another humble success from the crisis;

---

[46] "Record of Conversation with Zhou Enlai," 10/8/1962, *AVPRF*, f.0100, o.55, d.7, p.480, 59–60.

[47] Zhang, "Zai Mosike," 37–38.

[48] Westad, "Introduction," 28. MacFarquhar, *Origins*, vol. 3, 314.

[49] Nash, *Other Missiles*, 45–75.

[50] *PAAA-MfAA*, Konferenzen und Verhandlungen mit DDR-Beteiligung, Microfiche A 14702, 1349.

[51] Istochnik, "Doklad Prezidiuma TsK KPSS na oktiabrskom Plenume TsK KPSS," *Istochnik* 1998/2, 113.

[52] Aleksandr Fursenko et al., *One Hell of a Gamble* (New York: Norton, 1997), 288–89. Khrushchev, *Nikita S. Khrushchev*, 641–51.

while the American IRBMs (Jupiters) would soon be removed from Turkey, this would be done without public acknowledgment.[53]

There is no evidence that Moscow had informed Beijing of the Cuban operation before mid-October, when it promised support in the conflict against New Delhi.[54] But, apparently, the Chinese had good sources in Cuba and knew of the buildup early on.[55] Beijing's backing of Moscow during its conflict with Washington was negligible.[56] A Chinese government statement on October 25 protested against "U.S. piracy and war provocations" and supported "the Cuban people's struggle against U.S. aggression."[57] Wu Lengxi later claimed that "of course, we did not support Khrushchev's policy of stationing missiles on Cuba, but we also did not oppose it."[58]

It was only after the sudden end of the Cuban Missile Crisis that Chinese propaganda went into full swing. A media campaign denounced the withdrawal as a "Munich" and blasted Soviet revisionism for "show[ing] vacillation in a struggle and dar[ing] not to win a victory that can be won." The Chinese leadership staged mass rallies supporting Cuba's struggle and accusing the USSR of "adventurism" for sending the missiles and of "capitulationism" for withdrawing them.[59] The Soviet pullout from Cuba was a "cheap" propaganda victory for the Chairman, as Khrushchev complained to the CPSU plenum on November 23.[60] Beijing had nothing to lose in a nuclear confrontation on the other side of the globe.[61]

Mao's inability to keep his schadenfreude in check exasperated Khrushchev, who was still smarting from the humiliating withdrawal. In early January, he complained to John Gollan, a British communist leader, about the Chinese: "[W]e don't understand what they want. . . . [Their] position is confusing and inconsistent."[62] At the end of that month, he wrote Castro: "[O]nly God knows what moves them: ill-will or incomprehension."[63]

[53] Taubman, *Khrushchev*, 576–77. Nash, *Other Missiles*, 102–11, 118–71.

[54] Wang, *Zhonghua*, vol. 2, 248–49.

[55] MacFarquhar, *Origins*, vol. 3, 317.

[56] Prozumenshikov, "Sino-Indian Conflict," 254.

[57] Xinhua, *China's Foreign Relations*, 516.

[58] WLX, 504.

[59] Quoted in: Gittings, *Survey*, 176.

[60] "CPSU CC Plenum," 11/19–23/1962, RGANI, f.2, o.1, d.632, 103.

[61] Prozumenshikov, "Sino-Indian Conflict," 255–56.

[62] Quoted in: Sergey Radchenko, "The China Puzzle: Soviet Policy Towards the People's Republic of China in the 1960s" (diss., London School of Economics, 2005), 51.

[63] "Document 84: Premier Khrushchev's letter to Prime Minister Castro, reviewing the crisis, January 3, 1963," Laurence Chang et al., eds., *The Cuban Missile Crisis, 1962* (New York: New, 1992), 337.

After the Cuban Missile Crisis, Soviet support for China threatened to tilt back to neutrality in the Sino-Indian border war.[64] A November 3 letter from Khrushchev urged Nehru "to accept negotiations on the Chinese Communist terms."[65] And a *Pravda* editorial on November 5 called for a ceasefire and negotiations without preconditions.[66] In the first half of November, Moscow reversed the suspension of the MiG-21 sale.[67]

One cause of China's aggression in the Second Sino-Indian Border War might have been Mao's need for an external crisis in order to launch the SEM.[68] The documentary evidence for this link is certainly not as clear as in 1958, when he coupled the Second Taiwan Strait Crisis with the launching of the radical Great Leap Forward. The large rallies in support of revolutionary Cuba and against the defeatist Soviet Union, though, were undoubtedly Mao's attempts to instill revolutionary consciousness against revisionism in China's masses.[69] In the end, the two unrelated but concurrent crises in the fall of 1962 led to a resumption of Maoist ideological warfare against Khrushchevite revisionism. The attacks, however, were not well-received within the socialist camp, as the five European party congresses to which we now turn revealed.

FIVE EUROPEAN PARTY CONGRESSES

The series of communist party congresses in Bulgaria, Hungary, Italy, Czechoslovakia, and East Germany from early November 1962 to late January 1963 discloses, unmistakably, the Sino-Soviet ideological divisions that had deepened over Cuba and India. On the one hand, Mao used the confrontation as a means to render pressure on adversaries at home. On the other hand, Khrushchev was increasingly interested in a rapprochement with the United States, as described in chapter 8.

Before the first of the five party congresses, in early November, Khrushchev convened the Polish, East German, Czechoslovak, Hungarian, Romanian, and Bulgarian party leaders in Moscow to brief them on the international situation after the Cuban Missile Crisis. Because the gathering occurred on short notice, not all could attend at the same time.[70] The Soviet leader told his Czechoslovak guests that Soviet relations with the

[64] MacFarquhar, *Origins*, vol. 3, 317.
[65] *NYT*, 11/4/1962, 1, 3.
[66] *Pravda*, 11/5/1962, 1.
[67] Westad, "Introduction," 28.
[68] MacFarquhar, *Origins*, vol. 3, 297–99.
[69] Gittings, *Survey*, 176.
[70] Zhivkov, for example, left on November 3 while Gomułka arrived on that day: *NYT*, 11/4/1962, 35.

Chinese "could hardly be worse," but admitted that China's position in the Himalayas was "basically . . . correct . . . because India has taken an incorrect position in the recent period."[71]

Polemics resumed at the eighth Bulgarian Party Congress. The bad blood Chinese actions had engendered since the Soviet-Albanian split of 1961 now returned with a vengeance. On November 5, the congress convened to rubberstamp the victory of the pro-Soviet Zhivkov, who had defeated the Stalinist Prime Minister Anton Yugov.[72] The new Bulgarian leader endorsed Khrushchev's pursuit of de-Stalinization and peaceful coexistence, offered an olive branch to the Yugoslavs, sharply criticized the Albanians, and regretted the conflict between "the fraternal people—the Indians and the Chinese."[73] Soviet delegate Suslov followed with praise for the de-Stalinization of Bulgaria and a long-winded defense of Soviet policies in the Caribbean.[74]

Although the CCP had probably not anticipated Bulgaria's ideological about-face, it had expected such attacks from the Soviets.[75] Thus, the Chinese delegation adapted its behavior to whatever the Soviet comrades were doing. Expressing its "principled point of view," it would sit still if they clapped, and vice-versa.[76] When Wu Xiuquan got up to give his own speech, he lauded "heroic Cuba" for its struggle against "U.S. oppression and enslavement." Without even mentioning the missile crisis, he implicitly demanded that the Soviet comrades show a stiffer backbone in their struggle against American imperialism. In light of the Bulgarian criticism of Albania, Wu called for an end to these attacks and for the "redoubl[ing of] our efforts to safeguard the unity of the socialist camp."[77] In that vein, however, he failed to mention past Chinese propaganda attacks on the Soviets. The Chinese estrangement from the socialist camp also was obvious after the convention. During a courtesy call to Zhivkov, Wu painted India in the darkest colors.[78] Yet, his efforts could not make up for the previous lack of Chinese diplomatic lobbying.

The CCP delegation left Sofia for Bucharest in order to regroup, before continuing on to Budapest to attend the eighth Hungarian Party Congress

---

[71] "Czechoslovak Record of Conversation between Czechoslovak Party Leader Antonín Novotný and Soviet Leader Nikita Khrushchev, Moscow, October 30, 1962," Oldřich Tůma, ed., "Selected Czechoslovak Documents on the Cold War in Asia, 1962–1966," comp. and trans. for the conference "New Central and East European Evidence on the Cold War in Asia," Budapest, Hungary, 10/30–11/2/2003.

[72] Khrushchev, *Testament*, 275–78. *NYT*, 11/6/1962, 1, 4; 11/10/1962, 18.

[73] *Pravda*, 11/6/1962, 4–5.

[74] *Pravda*, 11/7/1962, 5.

[75] Wu, *Huiyi*, 346–47.

[76] Wu, *Huiyi*, 346–47.

[77] *SCMP* 2860, 25–29.

[78] Wu, *Huiyi*, 347–48. MacFarquhar, *Origins*, vol. 3, 318–19.

scheduled for November 20. When the delegation tried to book airplane tickets to Budapest, the Romanians claimed that all flights were full. Only after an appeal to the Hungarian embassy did the Chinese obtain the necessary tickets for a flight that turned out to be half-empty.[79]

The Hungarians must have soon regretted the fairness shown to the stranded CCP delegation, although, since they had anticipated a repetition of the Sino-Soviet clapping spectacle in Bulgaria, they had prohibited public expressions of support or opposition.[80] Party boss János Kádár and the CPSU representative, Kuusinen, made moderate speeches that did not mention China.[81] Wu's address, which, as usual, must have been prepared in Beijing, was even more antagonistic than his statements in Sofia. In light of Tito's impending trip to Moscow, it added to the earlier criticism of Soviet policy attacks on the "modern revisionists represented by the leading clique in Yugoslavia" who "carry on subversive work against the socialist camp and the world communist movement."[82]

Because his speech did not receive a friendly reception, Wu asked Beijing for instructions on "whether or not to declare where we stand." Under Mao's leadership, the Politburo quickly drew up a statement once again criticizing the Soviets and demanding a third Moscow-style meeting to solve the ideological disputes.[83] Since the official proceedings of the congress had already ended, the Chinese delegation decided that its interpreter should read the text, in Hungarian, to the farewell cocktail party. The Hungarians and Soviets were flabbergasted. Kádár quickly requested that the Chinese leave: "I never thought that your party delegation would say this, we can only express regret over your actions."[84] Wu and his staff immediately left for Warsaw to meet the Chinese ambassador to Poland, Wang Bingnan.[85] Wang had just returned from a conference of China's ambassadors in Beijing, where, following the Sixth All-Country Foreign Affairs Conference, they had been "instruct[ed] . . . [about] Peking's point of view for use when they return to their stations."[86]

On December 4, Tito arrived in Moscow for what was officially described as a vacation but was in reality his first official visit since 1956.[87] Khrushchev's personal welcome at the Kievskii Railway Station and his use of "comrade" as salutation were clear signs that he wanted to mend

[79] Wu, *Huiyi*, 348. MacFarquhar, *Origins*, vol. 3, 319.
[80] MacFarquhar, *Origins*, vol. 3, 319.
[81] *Pravda*, 11/21/1962, 6–7, 11/22/1962, 6.
[82] SCMP 2867, 20–24.
[83] WLX, 509.
[84] Wu, *Huiyi*, 348–49, 350–51.
[85] Wu, *Huiyi*, 352.
[86] NYT, 11/14/1962, 1, 9.
[87] NYT, 12/2/1962, 12; 12/5/1962, 4.

fences.[88] Tito's subsequent vacation trip to Volgograd was extensively covered in the Soviet media.[89] On December 13, in a "rare speech by a visiting foreign statesman in the Supreme Soviet," Tito endorsed the improvement of relations between Moscow and Belgrade.[90] Later, his Soviet host even accepted his invitation for a reciprocal visit.[91]

While Khrushchev feted Tito in Moscow, the Sino-Soviet ideological quarrel continued in Rome in early December. The Italian party leader Palmiro Togliatti and the Soviet representative, Kozlov, both took a harder line than Kádár and Kuusinen had a fortnight before, rigorously defending past Soviet policies and criticizing Chinese actions in the Himalayas.[92] The Chinese delegate Zhao Yimin responded by assailing Tito, the "100 per cent traitor to the cause of world Communism."[93] Obviously, the top Chinese leadership had decided to use Tito's visit as an opportunity to attack the revisionist twins, Yugoslavia and the USSR. Almost all delegates of the Italian party congress denounced Zhao's speech.[94]

As Zhao was toeing Mao's anti-revisionist line in Rome, Wu Xiuquan traveled from Warsaw to Prague to attend the twelfth Czechoslovak Party Congress on December 4. The same familiar spectacle unfolded. The leader of the host party, Antonín Novotný, and the Soviet representative, Leonid Brezhnev, defended Soviet foreign policies and criticized the Albanians. This time, the Sino-Indian border war only evoked expressions of regret.[95] Unlike the previous three party congresses, the Czechoslovak party had arranged for the Chinese to speak on the second day in order to reduce the time the CCP could use to rework its address.[96] Regardless, Wu's speech followed the same line as his earlier ones, attacking Soviet foreign policies, defending Chinese positions, accusing the host party for allowing its congress to be abused for attacks on other parties, and, ironically, calling for unity.[97] Clearly, the Chinese party did not mind its own internal inconsistencies nor did it care about the speech's reception. Wu was frequently interrupted by banging, trampling, hushing, and shouting.[98] Only the North Koreans supported the Chinese.[99]

[88] NYT, 12/5/1962, 1, 4 (quote); 12/6/1962, 8.
[89] NYT, 12/13/1962, 6.
[90] NYT, 12/14/1962, 1, 2; 12/24/1962, 2 (quote).
[91] NYT, 12/21/1962, 2.
[92] Pravda, 12/3/1962, 4–5; 12/4/1962, 3.
[93] NYT, 12/5/1962, 46; 12/6/1962, 16.
[94] NYT, 12/7/1962, 3.
[95] Pravda, 12/3/1962, 4–5; 12/6/1962, 3.
[96] WLX, 511.
[97] SCMP 2877, 27–31.
[98] WLX, 511–12. Wu, Huiyi, 353.
[99] WLX, 511. MacFarquhar, Origins, vol. 3, 321.

Informed by Wu about these developments, Mao convened the Politburo which decided to instruct the scholars to draft an aggressive statement in reply. It arrived in Prague on the last day of the congress, December 8.[100] Only minutes before the end of Novotný's closing address, Wu handed the statement over to the chairman of the congress, who passed it on to the speaker: "Novotný halted his final speech, looked at our statement, and got very angry. . . . he read our statement from head to tail."[101] It must have been strange to hear a defense of Albania, a stern blaming of the CPSU for the Soviet-Albanian split, and a censure of the "unusual manners [such] as shouting and hissing" displayed by his own comrades from Novotný's mouth.[102] Once again, the Chinese had not made new friends.

The Soviet party decided to inform its own people about the Sino-Soviet dispute with a propaganda campaign starting on December 10. Though lacking in much detail, it was the *first* time that Moscow notified its subjects about the developments of the last years.[103] On December 12, angered by Maoist propaganda on Cuba, Khrushchev also convened the Supreme Soviet to defend himself.[104] Given the secret U.S. assurances to abstain from an intervention in Cuba and to remove the Jupiters, the Soviet leader described the sudden end of the crisis as what it really was—a compromise. After criticizing Albania and mocking China's claims of leadership in decolonization, he lauded the Indians for their military action against the Portuguese imperialists in Goa the year before, while reminding the Chinese of their continued accommodation to British and Portuguese colonialism in Hong Kong and Macao, respectively.[105] Tito's presence at the Supreme Soviet was a compelling sign of the political changes in the socialist world, which included the possibility of rapprochement with the west.[106] The *New York Times* described Khrushchev's address "as a call for [a] Soviet-American alliance against China."[107]

Before the last party congress, in East Germany, the Chinese delegation returned home to Beijing to assess the situation. On December 15, *Renmin Ribao* published an editorial whose title—a slight variation of Marx's famous dictum—Mao had chosen personally: "Workers of All Countries, Unite to Oppose Our Common Enemy." According to Wu

[100] WLX, 512–13.
[101] WLX, 513–14. Wu, *Huiyi*, 354–55.
[102] SCMP 2883, 29–31.
[103] NYT, 12/11/1962, 2.
[104] NYT, 12/13/1962, 1, 2.
[105] *Pravda*, 12/13/1962, 1–5. NYT, 12/13/1962, 1, 2.
[106] NYT, 12/17/1962, 2, 9.
[107] NYT, 12/15/1962, 6.

Lengxi, this mix of justified criticism and Maoist hyperbole was a riposte to the so-called "encircle-and-destroy-campaign" of the CPSU.[108] Reviewing the major issues of the four party congresses, it insisted on putting an end to public disunity in the socialist camp because the public disputes only catered to the imperialists and reactionaries.[109] By publishing this editorial, however, the Chinese comrades demonstrated that they themselves did not take their own call for unity seriously.

Mao was eager to exploit the rifts that had opened during the four congresses. After quizzing Wu Xiuquan,[110] he forwarded his ideas for another propaganda strike to Liu Shaoqi. The Politburo coordinated the writing of a new polemic against the Soviets "without mentioning them by name," with the Chairman responsible for finalizing the text.[111] Published in *Hongqi* on December 31, it attacked Togliatti for "departing further and further from Marxism-Leninism."[112] The CPSU replied by announcing that Khrushchev would attend the impending East German party congress in person.[113] It was not a good omen; the last time he had attended a foreign congress was in Bucharest in June 1960.

Having drawn the battle lines, both sides tried to recruit supporters. During Prime Minister Yumjaagiyn Tsedenbal's trip to Beijing for the conclusion of the Sino–Outer Mongolian border treaty in late December, Zhou, in a tone "similar to a lecture," defended Chinese actions in the Himalayas and painted the "bourgeois" Nehru as a lackey of U.S. imperialism. According to the transcript, Zhou got "nervous" when his guest reminded him that "the Chinese-Indian border question must not be solved only in the interests of China, but also in accordance with the interests of the whole international communist movement."[114] Trying to pull the Mongolians to the Soviet side, Leonid Ilichev, the head of the CC Ideology Department, flew to Ulan Bator in early January to meet Tsedenbal. While there, he accused the Chinese of acting like "infallible Marxist-Leninists."[115] At midmonth, Andropov traveled to Hanoi to convince the Vietnamese Workers' Party (VWP), which, at that time,

---

[108] WLX, 515–17.

[109] CB 701, 1–9.

[110] Wu, *Huiyi*, 359.

[111] WLX, 517–20, 530–31.

[112] CB 702, 1–20.

[113] NYT, 12/15/1963, 6.

[114] First quoted in: "Record of Conversation by Chervonenko with D. Tsebegmid," 1/1/1963, AVPRF, f.0100, o.56, d.7, p.495, 3. "Record of Conversation (from East German Archives) between Chinese Premier Zhou Enlai and Mongolian Leader J. Tsedenbal," 12/26/1962, Hershberg, "New East-Bloc Documents," 265–69 (remaining quotes).

[115] "Information on the Consultations of the CPSU with the Communist and Workers' Parties," 4/9/1963, SAPMO-BArch, DY 30/IV A 2/20/42. NYT, 1/9/1963, 1, 2.

was toeing a middle line.[116] Before traveling to East Berlin, Khrushchev himself stopped over in Warsaw to work on the Polish comrades.[117]

The sixth congress of the East German Unity Party (SED) was thus convened under clearly unfavorable conditions. On the day of Wu Xiuquan's arrival, the party organ *Neues Deutschland* proclaimed that Chinese positions "must be opposed with all determination."[118] Ulbricht himself went to the railway station to greet Khrushchev, who, still on the platform, rebuffed the Chinese on peaceful coexistence: "We will not fight, we will not conduct war to set up a Socialist society in any country because we believe that this is a matter for the people concerned."[119]

As in preceding congresses, the local party boss opened the convention, followed by the Soviet delegate and then by Wu Xiuquan. While Ulbricht's January 15 speech was hard-hitting,[120] Khrushchev's address the next day was surprisingly conciliatory. In fact, by January 2, the CPSU Presidium had decided to seek reconciliation with the CCP.[121] After the Soviet leader himself had brought the world to the brink of nuclear war, he reflected pensively on the terrible consequences of such a war for mankind. When he addressed the problems affecting the socialist camp, he not only abjured any attempts to "excommunicate" either the Yugoslavs, who had been invited to East Berlin, or the Albanians, but also called for an end to these disputes for the sake of communism—"the most holy cause."[122]

Before Wu's January 18 speech, the Chinese delegation had to digest Khrushchev's unexpected speech. Together with the North Koreans and the North Vietnamese, the Chinese withdrew to Beijing's embassy for an assessment,[123] although Hanoi's delegates soon left out of fear of the negative public impression their attendance would make.[124] Wu denounced the speech, claiming that it put before the CCP a difficult choice: either accept the Soviet proposal of an ideological truce, which would mean

---

[116] The connection of Andropov's trip to the Sino-Soviet disputes is mentioned in: "Information on the Consultations . . . ," 3.

[117] *NYT*, 1/11/1963, 2. Khrushchev's visit mentioned in: "Information on the Consultations . . . ," 2.

[118] *NYT*, 1/14/1963, 1.

[119] *NYT*, 1/15/1963, 1.

[120] *Pravda*, 1/16/1963, 2–3.

[121] "Meeting of the CC CPSU Presidium," 1/2/1963, Fursenko, *Prezidium*, vol. 1, 669.

[122] *Pravda*, 1/17/1963, 1–4.

[123] "Report on the Participation of Delegations of Brother Parties from the Socialist Countries at the 6th Party Congress of Our Party," [no date], SAPMO-BArch, DY 30/IV A 2/20/14, 3–4. "On the Attitude of the Delegation of the Communist Party of China on the 6th Party Congress of the SED," [no date], PAAA-MfAA, Abteilung Ferner Osten-Sektor China, Microfiche A 6764, 2.

[124] "Report on the Opinions, which have been raised by the Vietnamese Comrades," 1/17/1963, SAPMO-BArch, DY 30/IV A 2/20/14, 1.

"sealing our mouths," or speak up and "lose [the support of] the masses and the sympathy of the other parties." He decided to play it safe and ask Beijing for instructions.[125] In Mao's absence from the capital, Liu determined to "change our speech . . . , adopt a magnanimous attitude, advocate unity, oppose false unity, and expose the trick of the so-called termination of public disputes."[126]

The East German comrades were ready for another Chinese provocation. Indeed, the SED Politburo ordered the chairman of that particular session to "switch off the microphones" in case of "provocations by the Chinese delegation" against the Yugoslavs.[127] Wu's speech on January 18 was *not* magnanimous. After some polite remarks about the achievements of the host party, he not only raised well-known Chinese positions but also declared that "the Tito-Clique defrauds the revolutionary people . . . under the cover of Marxism-Leninism." At that point, protests from the floor could be heard and, eventually, the chairman of the session requested—much to the applause of the audience—that Wu abstain from attacks on the Yugoslav guests. But Wu continued to denounce "the Tito-Clique . . . [as] the special squad of American imperialism," to which the hall immediately replied with booing and trampling. To the "laughter" of the audience, the Chinese delegate then proceeded to call for the "unity of the socialist camp."[128] Wu recollected that "my speech was rudely interrupted" but that he continued reading stubbornly except, at one point, in order to scold the East Germans for their booing: "You did that very well; this shows me the 'culture' of the East German comrades."[129] The CCP delegation had one last provocation in store. On the final day of the congress, when all the delegates sang the Internationale, the Chinese comrades walked out of the hall. They refused to intone the anthem of the world's oppressed people together with the "special squad of American imperialism."[130]

The Chinese comrades decided to keep up the pressure once their delegation had returned home. After debriefing Wu, the CCP leadership concluded that Khrushchev had organized "a new peak of revisionist attacks on China."[131] A *Renmin Ribao* editorial on January 27, 1963, accused

[125] Wu, *Huiyi*, 360–62.

[126] WLX, 521.

[127] "Final Protocol No. 57 of the Meeting of the Politburo," 1/10/1963, Meissner, *DDR*, 128.

[128] "Fourth Day: Friday," 1/18/1963, *SAPMO-BArch*, DY 30/IV 1/VI/4, 856–57.

[129] Wu, *Huiyi*, 262–63.

[130] "From: 'Cankao Xiaoxi' of February 5, 1963, page 3: The Delegate of the Treacherous Tito-Clique became the 'Favorite' on the Party Congress of the SED," 2/7/1963, *PAAA-MfAA*, Abteilung Ferner Osten-Sektor China, Microfiche A 6764, 1.

[131] WLX, 523.

the East German congress of "crude attacks . . . against the Chinese Communist Party" and condemned its "brazen attempts, which were in open violation of the Moscow Declaration [1957] and the Moscow Statement [1960], . . . to reverse the verdict passed on the Tito clique of renegades to Marxism-Leninism." After accusing the CPSU of starting the current ideological dispute at its twenty-second congress, the editorial claimed that the CCP had never favored or caused public disunity. In fact, the article claimed that, since April 1962, the CCP had actually called for an international meeting to overcome ideological conflict. The piece concluded by blaming the CPSU for pushing the international communist movement "to the precipice" of a split.[132]

This latest Maoist tirade was disingenuous. In claiming that it had proposed a Moscow-style meeting since early 1962, Mao's CCP tried to take credit for the initiatives of other parties and make positions Mao had *opposed* at the time their own, as related in chapter 6. In early 1962, the Chairman had been in self-imposed exile in Wuhan; the proposal for a new international gathering was not Chinese but was pushed by five other parties. Ultimately, Liu and Deng had agreed to it reluctantly while following Mao's harsh foreign policy line. The one person calling for a genuine rapprochement was Wang Jiaxiang, whom the Chairman had purged as a domestic revisionist in the late summer of 1962.

The Sino-Soviet Split Prepared

It was clear that Mao had no interest in solving the ideological conflict with Khrushchev. Aleksei Brezhnev, then working at the Soviet embassy, recalled his impression of a strong connection between Chinese foreign and domestic politics: "Mao Zedong created a smoke screen, under whose cover the reprisal against those whom the CCP CC Chairman considered to be his rivals was organized."[133] For example, the December 31 *Hongqi* article attacking Togliatti warned of the lack of ideological integrity within the Italian party and of the corresponding dangers this presented for other communist parties.[134] Peng Zhen, Wu Han's patron during the Great Leap Forward, indirectly confirmed the tightening of the ideological screws when he told the Romanian ambassador that the policies of the Great Leap Forward "had been correct."[135] But not all of

[132] *SCMP* 2908, 29–37.

[133] Brezhnev, *Kitai*, 83–84. Also: Lieberthal, "Great Leap," 297–98.

[134] *CB* 702, 1–20.

[135] "Record of Conversation with Gheorghiu Dumitru," 1/17/1963, *AVPRF*, f.0100, o.56, d.7, p.495, 30–33.

Mao's domestic antagonists toed the Chairman's line. In early February, Liu Shaoqi told an English party delegation that the USSR was central to the socialist camp,[136] warning how "harmful" a split "to the essential interests of the Chinese people [and] . . . to Soviet interests" would be.[137]

After his return to Beijing in early 1963 from a long stay in Wuhan and Hangzhou, Mao called for an "anti-revisionist struggle" at home— "we have to educate those cadres who do not or only little understand Marxism"—and for propaganda against Khrushchev's "anti-Chinese campaign."[138] While a February work conference prepared for the possibility of a "break in Sino-Soviet party relations," it eventually decided to sever "completely" the bonds with the CPSU revisionists *only* "if an open fascist dictatorship was established in the Soviet Union." In that case, the Chairman mused, war against the Soviet fascists would break out and "we withdraw from Beijing into the mountains, to Yan'an . . . [and] fight a guerilla war."[139] Despite Mao's premonitions, Deng proposed to stop the attacks after the publication of three planned polemics in order to see whether the Soviet revisionists were willing to come to terms with the Chinese Marxist-Leninists.[140]

It was at this time that Mao also formalized the writing unit of scholars that had been working on the polemics informally since November. The new "central anti-revisionist drafting group," headed by the ultraleftist Kang Sheng, included people from the liaison and ideology departments and was "power-driven" by Chen Boda. Before its collapse in May 1966, it drafted *all* anti-Soviet polemics; the Chairman personally reviewed and finalized every single one.[141]

The Chinese comrades wanted to publish the polemics before talking to the Soviets. While presented as replies to recent criticisms by the Italian, French, and American communist parties, they were in fact aimed at the Soviet revisionists, as Wu Lengxi recalled.[142] The last of the three polemics,[143] published on March 8, is especially noteworthy. On January 9, the American comrades had elaborated on Khrushchev's December criticism of Chinese accommodation of British and Portuguese imperialism.[144] In a

[136] "Note on a Talk with Stoev," 2/8/1963, *PAAA-MfAA*, Abteilung Ferner Osten–Sektor China, Microfiche A 6764, 1–3.

[137] Zhonggong zhongyang wenxian yanjiushi bian, *Liu Shaoqi nianpu*, vol. 2 (Beijing: Zhongyang wenxian, 1996), 570.

[138] WLX, 525, 537–38. Bo, *Ruogan*, vol. 2, 1146.

[139] WLX, 537–38.

[140] WLX, 538.

[141] WLX, 505–7, 540–541 (quotes). MacFarquhar, *Origins*, vol. 3, 360–62.

[142] WLX, 525–30.

[143] The first two articles: CB 706, 1–97. SCMP 2929, 25–39.

[144] Xiao, *Qiusuo*, vol. 2, 1027.

skillful rhetorical exercise, the CCP put Hong Kong and Macao into the context of the "unequal treaties . . . which the imperialists had imposed on China" and listed *all* Sino-Russian treaties from the nineteenth century.[145] Moscow was put on notice that Beijing had extended ideological conflict to territorial issues as well.

Soviet Ambassador Chervonenko was aware that the Chinese had launched a new propaganda campaign. On January 31, he complained to Foreign Minister Gromyko that the "Chinese side tries to use mistakes and shortcomings of some Soviet organizations and staff . . . for its political aims, and at the same time allows itself serious digressions from the obligations accepted." He proposed to set up a commission in Moscow responsible for tracking the contents and implementation of all Sino-Soviet agreements since 1950.[146] Chervonenko's advice went unheeded. According to Aleksei Brezhnev, "Moscow frequently acted on the principle of a fire-brigade."[147] Hence, when small-scale border clashes erupted shortly after Beijing had notified Moscow of its territorial issues, the Soviet comrades scrambled to get more information about the historical and current situation of their Far Eastern borders.[148]

With the prospect of a new Moscow-style meeting on the agenda, in early February the socialist camp faced the problem of how to bring the CCP and the CPSU together. Since December, the parties from New Zealand, India, the United Kingdom, North Vietnam, Japan, and Indonesia had tried to seize on Wu Xiuquan's November demand for such a meeting.[149] The North Vietnamese public call "for the unity of the international communist movement" on February 10 generated the momentum necessary for a new Sino-Soviet party meeting. Although Hanoi abstained from blaming either Beijing or Moscow for the disputes, the call clearly hinted at its desire for unity for its own sake—for the struggle against American imperialism in Vietnam.[150] However, at that very moment, the Vietnamese seemed to be internally split as to how to deal with Sino-Soviet disagreements over peaceful coexistence. In late January, Hanoi had backed Moscow's policy, but by March, First Secretary Le Duan openly rejected it.[151]

On February 21, the CPSU responded to the Vietnamese initiative by calling on the CCP to meet for talks. The Soviet comrades also pleaded

[145] *SCMP* 2936, 27–34.

[146] "To Gromyko," 1/31/1963, *AVPRF*, f.0100, o.56, d.22, p.498, 4–8.

[147] Brezhnev, *Kitai*, 85.

[148] "To CPSU CC," 3/21/1963, *RGANI*, f.5, o.30, d.424, 47–50.

[149] Gittings, *Survey*, 185.

[150] "Declaration by the Politburo of the VWP CC on the Unity of the International Communist Movement," 2/10/1963, *SAPMO-BArch*, DY 30/IV A 2/20/437, 1–6.

[151] Zhai, *China and the Vietnam Wars*, 122–24.

for an end to polemics in the "highest interest" of the common communist cause.[152] Two days later, after his receipt of the letter, Mao convened the CCP Politburo in his bedroom. Claiming that the Soviet revisionists finally had accepted his proposal from April of the year before, the Chairman announced that "we should seize this opportunity to relax tensions and achieve unity."[153] As further events revealed, however, he was not willing to honor his own words.

After the Politburo ended around 11 P.M., Mao—still lying in his bed in pajamas—received Chervonenko for a preliminary reply. According to Li Zhisui's memoirs, the Chairman had "rehearsed . . . several times" a prank; pretending to be gravely ill, he wanted to test the "Soviet reaction to his possible death."[154] Alas, his best efforts were in vain. As Chervonenko concluded his report of this bizarre encounter, "if compared with the impressions of him at the time of the two previous meetings, this time Mao Zedong looked much more energetic."[155]

Both the Chinese and Russian versions of the meeting reveal that Mao had no intention of engaging in a constructive conversation. Having accused the Soviet revisionists of starting the public polemics, Mao charged them with saying one thing and then doing the opposite, and also reserved the right "to answer all attacks against China by all 43 parties" at the recent congresses.[156] The Chairman eventually realized that he had gone too far, relented, and even agreed to a meeting of both parties. Before Chervonenko left, he countered Mao's invitation for Khrushchev to visit Beijing with an invitation for the Chairman to travel to Moscow, to which Mao tactfully replied that "he does not rule out the possibility of this happening."[157]

In his report to Gromyko some days later, Chervonenko complained about Mao's pomposity in talking about "equality" and the "'unilateral and great-power' violations of the Moscow documents by the Soviets," as well as the Chairman's attempt to cast himself in "the role of the 'rescuer' of the communist movement, as if it stood 'on the abyss.'" The ambassador noted with concern that "Mao's insistence that 'words have to be followed by deeds' in fact had a 'duplicitous character,'" since *Renmin Ribao* had published Albanian material attacking the CPSU on February 26." Ultimately, the Chinese invitation for Khrushchev to come to Beijing was nothing else but "a perfidy" designed only "to enhance Mao

[152] "To CCP CC," 2/21/1963, MOL, 288 f.9/1963/25 őe, 18–24.

[153] WLX, 543.

[154] Li, *Private Life*, 105. Brezhnev recounts Chervonenko's recollections: *Kitai*, 79.

[155] "Record of Conversation by Chervonenko with Mao Zedong," 2/23/1963, AVPRF, f.0100, o.56, d.7, p.495, 104, 121.

[156] WLX, 543–50.

[157] "Record of Conversation by Chervonenko with Mao Zedong," 98–121.

Zedong's role in resolving the Soviet-Chinese discord."[158] Chervonenko's skepticism was well founded; Mao did not want to stop the open polemics. With those against the French and Italian parties having already been published, Mao forged ahead with the publication of the long-planned article against the Communist Party of the United States of America (CP USA)—directed against Russian unequal treaties of the past—which was scheduled for release on March 8.

Upon the publication of the polemic against the CP USA, Mao convened the Politburo. While the meeting declared that the publication of the three polemics "was a good education for our people," it also agreed to the Soviet plea to stop polemics, if only because the CCP should "not use up all our bullets." The Chinese comrades understood that the Soviet leader would never fall for the Chinese invitation to come to Beijing; it was thus decided that neither Mao nor Liu, but, as in previous bilateral party meetings, Deng should go to Moscow. As for the ideological stance the mission should adopt, there was no doubt: for the sake of Marxist-Leninist purity, not one inch could be given to the Soviet revisionists. Mao, though, understood that his uncompromising stance threatened to split the communist movement. To evade the blame, he decided to "procrastinate" as much as possible: "We should not take the initiative to split. *We should make Khrushchev instigate the split*, let him assume the responsibility for it."[159]

While the CCP reply letter of March 9 sounded less venomous than its hidden objective, it nevertheless included unpleasant aspects. Despite having already decided to send Deng to Moscow, the letter claimed that this question was unsettled and thus invited a Soviet delegation to Beijing. It also asserted that the present disagreements were a matter of "principle" and that, as a result, the socialist camp was standing at the precipice of a split.[160] Clearly, the CCP was not willing to give reconciliation the slightest chance. For the next three weeks the "central anti-revisionist drafting group" met "day and night" to "*prepare the documents for the Sino-Soviet split.*"[161]

On April 1, Chervonenko tried to meet Mao for the delivery of the Soviet reply letter. The Chairman was not in the mood to see the ambassador, and ordered Deng and Zhou to step in for him.[162] The letter compared Mao's two visits to Moscow (1949–50 and 1957) with Khrushchev's three trips to Beijing (1954, 1958, and 1959) and thus

---

[158] "To Gromyko," 2/26/1963, *AVPRF*, f.0100, o.56, d.22, p.498, 24–42.

[159] WLX, 552–56 (italics mine).

[160] *SCMP* 2940, 26–29.

[161] WLX, 556–57 (italics mine).

[162] Mentioned in: "Record of Conversation with Zhou Enlai and Deng Xiaoping," 4/2/1963, *AVPRF*, f.0100, o.56, d.7, p.495, 130–34.

proposed that the Chairman should come to the Soviet capital as discussed on February 23. Most of the letter, however, somberly recounted Moscow's ideological positions.[163] Published in *Pravda* on April 3,[164] it was the Soviet attempt to frame the debate—just as the CPSU had tried to do at Bucharest and Moscow in 1960—and to portray itself as the reasonable side in the dispute. After Chervonenko handed over the Russian and Chinese versions of the letter, Zhou and Deng got acquainted with the Chinese text "in 50 minutes." While they were reading, Chervonenko observed that "they became visibly nervous." The Soviet reiteration of long-held ideological positions apparently annoyed the two so much that they decided to create one more artificial obstacle for the planned party talks. Despite the fact that the CCP Politburo had already decided to send a mission to Moscow, its designated head, Deng, accused the Soviets of a lack of goodwill because Khrushchev did not want to come to China.[165]

In a Politburo meeting chaired by Mao, the CCP leadership determined that "the Khrushchev group has still not changed its basic line." The Chinese comrades approached the letter in line with Russian intentions—as an attempt to define the framework of the debate on the basis of "their general line." Mao, however, realized that "we should not give the people the impression that we just repudiate their letter, because then we have no leverage in the talks." He thus decided to let the "central anti-revisionist drafting group" draft an article "based on Marxist analysis" in order to make clear "what [general] line the international communist movement should adopt." He also proposed the widespread publication of the Soviet letter in order to instruct the Chinese masses on the dangers of Soviet revisionism.[166]

Also in April, the Chinese comrades again took up Sino-Soviet territorial disagreements when the PRC notified the USSR of its desire to negotiate. The following month, Moscow indicated its readiness to do so.[167] Although the Chinese side had proposed to respect the status quo, Soviet memos from June and July indicated various incursions into Soviet-controlled territories by Chinese farmers and fishermen.[168]

At the same time, Mao continued to sharpen his ideological dagger against revisionists abroad and at home. Drafting documents for the SEM,

[163] "The Letter of the Central Committee of the C.P.S.U. to the Central Committee of the C.P.C., March 1963," Peter Berton, ed., *Chinese-Russian Dialogue*, vol. 1 (Los Angeles: Southern California, 1964), no page numbers.

[164] *Pravda*, 4/3/1963, 1–2.

[165] "Record of Conversation with Zhou Enlai Deng Xiaoping," 130–34.

[166] WLX, 558–92.

[167] Li, *Lengnuan*, 323. Wang, *Zhonghua*, vol. 2, 254.

[168] "Note by MID USSR," 6/11/1963, *AVPRF*, f.100, o.50, d.1, p.210, 29–30. "[Note by MID USSR]," 7/10/1963, *AVPRF*, f.100, o.50, d.1, p.210, 37–40.

he claimed that if the CCP ever forgot class struggle or proletarian dictatorship, then "a counterrevolutionary restoration on a national scale
would inevitably occur, [and] the Marxist-Leninist party will undoubtedly become a revisionist party or [even] a fascist party."[169] Hence, at the
Hangzhou work conference in the first half of May, the Chairman "made
anti-revisionism and opposition against 'peaceful evolution' the ideological
guiding line" for the CCP,[170] while pushing through the "Resolution on
Certain Problems of Rural Work at the Present Time," which asserted that
"both feudal and capitalist forces were attempting to stage a comeback in
the Chinese countryside."[171] In a circular to all provincial and local party
branches titled "On Class and Class Struggle," Mao warned that a lack
of ideological vigilance would inevitably lead to revisionism at home and,
eventually, to the restoration of capitalism in China.[172]

Finally, on June 14, the Chinese published the "Proposal Concerning
the General Line of the International Communist Movement," a highly
polemical reply to the March 30 Soviet letter. It was accompanied by a
series of eight supporting articles and radio broadcasts, which Aleksei
Brezhnev remembered to be "framed with pompous music," as if they
were "reports of military action" from the battlefront.[173] The twenty-five
points of the proposal were a long-winded and detailed proclamation of
an alternative general line for the international communist movement. It
recounted in detail Mao's ideological positions and, unlike Moscow's letter from March 30, listed alleged mistakes and "erroneous views" of the
other side. It also spoke of supposed Chinese attempts to keep the international communist movement together. Despite its final call for unity in
the struggle against imperialism, the Chinese open letter not only claimed
that factionalism was an objective necessity in the development of any
communist party, but also insinuated that the USSR had already ceased
to be a socialist country.[174]

The Chinese reply to the March 30 Soviet letter clearly achieved its
objective—to kill any prospect of a Sino-Soviet compromise. According
to Georgii Arbatov, who worked in the CPSU CC Liaison Department,
"the Soviet leadership took this as an open challenge and proof of the
irreconcilability of the Chinese leaders to some of our efforts." Moscow
understood Beijing's intention to use the proposal as both an ideological

[169] Li, "Study [I]," 68.

[170] Bo, *Ruogan*, vol. 2, 1147.

[171] Li, *Private Life*, 398. Also: *MZDDG*, 1094.

[172] Mao Zedong, "On Class and Class Struggle," [no date] (reprinted by Jiangsu Provincial Party on 5/17/1963), *JSSDAG*, 3011, zhang 1030, 1–2a.

[173] Brezhnev, *Kitai*, 86–87.

[174] *SCMP* 3003, 15–41.

Trojan horse abroad and a live-germ vaccination against the revisionist disease at home: "Obviously, this was a political platform intended
for export to the Soviet Union," Arbatov recalled, but added that "Mao
Zedong's main motives were domestic."[175]

The Soviet reaction was swift. In a brief CC resolution of June 18,
the Soviet comrades deplored the distortions of history outlined in the
Chinese proposal. It also announced that the CPSU would not publish
the Chinese communication in the USSR because this "would call for a
public reply which would [only] lead to a further aggravation of the polemics."[176] During the CPSU CC plenum from June 18 to 21, the CC secretaries Mikhail Suslov, Boris Ponomarev, and Yurii Andropov accused
the CCP of having fomented the ideological split since late 1959 when
"overt concepts of wrong views . . . factually emerged in the Chinese
leadership . . . [and since] April 1960 in connection with the 90th birthday of Lenin."[177] All three speeches were detailed indictments of Chinese
mistakes but, unlike the Chinese provocation, they were never published
in the Soviet media.[178] The plenum adopted a resolution that empowered
Khrushchev to defend the decisions of the twentieth, twenty-first, and
twenty-second CPSU congresses against the "slanderous attacks" of the
CCP in the impending party talks, scheduled to start in early July.[179] The
developments in Moscow were so rapid that they even surprised some
of the CPSU CC members. Kiev party boss Petro Shelest was shocked to
hear that "our relations with China had become complicated and sharp,
which could not but cause alarm."[180]

The CPSU CC resolution immediately became an object of intense
discussion in Beijing. The Chinese comrades concluded that it "bodes
ill rather than well for the [impending] talks." In a Politburo meeting,
Mao even announced that, without doubt, Khrushchev had decided
on the split. While in Moscow, Deng should thus "grasp the banner of
unity. . . . If they want the split, we will procrastinate to postpone the
split. . . . Even if the talks have no result, we should propose to convene
them again in Beijing."[181]

At the same time, in an attempt to circumvent the CPSU decision
to shield the Soviet population from Mao's ideological Trojan horse,

[175] Arbatov, *System*, 94–97.

[176] "Statement of CPSU Central Committee Concerning Letter of the CPC Central Committee," 6/18/1963, Berton, *Chinese-Russian Dialogue*, vol. 1, no page numbers.

[177] The three speeches are in: *AAN*, KC PZPR, XI A/81, 234–10 (quote on 237).

[178] Unlike all other speeches at the plenum, the three speeches were not published in
Pravda.

[179] "Decision of the CPSU CC Plenum," 6/21/1963, *RGANI*, f.2, o.1, d.658, 193.

[180] Petro Shelest, *Da ne sudimy budete* (Moskva: edition q, 1994), 168.

[181] WLX, 594–98.

the CCP began with the distribution of the June proposal in Moscow. While similar to the campaign in the summer of 1960, the new operation targeted the Soviet intellectual elite at institutions of higher learning and research. Twice throughout June, the Soviet foreign ministry protested against these "illegal" activities. Finally, on June 27, its protests unheeded, the Soviet government expelled three embassy staff and two Chinese citizens.[182] The PRC foreign ministry highlighted the alleged illegality of these actions, claiming that Soviet demands for a recall were "unreasonable and . . . untenable," and even that "it is normal and unimpeachable for the Chinese Embassy and Chinese personnel in the Soviet Union to distribute official documents of the CCP Central Committee." The five expelled Chinese returned to Beijing in early July to a heroes' welcome attended by Zhou Enlai and 7,000 cadres.[183]

Shortly before the start of party talks in early July 1963, it was clear that only a complete ideological surrender of one side could save Sino-Soviet relations. Moscow had certainly contributed to this sorry state of affairs. Khrushchev's Caribbean adventure had seriously undermined his standing in the socialist camp, and Soviet polemics during some of the European congresses had added fuel to the fire.

But this cannot explain the rapid deterioration of relations by spring 1963. Indeed, it was Mao's comeback in the late summer of 1962 that provided the impetus for renewed ideological radicalism in China's foreign policy. His return was based on frustrations with internal developments; he came to believe that revisionism was on the march in China and that the restoration of capitalism was in the making. His slogan *fanxiu fangxiu* (oppose revisionism abroad, prevent revisionism at home) connected for the first time *explicitly* China's foreign and domestic policies. Mao thus employed his dissatisfaction with Khrushchev as a political and ideological tool to attack the reformers Liu and Deng. Although documentary evidence is limited, the events from late summer of 1962 to the spring of 1963 suggest that Mao instigated the deterioration of Sino-Soviet relations precisely with domestic aims in mind. By 1959 Mao had already decided that China did not need the Sino-Soviet alliance anymore. The political developments after his resurgence in the late summer of 1962 suggested that a well-managed collapse of the partnership would be of much greater use than the renewal of the relationship with Moscow.

---

[182] "[Note by MID USSR]," 6/27/1963, *AVPRF*, f.100, o.50, d.1, p.210, 31–34. The bickering continued for a while: "[Note by MID USSR]," 8/28/1963, *AVPRF*, f.100, o.50, d.1, p.210, 44.

[183] *CB* 721, 47–48 (quotes). *SCMP* 3014, 38.

Accordingly, the Chairman exploited Khrushchev's blunders in the Caribbean and the Himalayas to his own benefit. While the Chinese provocations during the subsequent five party congresses were partially understandable given the ideological disagreements, their ferocity was disproportionate. As before, Maoist hyperbole negated the possibility of political pragmatism. Despite agreeing to convene conciliatory talks between the CCP and the CPSU, the Chairman did not even consider compromising for the sake of socialist unity. He had reserved for himself the right to judge who was a true Marxist-Leninist, and had clearly decided that the Khrushchevite traitors did not fit that role. For the Chairman, the Soviet comrades could only achieve true reconciliation with their Chinese brethrens through a complete ideological surrender to Maoist positions. And that, the Soviets determined, would never happen. By early June 1963, the Sino-Soviet rift was waiting to burst.

CHAPTER 8

The American Factor, 1962–1963

ON OCTOBER 2, 1964, the *New York Times* printed an article, probably based on U.S. governmental leaks, about the Soviet-British-American nuclear test ban talks from the previous year. It reported that, in the summer of 1963, Washington had proposed cooperation to Moscow in order "to prevent the Chinese Communist nuclear-weapons development, but received a cold response from Premier Khrushchev."[1] For years before, the U.S. government had been concerned about the dangers of a nuclear PRC. In 1962–63, in an attempt to undermine Sino-Soviet relations, U.S. President Kennedy courted the Soviet leader in the field of nuclear arms limitation. Despite Khrushchev's negative reply, U.S. planning for a military operation against the Chinese nuclear weapons program continued—without success. A fortnight after the *New York Times* article, the PRC exploded its first nuclear device in Lop Nor, Xinjiang.

July 1963 witnessed the merging of two larger developments in Sino-Soviet-American relations. While the first, Mao's ideological resurgence and its consequences, has been extensively covered in chapter 7, the second, Soviet-British-American nuclear arms limitation talks, is the central theme of this chapter. Although the negotiations had started in 1958, it was only in late 1962, following the Cuban Missile Crisis, that they entered their final stage. China's position on nuclear arms limitation had been ambiguous until early 1960; at that time, however, its indistinct attitude changed to a rigid, dismissive stance. Mao's ideological resurgence in the late summer of 1962 boosted Chinese radicalism on the issue as well. As Sino-Soviet relations continued to worsen until mid-1963, Soviet-American relations on nuclear arms testing improved so much that, in the spring, Khrushchev faced a difficult choice: ideological surrender or nuclear arms regulation.

The simultaneous Sino-Soviet party talks and Soviet-British-American test ban negotiations in Moscow linked the Sino-Soviet-American parties in more than geographic terms. The collapse of the party talks on July 20, and the conclusion of the Limited Nuclear Test Ban (LNTB) negotiations five days later, marked a major turning point in Beijing's relationship with Moscow. The Soviet decision to join the LNTB was partially the

[1] *NYT*, 10/2/1964, 13.

result of Mao's previous anti-Soviet propaganda. For the Chairman, it simply reinforced his assessment of Soviet revisionism. But in the end, it isolated China internationally and raised new security concerns at the Sino-Soviet border.

SOVIET-AMERICAN NUCLEAR RAPPROCHEMENT

It is too simplistic to see the changes in Sino-Soviet-American relations from mid-1962 to mid-1963 solely as the product of Kennedy's efforts to exploit the deteriorating relationship between the USSR and the PRC. Both Moscow and Washington had unrelated motives, such as moral considerations, environmental concerns, and domestic and international pressures, for pursuing nuclear rapprochement. But American worries also revolved around one important issue that could potentially undermine Sino-Soviet relations: nonproliferation of nuclear technology.

Even before the conclusion of the alliance in early 1950, American presidents had considered ways of splitting the Sino-Soviet partnership. The Truman Administration tried to tempt the Chinese Communists with aid, but abandoned this strategy after their intervention in the Korean War in November 1950. President Eisenhower's Secretary of State Dulles reversed the wedge strategy, pursuing a policy of confrontation toward the PRC and moderation toward the USSR. His aim was to strain the Sino-Soviet alliance by compelling the Chinese to increase economic and military demands for Soviet support to the point where Moscow would be forced to drop Beijing. Dulles eventually realized that Sino-Soviet ties were so solid that any hopes for a split were premature.[2] Nevertheless, the Eisenhower Administration tried to use nuclear threats during both Taiwan Strait Crises (1954–55 and 1958), as well as public criticism of Soviet positions during the First Sino-Indian Border War in 1959, to undermine the Sino-Soviet alliance. In general, though, the White House, the State Department, and Washington's intelligence community routinely dismissed signs of Sino-Soviet differences as insignificant or, in some cases, as communist propaganda designed to mislead the United States.[3]

---

[2] Gaddis, *Long Peace*, 147–94. Chang, *Friends*, 18–26, 46–48, 57, 60, 81–202. Zhang, *Economic Cold War*, 1–264.

[3] *FRUS 1952–1954*, XIV, 366, 611–24, 674–75, 689–701, 720–21, 827–42. *FRUS 1955–1957*, II, 147–48, 202–3, 210–12, 234–38, 251–59, 273–76, 289–91, 320–28, 368–72, 587–88. *FRUS 1955–1957*, III, 24–38, 79–81, 242–68, 425–41, 507–24. *FRUS 1958–1960*, X, 100–102, 118–22, 269–81, 284–86, 359–71, 485–92, 493–95, 545–46, 559–61, 561–63. *FRUS 1958–1960*, XIX, 23–27, 35–37, 548–50, 568, 577–81, 593–94, 639–40, 664–65, 675–83, 688–91, 703–5, 709–11, 721–23.

When the United States did finally receive evidence of Sino-Soviet ideological clashes during the Bucharest Meeting and over the Soviet withdrawal of specialists in mid-1960, Khrushchev's overreaction to the U-2 Incident had already precluded the possibility of a Soviet-American rapprochement.[4] Also, in early 1961, the incoming Kennedy Administration immediately reviewed its predecessor's China policy. Some advisers encouraged the president to chart a less confrontational policy toward the PRC, partially because of the impossibility of containing a rising China. Internal disagreements and the belief that once the Sino-Soviet Split had occurred, Beijing—but not Moscow—would turn toward Washington, left them waiting for events that would not occur.[5]

The Kennedy Administration found it difficult to grasp precisely what was happening in the socialist camp. The period from its inauguration to the late summer of 1962 paralleled, almost exactly, a phase of ambiguity in Sino-Soviet relations, as related in chapter 6. While intelligence estimates and internal papers provided the president with information about Sino-Soviet conflicts and speculations about their causes, they were usually sketchy.[6] In the end, the administration was left to follow the suggestion of the éminence grise of U.S. Sovietology, George Frost Kennan: "The question of Sino-Soviet relations appears to be one for intelligence analysis rather than planning. We cannot do much to influence these relations but we must constantly observe them."[7]

The Soviet-British-American negotiation process, which eventually led to the LNTB in the summer of 1963, had already started in late 1958, just after the Second Taiwan Strait Crisis. Its unusually long duration was due to a lack of consensus on the object of the talks: nonproliferation, arms reduction, a comprehensive or a limited test ban. Prior to the use of spy satellites, in an era of irregular and dangerous reconnaissance missions, disagreements also arose over implementation and verification. Finally, the three sides failed to settle the question of whether other nondeclared potential nuclear powers, like France and China, should be included in the negotiations.[8]

[4] FRUS 1958–1960, XIX, 713–15, 719–20, 729–30, 731, 739–41, 742–43.

[5] Chang, Friends, 217–24. Warren Cohen, Dean Rusk (Totowa: Cooper Square, 1980), 163–70. Dean Rusk, As I Saw It (New York: Norton, 1990), 282–87. "The Signs of Chinese Communist Friendliness," 6/17/1961, John F. Kennedy Library and Museum [JFK], National Security Files, box 22, "China General."

[6] FRUS 1961–1963, V, 17–19, 156, 378, 421, 484–85, 510.

[7] "Record of the PPS Meeting," 2/8/1961, FRUS 1961–1963, V, 62.

[8] Glenn Seaborg, Kennedy, Khrushchev, and the Test Ban (Berkeley: California, 1981), 1–158. Seaborg, Stemming the Tide (Lexington: Lexington, 1986), 25–93. Kendrick Oliver, Kennedy, Macmillan and the Nuclear Test-Ban Debate, 1961–1963 (Houndsmills: Macmillan, 1998), 4–103.

By the summer of 1962, continued nuclear testing and proliferation had arisen as the two most pressing issues. Regarding the first, the atmospheric testing of progressively larger devices raised questions about their environmental effects.[9] Public debates in the United States had already started after a 1954 U.S. H-bomb test contaminated Japanese fishermen in the Pacific.[10] In the USSR, nuclear scientists surreptitiously protested against what they believed were politically motivated but environmentally harmful and technologically redundant bomb tests.[11] Finally, in April 1962, eight nonaligned nations voiced their dissatisfaction with the frustratingly slow negotiation process, adding even more pressure.[12]

As for the second issue, the danger of nuclear proliferation was weighing heavily on Kennedy's mind in late July of 1962. The administration reckoned that by 1972 twenty more nations would acquire nuclear weapons, with China being the first. In general, the United States worried that such a spread of nuclear weapons would devalue its own stockpile; in particular, it feared that Chinese possession of nuclear weapons would render the American defense of its Asian allies unfeasible. Anxious about Moscow's export of nuclear know-how for peaceful purposes, Washington focused on mechanisms to prevent Beijing from acquiring dual-use technology for its own nuclear weapons program. The administration deemed a test ban treaty "a necessary, but not a sufficient condition" toward achieving this aim. At the same time, it also considered inserting an article that would render the treaty invalid in the event a nonsignatory power began conducting tests. The article was designed to pressure any aspiring nuclear power to abstain from testing unless it wanted to trigger another testing round by the existing nuclear powers.[13]

China had been an object of American concerns for some time. A National Security Council paper from May 1958 considered "hostile Soviet and Chinese Communist regimes" a *"basic threat* to U.S. security."[14] As early as July 1959—a month after the Soviet Union had rescinded its promise to deliver a model A-bomb—intelligence suggested that the "USSR is almost certainly reluctant to see the Chinese Communists acquire nuclear

[9] Gaddis, *We Now Know*, 223–57. Oliver, *Kennedy*, 4–5. Rebecca Strode, "Soviet Policy Toward a Nuclear Test Ban," Michael Mandelbaum, ed., *The Other Side of the Table* (New York: Council on Foreign Relations, 1990), 5–39.

[10] Oliver, *Kennedy*, 4.

[11] Andrei Sakharov, *Memoirs* (New York: Vintage, 1992), 188–232.

[12] Chang, *Friends*, 233–35. Seaborg, *Kennedy*, 161–62. Andreas Wenger et al., "John F. Kennedy and the Limited Test Ban Treaty," *Presidential Quarterly* 29/2, 467–69. Oliver, *Kennedy*, 100–108. Seaborg, *Kennedy*, 161–62. Gaddis, *Strategies*, 197–234.

[13] "Tape No. 2, 7/30/1962" (quote), and "Tape No. 6, 8/3/1962," *JFK*, President's Office Files, Presidential Recordings. Chang, *Friends*, 235.

[14] "NSC 5810/1," 5/5/1958," *FRUS 1958–1960*, III, 100–101 (italics original).

weapons under their own control."[15] Yet, during his visit to the United States in September, Khrushchev did not allay American concerns when he casually told his host that "China . . . within the next ten or fifteen years" could "make a bomb."[16] A National Intelligence Estimate from late 1960 reckoned "that the most probable date at which the Chinese Communists could detonate a first nuclear device is sometime in 1963, though it might be as late as 1964, or as early as 1962, depending upon the actual degree of Soviet assistance."[17] In reality, the Soviets had already minimized their assistance by 1960 and the first Chinese nuclear device did not explode until October 16, 1964.

Such fears made the inclusion of the PRC in nuclear arms limitation talks a central U.S. concern. An internal proposal from March 1958 spoke about "the installation of 70 observation stations in . . . the USSR and China."[18] Given Mao's furious rejection of Moscow's joint submarine fleet proposal as an infringement on his country's sovereignty, one can only wonder as to how this idea could have ever been implemented. Regardless, on August 18, 1958—five days before Mao started the Second Taiwan Strait Crisis—Eisenhower rejected the whole idea on the grounds that "he did not accept any implication of recognizing Communist China" for that or any other purpose.[19] Less than a year later, Secretary of State Christian Herter concluded that the PRC was "almost a *separate problem*" in the ongoing Soviet-American-British nuclear talks.[20]

So far, no evidence that Moscow and Beijing ever talked about Chinese participation in these negotiations has surfaced. Throughout the 1950s, the PRC officially supported *both* a test ban *and* continued Soviet testing of nuclear weapons.[21] On January 21, 1960, a Chinese public statement reconfirmed what Chen Yi had confidentially told the Soviet ambassador in mid-1958,[22] that "any international disarmament agreement which is arrived at without the formal participation of the Chinese People's Republic and the signature of its delegate cannot, of course, have any binding force on China."[23] As the Lenin Polemics of April 1960 revealed, Mao's peculiar views on nuclear war, which he had first stated publicly at

[15] "NIE 13–59," 7/28/1959, *FRUS 1958–1960*, XIX, 579.

[16] "Memorandum of Conversation," 9/17/1959, *FRUS 1958–1960*, X, 414.

[17] "NIE 13-2-60," 12/13/1960, *FRUS 1958–1960*, XIX, 746.

[18] "Report of the NSC Ad Hoc Working Group on the Technical Feasibility of a Cessation of Nuclear Testing," [no date], *FRUS 1958–1960*, III, 575.

[19] "Memorandum of Conference with President Eisenhower," 8/18/1958, *FRUS 1958–1960*, III, 648.

[20] "Memorandum of Conversation," 5/5/1959, *FRUS 1958–1960*, III, 740 (italics mine).

[21] Christer Jönsson, *Soviet Bargaining Behavior* (New York: Columbia, 1979), 86–122.

[22] Chen Yi's words in 1958: "Statements by Leaders of the PRC on Important Questions of Foreign Policy," 12/9/1960, *AVPRF*, f.0100, o.53, d.24, p.457, 236–37.

[23] *CB* 619, 6.

the Moscow Meeting in late 1957, also had not changed: "If the U.S. or other imperialists refuse to reach an agreement on the banning of atomic and nuclear weapons and should dare to fly in the face of the will of all humanity by launching a war using atomic and nuclear weapons, the result will be the speedy destruction of these monsters. . . . On the debris of a dead imperialism, the victorious people would create with extreme rapidity a civilization thousands of times higher than the capitalist system and a truly beautiful future for themselves."[24] The Kennedy Administration was aware of Mao's unusual views about nuclear war.[25]

By late August 1962, international public pressure, combined with Kennedy's concerns over China's nuclear capabilities, provided Washington with the impetus for action. U.S. Secretary of State Dean Rusk presented Soviet Vice–Foreign Minister Kuznetsov with two proposals: a comprehensive test ban treaty that would outlaw all nuclear testing and a limited test ban treaty that permitted only environmentally less harmful underground testing. The second proposal was less restrictive and thus politically more feasible. Both treaty proposals included a clause that stipulated the right to withdraw should a third party explode nuclear devices.[26]

On August 28, the Soviets agreed on the resumption of nuclear negotiations but rejected the two proposals.[27] There were several reasons for Moscow's qualified response. On the one hand, there were genuine security concerns. Khrushchev himself rejected Rusk's proposals on the basis of his long-held fears of U.S. espionage if on-site inspections designed to verify compliance were permitted.[28] Furthermore, as Soviet Ambassador Anatolii Dobrynin told Special Assistant to the National Security Council McGeorge Bundy, the proposals did not address recent Soviet apprehensions over the possibility of West German access to nuclear weapons through NATO's Multilateral Force (MLF) arrangements.[29] The MLF idea, raised as early as 1957, was designed to dissuade smaller NATO powers—West Germany and France, in particular—from developing their own nuclear capabilities by granting them partial access to American and British nuclear weapons systems. Negotiations over the Multilateral

---

[24] SCMP 2788, 32. For Mao's earlier views on nuclear weapons: Mao, On Diplomacy, 129–34; SW, vol. 5, 152–53; AVPRF, f.0100, o.50, d.3, p.423, 37–38; JYMW, vol. 6, 636.

[25] "NIE 4-2-61," 4/6/1961, FRUS 1961–1963, VII, 37.

[26] Oliver, Kennedy, 108–34. Seaborg, Kennedy, 161–71. Chang, Friends, 233–35.

[27] Oliver, Kennedy, 108–34.

[28] "Informal Communication from Chairman Khrushchev to President Kennedy," 9/4/1962, FRUS 1961–1963, VI, 149. Chang, Friends, 233–35.

[29] "Outgoing Telegram Department of State," Aug. 08 9:25 P.M. '62, "Outgoing Telegram Department of State," Aug. 23 8:02 P.M. '62, and "Department of State Airgram," 9/8/1962, JFK, National Security Files, box 185, "Dobrynin Talks-Rusk."

Force, which was supposed to serve on nuclear missile–carrying U.S. naval vessels and to consist of mixed crews from several NATO member states, including West Germany, started in 1962.[30] This was accompanied by public discussions within NATO, as well as Soviet and East European concerns about the possibility of West German access to nuclear weapons.[31] The USSR had canceled the delivery of a model A-bomb to China in 1959 because, among other reasons, it feared this would justify the American supply of nuclear weapons to West Germany.[32] By the fall of 1962, Soviet fears over nuclear access by supposedly revanchist West Germany grew parallel to American concerns over China's nuclear weapons project.

On the other hand, Moscow agreed, at least in principle, to the resumption of negotiations because it needed to reassure Washington for its own needs. *At that very moment*, Soviet ships were delivering nuclear IRBMs to Cuba behind the back—rather, under the nose—of the United States. This action not only triggered the Cuban Missile Crisis in October,[33] but also violated the spirit, though not the narrow definition, of nuclear nonproliferation. When, in late September, Rusk insisted on the withdrawal clause, Soviet Foreign Minister Gromyko—with Soviet missiles on the way to Cuba likely in mind—remarked "that test ban and proliferation were *two different things*."[34]

The Soviet agreement in principle prompted a rapid Sino-Soviet diplomatic exchange. Moscow justified it to Beijing by highlighting the need to prevent West Germany from obtaining nuclear weapons.[35] Although by the fall of 1962 the PRC had been developing its own nuclear arsenal for some years, the Chinese leaders must have picked up on suggestions in the Western media that Rusk's proposals were designed to stop proliferation.[36] The PRC thus notified the USSR on September 3 that the proposals "are mainly spearheaded against China,"[37] and that the Soviet Union

[30] Lawrence Kaplan, *NATO Divided, NATO United* (New York: Praeger, 2004), 38–41. Gregor Schöllgen, *Aussenpolitik der Bundesrepublik Deutschland*, 3rd, exp. and rev. ed. (München: Beck, 2004), 73–76. Bundy, *Danger*, 488–90.

[31] For the discussion on MLF between the United States and its NATO allies: *FRUS 1961–1963*, XIII, 250–640, and the almost weekly reports in the *NYT* throughout most of 1962. Soviet and East European concerns: *NYT*, 1/29/1962, 1; 3/13/1962, 1; 3/24/1962, 6; 4/8/1962, 19.

[32] Interview with Sergo Mikoyan, Reston, 6/6/2003.

[33] Taubman, *Khrushchev*, 547–51.

[34] "Memorandum of Conversation," 9/25/1962, *FRUS 1961–1963*, VII, 574 (italics mine).

[35] Westad, *Brothers*, 179–80. Liu, *Chushi*, 171.

[36] *NYT*, 8/28/1962, 25; 9/2/1962, 106.

[37] Li, *Lengnuan*, 320.

had no right to assume legal "responsibilities in lieu of China."[38] Given Mao's political resurgence since August, the Chinese reconfirmed their negative position in starker ideological tones on October 20: "The Soviet comrades have lost their class position in the question of the threat of nuclear war. . . . you betrayed the principle of proletarian international-ism."[39] With that, Sino-Soviet exchanges on the topic ended for the next six months.

The Cuban Missile Crisis represented an opportunity for Washington to get test ban negotiations started. In an October 27 letter to Khrushchev, Kennedy expressed his eagerness to end the arms race.[40] While the Soviet leader agreed "to continue the exchange of views,"[41] two days later he reaffirmed the old Soviet position: "We shall not accept inspection."[42]

Clearly, Washington was aware that Beijing's propaganda over Moscow's publicly humiliating withdrawal from Cuba presented a perfect opportunity to "*exacerbat[e] . . . the Sino-Soviet dispute.*"[43] Walt Rostow, national security adviser to the president, tried to apply pressure with a public call on the USSR "to accept the principle of international arms inspection or to go another round in the cold war tensions."[44] But the State Department was convinced that Khrushchev needed time to shore up support among his East European allies, whom he gathered in Moscow shortly after the end of the Cuban Missile Crisis.[45]

Mid-December witnessed the first time that Khrushchev, in Tito's presence, linked, however subtly, the Caribbean crisis, China's hard stance on war and peace, and the possibility of further nuclear arms limitation negotiations with the United States: "Some dogmatists . . . push the Soviet Union and other socialist countries on the path of unleashing a world war. . . . this extravagant attitude fails to attract the people of other countries to communism. . . . among the leading circles of the United States are some people, who judge the situation more soberly and, on the basis of the current balance of power in the international

[38] Dangdai, *Waijiao*, 119–20.

[39] Quoted in: Westad, "Sino-Soviet Alliance," 179–80.

[40] "Telegram from the Department of State to the Embassy in the Soviet Union," 10/27/1962, *FRUS 1961–1963*, VI, 182.

[41] "Letter from Chairman Khrushchev to President Kennedy," 10/28/1962, *FRUS 1961–1963*, VI, 185.

[42] "Letter from Chairman Khrushchev to President Kennedy," 10/30/1962, *FRUS 1961–1963*, VI, 192.

[43] "Memorandum Prepared by the Central Intelligence Agency," 11/29/1962, *FRUS 1961–1963*, V, 586–87 (italics mine).

[44] *NYT*, 11/13/1962, 5

[45] "Intelligence Note," 11/7/1962, *JFK*, National Security Files, box 179, "USSR General 11/62."

arena, realize that if they unleash war, the United States can neither win nor achieve their aims. . . . The Soviet government hopes that the commitments the United States has assumed with regard to Cuba will be strictly observed. The violation of these commitments . . . would not only destroy any trust in these commitments but also exclude *any future possibility to use this method of peaceful resolution.*"[46] The next day, Khrushchev told Norman Cousins, an American peace advocate, how desperately he wanted to avoid nuclear war: "If we don't have peace and the nuclear bombs start to fall, what difference will it make whether we are Communists or Catholics or Capitalists or Chinese or Russians or Americans? Who could tell us apart? *Who will be left to tell us apart?*" Chinese "dirty words" about his alleged "cowardice" during the Cuban Missile Crisis were simply "irresponsible."[47]

While Moscow signaled peace to Washington, Beijing was on the ideological warpath against nuclear arms limitation. The December 31, 1962, polemic against Togliatti denied that nuclear weapons had changed "the fundamental Marxist-Leninist theory on war and peace." Referring to Mao's belief that nuclear weapons were "paper tigers the U.S. reactionaries use to scare the people," it concluded that only struggle could save the world and that "in the end the nuclear teeth of imperialism . . . will be consigned by the people of the world to the museum of history, together with imperialism."[48]

In early 1963, with negotiations deadlocked over on-site inspections, Kennedy switched his focus to China. On January 9, the president told Kuznetsov that "he would hope the Chinese Communist political outlook, as expressed in recent editorials, would change as currently their attitude is a danger for all."[49] Two weeks later, Kennedy even indicated to the National Security Council that "the Chinese nuclear program was a principal driving force behind his quest for a test ban,"[50] designed "to halt or delay the development of an atomic capability by the Chinese Communists."[51] But the Soviets were not moved by such concerns; Kuznetsov replied to the president that he was not authorized to talk about the issue and that the "Soviet Government cannot speak for other socialist countries."[52]

[46] *Pravda*, 12/13/1962, 3 (italics mine).

[47] Norman Cousins, *Improbable Triumvirate* (New York: Norton, 1972), 45–46 (italics mine).

[48] CB 702, 5–9.

[49] "Memorandum of Conversation," 1/9/1963, *FRUS 1961–1963*, VII, 629.

[50] Seaborg, *Kennedy*, 181.

[51] "Notes on Remarks by the President Kennedy before NSC," 1/22/1963," JFK, National Security Files, box 314, "NSC Meetings 1963 No. 508, 1/22/1963."

[52] "Memorandum of Conversation," 1/9/1963, *FRUS 1961–1963*, VII, 629.

During his State of the Union Address on January 14, Kennedy highlighted Khrushchev's worsening relations with Mao, speaking about "strains and tensions within the Communist bloc," which provided "avenues of opportunity."[53] Two days later, in his conciliatory speech to the sixth SED Congress, Khrushchev commented on the Maoist vision of nuclear war, warning that the first nuclear exchange alone would kill "700 to 800 million people" and destroy "all the big cities not only of the two enemies conducting nuclear war—the USA and the USSR—but also in France, England, Germany, Italy, China, Japan, and many other countries of the world. . . . What concerns Marxist-Leninists, they cannot think to build a communist civilization on the ruins of the world's cultural centers."[54] While Khrushchev's speech contained a call for unity in the socialist world (as argued in chapter 7), it was in fact an olive branch extended to *both* Mao *and* Kennedy. The Chinese rejected it as fake, and the Americans were lukewarm.[55] After all, the speech did not offer a break in the negotiating deadlock over on-site inspections.[56] On February 1, the president announced the resumption of nuclear testing in Nevada,[57] designed to experiment with seismographic verification methods that could substitute for on-site inspections.[58] Not knowing the real purpose of the tests, Khrushchev was dismayed.[59]

Kennedy's announcement triggered Khrushchev's "conditioned reflex."[60] Eleven days after the Vietnamese call for unity on February 10, the CPSU sent a letter inviting the CCP to Sino-Soviet party talks.[61] Beijing and Washington immediately noticed changes in Moscow's behavior. Mao remarked that "Khrushchev was not ready to split with China because relations with America had *not yet improved*."[62] The CIA was concerned about what influence "a reconciliation or a suspension of the [Sino-Soviet] hostility" would have on "such matters as . . . nuclear testing."[63] The hardening of Soviet positions over the test ban treaty quickly became obvious. The counselor to the Soviet embassy in Washington,

[53] "Annual Message to the Congress on the State of the Union," 1/14/1963, John Kennedy, *Public Papers of the President*, vol. 3 (Washington: GPO, 1964), 11–19.

[54] *Pravda*, 1/17/1963, 3.

[55] *NYT*, 1/18/1963, 8. "Current Intelligence Weekly Review," 1/18/1963, *FRUS 1961–1963*, V, 606.

[56] Seaborg, *Kennedy*, 185.

[57] *NYT*, 2/2/1963, 1.

[58] Seaborg, *Kennedy*, 187–88.

[59] Khrushchev, *Nikita S. Khrushchev*, 693.

[60] Troyanovskii, *Cherez*, 231–32.

[61] "To CCP CC," 2/21/1963, MOL, 288 f.9/1963/25 őe, 18–24.

[62] WLX, 537.

[63] "Memorandum from Director of Central Intelligence McCone to the Executive Director of Central Intelligence (Kirkpatrick)," 2/25/1963, *FRUS 1961–1963*, V, 634.

Georgii Kornienko, told his American liaison that "it would make no difference if the Chinese did get nuclear weapons, 'everything would remain the same.'"[64] Nevertheless, Kennedy continued to insist on a test ban treaty—even an "unenforceable" one—as long as it *might* prevent the Chinese from acquiring nuclear weapons.[65]

Khrushchev spent much of the early spring at the Black Sea. According to a contemporaneous Kremlinologist, he "appeared more and more in disgrace."[66] As the designated successor, Kozlov had followed Khrushchev's policies loyally for years, but after the Caribbean humiliation he had started to mark out his own pro-Chinese, anti-American positions. On April 11, however, a debilitating stroke removed Kozlov from the political stage.[67] Washington was well aware of the Byzantine power struggles in Moscow. Kennedy thus urged caution in a late March letter to British Prime Minister Harold Macmillan: "Khrushchev probably has too many problems on his hands right now."[68]

To the surprise of the White House, however, Khrushchev himself seemed to take the initiative when, on April 1, before Kozlov's demise, he indicated that a U.S. effort to reach a test ban "would of course meet a positive response from us." But there were strings attached: no inspections and no West German access to nuclear weapons through MLF.[69] Since this message closely trailed the CPSU letter to the CCP, which not only called for party talks but also listed Soviet ideological positions, it seems that Khrushchev had finally recognized the necessity of a final decision between two incompatible alternatives: rapprochement with the Chinese comrades or détente with the American imperialists.

On the day of Kozlov's stroke, Kennedy replied to Khrushchev, firmly reiterating previous U.S. positions.[70] But in a conversation with Dobrynin just days before, Ambassador at Large Llewellyn Thompson had indicated greater flexibility and even offered to send, in secret, a high-ranking emissary to Moscow.[71] Whether any of these messages had reached Khrushchev at Gagri by April 12, when he received Norman Cousins, is

[64] "Nuclear Testing; Non-Dissemination of Nuclear Weapons," 2/19/1963, *JFK*, National Security Files, box 180, "USSR General 2/25–2/28/63."

[65] Quoted in: "Editorial Note," *FRUS 1961–1963*, VII, 645.

[66] Michel Tatu, *Power in the Kremlin* (New York: Viking, 1969), 312–43.

[67] Taubman, *Khrushchev*, 613–14. MacFarquhar, *Origins*, vol. 3, 357. Tatu, *Power*, 312–40.

[68] "Message from President Kennedy to Prime Minister Macmillan," 3/28/1963, *FRUS 1961–1963*, VII, 659.

[69] "Message from the Soviet Ministry of Foreign Affairs to the Soviet Ambassador to the United States" (Dobrynin), 4/1/1963, *FRUS 1961–1963*, VI, 250–62.

[70] "Message from President Kennedy to Chairman Khrushchev," 4/11/1963, *FRUS 1961–1963*, VI, 265–68.

[71] Anatoly Dobrynin, *In Confidence* (New York: Times, 1995), 105.

not known. Before his trip to the USSR, the peace activist had met with the president, who told him to inform the Soviet leader that the United States would continue to insist on a certain number of inspections.[72] Following the meeting with Khrushchev, Cousins conveyed to Thompson that, after the Cuban Missile Crisis, the Soviet leader had been suffering from a credibility problem within the socialist world and, as a result, could not make any concessions on inspections. Given the scheduling of Sino-Soviet reconciliation talks for the summer, Thompson concluded, "it is important to him [Khrushchev] at this juncture not to do anything which exposes him to further Chinese attack."[73]

In an April 15 letter to Khrushchev, Macmillan and Kennedy made an appeal to the joint "duty to humanity," and repeated their willingness to send a high-ranking delegation to Moscow for exploratory talks.[74] With his hands untied domestically after Kozlov's stroke, this request seemed to move Khrushchev. Five days later, the Soviet government replied to the Chinese October 20 note, which had accused Moscow of betraying its "class position,"[75] with the following rebuttal: "The Chinese comrades of course can try to develop their own nuclear weapons, but we have to be clear that in this case new, gigantic difficulties for the successful struggle of the socialist countries and the peace-loving forces against the nuclear armament of the capitalist world would arise."[76]

At the same time, in order to increase pressure on the U.S. imperialists and keep the Chinese comrades at bay, Khrushchev complained to an Italian *Il Giorno* news reporter about Western stinginess on inspections and refuted the idea that the "debate . . . between Moscow and Peking" was more than just "internal affairs."[77] This did not prevent him from agreeing to secret high-level talks with the Americans on April 23 and from telling the CPSU CC plenum two days later about his keen desire to come to an agreement on nuclear testing.[78] Despite what U.S. Ambassador Foy Kohler called Khrushchev's "entirely negative" attitude during the meeting,[79] his son's memoirs claim that the Soviet leader had in fact

[72] "Tape No. 82/2, 4/22/1963," *JFK*, President's Office Files, Presidential Recordings.

[73] "Memorandum from the Ambassador at Large (Thompson) to Secretary of State Rusk," 4/24/1963, *FRUS 1961–1963*, VII, 687.

[74] "Telegram from the Department of State to the Embassy in the Soviet Union," 4/15/1963, *FRUS 1961–1963*, VII, 268–70.

[75] Quoted in: Westad, "Sino-Soviet Alliance," 179–80.

[76] "Reply of the Soviet Government to the Memorandum of the Government of the PRC from October 20, 1962," 4/20/1963, *SAPMO-BArch, DY 30/3607*, 45–64.

[77] Interview excerpts were published: *NYT*, 4/22/1963, 12.

[78] "Stenographic Transcript of the CPSU CC Plenum," 4/25/1963, Fursenko, *Prezidium*, vol. 1, 702–6.

[79] "Telegram from the Embassy in the Soviet Union to the Department of State," 4/24/1963, *FRUS 1961–1963*, VII, 685–86.

decided "to move forward."[80] The same day, W. Averell Harriman, Kennedy's special envoy, left for Moscow to engage in preliminary talks. But Khrushchev still refused to accept anything more than a symbolic number of inspections and continually evaded Harriman's inquiries about Soviet worries on Chinese nuclear weapons.[81]

Five weeks later, the dynamics in the Sino-Soviet-American triangle changed. On May 30, Kennedy and Macmillan announced their readiness to "send highly placed representatives to Moscow" in late June or early July for frank negotiations.[82] On June 6, Beijing sent its reply to the Soviet April 20 letter, accusing Moscow of participating in a U.S. "conspiracy" directed "against China," of "catering to the desires of the U.S. government," and of trying to enter into treaty obligations in "China's name."[83] The Chinese communication sparked Khrushchev to action. Despite the obviously despondent tone of his June 8 letter to Kennedy, he accepted the proposal for high-level talks and proposed mid-July as a starting date.[84]

In a June 10 speech at American University, which was given on Cousins's advice with the intention to make a "dramatic peace offer" before the impending CPSU CC plenum,[85] the president sympathized with the Soviet people because "no nation in the history of battle ever suffered more," described the "devastation" after nuclear war, and concluded with the announcement of test ban negotiations in Moscow.[86] Khrushchev was delighted with what he heard: "The best speech by any president since Roosevelt."[87] In a memorandum two days later, Moscow rejected Beijing's allegations from June 6.[88] Kennedy's emotional address on world peace also stood in stark contrast to the hammer of political warfare which the CCP struck on June 14 with the "Proposal Concerning the General Line of the International Communist Movement."

To increase the chances for any treaty, Kennedy decided to give up his pursuit of a comprehensive test ban. His willingness to concede was

---

[80] Khrushchev, *Nikita S. Khrushchev*, 694.

[81] "Memorandum of Conversation," 4/26/1963, 12:45 A.M., *JFK*, National Security Files, box 187, "Khrushchev Talks (Harriman)."

[82] "Telegram from the Department of State to the Embassy in the Soviet Union," 5/30/1963, *FRUS 1961–1963*, VI, 290.

[83] "[Note]," 6/6/1963, *PAAA-MfAA*, VS-Hauptstelle, G-A 361, 1–14.

[84] "Letter from Chairman Khrushchev to President Kennedy," 6/8/1963, *FRUS 1961–1963*, VI, 292–96.

[85] Cousins, *Triumvirate*, 122.

[86] "Commencement Address at American University in Washington," 6/10/1963, John Kennedy, *Public Papers of the President*, vol. 3, 459–64.

[87] Quoted in: Taubman, *Khrushchev*, 602.

[88] "Memorandum," 6/12/1963, *MOL*, 288 f.9/1963/26 őe, 34–61.

undoubtedly buttressed by data from the most recent Nevada tests, which suggested that existing seismographic stations could pick up underground tests at almost any place in the world. It was a radical cure to a major headache: Khrushchev's hard stance on inspections.[89] But the PRC continued to haunt Kennedy when, in late June, he started to toy with the idea of getting an "assurance" from Moscow "that the Chinese Communists would not proceed with their nuclear weapon development."[90] Despite U.S. uncertainties over the positions the Kremlin might adopt, Khrushchev's agreement to install a hotline, a direct telephone link between the Kremlin and the White House, was a promising sign.[91]

While Kennedy was mulling over China, Khrushchev was explaining the latest changes in Soviet foreign relations to the Central Committee. Summing up a plenum that had dealt largely with cultural issues, the Soviet leader delivered another of his rambling speeches in which he criticized the Chinese comrades. Khrushchev finally turned to the test ban, calling Chinese views on nuclear war an "adventurist path that contradicts the essence of Marxism-Leninism. . . . One should ask the Chinese comrades, who propose to build a beautiful future on the ruins of the old world that has perished in thermonuclear war: have they consulted on this question with the working class of those countries, where imperialism still rules? . . . The atom bomb does not distinguish between an imperialist and a worker—it hits all places. . . . So, for example, if U.S. President Kennedy or his representative Harriman would come here, I would welcome him with the words: *our guest, a sort of a comrade.*"[92]

In the first three days of July, on the occasion of Walter Ulbricht's seventieth birthday, Khrushchev met some of the East European leaders in East Berlin.[93] There, the Soviet leader made a major speech on international relations that closely followed Kennedy's emotional "Ich bin ein Berliner" speech in West Berlin on June 28.[94] Although Khrushchev ranted against Western propaganda on the "so-called wall," he nevertheless lauded American acquiescence to an inspection-free test ban agreement, and renewed his 1958 proposal for a "non-aggression pact between . . . NATO countries and the Warsaw Pact member states."[95] U.S. reactions revealed

[89] Seaborg, *Kennedy*, 219–31. Oliver, *Kennedy*, 188–95.

[90] "Editorial Note," *FRUS 1961–1963*, VII, 735.

[91] Theodore Sorensen, *Kennedy* (New York: Smithmark, 1995), 727. Beschloss, *Crisis Years*, 602.

[92] "Seventh Session," 6/21/1963, *RGANI*, f.2, o.1, d.658 72–89a.

[93] *NYT*, 7/1/1963, 1, 4; 7/2/1963, 8.

[94] Sorensen, *Kennedy*, 601. Beschloss, *Crisis Years*, 606–8.

[95] *Pravda*, 7/3/1963, 2. *NYT*, 7/3/1963, 4.

satisfaction with Khrushchev's obvious eagerness to come to terms on the test ban, but were less favorable toward the pact.[96]

While Khrushchev's proposal of a nonaggression pact was likely related to Soviet MLF concerns, it was also the result of his attempt to reorient the Warsaw Pact against China. On July 10, the Soviet leader sent a circular to his East European allies supporting Outer Mongolia's request for Warsaw Pact membership.[97] Although archival evidence on whether Khrushchev raised this issue during his visit to East Berlin is inconclusive,[98] the proposal fit well with his harder stance toward Beijing and his softer course toward the West since early June.

The global importance of the Soviet-American nuclear rapprochement, made public by Kennedy on June 10, was not lost on the Chinese comrades. Since the previous August, when Rusk had tabled the test ban proposals, they had been suspicious. Due to the secret nature of the subsequent Soviet-British-American negotiations, the Chinese leaders had no knowledge of them and, as a result, Chinese polemics could not comment on them. Because the Soviets did not show any outward signs that they shared American concerns over the Chinese nuclear weapons program, the first polemic against the test ban was directed solely against the United States. A June 21 *Renmin Ribao* editorial ridiculed Kennedy's "strategy of peace" (quoting the three closing words of his American University speech) and claimed—not inaccurately—that the United States "laid great emphasis in its foreign policy on sowing discord between China and the Soviet Union and undermining the Socialist camp."[99]

Party Talks and Test Ban Negotiations, July 1963

Thus by mid-June 1963, two larger narratives in Sino-Soviet-American relations started to intersect. No evidence suggests that the U.S.-Soviet nuclear détente had any influence on Mao's preparations for the Sino-Soviet party talks. Indeed, his attempts to radicalize China's policies since early August 1962 clearly preceded Rusk's proposals for test ban negotiations later that month. And Khrushchev's warming to the idea of genuine

[96] "Editorial Note," *FRUS 1961–1963*, VII, 762–64. "Editorial Note," *FRUS 1961–1963*, V, 712–13. Rudy Abramson, *Spanning the Century* (New York: Morrow, 1992), 596. *NYT*, 7/3/1962, 1, 4, 26; 7/4/1963, 3.

[97] "Khrushchev to Ulbricht," 7/10/1963, *SAPMO-BArch*, DY 30/3387, 47–49.

[98] "Protocol no. 21/63," 7/4/1963, *SAPMO-BArch*, DY 30/J IV 2/2/885, 1. "Notes on a talk of the first secretaries of the CCs with comr. N.S. Khrushchev on 6/30/1963," *SÚA*, Archiv ÚV KSČ, f.07/16, Antonín Novotný—Zahraničí, karton 140, Návštěva s. Novotného u příležitosti 70. narozenin W. Ulbrichta v Berlíně—29.6.-1.7.1963, 1–7.

[99] Quoted in: *NYT*, 6/22/1963, 20.

test ban negotiations in April followed Mao's decision in March to work for the split while trying to deflect responsibility for it onto Khrushchev.

On July 5, the CCP delegation left Beijing for Moscow with apprehensions about Soviet attitudes. According to Wu Lengxi, the Chinese had "intelligence stating that the Soviet government and the Americans were negotiating, [and that they] wanted to conclude a test ban [treaty] with the purpose of pressuring and compelling us to abandon our nuclear program."[100] Apart from the impending test ban talks, the expulsion of Chinese embassy staff and citizens on June 27, as described in chapter 7, was another bad omen. Not a hardliner himself, Liu Shaoqi thus was pessimistic about any outcome of the talks, but admitted that *both* sides were "not ready" for constructive talks.[101] Consequently, following his own hard line as laid out since the spring, Mao convened a Politburo meeting on the evening of July 4 and declared that "the Soviet Union will not negotiate in good faith [with us,] . . . it wants us to surrender." The final instructions to the delegation again confirmed what Mao's fellows had decided many months before: "The delegation should not kneel down in front of Khrushchev."[102]

The delegation's welcome in Moscow was courteous. Politburo member Suslov came to greet them at the airport.[103] Khrushchev, however, made a point of being absent; on his way back from East Berlin, he stopped over in Kiev.[104] The CCP delegation was lodged in state guesthouses, but because it assumed—probably correctly—that the rooms were bugged, it moved the most important delegation members to the nearby embassy. Wu Lengxi recalled that "the Soviet side was cheerless, even the meals were neither very big nor very good." One day, in the car returning "from the canteen," Peng Zhen complained about the bad fare. "The next day, the food had improved." Even the car seemed to have had surveillance microphones![105]

The talks started on July 6. They were neither conversations nor negotiations, but a mutual lecturing about past mistakes, real and invented, of the other side. Witnesses called them a "dialogue of deaf people"[106] and remembered the "endless unilateral declarations intended . . . to rip the other side to shreds."[107] On the first day, Suslov lectured "for more

[100] WLX, 600.
[101] Zhonggong, *Mao Zedong zhuan*, 1281.
[102] WLX, 600.
[103] *NYT*, 7/6/1963, 1, 2.
[104] Michael Beschloss, *Crisis Years* (New York: HarperCollins, 1991), 618.
[105] WLX, 601–2.
[106] Wu, *Huiyi*, 372.
[107] Georgii Arbatov, *System* (New York: Times, 1993), 97.

than two hours" until the meeting was adjourned.[108] For the most part, he countered the Chinese "Proposal Concerning the General Line of the International Communist Movement" with long-held Soviet positions.[109] Afterward, the CCP delegation decided to use one of the speech drafts prepared beforehand, in Beijing, to address the historical roots of Sino-Soviet disagreements.[110] On July 8, Deng laid out a long list of labels the CPSU had allegedly tried to stick on the CCP, followed by a five-hour catalog of supposed Soviet mistakes committed since the twentieth CPSU congress.[111]

Meanwhile, in a July 9 meeting of the National Security Council, Kennedy again brought up the question of "how we thought the Russians would discuss a test ban treaty with the Chinese."[112] With Harriman's Moscow trip fast approaching, Washington started to contemplate other schemes of "removing the potential capability" or even "action to deny the ChiComs [Chinese Communists] a nuclear capability."[113] The president vaguely instructed Harriman that "he could go as far as he wished in exploring the possibility of a Soviet-American understanding with regard to China."[114]

Before Harriman's July arrival in Moscow, the Chinese and Soviets had met several times more to continue their bizarre exchange. On July 10, Suslov stated that Deng's laundry list of Soviet mistakes was a clear sign that the CCP "had in no way the wish to show good will." The Soviet chief ideologue's speech had compelling moments, especially when he spoke out emphatically against nuclear war and rejected Chinese charges of a Soviet "Munich conspiracy" in the Caribbean. Suslov also challenged the Maoist allegation that the CPSU had pushed the international communist movement "to the abyss."[115] But, on the whole, the speech was not great. Among themselves, the Chinese comrades derided the "Soviet 'authority' on theory" for "sophistry," and decided to use the momentum to charge the CPSU with "splittism."[116] On July 12, Deng accused Suslov of defending "mistaken positions . . . which the CPSU

---

[108] WLX, 604.

[109] "Meeting of the Delegations of the CPSU and the CCP in July 1963: First Session," 7/6/1963, *SAPMO-BArch*, DY 30/3608, 1–64.

[110] WLX, 604.

[111] "Second Session," and "Third Session," 7/8/1963, *SAPMO-BArch*, DY 30/3608, 65–102.

[112] "Summary Record of the 515th Meeting of the NSC," 7/9/1963, *FRUS 1961–1963*, VII, 783.

[113] Quoted in: Chang, *Friends*, 241.

[114] Quoted in: Arthur Schlesinger, *Thousand Days* (New York: Fawcett Premier), 825.

[115] "Fourth Session," 7/10/1963, *SAPMO-BArch*, DY 30/3608, 103–45.

[116] WLX, 605–6.

champions so stubbornly." He concentrated on the most recent Soviet-American rapprochement and criticized peaceful coexistence as a "rightist opportunist line, a line that rejects revolution."[117]

While Deng's rhetoric was skillful, he could not convince the Soviet splitters of the essential point of his diatribe. On the contrary, that very day, the Soviet government presented its Chinese counterpart with a memorandum defending Soviet-American nuclear rapprochement. Although it rejected the Chinese charge that the Soviet government had assumed "duties . . . in lieu of China," its argument pointed to the reasons why Moscow believed Beijing should *not* have nuclear weapons: the precedent it would set could justify the American imperialist arming of West Germany.[118]

Chinese public polemics resumed on July 13 with a *Renmin Ribao* editorial, mistitled: "We Want Unity, Not a Split." A reply to the Soviet memorandum, it vigorously claimed that the "imperialists headed by the United States, the reactionaries of all countries and the modern revisionists represented by the Tito group are counting on the failure of the Sino-Soviet talks."[119] An editorial published the next day—"Do Not Allow U.S. Imperialism to Meddle in Sino-Soviet Divergence"—referred to specific American newspaper articles that had linked the test ban treaty to the Sino-Soviet dispute.[120]

At the same time, the CPSU was preparing its own polemical reply to the "Proposal Concerning the General Line of the International Communist Movement." Right before Deng's July 12 speech, Suslov had announced to some advisers of the CC apparatus that he wanted "to prepare a document urgently, that very day, expressing the Soviet Communist Party's position in the quarrel with Chinese leaders." Fedor Burlatskii recalled his superior's justification: "We must inflict a blow on them suddenly while they are unprepared." The Soviet chief ideologue then left to attend that day's session while Andropov instructed Burlatskii to draft "an outline for an open letter on China's position." After sitting through Deng's second diatribe, "our delegation . . . arrived . . . before I [Burlatskii] had finished." Suslov was not satisfied with the "two or three initial questions worked out in detail," and pointed out a whole string of issues he wanted to be covered.[121] Georgii Arbatov recalled that "we worked in the Central Committee building for about thirty hours straight and handed

---

[117] "Sixth Session," 7/12/1963, *SAPMO-BArch*, DY 30/3608, 145–90. This was the fifth session; the transcript misnumbers all following sessions.

[118] "Memorandum," 7/12/1963, *SAPMO-BArch*, DY 30/3607, 100–138.

[119] *PR* 29 (7/19/1963), 8.

[120] *SCMP* 3024, 32–33.

[121] Fedor Burlatskii, *Khrushchev and the First Russian Spring* (New York: Scribner's, 1988), 137, 184–86.

in the draft, page by page, to the secretaries of the Central Committee for editing."[122]

The new focus of the CPSU apparatus inevitably showed in the Sino-Soviet party talks. On July 13, it was the Soviets' turn to lecture the Chinese comrades. The CCP delegation "had expected, they would just refute Deng straight away," but when Ponomarev read a tame and short speech addressing only some of the points raised earlier, the Chinese side felt let down. The speech was "feeble, only posturing."[123]

The Soviet reply to the Chinese "Proposal" of June 14 was published in *Pravda* on July 14 as "Open Letter of the Central Committee of the Communist Party of the Soviet Union."[124] It was the *very first time* that the Soviet people could read about the *details* of the ideological disagreements.[125] The letter claimed that the CPSU had struggled to end the polemics, charged the CCP with publicizing the rift with its June 14 proposal, asserted that the disagreements were published first by the CCP in April 1960, and rebutted Chinese views on nuclear war and arms limitation.[126] The following morning, five days after the July 10 dispatch mentioned above, Khrushchev sent out a second circular letter to the WAPA allies, in which he once again underscored the importance of Outer Mongolian membership and called for a PCC meeting in Moscow on July 26 and 27 to discuss the issue.[127] Khrushchev was determined to turn the Warsaw Pact against the PRC—an act the Sino-Soviet alliance treaty explicitly prohibited.[128]

That the CPSU published the open letter one day before the Soviet-American-British nuclear test ban talks were to begin was, in itself, remarkable. The *New York Times* called it "a political explosion of historical importance."[129] The Kennedy Administration happily suggested that "the Kremlin's latest criticism of the Chinese Communist regime has enhanced the chances of a positive outcome of the East-West talks."[130] The CCP delegation, meanwhile, was taken aback by these developments, especially since it had only heard of the open letter through a Soviet radio broadcast. Internally, it accused Khrushchev of repeating "the old trick" from before "Camp David," when he "had joined the United States in order to oppose China." Not knowing what to do, the

[122] Arbatov, *System*, 98.
[123] WLX, 608. "Seventh Session," 7/13/1963, *SAPMO-BArch*, DY 30/3608, 191–215.
[124] *Pravda*, 7/14/1963, 1–7.
[125] NYT, 7/21/1963, 1.
[126] *Pravda*, 7/14/1963, 1–7.
[127] "Khrushchev to Ulbricht," 7/15/1963, *SAPMO-BArch*, DY 30/3387, 52–53.
[128] Article III of the treaty in: Hinton, *People's Republic*, vol. 1, 123.
[129] NYT, 7/15/1963, 10, 28.
[130] NYT, 7/15/1963, 1.

delegation asked Beijing for instructions.[131] The next day, *Renmin Ribao* published a tough editorial: "The essential problem of the Sino-Soviet talks lies *not in one making concessions to the other*, but in that both must adhere to the fundamental principles of Marxism-Leninism."[132]

Khrushchev personally attended the Soviet-American-British negotiations during the first three days, July 15–17.[133] The talks proceeded quickly, although Harriman continued to insist on the withdrawal clause while Gromyko adhered to the nonaggression pact.[134] After the first day of negotiations, Harriman reported to Kennedy that he had also "open[ed] up problems with China," and that Khrushchev's response was heartening: "It will be some years off before China is a nuclear power."[135] Kennedy, however, replied "that Chinese problem is more serious than Khrushchev comments . . . suggest, and [I] believe you should press questions in private meeting with him." He reminded Harriman that "relatively small [nuclear] forces in hands of people like ChiComs could be very dangerous to us all."[136] The telegram ended: "You should try to elicit Khrushchev's view on means of limiting or preventing Chinese nuclear development and his willingness *either to take Soviet action or to accept US action aimed in this direction*."[137] It was not until the very end of the negotiations, however, that Harriman would be able to meet the Soviet leader in private.

While Soviet-British-American test ban negotiations went smoothly, Sino-Soviet party meetings continued to be dominated by the same unforgiving tones. As early as July 13, the Chinese delegation had realized "that the tripartite talks were not a good portent," and decided to rewrite Peng Zhen's speech scheduled for two days later.[138] It responded to the points Ponomarev had raised with well-known arguments.[139] On July 17, Andropov recounted the Chinese mistakes responsible for the rift in as much detail as Deng had done nine days before. As usual, the two delegations adjourned the meeting without having had any constructive discussion.[140]

[131] WLX, 611.

[132] Quoted in: *NYT*, 7/16/1963 (italics mine).

[133] Abramson, *Spanning*, 596.

[134] Chang, *Friends*, 245–47. Seaborg, *Kennedy*, 243–47. Dobrynin, *In Confidence*, 107–8. Abramson, *Spanning*, 596–97.

[135] "Telegram from the Embassy in the Soviet Union to the Department of State," 7/15/1962, *FRUS 1961–1963*, VII, 800.

[136] "Telegram from the Department of State to the Embassy in the Soviet Union," 7/15/1963, *FRUS 1961–1963*, VII, 801.

[137] The last part is not published in *FRUS*, but has been quoted on the basis of archival sources: Chang, *Friends*, 243 (quote; italics mine). Seaborg, *Kennedy*, 239.

[138] WLX, 613.

[139] "Eighth Session," 7/15/1963, *SAPMO-BArch*, DY 30/3608, 216–43.

[140] "Ninth Session," 7/17/1963, *SAPMO-BArch*, DY 30/3608, 244–69.

On July 18, Harriman reported to Kennedy that he was slowly coming to understand "why Khrushchev is interested in a test ban."[141] For days, the Soviet leader had demanded French accession.[142] "Obviously, his first preoccupation is his battle with ChiComs . . . Since he is unable to get the ChiComs to agree to join the test ban, he will attempt to isolate them . . . , thus leaving the Chinese isolated if possible as the only nation refusing to cooperate on this highly emotional subject to the underdeveloped nations." Harriman bolstered his observation with a reference to China's propaganda on national liberation wars that provided the PRC with an advantage in its "competition with the Soviet Union" for the support of the Third World.[143]

On July 19, the CCP published two more polemics. The first criticized the CPSU open letter as "superlative material for learning by negative example"; the second called the negotiated Limited Nuclear Test Ban a "U.S. nuclear fraud" which "will not stop U.S. nuclear proliferation . . . among its allies" and, worse, was designed to "manacle the socialist countries."[144] Indeed, by that point, and unbeknownst to the Chinese, the Soviets had ceased to pursue the MLF issue in negotiations.[145]

The CCP Politburo had also decided that its delegation in Moscow "should meet one or two times more and then terminate the talks." The delegation not only got "a free hand . . . to criticize the mistakes of Khrushchev and other Soviet leaders," but was also urged "not to fear a split." It was thus that, on July 19, Kang Sheng delivered the "Stalin speech," which had been "prepared in Beijing but amended after the [Soviet] open letter."[146] It was nothing but a reiteration of Mao's 70 percent—30 percent evaluation of Stalin from 1956.[147] Afterward, in a telegram to Beijing, the CCP delegation proposed to invite "the Soviet side to send a delegation to Beijing, but especially to propose that Khrushchev come." The Chinese side wanted not only to keep up the

---

[141] "Telegram from the Embassy in the Soviet Union to the Department of State," 7/18/1963, *FRUS 1961–1963*, VII, 808.

[142] "Telegram from the Embassy in the Soviet Union to the Department of State," 7/15/1963, *FRUS 1961–1963*, VII, 800. "Telegram from the Embassy in the Soviet Union to the Department of State," 7/16/1963, *FRUS 1961–1963*, VII, 803–4.

[143] "Telegram from the Embassy in the Soviet Union to the Department of State," 7/18/1963, *FRUS 1961–1963*, VII, 808–809.

[144] *PR* 30 (7/26/1963), 9, 47–48.

[145] Khrushchev raised MLF only at the beginning: "Incoming Telegram Department of State," 7/16/1963, 8:30 A.M., *JFK*, National Security Files, box 187, "Khrushchev Talks (Harriman)," 24. Harriman's reports from the talks suggest that the Soviets hoped to address West German nuclear access through a nonaggression pact: *JFK*, National Security Files, box 187, "Khrushchev Talks (Harriman)."

[146] *WLX*, 614–15.

[147] "Tenth Session," 7/19/1963, *SAPMO-BArch*, DY 30/3608, 270–78.

façade of possible future cooperation, but also to induce Khrushchev to make a pilgrimage to Beijing. That evening, Zhou agreed to the idea over the phone.[148]

July 20 began with renewed Chinese press polemics calling on the people of the world to resist the U.S. nuclear fraud.[149] Later that day, the two party delegations met in Moscow for the last time. Suslov and Deng mocked each other, while the Chinese refused to heed the Soviet call to end polemics. The head of the Chinese delegation claimed that the CCP had not "provoked the open polemics," and thus retained the right to respond to the CPSU open letter.[150] After a frosty dinner with Khrushchev—this was the only the time he met with the CCP delegation—the Chinese left for Beijing.[151]

But Khrushchev had not yet brought the full harvest into the barn. Although the Soviets, British, and Americans had announced a tentative agreement on the twentieth,[152] Harriman still sought the withdrawal clause.[153] By now, U.S. resolve seemed to exasperate the Soviets. Gromyko, it appears, had complained at home to his wife, and so, on the twenty-second, she conveyed to U.S. Ambassador Kohler at a reception in the Polish embassy: "You tell Mr. Harriman that he has to do everything that is necessary to get this (test ban) treaty. We have to have this so that when those Chinese have their first nuclear explosion, we will have a basis on which to call them to account."[154] That same day, Harriman received new instructions from Kennedy to "try as soon as possible to reach agreement with Gromyko." The president once more reiterated his desire that his envoy approach Khrushchev, confidentially, on the issue of action against the Chinese nuclear weapons program.[155] Harriman, however, was still unable to talk discreetly with the Soviet leader about that issue. Furthermore, since both sides now wanted as many nations as possible to sign, they agreed that those countries not recognized by all other signatory states—such as the PRC and Taiwan, or East and West Germany—could accede as well.[156]

[148] WLX, 615–16.

[149] Chang, *Friends*, 242.

[150] "Eleventh Session," 7/20/1963, *SAPMO-BArch*, DY 30/3608, 279–87.

[151] *SCMP* 3026, 36–37. WLX, 621–23.

[152] Chang, *Friends*, 246.

[153] "Telegram from the Embassy in the Soviet Union to the Department of State," 7/20/1962, *FRUS 1961–1963*, VII, 816.

[154] *FRUS 1961–1963*, VII, 645, n. 1 (parentheses in original).

[155] "Telegram from the Department of State to the Embassy in the Soviet Union," 7/22/1962, *FRUS 1961–1963*, VII, 832.

[156] "Telegram from the Embassy in the Soviet Union to the Department of State," 7/23/1962, *FRUS 1961–1963*, VII, 833. "Telegram from the Embassy in the Soviet Union to the Department of State," 7/25/1962, *FRUS 1961–1963*, VII, 842–44. Seaborg, *Kennedy*, 249–50. Rusk, *As I Saw It*, 287.

The Soviets had been moving so fast that the sudden emergence of a final agreement caught Harriman unprepared. To get Washington's quick approval without going through the cumbersome process of exchanging telegrams, he called Kennedy on the newly installed phone line and, within minutes, received the president's endorsement.[157]

The treaty, initialed on July 25, was the bare minimum the tripartite talks could have produced. It outlawed nuclear testing in the atmosphere, outer space and under water "at any place under [the] jurisdiction or control" of the signatories, and also required them "to refrain from causing, encouraging, or in any way participating in, the carrying out of any nuclear weapon test explosion, or any other nuclear explosion, *anywhere*."[158] A year of tedious negotiations over inspections and American concerns about the Chinese nuclear weapons program had only produced a short text that did not even include the term "nonproliferation."

Only on the day after the official ceremony, July 26, did Harriman have the chance to talk with Khrushchev in private. When the American envoy implored Khrushchev over Moscow's assistance to Beijing's bomb project, the Soviet leader indicated that this had happened only "at [an] initial stage." Upon Harriman's questioning as to whether the Soviet Union "was not concerned that China would explode [a] nuclear device soon," Khrushchev gave a short, negative reply.[159] The published American transcript does not indicate whether Harriman ever asked Khrushchev for action against the Chinese bomb project, as requested by the president.[160] The Kennedy Administration and, after late 1963, its successor under Lyndon Johnson, continued to work on military plans to attack the Chinese nuclear weapons project, despite Soviet diffidence on the issue.[161] In a discussion with Soviet Ambassador Dobrynin on September 25, 1964, Bundy got the impression that the USSR believed the "Chinese nuclear weapons had no importance against the Soviet Union or against the U.S."[162] This may have sparked the leak to the *New York Times* mentioned at the beginning of this chapter.[163] Regardless, with the first Chinese nuclear test on October 16, 1964, the American project became obsolete.[164]

---

[157] Abramson, *Spanning*, 598–99. Oliver, *Kennedy*, 204–5.

[158] Text in: U.S. Arms Control and Disarmament Agency, ed., *Arms Control and Disarmament Agreements, 1959–1972* (Washington: GPO, 1972), 14–15.

[159] "Telegram from the Embassy in the Soviet Union to the Department of State," 7/27/1962, *FRUS 1961–1963*, VII, 856–57.

[160] Chang makes a similar point: *Friends*, 246–47.

[161] William Burr et al., "Whether to 'Strangle the Baby in the Cradle,'" *International Security* 25/3, 72–99.

[162] "Memorandum of Conversation," 9/25/1964, *FRUS 1964–1968*, XXX, 104–5.

[163] *NYT*, 10/2/1964, 13.

[164] Seaborg, *Stemming*, 111–18.

Khrushchev received his East European allies for the PCC meeting of the Warsaw Pact two days after the LNTB was initialed. While his July 10 proposal to turn the pact against China had not attracted much attention, his second circular five days later, which called for the WAPA meeting on July 26 and 27, caused concern. It put the Romanians under pressure to formulate, rather quickly, a clear position. On the eighteenth, they concluded that Khrushchev's ideas would create "military blocs within the framework of the socialist camp."[165] Two days later, a Polish memorandum notified the Soviets that the proposal's "thrust is directed against the PRC."[166] Both Bucharest and Warsaw thereby indicated that they had no intention of assuming alliance obligations outside Europe. During the actual PCC meeting, only the Romanians dared to speak against Outer Mongolian membership. Aware of the political complications presented by his request, the Mongolian party boss Tsedenbal offered to suspend it "until the conditions become more favorable."[167]

After the breakdown of the Sino-Soviet party talks, the CCP delegation was greeted to a heroes' welcome at Beijing airport; Mao Zedong, Liu Shaoqi, Zhou Enlai, Zhu De, and another five thousand cadres participated. The reunited Chinese leadership proceeded to Zhongnanhai to celebrate "complete victory." There, Mao announced that "we are close to the split, we have already reached the brink."[168]

In reality, China was swept away by a tidal wave of defeat. After the three original negotiating parties had signed the LNTB treaty in Moscow on August 5, 1963, another eighty-two nations followed that month alone, with twenty-four more acceding before the end of the year. While the majority of socialist countries acceded, the PRC, North Vietnam, North Korea, Albania, and Cuba refused to do so.[169] Among the nonsocialist

---

[165] English translation of "Stenographic Record of the Meeting of the Politburo of the Romanian Workers' Party Central Committee," 7/18/1963, in: http://www.isn.ethz.ch/php/collections/coll_11.htm#RealtedDocuments, accessed on 2/25/2004.

[166] English translation of "Memorandum by the Polish Foreign Minister (Rapacki), 7/20/1963," in: http://www.isn.ethz.ch/php/collections/coll_11.htm#RealtedDocuments, accessed on 2/25/2004.

[167] Quoted in: Carmen Rijnoveanu, "A Romanian Perspective on the Sino-Soviet Conflict, 1960–1968," paper presented at the conference "New Central and East European Evidence on the Cold War in Asia," Budapest, Hungary, 10/30–11/2/2003, 9. Also: "Excerpts of Report to the Hungarian Politburo on the PCC Meeting by the First Secretary of the MSzMP (János Kádár), July 31, 1963," http://www.php.isn.ethz.ch/collections/colltopic.cfm?ord216=Date&q216=Politburo&lng=en&id=17907, accessed on May 11, 2006. According to the Hungarian document, Khrushchev himself had second thoughts about Outer Mongolian membership once the Romanians had lodged their disapproval.

[168] WLX, 623–24.

[169] For the list of signatory nations: U.S., *Arms Control*, 18–23.

countries, only France, Saudi Arabia, Cambodia, Guinea, the two Congos, Zanzibar, and the Vatican abstained.[170]

Beijing tried to get international support for its unusual position. However, Zhou's open August 2 letter, calling for the "complete, thorough, total and resolute prohibition and destruction of nuclear weapons" was only a cheap propaganda ploy.[171] In fact, at that time, the Chinese leaders accelerated work on the Chinese A-bomb project.[172]

Despite recent Chinese historiographical claims that the LNTB treaty "deprived China of the right to test above-ground,"[173] the Chinese leaders of the day clearly understood the real implications of August 5. Of course, the treaty did *not* deprive any nonsignatory state of the right to any kind of nuclear testing. Zhou grudgingly acknowledged that: "Khrushchev scored a major *political* victory." In fact, the treaty was an attempt to prevent the international flow of nuclear technology: "They are trying to stop everyone else from having *nuclear know-how*."[174] Despite all the propaganda, the Chinese leadership knew that it could continue to build its own nuclear weapons. On October 16, 1964, the PRC exploded its first nuclear device—in the face of the LNTB.[175]

In a September circular to all provincial party branches, the CCP leadership explained the new international situation. Accusing the USSR for the "surrender of revisionism to imperialism," it announced that "China will become the world's revolutionary center" armed with "nuclear weapons and Marxism-Leninism" after "ten years" of isolation. In the short term, as the circular happily pointed out, Khrushchev had failed to secure the nonaggression pact that "would have allowed the Soviet Union to withdraw troops from Eastern Europe."[176] Nevertheless, by late July 1963, the security environment of the PRC had become more hostile. The Chinese leadership thus decided "to strengthen its northern defense."[177]

Initially, the *primary* motives for the LNTB treaty were public pressures, environmental concerns, and a genuine desire on the part of almost all nations to limit the arms race. The treaty capped eighteen years of attempts

---

[170] I identified these states through comparison of a list of the signatory states and a list of the U.N. member states (ordered according to admission): Peter Stearns, *The Encyclopedia of World History*, 6th ed. (Boston: Houghton Mifflin, 2001), 1078–79. Switzerland, the only U.N. non-member state, joined the NTB in the fall of 1963.

[171] *PR* 32 (8/91963), 7.

[172] Li, *Lengnuan*, 321–22.

[173] Dangdai, *Waijiao*, 120. Li, *Lengnuan*, 320–22. WLX, 628–30.

[174] Han, *Eldest Son*, 295 (italics mine).

[175] Lewis, *China Builds the Bomb*, 192–93.

[176] "[No title]," September 1963, JSSDAG, 3124, zhang 177, 1–25.

[177] Li, "ZhongSu," 115–16.

to outlaw nuclear weapons. The rapid signing of the vast majority of countries in the world revealed the universal desire for arms limitation.

Until 1962, worries about Beijing had been a *secondary* concern in Washington's thinking about a nuclear test ban treaty. After the Cuban Missile Crisis, however, they rose increasingly higher *within* that second tier. In late 1962, Washington saw the test ban negotiations as a tool to apply the wedge strategy against the Sino-Soviet alliance. By early 1963, Kennedy was obsessed with the Chinese nuclear weapons project and its implications for American security. Over the spring and summer, the U.S. president was willing to make a substantial number of concessions to get any treaty that would slow down China's acquisition of nuclear weapons. No wonder that the final agreement represented the lowest common denominator for a nuclear test ban. It neither was comprehensive nor called explicitly for nuclear nonproliferation. In fact, it took another five years of negotiations, interrupted by the Vietnam War, to reach a nonproliferation agreement. Kennedy was similarly unable to obtain Khrushchev's agreement over joint action against the Chinese nuclear weapons project. In the end, the LNTB neither prevented nor deterred the Chinese from working toward their own nuclear bomb.

For a long time, the USSR did not seem to share American concerns over China's nuclear weapons program; instead, it was worried by West German access to nuclear weapons and by on-site inspections. It was only after the Cuban Missile Crisis that the Soviet leader, having been shaken by the events in the Caribbean that he himself had brought about, started to link his criticism of Chinese ideological extremism to the environmental dangers of nuclear war. Given Mao's hard-line ideological position in June of 1963, Khrushchev eventually decided on nuclear rapprochement with the United States at the expense of ideological reconciliation with the Chinese comrades, especially once the United States ceased to insist on on-site inspections. Succumbing to his tendency to carry things to extremes, the Soviet leader even was willing not only to sacrifice his security concerns over West German access to nuclear weapons, but also to reorient the Warsaw Pact away from NATO against the PRC. In the end, like Kennedy, he did not get all that he wanted. While he did obtain an LNTB treaty that was signed by the vast majority of states and that simultaneously isolated China, Khrushchev did not achieve the strategic redirection he had hoped for. His East European allies either opposed additional responsibilities outside of Europe or were sympathetic to China.

In Mao's mind, as far as Chinese evidence suggests, Sino-Soviet differences and Soviet-American nuclear rapprochement did not merge before June 1963. Although, in the fall of 1962, Beijing's diplomatic notes to Moscow claimed that the American treaty proposals were directed against China, no PRC statement before late June of 1963 accused the

USSR of abetting the U.S. wedge strategy by participating in test ban talks. But since the Chairman had decided to seek the split anyway at that time, Soviet-British-American test ban negotiations were only additional water through his ideological mill. In the end, Mao's renewed radicalism had prepared the ground for the Sino-Soviet rift; the LNTB treaty simply helped it to burst into the open.

CHAPTER 9

Khrushchev's Fall and the Collapse of Party Relations, 1963–1966

EDUCATED IN THE U.K. and the United States, Wu Ningkun decided to follow the call of the new regime to return to China in 1951. After running afoul of the Anti-Rightist and anti-American Campaigns of the 1950s, he was lucky enough to find a teaching job in the English Department of Hefei (Anhui) Teachers College. In late 1965, newspapers began carrying articles denouncing Wu Han for his 1959 attacks on the "Great Leader." When Wu entered the Liberal Arts Building to teach his class on June 1, 1966, he passed *dazibao* (big-character posters) attacking an English and a Russian professor for counterrevolutionary activities. Some nights later, his own students came to his apartment and assaulted him. He was, they claimed, an enemy of the people. In August, after Mao had intentionally exacerbated teenage unrest at several mass rallies on Tiananmen Square, student Red Guards from the "center of world revolution" arrived in provincial Hefei to instigate proletarian "dictatorship" on the basis of the "wisdom of Mao Zedong." Over the next two years, local student Red Guards terrorized the faculty members of the Russian and the English departments, accusing them of being "Soviet revisionists" and even "Soviet spies."[1]

From mid-1963 to mid-1964, Mao supervised the publication of nine anti-Soviet polemics. While the primary intention was to discredit the Soviet leadership further, they were also responsible for intensifying the domestic debate on ideology and policies. It was also during this period that incidents at the Sino-Soviet border occurred on a regular basis. Although the evidence is ambiguous, it seems that Beijing instigated these conflicts in order to pressure Moscow to make concessions during the border talks of 1964.

By mid-1964, the polemics had clearly defined Mao's ideological yardstick. The Chairman was betting on the return of the Soviet comrades to these—his own—positions, which would have also forced his alleged domestic opponents into acquiescence. However, Mao's long-term hopes were disappointed when, in October 1964, Khrushchev's fall failed to

---

[1] Wu Ningkun, *Single Tear* (New York: Atlantic Monthly, 1993), 192–211.

terminate Soviet revisionism. Fearing its effects on China, Mao decided to turn against the party he had helped to create over the preceding four decades. This turn was clearly an attempt to forestall what he feared might have been his own removal. The final collapse of Sino-Soviet relations in the spring of 1966 thus was a function of Chinese domestic politics. Without the break in relations with the Soviet comrades, the Chairman would have been politically unable to launch the party purge that set off the Cultural Revolution.

POLEMICS AND BORDERS

While Chinese propaganda against the LNTB continued, the CCP prepared, under Mao's personal supervision,[2] a new round of nine polemics to be published from September 6, 1963, to July 13, 1964.[3] They covered the origins of the Sino-Soviet differences, the Stalin question, Yugoslavia, the Soviet defense of colonialism, questions of war and peace, peaceful coexistence, Soviet splittism, Khrushchev's revisionism, and his "phoney communism."[4] Apart from more hyperbolic personal attacks on the Soviet leader, they did not add anything new to the ideological disagreements that had been growing since 1956.[5] Nor did they succeed in convincing anybody in the socialist camp of the ideological correctness of the Chinese party. The pro-Chinese parties remained on Beijing's side (Albania, Korea, Vietnam, Japan, and Indonesia) while the pro-Soviet parties remained committed to Moscow (almost all of Europe, Africa, and the Americas). The Romanians, who for their own reasons were moving away from the Soviets, told the Chinese that the polemics "are at any rate not serious, that nobody believes them and will ever believe them."[6]

As Hu Qiaomu recollected, the polemics were primarily aimed at the domestic front.[7] Since the late summer of 1962, as described in chapter 7, Mao had stressed the new slogan of *fanxiu fangxiu* (oppose revisionism

[2] WLX, 639.

[3] Originally, ten polemics were planned. The tenth polemic was canceled in October 1964 after Khrushchev fell. Parts of the tenth draft polemic were inserted into "Why Khrushchev Fell," published in November 1964: Wu, *Huiyi*, 375–76.

[4] WLX, 633–39. The polemics are in: *PR* 37 (9/13/1963), 6–23; 38 (9/20/1963), 8–15; 39 (9/27/1963), 14–27; 43 (10/25/1963), 6–15; 47 (11/22/1963), 6–16; 51 (12/20/1963), 6–18; 6 (2/7/1964), 5–21; 14 (4/3/1964), 5–23; 29 (7/17/1964), 7–28 (quote).

[5] For a Soviet analysis: "The position of the CPSU in the struggle with the leaders of the CP China," [no date], *SAPMO-BArch*, DY 30/IV A 2/20/157, 4.

[6] "Record of Conversation with Gheorghiu Dumitri," 10/3/1963, *AVPRF*, f.0100, o.56, d.8, p.496, 29.

[7] 'Hu' zhubian, *Hu Qiaomu*, 70–71.

abroad, prevent revisionism at home).[8] In early 1963, Mao took the first steps toward the Cultural Revolution by permitting his wife, Jiang Qing, and Shanghai party boss Ke Qingshi to publish a report critical of ghost plays on China's theater stages. The report referred to Mao's 1961 pamphlet "Don't Fear Ghosts," in which the Chairman declared imperialism and revisionism as the main ghosts of the current period (see chapter 6). It was the opening shot in the emerging conflict over culture. The preliminary culmination of this struggle was the Beijing Opera Festival in mid-1964, during which a new model of revolutionary operas was launched. Until the Cultural Revolution, this conflict led to the rectification of cultural politics.[9]

The nine polemics also played a crucial part in rendering pressure on what Mao increasingly considered his opponents within the central party leadership and in the lower ranks. It is within this domestic context that the second polemic—on the Stalin question—was of particular importance. Its assertion that Khrushchev's opposition to the personality cult was wrong and harmful reinforced the Mao worship.[10] The Chairman subsequently claimed that Stalin had failed to acknowledge the existence of class struggle in the entire period of proletarian dictatorship. This enabled him to assert that the late Soviet leader had failed to suppress *all* counterrevolutionaries, especially Khrushchev. Once he had established the fact of Stalin's right deviation, he had a free hand to call those who did not agree with his views revisionists and capitalists.[11]

Simultaneously, the propaganda war over Sino-Soviet border questions turned into conflict on the ground. While Moscow's diplomatic notes from the summer and the fall of 1963 suggest that these incidents were the result of transgressions by Chinese border guards, farmers, and fishermen,[12] the reasons for these border problems are difficult to gauge in the absence of any Chinese documentation. Their sudden occurrence implies, however, that the Chinese wanted to create a record of border problems before the PRC notified the USSR of its desire to settle the Sino-Soviet borders in late 1963.[13] While the Soviets agreed to talks, they indicated that they would negotiate only on those areas where incidents had occurred. Moscow was not willing to heed Beijing's call for a renegotiation of all unequal treaties from the nineteenth century.[14]

---

[8] Cong, *Quzhe*, 518–22, 576.

[9] Li, "Study [I]," 74. MacFarquhar, *Origins*, vol. 3, 21–22, 334–39, 381–98.

[10] Li, "Study [I]," 75.

[11] Li, "Study [I]," 75–76. *PR* 38 (9/20/1963), 9–10.

[12] For the Soviet diplomatic protests: *AVPRF*, f.100, o.50, d.1, p.210, 29–30, 37–40, 55–61, 64–65.

[13] Xiao, *Qiusuo*, vol. 2, 1027–28.

[14] "[Note]," 12/14/1963, *AVPRF*, f.100, o.51, d.3, p.215, 1–4.

Border negotiations on the eastern sector (the border stretching from Vladivostok to Outer Mongolia, comprising roughly the Ussuri, Amur, and Argun rivers) started on February 23, 1964, in Beijing, and lasted until August. On the one hand, according to Chinese historiography, the PRC demanded that the USSR "acknowledge" that the old border treaties from Tsarist times were "unequal," but also indicated that it did not want to have any territory back.[15] On the other hand, Soviet memoirs claim that China demanded the return of Vladivostok and the territories east of the Ussuri and north of the Amur rivers.[16] Clearly the demands were negotiation tactics designed to play on Soviet feelings of guilt. Despite all the Chinese hyperbole, the two sides eventually agreed on the border line—with the exception of Zhenbao/Damanskii Island, which would be at the heart of the 1969 border clashes, and some other islands. Negotiations were suspended in August 1964, with an agreement to meet again for talks on the western sector (Xinjiang). However, due to Khrushchev's October removal from office and the subsequent collapse of the remainder of Sino-Soviet relations, negotiations did not resume until late 1969.[17]

In July 1964, despite having agreed with Stalin in 1950 that the PRC would recognize its independence, Mao reopened the question of Outer Mongolia.[18] His action might have been a response to the signing of a Soviet–Outer Mongolian defense agreement that same month.[19] In a July meeting with Japanese socialists, he demanded Soviet territory from Lake Baikal to Vladivostok, supported Japanese claims on the Kurile Islands, and called for the return of Soviet-occupied Polish and German territories.[20] While Moscow was unable to verify Mao's statements for several weeks, once it had done so, it began its own propaganda campaign in reply.[21] In early September, *Pravda* shocked its readers with a report on Mao's demand for 1.5 million square kilometers of Soviet territory, calling it an "aggressive threat against the USSR."[22] On September 15, Khrushchev told Japanese reporters that "the Chinese emperors were not inferior to the Russian Tsars in plundering. . . . [They] seized Mongolia,

[15] Li, "1969," 42.

[16] Semichastnyi, *Bespokoinoe*, 323–25. Khrushchev, *Khrushchev Remembers*, 474.

[17] Gittings, *Survey*, 158–61. Khrushchev, *Testament*, 287–89. Wang, *Zhonghua*, vol. 2, 254–55.

[18] Pei, *Zhonghua*, vol. 1, 20–21. O. Arne Westad, ed., "Fighting for Friendship," *CWIHP Bulletin* 8–9, 229. Shi, *Zai lishi*, 400–403. Xu, *Wang*, 497.

[19] Li, "1969," 43.

[20] Mao, "Interview with Personage of the Japanese Socialist Party," 7/10/1964, *MZDSW 1969*, 532–45.

[21] Heinz Brahm, *Pekings Griff nach der Vormacht* (Köln: Wissenschaft und Politik, 1966), 31.

[22] *Pravda*, 9/22/1964, 2–3.

Tibet and Xinjiang."[23] The Soviet foreign ministry lodged a formal protest in Beijing.[24] Yet, all the hyperbole, as Mao told French visitors, was "just idle talk" in order to make "Khrushchev a little tense. . . . Its goal is to obtain a reasonable . . . border treaty."[25] Mao was unclear as to what he considered reasonable.

Although Moscow had agreed to border talks by the end of 1963, Khrushchev made one more attempt to curb Chinese polemics. The rash publication, extent, and hyperbole of the first five polemics had surprised the Soviets. Already four days after the publication of the first polemic, on September 10, he wondered: "What precisely do they accuse us of?"[26] Mao's implicit claim that the center of world revolution had shifted from Moscow to Beijing angered Khrushchev.[27] His initial reaction was to engage in public polemics as well, and to have calls by foreign parties for a new international meeting of all communist parties reprinted in the Soviet press.[28] However, in a late October interview in *Pravda*, the Soviet leader reversed course, calling for an end to the public debates.[29] Soviet polemics quickly disappeared from Soviet media.

On November 29, the CPSU formally proposed the termination of polemics, stating that all sides had aired their positions, offered improved economic cooperation, and called for another meeting of all communist parties designed to achieve unity.[30] Khrushchev privately was not hopeful about reconciliation,[31] but he nevertheless told the Presidium at the end of the year that economic needs would ultimately force China to mend relations with the Soviet Union.[32] In his speech to the December 13 CC plenum, the Soviet leader reviewed old Soviet positions and claimed that "we love the Chinese people" while blasting the CCP leadership

[23] Quoted in: Li, "1969," 43. Also: "Stenographic Record of the CPSU CC Presidium Session on N. S. Khrushchev's Trip to several Regions of the Country," 8/19/1964, Fursenko, *Prezidium*, vol. 1, 849–50.

[24] "[Note PRC]," 9/16/1964, AVPRF, f.100, o.51, d.1, p.215, 30–35.

[25] Li, "1969," 43.

[26] "Protocol No. 114a: Session of September 10, 1963 (sequel)," Fursenko, *Prezidium*, vol. 1, 758.

[27] Semichastnyi, *Bespokoinoe*, 318–19. An internal CCP circular even explicitly stated that "China will become the world's revolutionary center": "[No title]," September 1963, *JSSDAG*, 3124, zhang 177, 25.

[28] "Protocol No 114a: Session of September 10, 1963 (sequel)," Fursenko, *Prezidium*, vol. 1, 757–60. Gittings, *Survey*, 212. *Pravda*, 9/21/1963, 1–2; 9/22/1963, 1–2. *Kommunist*, 14 (October 1963), 3–62.

[29] *Pravda*, 10/27/1963, 1–3.

[30] "Letter of CPSU CC to CCP CC," 11/29/1963, AAN, KC PZPR, XI A/9, 639–47.

[31] Troyanovskii, *Cherez*, 349.

[32] "Stenographic Record of the CPSU Presidium Session," 12/23/1963, Fursenko, *Prezidium*, vol. 1, 786.

for trying "to make the Soviet Union responsible for its own domestic economic policies." The plenum decided to distribute its official record, including speeches critical of China by other Soviet leaders, to all party members, beyond the usual list of top level recipients.[33]

The Chinese reaction to the November 29 letter was not favorable. The CCP maintained that the CPSU had again "adopted a big stick and carrot policy." Mao also refused to stop polemics because the Chinese side had still not answered all previous criticisms. Since the current situation was "beneficial" to the Chinese side, he claimed, the CCP should "not be eager to reply" but continue with polemics.[34] Mao wrote Ho Chi Minh that Sino-Soviet talks were "not suitable" in the near future, and that it could take "some years or some decades in order to come to a result beneficial for the revolution and for real unity."[35] Formally, the CCP rejected the proposal to stop polemics on the ground that Khrushchev's proposal was "personal" and not "issued in the name of the [Soviet] party."[36]

The Chairman interpreted contemporaneous developments as evidence for the correctness of his tough stance. In mid-December, the Romanian party had indicated that it would no longer attend any international meeting that China refused to attend or that it considered to be anti-Chinese.[37] The "phenomenon of continuing leader substitutions in the Soviet Party, the Bulgarian Party, the Hungarian Party and the Czech Party" also indicated to Mao that "Khrushchev's days are numbered."[38] In late 1963, in an attempt to encourage such developments, *Xinhua* published a piece that explicitly called for factionalism in other communist parties.[39]

Once again, Mao linked events abroad with those at home. On December 11, the very day the sixth polemic on peaceful coexistence was published, he ordered low-level party committees to set up study circles for ideological training, explaining "that the enlarged international anti-revisionist struggle was an advantageous and beneficial exercise for the ranks, and could teach the masses."[40] In January, he even warned that, lest this ideological work be taken seriously, "each level of leadership" of

---

[33] "Stenographic Report of the CPSU CC Plenum, December 1963" (quote), and "Decision of the CPSU CC Plenum," 12/13/1963, *RGANI*, f.2, o.1, d.696, 2, 101a–18.

[34] WLX, 655–62.

[35] "Remarks on the Reply Letter to Ho Chi Minh," 12/26–27/1963, *JYMW*, vol. 10, 465–66.

[36] "Information," 12/20/1963, *AMVnR*, o.20a, a.e.1083, 2.

[37] Wang, *Zhonghua*, vol. 2, 324.

[38] Mao, "Khrushchev Is Having a Hard Time," 1/17/1964, Mao, *On Diplomacy*, 392–95.

[39] Gittings, *Survey*, 213.

[40] Xiao, *Qiusuo*, vol. 2, 1020.

the party "will be seized by revisionists" and lead China "to walk on the road restoring capitalism."[41]

The seventh polemic—published on February 3 under the title "The Leaders of the C.P.S.U. Are the Greatest Splitters of Our Times"—reached a new level of hyperbole and provocation. It not only predicted that the communist international movement would soon split, as the First and Second Socialist International had in the past, but also declared that such a split was the only way to carry "the international working-class movement forward to a new stage." Although the Chairman had thereby given himself a carte blanche to work toward a split, he refused to assume any responsibility for the law of revolutionary progress he had just proclaimed. The polemic also stood out for its heightened level of personal attacks on Khrushchev.[42] Only after its publication did Mao turn to writing a reply to the CPSU letter of November 29.[43]

Mao had certainly achieved his goal—the CPSU was fuming. On February 12, the Soviet party informed some of its East European counterparts that "the CPSU CC has decided to deal with the splittist activities [of the CCP] . . . at the impending plenum," and declared that it was "necessary to unfold the struggle against . . . the splittist, subversive actions of the Chinese leaders."[44] Two days later, Suslov told the plenum that the "Chinese leaders have once more gone further and provoked the immediate danger of a split." He called on the CPSU to take "an open and decisive stand against the dangerous actions of the CCP leadership."[45]

On February 14, fearing a decisive split, the Romanians asked the Soviets to reverse their previous decision to publish the CC material; they also sent a letter to the Chinese comrades requesting the immediate cessation of all polemics.[46] While the Soviets agreed,[47] the Chinese comrades tried to use the momentum generated by their provocations. On February 18, following Mao's instruction, Peng Zhen summoned Chervonenko for a meeting. First, he complained that the CPSU had not sent the letter

---

[41] "A Part of a Speech added to Xu Bing's 'On a Summary . . . ,'" January 1964, *JYMW*, vol. 11, 17–19 (quotes). Also: "Outline of the Propaganda on Anti-Revisionism," 1/26/1964, *JSSDAG*, 3011, zhang 1130, 3–21a.

[42] *PR* 6 (2/7/1964), 5–21 (quote). "Circular by the CC to Grass-Root Cadres, Party Members, and the People's Masses Carrying Out anti-Revisionist Education," 1/26/1964, *JSSDAG*, 3011, zhang 1130, 1–2a.

[43] WLX, 666.

[44] "Letter by the CPSU CC," 2/13[12]/1964, *SAPMO-BArch*, DY 30/3609, 4.

[45] "Report by Suslov," 2/14/1964, *RGANI*, f.2, o.1, d.743, 103–21.

[46] Interview with Ioan Romulus Budura, Bucharest, 7/10/2004. Both letters are reprinted: "RWP CC to SED CC," 2/18/1964, *SAPMO-BArch*, DY 30/3655, 112–17.

[47] "[Letter by the CPSU CC]," 2/15/1964, *SAPMO-BArch*, DY 30/3609, 10–11. "Note," 2/24/1964, *SAPMO-BArch*, DY 30/3655, 130–31.

about the February plenum to the Chinese comrades and then charged the Soviets with delivering an "ultimatum" in the form of the November 29 letter, while "behind our back [at the February plenum] . . . you are conducting splittist activities." Since Chervonenko had not yet seen the plenum documents, he was first flabbergasted by the ferocity of Peng's verbal assault, but then held his own. He rejected all accusations, reminding Peng that the CCP had failed to reply to the November 29 letter for almost four months while continuing to publish polemics, and told his interlocutor bluntly: "If you, comrade Peng Zhen . . . and other Chinese comrades would toil to write out from your articles only those insulting terms and epithets and those rude abuses, to which you all most often resort in your statements, . . . you could carpet over all of Tiananmen Square with these statements."[48]

On February 29, the CCP finally replied to the Soviet letter of November 29. After a long list of supposed past Soviet mistakes, the Chinese comrades agreed to a new international meeting—but only under certain conditions. Although until mid-1963, the CCP had consistently called for a repeat of the three-level process of the 1960 Moscow Meeting (first Sino-Soviet talks, then the Editorial Board comprising the same twenty-six parties and, finally, a convention of all communist parties), it now tried to change the format, demanding a reduction of the number of parties attending the Editorial Board (from twenty-six to seventeen), the replacement of nine pro-Soviet with pro-Chinese members in it, and an extended schedule of the process.[49]

On March 2, the Romanian mediators—the Chairman of the State Council Chivu Stoica, its Vice-Chairman Ion Maurer, and Politburo members Emil Bodnăraş and Nicolae Ceauşescu—arrived in Beijing. Their declared desire was to help end the Sino-Soviet polemics and to improve Sino-Romanian relations. Mao agreed to stop polemics for the duration of the Romanian visit, but insisted on the right to respond to all previous public criticism of the CCP. After some days of talks, Mao complained to Kim Il-sung, who was present in Beijing but did not participate in the talks, about the "endless pestering" of the Romanian guests. After the East Europeans had left China on March 12, the CCP immediately resumed polemics.[50]

While the Sino-Romanian talks were under way in Beijing, the CPSU replied to the late February CCP letter regarding the meeting of all

[48] "Record of Conversation by Chervonenko with Peng Zhen," 2/18/1964, *AVPRF*, f.0100, o.57, d.6, p.508, 36–59.

[49] *CB* 733, 10–18.

[50] WLX, 688–723. About the Romanian desire to end the polemics: "Dölling to Florin," 2/25/1964, *SAPMO-BArch*, DY 30/IV A 2/20/354, 1–2. "Note on a Talk with Lazarescu," 3/11/1964, *SAPMO-BArch*, DY 30/IV A 2/20/354, 1–4.

communist parties. The Soviet side stated that "the polemics you are conducting have long ago gone beyond the bounds of an ideological dispute." The letter also contrasted CPSU "self-restraint" with the CCP's public call for the Soviet people to fight against their leaders. Finally, it proposed to carry out the three-level process of talks—unchanged from their previous format—within eighteen months.[51] This was not the kind of letter the Chinese wanted to receive, as CC member Wu Xiuquan told Chervonenko when the Soviet ambassador handed it over on March 8.[52]

Once the Romanians had left Beijing, Mao convened the CCP Politburo to discuss the Soviet letter. While conveniently disregarding his own provocative actions since mid-1963, the Chairman argued that the Soviet reply was proof that their November 29 letter calling for an end to polemics was a "dupe" and that the Soviets actually "wanted" a split. Despite this deliberate distortion, Mao considered, correctly though not knowingly, Khrushchev's domestic situation "unstable."[53] By that time, the conspiracy to remove Khrushchev had already started among the Soviet leadership.[54] But Mao's conclusion that the failure of Khrushchev's policies was the main reason why the Soviet leader wanted the split originated in his fantasy. He continued to insist on more public polemics designed to make "Khrushchev . . . stamp with fury," although he professed that he wanted to delay the split and preserve unity by postponing the reply to the Soviet letter for some time.[55]

In late March, the Romanians once again tried to stop the polemics.[56] While the CPSU agreed on the twenty-eighth, under the condition that the CCP consent to "stop immediately polemics in any form,"[57] the Chinese simply ignored the Romanian plea by publishing the eighth polemic, which contained more vicious personal attacks on Khrushchev, two days later.[58] The CPSU rescinded its pledge,[59] and, on April 3, published the materials of the February plenum that it had promised the Romanians it would temporarily withhold.[60] Mao had again displayed a remarkable sense of timing and provocation. He clearly enjoyed it: "Now we

[51] "To CCP CC," 3/7/1964, AAN, KC PZPR, XI A/10, 50, 55–56.
[52] "Record of Conversation with Wu Xiuquan," 3/8/1964, AVPRF, f.0100, o.57, d.6, p.508, 75.
[53] WLX, 729–33.
[54] Taubman, Khrushchev, 615.
[55] WLX, 729–33.
[56] "Gheorghiu-Dej to CPSU CC," 3/25/1964, SAPMO-BArch, DY 30/3655, 139–40.
[57] "Khrushchev to RWP CC," 3/28/1964, SAPMO-BArch, DY 30/3655, 161.
[58] PR 14 (4/13/1963), 5–6.
[59] "Khrushchev to RWP CC," 3/31/1964, SAPMO-BArch, DY 30/3655, 166–70.
[60] Pravda, 4/3/1964, 1–8. Brahm, Pekings Griff, 22.

command Khrushchev; when we shout: 'jump,' he jumps, when we shout: 'laugh,' he laughs."[61]

In late April, Mao's CCP finally turned to the composition of a reply to the Soviet letter from early March. The final version claimed that because the Chinese party wanted "to uphold unity and oppose a split," it could not agree to any talks that would "only lead to a split." Instead, the Chinese comrades reiterated their demand for a review of the three-level process of the talks, including the removal from the Editorial Board of parties that had degenerated into "renegades of communism."[62] Internally, Mao made clear that he "originally had wanted to delay the international meeting for three years, [but] that's now not enough, four or five years, or even longer" would be better.[63] Although Mao had convinced himself that Khrushchev would soon fall in a coup d'état, he feared that his successors might be worse: "Therefore, we should be friendly to Khrushchev."[64]

The Soviet mid-June reply called the new Chinese "proposal for putting off a new world conference . . . particularly unacceptable." Since such a gathering was "indispensable" to overcome the disputes, "the question of convening . . . cannot be shelved." It rebutted the Chinese argument that it could be convened only when all parties agreed, by making the counterargument that no single party could block its convocation.[65]

Mao's CCP decided to "shelve" the Soviet letter, since it was preparing the ninth polemic for its July 13 publication, after three months or preparation.[66] Unlike its two predecessors, it concentrated less on Khrushchev but directed most of its attention on demonstrating that "antagonistic classes and class struggle exist in the Soviet Union." The new polemic had a clear domestic purpose. Since 1962, Mao had become obsessed with the march of the counterrevolution—a theme echoed in the ninth polemic when it called for an "extensive socialist education movement . . . in the cities and the countryside" to root out "anti-socialist, capitalist, and feudal forces."[67]

The ninth polemic was also closely connected to two issues that would become central elements of the Cultural Revolution two years later. In June and July 1964, the Chinese capital hosted the Beijing Opera Festival. Mao used the event to provide his wife, Jiang Qing, with a platform to attack ghost plays—historical, counterrevolutionary, and bourgeois

[61] Quoted in: Xiao, *Qiusuo*, vol. 2, 1024.

[62] *PR* 19 (5/7/1964), 8–9.

[63] WLX, 734, 770.

[64] Mao, "Remarks and Revisions on a CCP CC Draft Reply Letter to the CPSU Letter," 4/30/1964, *JYMW*, vol. 11, 68.

[65] "To CCP CC," 6/15/1964, MOL, 288 f.9/1964/22 őe, 37–56.

[66] WLX, 792, 796.

[67] *PR* 29 (7/17/1964), 7–28 (quotes). Wu, *Yi Mao zhuxi*, 148.

operas—and link them to Khrushchev's revisionism.[68] Accordingly, on July 2, the Chairman claimed that unless the CCP Politburo worked to rectify China's cultural organizations, "they will certainly change into organizations like the Hungarian Petőfi clubs."[69] At the same time, Mao endorsed the public emphasis on China's youth as the future guardians of the revolution. As the ninth polemic declared, "the question of training successors for the revolutionary cause of the proletariat is . . . whether or not we can prevent successfully the emergence of Khrushchevite revisionism in China."[70] The first edition of the *Little Red Book* had already been published in May. Edited by Lin Biao, this collection of Mao's sayings from the pre-1949 period would eventually become the indispensable ideological survival tool for each Red Guard during the Cultural Revolution. To Mao's dissatisfaction, however, some of his fellow central comrades—Deng Xiaoping and Lu Dingyi, in particular—did not agree with this new expression of Mao's personality cult.[71] In mid-June, the official campaign "to foster and train eleven million successors for the undertakings of the proletarian revolution" was launched.[72] The Chairman also pressed for the devolution of central power: "If Khrushchev's revisionism should emerge at the center, then each province will resist." From there, it was not an unimaginable ideological stretch for Mao to call on the student Red Guards to "bombard the headquarters" two years later.[73]

Two weeks after the publication of the ninth polemic, the CCP replied to the CPSU's June letter that had pressed for an early international meeting. Addressing the Soviet claim that no party could block an international meeting of all communist parties, the letter concluded mockingly that "you are caught in an insoluble dilemma. You are falling into a trap of your own making and will end by losing your skin. If you do not call the meeting, people will say that you have followed the advice of the Chinese and the Marxist-Leninist Parties, and you will lose face. If you do call the meeting, you will land yourselves in an impasse without any way out. In the present historical juncture this is a grave crisis for you modern revisionists, a crisis of your own making!"[74] Mao was delighted that he had "stimulated him [Khrushchev] to convene it, stimulated him

[68] MacFarquhar, *Origins*, vol. 3, 387–90. Ansley, *Heresy*, 89.

[69] Wu, *Yi Mao zhuxi*, 148.

[70] *PR* 29 (7/17/1964), 26.

[71] Li, *Private Life*, 412–13.

[72] Quoted in: Si, "Zhonggong," 63.

[73] Bo, *Ruogan*, vol. 2, 1148. Mao, "Bombard the Headquarters: My Magnificent Big-Character Poster," August 5, 1966, *JYMW*, vol. 12, 90–92. Also: *JYMW*, vol. 12, 135–36.

[74] *PR* 31 (7/31/1964), 5–11.

to assume responsibility for the public split." The Chairman could not hide his schadenfreude when he remarked to his fellow leaders that he was looking forward to how "Khrushchev would burn in anger" upon receiving the Chinese letter.[75]

Khrushchev, however, did not blink. On July 30, he called for the original twenty-six members of the 1960 Editorial Board "to come to Moscow by December 15."[76] In a meeting with Gomułka, Novotný, and Ulbricht a week before, Khrushchev had complained about Chinese attempts to isolate the CPSU within the communist movement. He also claimed—with an alarming prescience of China's domestic carnage to come—that Mao "has entirely gone crazy" by following "a policy of bloodshed, animal hatred, and the killing off of his opponents."[77] In the following weeks, most parties invited to attend the Editorial Board reacted in a predictable manner; the Albanians, North Koreans, North Vietnamese, Japanese and Indonesians refused to attend, while the Italians, the Romanians, the English, and the Cubans voiced reservations about the convention of the meeting. The other fifteen parties invited agreed to attend.[78]

In early August, Mao convened the Politburo at Beidaihe to discuss the new Soviet announcement. He opened the meeting by remarking that "we estimated correctly that Khrushchev, once hit, would jump."[79] When, in mid-August, the North Vietnamese First Secretary Le Duan passed through Beidaihe after a visit to Pyongyang, the Chairman decided to reject the Soviet invitation, though he still wanted to avoid providing the CPSU with evidence that the CCP was pushing for the split.[80] Accordingly, the number of anti-Soviet publications fell sharply after mid-August. The Chairman also decided not to follow an Albanian proposal to use the impending fifteenth anniversary of the PRC for a meeting of all leftist parties. He did not want to provide the Soviets with any evidence that the CCP had convened a splittist meeting first.[81] However, according to information later passed on by the North Vietnamese to the Soviets, such a meeting actually did occur secretly on China's National Day.[82]

[75] WLX, 793, 797, 800.

[76] PR 36 (9/4/1964), 8–9.

[77] "Report on a Meeting of Khrushchev, Novotný, Gomułka, and Ulbricht in Warsaw," [no date], SÚA, Archív ÚV KSČ, f.02/1, Předsednictvo ÚV KSČ, 1962–66, 73/77/20, 3–14. Translation by Mike Hornacek.

[78] Brahm, Pekings Griff, 27. The parties that accepted to attend were from: Poland, GDR, Czechoslovakia, Hungary, Bulgaria, Outer Mongolia, Yugoslavia, West Germany, France, Syria, India, Argentia, Brazil, Australia, and the United States.

[79] WLX, 810.

[80] WLX, 818. PR 36 (9/4/1964), 6–7.

[81] WLX, 811.

[82] "Note no. 131/64 on a Talk between Privalov and Bibow," 12/10/1964, SAPMO-BArch, DY 30/IV A 2/20/442, 1–5.

The public polemics of 1963 and 1964 were devastating to the international communist movement. Without a doubt, most of the polemics emanated from Mao's CCP. Unlike Khrushchev's CPSU, it consistently refused to stop polemics. The Chairman had decided that he wanted either a complete break with the CPSU or a complete Soviet surrender. Compromise was simply not an option. For Mao, this course of action not only had an external rationale—leadership of the international communist movement would be his—but also an internal purpose: Once he had achieved international leadership, who would dare oppose him at home? In the end, the nine polemics worked to define Mao's ideological yardstick against which any communist party or socialist country would be measured. Of course, Khrushchev's revisionist CPSU and USSR had failed. But what about the CCP and the PRC? Those who did not measure up would soon succumb to Khrushchev's cruel fate. Many of those who had supported Mao in writing the nine polemics against the Soviets probably did not realize that the demons they helped to raise would return to haunt them during the Cultural Revolution.

KHRUSHCHEV'S FALL AND THE COLLAPSE OF SINO-SOVIET PARTY RELATIONS

Khrushchev's removal at the October 1964 CPSU CC plenum led neither to a reversal of revisionism nor to the submission of the Soviet party to Mao's will. The fact that revisionism continued to be alive in the USSR after Khrushchev's demise, combined with his fear that it would prosper in China, convinced the Chairman to take radical measures at home. In 1965, he adopted a set of confrontational policies which led to the purging of domestic opponents—real or imagined—when the Cultural Revolution began a year later. Because Mao rhetorically linked his internal adversaries to Soviet revisionism, the final collapse of Sino-Soviet party relations in March 1966 was primarily a function of his domestic politics.

Khrushchev was dismissed *neither* for his theoretical novelties *nor* for the general direction of his foreign policy.[83] While the original documents from the fateful Presidium meeting on October 13, 1964, reveal, in great detail, the dissatisfaction felt by Khrushchev's fellow leaders—among the reasons for his dismissal were problems with party reorganization, the personality cult, agriculture, the Cuban Missile Crisis, and nepotism—criticism of his China policy was *not* among them. A review of the report

[83] Pikhoya, *Sovetskii Soyuz*, 228–39. Volkogonov, *Autopsy*, 252–55. Taubman, *Khrushchev*, 4, 10–13.

to the CC plenum the next day reveals a slightly different emphasis. Although Khrushchev was accused of some mistakes in his policy toward the Chinese party, the only example mentioned explicitly was Khrushchev's characterization of Mao as an "old galosh" in February 1960. The report did, however, spell out, unmistakably, that *the leadership of the CCP . . . worked out a plan, [and] carefully prepared and carried out an attack against us.*[84]

The new Soviet leadership under First Secretary Brezhnev and Prime Minister Kosygin—the CPSU decided to split party and government functions—only made a few changes in Khrushchev's policies. The most important concerned agriculture and Soviet policy toward the escalating conflict in Vietnam.[85] Although the new leaders denounced Khrushchev's "harebrained scheming" in public, from the very beginning they reaffirmed their intentions to continue his policies. On October 17, the *New York Times* thus wondered what "Khrushchevism Sans Khrushchev" meant.[86]

Of course, the removal of the Soviet leader had immediate repercussions within the socialist camp. Like Khrushchev's Secret Speech in early 1956, it shattered a seemingly clear alignment of forces.[87] Pyongyang terminated all polemics.[88] Hanoi was simply perplexed.[89] Bucharest did not react. Only Tirana continued with polemics.[90]

Although there is no evidence that Mao knew anything about the monthslong preparations for Khrushchev's removal,[91] the Chairman had hoped for the fall of the Soviet leader since 1959. This conviction was based on Mao's belief that the Soviet leader did not represent the healthy forces in the Soviet Union,[92] and that the CPSU and the Soviet people actually shared *his* views.[93] Because Mao had been *personalizing* the conflict with the CPSU for years, he envisioned Khrushchev's fall as his own victory, both abroad and at home.

Barely twelve hours after Khrushchev's forced resignation, Chervonenko informed the CCP leadership about the events in Moscow. The new Soviet leaders had instructed the ambassador to tell the Chinese comrades "that the CPSU CC plenum stressed unanimously that the CPSU

[84] Istochnik, "Zapisi V. Malina na zasedanii Prezidiuma TsK KPSS," *Istochnik* 1998/2, 125–43. Istochnik, "Doklad," 102–25 (italics mine).

[85] Pikhoya, *Sovetskii Soyuz*, 239.

[86] *NYT*, 10/17/1964, 28.

[87] MacFarquhar, *Origins*, vol. 3, 367.

[88] "Information about some Aspects of the Conflicts with the Chinese Leadership," 11/26/1964, *PAAA-MfAA*, Abteilung Ferner Osten—Sektor China, Microfiche A 6835, 3.

[89] For Vietnamese reaction: chapter 10.

[90] WLX, 850.

[91] Taubman, *Khrushchev*, 615.

[92] Delyusin, "Guanyu," 108–9.

[93] WLX, 798–800. Brezhnev, *Kitai*, 111–12. Semichastnyi, *Bespokoinoe*, 318.

will continue to conform steadily to the decisions of the 20th, 21st, and 22nd congresses."[94] While the Soviets informed some of its East European allies, and even the Americans, about the reasons for Khrushchev's fall,[95] it left the Soviet embassy in Beijing and, as a result, the Chinese comrades in the dark. Thus, in late October 1964, Chervonenko decided to send the embassy's Party Secretary Aleksei Brezhnev to Moscow to gather information.[96]

In a state of ignorance, the CCP PB attributed Khrushchev's fall to what Mao had, for a long time, denounced as the Soviet leader's "revisionist path . . . both in domestic and foreign policies." The Chairman's joy over the fall of his personal enemy must have doubled with news of the October 16 success of the first Chinese nuclear test. Eleven days later, Mao proposed that the Politburo "seize the initiative" by sending a delegation to Moscow for the forty-seventh anniversary of the October Revolution. The goal of the mission, according to the Chairman, was to bring the Soviet leadership back on the correct ideological path. Mao was cautious of quick changes, however, because he believed that "many problems have accumulated" which the new Soviet leaders needed to sort out.[97]

On October 28, Zhou Enlai officially proposed Mao's idea to Chervonenko. The Soviet ambassador was immediately suspicious of Chinese motives, arguing that this proposal amounted to nothing more than an attempt to improve relations on Beijing's terms. Chervonenko bluntly told Zhou that the Soviet embassy had seen no changes in Chinese behavior since Khrushchev's resignation. He concluded "that a trip to Moscow by a Chinese delegation alone . . . would not be desirable, as this would be used by the Chinese side for its own aims."[98]

The Chairman convened another Politburo meeting on the morning of October 29, during which he accepted Chervonenko's stipulations but decided to preempt the Soviet ambassador from raising new objections. Zhou Enlai was sent to inform the ambassadors of the pro-Chinese socialist countries and ask them to send a delegation to Moscow in order to "use this opportunity for contacts and exchanges of opinions." The

[94] "Record of Conversation with Wu Xiuquan," 10/15/1964, *AVPRF*, f.0100, o.57, d.7, p.508, 50–51.

[95] "Note on a Telephone Conversation between Brezhnev Honecker on 10/15/1964, between 12:55 and 13:25 P.M.," 10/16/1964, *SAPMO-BArch*, DY 30/3514, 155–56. "On the Changes in the Leadership of the Soviet Union," 10/22/1964, *SAPMO-BArch*, DY 30/J IV 2/2J/1316. "Telegram From the Embassy in the Soviet Union to the Department of State," 10/23/1964, *FRUS 1964–1968*, XIV, 152–56.

[96] Brezhnev, *Kitai*, 90–93.

[97] WLX, 831, 833, 841–42.

[98] "Record of Conversation with Zhou Enlai," 10/28/1964, *AVPRF*, f.0100, o.57, d.7, p.508, 68–74.

prime minister speculated that "some [people] think that the new Soviet leaders are companions-in-arms of Khrushchev, [and] therefore we should not wait for a fundamental change in the foreign policy of the CPSU." But he was optimistic, asking rhetorically: "If this were so, then why throw out Khrushchev?"[99] When Zhou eventually informed Chervonenko,[100] the Soviet ambassador realized that the Chinese had again tried to set the agenda by excluding Yugoslavia from the list of invitees. He proposed to Moscow to invite both a Yugoslav delegation and representatives from neutral African or Asian countries in order "to prevent the Chinese from creating the impression in world public opinion of any unity among communist parties." He clearly feared that if only the twelve ruling communist parties were represented in Moscow, the CCP would proclaim this convention a meeting of all communist parties and, in turn, try to denounce the Editorial Board meeting in December.[101]

Also, on October 29, Chervonenko briefly reported to Moscow about the latest developments. The CPSU Presidium professed not to understand "what aims the CCP leadership was pursuing," but was euphoric about the visit of the Chinese delegation.[102] According to Troyanovskii, Moscow believed that this was a "show [of] support for the post-Khrushchev leadership"[103] and decided "to use Khrushchev as a scapegoat for past conflicts."[104] Chervonenko was instructed to transmit the official invitation to the CCP on October 31.[105]

Following Khrushchev's fall, the new Soviet leadership had started to think about ways to improve relations with the Chinese. While Prime Minister Kosygin was the most optimistic—he could not understand why the two communist powers were quarreling in the first place—the head of the CC Liaison Department, Andropov, was skeptical, and First Secretary Leonid Brezhnev did not raise any opinion.[106] Some members of the Soviet embassy in Beijing did not share any of the optimism: "In Moscow many did not have . . . a complete understanding of the actual

---

[99] WLX, 842–43.

[100] "Record of Conversation with Gheorghiu Dumitri," 11/1/1964, *AVPRF*, f.0100, o.57, d.7, p.508, 90–104.

[101] "Record of Conversation with Zhou Enlai," 10/29/1964, *AVPRF*, f.0100, o.57, d.7, p.508, 75–79.

[102] "Note on a Telephone Conversation with Comrade Podgorny on 10/29/1964," 11/3/1964, *SAPMO-BArch*, DY 30/3609.

[103] Troyanovskii, *Cherez*, 349.

[104] Interview with Oleg Troyanovskii, Moscow, 6/8/2002.

[105] "Record of Conversation with Zhou Enlai," 10/31/1964, *AVPRF*, f.0100, o.57, d.7, p.508, 84 .

[106] A. M. Aleksandrov-Agentov, *Ot Kollontai do Gorbacheva* (Moskva: Mezhdunarodnye otnosheniya), 167–68.

situation of affairs in China . . . and of the intentions of the top Chinese leadership."[107]

In early November, after Chervonenko had told Zhou that the CCP should not expect to use the impending meeting to spread its ideological positions,[108] Mao called several Politburo meetings to discuss the new situation. The prime minister accused the Soviet ambassador of being "Khrushchev's trusted follower." The Chairman pessimistically asserted that the CCP would send a delegation to Moscow only "to see what trends there are, to understand why they made Khrushchev fall from power, and what they are ready to do. But we also don't want to take it too seriously." With regard to the Editorial Board meeting called for December, Mao insisted that the PRC had "never surrendered," and would not surrender to Soviet "great power chauvinism."[109] The growing rift did not remain hidden. As the *New York Times* reported on November 2, "Peking indicated . . . that [the] present truce in its ideological dispute with Moscow might be shortlived."[110]

Although Kosygin continued to be optimistic even after Zhou's November 5 arrival,[111] memoirs from both sides testify that the atmosphere was full of tension. Yu Zhan recalled a certain stiffness and coolness on the Soviet side,[112] while Aleksei Brezhnev remembered "the uncommonly arrogant tone of Zhou Enlai."[113] Leonid Brezhnev's polite but clear refusal of Zhou's last-minute request for a public speech—prepared beforehand, and calling for "the Chinese and Soviet party to unite on the basis of Marxism-Leninism and proletarian internationalism"—certainly did not improve the hostile atmosphere.[114]

November 7 fully revealed the gap between the Chinese and the Soviet positions. When Leonid Brezhnev, in his official anniversary speech, called for "a new international meeting of the fraternal parties," the "audience broke into thundering applause. . . . [while] Premier Chou [Zhou] sat quietly and fiddled with the earphones."[115] A personal insult followed this political affront. At a relaxed cocktail party later that evening, the

[107] Brezhnev, *Kitai*, 90–93.

[108] "Record of Conversation with Zhou Enlai," 10/31/1964, *AVPRF*, f.0100, o.57, d.7, p.508, 84–87. "Record of Conversation with Zhou Enlai," 11/1/1964, *AVPRF*, f.0100, o.57, d.7, p.508, 88–89.

[109] WLX, 847, 848, 853.

[110] *NYT*, 11/3/1964, 3.

[111] Troyanovskii, *Cherez*, 349–50.

[112] Yu Zhan, "Yici bu xunchang de shiming," Pei, *Zhongguo waijiao feng yun*, vol. 3, 22–23.

[113] Brezhnev, *Kitai*, 96.

[114] ZELNP2, 685.

[115] Parts of Brezhnev's speech in: *NYT*, 11/7/1964, 1, 8.

drunken Soviet minister of defense, Malinovskii, offended the Chairman: "I do not want any Mao and Khrushchev to hamper us . . . We already did away with Khrushchev, now you should do away with Mao."[116] After a sharp protest, the Chinese left the cocktail party and returned to the embassy. There, the delegation stayed up until three in the morning reconstructing what happened in order to inform Beijing.[117]

The CCP delegation was convinced that Malinovskii's words were a planned provocation. Before Zhou had left, Leonid Brezhnev stressed that this was not the official Soviet position and that Malinovskii had made "an indiscreet remark after drinking." Zhou replied that "this essentially is not an indiscreet remark after drinking; since true words are spoken after drinking, he [Malinovskii] had said words from his heart."[118] In the Chinese embassy, the prime minister told his staff that this incident "could not be tolerated . . . [as it] aimed at openly subverting our party's and country's leader." The delegation proposed to the Chinese leadership in Beijing to lodge a formal protest.[119] Mao agreed. Since the new Soviet leaders "do Khrushchevism without Khrushchev," the Chinese side should not only "demand an apology" but also refuse to compromise in the talks.[120]

The Soviet side was shocked by Malinovskii's faux pas. The remark was tactless and did not represent the official Soviet position. Nonetheless, Andropov told Arbatov that he hoped that things could be patched up in upcoming talks.[121] But consternation quickly spread through the apparatus. Delyusin, who worked in the Far Eastern Department of the Foreign Ministry, recalled that "everybody discussed how to improve relations with China, then this bastard comes, makes a rude speech, and destroys everything."[122]

On November 8, Leonid Brezhnev, Mikoyan, and Kosygin met the CCP delegation to apologize on behalf of the CPSU CC. But since the delegation had just received Mao's instructions,[123] Zhou was hardly conciliatory. He dismissed the explanation that Malinovskii had only spoken nonsense while drunk, claiming that "truth lies in wine."[124] Given the

[116] Yan Mingfu, "Yi Zhou zongli 1964nian fang Su," *Zhonggong dangshi ziliao* 65, 14. Kapitsa remembered Malinovskii's words similarly: "We removed our fool, remove yours, and the relations between our countries will be friendly." See: Kapitsa, *Na raznykh parallelyakh*, 76.

[117] Yan, "Yi Zhou," 14–15.

[118] WLX, 861.

[119] Yu, "Yici," 23.

[120] WLX, 862–63.

[121] Arbatov, *System*, 113–15.

[122] Ding, "Huigu," 34.

[123] WLX, 865.

[124] Yu, "Yici," 24

negative Soviet attitude, he announced, China would not stop the polemics. In subsequent talks, the Chinese delegation accused the CPSU of "ignoring the good faith of the CCP."[125] Kang Sheng even complained that, at the November 7 reception, Kosygin had been excessively "friendly" to U.S. Ambassador Kohler, which, given the self-professed Soviet position of anti-imperialsim, proved that, in fact, "the Soviet government has two positions . . . in front of imperialism."[126]

On November 10, Mao informed the Chinese delegation that it now had "a free hand to counterattack . . . [and] to refuse firmly . . . to attend the Editorial Board in December." He further instructed the delegation "to ask whether or not the Soviet side will change the anti-Chinese line . . . [and] the line of splitting the socialist camp."[127] According to later Soviet reports to the Hungarians, the Chinese announced that if the CPSU comrades "pursue the old policy, 'they will also be dismissed.'" The Soviets in turn rejected the Chinese demand for "CPSU changes in the political line" as a precondition for unity.[128] On November 11, Mikoyan even told the CCP delegation bluntly: "On the question of the disagreements with the CCP, we totally agree with Khrushchev, even to the point that we can state that there is not the slightest difference."[129] Zhou Enlai, however, tried to end the talks on an upbeat note when he declared that "our quarrel is a temporary phenomenon, our unity should be eternal."[130]

Even before the start of the meeting in Moscow, both sides occupied irreconcilable positions. The Malinovskii incident merely served as the catalyst for the revelation of these basic disagreements. In light of Mao's excessive personality cult, the Chinese delegation in Moscow had no choice but to *overreact* to the incident in order to cover its back at home. Yet, the Chinese claim that "truth lies in wine" contained a kernel of truth. Malinovskii's tactless remark indicated that it was not only the

[125] WLX, 866.

[126] "Stenographic Report of the CPSU CC Plenum, November 16, 1964," *RGANI*, f.2, o.1, d.764, 76. Also:"Talk of the Party and Government Delegation of the GDR with the Party and Government Delegation of the People's Republic of China (11/19/1964 in the Embassy of the GDR in Moscow)," *SAPMO-BArch*, DY 30/J IV 2/201/712.

[127] WLX, 873–74.

[128] "Report on the Talks of the Hungarian Party and Government Delegation in Moscow between 6–12 November 1964 (16 November)," Zsófia Zelnik et al., eds. "Selected Hungarian Documents on China, 1964–1968," comp. and trans. for the conference "New Central and East European Evidence on the Cold War in Asia," Budapest, Hungary, 10/30–11/2/2003.

[129] WLX, 875.

[130] Quoted in: "From a Draft Speech pf the First CPSU CC Secretary L. I. Brezhnev on the CPSU plenum (titled) 'On the Negotiations and Consultations with some Fraternal Parties,'" 11/14/1964, *Istoricheskii Arkhiv* 2006/5, 22.

Chairman who had personalized Sino-Soviet discord, but officials on the Soviet side as well. The CCP resumed open polemics with the November 21 publication of "Why Khrushchev Fell," showering more abuse on the "modern revisionists . . . [who] are continuing to pray . . . so that 'Khrushchevism without Khrushchev' may prevail."[131]

Despite this new round of hyperbole, Mao faced an inauspicious puzzle. What was the larger meaning of "Khrushchevism without Khrushchev"? Although he had just won a battle abroad, he began to fear that he was losing the war at home. Victory over revisionism abroad would have meant victory over his opponents at home. "Khrushchevism without Khrushchev," however, not only denied him *precisely* that, but also raised the specter of "Maoism without Mao."[132]

The Chairman thus decided to revisit the personality cult issue. In an interview with the American journalist Edgar Snow in January 1965, he maintained that "it is alleged that Stalin had a personality cult, Khrushchev had not in the least, and the Chinese have one. . . . Khrushchev was ousted most probably because he lacked a personality cult."[133] Although the Chairman was wrong with regard to Khrushchev's cult—among other reasons, he was sacked for his personality cult—the implication of his words was clear: Mao apparently believed he needed *more* of the personality cult because it served as a shield against domestic challenges.[134] It was also around this time that the Chairman started to view his opponents within the CCP leadership with a heightened sense of suspicion. When he fell ill at the beginning of the CCP Politburo work conference in Beijing over the New Year, he misinterpreted Deng's advice to rest and not attend the conference as an attempt to sideline him. Mao participated and accused Liu of trying to be the "whole person of authority" and Deng of creating an "independent kingdom."[135]

The discussions at the work conference further poisoned relations between Mao and the other Chinese central leaders. Although Mao's original idea in 1962 was to use the SEM to get control over rural party cadres, Liu and Deng had been able to rein in his extreme proposals in order to prevent damage to agricultural production.[136] Instead, in early 1965, disagreement arose over the underlying class antagonisms the SEM was supposed to address. While Liu proposed a political campaign in the countryside, Mao, who was concerned over the emergence of revi-

---

[131] *PR* 48 (11/27/1964), 6–9.

[132] MacFarquhar, *Origins*, vol. 3, 416–17.

[133] Mao, "Talk with Edgar Snow on International Issues," 1/9/1965, Mao, *On Diplomacy*, 424–25.

[134] Li, *Private Life*, 416–17.

[135] Cong, *Quzhe*, 602, 604.

[136] MacFarquhar, *Origins*, vol. 3, 334–48. Han, *Eldest Son*, 315–17.

sionism in the CCP after the meeting in Moscow, pushed for a shakeup of the rural party organizations.[137] Given this deadlock, the Chairman made a new proposal that no longer spoke of the "regulation" of local party organizations but of the "correction of those who hold power in the party and walk the capitalist path."[138] It was aimed specifically at Liu and Deng, both of whom had promoted agricultural reform with the field responsibility system (family farming) since 1962.[139] Because Liu was trying to block Mao's new proposal at the January 1965 Politburo meeting, the Chairman decided for himself, as he claimed in 1970, that Liu "had to go."[140] Although this was probably a simplification of what transpired in early 1965, it pointed to changes in Mao's attitude that other witnesses had also noticed. Zhou Enlai was concerned about the mounting differences between Mao and Liu,[141] while Bo Yibo recollected that "starting in 1965, Mao more and more took the problem of revisionism at the center seriously."[142]

Even as Mao was convinced that Khrushchev's spirit still haunted the Kremlin, Kosygin tried to mend fences with the Chinese comrades.[143] When he again turned to Leonid Brezhnev with the idea of approaching the Chinese, the Soviet party leader's response was hesitant: "If you think this is necessary, then you go by yourself."[144] But Kosygin was not sure how best to proceed. Afraid that the CCP leadership would turn down a Soviet proposal for an official visit to the PRC, he decided to stop over in Beijing on the way back from Hanoi in early February.[145]

Kosygin and Zhou were able to solve a series of smaller issues in a constructive manner. They agreed to celebrate the fifteenth anniversary of the Sino-Soviet alliance on February 14, to develop trade on a long-term basis, to cancel the sixty-six projects agreed upon in 1961, and to solve other technical matters.[146] But the Soviet and Chinese sides could not settle the row over the Editorial Board. After the November encounter in Moscow, the CPSU had decided to postpone the Board's meeting to March 1—the Soviet letter announcing the postponement was immediately published in China under the title "Order No. 2 of the C.P.S.U.

[137] MacFarquhar, Origins, vol. 3, 419–21.

[138] Sladkovskii, Ocherki, 405.

[139] MacFarquhar, Origins, vol. 3, 428–30.

[140] Edgar Snow, Long Revolution (New York: Random, 1971), 17.

[141] Wang Yongqin, "Mei xiangdao," Dangshi zongheng 2000/7, 32.

[142] Bo, Ruogan, vol. 2, 1149.

[143] Troyanovskii, Cherez, 350–51.

[144] Aleksandrov-Agentov, Ot Kollontai, 169.

[145] Interview with Oleg Troyanovskii, Moscow, 6/8/2002.

[146] Zhou, Zhou Enlai waijiao wenxuan, 445–47. Zhonghua, Zhou Enlai waijiao huodong dashiji, 435–36.

Leadership."[147] Zhou told Kosygin that Sino-Soviet disagreements were deep, and that any rapprochement could occur only gradually. Even after the Soviet prime minister had told his Chinese counterpart that the March meeting had been downgraded to consultative, Zhou replied that the CCP would "not attend this meeting, no matter what it is called," urging the CPSU to cancel this splittist meeting.[148]

Kosygin met Mao on February 11, shortly before his departure for Pyongyang.[149] For a long time, the Chairman did not want to meet the Soviets at all. It was only Zhou's intensive prodding that finally convinced Mao to receive the Soviet prime minister.[150] Regardless, he left his guest in the dark as to whether he would receive him until the very last moment.[151]

The Mao-Kosygin talk was a verbal wrestling match about well-known ideological disagreements. Mao was not only obsessed by the ideological squabbles with the Soviets but also little in command of the details of daily politics. After briefly discussing Vietnam, he turned to the impending meeting on March 1. "Beg[ging the Soviets] to carry out this conference," he professed his advance joy about the new polemical article the CCP would write about it afterward. He later consented to attend on the condition that "you state that your letter of July 14 [1963] and your February plenum [of 1964] were errors, that you annul them." Kosygin, however, was not willing to surrender to Mao's demands; again, he raised the need to overcome the polemics. Unity, he claimed, would be much more beneficial for the socialist camp in its conflict with imperialism. Mao could not be swayed.

The Mao-Kosygin talk then turned to global strategy. The Chairman again stressed people's war as a viable military strategy in conflicts with imperialism, and called Soviet foreign policy an "illusion." He then proceeded to claim that the Chinese, "as belligerent people" and "dogmatists," were supporting national liberation wars much more than the Soviets. Yet, as the subsequent exchange indicated, Mao actually thrived on *illusions* about Soviet foreign policy. With large-scale Soviet military assistance to the Congolese insurgents in mind, Kosygin immediately derided Mao's charge. "Meanwhile," he asserted, "it is a fact that nowhere is a fight against imperialism taking place without our participation. . . . However, your special soldiers are nowhere, except in words; we don't see

[147] *PR* 13 (3/26/1965), 21–22 (italics mine).

[148] *ZELNP2*, 706, 708.

[149] About the methodological problems of the sources on the Mao-Kosygin meeting, see my dissertation: "The Sino-Soviet Split, 1956–1966" (Yale University, 2003), 513–14.

[150] *ZELNP2*, 708.

[151] Troyanovskii, *Cherez*, 351.

them. They are too little displayed in reality, and even in the fight against imperialism they are not numerous." The Chairman had no reply.

The meeting with Kosygin revealed Mao's political insecurities. The man who, in 1959, had bent the Lushan meeting to his will had become a shadow of his former self. He frequently allowed the Soviet prime minister to define the content and direction of the talk. Occasionally, the Chairman even cornered himself with his own extravagant claims. Mao paid a heavy price for his ideologically distorted worldview. Although he jokingly claimed that the polemics would continue for "ten thousand years," he in fact mentioned several times that they would stop after ten or fifteen years as "the imperialists will force us to unite"—supposedly around his own ideological positions.[152]

But this was no reason for Mao to cease polemics *right then*.[153] Chinese polemics resumed after Kosygin's departure with the February 25 publication of a volume of Khrushchev speeches, prefaced by Mao's words: "History shows that each advance of Marxism-Leninism is won in the struggle against antagonistic ideology. . . . We also have teachers by negative example in Chiang Kai-shek, the Japanese imperialists, the U.S. imperialists, *and those people in our Party who made the mistake of adopting 'Left' or Right opportunist lines.*"[154] It was no accident that, in a volume deriding the speeches of his Soviet archenemy, Mao referred to the incorrect positions of past intraparty struggles.

Nineteen of the twenty-six invited parties attended the Editorial Board meeting in early March, with the Chinese, Albanians, Romanians, North Koreans, Indonesians and Japanese refusing to show. The North Vietnamese indicated that, while they had nothing against the meeting, they were under pressure from the Chinese not to attend. The final communiqué was a toothless declaration that reflected the disagreements of those who had come to Moscow; it did not even call for a new gathering of all communist parties. The only success the meeting produced was a declaration on Vietnam targeting the U.S. escalation of conflict in Indochina since August 1964.[155]

---

[152] "Record of Conversation of Kosygin with Mao Zedong," 2/11/1965, *AAN*, KC PZPR, XI A/10, 517–24.

[153] WLX, 906.

[154] *PR* 10 (3/5/1965), 11–12.

[155] Summaries of the March meeting in: "Report on the consultative Conference of the 19 Communist and Workers' Parties from March 1st to 5, 1965, in Moscow," *SAPMO-BArch*, DY 30/J IV 2/201/720, 4. "Plenum of the CC of the Bulgarian Communist Party, which occurred on March 23, 1965," *TsDA*, TsPA, f.1B, o.34, a.e.3, 1–39. "Meeting of the Directorate of the Party," 3/8/1965, *FIG*, APC, Direzione 1965, vol. 29, 608–23. Also: Brahm, *Pekings Griff*, 43–45, 53, 233–37.

Chinese propaganda haunted the meeting.[156] While the CCP accused the Soviets of issuing anti-Chinese publications, the People's Publishing House in Beijing released a volume of the June 1963 Chinese proposal on a new general line, as well as all nine polemics.[157] Finally, the CCP published its own "comment on the March Moscow Meeting" calling it "schismatic" and announcing polemics for "ten thousand years."[158]

With that, though, came the end of the period of the great Sino-Soviet public ideological disputes. This change was not only the result of the Chinese view that the lines had finally been drawn, but also of the PRC's continuing turn inward.[159] In June, Mao revealed his growing apprehensions over revisionism in China. He answered his own questions "What is to be done if a Khrushchev emerges? What shall the Central Committee do if revisionists emerge in China?" with: "Every provincial party committee must stand up against the revisionist Central Committee."[160]

The struggle for domestic supremacy in the PRC had entered its final phase. Late in the summer, Mao demanded that the Politburo investigate Wu Han's counterrevolutionary writings. The Politburo created the Cultural Revolution Small Group (CRSG) under Peng Zhen, a close ally of Liu Shaoqi and Deng Xiaoping. Peng was instructed to judge the revolutionary credentials of his protégé Wu Han and thereby—at least indirectly—his own. It was a brilliant tactical move by Mao. Having dragged its feet for a long time, in February 1966, the CRSG concluded that Wu Han's plays were not counterrevolutionary. In November, however, the Chairman had moved from Beijing to Shanghai, where he started to prepare his next move against his political opponents in the capital. While there, Mao set up his own CRSG in Shanghai under the chairmanship of his wife, Jiang Qing.[161]

In late February of 1966, the CPSU sent a letter to the CCP inviting it to send a delegation to the twenty-third CPSU congress in April.[162] The Soviet party, however, had decided that its party convention would look ahead to the future, not back to the past: "The CPSU is completely committed to the line of not starting any polemics against the Chinese leaders before and during the congress, [and] of keeping open the opportunity

---

[156] PR 10 (3/5/1965), 27–30.

[157] Brahm, Pekings Griff, 45.

[158] PR 11 (3/12/1965), 11–13; 13 (3/26/1965), 7–13 (quotes).

[159] Sladkovskii, Ocherki, 413–14.

[160] Li, "Study [I]," 69.

[161] MacFarquhar, Origins, vol. 3, 443–45. Ansley, Heresy, 89–90. Li, Private Life, 440–42. Wu, Yi Mao zhuxi, 149–51. Roderick MacFarquhar et al., Mao's Last Revolution (Cambridge: Belknap, 2006), 15–17.

[162] SCMP 3666, 37–38.

for the Chinese to send a delegation to the congress and to talk with the CPSU."[163] Although Peng Zhen urged the dispatch of a delegation to Moscow, the Politburo in Beijing was not sure what to do in Mao's absence.[164] When, some days later, Peng approached the Chairman with his idea, Mao accused him of being pro-Soviet.[165] On March 15, the Chairman called the Politburo to Shanghai, ostensibly to decide the question. Once it had convened, however, Mao changed the topic; he singled out Wu Han and proposed to launch the Cultural Revolution in literature, history, economics, and law.[166] Peng Zhen was warned that he could be next.

On March 18, Mao chaired another Politburo meeting in Hangzhou. With many of its members on inspection tours, the meeting was attended only by Mao, Liu Shaoqi, Zhou Enlai, and Peng Zhen as members, Kang Sheng and Chen Boda as alternates, and Wu Lengxi. Mao began with a purge of Wu—who had been in charge of running *Xinhua* and *Renmin Ribao* since the mid-1950s—for failings in cultural work. The Chairman then decided not to send a delegation to Moscow. The official reply letter explained that the CCP could not attend the Soviet party congress until the CPSU had "openly admitted" past mistakes.[167]

Eighty-six parties sent delegations to the twenty-third CPSU congress from March 29 to April 8. Only four parties refused to attend: China, Japan, Albania, and New Zealand.[168] The club of naysayers was dwindling rapidly. It was a late victory for the Soviets. Leonid Brezhnev's official report to the congress hardly touched the Sino-Soviet Split.[169] Beijing reacted to the twenty-third CPSU congress with a subtle polemic comparing Communist China to the Paris Commune of 1871 and justifying "the use of revolutionary violence to seize power."[170] The CCP also refused to receive Chervonenko for a briefing on the twenty-third CPSU congress: "The information is not needed."[171] The Chinese Communist Youth League similarly rejected an invitation from its Soviet counterpart to send a delegation to the impending Komsomol congress: "The Communist Youth League of China, as an assistant to the great

[163] "Note on a Talk by Knobbe with Senin," 2/17/1966, *SAPMO-BArch*, DY 30/3518, 22–26.

[164] WLX, 935–37.

[165] Interview with Ioan Romulus Budura, Bucharest, 7/10/2004.

[166] Li *Private Life*, 454–55.

[167] Wu, *Yi Mao zhuxi*, 151–52. WLX, 937–39. PR 13 (3/25/1966), 6 (quote).

[168] *NYT*, 4/9/1966, 2.

[169] "Stenographic Report of the CPSU CC Plenum, March 1966," *RGANI*, f.2, o.1, d.822, 2–9.

[170] *PR* 14 (4/1/1966), 23–26 (quote); 15 (4/8/1966), 17–18, 25; 16 (4/15/1966), 23–29.

[171] "Soviet-Chinese Relations (January–June 1966)," 10/13/1966, *AVPRF*, f.0100, o.59, d.16, p.526, 72.

Marxist-Leninist Communist Party of China, must draw an outright, clear-cut line of demarcation between itself and you."[172]

The increasingly confrontational Chinese behavior in external affairs was related to the rapid unfolding of the Cultural Revolution at home. Two days after Liu Shaoqi had left China on a three-week trip to South East Asia on March 26, Mao gathered Kang Sheng, Jiang Qing, Zhang Chunqiao (later a member of Jiang's notorious Gang of Four) to denounce Peng Zhen for protecting bad people—Wu Han, in particular—and to demand that the Beijing CRSG be disbanded.[173] The Chairman also announced that he would soon call for an "attack on the Central Committee."[174] When Liu returned, Mao presented him with the fait accompli decision to purge Peng. The publication of the "May 16 Notification," revised by Mao personally, sealed Peng's fate: "[R]epresentatives of the bourgeoisie . . . have sneaked into the party, the government, the army and various cultural circles. . . . Some are still trusted by us and are being trained our successors, persons like Khrushchev, for example, who are still nestling beside us."[175]

Having aroused the fears and emotions of party members, Mao's ominous retreat to southern China on May 17 suggested his desire to observe, from afar, how factional conflict erupted in the Chinese capital.[176] At that time, through the coaxing of Kang Sheng's wife, Cao Yiou, Beijing University teachers accused the school administration of counterrevolutionary activities. In the face of this sudden defiance, Liu and Deng sent in work teams to contain the unrest.[177]

After Mao returned to Beijing in the second half of July, he announced that Liu and Deng had suppressed revolutionary action as much as the feudal Qing dynasty and the reactionary Guomindang had in the past.[178] On August 1, Mao told a student who had formed a group of Red Guards at a middle school run by Qinghua University that "to rebel is justified."[179] Some weeks later, Red Guards—armed with Mao's *Little Red Book*—started to persecute persons of authority. On August 5, the Chairman called the first CC plenum since 1962; it was stuffed with Mao's supporters. At the gathering, he read his August 5 big-character poster "Bombard the Headquarters," thereby explicitly calling for the

[172] *PR* 21 (5/20/1966), 3–4, 20.

[173] MacFarquhar, *Origins*, vol. 3, 456, 458.

[174] Li, "Study [I]," 69.

[175] Quoted in: Dietrich, *People's China*, 182. Li, *Private Life*, 455, 457–58. Macfarquhar, *Last Revolution*, 32–44.

[176] Li, *Private Life*, 459.

[177] MacFarquhar, *Origins*, vol. 3, 461.

[178] MacFarquhar, *Origins*, vol. 3, 462.

[179] Li, *Private Life*, 463, 471.

open public criticism of his fellow central leaders.[180] The plenum decided: "The main target of the present movement are those within the Party who are in authority and are taking the capitalist road.[181] Liu and Deng, although still CC members, were demoted from their party positions. They would soon emerge as the prime capitalist roaders.[182]

The CPSU observed the rapid self-mutilation of the CCP from the sideline. The Soviet China specialist Mikhail Kapitsa told the East Germans that the Cultural Revolution "carries explicit . . . semi-fascist . . . characteristics."[183] Vladimir Semichastnyi, the KGB chief, recalled that the Soviet leadership suffered through sleepless nights: "What if a storming crowd of Chinese moved on foot and without any armament to the north, to our border? . . . what could be done against the storming of a fanatical crowd, against people, who were resentful and not predictable?"[184] Of course, this never became a reality, despite the fact that a Soviet foreign ministry report from November 1966 stated that the PRC "in fact propagate[s] that the basic intergovernmental act—the Treaty on Friendship, Alliance, and Mutual Assistance between the USSR and the PRC of February 14, 1950—has lost its meaning."[185]

Foreign parties were equally critical. The Hungarians saw "parallels between the actions of the Red Guards and the counterrevolution in Hungary in 1956," while Hanoi expressed "alarm over the actions of the 'young guards.'" The North Koreans, meanwhile, rejected the Chinese claim that a single party or a single country could be the "center of world revolution."[186] Even Hoxha—Mao's only friend—distanced himself from the Chairman, calling the actions of the Red Guards "dangerous" and the Cultural Revolution a "rectification of the entire line of the party . . . undertaken outside the Leninist norms of the party and the laws of the dictatorship of the proletariat."[187] The Cultural Revolution, as Hoxha judged correctly, had led the PRC into total "self-isolation."[188]

---

[180] Jin Qiu, *The Culture of Power* (Stanford: Stanford 1999), 85. Mao, "Bombard the Headquarters: My Magnificent Big-Character Poster," August 5, 1966, *JYMW*, vol. 12, 90–92. Also: *JYMW*, vol. 12, 135–36.

[181] "Decision of the Central Committee of the Chinese Communist Party Concerning the Great Proletarian Cultural Revolution," August 5, 1966, *PR* 33 (8/12/1966), 8.

[182] MacFarquhar, *Origins*, vol. 3, 462–63.

[183] "Extracts from a Note on Talks of Quilitzsch and Comrade Seidel," 8/31/1966, *PAAA-MfAA*, Botschaft Moskau—Politische Abteilung, Microfiche 001170, 136.

[184] Semichastnyi, *Bespokoinoe*, 328.

[185] "Inter-Governmental Relations of the PRC with the Soviet Union," 11/11/1966, *AVPRF*, f.0100, o.59, d.16, p.526, 117.

[186] "Information No. 68/66," 9/23/1966, *SAPMO-BArch*, DY 30/IV A 2/20/991, 3, 4.

[187] Hoxha, "Some Preliminary Ideas about the Chinese Proletarian Cultural Revolution," 10/14/1966, Hoxha, *Selected Works*, vol. 4, 108–11.

[188] Enver Hoxha, *Reflections on China, 1962–1977*, vol. 1 (Tirana: Nentori, 1979), 181.

After the collapse of the Sino-Soviet party talks in Moscow in mid-1963, Mao Zedong used the nine polemics to sharpen the conflict with the Soviet revisionists. There is no doubt that he was a true communist believer and that he was convinced that Khrushchev's political problems in the USSR were a sign that the CPSU and the Soviet people were turning against the Soviet leader's revisionism. However, as in 1962–63, the extremism and hyperbole of the nine polemics went beyond the boundaries of reason. Witnesses from the time, as well as an analysis of the polemics themselves, suggest that they served the domestic purpose of rendering pressure on Mao's internal opponents, such as Liu Shaoqi, Deng Xiaoping, and other like-minded CCP leaders. In light of his belief that Khrushchev's impending fall, which he had hoped for since late 1959, would mean ideological victory abroad, the Chairman linked his anti-Soviet polemics to domestic policy problems and to his internal rivals. In this context, any attempts by the Soviets, or by outsiders such as the Romanians, to seek an end to the ideological attacks were condemned to failure. As a matter of fact, Mao even displayed a keen ability to exploit these attempts for his own political needs.

The increasing frequency and timing of the incidents at the Sino-Soviet border in the second half of 1963 also suggest that Mao wanted to increase the pressure on the Soviet revisionists over territorial issues. Excessive demands on the Soviet Far East were his preferred method of making Khrushchev uneasy. Although there is no hard evidence, Mao's use of the border issue might have also had the purpose of stirring nationalism in order to mobilize the Chinese people, as in the Second Taiwan Strait Crisis. In the end, though, Beijing and Moscow were able to disentangle their competing claims for most of the eastern sector of their border.

While Mao was convinced that Khrushchev's removal was the result of his revisionism in domestic and foreign policies, Soviet documentation reveals a different story. In order to exploit the momentum generated by Khrushchev's departure, Mao tried to use the upcoming celebrations for the anniversary of the October Revolution to push the new Soviet leaders to accept correct—that is, his own—ideological positions. However, Khrushchevism was not finished in Moscow, as Mao soon would realize.

When, by mid-November of 1964, Mao realized that his strategy had failed, the Chairman was unable to celebrate his leadership of the socialist world to which he aspired. Khrushchev's fall, for reasons unrelated to his revisionist policies, seemed to generate a feeling of insecurity in Mao, especially given the domestic leadership struggle over rural politics. In early 1965, Mao thus turned against his fellow leaders in order to secure the political supremacy he feared was being threatened. Using alliances outside the official party structures he had established since 1962, and exploiting the gullibility and revolutionary idealism of young people, he instrumentalized ideological conflict with the Soviet comrades in order to justify a party purge in mid-1966. The complete collapse of Sino-Soviet party relations thus was the necessary prerequisite for the start of the Cultural Revolution. It was for this reason that, by the summer of 1966, Mao had pushed Sino-Soviet party relations to its definitive split.

CHAPTER 10

Vietnam and the Collapse of the Military Alliance, 1964–1966

IN THE MID-1960S, American historian Douglas Pike interviewed over one hundred North Vietnamese officials and ordinary communist guerilla fighters who had been taken prisoner or had deserted. In one of the interviews, he asked: "You don't feel the Chinese and the Russians are supporting you and your war sufficiently?" and got as a reply: "No, they are not. They don't care about us. *They are only interested in their arguments.*"[1] Although the answer simplified Sino-Soviet-Vietnamese relations, it pointed to one of the major problems vexing the Vietnamese conduct of war: the Sino-Soviet ideological dispute. Even low-level guerilla fighters and officials were aware of the problem.

Conflict between Beijing and Moscow over the Second Vietnam War (1964–75) emerged over their historically disparate support for Hanoi, contrary visions of how the war should be fought militarily and diplomatically, Chinese security needs, and continued ideological disputes. The PRC had always been the staunchest ally of the DRV. Chinese military and economic support dated back to 1949 and was renewed in the summer of 1964 in anticipation of the American escalation of the Vietnam conflict. In comparison, the USSR under Stalin and Khrushchev showed little interest in the Vietnamese Revolution. Even after the Gulf of Tonkin Incident, which triggered the American escalation of war in August of 1964, Moscow continued its hands-off policy. Only Khrushchev's fall two months later led to an overhaul in Soviet policy toward the war in Indochina.

From mid-October 1964 to mid-February 1965, Soviet support for the DRV increased rapidly while China's policy blended commitments to North Vietnam with attempts at finding a negotiated solution to the new Indochina conflict. Against the background of Mao's further ideological radicalization since early 1965, China's attitude toward the Second Vietnam War hardened. The intensification of the American air war after the Pleiku Incident in early February, the Soviet promotion of four political and military initiatives designed to strengthen the North Vietnamese

---

[1] Quoted in: Eugene Lawson, *Sino-Vietnamese Conflict* (New York: Praeger, 1984), 159 (italics mine).

ability to counter this escalation, and the dispatch of U.S. ground troops to South Vietnam in early March greatly increased Chinese security fears. Although Beijing responded by intensifying its national defense preparations and even tried to signal to Washington its willingness to keep the conflict limited to Vietnam, it did not seek a rational cooperation with Moscow to support Hanoi. Chinese mistrust of Soviet motives and ideological hyperbole hampered the North Vietnamese military and diplomatic struggle in the spring and summer of 1965, and continued to complicate Sino-Soviet–North Vietnamese relations even beyond. In the end, the unconstructive Chinese attitude that emerged in late February laid the Sino-Soviet military alliance to rest.

Before Tonkin

The Sino-Soviet alliance was originally directed against Japanese militarism and its allies, that is, the United States. On this basis, Moscow had supplied Beijing with military hardware and know-how since 1950. Even after the withdrawal of the Soviet military specialists in the summer of 1960, Sino-Soviet military cooperation continued, though on a much smaller scale, as described in earlier chapters. For Mao, the Sino-Soviet alliance primarily served as a means to provide security at China's three potential points of conflict with the American imperialists: on the Korean Peninsula, in the Taiwan Strait, and in Vietnam. The Korean War seemed to fulfill his prophecies of inherent American aggressiveness when the U.S.-led United Nations intervention threatened to carry the war into Manchuria. Increased American military and economic support for South Korea and Taiwan after the outbreak of the war militarized the Korean peninsula and the Taiwan Strait. For various reasons, however, Soviet military support at these two fronts turned out to be less than what the Chinese had expected, as covered in chapters 1 and 3. Yet, the collapse of the Sino-Soviet military alliance in the early Second Vietnam War was not due to renewed Soviet reluctance to provide military aid—on the contrary, Moscow offered much aid—it was, rather, global and military strategy that caused the breakdown.

Mao's decision in 1961 to cut China's formal ties to the socialist camp (WAPA and COMECON) and his resolution to reposition the PRC in the Asian-African-Latin American intermediate zone the following year changed his views on world revolutionary strategy. In his eyes, the USSR had ceased to be anti-imperialist because it pursued peaceful coexistence and superpower cooperation to solve international problems. Mao believed that the Asian-African-Latin American intermediate zone had to carry on the anti-imperialist struggle on its own. As the largest country in that zone, China presented itself as a natural leader. Moreover, as a result of Lin Biao's indoctrination of the PLA with *Mao Zedong Military Thought* in 1958, China's military strategy had embraced principles that favored people's war (guerilla warfare) over the use of modern technology. Ultimately, Mao's rejection of the anti-imperialist role of the socialist camp, his stress on national liberation movements, and his advocacy of people's war had a significant combined influence on China's approach to the early Second Vietnam War.

The emerging disagreements over global strategy crystallized over Chinese and Soviet aid to Vietnam. The PRC had been supporting the DRV since its foundation. China was the first country to recognize North Vietnam diplomatically, in early 1950, and Mao was instrumental in convincing Stalin to follow suit.[2] In the early 1950s, Beijing provided Hanoi with significant amounts of artillery, firearms, and ammunition.[3] Chinese military aid was critical to the North Vietnamese victory at Dien Bien Phu in the spring of 1954, enhancing Hanoi's negotiating position at the Geneva Conference, which ended the First Vietnam War (1945–54) against France that summer.[4]

Sino-Soviet cooperation at the conference was crucial for the pacification of the country. However, it also led to its partition into the communist Democratic Republic of Vietnam (DRV) north of the 17th parallel and the U.S.-backed Republic of Vietnam (RVN) in the south. Saigon's policy, endorsed by Washington, to thwart nationwide elections in 1956—out of fear that they could lead to a communist takeover of the RVN—convinced Hanoi to seek reunification through a military solution.[5] It was the point of departure for the Second Vietnam War.

While still difficult to assess in monetary terms, Chinese economic aid from 1954 to the early 1960s was enormous. Much of it consisted of foodstuffs, assistance to repair the agricultural, economic, and transportation infrastructure damaged by the war against France, know-how transfers, and the dispatch of technical specialists and a labor force.[6] Until 1962, however, Chinese fears of U.S. aggression had discouraged the PRC from directly helping the DRV to liberate the South by military force. Nevertheless, from 1956 to 1963 Beijing had given 320 million yuan (approximately 193 million transfer rubles according to the noncommercial exchange rate adopted on January 1, 1961) of military aid

---

[2] Lawrence, *Assuming*, 260. Gaiduk, *Confronting*, 4–5. Westad, *Decisive*, 317.

[3] Christensen, "Worse," 90.

[4] Chen Jian, "China and the First Indo-China War," *China Quarterly* 133, 103–4. Christensen, "Worse," 96.

[5] Gaiduk, *Confronting*, 28–204. Zhai, *China*, 49–129.

[6] Zhai, *China*, 69–71.

to Hanoi.[7] When Mao started to stress national liberation movements in 1962, political support for military reunification increased as well.[8] In comparison, the USSR assisted the DRV almost exclusively through economic aid, though on a smaller scale than the PRC.[9] According to Soviet sources, from 1955 to 1964 the USSR sent over two thousand specialists and provided 317 million transfer rubles in aid to the DRV, 70 percent of which were for industrial development.[10] Like China, though, the USSR also feared that military assistance to the DRV would negatively influence its relations with the United States.[11]

Sino-Soviet differences on global strategy had a significant influence on the North Vietnamese position. Since 1960, the VWP had tried to mediate the ideological dispute for its own sake, as described in chapters 5 and 6. However, once it had become clear, in the spring of 1963, that the CPSU and the CCP were unable to bridge their differences, the VWP moved closer to its Chinese brother. In March 1963, First Secretary Le Duan openly rejected the Soviet position on peaceful coexistence and at the ninth plenum late that year, the VWP formally turned toward Mao's concept of national liberation wars. Unlike Mao, however, Le Duan had no desire to break completely with the Soviet comrades.[12]

AFTER TONKIN

A North Vietnamese torpedo boat attack on the U.S. destroyer *Maddox* on August 2, 1964, in the Gulf of Tonkin, and American claims of another attack that had supposedly occurred two days later, precipitated the U.S. escalation of the Second Vietnam War. Although the details remain murky, it is certain that, on August 2, a local commander made the decision to attack without the knowledge of the central military leadership in Hanoi. The second attack on August 4 probably never happened. Even though Washington had only sketchy details about the incident, the White House used the episode to get congressional approval to take all necessary measures to repel more armed attacks against U.S. forces and

[7] Chen, *Mao's China*, 205–7, 211. Chen does not mention the ruble rate, but I arrived at this sum in transfer rubles according to the exchange rate listed in a Soviet document from early 1961: *AVPRF*, f.100, o.48, d.1, p.199, 3–4. Also: Christensen, "Worse," 102.

[8] Chen, *Mao's China*, 207.

[9] Zhai, *China*, 71, 73. Ilya Gaiduk, *Soviet Union and the Vietnam War* (Chicago: Dee, 1996), 5.

[10] "Information," [no date], *AAN*, KC PZPR, XI A/66, 412–20.

[11] Gaiduk, *Confronting*, 95, 107, 113.

[12] Zhai, *China*, 123, 125. "Report by Dimitr Grekov," 1/29/1965, *AMVnR*, o.21, a.e.749, 1–12. Radchenko, "China Puzzle," 102.

to prevent further aggression against the RVN. It was a *carte blanche* to widen the war. In view of the impending presidential election, however, the Johnson Administration did not yet decide to dispatch ground troops. In August of 1964, the United States limited the escalation to retaliatory air strikes.[13]

The Gulf of Tonkin Incident reinforced Chinese support for the DRV. Given the signs of rapidly increasing American military assistance to the RVN following the overthrow and assassination of South Vietnam's President Ngo Dinh Diem on November 1, 1963, the PRC had already announced additional military and economic aid to the DRV by the summer of 1964.[14] On June 24, Mao had even promised Korean War–style volunteer troops to Van Tien Dung, chief of the General Staff of the North Vietnamese Army.[15] Half a month later, Zhou had warned that "if America wants to widen the war, by attacking the DRV, or perhaps by sending troops itself, [thereby] bringing fire to China's periphery, we simply cannot sit by watching."[16]

No surprise, then, that on August 6, one day after the first American retaliatory bombings,[17] *Xinhua* publicly accused Washington of fabricating the Gulf of Tonkin Incident, announcing that "no Socialist country can sit idly by while it [Vietnam] is being subjected to aggression."[18] At the same time, Beijing ordered air force and navy units in Yunnan and Guangxi to prepare for combat.[19] Within a couple of days, China also transferred older MiG-15 and MiG-17 fighter planes to the Phuc Yen airfield near Hanoi.[20] Although the PRC did not provide its own pilots, it agreed to train Vietnamese pilots and to build supply and repair stations close to the Vietnamese border.[21] In light of the U.S. reluctance to dispatch ground troops until March 1965, negotiations on troop commitments dragged on until December, when the PRC and the DRV signed a military assistance treaty. It stipulated the sending of 300,000 regular PLA infantry and anti-aircraft troops to the northern DRV to replace the Vietnamese troops moved farther south.[22] But Hanoi and Beijing agreed

[13] Fredrik Logevall, *Choosing War* (Berkeley: California, 1999), 193–221, 333–74. Chen, *Mao's China*, 213.

[14] Chen, *Mao's China*, 209.

[15] Li, "ZhongSu," 112.

[16] ZELNP2, 655.

[17] Christensen, "Worse," 107.

[18] Official English version: *NYT*, 8/7/1964, 7.

[19] Chen, *Mao's China*, 212–13.

[20] Logevall mentions "three dozens" of aircraft (*Choosing War*, 207), while Zhai only "approximately fifteen MIG-15 and MIG-17 jets" (*China*, 132).

[21] Zhai, *China*, 132.

[22] Ilya Gaiduk, ed., "Vietnam War and Soviet-American Relations, 1964–1973," *CWIHP Bulletin* 6–7, 250.

on the details only in late April of 1965.[23] The first Chinese units arrived in June.[24]

Apart from military assistance, Mao also provided political advice. On August 13, 1964, he was skeptical whether the United States, the DRV, or the PRC wanted large-scale war, asserting that the Gulf of Tonkin Incident was the result of mistaken judgment and incorrect information. However, the Chairman suggested, in the event of an American dispatch of troops, North Vietnam should withdraw into the mountains and engage in people's war.[25] In talks with Vietnamese Prime Minister Pham Van Dong and Politburo member Hoang Van Hoan on October 5, Mao also counseled against rejecting negotiations with the Americans, but warned not to expect any quick results.[26] Nonetheless, Beijing was willing to endorse publicly Hanoi's negative position on this issue.[27]

Despite these commitments to the DRV, Mao was cautious in light of the brewing conflict in Southeast Asia. He understood that Chinese military and political support for the DRV raised the possibility of direct military conflict with the United States. Indeed, since the late spring, he had been concerned about the possibility of large-scale war and its consequences for the PRC. A report by the War Planning Office of the PLA General Staffs, prepared for the First Vice-Chief of Staff Yang Chengwu on April 25, had identified structural defense problems—for example, the overconcentration of population and industrial centers in vulnerable border or seashore provinces—and proposed to relocate people as well as industrial and strategic military assets along a three-line defense concept to the rear, that is, China's mountainous interior.[28] Mao explicitly promoted this idea during a CC work conference on the Third FYP from May 15 to June 17, stating that "in an age of nuclear weapons, it was not acceptable that China has no rear."[29] The Gulf of Tonkin Incident and American retaliatory bombings emphasized that point. Already on August 10, Mao Zedong instructed PLA Chief of Staff Luo Ruiqing and his deputy Yang "to implement step-by-step" the April 25 report.[30] Despite the fact that,

[23] Zhang Xiaoming, "The Vietnam War, 1964–1969," *Journal of Military History* 60/4, 748.

[24] Zhai, *China*, 135.

[25] Chen, *Mao's China*, 213.

[26] "Mao Zedong and Pham Van Dong, Hoang Van Hoan, Beijing, 5 October 1964 7–7:50 (P.M.?)," O. Arne Westad et al., eds., "77 Conversations between Chinese and Foreign Leaders on the Wars in Indochina, 1964–1977," *CWIHP* Working Paper 22, 76.

[27] *NYT*, 10/7/1964, 10.

[28] "Report of the War Planning Office of the [PLA] Headquarters," 4/25/1964, *Dangde wenxian* 1995/3, 34–35.

[29] Li Chen, ed., *Zhonghua Renmin Gongheguo shilu*, vol. 2/2 (Changchun: Jilin renmin, 1994), 953.

[30] *Dangde wenxian* 1995/3, n. 33.

on August 13, Mao had told Le Duan that neither the United States nor the DRV, nor the PRC wanted to escalate the conflict in Vietnam, Mao warned during a CCP Central Secretariat conference four days later that "we must prepare for the possibility that imperialism starts an aggressive war."[31] The conception of the national three-line defense lasted into October.[32] American threats to pursue DRV planes into PRC territory, or what the U.S. called "privileged sanctuary,"[33] seemed to increase the possibility of an escalation to nuclear war, as Mao feared in October.[34] At the end of that month, the CCP CC sent out instructions to all provinces to implement the countrywide three-line defense plan and to carry out defense preparations.[35]

Until early 1965, however, the PRC seemed willing to keep the door open to a negotiated solution of the Vietnam crisis. In early October of 1964, Mao had counseled Pham and Hoang not to give up on the idea of talks with the Americans.[36] In an interview with Edgar Snow on January 9, 1965, the Chairman brought up the idea of a conference on the Vietnam War.[37] Six days later, the PRC embassy in Paris, "on instruction from Peiping [Beijing]," approached the French government in an attempt to find out "whether France would assume a more active role in Viet-Nam and would approach the US with a view to discussing a negotiated settlement."[38] On February 13, the Chinese ambassador conveyed to the French Foreign Minister Maurice Couve de Murville that "the thing to do in Southeast Asia was to go back to the Geneva Agreement of 1954 as a basis for negotiations."[39]

While Beijing maneuvered cautiously between increased commitments to the DRV, guarding its own security, and trying to defuse the crisis through diplomatic action, Moscow increased its political and military support for Hanoi on a massive scale. In fact, Khrushchev's fall ended Moscow's hands-off policy toward South East Asia.

---

[31] Sun Dongsheng, "Woguo jingji jianshe zhanlüe buju de da zhuanbian," *Dangde wenxian* 1995/3, 45.

[32] Li, *Zhonghua*, vol. 2, 1015, 1022, 1025, 1029. Sun, "Woguo," 44–45. Several documents in: *Dangde wenxian* 1995/3, 33–35.

[33] *NYT*, 9/27/1964, 1.

[34] Zhang, "Vietnam War," 742.

[35] CCP CC, "Instruction with Regard to the Construction of the First and Second Rear Line Defense and the Preparations for War," 10/29/1964, *Dangde wenxian* 1995/3, 35–37.

[36] "Mao Zedong and Pham Van Dong, Hoang Van Hoan, Beijing, 5 October 1964 7–7:50 (P.M.?)," Westad, "77 Conversations," 76.

[37] Logevall, *Choosing*, 365.

[38] Quoted in: "Draft Paper Prepared by the Assistant Secretary of State for Far Eastern Affairs (Bundy)," 2/23/1963, *FRUS 1964–1968*, II, 353.

[39] Quoted in: "Memorandum of Conversation," 2/19/1965, *FRUS 1964–1968*, II, 332.

Soviet-Vietnamese relations in the late Khrushchev era had been cool. In January of 1963, for example, Le Duan had flown to Moscow to reveal Vietnamese approval of Mao's radical ideas on national liberation. Khrushchev upheld peaceful coexistence with the United States, defended the Soviet record of assistance to national liberation movements, and criticized the Chinese for boisterous but empty rhetoric.[40] Nevertheless, he decided to reduce support to North Vietnam to mere propaganda.[41]

Even after the Gulf of Tonkin Incident, Khrushchev remained wary of supporting the Vietnamese cause. On August 5, the Soviet government denounced the "aggressive actions of the United States," but did not announce any further steps.[42] Moscow even joined Washington's call to take the Vietnam issue to the United Nations Security Council, for which it promptly received a stern criticism from Beijing.[43] Only on August 8 did Khrushchev warn "that if the Western powers sought to impose war on the Communist camp, they would find the USSR willing and ready to fight for itself and other Communists."[44] Frustrated about Khrushchev's vacillation, Le Duan complained to Mao five days later that "the Soviet revisionists want to use us as a bargaining chip."[45]

Moscow's reluctant position derived from its doubt about Hanoi's battlefield chances. The Soviet embassy in the DRV believed that the country and its military arm in the RVN, the National Liberation Front (NLF), were overly optimistic about the possibility of winning a war against the United States.[46] The North Vietnamese indeed believed that the U.S. escalation was due to American failures in the south.[47] Nor did the commitments to the DRV made by the PRC since early August convince the USSR. Moscow mocked Beijing's claims to aid Hanoi militarily and economically as "noise," because, it claimed, "the Chinese have done little for the communist movement" on a global scale in the past.[48]

---

[40] "Note no. 27/64," 3/6/1964, *SAPMO-BArch*, DY 30/IV A 2/20/442. Zolotarev, *Rossiya*, 80. Zhai, *China*, 128. Gittings, *Survey*, 254.

[41] Gaiduk, "Vietnam War," 250.

[42] *NYT*, 8/5/1964, 8.

[43] Gittings, *Survey*, 254.

[44] *NYT*, 8/9/1964, 1, 37.

[45] Quoted in: Chen Jian, "Personal-Historical Puzzles about China and the Vietnam War," Westad, "77 Conversations," 30.

[46] "Notes of Conversation at the Embassy of the USSR in Hanoi," 9/2/1964, *AMSZ*, Departament II, zespol 24/71, wiazka 2, teczka D. II Wietnam 2421, 1–4.

[47] Logevall, *Choosing*, 208–9. Robert McNamara et al., eds., *Argument without End* (New York: Public Affairs, 1999), 195.

[48] "Information," [no date], *AMSZ*, Departament II, zespol 26/67, wiazka 1, teczka D. II Wietnam 241-29-64, 1–6.

Khrushchev's removal from power in mid-October perplexed the North Vietnamese. A late October article in the party journal *Hoc Tap*, clearly critical of recent Soviet policies, revealed that the Vietnamese party was divided. The piece warned of "subjectivism and arbitrariness . . . , the removal from reality, boasting, empty promises, [and] a tendency toward administrating and bureaucraticism"—all code words for Khrushchevism. However, it apparently did not conform to the new line taken by the party leadership.[49] On November 3, Le Duan apologized to Soviet Ambassador Ilya Shcherbakov, claiming that "some communists [in the party] do not agree with the line of the VWP CC."[50] Subsequently, the article was cut from the remaining copies of *Hoc Tap*.[51]

At the same time, the new Soviet leadership started to revise Khrushchev's Vietnam policy. After the signing of a credit and loan agreement in early November,[52] Kosygin and Pham Van Dong, who had come to Moscow for the celebrations of the October Revolution, discussed economic and military aid, as well as a possible visit by the Soviet prime minister to Vietnam.[53] Nonetheless, the North Vietnamese returned from the meeting in Moscow in an ambivalent mood. When Pham Van Dong passed through Beijing, he curtly told Deng Xiaoping, who met him at the airport, that "he and the delegation had no questions" to discuss.[54] The Soviet embassy in Hanoi was irritated that the North Vietnamese prime minister was "cool" and "evasive," and it even feared that the VWP would republish the *Hoc Tap* article.[55]

The North Vietnamese, however, did not turn against the Soviets, as the late November Solidarity Conference for Vietnam in Hanoi revealed. While the Chinese had hoped to exploit it for the purpose of an ideological struggle against "the views of the Soviet Union and the other 'representatives of modern revisionism,'" the North Vietnamese, at the last minute, told the Chinese not to provoke and the Soviets not to react to

[49] "Excerpts from the article, originally published in no. 11 of the Journal 'Hoc Tap' and then withdrawn," [no date], *PAAA-MfAA*, Abteilung Ferner Osten—Sektor Vietnam, Microfiche C 933/76, 67–68.

[50] "Record of Conversation with Le Duan," 11/3/1964, *AVPRF*, f.079, o.19, d.8, p.40, 92.

[51] "GDR Embassy to Ministry for Foreign Affairs," 11/14/1964, *SAPMO-BArch*, DY 30/IV A 2/20/442, 57–58.

[52] "Record of Conversation with Nguyen Duy Trinh," 11/6/1964, *AVPRF*, f.079, o.19, d.8, p.40, 96–97.

[53] Gaiduk, *Soviet Union*, 19–20.

[54] "Information about Some Aspects of the Conflicts with the Chinese Leadership," 11/26/1964, *PAAA-MfAA*, Abteilung Ferner Osten—Sektor China, Microfiche A 6835, 3.

[55] "Note no. 131/64," 12/10/1964, *SAPMO-BArch*, DY 30/IV A 2/20/442, 1–5.

any polemics. Unable to exploit the conference for anti-Soviet propaganda, the CCP delegation "left Hanoi by plane not very happy."[56]

The Vietnamese-Soviet rapprochement gathered momentum to the detriment of a Soviet-American nuclear understanding. Two weeks after the Chinese A-bomb test in mid-October, the Johnson Administration had tried to engage the post-Khrushchev Soviet leadership in a dialogue on nuclear nonproliferation. However, the U.S. escalation of the Second Vietnam War and the increasingly assertive Soviet position on the issue prevented the possibility of reaching any agreement on nonproliferation quickly.[57] On November 27, Soviet Foreign Minister Gromyko sent a telegram to his North Vietnamese counterpart, Xuan Thuy, stating that "the USSR will not remain uninvolved in the fate of a fraternal socialist country and is ready to render the necessary aid to the DRV if the aggressors dare to encroach on its security and sovereignty." The day before, Moscow had issued a *TASS* announcement to the same effect.[58] The following month, Shcherbakov told the East German embassy that "since October 15" twenty-six delegations had been sent to Moscow or come to Hanoi, which would "have been unthinkable only some months ago." He explained this change as the result of "doubts [that] had arisen among some Vietnamese cadres as to the sincerity of the Chinese leaders." The root of these doubts lay in "insufficient" Chinese military and economic aid since August, or so the ambassador claimed.[59] On December 12, the Soviet government also allowed the NLF to open an office in Moscow.[60]

As a result of the rapprochement between the USSR and the DRV, Kosygin accepted an invitation to visit Hanoi from February 6 to 10.[61] Although the North Vietnamese capital appeared to the Soviet visitors to be "at peace,"[62] the U.S. air raids on February 7 and 9, following the NLF attacks on the Pleiku U.S. helicopter base in the RVN, reminded them that they were in fact in a war zone.[63] The Soviet government considered the American bombing of its prime minister an "unfriendly act."[64] At an embassy reception on February 8, Kosygin "called for a United States

---

[56] "Note no. 1/65," 1/5/1965, *SAPMO-BArch*, DY 30/IV A 2/20/442, 1–5.

[57] *FRUS 1964–1968*, XI, 203–5; XIV, 165–68, 168–70, 172–76, 176–78, 178–80, 182–83, 184–85, 193–200, 210–12. Seaborg, *Stemming*, 158–60.

[58] *NYT*, 11/27/1964, 1.

[59] "Note no. 2/65," 12/22 & 28/1964, *SAPMO-BArch*, DY 30/IV A 2/20/442.

[60] Gaiduk, *Soviet Union*, 20.

[61] A Soviet document sent to the Poles mentions that the Vietnamese party had invited the Soviet party to send a delegation: "Information," [no date], *AAN*, KC PZPR, XI A/10, 534.

[62] Interview with Oleg Troyanovskii, Moscow, 6/8/2002.

[63] Zhai, *China*, 133. McNamara, *Argument*, 172.

[64] Quoted in: Gaiduk, *Soviet Union*, 30.

withdrawal from Vietnam,"[65] and in the ensuing negotiations offered "modern means of anti-aircraft and coastal protection." When the Soviet prime minister touched the possibility of a "joint action of the USSR, China, the DRV, and other socialist states as well as some countries of Asia," his Vietnamese hosts indicated immediately that they would soon present a draft for a joint declaration.[66]

The Kosygin visit revealed that Hanoi was moving toward a middle position in the Sino-Soviet ideological disputes. When the two sides talked about the March Meeting in Moscow (see also chapter 9), the North Vietnamese explained that "all in all they had nothing to say against the meeting on March 1, but for understandable reasons they could not participate."[67] The North Vietnamese also made clear that they would "not participate in any counter-meeting in Beijing likely to be organized by the Communist Party of China." The Soviet delegation was content with the modified stance of the VWP.[68]

On his stopover in Beijing, the Soviet prime minister briefed his Chinese counterpart about the agreements reached in Hanoi. Zhou remarked that "the positions of the CCP and the CPSU have come close," and promised to have Soviet arms shipments transported, at no cost, on Chinese railroads to Vietnam.[69] But disagreements lurked behind this façade of unity. The Soviets were irritated that, despite revealing the extent of their aid, the Chinese "did not inform [us] about their steps and measures to render concrete aid to the Vietnamese people." Also, Zhou announced that Beijing would not sign any joint statement in support of Hanoi, justifying the refusal with the "differences in opinion on the question of . . . the consultation by representatives of the fraternal parties on March 1st" in Moscow.[70]

During his meeting with Mao on February 11, Kosygin briefed the Chairman about the Soviet decisions to send, at no cost, ground-to-air missiles, artillery and tanks, as well as Soviet military specialists to train the Vietnamese "to master these weapons." Mao agreed. But when he later accused the Soviets of doing "too little," Kosygin's reply touched a sensitive spot in Chinese policy: "We help . . . as much as our geographical position allows us. Unfortunately, we have no air force there, which

[65] *NYT*, 2/9/1965, 1, 12.

[66] "Information," [no date], *AAN, KC PZPR*, XI A/10, 534–35.

[67] "Information," [no date], *AAN, KC PZPR*, XI A/10, 535–36.

[68] "Report on the Consultative Conference of the 19 Communist and Workers' Parties from March 1 to 5, 1965, in Moscow," *SAPMO-BArch*, DY 30/J IV 2/201/720, 2.

[69] Wang, *Zhonghua*, vol. 2, 265.

[70] "Information," [no date], *AAN, KC PZPR*, XI A/10, 538. Also: "About the Question of Some Measures . . . of the Soviet Government on the Vietnam Problem (Reference)," 4/11/1965, *AVPRF*, f.079, o.20, d.12, p.46, 76.

could come forward with counter strikes against American bases. Only you could do this, but you don't do it, and [thereby] you do not give an appropriate rebuke to the American imperialists, although you could do it." With fears about a military confrontation with the United States in mind, Mao instead stressed the idea of people's war: "The South Vietnamese people . . . will drive away the Americans by themselves." Kosygin was not convinced, continuing to insist that "it is necessary to give the Americans a rebuke."[71]

FOUR SOVIET INITIATIVES AND CHINESE RESPONSES

Four major Soviet initiatives emerged from Kosygin's trip: the promotion of a negotiated settlement for the Vietnam War, the shoring up of diplomatic and political support for North Vietnam within the socialist camp, and two initiatives with regard to practical military aid to Hanoi. Yet, the subsequent—and sometimes bitter—exchanges between Moscow and Beijing about these four proposals revealed how Sino-Soviet ideological disagreements as well as China's security concerns negatively influenced diplomatic and military assistance to the DRV.

As soon as Kosygin was back from East Asia, he started to promote the first of the four initiatives by calling for a new Indochina conference under the condition that the United States stop escalation. The Soviets thereby took up a February 10 suggestion of French President Charles de Gaulle,[72] which followed a North Vietnamese request and the Chinese initiative from a month earlier, mentioned above.[73] On February 16, Chervonenko proposed to Vice-Foreign Minister Liu Xiao convening the 1954 Geneva conference, but Liu conveyed little enthusiasm.[74] Pham Van Dong told the Soviets that his government was "in principle" in favor of a new conference, but also mentioned that the DRV had "to consult with the PRC" first.[75] Apparently, Hanoi's hands were not totally free.

The tentative nature of Pham Van Dong's approval was probably also linked to ongoing internal discussions by the North Vietnamese leadership. The U.S. bombing of Hanoi had an effect on the Vietnamese similar to the one that the German air raids of London during the Second World

---

[71] "Record of Conversation of Kosygin with Mao Zedong," 2/11/1965, AAN, KC PZPR, XI A/10, 526–27.

[72] NYT, 2/9/1965, 12.

[73] North Vietnamese request mentioned in: NYT, 2/23/1965, 1.

[74] "Record of Conversation with Liu Xiao," 2/16/1965, AVPRF, f.0100, o.58, d.5, p.516, 28–32.

[75] "About the Question of Some Measures . . . ," 77.

War had wrought on the British—it strengthened their resolve to carry on the war. The North Vietnamese believed that the air strikes were an *implicit* admission that the war in the South against the NLF was not going well. Together with the military support promised by Kosygin, this belief probably led Hanoi to up the ante with regard to a negotiated settlement. Starting in mid-February, Ho Chi Minh, Le Duan, Pham Van Dong, and a special drafting committee discussed the so-called Four Points, which were presented to the public on April 8: U.S. troop withdrawal from South Vietnam, respect for the 1954 Geneva agreements, the demand that internal affairs of South Vietnam must be settled by the South Vietnamese themselves, and the requirement that the peaceful reunification of Vietnam be settled by the Vietnamese people alone.[76]

While Beijing and Hanoi were still considering how to respond to Moscow's February 16 proposal, the Soviet ambassador in Paris, Sergei Vinogradov, had a short conversation with de Gaulle about Vietnam on February 23. In a position paper dated six days earlier, and approved subsequently by the CPSU Presidium, Gromyko had proposed to use the French to communicate to the Americans "the determination of the Soviet Union to render practical aid to the DRV government." The Soviet foreign minister considered this announcement both a warning to the Americans and a way to spell out Moscow's preconditions for negotiations on Vietnam: "The U.S. must stop bombing."[77] However, the Vinogradov initiative was limited; Moscow did not seek any superpower understanding on Vietnam. When the French Foreign Ministry conveyed the contents of the Vinogradov–de Gaulle talk to the British ambassador three days later, it stressed that "the Russian Ambassador's demarche was pitched in *a minor key*" and "was *not* an invitation to press ahead with the idea of a conference."[78] Moscow also informed Hanoi about the exchange, revealing that both the French and the Soviet sides had blamed the Americans for renewed war in Indochina, and that "de Gaulle was told that no talk on negotiations will occur as long as the aggressive [U.S.] policy against Vietnam exists."[79] But the Soviets did not inform the Chinese, who got their information from the Western press.[80] Lacking the specific details of the Vinogradov–de Gaulle exchange, the *New*

---

[76] McNamara, *Argument*, 188–95, 216, 223–24.

[77] "CPSU CC," 2/17/1965, *AVPRF*, f.079, o.20, d.12, p.46, 12–17.

[78] "From Paris to Foreign Office," 2/26/1965, *Public Records Office*, Foreign Office, FO 371/180582 (italics mine). Fredrik Logevall kindly provided me with this document.

[79] "Oral Communication to the Ambassador of the DRV in Moscow (draft)," [February 1965], *AVPRF*, f.079, o.20, d.12, p.46, 24–25.

[80] That Beijing got its information from the Western press is revealed: "Record of Conversation by Lapin with Zhou Enlai," 5/15/1965, *AVPRF*, f.0100, o.58, d.5, p.516, 202.

York Times, for example, erroneously portrayed the talks as a NATO-approved French initiative and even went so far as to assert that Paris "doubt[ed] . . . that Moscow would cling to its demand for an end to American air strikes if a conference was clearly in view."[81]

On February 27, two days after Washington had already rejected de Gaulle's February 10 proposal to convene a new Indochina conference because North Vietnam continued "its aggression against South Vietnam,"[82] Hanoi and Beijing replied to Moscow's February 16 initiative for a new Indochina conference in similarly negative tones. Liu Xiao curtly informed the Soviet embassy that the "Chinese government cannot agree to it" as long as the United States refused "to adhere strictly to the Geneva Agreement and to withdraw from the region all its armed forces."[83] Xuan Thuy sent Gromyko a letter demanding that the United States must "completely" honor the 1954 agreements before any conference. The DRV foreign minister, however, was not entirely dismissive about the Soviet idea since, as he indicated, the North Vietnamese leadership was still discussing what would become the Four Points.[84] Moscow understood that Hanoi considered "a new conference on Vietnam . . . not timely."[85]

These developments reveal that, midmonth, Beijing's position on negotiations had changed. As late as February 13, the PRC embassy in Paris had pushed for a negotiated solution, as related above. However, on the eighteenth, two days after the Soviets had made the proposal for a new Indochina conference, Chen Yi stated publicly that it "is imperative today . . . to force the United States imperialists into withdrawing all their aggressive forces from Indochina. *Only thus can peace in Indochina be insured.*"[86] On February 27, Liu Xiao told the Soviet embassy that the resumption of the 1954 conference was "a manifestation of weakness before American imperialism."[87] Four weeks later, he made clear to Chervonenko why the Chinese had refused to accept the Soviet proposal. Reciting the erroneous press reports on the Vinogradov–de Gaulle talks, he claimed that the USSR "carries out negotiations with the USA on Vietnam behind the back of China and Vietnam."[88]

[81] *NYT*, 2/26/1965, 2, 4.

[82] *NYT*, 2/26/1965, 1, 2.

[83] "Text of the Oral Statement of the Government of the PRC," 2/27/1965, *AVPRF*, f.0100, o.58, d.1, p.516, 1–2.

[84] "To Gromyko," 2/27/1965, *AVPRF*, f.079, o.20, d.12, p.46, 38–39.

[85] "About the Question of Some Measures . . . ," 77.

[86] *NYT*, 2/19/1965, 11 (italics mine).

[87] "Text of the Oral Statement of the Government of the PRC," 2/27/1965, *AVPRF*, f.0100, o.58, d.1, p.516, 1.

[88] "Record of Conversation with Liu Xiao," 3/23/1965, *AVPRF*, f.0100, o.58, d.5, p.516, 48. Wang, *Zhonghua*, vol. 2, 266.

Why did the Chinese position on negotiations change so suddenly? In the absence of Chinese documentary evidence, three rationales seem to be likely. First, since the turn of the year, Mao had sought a confrontation with his opponents in the CCP leadership, as covered in chapter 9. Accusing them of being Khrushchevite revisionists, the Chairman could not appear to be cooperating with the Soviets. Second, the February 7 Pleiku Incident led to the U.S. escalation of the war. Once Johnson had ordered daily retaliatory attacks on the DRV,[89] he publicly mulled over the sending of ground troops to the RVN.[90] The White House eventually announced the dispatch of U.S. Marines on March 1.[91] Three thousand five hundred troops landed at Danang Bay in central Vietnam a week later.[92] By the end of the month, 30,000 more had arrived, with another 45,000 to 50,000 to follow by the summer. Over the course of 1965, American military personnel in the RVN had grown from 23,500 military advisers and pilots to 184,500 servicemen, mostly ground troops.[93] Against the background of the U.S. air raids and public hints by the Johnson administration regarding troop dispatches, Chen Yi warned at a reception at the Soviet embassy in mid-February—on the fifteenth anniversary of the Sino-Soviet treaty—that "peaceful coexistence with the United States was 'out of question'" because "Johnson, the pirate chieftain, personally ordered the bombing of the Democratic Republic of Vietnam. . . . Only in concrete action against the United States imperialism and its followers *can the Chinese-Soviet alliance be tested and tempered*."[94] Finally, Beijing's position on negotiations changed, on February 16, once the Khrushchevite revisionists in Moscow started to promote the conference the PRC itself had advocated in Paris only three days before.

The prospects for a negotiated settlement worsened in March. During the visit of Pakistani President Mohammad Ayub Khan, the Chinese hosts remained silent about their guest's call for a negotiated settlement.[95] Given the U.S. escalation, Gromyko, too, stonewalled during his London talks with Prime Minister Harold Wilson and Foreign Secretary Michael Stewart, who both had the "strong impression . . . that the Soviet Union

[89] Logevall, *Choosing*, 326–32.

[90] *NYT*, 2/14/1965, 1; 2/23/1965, 1.

[91] *NYT*, 3/2/1965, 1.

[92] *NYT*, 3/8/1965, 1.

[93] James Hershberg et al., "Reading and Warning the Likely Enemy," *International History Review* 27/1, 56–57. For the number of military personnel before March 8: *NYT*, 3/7/1965, 1.

[94] *NYT*, 2/16/1965, 1 (italics mine).

[95] *NYT*, 3/8/1965, 2.

was unwilling to take any step on Vietnam without first obtaining some sign of cooperation from . . . North Vietnam and China."[96]

The U.S. escalation also raised American public pressure on President Johnson to negotiate. In an April 7 speech delivered in Baltimore, he made a proposal for "unconditional discussions." The offer, however, was not unconditional. He announced that the United States would continue to defend the "independence" of South Vietnam against any attack, at all cost.[97] Almost simultaneously, Pham Van Dong proclaimed the Four Points, which had been in the works for over two months.[98] As the North Vietnamese chargé d'affaires in Beijing, Hoang Bac, told Chervonenko, the DRV did not believe the Johnson proposal to be sincere: "It is so far not evident that the U.S. wants to decide the problem in a political way." Hoang also referred to Johnson's "conditions" and to "press reports . . . that the U.S. is pouring in more means into South Vietnam."[99]

In subsequent weeks, the PRC and the DRV continued to reject all calls for negotiations. On April 12, Zhou Enlai dismissed a British initiative from earlier that month. He went so far as to declare a visit by a delegation unwelcome in Beijing as long as London failed to assume its responsibilities as cochair of the 1954 Geneva conference and thus condemn Washington's aggression.[100] Peace initiatives by the United Nations, India, Britain, Nigeria, Ghana, France, and others, which all had used the Johnson proposal as a starting point, ran into fierce Chinese and North Vietnamese opposition.[101]

Although the Chinese rejection of any negotiations was categorical, the Vietnamese position was more flexible than it suggested to the outside. Le Duan, in a letter to NLF leaders in May, admitted that the Four Points were a retreat from the categorical demand that the United States must honor the 1954 Geneva agreements first.[102] Also, the points were not as nonnegotiable as the Johnson administration repeatedly claimed they were. On May 19, Mai Van Bo, the head of the North Vietnamese commercial delegation in Paris, indicated to the Americans through the French Foreign Ministry that the Four Points were working principles

[96] NYT, 3/17/1965, 6.

[97] NYT, 4/8/1965, 16.

[98] The Four Points were not a reply to the Johnson announcement: McNamara, Argument, 227.

[99] "Record of Conversation with Hoang Bac," 4/13/1965, AVPRF, f.0100, o.58, d.5, p.516, 98.

[100] Zhai Qiang, "Beijing and the Vietnam Peace Talks, 1965–1968," CWIHP Working Paper 18, 3–4.

[101] Zhai Qiang, China, 158–62.

[102] McNamara, Argument, 231.

and final objectives. The DRV, however, would not abandon its ally in the South, the NLF, as demanded by the Americans.[103]

While Moscow's February 16 initiative for a new Indochina conference was a complete failure, Hanoi reacted positively to the three remaining Soviet initiatives. Beijing's response, in contrast, was entirely unconstructive. The second Soviet initiative called for a joint statement by all socialist countries in support of the DRV, as proposed by Kosygin on February 7.[104] Pham Van Dong handed over a draft to the Soviet ambassador on the twenty-second.[105] It already encompassed some of the Four Points the VWP leadership was discussing at the time.[106] But on February 28, one day after it had rebuffed the Soviet Union's call for a new Indochina conference, the PRC rejected the joint statement as well.[107] Zhou had already indicated to Kosygin earlier in the month that the PRC could not sign such a statement because the Soviets were convening the March Meeting. On March 1, the Chinese prime minister warned Ho Chi Minh that the "new Soviet Party leadership is carrying out nothing but Khrushchevism. It is absolutely impossible for them to change."[108] And Mao reminded the Vietnamese leader that the call of the Soviet revisionists for "united action" was only a ruse "to use this war for their own purposes."[109] Pham Van Dong informed Shcherbakov on March 7 that "the question on the joint statement by the socialist countries in support of Vietnam can be considered decided."[110]

The third Soviet initiative was much more practical. During his February talks in Hanoi, Kosygin had promised military assistance to the North Vietnamese and, afterward, Zhou agreed to permit arms shipments on railroads across the PRC. On February 19, desperate for protection against daily U.S. bombing raids, Pham Van Dong "turn[ed] to the Soviet government with the request to send to the DRV a part of the anti-aircraft armament in accelerated form by air." On February 27, Moscow asked Beijing for permission "to send immediately 45 An-12 transport planes from the Soviet Union through China to Hanoi, providing 75 high-altitude missiles and 18 M-37 high-altitude missiles."[111] A day later, the

---

[103] "Telegram from the Embassy in France to the Department of State," 5/19/1965, and "Memorandum from Chester L. Cooper of the National Security Staff to President Johnson," 5/25/1965, *FRUS 1964–1968*, II, 673–74, 685–89. McNamara, *Argument*, 269, 271.

[104] "About the Question of Some Measures . . . ," 76.

[105] "CPSU CC," February 1965, *AVPRF*, f.079, o.20, d.12, p.46, 20.

[106] "Joint Statement (draft)," 2/22/1965, *AVPRF*, f.079, o.20, d.12, p.46, 26–31.

[107] SRV Ministry of Foreign Affairs, *Truth about Vietnam-China Relations over the Last Thirty Years* (Hanoi: SRV Ministry of Foreign Affairs, 1979), 33.

[108] "Zhou Enlai and Ho Chi Minh, Hanoi, 3/1/1965," Westad, "77 Conversations," 77.

[109] Han, *Eldest Son*, 304.

[110] "About the Question of Some Measures . . . ," 76–77.

[111] Wang, *Zhonghua*, vol. 2, 265.

PRC refused the Soviet request on the grounds that "the Americans could find out about this operation, and this might lead to victims." Despite this rejection, the Chinese foreign ministry proposed the delivery of an "urgent part of [Soviet] anti-aircraft armament by land."[112] Soviet 37mm and 57mm anti-aircraft guns appeared in North Vietnam in March.[113]

The Sino-Soviet battle over military transport had only just started. On March 3, the USSR thanked the PRC for the railroad transport of the urgently requested arms, but rejected China's reasoning for the refusal to send them by air.[114] A week later, Beijing delivered another excuse, claiming that Moscow had made the arms shipment public. It further accused the Soviets of "imposing [themselves] on other people" instead of negotiating with the Chinese and North Vietnamese first. Liu Xiao maintained that granting overflight rights "would put the DRV and the PRC under the control of the USSR."[115] Realizing that he had overplayed his hand, the Chinese vice–foreign minister told some East European diplomats in late March that "we still have to talk [about air transport] and formalize it in a protocol."[116] Eventually, in early 1966, the PRC allowed selected air transports.[117] When Shcherbakov told Pham Van Dong on April 2, 1965, about the unconstructive Chinese position, the Vietnamese prime minister "was discouraged and shook his head."[118] Three days before, China at least had agreed to formalize railroad transport for future arms shipments.[119]

Sino-Soviet polemics about military deliveries continued for years, fueled by the Chinese refusal to let the Soviets know exactly what they supplied to the North Vietnamese, by the simultaneous Chinese request that the Soviets account in detail for everything they wanted to ship through the PRC, and by the Chinese insistence on checking the necessity of each Soviet military delivery with the Vietnamese side first.[120] But the sharp, reciprocal accusations could not hide the fact that all three sides contributed their share to the problem. Although Moscow repeatedly accused Beijing of obstructing arms shipments, it did not fully use the railroad capacity allotted by the Chinese and its trains frequently

[112] "About the Question of Some Measures . . . ," 74–75.

[113] Zolotarev, *Rossiya*, 86.

[114] "About the Question of Some Measures . . . ," 75.

[115] Wang, *Zhonghua*, vol. 2, 266–67.

[116] "Record of Conversation with Kohrt, Halasz, and Stachowjak," 4/11/1965, *AVPRF*, f.0100, o.58, d.5, p.516, 80.

[117] "Chronicle of Soviet-Chinese Relations (for April 1966)," 5/5/1966, *AVPRF*, f.0100, o.59, d.16, p.526, 24.

[118] "Note on a talk with the Ambassadors of the Other Socialist States in the Embassy of the USSR on 4/2/1965," 4/25/1964, *PAAA-MfAA*, VS-Hauptstelle, Microfiche G-A 331, 3.

[119] Wang, *Zhonghua*, vol. 2, 267.

[120] "Record of Conversation with Zhao Yimin," 11/6/1965, *AVPRF*, f.0100, o.58, d.6, p.516, 12–16. *SCMP* 3692, 33–35.

arrived off schedule.[121] Similarly, the Chinese border guards were overly bureaucratic with their controls and their insistence on the letter of agreements.[122] The bottlenecks in the Vietnamese narrow-gauge railroad system, however, were beyond the control of Beijing and Moscow.[123]

The fourth initiative—the Soviet proposal to station military personnel in southern China and North Vietnam—was the most controversial. On February 19, Pham Van Dong had also appealed for more military technology.[124] On the twenty-fifth, Moscow asked Beijing to allow the transport of four thousand Soviet anti-aircraft missile troops, including their weapons systems, through the PRC and to provide two airfields near Kunming for the stationing of modern MiG-21s, including five hundred Soviet personnel.[125] Only two days later, the North Vietnamese commander-in-chief, General Vo Nguyen Giap, thanked the Soviets for the offer, mentioning that the Politburo was already considering the logistics of quartering such a great number of people.[126]

The Chinese were not at all enthusiastic. On March 1, Zhou told Ho Chi Minh that "we oppose . . . the sending of missile battalions and [1]2 MiG-21 aircraft." He warned the Vietnamese not to accept the Soviet offer: "Relations between our two countries may turn from good to bad."[127] Zhou justified his admonition by citing the untrustworthiness of the "Khrushchevites" in the Kremlin.[128] Later, he reminded Ho about "the terms, the conditions," under which the Chinese would help the Vietnamese: "It [the war] could *only be won* if it was played the way China had outlined: Mao's strategy of a people's war."[129] Since the North Vietnamese had no choice, they rejected the Soviet offer. They did, however, propose to send their own MiG-17 pilots to the USSR for training on MiG-21s that, afterward, "should return together" to Vietnam. Moscow agreed.[130] Regardless, on March 10, Liu Xiao justified the Chinese refusal with the false assertion that "the Vietnamese comrades said they were against the sending of Soviet personnel to the DRV." Beyond that, he claimed, the Soviet proposal was part of a greater scheme to "reach

---

[121] SCMP 3692, 33–35. "CCP CC to CPSU CC," 11/5/1965, SAPMO-BArch, DY 30/3610.

[122] "Note on a Talk in the Foreign Ministry of the PR China," 2/12/1966, SAPMO-BArch, NY 4182/1222.

[123] "Note no. 53/66," 3/25/1966, PAAA-MfAA, VS-Hauptstelle, Microfiche G-A 354.

[124] "About the Question of Some Measures . . . ," 74.

[125] Wang, Zhonghua, vol. 2, 265. Ding, "Huigu," 32.

[126] "About the Question of Some Measures . . . ," 74.

[127] "Zhou Enlai and Ho Chi Minh, Hanoi, 3/1/1965," Westad, "77 Conversations," 78 (brackets in original).

[128] Zhonghua, Zhou Enlai waijiao huodong dashiji, 438.

[129] Han, Eldest Son, 304 (italics original).

[130] "Draft," 6/17/1965, AVPRF, f.079, o.20, d.12, p.46, 167.

control over Vietnam and China," designed to "negotiate easily with America on the back of Vietnam and China."[131] Two weeks later, Zhou explained to the visiting Ceauçescu that Moscow wanted to send four thousand troops to the DRV "not for training purposes" but to "control the country." As in Cuba in October 1962, Zhou falsely claimed, Soviet missile troops would refuse to shoot down any American planes once stationed in North Vietnam. Nevertheless, on March 23, the PRC had allowed for 260 Soviet missile instructors to pass through China by train, together with their missiles.[132]

The issue of Soviet troops in Vietnam continued to vex Sino-Soviet relations. On March 22, the NLF requested "to send to South Vietnam its youth and soldiers" from the countries of the world.[133] Leonid Brezhnev swiftly proposed to fulfill this request.[134] The Chinese leaders were equally quick, offering "men and war matériel."[135] The Sino-Soviet competition to support the NLF made Hanoi uneasy. The DRV made clear that Vietnam had enough people, but needed weapons.[136]

Chinese historiography to this day emphasizes that the PRC "destroyed the [four] Soviet initiatives."[137] Beijing had some justified security concerns, given the possibility of a military confrontation with Washington since the arrival of the first American troops on March 8. In his memoirs, the Soviet Embassy Secretary Aleksei Brezhnev acknowledged that "a more subtle policy would have been required from us" to overcome Chinese fears.[138] Indeed, Mao told foreign visitors in March that concerns over Soviet-American collusion over Vietnam led the PRC to prepare for the possibility of a U.S. attack.[139] That month, China embarked on a two-pronged strategy to counter the perceived American threat to its security. While it accelerated its defense preparations, it tried to signal to the United States that it wanted to keep the war limited to Vietnam.

[131] Wang, *Zhonghua*, vol. 2, 266–67.

[132] "Minutes of Conversation Between the RCP Leadership led by Nicolae Ceausescu and the CCP Leadership led by Zhou Enlai," 3/26/1965, Mirca Munteanu, ed.,"Documents from the Romanian Communist Party Archive and the Archive of the Romanian Ministry of Foreign Affairs on the Vietnam War, 1965–1966," compiled for the International Conference "The Vietnam War: Thirty Years On," Temple University, Philadelphia, June 20–21, 2005, no page number. In fact, Soviet troops *did* shoot down a U-2 in Cuba on 10/27/1962, see: Fursenko, *One Hell of a Gamble*, 277–78.

[133] "CPSU CC," 3/27/1965, *AVPRF*, f.079, o.20, d.12, p.46, 69.

[134] Gaiduk, *Soviet Union*, 62.

[135] *NYT*, 3/25/1965, 1.

[136] Gaiduk, *Soviet Union*, 63.

[137] Li, *Lengnuan*, 338.

[138] Brezhnev, *Kitai*, 104.

[139] Christensen, "Worse," 111.

Only four days after the March 8 landing of U.S. Marines near Danang, Zhou revisited the construction of the three-line defense.[140] On March 14, the Office of Defense Industry Works of the PRC State Council sent out instructions on organizing provincial three-line defenses.[141] At a Politburo meeting on April 12, Liu Shaoqi warned of the possibility of the "U.S. sending ground troops to North Vietnam," as well as the possible expansion of the war into China. Deng Xiaoping declared the current defense preparations "urgent," announcing that "we must prepare against American imperialism fighting a war in all our country."[142] Zhou called for the further acceleration of the construction of the nationwide three-line defense.[143] The Politburo eventually dispatched instructions to all provinces to augment defense preparations.[144] On the twentieth, the State Council ordered the relocation, and, in some cases, the new construction of strategic oil reserves away from population centers, as well as their protection through anti-aircraft artillery.[145] A day later, it ordered the resurrection of provincial anti-aircraft defense militias, which had fallen in disorder after the Great Leap Forward, and the creation of provincial emergency plans in case of an American attack on the PRC.[146] A team of specialists traveled to Hanoi to study the North Vietnamese experience with anti-aircraft defense militias.[147] The implementation of these civilian and military defense measures lasted into the summer.[148]

While China increased its defense preparedness, Beijing also sent out signals to Washington about its desire to keep the conflict contained to

[140] Zhou Enlai, "Outline of a Report," 3/12/1965, *Dangde wenxian* 1995/3, 37–38.

[141] PRC, State Council, Office of Defense Industry Works, "Focal Points on the Construction of the 1st and 2nd Rear [Defense] Line of Each Province," 3/14/1965, *Dangde wenxian* 1995/3, 38.

[142] "Comrade Wang Wei Communicates the Speeches of Some Responsible Comrades Discussing the 'War Preparedness Instructions' in the Politburo," 4/12/1965, *JSSDAG*, 3011, zhang 1162, 43–49. Also: Hershberg, "Reading," 63.

[143] Zhou Enlai, "Some Problems with Regard to Capital Construction," 4/12/1965, *Dangde wenxian* 1995/3, 39.

[144] Zhang Baojun, "1969nian qianhou dang dui waijiao zhanlüe de zhongda tiaozheng," *Zhonggong dangshi yanjiu* 1996/1, 61–67.

[145] "Comments by the State Council on the Report by Commercial Department on Strengthening the Air Defense and War Preparation Measures of the Oil Depots of the Commercial System," 4/20/1965, *JSSDAG*, 3072, zhang 1864, 5–10.

[146] Order mentioned: "Circular on Participating in the Work of the People's Anti-Air Defense," 5/6/1965, *JSSDAG*, 3072, zhang 1879, 9–10.

[147] "Report on Studying and Inspecting the Experience of the Vietnam People's Air Defense Work," 8/29/1965, *JSSDAG*, 3011, zhang 1879, 15a–21.

[148] *JSSDAG*, 3072, zhang 1860, 3–6; 3011, zhang 1162, 66–71; 3072, zhang 1879, 1–2, 10–15. Cong, *Quzhe*, 467.

Vietnam. As early as the last week of March, Chinese public statements warned the United States that the PRC was ready to send troops and war material to the DRV.[149] During a visit to Pakistan on April 2, Zhou Enlai asked Ayub Khan, who was scheduled to visit Washington later that month, to convey to Johnson that China would "not take the initiative to provoke a war against the United States," but was "prepared" if the United States attacked.[150] The message never arrived because Johnson unexpectedly postponed Ayub Khan's visit.[151] On May 31, after unsuccessful attempts to send signals through Burma and Cambodia, Chen Yi approached the British chargé d'affaires in Beijing, Donald Hopson, to relay a message similar to the one given to the Pakistani president almost two months earlier.[152] Seven days later, the British diplomat told a Chinese Foreign Ministry official that the message had been delivered to Dean Rusk. The Chinese leaders hoped that the Americans would be sufficiently deterred.[153]

Neither China's increased war preparations nor its signaling to the United States, however, can fully explain Beijing's unconstructive attitude toward Moscow's requests for cooperation to support Hanoi. Mao's ideological fervor simply did not permit the CCP leaders to acknowledge changes in Soviet policy toward Vietnam. Committed to the view that whatever the comrades in Moscow said was dubious, Beijing started to question the validity of the security alliance with the Soviet Union, as Deng Xiaoping told a gathering of regional and provincial leaders on April 12: "We should ponder if revisionism will not only not support us but even obstruct us."[154]

Indeed, North Vietnam started to rethink its relationship with the Chinese neighbor to the north and the Soviet ally beyond. The eleventh plenum in late March promoted "centrist" cadres who had "not exposed themselves in the last years against the Soviet Union or P[eople's] R[epublic of] China."[155] But it was difficult for Hanoi to establish a middle ground. In late April, Ho Chi Minh and Pham Van Dong admitted to Giancarlo Pajetta, a visiting CC member of the Italian Communist Party,

[149] Hershberg, "Reading," 64–65.

[150] "Zhou Enlai and Pakistani President Ayub Khan; Karachi, 4/2/1965," Westad, "77 Conversations," 82–83.

[151] Hershberg, "Reading," 68–69.

[152] Hershberg, "Reading," 69–73.

[153] Hershberg, "Reading," 78.

[154] "Comrade Wang Wei Communicates the Speeches of Some Responsible Comrades Discussing the 'War Preparedness Instructions' in the Politburo," April 12, 1965, *JSSDAG*, 3011, zhang 1162, 44.

[155] "Note on a Talk between Jarck and Svervev," 4/14/1965, *PAAA-MfAA*, VS-Hauptstelle, Microfiche G-A 331.

that "they did not want Vietnam to become a source of new disagreements between the USSR and China, which is what they keep in mind when they seek aid."[156]

CONTINUED LACK OF COOPERATION

After the failure of its four initiatives, the Soviet government decided to start anew; this time, it focused on Sino-Soviet-Vietnamese talks on military aid. On April 2, Shcherbakov sought out Pham about the possibility of trilateral negotiations. While Hanoi's prime minister complained about Chinese obstruction, he promised to talk once more to the comrades in Beijing.[157] The following day, the USSR sent out official invitations to the DRV and to the PRC.[158] The North Vietnamese—"especially comrade Le Duan," as the Soviets later claimed—eagerly agreed,[159] but, on April 8, when the first secretary of the VWP traveled to Beijing to persuade the Chinese comrades to participate, he received a rejection. Le later told the Soviets that the Chinese side "justified . . . its refusal with the disputes between the CPSU and the CCP" and indicated that talks can "only run on a bilateral basis."[160] That was a bitter blow for the Vietnamese, who obviously had anticipated China's endorsement of the new Soviet proposal. Before Le's departure from Hanoi, the VWP had left space open in the new issue of its central organ, *Nhan Dan*, for the publication of the expected statement on trilateral talks.[161]

Since Beijing had torpedoed almost all trilateral agreements, it could not leave the Vietnamese without any real commitments. On April 20 and 21, Vo Nguyen Giap was able to get an agreement from Luo Ruiqing and Yang Chengwu on the precise tasks of Chinese troops, promised since late 1964, in the DRV.[162] Yet, after several North Vietnamese leaders failed to receive China's endorsement for requests regarding aid for railway and

---

[156] "Directorate of the PCI," 5/21/1965, *FIG*, APC, Direzione 1965, vol. 29, 759. For the date of the visit: *NYT*, 4/23/1965, 3.

[157] "Note on a Talk with the Ambassadors of the Other Socialist States in the Embassy of the USSR on 4/2/1964," 4/2/1964, *PAAA-MfAA*, VS-Hauptstelle, Microfiche G-A 331, 3.

[158] The Soviet letters are in *AVPRF*, f.079, o.20, d.12, p.46, 72–73, and f.100, o.52, d.13, p.220, 18–19.

[159] "Note on a Joint Talk with the Ambassadors from Other Socialist Countries in the Hungarian Embassy," 5/12/1965, *PAAA-MfAA*, VS-Hauptstelle, Microfiche G-A 319, 1.

[160] "Information on the Visit to Moscow of the Delegation from the DRV," [no date], *AAN*, KC PZPR, XI A/76, 103.

[161] "Note on a Joint Talk with the Ambassadors from Other Socialist Countries in the Hungarian Embassy," 1.

[162] Zhang, "Vietnam War, 1964–1969," 742.

road construction, Ho Chi Minh was forced to travel to Changsha in May and June for talks with Mao. Following the finalization of the agreement in June, the PRC eventually sent Chinese road and railways engineering troops, anti-aircraft artillery, and military equipment to the DRV.[163] Ultimately, Chinese engineering troops built, within the territory of the DRV, important roads connecting North Vietnamese supply routes with the Ho Chi Minh trail.[164] On July 16, however, the PRC informed the DRV that "the time was not appropriate" to send Chinese pilots,[165] which Le Duan had asked for on April 8.[166] A year later, Beijing even claimed that it "has not enough air power to help defend Ha Noi."[167]

North Vietnam's struggle to reach an agreement with China over its military aid did not prevent the CCP from sending a letter to the CPSU on April 11 that attempted to justify its refusal to cooperate on a trilateral basis. According to the letter, "the Chinese and the Vietnamese side . . . have reached complete concord of opinion" in their most recent negotiations: "[There] is no necessity to conduct trilateral negotiations." The letter even tried to create the impression that *only* Beijing, and not Moscow, was aiding Hanoi, calling Soviet support "insignificant."[168] The message obscured the fact that, since February, China's obstruction had been the *main cause* of the allegedly insignificant amount of Soviet aid.

On April 10, Le Duan flew from Beijing to Moscow. The Kremlin "satisfied concrete requests by the Vietnamese comrades[169] and agreed to station in Vietnam various kinds of arms and military technology" worth "hundreds of millions of rubles." Le reportedly thanked the Soviet government for its "ample" aid.[170] The USSR committed military specialists and fighter aircraft. Until mid-1966, these specialists helped to create ten Vietnamese anti-aircraft missile regiments, three radio communication regiments, and two fighter aircraft regiments.[171] In Moscow, Le Duan "did not hide his dissatisfaction with the Chinese leaders," confessing that he could not understand why they "so stubbornly" rejected any joint action, why they considered the role of national liberation movements, such as the NLF, more important than the role of the socialist camp, or

[163] MacFarquhar, *Origins*, vol. 3, 371. Chen, *Mao's China*, 219.

[164] Chen, *Mao's China*, 221–29. McNamara, *Argument*, 264.

[165] SRV, *Truth*, 33.

[166] "Liu Shaoqi and Le Duan, Beijing, 4/8/1965," Westad, "77 Conversations," 85.

[167] SRV, *Truth*, 33.

[168] "CCP CC and PRC State Council to CPSU CC and USSR Minister Council," 4/11/1965, *SAPMO-BArch*, DY 30/3610, 6.

[169] "Information on the Visit to Moscow of the Delegation from the DRV," [no date], *AAN*, KC PZPR, XI A/76, 102.

[170] "CPSU CC to SED CC," 4/20/1965, *SAPMO-BArch*, DY 30/3610, 25.

[171] Zolotarev, *Rossiya*, 83, 85.

why they "considered themselves to be the sole true Marxists."[172] Finally, he did not rule out "political methods for the solution of the Vietnamese problems," even indicating that he was ready "to sit down . . . at the negotiation table with the USA." His only condition was the cessation of U.S. air raids.[173]

On the way home, Le Duan stopped over in Beijing. There, the Chinese criticized him for "allowing himself to get too close to modern revisionism." The Vietnamese first secretary replied curtly that "the CCP itself has entered a pact with Chiang Kai-shek against the Japanese [in 1937], and [that] he did not understand why the DRV should not expand and solidify its relations with another socialist country." But the Chinese continued to reject trilateral agreements on the grounds that "the differences in opinion with the CPSU are so big that it is impossible to sit down at one table."[174]

While Moscow was pledging vast sums of military aid to Hanoi, Beijing continued to speak of a Soviet sellout of Vietnam during the farewell talks of Soviet Ambassador Chervonenko in April. These meetings included a bizarre lunch between Zhou and Chervonenko on the thirteenth, which was being taped, probably so the Chairman could listen in. No wonder, then, that the Chinese prime minister ended each of his statements with a reference to "well-known sayings made by Mao Zedong."[175] The lunch was followed by a chat with Liu and Deng eight days later. Instead of microphones, Mao's left hand, Kang Sheng—"his majesty's eye"—was present, silently puffing one cigarette after another.[176]

While the second meeting was not particularly contentious, the talks with Zhou ended in a shouting match. Despite the fact that the Chinese prime minister had just been to Pakistan with the aim to use Ayub Khan as an intermediary to warn the United States not to carry the war into China,[177] he accused the Soviets of "treason" because they had supposedly contacted the Americans "behind the back of China and Vietnam" during the Vinogradov–de Gaulle talks on February 23. The rest of the

---

[172] "Note on a Joint Talk with the Ambassadors from Other Socialist Countries in the Hungarian Embassy," 4.

[173] "Information on the Visit to Moscow of the Delegation from the DRV," [no date], *AAN*, KC PZPR, XI A/76, 100.

[174] "Note on a Talk of Jarck with Freybort," 6/3/1965, *PAAA-MfAA*, VS-Hauptstelle, Microfiche G-A 331, 83.

[175] "Record of Conversation by Chervonenko with Zhou Enlai," 4/13/1965, *AVPRF*, f.0100, o.58, d.5, p.516, 101, n. 1.

[176] Brezhnev, *Kitai*, 103 (quote). The record of the second meeting: *AVPRF*, f.0100, o.58, d.5, p.516, 133–52.

[177] Zhai Qiang, "Beijing and the Vietnam Conflict, 1965–1968," *CWIHP Bulletin* 6–7, 233–50.

Chinese and Soviet delegations joined in, calling each other names. This ended only when food was served.[178]

Zhou's criticism of alleged Soviet revisionism was even more pronounced in his talk with Sergei Lapin, the new Soviet ambassador, in mid-May. The prime minister protested against "intimate" relations between Moscow and Washington: "The [Sino-Soviet alliance] treaty is directed against Japanese imperialism and its allies. That is American imperialism. [If the treaty] . . . is still in force, how then can one not oppose American imperialism, particularly when the Americans unleash a war in the Far East . . . ?" Zhou further charged that "the French public and the whole world press have been speaking about the proposed [peace] negotiations" after the Vinogradov—de Gaulle talks. Lapin, who had listened silently to Zhou's allegations, jumped in at this point, declaring that "the French press . . . had distorted" the talks. He even offered to request a copy of the transcripts for Zhou's use, but the prime minister could not be swayed.[179]

The Chinese subsequently tried to convince the North Vietnamese that the Soviets were untrustworthy because of their alleged contacts with the Americans on Vietnam. During Ho Chi Minh's visit to Beijing two days later, Zhou declared Moscow had "sold out its brothers" when, in February, it had pushed Hanoi to enter peace talks. Deng even claimed that the Soviets "provide you some aid for their own purposes. . . . If Vietnam finds it inconvenient to expose this fact, let us do it for you."[180] Chinese assertions, however, were increasingly removed from reality. During a meeting two days before, Gromyko had not even bothered to reply to Wilson's proposal for a new Indochina conference.[181]

After the Chinese had tried, unsuccessfully, to block the flow of parts of Soviet military technology to North Vietnam, it switched tactics to prevent their use on the battlefield. In June 1965, the first anti-aircraft missile SA-2 sets had arrived in the DRV.[182] Chinese military specialists in North Vietnam tried to denigrate Soviet missile technology as "unreliable and old."[183] For some weeks, field commanders decided not to use them against U.S. planes since, according to the Soviets, the Chinese had put

[178] "Record of Conversation by Chervonenko Zhou Enlai," 4/13/1965, AVPRF, f.0100, o.58, d.5, p.516, 102–105, 114–27.

[179] "Record of Conversation by Lapin with Zhou Enlai," 5/15/1965, AVPRF, f.0100, o.58, d.5, p.516, 191–227.

[180] "Zhou Enlai, Deng Xiaoping, and Ho Chi Minh, Beijing, 5/17/1965," Westad, "77 Conversations," 87.

[181] Mentioned in: NYT, 6/4/1965, 3. Christensen, "Worse," 90.

[182] Zolotarev, Rossiya, 86.

[183] Pikhoya, Sovetskii Soyuz, 266.

the North Vietnamese under pressure not to deploy them at all.[184] Chinese behavior was indeed curious since the PRC had successfully used the same missile to shoot down high-flying Taiwanese, U.S.-built spy planes since 1959.[185]

Once the North Vietnamese army decided to use the missiles in combat, Soviet technology proved to be too successful for its own good. On July 24, at their very first launching, Soviet missiles scored a double kill.[186] Subsequently, U.S. military planners ordered war planes to attack missile sites in the DRV systematically.[187] American pilots also learned to fool the SA-2 radar guidance systems through sharp maneuvers or low approaches.[188] By December, only 9 of 150 missiles launched had hit their target.[189] The Chinese were more than happy to utilize this development for their own propagandistic purposes.[190]

Beijing's joy over the supposedly antiquated Soviet military technology, however, could not conceal the fact that its strategy of fomenting national liberation and people's war in the Asian-African-Latin American intermediate zone had hit a dead end. In June, on the eve of the Second Afro-Asian Conference to be held in Algiers, the Algerian President Mohamed Ahmed Ben Bella, one of China's allies in that intermediate zone, was overthrown. Despite the political instability of Algeria, the PRC pushed for convening the conference in Algiers in order to exploit its numerical support within the Afro-Asian Movement. The conference, however, was ultimately postponed to early November 1965. Then, to insult came injury. In September, a right-wing coup in Indonesia not only removed Sukarno but wiped out the pro-Chinese Communists. And in the same month, India defeated China's ally Pakistan in a short war over Kashmir.[191]

China's response to these events reflected its ideological discourse in the run-up to the Cultural Revolution. In late September, Foreign Minister Chen Yi declared that the Chinese people were ready to make "giant sacrifices" in the "fight against U.S. imperialism" and against the "Indian and Japanese militarists." He even stated that the Afro-Asian Conference in November would "open up a new front in the struggle against 'cur-

[184] "Note on a Talk with an Employee of the International Department of the CC of the CPSU on the Situation in Vietnam," 7/9/1965, SAPMO-BArch, DY 30/3667.

[185] Fu, "Zuotian," 113–14.

[186] Gaiduk, Soviet Union, 59.

[187] NYT, 10/18/1965, 1, 6.

[188] NYT, 11/6/1965, 2.

[189] NYT, 12/8/1965, 16.

[190] "Record of Conversation with Zhao Yimin," 11/6/1965, AVPRF, f.0100, o.58, d.6, p.516, 12–16.

[191] Gittings, Survey, 247–48. Zhai, "Beijing and the Vietnam Conflict," 240. Zhai, "Beijing and the Vietnam Peace Talks," 24. Han, Eldest Son, 306.

rent revisionism.'"[192] China's attempt to mobilize the Asian-African-Latin American intermediate zone against Soviet revisionism, however, was not well received in the Afro-Asian countries.[193] The Second Afro-Asian Conference was never convened because the PRC ultimately chose to denounce what it could not completely control.[194]

Thus, in the late summer of 1965, the North Vietnamese leadership faced difficult choices. The VWP was internally split, as Le Duan had bemoaned in a *Hoc Tap* article published in July.[195] The Minister of Internal Affairs Ung Van Khiem, who was known for his pro-Soviet views, told the Hungarian Ambassador Imre Pehr that the Chinese "theory of 'modern revisionism' is a big lie, for no revisionist would have given such a support to the revolutionary struggle of a socialist country as the Soviet Union did."[196] An East German report of August 19 claimed that while the "fighters of the National Liberation Front still believe that only the PRC renders aid," Soviet military aid, worth one million rubles per day, had caused "Chinese propaganda about the lack of Soviet aid to lose ground" in the DRV. As a result, some of the "sensitive key comrades" in Hanoi were considering the "thought of negotiations." They were increasingly convinced, the report continued, that: *"The Chinese are ready to fight to the last Vietnamese, but otherwise are content to be left alone by the Americans."*[197] The PRC did not fail to note these changes in Hanoi. In a circular, also dated August 19, the Chinese Foreign Ministry noted that North Vietnam was under the influence of "Soviet revisionism," and had not "completely closed the door on peace talks."[198]

In the first half of October, Pham Van Dong traveled to Beijing and Moscow to "counsel with the fraternal parties." By then, the VWP had decided to continue the war "with military means," because it did not want to negotiate with the United States from a position of inferiority.[199] On Pham's first stopover in Beijing, Zhou asserted that "during the

[192] Speech abbreviated: "Information No. 51/65," 10/2/1965, *SAPMO-BArch*, DY 30/IV A 2/20/220, 2.

[193] *NYT*, 10/29/1965, 42.

[194] *NYT*, 11/7/1965, E3.

[195] *NYT*, 8/1/1965, 4.

[196] "Hungarian Embassy to North Vietnam Report, 9/1/1965," Balazs Szalontai, ed., "Selected Hungarian Documents on Vietnam, 1954–1966: Summaries," comp. and trans. for the conference "New Central and East European Evidence on the Cold War in Asia," Budapest, Hungary, 10/30–11/2/2003.

[197] "Note," 8/19/1965, *PAAA-MfAA*, Minister Kiesewetter, Microfiche A 17445, 2–3 (italics mine).

[198] Chinese Foreign Ministry Circular, "Vietnam 'Peace Talk' Activities," 8/19/1965," Zhai, "Beijing and the Vietnam Peace Talks," 33–34.

[199] "On the Policy of the Democratic Republic Vietnam," 12/8/1965, *SAPMO-BArch*, DY 30/J IV 2/2J/1559, 1–3.

time Khrushchev was in power, the Soviets could not divide us because Khrushchev did not help much. The Soviets are now assisting you. . . . The U.S. likes this very much." He concluded that the DRV "will be better without Soviet aid" because the latter provides Moscow with control over Hanoi's foreign policy. He reassured Pham that, unlike the USSR, the PRC "never think[s] of selling out Vietnam," but he bemoaned that, alas, "we are always afraid of the revisionists standing between us."[200]

In Moscow some days later, Pham accepted the offer to supply "some more hundreds of millions of rubles in aid," although the Soviets had the strong impression that the Chinese had tried to render pressure to the contrary on the North Vietnamese. While Moscow agreed with Hanoi's estimate that Washington did not want serious negotiations, it maintained that the refusal to negotiate was imprudent. In order to mobilize "support among Afro-Asian nations," the DRV should go on public record with a proposal for negotiations and let the subsequent, negative American attitude speak for itself. The stiff Vietnamese position, the Soviets argued, reminded too many Third World countries of China's current unconstructive position with regard to the Second Afro-Asian Conference.[201]

Soviet advice did not conform to Mao's vision. On October 20, he told Pham, who passed through Beijing en route to Hanoi, that negotiating with the Americans was useless. The PRC, Mao claimed, had been wasting time in low-level diplomatic talks with the United States on Taiwan for ten years.[202] During Ho Chi Minh's visit to Beijing in early November, the Chairman asserted that the DRV should not negotiate with the United States because "Vietnam will win" the war anyway. Thus, China would give only relatively little aid to the DRV, Mao continued, explaining his vision of joint national revolutions in the Asian-African-Latin American intermediate zone: "The largest [part of Chinese] assistance will be rendered through support for active military action against the U.S. in South East Asia (Laos, Thailand, Cambodia). With that, we will widen the anti-American front and thereby reduce the burden on the conduct of war by the DRV." The Chairman also urged Ho to cut all ties with the revisionist Soviets, warning the VWP about "the position it would get in, once revisionism had left the stage." After his return to Hanoi, Ho told a VWP plenum that he was "disappointed" with Beijing: "[It is] . . . astonishing that those who do not agree with the attitude of

[200] "Zhou Enlai and Pham Van Dong, Beijing, 4 P.M. 10/9/1965," Westad, "77 Conversations," 89–90.

[201] "On the Policy of the Democratic Republic Vietnam," 1–3.

[202] "Mao's Conversation with the Party and Government Delegation of the Democratic Republic of Vietnam, 10/20/1965," Zhai, "Beijing and the Vietnam Conflict," 245–46.

the VWP in all questions . . . supply greater and more unselfish aid. Those forces, with which the VWP has a lot of common points of view, . . . at the moment render less support than they are capable of."[203]

THE MICHAŁOWSKI AND SHELEPIN MISSIONS

In late 1965, the Johnson White House looked at Vietnam in gloom following an intense military clash between U.S. and DRV troops in Ia Drang Valley near the Cambodian border. The incident, which lasted from November 13 to 19, revealed the high degree of Northern infiltration into the South. It was against this background that, on December 29, the Johnson administration presented the Fourteen Points, which were much closer to the Four Points than Johnson's Baltimore speech. A thirty-seven-day American bombing pause of the DRV followed.[204]

As a part of Johnson's strategy to shore up international support for the Fourteen Points by sending U.S. diplomats to 145 countries, W. Averell Harriman, one of the president's top diplomats, turned to the Polish leader, Władysław Gomułka. In the past, Warsaw not only had been highly critical of China's stand on military aid and peace negotiations, but had also shown a particular interest in a new Indochina conference.[205] The Poles decided to send secretly a high-ranking Foreign Ministry representative, Jerzy Michałowski, to the Soviet Union, China, and North Vietnam with their own version of the Fourteen Points.[206] In Moscow, Gromyko welcomed the Polish mission in principle, but warned of too much enthusiasm. The Soviet foreign minister not only predicted Chinese "sabotage" attempts of the mission, but also was doubtful about any success in the DRV given that Hanoi had already indicated its opposition to the Fourteen Points.[207]

The talks Michałowski had with Wang Bingnan, newly appointed vice–foreign minister, and Yu Zhan in early January 1966 did not go well. The Chinese side called the Fourteen Points President Johnson's "new trick." Wang Bingnan—who had negotiated on the Taiwan issue

[203] "Winzer to Ulbricht, Stoph, Honecker," 12/21/1965, *SAPMO-BArch*, NY 4182/1222, 95–96. A similar report: "Report by Ivan Dimitrov—adviser," 12/14/1965, *AMVnR*, o.22, a.e.1549, 7–9.

[204] McNamara, *Argument*, 232–33, 236, 273–74.

[205] *NYT*, 12/4/1965, 2. McNamara, *Argument*, 233, 275. Gaiduk, *Soviet Union*, 83.

[206] "PUWP CC to CCP CC," 12/28/1965, *SAPMO-BArch*, DY 30/3654. "To VWP CC," 12/28/1965, *AAN*, KC PZPR, XI A/10, 681–82. James Hershberg, "Peace Probes and the Bombing Pause," *Journal of Cold War Studies*, 5/2, 51.

[207] Jerzy Michałowski, "Polish Secret Peace Initiatives in Vietnam," *CWIHP Bulletin* 6–7, 258.

with the Americans for many years without any result—told Michałowski that "peaceful negotiations are possible in principle, but only after a military victory, because nobody has ever won 'at the green table.'" When Wang started to abuse Michałowski verbally, the Polish diplomat decided to end the discussion.[208] After his departure, the CCP CC sent a letter to its Polish counterpart, accusing Poland of "cooperating with imperialism, . . . weakening the anti-imperialist activities of the Asian people, [and] isolating and opposing China." It concluded that China could never attend any conference on Indochina.[209]

Michałowski's meetings in Hanoi left him with the impression that the North Vietnamese leaders were divided about negotiations. Pham Van Dong claimed that they were "day and night think[ing] about how to end the war," but also remarked that the Americans had so far not fully realized "how difficult this war is for them." Ho Chi Minh and Foreign Minister Nguyen Duy Trinh refused the Fourteen Points, demanding another "Dien Bien Phu" as the basis for a new Indochina conference.[210] In late January, the North Vietnamese minister in Pyongyang told the East Germans that the DRV would attend a conference only together with the PRC and the USSR. No conference at all was still better than a failed one, because the latter would have "very disadvantageous consequences for the struggle in Vietnam."[211]

On January 15, on his way home, Michałowski stopped briefly in Moscow to report his own impressions to Vice-Foreign Minister Kuznetsov. The southern guerillas apparently were frightened of any negotiated settlement, because this would "lessen the influence of the NLF." Given that they were largely equipped with Chinese weaponry, they were also very receptive to Beijing's uncompromising stand on negotiations. As Michałowski claimed, "relations between the DRV and the National Liberation Front of South Vietnam . . . are highly complicated."[212]

While Michałowski believed that one of the major stepping stones to negotiations was the NLF, he probably exaggerated the possibility of conflict between Hanoi and the southern guerillas. Although the PRC had supported the NLF with military equipment, the building of transportation links to the Ho Chi Minh trail, and—above all—the ideological basis for the national liberation war, the chances of Beijing assuming political

[208] "Reception for Michałowski," 1/15/1966, *AVPRF*, f.0100, o.59, d.5, p.525, 2.

[209] Wang, *Zhonghua*, vol. 2, 272.

[210] "Reception for Michałowski," 2–3.

[211] "Note on Two Talks with the Minister Counselor of the DRV Embassy, Comrade Huon Muoi, on January 26, 1966 in the Cuban Embassy and on January 27, 1966 on the Occasion of a Farewell Visit in our Embassy," 1/27/1966, *PAAA-MfAA*, VS-Hauptstelle, Microfiche G-A 332.

[212] "Reception for Michałowski," 3–4.

domination over it were smaller than Michałowski imagined. In the end, the southern guerillas were the only leverage the DRV had in any negotiations. Hanoi simply could not accept point thirteen of Johnson's Fourteen Points, which demanded the end of North Vietnamese aggression against the south. For the DRV, this would have meant the abandonment of the NLF and, by extension, a loss of political influence in the RVN.[213]

Even before the Michałowski mission, Moscow had toyed with the idea of sending its own mission to Beijing and Hanoi, but had encountered Chinese resistance in the form of ideological warfare. In late September, Chinese propaganda denounced "the Soviet revisionist leading group" of taking "another step . . . in becoming an accomplice of U.S. imperialism," referring to the discussion between Soviet and American United Nations diplomats on Vietnam.[214] On the occasion of the forty-eighth anniversary of the October Revolution, Beijing announced that "compromise between the two lines is out of question."[215] But Moscow refused to accept silently Beijing's polemics any longer. In late November, *Pravda* remarked that the CPSU had been "striving for the cohesion of revolutionary forces" by "refrain[ing] over a year from open polemics." Now, it charged the CCP with harming "the entire international Communist and liberation movement."[216]

On November 28, Leonid Brezhnev wrote to Mao that he rejected "assisting" the PRC in allowing these "unprincipled squabbles" to become a justification for China's "refusal to defend fraternal Vietnam." He called on the Chinese to stop providing the Americans a pretext for escalating the war in Vietnam through the public display of disunity in the socialist camp. Instead, he concluded, "the CPSU and the CCP, the Soviet and the Chinese people as well as the peoples of the socialist camp" should act together "in the struggle for the liberation of [all] peoples from the yoke of exploitation and for the construction of a communist society."[217]

It was in this context that Moscow sent its own mission, headed by CPSU CC members Aleksandr Shelepin and Dmitrii Ustinov, to Beijing and Hanoi in early January 1966. On the way to Hanoi, the delegation stopped over in Beijing for a fifty-minute refueling break, during which Li Xiannian and some foreign ministry personnel, but no official party representatives, showed up.[218] That very day, the CCP also replied to Brezhnev's letter to Mao, accusing the Soviets of "clinging firmly to

[213] McNamara, *Argument*, 236–37.

[214] Quoted in: Zhai, "Beijing and the Vietnam Peace Talks," 10–11.

[215] *NYT*, 11/7/1965, E3.

[216] *NYT*, 11/28/1965, 1, 3.

[217] "CPSU CC to CCP CC," 11/28/1965, *SAPMO-BArch*, DY 30/3610.

[218] "Soviet-Chinese Relations (January–June 1966)," 10/13/1966, *AVPRF*, f.0100, o.59, d.16, p.526, 72. *SCMP* 3615, 33.

Khrushchev's policy of appeasing the American aggressors," for trying to win a "right of control, a right of a vote, and a right of representation" in the Vietnam question, and for trying to implement "great power chauvinism and to split the international communist movement."[219]

In Hanoi, Shelepin conferred primarily with Pham Van Dong, while Le Duan, Ho Chi Minh, and Politburo member Le Duc Tho stayed in the background. The Soviets had the impression that some pro-Chinese comrades in the VWP resented this visit, because they believed that the USSR was trying to "detach the DRV from the PR China." Yet, the Vietnamese central leaders made clear that "it was now the moment . . . to demonstrate a close relationship with the Soviet comrades."[220] Both sides agreed that only the Four Points should be the basis for negotiations. Pham explained that the DRV was not inflexible; it was internally discussing how it could determine "the advantageous moment" to bring about a negotiated settlement.[221] The Soviets agreed but, again, urged the North Vietnamese to do more "to explain the four points . . . to world public opinion." But the North Vietnamese and the Soviets differed on how to judge the role of the NLF in the war effort. The DRV leadership was convinced that NLF activities had thwarted major U.S. military actions. However, because the U.S. war potential was great, the Vietnamese comrades readily admitted to the Soviets that the NLF fighters "were unable to create a Dien Bien Phu."[222]

Finally, the talks turned to the role of the PRC in the war effort. The Soviets urged the Vietnamese to assert themselves against the Chinese, because Beijing's unconstructive position damaged Hanoi's cause. The Vietnamese replied, however, that the DRV was both too small and too dependent on Chinese economic assistance to assert itself. Ho Chi Minh, though, asserted privately that the current "military aid of the Chinese was insignificant."[223] The Vietnamese thus urged the Soviets to improve relations with the Chinese—for Vietnam's sake—although they admitted that "China's objections to Soviet aid are unjustified,"[224] and that the DRV "agreed completely with the Soviet policy toward America."[225]

[219] "CCP CC to CPSU CC," 1/1/1966, SAPMO-BArch, DY 30/3611.

[220] "Winzer to Ulbricht, Stoph, Honecker, Axen," 3/8/1966, SAPMO-BArch, DY 30/3667, 197–204.

[221] "Note on Two Talks with the Minister Counselor of the DRV Embassy, Comrade Huon Muoi, on January 26, 1966 in the Cuban Embassy and on January 26, 1966 on the Occasion of a Farewell Visit in our Embassy," 46.

[222] "Winzer to Ulbricht, Stoph, Honecker, Axen," 203.

[223] "Winzer to Ulbricht, Stoph, Honecker, Axen," 203.

[224] "Note on Two Talks with the Minister Counselor of the DRV Embassy, Comrade Huon Muoi, on January 26, 1966 in the Cuban Embassy and on January 26, 1966 on the Occasion of a Farewell Visit in our Embassy," 47.

[225] "Winzer to Ulbricht, Stoph, Honecker, Axen," 202–203.

The PRC was still unwilling to stop its polemics. During another stop-over in Beijing on January 13 and 14, Shelepin again suggested joint action. Li Xiannian rejected the proposal immediately and instead demanded that the USSR bring pressure on the Americans in West Berlin and West Germany.[226] Some days later, *Renmin Ribao* propaganda asserted that "the Soviet leaders . . . have actively peddled the peace talks swindle."[227] It was in this antagonistic context that, on January 18, Zhou Enlai demanded that the North Vietnamese cut all ties with the Soviet Union.[228]

The failure of the Miyamoto mission from February 10 to April 4 revealed Mao's hand in these accusations. The secretary general of the Japanese Communist Party, Kenji Miyamoto, visited the PRC with the purpose of promoting a socialist united front against U.S. imperialist aggression in Indochina. The trip included a ten-day visit to Hanoi at the end of February, during which Le Duan bemoaned how socialist disunity undermined his country's war effort: "We will be able to effectively counterattack if the Soviet Union and China take joint action with Vietnam."[229] In two rounds of talks with Liu Shaoqi and Deng Xiaoping at the beginning and the end of March, Miyamoto was able to work out an agreement for an anti-American united front in Asia, although his hosts initially demanded that the USSR open up a second front in Europe.[230]

With the political support which he got from the North Koreans for his mission during a eleven-day trip to Pyongyang,[231] Miyamoto flew to Shanghai to finalize the text of the accord with Mao. In the March 28–29 talks, however, the Chairman insisted that neither Liu nor Deng was authorized to work out such an agreement. Claiming that the Soviet Union had ceased to be a socialist country, he instead urged the formation of an anti-imperialist *and* anti-revisionist united front, denigrated Soviet aid to Vietnam, and accused his guests of pursuing a strategy in Indochina that could only please the revisionists. Although the Japanese party was among the few naysayers that had followed Mao's boycott of the concurrent twenty-third CPSU congress, its delegation realized only later how ill-timed the visit to Shanghai was. As a matter of fact, the talks with Mao occurred *immediately* after the Chairman's March 28 decision to

---

[226] Zhai, *China*, 165.

[227] *NYT*, 1/19/1966, 9.

[228] ZELNP3, 4.

[229] Masaru Kojima, ed., *The Record of the Talks between the Japanese Communist Party and the Communist Party of China* (Tokyo: Central Committee of the Japanese Communist Party, 1980), 57.

[230] Kojima, *Record*, 63–163, 169–69. Zhai, *China*, 154.

[231] Kojima, *Record*, 163–68.

attack Peng Zhen's CRSG in Beijing and his announcement to call for an attack on the Central Committee, as related in chapter 9.[232]

China's antagonistic attitude toward negotiations was rooted in Mao's view of the country's place in the world and, ultimately, its domestic politics. Starting in 1962, the Chairman had emphasized the Asian-African-Latin American intermediate zone and subsequently implemented policies to exclude Soviet influence. Also, since the fall of 1965, the theme of a hostile encirclement had become obvious in Chinese public statements. A *Peking Review* article titled "Trends of Imperialism" spoke of an "Anti-China Holy Alliance" encompassing the United States, the USSR, Japan and India.[233] The rhetorical creation of a besieged fortress thus became a rationale for domestic action. The Chairman had already used this device during the Second Taiwan Strait Crisis. In 1966, the alleged anti-imperialist conflict abroad created the background for the struggle against revisionists and capitalists at home. Ostensibly, Mao opposed a socialist united front not on the ground of real evidence that Moscow was colluding with Washington, but on the basis of his own ideological and rhetorical needs in the run-up to the Cultural Revolution.

VIETNAM AND THE TWENTY-THIRD CPSU CONGRESS

Against CCP pressure, the VWP sent a delegation to the twenty-third CPSU congress. On the way to Moscow, Le Duan passed through Beijing on March 22–25.[234] Zhou warned him of Soviet attempts "to win your trust in a deceitful way," which aimed at "split[ting] Vietnam and China . . . [and] obstructing the struggle and revolution of the Vietnamese people." He apparently believed that Le Duan was flying to Moscow for another round of Soviet-Vietnamese military talks. In the end, the Chinese prime minister claimed that "opposing the US should necessarily go hand in hand with opposing revisionism."[235] According to rumors at the time, the Chinese side tried to punish the Vietnamese for their independence by curtailing the transport of Soviet military and economic aid through the PRC for some weeks.[236]

At the congress, both the Soviets and the Vietnamese decided not to pour more fuel on the fire. In his official report on March 29, Leonid Brezhnev did not mention China at all when addressing Soviet support

[232] Kojima, *Record*, 197–231. Zhai, *China*, 154. SRV, *Truth*, 39.

[233] *PR* 7 (2/11/1966), 17.

[234] *NYT*, 4/1/1966, 6.

[235] "Zhou Enlai and Le Duan, Beijing, 3/23/1966," Westad, "77 Conversations," 93–94.

[236] *NYT*, 3/20/1966, 1, 9.

for national liberation movements.[237] The next day, Le Duan read Ho Chi Minh's greetings, giving thanks for the "warm support and valuable assistance of the Soviet Union, China, and other socialist countries," to which the congress responded with "thunderous and extended applause."[238] In a personal meeting on April 11, Brezhnev asked Le Duan to convey a message to Mao that he was ready "to meet with him at any time and in any form," stressing that "improvement of relations between the USSR and the PRC would be an effective step to the strengthening of the general struggle against imperialism."[239]

Le Duan's meetings with the Chinese comrades during his stopover in Beijing were unpleasant. Having allegedly called the Soviet Union his "second motherland" during the CPSU congress,[240] the Vietnamese party leader was confronted with a "list with all dates and locations, at which . . . [he] had made remarks against the Chinese leaders."[241] Zhou prohibited Le from "mention[ing] Chinese aid at the same time as Soviet aid." The PRC, he claimed, considered this "an insult." Seemingly fed up with Chinese accusations, Le Duan rejected the Chinese accusation "that the Soviets are selling out Vietnam."[242] In light of the clashes between Le and the Chinese leaders, the Vietnamese party subsequently decided not to send its own first secretary to Beijing for further negotiations. It wanted to preclude the possibility "that the attitude of the Chinese toward the DRV worsens."[243] China's ideological radicalization in the run-up to the Cultural Revolution and its impact on the North Vietnamese war effort frustrated Ho Chi Minh, who "expressed disagreement with the developments in China" to Shcherbakov.[244]

In the context of its ideological chimeras on world affairs, the Chinese side had long since been chipping away at the Sino-Soviet alliance treaty. Since the fall of 1965, Chinese comrades had insinuated that, in league with the American imperialists and the Japanese and Indian militarists, Soviet revisionists were trying to encircle the PRC.[245] Starting in late February 1966—after the Michałowski and the Shelepin missions—the Chinese press carried articles that implicitly compared "Soviet . . .

[237] "Report by Brezhnev," 3/29/1966, *RGASPI*, f.593, o.1, d.1, 45–56.

[238] "[Speech by] Le Duan," 3/30/1966, *RGASPI*, f.593, o.1, d.3, 48.

[239] Istochnik, "Zapis Besedi," *Istochnik* 1998/3, 129.

[240] Quoted in: Chen, *Mao's China*, 232.

[241] "Note of Conversation by Bergold with Siedliecky," 11/10/1966, *SAPMO-BArch*, DY 30/3667, 213.

[242] "Zhou Enlai, Deng Xiaoping, Kang Sheng and Le Duan, Nguyen Duy Trinh, Beijing, 4/11[?]/1966," Westad, "77 Conversations," 96, n. 145, and 97.

[243] "Note of Conversation by Bergold with Siedliecky," 213.

[244] "Report by Vasil Dimitrov," 7/8/1966, *AMVnR*, o.22, a.e.779, 58–61.

[245] "Information No. 51/65," 10/2/1965, *SAPMO-BArch*, DY 30/IV A 2/20/220, 2.

collaboration with the United States in a military encirclement of Communist China" with the "'capitalist encirclement' propounded by Stalin after the Bolshevik Revolution."[246] On May 17, in an interview with Scandinavian journalists, Chen Yi went further, stating that in case of a military aggression against the PRC, China "will be forced to wait for aid from the USSR."[247] Although the Sino-Soviet military alliance had been in dire straits for many years, by 1966 it had effectively died over diplomatic and military strategy in Vietnam.

In *Argument without End*, a collection of edited transcripts from two conferences held in the 1990s, American and Vietnamese scholars, together with participants in the events of almost forty years ago, tried to come to terms with why the United States and the DRV had been unable to prevent the tragedy of the Vietnam War. While they identified many missed opportunities, strangely, they did not address the Soviet and the Chinese influence.[248] Indeed, in the crucial time after the Gulf of Tonkin Incident, Moscow and Beijing were important players in the wings.

The PRC had made commitments to the DRV almost since its foundation on October 1, 1949. They were rooted in both ideological affinities and in Mao's decision to engage in an active defense against supposed American imperialist aggression at three fronts: Korea, Taiwan, and Vietnam. This commitment included diplomatic recognition in early 1950, military aid during the First Vietnam War, substantial economic aid afterward, and renewed military commitments since mid-1964. Yet, from the Gulf of Tonkin Incident to mid-February of 1965, Mao remained convinced that the door to an international conference should be kept open. Following a change of mind, however, Beijing pursued a hard line, rejecting any negotiated settlement, advocating people's war as the only method to fight the war, and attempting to control, and even limit, Soviet military and diplomatic assistance.

In comparison, Soviet economic and military aid to Vietnam from 1950 to late 1964 was much smaller than that of the Chinese. In the late years of Khrushchev's rule, Soviet support dwindled, largely as a result of the North Vietnamese support for Chinese ideological positions on world revolution. This hands-off policy remained in place after the Gulf of Tonkin Incident until Khrushchev's removal from office. Although Mao held Khrushchev's successors to be ideological carbon copies of the fallen leader, in fact, they radically overhauled Soviet policy toward the

[246] *NYT*, 2/6/1966, 1.
[247] "Inter-Governmental Relations of the PRC with the Soviet Union," 11/11/1966, *AVPRF*, f.0100, o.59, d.16, p.526, 117–18. Also: Kapitsa, *Na raznykh parallelyakh*, 76.
[248] McNamara, *Argument*, 399–408.

Second Vietnam War, much to the detriment of relations with the United States. Indeed, Moscow's 180-degree turn was so rapid that it surprised, and even worried, Beijing.

China's hard-line policy combined with the rapidly increasing Soviet engagement in Vietnam after mid-February of 1965 exacerbated the existing Sino-Soviet disagreements. While Mao had always been quick to accuse the Soviet Union of great power chauvinism in its relations with other socialist countries, China's policy of trying to define the military and political terms of the Second Vietnam War on behalf of the DRV was similarly high-handed. Simultaneously, Beijing asserted the right to define Sino-Soviet alliance obligations on its own terms. It not only demanded that Moscow cut all its relations with Washington, but in early 1966 also requested the USSR put pressure on the United States in Berlin and West Germany; unless, that is, the Soviet leaders wanted to go down in history as traitors to the alliance and to world revolution. The Sino-Soviet treaty, however, did not include any provisions that the PRC could invoke if a third fraternal country fought with imperialism. It only stipulated "military and other assistance" in the event that "*one of the High Contracting Parties* [is] being *attacked* by Japan or states allied with it."[249] Vietnam was not a party to the Sino-Soviet alliance.

Although Moscow lacked sensitivity toward Beijing's justified security needs, the Chinese accusation of Soviet treason was far-fetched. In fact, the post-Khrushchev leadership was willing to engage in the DRV, to risk its own specialized troops, its air force, and much aid while endangering relations with the United States with which it was negotiating a Nuclear Proliferation Treaty. Concerns over security thus only partially explain Chinese hyperbole. In reality, the accusation was politically useful to Mao. It prevented Moscow from what he feared was an attempt to wrest control over the Vietnam War from Beijing. It also aligned with the intensifying ideological struggle abroad and at home in the run-up to the Cultural Revolution. Ultimately, these accusations buried the Sino-Soviet military alliance, which Mao had already started to deride years before. The Vietnam War simply served as the catalyst for the final collapse of the Sino-Soviet military partnership.

[249] Article I of treaty in: Hinton, *People's Republic*, vol. 1, 123–24 (italics mine).

Conclusion

BUTTRESSED by the Soviet–Outer Mongolian alliance of January 1966 and following the final deterioration of Sino-Soviet relations shortly thereafter, the USSR stationed troops, heavy weaponry, and even missiles at the Chinese border. By 1968, six divisions were stationed in Outer Mongolia[1] and another sixteen were stationed at the Sino-Soviet border. They faced forty-seven lightly armed Chinese divisions.[2]

In November 1967, border skirmishes occurred on the frozen rivers of the eastern sector.[3] After the first (Chinese) fatalities on January 5, 1968,[4] the CCP MAC cabled instructions to the Shenyang military region on the planning of a "counterattack in self-defense" at a "politically opportune moment." While no more clashes occurred before the ice thawed,[5] incidents did resume the following winter.[6] On February 19, 1969, the PLA General Staff and the PRC Foreign Ministry agreed to an ambush on Zhenbao/Damanskii Island planned by Heilongjiang provincial military command.[7]

On March 2, Soviet border troops opened fire as soon as they realized that they were facing an ambush. At least thirty-one Soviet border guards were killed; the number of Chinese troops lost is unknown.[8] Suddenly fearing a "large-scale conflict,"[9] the PRC wanted to limit the scale of the confrontation, as Zhou told Chen Xilian, the commander of the Shenyang military region: "We are rational, . . . if we start war it will be part of a world war, we don't want to expand the conflict."[10]

---

[1] Thomas Robinson, "The Sino-Soviet Border Conflict," Stephen Kaplan, ed., *Diplomacy of Power* (Washington: Brookings, 1981), 272.

[2] Thomas Robinson, "China Confronts the Soviet Union," Roderick MacFarquhar et al., eds., *The Cambridge History of China*, vol. 15 (Cambridge: Cambridge, 1991), 292, 299.

[3] Li Ke et al., *Wenhua dagemingzhong de renmin jiefangjun* (Beijing: Zhonggong dangshi ziliao chubanshe, 1989), 317.

[4] Gong Li, "Chinese Decision Making and the Thawing of U.S.-China Relations," Ross, *Re-examining the Cold War*, 329. Yang Kuisong, "The Sino-Soviet Border Clash of 1969," *Cold War History* 1/1, 24–25.

[5] Xu Yan, "1969nian ZhongSu bianjie de wuzhuang chongtu," *Dangde yanjiu ziliao* 1994/5, 5.

[6] Yang, "Border Clash," 25.

[7] Li, *Wenhua*, 319.

[8] Barbara Barnouin et al., *Chinese Foreign Policy during the Cultural Revolution* (London: Kegan Paul, 1998), 88.

[9] *ZELNP3*, 284–85.

[10] Gao, *Wannian Zhou Enlai* (New York: Mingjing, 2003), 402.

The March 2 incident completely surprised Moscow.[11] Although the USSR informed its East European allies about "necessary steps to prevent further border violations,"[12] Soviet border troops and regular units were ordered to counterattack. The Soviet ambush in the early morning hours of March 15, however, did not go as planned.[13] Although the Chinese lost a high but unsubstantiated number of lives while the Soviets suffered relatively few fatalities, the PRC was able to maintain its positions on the island.[14]

The failure to retake Zhenbao/Damanskii Island came as a shock to the Soviet leadership. As early as the afternoon of March 15, Soviet radio stations beamed Chinese-language broadcasts into the PRC elaborating on the capabilities of the Soviet nuclear missiles.[15] Although no more clashes occurred on the frozen rivers in the Eastern sector, both sides continued to militarize the entire length of the border.[16]

Beijing was equally concerned about its international position. On March 14 (American time), at almost the same time as the Soviet ambush in the early morning of March 15 (East Asian time), U.S. President Richard Nixon officially announced the establishment of a new Anti-Ballistic Missile system. In an attempt to ensure continued nuclear negotiations with the Soviets, the president publicly justified this system not as a safeguard against a Soviet strike but as one against "any attack by the Chinese Communists that we can foresee over the next 10 years."[17] This revelation disturbed Mao greatly. In a meeting of the Cultural Revolution leadership on the afternoon of March 15, he admitted: "We are now isolated. No one wants to make friends with us."[18]

A March 21 attempt by Kosygin to reach Mao by the high-frequency phone line failed because the Chinese operator refused to connect the

[11] Shevchenko, *Breaking*, 164–65.

[12] "Document No. 1: Soviet Report to GDR Leadership on 2 March 1969," Christian Ostermann, ed., "East German Documents on the Sino-Soviet Border Conflict, 1969," *CWIHP Bulletin* 6–7, 189–90.

[13] Li, *Wenhua*, 321–23.

[14] A Russian source mentions forty-eight Soviet and eight hundred Chinese troops killed: "Itar-Tass Weekly News," 2005-03-03 ITA-No., http://dlib.eastview.com.ezp2.harvard .edu/searchresults/article.jsp?art=16, accessed on June 10, 2005.

[15] *Guardian*, 3/20/1969, 1.

[16] "Memorandum for Col. Haig," 3/27/1969, *National Archives and Record Administration* [*NARA*], NIXON, NSC, Box 711, USSR Vol. 1 [Dec 68–Dec. 69] [3 of 3]. "From American Embassy in Moscow to Department of State," 4/5/1969, NARA, State Department, RG 59, Central Files, 1967–1969, Box 1850, POL—POLITICAL AFF. & REL. ASIA 1-1-67.

[17] *NYT*, 3/15/1969, 16.

[18] Gong, "Chinese Decision Making," 323.

call, cursing the Soviet prime minister as a "revisionist element."[19] Zhou was aghast: "The two countries are at war, one cannot chop the messenger."[20] He proposed to Mao to keep the communication channels of the foreign ministry open. The Chairman agreed: "Immediately prepare to hold diplomatic negotiations."[21] No high-level negotiations, however, materialized.

Under Soviet prodding,[22] the two sides eventually agreed to fifteen rounds of talks by the low-level Sino-Soviet Commission on the Navigation of Boundary Rivers between June 18 and August 8.[23] Five days after their collapse, another major border clash occurred at the western sector of the Sino-Soviet border.[24] In its immediate aftermath, the USSR again threatened nuclear war.[25] In reality, though, the Soviet leadership was in a stalemate over the use of nuclear weapons and would eventually dismiss it as an unfeasible option against a populous country like China.[26]

At an August 18 lunch meeting, Boris Davydov, the second secretary of the Soviet Embassy in Washington, asked William Stearman, a midlevel State Department official, "point blank what the US would do if the Soviet Union attacked and destroyed China's nuclear installations."[27] The lack of Soviet documentation, however, makes it difficult to assert whether this was a bluff or actual policy. Anyway, nine days later, the State Department and the CIA announced that the USSR had reportedly sounded out its Warsaw Pact allies about "a conventional attack to destroy China's nuclear weapons center at Lop Nor."[28] The following day, once Beijing had received the news,[29] it ordered the general mobilization of the PLA and massive civilian and military preparations against a Soviet attack.[30]

[19] "Dear Comrades," 4/2/1969, *SAPMO-BArch*, DY 30/3613, 16–17. Yang, "Border Clash," 32. Wang Yongqin, "1966–1976nian ZhongMeiSu guanxi jishi (lianzai yi)," *Dangdai Zhongguo shi yanjiu* 1997/4, 119 (quote).

[20] Gao, *Wannian*, 402–3.

[21] ZELNP3, 286.

[22] *Pravda*, 3/30/1969, 1. *NYT*, 5/5/1969, 3.

[23] Liu Zhinan, "1969nian, Zhongguo zhanbei yu dui MeiSu guanxi de yanjiu he diaozheng," *Dangdai Zhongguo shi yanjiu* 1999/3, 54.

[24] Yang, "Border Clash," 34.

[25] Xiong Xianghui, "Dakai ZhongMei guanxi de qianzhou," *Zhonggong dangshi ziliao* 42, 79–80. Liu, "1969nian," 45.

[26] Shevchenko, *Breaking*, 165–66.

[27] "Memorandum of Conversation," 8/18/1969, *NARA*, State Department, RG 59, Central Files, 1967–1969, Box 1529, DEF 12 CHICOM.

[28] *NYT*, 8/28/1969, 8; 8/29/1969, 5.

[29] Wang Yongqin, "1969nian: ZhongMei guanxi de zhuanzhedian," *Dangde wenxian* 1995/6, 78.

[30] "The CCP Central Committee's Order for General Mobilization in Border Provinces and Regions, 28 August 1969," Chen Jian et al., eds., "All under Heaven Is Great Chaos," *CWIHP Bulletin* 11, 168–69.

On September 9, 1969, under pressure from the communist parties of Romania, North Vietnam, and Italy to find a negotiated solution,[31] Kosygin tried to contact the Chinese delegation during Ho Chi Minh's funeral service in Hanoi.[32] The Soviet prime minister met his Chinese counterpart two days later at Beijing Airport. After reviewing Sino-Soviet relations,[33] Kosygin and Zhou agreed to normalize governmental relations and to seek a negotiated solution to the border problems.[34] In the immediate aftermath, Mao and Zhou were hopeful that the prospect of negotiations would diffuse the border conflict.[35] The Chinese prime minister even started to draft a letter with concrete proposals to relax the situation.[36]

On September 16, however, Soviet leaks on preparations for an air raid on the PRC nuclear weapons test site alarmed the Chinese leadership yet again.[37] Although the U.S. embassy in Moscow assumed that they were a part of psychological warfare,[38] Mao and Zhou grew suspicious about the motives behind Kosygin's visit to China. Comparing it with Japan's duplicitous behavior before the attack on Pearl Harbor, the Chinese leadership came to believe that the USSR was using diplomacy to mask its war preparations.[39] Of particular concern to Beijing was the fact that Washington had not indicated where it stood on the matter after it had revealed Moscow's supposed diplomatic inquiries in East Europe on August 27. In another instance of erroneous historical analogy, the Chinese leadership concluded that the United States not only supported Soviet policies but deliberately waited for war to break out, as it had in both world wars, in order to reap the spoils after joining in later.[40] The final version of Zhou's letter to Kosygin, sent on September 18, included

---

[31] According to what the Romanians told the Americans later: "Airgram from U.S. UN delegation to Department of State," 10/2/1969, *NARA*, State Department, RG 59, Central Files, 1967–1969, Box 1974, POLITICAL AFF. & REL. CHICOM-USSR 10/1/1969.

[32] Cong Wenzi, "Zhongshi waijiao diaoyan, shanyu zhanlüe sikao," *Waijiao xueyuan xuebao* 2001/4, 8.

[33] Kapitsa, *Na raznykh parallelyakh*, 81–92.

[34] "Document No. 3: Soviet Report on 11 September 1969 Kosygin-Zhou Meeting," Ostermann, "East German Documents," *CWIHP Bulletin* 6–7, 191–93.

[35] *ZELNP3*, 321. Gong, "Chinese Decision Making," 335.

[36] Niu Jun, "1969nian Zhongguo bianjie chongtu yu Zhongguo waijiao zhanlüe de tiao-zheng," *Dangdai Zhongguo shi yanjiu* 1995/6, 73.

[37] *London Evening News*, 9/18/1969, 7.

[38] "From American Embassy in Moscow to Secretary of State," September 19, 1969, *NARA*, State Department, RG 59, Central Files, 1967–1969, Box 1975, POLITICAL AFF. & REL. 8/1/69.

[39] Yang, "Border Clash," 39. Niu, "1969nian," 74.

[40] Liu, "1969nian," 46.

not only proposals on border negotiations but also the demand to stop threats against China's nuclear weapons project.[41]

At the same time, the Chinese leadership started with emergency preparations for war. When Moscow's September 26 reply asked for negotiations to begin in the Chinese capital on October 10, Beijing believed this reply indicated the approximate date when war would begin. While Zhou immediately responded with a request to postpone the talks for another ten days,[42] presumably to gain more time for war preparations, Lin Biao nevertheless ordered the PLA on full alert on September 30 in anticipation of a Soviet attack on China's National Day, October 1.[43]

Although the Chinese leadership was surprised when the Soviet attack did not come on October 1, it remained suspicious.[44] War preparations continued.[45] In the expectation of a Soviet attack around the start of the border negotiations on October 20, the top Chinese leaders left Beijing for different locations throughout the PRC with the dual purpose of escaping possible capture and of being in the right places to lead local guerilla wars after the Soviet invasion.[46] Simultaneously, a mass campaign to build air-raid shelters gathered momentum in urban centers.[47] On October 17, Lin Biao ordered the PLA on emergency alert.[48]

The Soviet Union, however, attacked neither after the start of the Sino-Soviet border talks nor after their failure on December 11.[49] Nevertheless, the PRC continued to suffer from a "war psychosis" given that the border rivers would soon freeze.[50] The relative quiet on the Sino-Soviet borders in the winter of 1969/70 eventually convinced the Chinese leadership that the worst was over. On May 1, Mao Zedong received the head of the Soviet border negotiation delegation on Tiananmen—a rare honor—announcing: "We should negotiate well, should have good-neighborly relations, should be patient, and only fight with words."[51]

[41] "Letter, Zhou Enlai to Alexei Kosygin, 18 September 1969," Chen, "All under Heaven," 171–72.

[42] ZELNP3, 322–23.

[43] Liu, "1969nian," 48. Zheng Qian, "Zhonggong dajiu qianhou quanguo de zhanbei gongzuo," Zhonggong dangshi ziliao 41, 219.

[44] Yang, "Border Clash," 40.

[45] Zheng, "Zhonggong," 221.

[46] Liu, "1969nian," 48–49. Zheng, "Zhonggong," 219. Xiong, "Dakai," 91. ZELNP3, 329.

[47] Yang, "Border Clash," 41.

[48] Wang, "1966–1976nian," 124–25. Yang, "Border Clash," 41.

[49] Li, "Changes," 313. ZELNP3, 338.

[50] "Dear Comrade Fischer," 11/28/1969, PAAA-MfAA, Abteilung Ferner Osten -Sektor China, Microfiche C 186/74, 86.

[51] Zhang Baojun, "1969nian qianhou dang dui waijiao zhanlüe de zhongda tiaozheng," Zhonggong dangshi yanjiu 1996/1, 63.

. . .

In a narrow sense, the Sino-Soviet crisis in 1969 was the product of a limited, premeditated border skirmish gone awry. The combination of hardball tactics by the Soviets and of the negative impact of China's self-isolation on its ability to function in international relations helped to bring about a veritable war scare in the PRC. In a larger perspective, the border conflict was the consequence of territorial disputes that predated, but were exacerbated by, the Sino-Soviet ideological disputes. The border clashes were *not* a part of the Sino-Soviet Split, just its most visible consequence.

What caused the Sino-Soviet Split? While many factors were significant, this book has argued that among all the causes, ideology was the most important. Ideological disagreements revolved around three issues: economic development, de-Stalinization, and international relations—peaceful coexistence and world revolution.

As early as 1955, Mao had rejected the socioeconomic development model (Bureaucratic Stalinism) the PRC had adopted from the USSR. The structural economic crisis China faced in the mid-1950s was genuine. While the industrial sector had grown as a result of Soviet investments, agriculture continued to lag behind and thus threatened the country's economic health. Because Soviet credits were ending in the late 1950s, a surplus of agricultural products was supposed both to maintain the industrial sector *and* to repay the loans. Mao thus concluded that only rapid agricultural development could fulfill both these needs. However, the solution—Mao's promotion of rural policies similar to Revolutionary Stalinism—was highly ideological rather than pragmatic. It is important to note that there was no absence of alternatives; the Chinese leadership discussed Bukharinite, Titoist, and Bureaucratic Stalinist solutions, but Mao rejected all of them for ideological reasons. Nonsocialist policies, as adapted after his death, did not even cross his mind. The Socialist High Tide was eventually launched in the second half of 1955 but ran into problems similar to, though not as severe as, those of Stalin's agricultural policies from the early 1930s.

The failure of the Socialist High Tide became apparent in early 1956, at the same time that Khrushchev began criticizing Stalin. At its eighth congress in September, the CCP returned to Bureaucratic Stalinist socioeconomic policies. Under the influence of the Hungarian Revolution, however, Mao again rethought that development model. Unlike Khrushchev, who promoted de-Stalinization in the political and ideological sphere (see below), the Chairman was willing to consider the de-Stalinization of China's economic system. The resulting liberal political and economic experiments in early 1957, however, did not survive the

Anti-Rightist Campaign of the summer. Criticism raised by intellectuals and technical specialists during the Hundred Flowers Campaign discredited both Bureaucratic Stalinism and these experiments.

The Great Leap Forward was a great flight away from the problems that had emerged in the 1955–57 period. Even more radical than the Socialist High Tide, it took inspiration from Revolutionary Stalinism, the Yan'an myths, and Mao's criticism of Bureaucratic Stalinism. Its collapse in late 1960 triggered a short period of sensible reform, which Mao increasingly considered a reintroduction of capitalism in China. The debates on economic policy from 1962 to 1966 were largely a function of the Chinese leadership struggle before the Cultural Revolution.

The Sino-Soviet disputes over political and ideological de-Stalinization that emerged in 1956 quickly overshadowed the Chinese disagreement with the Bureaucratic Stalinist economic development model. Khrushchev's condemnation of Stalin's personality cult threatened to undermine the domestic position of the Chairman. Mao thus tried to pursue the double strategy of limiting the discussion of de-Stalinization in the PRC and using Stalin's supposed mistakes in the Chinese revolution to protect his own personality cult. The eighth CCP congress, however, undercut some of Mao's prerogatives for a brief time. While considering the de-Stalinization of China's economy, the Chairman blamed Khrushchev's political and ideological de-Stalinization for the Polish October and the Hungarian Revolution. Using his extraordinary skill at political maneuvering and manipulation, he was eventually able to overturn the decisions of the eighth CCP congress. Simultaneously, he launched the Great Leap Forward with the stated aim of avoiding the mistakes Stalin had committed in the early 1930s.

By 1959, Mao's personal and political ambitions triggered criticism both at home and abroad. As the Lushan conference in mid-1959 revealed, several Chinese leaders disagreed both with his Stalin-like personality cult and his deceptively positive portrayal of the Great Leap Forward. Fearing for his political survival, Mao turned this well-founded criticism into a supposed conspiracy against him. While he was able to overcome his mostly imaginary foes at home, the Soviet comrades increasingly saw him as a second Stalin. De-Stalinization subsequently disappeared, almost completely, as a topic in the Sino-Soviet debates, with the exception of the twenty-second CPSU congress in 1961 and the Stalin polemic of 1963.

The major issue that dominated Sino-Soviet debates in the 1960s—the correct policy line in international relations—had been only a minor irritant in Sino-Soviet disagreements during most of the 1950s. In 1954, together with India, China had proclaimed peaceful coexistence—Pancha Shila. Khrushchev's proposal for peaceful coexistence at the twentieth

CPSU congress in early 1956 expanded this idea into the arena of super-power conflict. Initially, the PRC supported Khrushchev's new policy in the hope that it might solve the Taiwan Question. However, the Polish October and the Hungarian Revolution prompted the first doubts, which were eventually reinforced by the failure of Khrushchev's peaceful co-existence policy to produce tangible results in the Taiwan Question. The Second Taiwan Strait Crisis in 1958 was Mao's deliberate challenge to Khrushchev's strategy of peaceful coexistence.

During 1959, Mao's criticism of Khrushchev's conduct in international affairs changed from the rejection of peaceful coexistence to radical support for world revolution. This change of heart was the result of two mutually enforcing developments. On the one hand, China's hard-line response to the Tibetan Uprising not only destroyed Pancha Shila but also provoked the Sino-Indian Border War. On the other, Mao's views on international relations had been radicalized since early 1959. Although the Second Taiwan Strait Crisis had sorted out some of the issues between the United States and China, the Chairman, more strongly than before, saw American imperialism in the darkest colors.

After the Lushan meeting, Mao developed uncompromising views on the correct kind of relationship that socialist countries could have with imperialist ones. This, however, did not prevent the PRC from cooperating with them economically after the 1960 withdrawal of the Soviet specialists. By 1962, the Chairman discarded the socialist camp as the primary agent in world revolution and, instead, turned his sights on national liberation movements in the Asian-African-Latin American intermediate zone. In turn, he accused the Soviet Union of selling out world revolution and of instigating the restoration of capitalism.

The ideological debates on economic development, de-Stalinization, and world revolution raise a fundamental question: did the Chinese leaders in general, and Mao in particular, use ideology as a genuine belief system or as an instrumental device? Clearly, the Chinese leaders were committed communists from a very early point in their political careers, though their individual understanding of Marxism-Leninism varied. There is no evidence that they were pure cynics who used ideological claims in a deceitful manner to achieve goals contrary to larger Marxist-Leninist postulates.

There are several clear instances when ideology served either as a belief system or as an instrumental device. The basic conception of the Great Leap Forward, on the one hand, grew out of a genuine belief in its ideological correctness. This does not contradict the fact that it was foolish, because a lack of understanding of Marxism-Leninism does not preclude a sincere belief in it. There are several instances, on the other hand, in which Mao used ideological arguments to protect his own position, such as in the spring of 1956 or in the summer of 1959. During the Anti-Rightist Campaign of 1957, the Chinese leadership collectively used pronunciations of ideological correctness to smother political dissent inside and outside of the party. And in mid-1959 and after the summer of 1962, Mao used the same tactic to attempt to silence dissent within the party leadership.

De-Stalinization, from the Secret Speech to the Anti-Party Incident to the twenty-second CPSU congress, rattled Sino-Soviet relations, although it was primarily rooted in genuine Soviet internal debates between old Stalinist stalwarts and reformers over the future of the USSR. In comparison, Mao's instrumental use of ideology in domestic politics contributed to the worsening of Sino-Soviet relations to a much greater degree. His increasing, though probably unfounded, suspicion during the first half of the 1960s that his fellow leaders were out to depose him led the Chairman to exaggerate Soviet revisionism for domestic political purposes.

Yet, the mutual influence of domestic and foreign policy was a two-way street, particularly in China. Events in Hungary in late 1956, for example, greatly influenced Mao's thinking on reform at home. Without the Hungarian Revolution, he would not have revisited the viability of Bureaucratic Stalinism for China nor would he have been willing to engage in liberal experiments. Conversely, the extremism of the Great Leap Forward demanded the instigation of a foreign policy crisis for mobilization purposes. Indeed, the timing of the Second Taiwan Strait Crisis was closely linked to the launching of the commune movement and other radical policies in the later summer of 1958. Similarly, in the mid-1960s, Mao seemed to accelerate the Sino-Soviet split for his domestic agenda in the run-up to the Cultural Revolution.

Apart from ideology and its connections to domestic politics, several other factors helped to intensify Sino-Soviet antagonism. There is no doubt that the newly established PRC sought security in an alliance with the USSR against what it perceived as an inherently aggressive, revanchist, and imperialist United States. Yet, this ideologically distorted view of the world only helped to create greater security problems after 1949. China's recognition of the DRV and its commitment to the Korean War even before its outbreak elicited the stiffening of American positions on Vietnam, Taiwan, and Korea. Not only did the continued militarization of these three fronts over the following two decades exacerbate the negative consequences of the country's increasing self-isolation but it also threatened to undermine the Sino-Soviet alliance. After provoking the Second Taiwan Strait Crisis in 1958, the PRC tried to involve the Soviet Union in a nuclear war with the United States. It was one of the reasons why Moscow approved nuclear negotiations with Washington. Although the ensuing LNTB did not restrict the PRC from developing its own nuclear weapons, it was a major political blow for the country and its place in world affairs. Finally, China's active defense of Vietnam since 1950, as well as its constant emphasis on national liberation since 1962, helped to undermine its security after the Gulf of Tonkin Incident in August 1964.

In addition, the unequal positions of the two alliance partners within the international system increasingly separated them. On the one hand, the Soviet Union was a world power with an increasing number of commitments. These obligations, such as the Soviet-Indian friendship and superpower rapprochement over nuclear weapons, were at the root of some of the problems in the Sino-Soviet alliance. The PRC, on the other hand, was a regional power with a limited number of commitments; it was also a country that became increasingly isolated after the late 1950s, largely on account of Mao's choice. Despite claims of equality within the socialist camp and despite its difference in size from most other socialist states, the PRC was *never* equal to the Soviet Union in either the socialist camp or in world affairs. Although Chinese claims to that effect gained acceptance among some socialist states and a small number of communist parties, the majority of the international communist movement regarded Mao's China as the odd man out.

What set Mao apart from other wannabe leaders of the socialist camp was not only the size of the country he headed or the ideological pretensions he entertained, but the talent and tenacity with which he exploited conflict among diverse Soviet commitments across the world. Soviet-American rapprochement in 1959–60 served Mao to launch public polemics in early 1960, the LNTB helped him to prove the revisionism of the Soviet leadership, and the Second Vietnam War, despite Moscow's support of Hanoi, provided a platform from which the Chairman could accuse Soviets of duplicity. Mao's skills were almost matched by Khrushchev's clumsiness. The USSR was imprudent in responding so negatively to both the Sino-Indian Border Wars and the Chinese polemics of 1963–64. Soviet reactions were also often disproportionate, as revealed by the withdrawal of the specialists in 1960.

There is no doubt that personality issues contributed to the worsening of the Sino-Soviet alliance. Mao's eccentricity and megalomania irritated the Soviets. His claim that the Great Leap Forward would enable the PRC to enter communism before the Soviet Union was galling to Khrushchev. The Chairman's arrogance peaked in 1963 when he claimed that Beijing had become the center of world revolution. Khrushchev's behavior, however, could be equally harmful to Sino-Soviet relations. As his 1958 proposal to station submarines in China revealed, he did not fully understand Chinese sensitivities over sovereignty. The Soviet leader could also be brash and downright rude, especially when, in early 1960, he compared Mao to an old pair of discarded shoes, or, the following year, he told Zhou that the CPSU no longer needed the advice of the CCP.

Territorial conflicts, by contrast, were not at the root of the Sino-Soviet conflict. Although the mutual border was partially unmarked and the PRC had not really relinquished its claim on Outer Mongolia, conflicts emerged only in the wake of the ideological disputes that began in 1960. Tenuous evidence suggests that China instigated border incidents in order to exploit them in ongoing Sino-Soviet negotiations, regardless of their relation to or independence of the border issues.

Finally, accidents contributed to the collapse of the Sino-Soviet partnership. Most importantly, the U-2 Incident was a propaganda boon for the CCP, which did not waste any time to press its radical ideological points while alienating the CPSU and its allies in the process. The Cuban Missile Crisis in 1962 and the Malinovskii incident two years later had a similarly inadvertent negative impact. However, had it not been for Mao's willingness to use them for his own needs, they would not have had such disproportionably negative effects on Sino-Soviet relations.

This all brings us to a crucial question: could the split have been avoided if the one or the other factor had been removed from these events? Obviously, counterfactuals are not hard evidence; they are only argumentative devices that, if applied carefully, help us to consider possible alternatives. What if, for example, Stalin had not died but continued to live into old age, been intellectually alert, and remained politically active? In that case, the ideological disagreements would not have emerged, or at least not in such an acute form. Mao would certainly not have enjoyed the same room to maneuver that Khrushchev unwittingly allowed him to occupy. Indeed, Stalin's seniority, combined with his distinctively central position in the communist world, would have hardly allowed for ideological or political plurality. Given that Khrushchev played the China card in 1954 and 1957 in order to buy Chinese support for his struggle against the remaining Stalinist stalwarts, Stalin's continued presence at the helm of the Soviet Union would probably not have led to the greater economic assistance that the PRC actually received after his death. Even if the great Soviet dictator was not prone to committing gaffes or embarking on adventurous policies as Khrushchev repeatedly did, he still had his track record of devastating blunders that might have had a negative effect on his relations with Mao. Furthermore, his history of selling out foreign communist parties whenever it served his purposes might not have boded well for China. Stalin was an international leader who demanded loyalty from everybody else but was loath to return any.

What if Khrushchev had not come to power but the Soviet Union had been run by another leader closer to Stalin's outlook? While many of the considerations in the paragraph above probably apply, developments in Sino-Soviet relations after 1953 would have also been dependent on who exactly succeeded Stalin. One of Stalin's closest associates that had participated in the October Revolution certainly would have commanded a great degree, though not all, of Stalin's authority in the communist world. A junior leader, by contrast, would have faced Mao's scrutiny, given that the Chairman dismissed the younger Khrushchev as immature as early as 1956. Such a successor might also have initiated necessary domestic reforms to shore up popular support, though on a smaller scale and with greater caution than Khrushchev. This might have led to a limited pluralism within the socialist world that, in turn, may have provided Mao with enough leeway to push through his own radical ideas. Regardless, the potential for conflict would certainly have been smaller.

What if Mao had died early or had been removed from power between 1956 and 1966? Since he was the dominant person in the worsening Sino-Soviet relationship, this is probably the most significant counterfactual consideration. As in Lenin's case, Mao's early death would have enabled him to enter history as a great revolutionary without being blamed for his subsequent mistakes while running China. Similarly, his removal for political mistakes at the eighth CCP congress in 1956, at the Lushan meeting in 1959, or at the 7,000-Cadres Conference in 1962 would have prevented him from causing further damage to the economic health and physical security of the PRC. There is little doubt that Mao was one of the most radical among the Chinese top leaders. Although Zhou, Liu, and Deng repeatedly sided with the Chairman by supporting his extreme policies, there is enough evidence to suggest that all three were comparatively moderate leaders who were capable of implementing reasonable policies. They also lacked the inflated ego of the Chairman, which made collective decision making in China so difficult and teamwork almost impossible. While Sino-Soviet disagreements may have been much less confrontational, the alliance might still have lost its internal glue over time. It would have been unlikely, however, for the alliance to degenerate into outright hostility.

What were the actual chances for Mao to be removed from power? In fact, they seemed to be limited from the beginning and were getting progressively smaller as the Sino-Soviet disagreements continued. Mao's personality cult, which the party had nourished since 1945 for political reasons, had, in the mind of many Chinese citizens, inextricably linked the Chairman to the new regime. As Zhang Wentian realized in 1959, Mao's removal may have meant a mortal blow to the party and, in turn, to the communist regime at large. In a perverse sense, then, the CCP was stuck with Mao; even if many party members might have disagreed with his radical positions, he had become indispensable to the continuation of communist rule.

Finally, was there anything Khrushchev could have done to prevent the Sino-Soviet split after his delivery of the Secret Speech? Although the Soviet leader should have done many things differently, it still does not mean that an alternative course of action could have prevented the alliance from collapse. Khrushchev's impulsiveness, his lack of consideration, and his propensity to make unfounded claims or embark on adventurous but potentially damaging policies all contributed to the split. However, they were *not* major factors in bringing about the split. The principal problem was that once he had let the genie of ideological pluralism out of the bottle, only a master politician could have tempted it back in. Thus, with de-Stalinization, the Soviet empire of ideological unity had vanished forever. Yet, as the worsening of Sino-Soviet relations continued, there was increasingly less left for Khrushchev to keep the alliance alive—short of complete ideological surrender. Of course, no great power would have ceded leadership of its domain to an ally that was militarily less powerful, economically weaker, and run by a radical megalomaniac. Only in Mao's fantasy world was this possible; few inside the PRC and even fewer outside, however, shared the Chairman's monumental delusions.

Essay on the Sources

AFTER MUCH THOUGHT, I decided to replace a conventional bibliography with an essay on the most important sources. The inclusion of a chapter-length, comprehensive bibliography in this book would have required substantial cuts to all chapters. A complete bibliography is available for downloading on the PUP website as long as this book is in print (http://pup.princeton.edu/) and on my own official university website.

I had the good fortune of using a unique combination of archival sources and published material from China, the former Soviet Union, Poland, former East Germany, the Czech Republic, Hungary, Bulgaria, Italy, and the United States. Many of these sources became available either after the end of the Cold War or only very recently.

For the Chinese side, published documents and memoirs have been the most important basis for this book. Particularly useful were *Jianguo yilai Mao Zedong wengao* (*JYMW*),[1] which reproduces many internal documents, and *Neibu cankao* (NC),[2] the confidential news bulletin for the top party leadership, which contains intelligence on domestic events and translations of foreign news reports. *Neibu cankao* provides unique insights into what information China's central leaders received on a daily basis.

Although no personal recollection by any of China's highest leaders has surfaced, many of their immediate subordinates and assistants have published memoirs. They are frequently Sino-centric and unapologetic, but they nevertheless contain interesting details on Sino-Soviet relations. The most important personal recollection is Wu Lengxi's *Shinian lunzhan* (WLX).[3] Wu attended many of the Politburo meetings relevant to foreign relations as the semi-official note taker and debriefed Chinese leaders after meetings with Soviet leaders. Despite its Mao-centered outlook, it will remain the most important source on the making of Chinese foreign relations for the 1956–66 period in the near future.[4] Other important,

---

[1] Mao Zedong, *Jianguo yilai Mao Zedong wengao*, 13 vols. (Beijing: Zhongyang wenxian, 1987–98).

[2] Xinhua tongxunshe, *Neibu cankao* (Beijing: Xinhua tongxunshe, 1949–).

[3] Wu Lengxi, *Shinian lunzhan, 1956–1966* (Beijing: Zhongyang wenxian, 1999).

[4] John Garver, "Review Article: Mao's Soviet Policies," *China Quarterly* 173 (March 2003), 197.

though less detailed, memoirs come from Russian language interpreters,[5] Mao's secretaries,[6] economic specialists,[7] party and governmental diplomats,[8] and interview projects.[9] Despite some initial doubts, the occasionally sensational memoirs of Mao's personal physician Li Zhisui turned out to be a relatively reliable source that I could verify through comparisons with other Chinese memoirs and even Russian documents.[10]

Political considerations and restricted access to original documentation pose great problems for Chinese secondary literature. Nevertheless, several insightful and critical analyses of China's foreign relations[11] and

[5] Li Yueran, "Huiyi Mao Zedong Zhuxi," Pei Jianzhang, ed., Xin Zhongguo waijiao feng yun, vol. 2 (Beijing: Shijie zhishi, 1991), 1–14. Li, Waijiao wutai shang de Xin Zhongguo lingxiu (Beijing: Jiefangjun, 1989). Li, "Woguo tong Sulian shangtan," Jianzhang, Xin Zhongguo, vol. 2, 15–18. Li, "Wo zai Zhou Enlai shenbian gongzuo de pianduan huiyi," Jianzhang, Xin Zhongguo, vol. 1, 86–98. Shi Zhe, "With Mao and Stalin," Chinese Historians 5/1, 35–46. Shi, and Li Haiwen, Zai lishi juren shenbian, rev. and exp. ed. (Beijing: Zhongyang wenxian, 1998). Yan Mingfu, "Huiyi liangci Mosike huiyi he Hu Qiaomu," Dangdai Zhongguo shi yanjiu 1997/3, 6–21. Yan, "Peng Zhen zai Bujialeisite huiyi shang," Dangdai Zhongguo shi yanjiu 1998/3, 71–86. Yan, "Yi Zhou zongli 1964nian fang Su," Zhonggong dangshi ziliao 65, 7–19.

[6] Hu Qiaomu, Hu Qiaomu huiyi Mao Zedong (Beijing: Renmin, 1994). Li Rui, Li Rui wenji, 3 vols. in 4 books (Haikou: Nanfang, 1999). For Lin Ke: Wang Fang, ed., "Mao Zedong bang le lao Jiang yi ba," Chang Cheng, ed., Zhiqingzhe shuo, vol. 1 (Zhongguo qingnian, 1995), 125–48. Wang, ed., "Xiaosa moru Mao Zedong," Cheng, Zhiqingzhe shuo, vol. 1, 95–124.

[7] Bo Yibo, "The Making of the 'Lean-to-One Side' Decision," Chinese Historians 5/1, 57–62. Bo, Ruogan zhongda juece yu shijian de huigu, 2 vols. (Beijing: Zhonggong zhongyang dangxiao, 1991–93).

[8] Hao Deqing, "Waijiao gongzuo sanshinian," Waijiaobu waijiaoshi yanjiushi bian, Dangdai Zhongguo shijie waijiao shengya, vol. 2 (Beijing: Shijie zhishi, 1995), 63–70. Liu Xiao, Chushi Sulian banian (Beijing: Dangshi ziliao, 1998). Liu Ying, "Bu xunzhang de dashi," Waijiaobu, Dangdai, vol. 2 (Beijing: Shijie zhishi, 1995), 1–29. Su Shifang, "Guanyu 50-niandai wo guo cong Sulian jinkou jishu he chengtao shebei de huigu," Dangdai Zhongguo shi yanjiu 1998/5, 48–50. Wu Xiuquan, Eight Years in the Ministry of Foreign Affairs (Beijing: New World, 1985). Yu Zhan, "Yici bu xunchang de shiming," Jianzhang, Xin Zhongguo, vol. 3, 14–30. Zhang Dequn, "Zai Mosike liunian ban," Zhonggong dangshi ziliao 58, 31–41. Zhu Zhongli, "Wang Jixiang waijiao shengya zong yi," Waijiaobu, Dangdai, vol. 1 (Beijing: Shijie zhishi, 1994), 1–33.

[9] Ding Ming, ed., "Huigu ge sikao," Dangdai Zhongguo shi yanjiu 1998/2, 20–36.

[10] Li Zhisui, The Private Life of Chairman Mao (New York: Random, 1994).

[11] Cong Jin, Quzhe fazhan de suiyue (Zhengzhou: Henan renmin, 1989). Dangdai Zhongguo congshu, Dangdai Zhongguo waijiao (Beijing: Zhongguo shehui kexue, 1988). Li Lianqing, Lengnuan suiyue: yibosanzhe de ZhongSu guanxi (Beijing: Shijie zhishi, 1998). Li Danhui, "1969nian ZhongSu bianjie chongtu," Dangdai Zhongguo shi yanjiu 1996/3, 39–50. Li, "Dui 1962nian Xinjiang Yita shijian qiyin de lishi kaocha," http://www.shenzhihua.net/muluzhong.htm, accessed on November 15, 2004. Li, "Genyu shijie gonglian Beijing huiyi de ruogan wenti," http://www.shenzhihua.net/muluzhong.htm, accessed on November 15, 2004. Li, "ZhongSu guanxi yu Zhongguo de yuanYue kangMei," Dangdai Zhongguo shi yanjiu 1998/3, 111–26.

the history of the PRC[12] have been published. *Nianpu* (life chronicles) of Peng Dehuai (*PDHNP*) and Zhou Enlai (*ZELNP*1-3)[13] are obviously based on archival documentation otherwise not available, as are the biographies of Mao Zedong and Wang Jiaxiang.[14]

On the whole, Chinese published sources are especially strong for the 1950s and the early 1960s. For the period after 1964, however, the quantity and quality of primary documentation, memoirs, and secondary works quickly decline. Particularly with regard to foreign relations, the inward turn of the PRC in the run-up to and during the Cultural Revolution was devastating. More generally speaking, Chinese authorities seem still reluctant to allow research on one of the darkest phases in modern Chinese history.

Unfortunately, the *Zhongyang Dang'anguan* (*CCP Central Archive*), which contains the most important primary documentation on the history of the PRC, is still closed. Nevertheless, I found very interesting sources in the *Jiangsu Sheng Dang'anguan* (*Jiangsu Provincial Archives*; *JSSDAG*), including transcripts of Politburo meetings, speeches and reports by central leaders, CC directives, and memoranda. The holdings at *JSSDAG* on foreign relations are particularly strong for the 1958–64 period, during which the central leadership tried to mobilize the provincial party for its domestic and foreign policies. Apart from an interesting group of documents on the war preparations of 1965, very few documents on foreign relations are available for the 1964–68 period, with none accessible for subsequent years. By mid-2006, just as this manuscript entered its final writing stage, the *Waijiaobu Dang'anguan* (PRC Foreign Ministry Archive) opened selected holdings for the 1956–60 period. After consulting several historians who were among the first to work with the newly opened collections, I concluded that these documents, which mostly stem from the bureaucracy but occasionally include conversations by Mao and Zhou with foreign (but *not* Soviet) representatives, would only add more detail rather than additional substance to the manuscript. In the end, historical monographs are always unfinished construction sites.

[12] Chen Shihui, "1959nian Lushan huiyi jishi," *Zhonggong dangshi ziliao* 28, 111–49. Pei Jianzhang and Wang Taiping, *Zhonghua renmin gongheguo waijiaoshi*, 3 vols. (Beijing: Shijie zhishi, 1994). Xiao Donglian, *Qiusuo Zhongguo*, 2 vols. (Beijing: Hongqi, 1999). Zhu Ren, "Lishi zai zheli guaiwan," Chang, *Zhiqingzhe shuo*, 2nd ser., vol. 4 (Zhongguo qingnian, 1999), 93–143.

[13] Wang Yanzhu, ed., *Peng Dehuai nianpu* (Beijing: Shijie zhishi, 1998). Zhonggong zhongyang wenxian yanjiushi bian, *Zhou Enlai nianpu, 1949–1976*, 3 vols. (Beijing: Zhongyang wenxian, 1997).

[14] Zhonggong zhongyang wenxian yanjiushi bian, *Mao Zedong zhuan (1949–1976)*, 2 vols. (Beijing: Zhongyang wenxian, 2003). Xu Zehao, *Wang Jiaxiang zhuan* (Beijing: Dangdai Zhongguo, 1996).

Similar to the *Zhongyang Dang'anguan* (*CCP Central Archive*), the most important Russian archive, the *Arkhiv Prezidenta Rossiiskoi Federatsii* (*Presidential Archive of the Russian Federation*), which holds the Presidium records and the papers of the most important Soviet leaders, is no longer accessible to researchers. At the CPSU archives, the situation was mixed when I conducted research in 2002. The *Rossiiskii Gosudarstvennyi Arkhiv Sotsialno-politicheskoi Istorii* (*Russian State Archive of Socio-Political History*; *RGASPI*), which holds most, though not all, of the documentation until 1953, contained interesting records such as the Otto Kuusinen files (fond 522, opis 3), materials on the genesis of the third CPSU party program of 1961 (fond 586, opis 1), and documents on the twenty-third CPSU congress in 1966 (fond 593, opis 1). The *Rossiiskii Gosudarstvennyi Arkhiv Noveishei Istorii* (*Russian State Archive of Contemporary History*; *RGANI*), which maintains mostly documents for the post-Stalin period, was virtually inaccessible, with the exception of the files of the Party Control Commission (fond 6). Luckily, several holdings that were closed in 2002 are available in German and American research libraries in the form of incomplete microfilm collections, such as the files from various CPSU congresses (fond 1), transcripts of CC plena (fond 2), and files of the Department for Relations with Foreign Communist Parties, 1953–57 (fond 5, opis 28; unfortunately, some important files, such as delo 407 with information on the impact of Khrushchev's Secret Speech on China, are not available on microfilm). The *Gosudarstvennyi Arkhiv Rossiiskoi Federatsii* (*The State Archive of the Russian Federation*; *GARF*) and the *Rossiiskii Gosudarstvennyi Arkhiv Ekonomiki* (*Russian State Archive of the Economy*; *RGAE*) offer records on economic cooperation, but usually run out of material by the mid-1950s. The *Arkhiv Vneshnei Politiki Rossiiskoi Federatsii* (*Archive of Foreign Policy of the Russian Federation*; *AVPRF*) mostly holds documentation on meetings between Soviet diplomats and Chinese leaders, diplomatic traffic, and internal reports on foreign relations. Despite the inaccessibility of the most important files, such as the office of the foreign minister, *AVPRF* turned out to be the most important Russian archive for this book. I was able to push declassification of the files on China (fond 100/0100) and Vietnam (fond 79/079) up to 1966, but was unable to gain access to the collections on India (fond 90/090) and Albania (fond 67/067). Materials on Tibet were closed for political reasons.

Some Soviet primary documents have been published in Russian-language editions. A collection of complete and fragmentary CPSU Presidium records provides some information on China.[15] All other document

---

[15] Aleksandr Fursenko, ed., *Prezidium TSK KPSS 1954–1964*, 2 vols. (Moskva: ROSSPEN, 2003–6).

publications relevant to this book focus only on one aspect of Soviet foreign relations, such as de-Stalinization, the Polish October, the Hungarian Revolution, the Anti-Party Incident, or Khrushchev's fall.[16]

Compared to China, Russia has produced only a small number of memoirs and secondary sources on Sino-Soviet relations. Apart from several memoirs that raise relations with China in passing,[17] only three explicitly deal with the relationship between Moscow and Beijing.[18] Boris Kulik is the only Russian to publish an analysis of Sino-Soviet relations after the end of the Cold War.[19] A former Soviet diplomat, he is wedded to a Marxist interpretative framework and largely bases his arguments on Chinese published sources.

Throughout my research, the problem of accessibility to China's and Russia's central archives was so serious that it called for imaginative solutions. Archives of the former fraternal countries and parties provided a great amount of evidence for this book. Transcripts of meetings between Chinese and Soviet leaders, protocols of conferences attended by parties from the entire socialist camp, memoranda of conversations, and letters are available in either the original language (Russian, Chinese, and French in the case of letters from North Vietnamese leaders) or translations into the local languages in Bulgaria (*Tsentralen Drzhaven Arkhiv* [*Central State Archive*; *TsDA*]), the Czech Republic (*Státní Ústřední*

[16] A. Artizov et al., *Reabilitatsia* (Moskva: Mezhdunarodnyi fond 'Demokratiya,' 2000). Istoricheskii Arkhiv, red., "SSSR i Polsha: oktyabr 1956-go," *Istoricheskii Arkhiv* 5–6, 178–91. Tofik Islamov et al., eds., *Sovetskii Soyuz i vengerskii krizis 1956 goda* (Moskva: ROSSPEN, 1998). N. Kovaleva et al., eds. *Molotov, Malenkov, Kaganovich, 1957* (Moskva: Mezhdunarodnyi fond 'Demokratiya,' 1998). Istochnik, "Doklad Prezidiuma TsK KPSS na oktiabrskom Plenume TsK KPSS," *Istochnik* 1998/2, 102–25. Istochnik, "Zapisi V. Malina na zasedanii Prezidiuma TsK KPSS," *Istochnik* 1998/2, 125–43. Istochnik, "Zapis Besedi," *Istochnik* 1998/3, 124–30.

[17] A. Aleksandrov-Agentov, *Ot Kollontai do Gorbacheva* (Moskva: Mezhdunarodnye otnosheniya, 1994). Georgii Arbatov, *The System* (New York: Times, 1993). Fedor Burlatskii, *Khrushchev and the First Russian Spring* (New York: Charles Scribner's Sons, 1988). Anatolii Dobrynin, *In Confidence* (New York: Times, 1995). Nikita Khrushchev, *Khrushchev Remembers*, 3 vols (Boston: Little, Brown, 1970–90). Anastas Mikoyan, *Tak bylo* (Moskva: Vagrius, 1999). Vladimir Semichastnyi, *Bespokoinoe serdtse* (Moskva: Vagrius, 2002). Petro Shelest, *Da ne sudimy budete* (Moskva: edition q, 1994). Arkadii Shevchenko, *Breaking with Moscow* (New York: Knopf, 1985). Oleg Troyanovskii, *Cherez gody i rasstoyaniya* (Moskva: Vagrius, 1997).

[18] Aleksei Brezhnev, *Kitai* (Moskva: Mezhdunarodnye otnosheniya, 1998). Lev Delyusin [Jieliuxin Lie Bie], "Guanyu SuZhong chongtu qiyin de ruogan sikao," *Dangdai Zhongguo shi yanjiu* 1998/3, 100–10. Delyusin, "Nekotorye razmyshleniya o nachale sovetsko-kitaiskogo konflikta," paper presented at the conference "Sino-Soviet Relations and Cold War: International Scientific Seminar," Beijing, China, October 1997. Mikhail Kapitsa, *Na raznykh parallelyakh* (Moskva: Kniga i biznes, 1996).

[19] Boris Kulik, *Sovetsko-kitaiskii raskol* (Moskva: RAN, Institut Dalnego Vostoka, 2000).

Archiv [*Central State Archiv*; *SÚA*]), (former East) Germany (*Stiftung Archiv der Parteien und Massenorganisationen der DDR im Bundesarchiv* [*Archive of the Parties and Mass Organizations of the GDR in the Federal Archives*; *SAPMO-BArch*]), Hungary (*Magyar Országos Levéltár* [*Hungarian National Archives*; *MOL*]), Italy (*Fondazione Istituto Gramsci* [*Foundation Institute Gramsci*; *FIG*]), and Poland (*Archiwum Akt Nowych* [*Archive of Modern Records*; *AAN*]). Transcripts of meetings with Soviet and Chinese leaders by representatives of third parties, reports on conversations with the Soviet ambassadors in Beijing and Hanoi, and embassy reports on the situation in the PRC and the DRV are widely available in the foreign ministry archives in Bulgaria (*Arkhiv na Ministerstvoto na Vnshnite Raboti* [*Archive of the Ministry of Foreign Relations*; *AMVnR*]), (former East) Germany (*Politisches Archiv des Auswärtigen Amtes, Bestand: Ministerium für Auswärtige Angelegenheiten* [*Political Archive of the Office for Foreign Affairs, Files: Ministry for Foreign Affairs*; *PAAA-MfAA*]) and Poland (*Archiwum Ministerstwa Spraw Zagranicznych* [*Archive of the Ministry for Foreign Affairs*; *AMSZ*]). Some of the archival documentation mentioned above is also available in the Russian and East European Archive Documents Database (RADD) at the *National Security Archive* (*NSA*), where historians have generously donated copies of the documents they found in Soviet and East European archives.

The quantity and quality of documents from the fraternal archives is particularly strong for the time after the mid-1950s, mainly for three reasons. First, the Soviet Union started to trust its East European satellite states in the late 1950s to a much greater degree than during the Stalin period and the years immediately thereafter. Second, documentation from archives of East European foreign ministries reflects the gradually increasing professionalization of their diplomatic corps over the course of the 1950s. This is particularly true for East Germany, which, after 1949, had to build up its foreign policy apparatus from scratch. However, no East European country had an extensive history of relations with East Asia until the PRC and the DRV joined the socialist camp in 1949/50. Because it took most of the 1950s to educate and prepare specialists for diplomatic duties in East Asia, including interpreters, it is no surprise that archival documentation for the initial period is rather weak. Finally, it is also clear that the Soviet Union tried to mobilize its fraternal allies once the Sino-Soviet disagreements began in the late 1950s. Soviet material, in the form of memoranda or transcripts of conversations between Russian and Chinese representatives, frequently emerges in various archival collections in East Europe. By the early 1960s, the Soviet ambassador and his East European counterparts also worked as a team in Beijing and Hanoi, regularly exchanging information.

A small but significant number of translated primary and secondary sources from China, the former Soviet Union, and East Europe has been published. The bulletin and the working papers of the *Cold War International History Project* (*CWIHP*) have pioneered this undertaking, providing numerous documents from China, Vietnam, and the Soviet Union that have only recently been declassified. Two older publications provide excellent material on the Sino-Soviet polemics in the 1960s.[20] A more recent volume edited by O. Arne Westad combines newly released internal documentation with articles by specialists on various aspects of the Sino-Soviet alliance in the 1950s and 1960s.[21] Harold Hinton has produced an excellent three-volume collection of documents on the domestic and foreign policies of the PRC.[22] Speeches by Mao have been published in English, both in official[23] and unofficial translations.[24]

Several German and English translations of Soviet and East European material focus on individual events or particular aspects of Sino-Soviet relations: Sino–East German relations including materials on the Sino-Soviet split,[25] the Warsaw Pact decision to build the Berlin Wall, including its connections to China,[26] and documents on the Hungarian Revolution that shed some light on Sino-Hungarian relations in late 1956.[27] Two conference readers with translated documents from the Hungarian and Romanian archives provide insight into the Sino-Soviet split and its impact on Vietnam.[28]

---

[20] Peter Berton, *The Chinese-Russian Dialogue* (Los Angeles: Southern California, 1964). John Gittings, *Survey of the Sino-Soviet Dispute* (London: Royal Institute of International Affairs, 1968).

[21] O. Arne Westad, ed., *Brothers in Arms* (Washington: Woodrow Wilson Center, 1998)

[22] Harold Hinton, ed. *People's Republic of China, 1949–1979*, 5 vols. (Wilmington: Scholarly Resources, 1980).

[23] Mao Zedong, *Selected Works*, 5 vol. (Beijing: Foreign Languages, 1961–1977). Mao, *On Diplomacy* (Beijing: Foreign Languages, 1998).

[24] Roderick MacFarquhar et al., eds., *The Secret Speeches of Chairman Mao* (Cambridge: Harvard, 1989). Mao Zedong, *Miscellany of Mao Tse-tung Thought* (Washington: JPRS, 1974). Also various issues of the journal *Chinese Law and Government*.

[25] Werner Meissner et al., eds., *Die DDR und China 1949 bis 1990* (Berlin: Akademie, 1995).

[26] Bernd Bonwetsch et al., eds., "Chruschtschow und der Mauerbau," *Vierteljahresheft für Zeitgeschichte* 48/1, 155–98.

[27] Csaba Békés et al., eds., *The 1956 Hungarian Revolution* (Budapest: Central European, 2002).

[28] Balazs Szalontai, ed., "Selected Hungarian Documents on Vietnam, 1954–1966," comp. and transl. for the conference "New Central and East European Evidence on the Cold War in Asia," Budapest, Hungary, October 30–November 2, 2003. Mirca Munteanu, ed., "Documents from the Romanian Communist Party Archive and the Archive of the Romanian Ministry of Foreign Affairs on the Vietnam War, 1965–1966," comp. for the International Conference "The Vietnam War: Thirty Years On," Temple University, Philadelphia, June 20–21, 2005.

For chapter 8, I used the *John F. Kennedy Library and Museum* which provided fascinating materials on Kennedy's obsession with the Chinese nuclear weapons project in 1962 and 1963. The *Foreign Relations of the United States (FRUS)* series supplied many important documents on U.S. policy toward China in general. State Department holdings and the Nixon Papers at the *National Archives and Records Administration (NARA)* in College Park, Maryland, contain important materials on the Sino-Soviet border conflict in 1969.

In the end, newspapers turned out to be very important sources. Western newspapers, which at the time employed well-connected correspondents in the Soviet Union, East Europe, and Hong Kong, often provide important background information as well as date verifications. The *Survey China Mainland Press (SCMP)* and *Current Background (CB)*, compiled at the time by the U.S. Consulate General in Hong Kong, contain many official and unofficial English translations of Chinese government statements and newspaper reports. *Pravda* was an indispensable source for official speeches by Soviet leaders that are otherwise unavailable.

Index